ROUTLEDGE LIBRARY EDITIONS:
BANKING & FINANCE

BANKING POLICY AND STRUCTURE

BANKING POLICY AND STRUCTURE

A Comparative Analysis

J. S. G. WILSON

Volume 34

LONDON AND NEW YORK

First published in 1986

This edition first published in 2012
by Routledge
2 Park Square, Milton Park, Abingdon, Oxfordshire OX14 4RN

Simultaneously published in the USA and Canada
by Routledge
711 Third Avenue, New York, NY 10017

First issued in paperback 2014

Routledge is an imprint of the Taylor and Francis Group, an informa company

British Library Cataloguing in Publication Data
A catalogue record for this book is available from the British Library

ISBN: 978-0-415-53852-7 (Volume 34)
ISBN: 978-0-415-75163-6 (pbk)

Publisher's Note
The publisher has gone to great lengths to ensure the quality of this reprint but points out that some imperfections in the original copies may be apparent.

Disclaimer
The publisher has made every effort to trace copyright holders and would welcome correspondence from those they have been unable to trace.

Banking Policy and Structure

A COMPARATIVE ANALYSIS

J.S.G. WILSON

CROOM HELM
London & Sydney

Croom Helm Ltd, Provident House, Burrell Row,
Beckenham, Kent BR3 1AT
Croom Helm Australia Pty Ltd, First Floor, 139 King Street,
Sydney, NSW 2001, Australia

British Library Cataloguing in Publication Data

Wilson, J.S.G.
Banking policy and structure: a comparative analysis.
1. Banks and banking
I. Title
332.1 HG1601

ISBN 0-7099-2783-5

Printed and bound in Great Britain by
Biddles Ltd, Guildford and King's Lynn

CONTENTS

Preface
Introduction 1
1. The Evolution of Deposit Banking 7
2. Financial Concentration and the Extension of Branch Banking 12
3. Unit Banking: the Experience of the USA 64
4. Hybrid Banking Systems 134
5. The Nordic Countries: Banking Structures 206
6. The Business of Banking 221
7. Industrial Banking 333
8. Assets and Liabilities Management 346
9. The Role of a Money Market 361
10. The Principles of Central Banking 385
11. The Techniques of Credit Control 398
12. Conclusion 424
Postscript – Australia 430
Index 432

To BMW

PREFACE

This book provides – I believe for the first time – a framework within which it is possible to analyse comparatively banking structure, the business of banking, money markets (on which is it proposed to publish a more detailed sister volume) and central-banking arrangements. It also provides a framework of particular interest to teachers of banking subjects. There are no doubt many ways in which this subject may be approached. This is one of them; hopefully, it will be regarded as a useful framework for the wider discussion of banking arrangements. We live now in a world where banking has become increasingly internationalised, with banks trading across borders – foreign banks competing actively with domestic banks and other financial institutions. It is important not only that bankers and students of banking should understand how banking systems work in other countries, how money markets operate, and how central banks seek to regulate and influence the activities of their banking and financial communities, but also that an interest should be stimulated in the comparative study of these matters. Furthermore, although over time the factual content of this book will become dated, it will always have an importance as a method of comparative study and an approach to the subject that has a permanent value and a historical significance.

I first became interested in this field when – as Reader in Money and Banking at the University of London – I inherited a course on Comparative Banking Institutions from Paul Bareau (a part-time lecturer at the London School of Economics and a distinguished financial journalist). Initially – as so many before me – I taught the subject country by country. What was comparative about this treatment was only incidental. Soon, however, I began to look for a framework within which to find patterns of behaviour that had a wider relevance in commercial banking, money-market arrangements, and central banking. The structure and content of the present book is a result of methods of teaching first developed at the London School of Economics and continued in later years at the University of Hull.

In any work of this kind, one is greatly indebted to a large number of people – more than can be mentioned by name. However, there are certain debts greater than others, especially to my wife, who has kept my research files for over 40 years. Others to whom I owe a special debt are, first, Dr H.C. Coombs (former Governor of the Reserve Bank of Australia), who taught me my first Economics at the Perth Technical College prior to my studying at the University of Western Australia; as he developed as a central banker, I, like many others, was influenced by his many contributions to the subject, but I did not realise how much I was indebted to him in my understanding of central banking, until I read his autobiography, *Trial Balance: Issues of my Working Life* (1981), and was reminded of the origin of some of the ideas that have now become commonplace; second, I owe a considerable debt to Professor R.S. Sayers, with whom I worked over a period of years at the London School of Economics – initially for allocating to me the teaching of Comparative Banking Institutions at the School and for giving me full freedom to develop the subject as I wished; third, I will always be grateful to Professor C.R. Whittlesey of the Wharton School in Philadelphia, who over many years of friendship encouraged me time and time again to write a book on comparative banking institutions; indeed, he was kind enough to suggest that I had much to offer to others interested in this field.

Although – as my wife will testify – much of our annual income over the years went into financing field work in many countries, the enterprise could not have been consummated without much generous supplementary support from a number of sources. These included the Houblon-Norman Fund of the Bank of England, which at various times between 1949 and 1968 made grants towards the expenses of field work in India and Pakistan (twice), France (twice), The Netherlands, the United States and Canada; the Leverhulme Trust, which financed my first field trip to the United States and Canada in 1955-6 and awarded me an Emeritus Fellowship in 1983-4 to provide secretarial support after retirement and during the closing stages of the work; the Ministry of Agriculture, which in the early 1970s financed an enquiry (headed by myself) into the availability of capital and credit to United Kingdom agriculture (this enabled me to undertake an extensive study of a wide range of UK financial institutions at all levels – head office, regional and district, and including branch managers); the Social Science Research Council, which made an award which contributed during 1980-2 to the financing of field work in a large number of countries around the world; the OECD (for which I worked as consultant in 1965-6 and again in 1979-81), which enabled me to undertake a large amount of field work in Western Europe; the Harvard Advisory Development Service which in 1967 invited me to survey banking arrangements in Liberia and to advise on the setting up of a central bank there; the American Philosophical Society, which in 1978 supplemented my funds with a small grant to assist with field work in the United States; the British Council, in cooperation with the universities in South Africa, which in 1979 made it possible for me to study banking and financial institutions in that country; and the Reserve Bank of New Zealand, which, in 1978, in collaboration with the universities in New Zealand, provided similar financial support. In 1980, The British Academy awarded me a grant to assist in financing a visit to most of the countries of South America.

Also, over these years, I was greatly assisted both by the London School of Economics and the University of Hull by generous grants of leave and by secretarial support. In this context, a first draft was prepared by Mrs Linda Kendall (née Bolton), research drafts by Mrs Kathleen Chatfield and Miss Zena Sinclair, who with Miss Joan Walton also typed the final version of the book. Their help and support is very much appreciated.

I am equally indebted to a large number of central bankers (including many Governors and other senior officials), commercial bankers (at all levels), and officers of a range of other financial institutions throughout the world; I have been greatly helped, too, by officials in ministries and government departments and by my Council colleagues in the Société Universitaire Européenne de Recherches Financières (SUERF), who have assisted in arranging interviews for me and have often also commented on my drafts. If I have a gift, it has been an ability to talk to bankers – and to persuade them to talk to me – and for all their assistance over many years I am immensely grateful; also for my seven years as a young man in the service of the old Commonwealth Bank of Australia, where I was first trained in banking principles and acquired some experience of practical banking. It is impossible, however, to acknowledge in detail the help of those many persons who have contributed in some measure to the present study. To my many banking friends around the world, I owe more than can be expressed in mere words. Nevertheless, for the accuracy of the text and for interpretations of the facts I alone must accept full responsibility.

Finally, there were two earlier versions of this type of study – my contributions on 'Banking' in the *International Encyclopaedia of the Social Sciences* published in 1968 and on 'Banks and Banking' published in the 15th edition of the *Encyclopaedia Britannica* in 1974. In important respects, Chapter 1 on 'The Evolution of Deposit Banking' and Chapter 10 on 'The Principles of Central Banking' have been based on the latter text. In a number of instances, I have chosen to retain non-English terms and expressions. This has been deliberate: there have been a number of reasons for doing so. In the case of direct quotation, the reason is obvious. In addition, certain terms did not lend themselves to exact translation and a literal translation would have been inappropriate. Furthermore, it was thought that readers of English might wish to acquaint themselves with the original terms, which are in all cases explained in the text. It is hoped that for bankers, teachers, and students alike this book will stimulate a continuing interest in the comparative study of banking and financial institutions.

J.S.G. Wilson
The University of Hull
England

INTRODUCTION

The comparative study of banking institutions is concerned with discovering both the extent to which arrangements in different countries are similar and the material respects in which they differ from the forms of organisation adopted elsewhere. However, in addition to merely factual inquiry, an attempt must also be made to establish the reasons for these similarities and differences. It is not so remarkable that there should be similarities. All banks deal in money and in money substitutes, and the peculiar characteristics of the 'commodities' in which they do business is a sufficient reason to explain the emergence of certain common elements basic to all banking business, even when that is undertaken in what appear to be strikingly dissimilar environments. Thus, in any well-run bank, no matter where it is situated (with the partial exception of Soviet-type institutions), there must be a certain amount of emphasis on liquidity and on margins of safety in lending. The broad objectives and 'rules of the game' will be essentially similar. It is in the details of organisation and technique that one tends to find the differences of emphasis. Although the problems that face these institutions appear to be much the same, there is in fact a considerable degree of variety in the solutions offered to resolve them.

Yet in more recent years there has been some evidence to suggest that differences between banking systems are now becoming much less pronounced than was formerly the case and, in a variety of ways, monetary authorities and commercial banks alike have shown a disposition to emulate practices that have proved successful elsewhere. There has been a tendency to modify, if not remove, some of the sharper contrasts that once obtained. This is no doubt due to the increasingly frequent exchange of views between the personnel both of central banks and of commercial institutions whether as a result of individual visits or group meetings in conferences and summer schools, not to mention the rising flood of publications that sometimes threatens to engulf all of us. It has been due in brief to the growth in the volume and efficiency of international communication. At the same time, the differences that still remain are sufficiently important to make a comparative study of banking institutions a significant and worthwhile undertaking.

In general terms, such differences as we find are due to environmental influences. The most obvious ingredient in environment is the nature of the country's economy. It may be a highly industrialised country, or it may be primarily agricultural; it may be relatively self-sufficient and have to import little, or it may depend for a significant proportion of its income on exports. But the character of the local economy will be only one of many ingredients in its environment, which in total is likely to be a very much more complex thing. The course of economic development and organisation will have been influenced by the whole stream of a country's history and it will therefore be necessary to look back to such traditions as might have been inherited from the past and/or from some other country. Linked with this will be questions of political philosophy. The political views that have been or are dominant in a country can exert a very important influence on the structure of its banking system, as witness – in their different ways – the very direct effects of political climate on banking structure in the United States and in the Soviet Union, with, on the one hand, the emphasis on the rights of the individual and the related survival of a large number of unit banks and, on the other, the application of a collectivist philosophy which sees the banking system as an instrument that can be employed to implement a national plan. Again, in the case of the so-called 'new' countries, the manner in which they were opened up has often been influential in forming their particular choice of banking organisation. In brief, one must always bear in mind the importance of historical evolution in providing the basic framework within which the banking organism grows up and has its being.

Indeed, on those occasions when an attempt has been made to impose from without institutions not in sympathy with the relevant environment, they have either broken down, become inoperative, or been so modified in the course of time as to lose their original form. Thus, traditional central banking techniques (such as discount policy) have failed to work in certain of the 'new' countries where the attempt was made to introduce them and subsequently the original arrangements have had to be modified to suit their specific requirements. The evolution of central banking in Australia is a case in point. Although the Commonwealth Bank (which was to fulfil the functions of a central bank) was given authority in 1924 to fix a discount rate, it never did so. Nor does the Reserve Bank of Australia, established in 1960, publish a Bank or discount rate, though it does act as a lender of last resort and there is therefore a kind of *de facto* Bank or discount rate in operation. It is true that another of the traditional techniques, namely, open-market operations, has been employed in Australia over a period of some years; the scope for market operations has gradually expanded, but this has remained a secondary means of credit control and more direct measures (e.g., statutory reserve deposits and the LGS convention[1]) have been found to suit the Australian environment better. Again, where economic forces have proved strong enough, a political philosophy of individualism and decentralisation may in practice have to be sacrificed, at least in part, in the interests of workability and efficient organisation. In this context, one might quote the several ways (e.g., correspondent banking and holding companies) in which banks in the United States have attempted to overcome the inconveniences imposed by legal barriers to the development of inter-state (and sometimes intra-state) branch systems. Again, during the period of Allied occupation of Germany following World War II, there was an attempt to impose an alien system from without, but the difficulties of making effective a policy of 'de-concentration' very soon resulted in the making of concessions by the Allied authorities. These permitted a limited return to larger units of operation and, subsequently, when sovereignty was finally restored to Germany, the emphasis was on re-concentration, with the result that in the commercial banking field evidence of Allied influence all but disappeared.[2] These are merely a few of the examples from the pages of banking history that emphasise the truth of Bagehot's dictum: 'New wants are mostly supplied by adaptation, not by creation or foundation.'[3] Furthermore, it is the influence of environment, in its broadest sense, which is the basis of the variety of banking organisation and technique that is to be found in the world at large and which offers the occasion for this attempt to treat the comparative study of banking as a subject in its own right.

In introducing a comparative study of banking institutions, it would be foolish to suggest that there are any watertight compartments into which banking systems can be divided. Undue formalism is dangerous. Yet, while avoiding set categories, it may still be possible to offer certain generalisations which will serve to describe the degree of concentration or, alternatively, of decentralisation in this or that banking system. To put it more concretely, why have some countries favoured and retained elements of a 'unit-banking' system, while others have evolved developed branch banking systems and yet others have elements of both? Further, is there evidence of any general trend in these matters? These are not altogether easy questions to answer and, in any event, many would question the attempt to find a 'trend' in any process as complex as socio-economic growth. Nevertheless, between the two extremes of 'unit banking', on the one hand, and a developed system of branch banking, on the other, there are to be found many instances of what for want of a better term one might call 'hybrid' systems, where the services of banks, which have nationwide branch networks, are supplemented by those that restrict their activities either to a region or to a locality. Is one to think of these 'hybrid' systems as half-way houses – as merely a stage in the evolution of a small number of large institutions with far-flung networks of branches? Will these 'hybrid' systems prove to be stable or will the smaller banks in the course of time disappear altogether or be absorbed by larger ones? To these questions there can again be no categorical answer. Nevertheless, there did seem to be an increasing amount of evidence to suggest as the general rule a gradual reduction in the number of banking units, growth in their average size, and a more widespread resort to branch banking, but this has not always been so – in some countries, the tendency has been for the number of banks to increase and this has not been confined to an influx of foreign banks. In addition, there has been an increasing degree of competition between different types of banks and other financial institutions for what are essentially similar kinds of business, each invading the domains of the others.

The banking system of the United Kingdom was generally regarded as evidencing a high degree of concentration, but within the banking community there has been an increasing number of small banks to be found, though at times these have tended to amalgamate into bigger units. It is true that many of the smaller institutions have survived largely on the basis of providing specialised services and have not therefore been in direct competition with the big banks and it may be argued that this is not a true 'hybrid' system in the sense of our definition. Other examples of banking systems that feature a high degree of concentration would include Canada, Australia, and South Africa, which in this matter have all been subject to British influence, and their experience may be compared with that of a number of Western European countries. The United States, on the other hand, is usually considered to be the home of 'unit banking', though this description tends to obscure both the degree to which large concentrations of financial power have developed in fact and the extent to which branch banking already exists. The United States may be something of a special case, because constitutional and legislative barriers exist to impede the strong forces that are working in the direction of greater concentration. Yet the very survival of these barriers reflects a still deeply-rooted political philosophy that favours individualism and decentralised financial control. Another country that had elements of 'unit banking' was Norway. There the strength of the local banks may have been largely attributable to the accidents of geography and the very mountainous terrain. At the same time, and even before bank amalgamations began to become more common, Norway could never be described as a true 'unit banking' system, and there is in fact no sharp dividing line between the so-called 'unit-banking' systems and the 'hybrid' systems of our attempted classification. Thus, in three fairly typical 'hybrid' systems – France, West Germany, and India – both local and regional banks appear to flourish side by side with those operating through networks of branches nationwide.

The obvious question to ask is whether these systems are merely in a state of transition to a more concentrated form of bank organisation. There is an increasing amount of evidence to suggest that this is so, but the process of change has so far been somewhat gradual and it may be that these 'hybrid' systems will continue to retain some degree of stability in their banking structures, at least for some time longer. Such questions cannot be answered dogmatically. The factors that must be taken into account are so numerous and so varied that each case study will be found to present its own unique combination of forces. Some of these will tend to make for a greater degree of concentration, while others will operate to oppose its development. The banking structure that emerges eventually will be the net result of a balancing-out process. Moreover, it is a process that is scarcely ever completed, though at some stage a pattern will usually become apparent and this may well remain dominant over a period of many years, subject only to very gradual modification. It is on this basis that a classification by categories becomes possible. Yet even within categories there will remain differences of degree and it could reasonably be claimed that all commercial banking structures are 'hybrids' to some extent.

The precise character of this or that banking system can best be sought in descriptive studies. Analysis of the way in which any such system has evolved is a task for the banking historian. What it is proposed to do in this volume is to abstract from both these branches of knowledge and to attempt a catalogue of the operative forces themselves, indicating rather by way of illustration when and where one might seek leading examples of their influence. Only in this way is it possible to achieve some kind of synthesis and to provide a framework within which to study the numerous individual banking systems of various countries. Because it is believed that in any dynamic society the general trend is towards greater concentrations of financial power and larger banking units with developed branch systems, it is proposed to consider first the forces that make for greater concentration. Nevertheless, there are also strong countervailing influences that sometimes swamp or considerably impede these developments and, in particular contexts, these must be accorded their full weight. Only when both sets of forces have been evaluated can a balance be struck and it is therefore essential to avoid premature judgements.

After a brief historical introduction, this book is concerned, firstly, with the structure of banking and similar institutions in a number of countries, treated comparatively; secondly, an attempt is made to study the business of banking within the framework of a simplified bank balance sheet; two special studies will follow– industrial banking and assets and liabilities management; thirdly, in order to establish the kinds of relationships that exist between the several banking and financial institutions, it is proposed to summarise the position with respect to the structure of money markets; finally, and within this framework, one can then discuss the principles of central banking and what the authorities attempt to do by way of monetary and credit policy. Throughout, an attempt will be made to deal with these matters comparatively.

Notes

1. LGS assets are liquids and government securities.
2. Japan was treated rather more leniently. Since 'large financial institutions were considered essential for Japan's reconstruction, they were not required to undergo any structural changes . . . Measures were taken, however, to sever some of the ties between the big banks and the industrial commercial and other financial enterprises of the former Zaibatsu; these included the removal of officers who had exercised power on behalf of the Zaibatsu, the elimination of Zaibatsu ownership of bank stocks, the limitation of the amount of stock which one individual or company could hold in a financial institution, the elimination of interlocking directorates between financial institutions and other juridical persons, and the termination of contractual service arrangements or other alliances between financial institutions and industrial and commercial organisations.' But it was 'questionable whether these measures actually achieved the purpose intended'. (Edna E. Ehrlich and Frank M. Tamagna, in 'Japan' in Benjamin Haggott Beckhart (ed.), *Banking Systems* (New York, 1954), p. 539.)
3. W. Bagehot, *Lombard Street: A Description of the Money Market*, new and revised edition (London, 1900), p. 79.

1 THE EVOLUTION OF DEPOSIT BANKING

Banking is known to have a long history, though little documentation exists prior to the thirteenth century. Many of the early 'banks' were not really banks at all and dealt primarily in coin and bullion, a good deal of their business being concerned with money-changing and supplying lawful foreign and domestic coin of the correct weight and fineness. Another and important early group of banking institutions comprised the merchant bankers; they dealt not only in goods but also in bills of exchange, and thereby provided for the remittance of money and payment of accounts at a distance, but without shipping actual coin. Such business was based on the fact that many of these merchants traded internationally and held assets at different points on the medieval trading routes. For a certain consideration, a merchant stood prepared to accept instructions to pay out money to a named party through one of his agents elsewhere, when the amount of the bill of exchange would be debited by the agent to the account of the merchant banker, who would also hope to make an additional profit from exchanging one currency against another and, because there was a possibility of loss, any profit or gain was not subject to the medieval ban on usury. Likewise there were techniques for concealing a loan by making foreign exchange available at a distance but deferring payment for it to a later date. In this way, the interest charged could be camouflaged by fluctuations in the rate of exchange between the date of ordering goods and the date of payment for them.

Another form of early banking activity was the acceptance of deposits. In origin, these might derive either from the deposit of money or valuables initially for safe keeping or for purposes of transfer to another party or, more straightforwardly, from the deposit of money in current account. But a balance in current account could also represent the proceeds of a loan that had been granted by the banker. Such loans might be based on an oral agreement between the parties (recorded of course in the banker's journal), whereby the customer might be allowed to overdraw his account. In all such cases, the banker was liable to pay on demand the claims of his customers.

English bankers in particular had by the seventeenth century begun to develop a deposit banking business and the techniques they evolved were in due course to prove influential elsewhere. Because they were men of wealth and reputation, the London goldsmiths already kept money and other valuables in safe custody for their customers. In addition, they dealt in bullion and foreign exchange; hence their acquiring and sorting coin for profit. Furthermore, as a means of attracting coin for sorting, they were prepared to pay a rate of interest. Indeed, it was largely in this way that they began to supplant as deposit bankers their great rivals the 'money scriveners', who were notaries that had come to specialise in bringing together borrowers and lenders; they had also themselves been accepting deposits.

Soon it was discovered that when money was deposited by a number of people with a goldsmith or a scrivener a fund of deposits came to be maintained at a fairly steady level – as a rule and over a period, money tended to come in steadily and in that way compensated for withdrawals. In any event, customers preferred to leave their surplus money with the goldsmith, only themselves holding sufficient for their everyday needs. As a result, there was likely to be a fund of idle cash, which could be lent out at interest to other parties in a position to use such money to advantage.

At about the same time, there grew up a practice whereby a customer could arrange for the transfer of part of his credit balance to another party by addressing to the banker an order to this effect. This was the origin of the modern cheque (the earliest known example in England is dated 1670). Moreover, it was only a short step from making a loan in specie (or coin) to allowing customers to borrow by issuing cheques. In this respect, either a loan account might be debited with the full amount borrowed and the amount credited to a current account against which cheques could be drawn or the customer could be allowed to overdraw his account up to a specified limit. In the first case, interest was charged on the full amount of the debit to loan account and, in the second, the customer only paid interest on the amount actually borrowed. However, in both cases, the customer was able to borrow by issuing cheques in payment for goods and services. The cheques represented claims against the bank, which had a corresponding claim against its customer.

An alternative means whereby a bank could create claims against itself was by issuing bank notes and, if the volume of notes issued exceeded the amount of specie or bullion held, additional money would have been created. The amount that would actually be issued depended on the banker's judgement of the possible demand for specie and this depended in large part on public confidence in the bank itself. In other words, the public would only accept such notes on the basis of the banker's known integrity and soundness. In London, goldsmith bankers were probably developing the use of the bank note at about the same time as the cheque, but the first bank notes actually issued in Europe were issued in 1661 by the Bank of Stockholm (which later became the Bank of Sweden). A number of commercial banks are still permitted to issue their own notes, but most of these issues have now been taken over by the central bank in the country concerned.

In Britain (because these developments were also being paralleled in Scotland), the cheque soon proved to be such a convenient means of payment that the public began to prefer the use of cheques for the larger part of their monetary transactions, coin only being used (and later, notes) for the smaller kinds of payments. As a result, banks began to grow bold and granted their borrowers the right to draw cheques much in excess of the amounts of cash actually held. Banks were now 'creating money', i.e. claims that were generally accepted as means of payment – money which came to be known as 'bank money' or 'credit'. If we exclude bank notes, this money consisted of no more than figures in bank ledgers, but it was money because of confidence in the ability of the bank to honour its liabilities when called upon to do so.

When a cheque is drawn and passes into the hands of another party in payment for goods or services, usually that cheque will be paid into another bank account, though some cheques will no doubt be cashed by direct presentation. Assuming that the overdraft technique is employed, if the cheque has been drawn by a borrower, the mere act of drawing and passing the cheque will create a loan as soon as the cheque is paid by the borrower's banker. Moreover, since every loan so made tends to return to the banking system as a deposit, for the system as a whole, deposits will tend to increase, or to decrease, more or less to the same extent as loans. On the other hand, if the money lent has been debited to a loan account and the amount of the loan has been credited to the customer's current account, a deposit will have been created immediately.

Mercantile courts in England have long had greater scope than on the Continent of Europe and, without doubt, one of the most important factors in the development of banking in England was the early legal recognition of the negotiability of credit instruments. The first orders for payment in Europe were non-negotiable, but in England many of these orders were drawn up in terms similar to those of a bill of exchange and, when the doctrine of negotiability had been established and accepted by the courts of common law, the cheque was expressly defined as a bill of exchange and recognised as a negotiable instrument.

This does much to explain some of the differences between banking arrangements in Continental Europe and in Britain, as well as in countries influenced by British traditions. For example, Continental limitations on the negotiability of an order of payment stood in the way of the extension of deposit banking based on the cheque that became such a feature of British banking developments in the eighteenth and early nineteenth centuries. On the other hand, Continental countries were meanwhile developing a system of giro payments whereby transfers were effected on the basis of written instructions to debit the giro account of the payer and to credit that of the payee. Only much more recently – from the early 1960s onwards – were giro-type transactions operated by the British banks (they were called 'credit transfers'); a Post Office National Giro was also set up in 1968.

These then were the ways in which deposit banking evolved. Its characteristics were as follows. A deposit bank is always under an obligation to repay the credit balances of its customers either on demand or when the amounts credited to them become due. A bank must, therefore, itself hold some cash balances (both in the till and as balances at a bankers' bank, like a central bank). Furthermore, it must keep a proportion of its assets in forms that can readily be converted into cash. Only in this way can confidence in the banking system be maintained. Confidence is likewise the basis of 'credit'. Provided it always honours its promises (e.g. to provide cash in exchange for deposit balances), a bank can 'create credit' for use by its customers. It may do this by issuing additional notes or by making new loans, which in their turn become new deposits. But a bank will only be able to do this as long as the public believes that the bank can and will without question honour its obligations, which will then be accepted at face value and circulate as money. So long as they remain outstanding, these promises or obligations will continue to constitute claims against that bank and can be transferred by means of cheques or other negotiable instruments from one party to another. In all essentials, this is what is known as 'deposit banking'. Although there are variations in detail, and with the partial exception of Soviet-type institutions, it is the accepted basis of commercial banking as practised in the world today.

Moreover, despite some differences, the banking systems of the world have many similarities. This is to be attributed to the fact that all banks trade in a type of commodity (money or money substitutes) that has peculiar characteristics. Thus, in all banking institutions (again with the partial exception of those in the USSR and those based on a similar system), there is some emphasis on the need for liquidity (or the ease with which assets can be converted into cash without risk of substantial loss) and on margins of safety in lending. Even where certain of the commercial banks are state-owned (e.g., in Australia, Egypt, France and India), this has remained true.

2 FINANCIAL CONCENTRATION AND THE EXTENSION OF BRANCH BANKING

The United Kingdom

The demand for larger banking units is generally a concomitant of economic growth. In this connection, there appear to have been two factors that historically were of overriding importance. The first and proximate reason for larger banks is probably to be found in the growth of population and, more especially, its aggregation in industrial centres. Given adequate natural resources and capital, an increasing population is a most potent growth factor and with it tends to be associated a rising level of production and expanding trade. Increasing wealth permits the more rapid accumulation of capital and there tends to be an increase in the size of the business unit both in the industrial and in the agricultural sectors of the economy, though in the latter case the evidence is still perhaps rather less clear-cut.

A second but prior condition not only of the growth but also of the integration of an economy (without which larger business units could scarcely emerge) is the development of adequate basic communications – roads, canals, railways, postal services, the telegraph and telephone, and, ultimately, airways, radio and television, telex, links with central computers, and so on. If banking empires are to increase the range and scope of their operations, they must be able to effect remittances easily and rapidly. Likewise with the transmission of information relating to accounting procedures. These again depend on a widespread network of efficient communications. Furthermore, while branch banking is not necessarily a function of growth, it was in England directly associated with it and good communications were again an essential condition of such development. As long as communications remained primitive, control over branches at a distance was almost impossible. The rapid transfers of specie and documents, and a regular and expeditious postal service were essential to an extension beyond purely local boundaries. In the 1860s, the telegraph made possible even more rapid communication and easier contact in emergency. Only then did a system of widely scattered branches at last become a practicable proposition.

In Scotland, the early corporate banks (the first – the Bank of Scotland – was founded in 1695) favoured the establishment of branches from the very beginning, but their initial attempts were not particularly successful, again because of poor communications and the difficulty of moving adequate supplies of coin. It was not until after the Napoleonic Wars that these banks began to expand their branches with vigour. Although communications were still capable of considerable improvement, they sought to overcome their difficulties at least in part by appointing as 'agents'[1] to take charge of their branches men of standing in their local communities, for whom banking was often merely a sideline.[2] It was only much later, when communications improved, that the responsibility for authorising advances was gradually shifted from the 'agent' to Head Office.

What greatly assisted the spread of branch banking throughout Scotland was the right to issue notes of less than £1, which enabled the banks to draw on the financial resources of a large number of small communities by putting their notes into circulation over a wide area and helping to finance the establishment of their branches at the same time.[3] The growth of networks of branches was also effected by the absorption of local banks and private banking houses by the larger banks, as well as by amalgamations between small units to form bigger banking units. In this way, the number of banks was gradually reduced – by 1865 it had fallen to 12 – while each institution was represented by branches spread across the country. In this matter, Scotland was at that time well ahead of England.

Yet it is in England that we find a better illustration of the main forces that operate to bring about greater concentration in banking. By the 1830s, the stream of industrial progress was running fast and the size of the business unit was growing. A system of banking conducted on the basis of a large number of small private banks was already proving less than adequate to meet the requirements of an industrial structure no longer capable of financing itself largely by ploughing back profits. Bigger industrial units began to need larger financial units. Small banks could not stand the strain of this enlarged demand and, in attempting to meet it, often became over-extended and failed. Hence, the strains that attended rapid industrialisation were accentuated during the early part of the nineteenth century by a chronic instability in the banking system. This was the economic basis for the growth in size of banks that was encouraged by legislation which (beginning in 1826) permitted joint stock ownership and made possible a more widely spread proprietary. This increase in size and in the area served by individual banks accelerated greatly as the amalgamation movement got under way during the second half of the nineteenth century.

In attempting to establish the reasons for the increase in the size of banks in England, too much importance cannot be attached to the invention of the joint-stock company and its general application as a dominant form of business organisation to banks as well as to other types of business unit. It was true that the vagaries of human experience could scarcely guarantee perpetual existence even to a joint-stock company, but such institutions could at least look beyond the lives and fortunes of individual partners. In addition, it was anticipated that a widely based proprietary was more likely than a small partnership to engender confidence and would of itself assist in attracting deposits from those with temporarily surplus funds. In this way it was hoped – in nineteenth century England – to augment considerably the supply of resources available to meet the enlarged and enlarging credit requirements of the industrial community.

Although limited liability could not be availed of generally in England prior to 1862, joint-stock organisation itself conferred tangible advantages. The unlimited liability of a number of men of substance was not only calculated to build up local confidence in a banking enterprise, but also effectively widened the area from which banks could draw funds. The transactions of a joint-stock bank carried the guarantee of all shareholders and the names of joint-stock banks on bills of exchange were therefore readily accepted in the London bill market. As a result, local requirements had no longer to be financed out of local resources. The latter could now be supplemented, when necessary, by borrowing on the basis of bills either by discounting in London, or with other banks elsewhere in the country. Indeed, even when it became possible to incorporate banks with limited liability, managements were slow to adopt it, though subsequently (during the 1880s following the failure of the City of Glasgow Bank in 1878)[4] its advantages came to be appreciated and it rapidly became general.[5]

The joint-stock company form of business organisation made generally possible the large business unit, but it should not be forgotten that most of the early joint-stock banks in England, as elsewhere, tended to be both local in origin and localised in the emphasis of their business. Their activities were certainly on a larger scale, but at first they were little more than a broadened and improved type of private bank. In some cases, this remained true for many years. Yet without the joint-stock form of organisation, latterly with limited liability, there would have been no adequate basis for the subsequent growth of the English banks both in the size of their resources and in the geographic coverage of their operations.

Once the assurance of adequate communications permits an extension of the area of operation of a bank, there are usually opportunities for securing a better spread of risks in the distribution of loans and investments. This does not necessarily follow. A relatively small area may enjoy a considerable diversification of industry and of economic activity (e.g., northern France and Alsace), and even relatively small banks operating in such an environment may be able to secure an effective spread of risks. Alternatively, this may be achieved by banks in a leading financial centre without resort to branches, in virtue of their specialised knowledge (e.g., the merchant banks in London) or on the basis of limited branching by means of a developed system of nationwide correspondents (e.g., the big 'money-market' banks in New York). In this way, such institutions are able to build up a nicely balanced loan portfolio that in effect reflects a good geographic and industrial spread. Yet there was much evidence in English experience to suggest that a local bank, whether joint stock or not, did tend to suffer from an undue concentration of risks. Any economic collapse affecting the main industry or industries of a particular district would almost certainly drag the local banks down with it. Quite apart from the concentration of industrial interest, over-concentration in a particular locality accentuated the risk that too much might be lent to particular firms, sometimes the firms concerned being those of the directors themselves. In the past, this has been a not uncommon experience in a number of countries (examples might be drawn from experience in England, the United States, France, Germany, and India) and it is still not unknown in some parts of the world.

An even more powerful factor in promoting measures to secure access to a wider geographic area, particularly by building up a network of branches, is the necessity for a bank to secure the resources required to support an expanding loan business. Frequently, the main objective in establishing branches is the attraction of additional deposits. This was true of branch development both in France and in Germany and, latterly, it has also been true of banks in the United States.

There are alternative means of securing access to supplementary resources, but on the whole such techniques have usually proved less reliable than branch expansion. Thus, in nineteenth-centiry England, as local industries began to expand rapidly, the local banks which served them sought to exploit the unlimited liability of their shareholders by relying to an excessive extent upon the resources of the London discount market. Indeed, so long as banks continued to be largely local concerns, the existence of such a highly organised bill market was for them an absolute necessity. Furthermore, any failure by some such means to divert the surplus funds of agricultural areas to meet the expanding demands of the manufacturing centres would have constituted an intolerable waste of resources. Yet in a period of rapid expansion, even a market capable of drawing funds from all over the country was likely to become occasionally over-strained. Nor was London always sufficiently careful in scrutinising the paper it was prepared to discount.[6] It was only slowly that these weaknesses were eliminated and, in any event, with the course of time, the extension of branch networks (mainly by way of amalgamation, or the outright purchase of private banking businesses) reduced the necessity of the banks to rediscount in London. In their turn, the joint-stock banks had found that their resources had become inadequate to meet the demands being made upon them and it was this that lay behind the movement towards 'consolidation', whereby banks joined together in their search for strength and stability. As the nineteenth century drew to a close, this process quickened and reached its zenith in the first two decades of the twentieth century.

By 1918, with the emergence of a 'Big Five' (Barclays, Lloyds, Midland, National Provincial and Westminster) whose resources constituted nearly two-thirds of the total for the whole country and which now boasted nationwide networks of branches, it was thought that the process had worked itself out. Moreover, the size of the later amalgamations prompted fears of the emergence of a 'money trust', 'invested with all the sinister power of a monopoly'. To allay the general feeling of unease, a Treasury Committee on Bank Amalgamations was appointed in 1918. Members of this Committee

> were agreed on the possibility that the process of concentration might produce an enormous institution menacing the supremacy of the Bank of England . . . and possibly even the Government itself. A bill was drawn up to incorporate the committee's recommendations, but was set aside in favour of a general undertaking given to the Government by the banks. Thereafter all proposed amalgamations or arrangements for joint working were to be submitted to the Treasury and Board of Trade and concluded only with their consent.[7]

It was on this basis that the banking structure took on the shape that was to remain substantially unchanged over a period of many years. A few remaining small joint-stock banks were absorbed or consolidated, some further 'affiliations' were arranged, and the last survivor among country note issues lapsed.[8] Apparently, the Treasury was prepared to acquiesce in all proposals for the absorption of small banks by bigger institutions, but it was the general understanding that the amalgamation of two giants would not be permitted.[9]

Apart from some further small amalgamations in England, there was the move by several of the English banks either by way of affiliation or ownership to penetrate Northern Ireland and Scotand, but for a long time it was believed that any further major amalgamation in England would virtually be prohibited by the Treasury. However, especially in the period after World War II, some amalgamations were taking place in Scotland. Thus, the two banks owned by the Midland were amalgamated in 1950 to form the Clydedale and North of Scotland Bank Limited (later to be renamed the Clydesdale Bank); the Bank of Scotland absorbed the Union Bank of Scotland in 1955; and the National Bank of Scotland and the Commercial Bank of Scotland amalgamated to form the National Commercial Bank of Scotland Limited in 1959. Meanwhile, during the inter-war period, the Royal Bank of Scotland had moved south across the border to absorb Drummond & Company (1924) and to acquire Williams Deacon's (1930), and Glyn Mills & Company (1939). Subsequently, these banks – the Royal Bank of Scotland, Williams Deacon's and Glyn Mills – were formed into the Three Banks Group. A further consolidation was announced in February, 1968, when it was disclosed that the Royal and National Commercial Banks were to amalgamate and also to form a holding company. The latter was called the National and Commercial Banking Group Limited and it was to control the Royal Bank of Scotland as well as three English banks – Glyn Mills & Company, National Bank (minus its former Irish branches), and Williams Deacon's. Subsequently, in April 1969, the merger of the last three banks was announced. This took place in September 1970, when a new bank – Williams & Glyn's Bank Limited – was formed.[10]

Only the British Linen Bank (owned by Barclays) remained outside these moves. But it was clear that this situation could not continue indefinitely and in May 1969, Barclays Bank and the Bank of Scotland announced that the Bank of Scotland would take over Barclay's British Linen Bank subsidiary in exchange for shares of £20 million. This gave Barclays a 35 per cent stake in the capital of the Bank of Scotland. This was sold to Standard Life Assurance, a leading Edinburgh-based mutual life assurance company, in 1985.[11] One might note, too, the interest of Lloyds Bank in the Royal Bank of Scotland. Initially, this represented the diluted value of their holding in the National Bank of Scotland following the merger of the National Commercial Bank and the Royal Bank of Scotland in 1969. Subsequently, Lloyds lifted their stake to 21.3 per cent in December 1983. These operations reduced the number of Scottish banks from four to three, of which the Bank of Scotland was the second largest, and were prompted by the need to continue the process of bank rationalisation in Scotland and the possibility of reducing the costs of computerisation. The merged institutions now had a much better geographic spread. However, to the extent that certain areas were 'over-banked', there was subsequently some reduction in the number of branches. Latterly, the Royal Bank of Scotlad Group has reorganised itself and, on the basis of a private Act of Parliament, has converted itself into the first truly UK bank trading on both sides of the border under the name of the Royal Bank of Scotland. The change became effective as from 1 October 1985.

Meanwhile, in England, another big bank merger had been announced – between, on the one hand, the Westminster and, on the other, the National Provincial and its subsidiary the District Bank. The National Westminster Bank Limited was formed in 1968 and acquired on 8 July 1968 the capital of Westminster Bank and National Provincial Bank; the latter had previously (in 1962) acquired District Bank. The business of all three banks was transferred to National Westminster on 1 January 1970. Coutts, which had been a wholly-owned subsidiary of National Provincial since 1920, became a subsidiary of National Westminster but retained its separate identity. This created a unit with deposits of £3,400 million and 3,057 branches. Almost immediately afterwards (in early February) it was intimated that Barclays, Lloyds and Martins planned to combine in a group that would have deposits of £4,800 million and 5,500 branches. It was at this stage that the Monopolies Commission was brought into the picture, the majority of the relevant committee being of the view that it was against the public interest to permit this merger, though a merger of Barclays with the much smaller Martins might be permitted. In November 1968, Barclays acquired the share capital of Martins Bank; the business of Martins was transferred to Barclays on 15 December 1969 by private Act of Parliament.

In November 1982, Barclays Bank PLC announced that after passage of a private Act of Parliament it would merge with Barclays Bank International Limited in order to coordinate business development and to reduce capital and tax problems. The Act was given the Royal Assent in June 1984 and the merger was effective as from 1 January 1985. Subject again to a private Act of Parliament, Lloyds Bank PLC in October 1984 likewise announced a merger with Lloyds Bank International Limited 'to improve service to customers by integrating operations more closely, cutting out duplication and reducing costs in various areas'. This was to become effective in January 1986.

Of the several possible reasons why further bank mergers might be favoured in the United Kingdom, the desirability of integrating complementary operations and spreading the overheads that derive from computer installations is probably the most relevant to British experience, where concentration has already progressed quite far and where further mergers between large banks may only result in acute problems of assimilation which could take years to overcome. What has tended to happen in more recent years is for banking groups to become more common and, for the big banks and some foreign banks, often through a holding company, to acquire interests in finance companies, merchant banks, leasing firms, even stockbrokers.

So far as competition is concerned, Britain's Big Four are sufficiently large to hold their own internationally, even allowing for contemporary mergers in France and the Netherlands. As for the United States, it is important to remember that, although the largest American banks are in absolute terms the biggest in the world, they are smaller in relation to the gross national product than would have been the proposed merger between Barclays, Lloyds, and Martins in relation to Britain's gross national product.

More than that; while in Britain a further large bank merger might lead to greater profits, there was little evidence to suggest that it would result in greater competition, or the provision of a markedly better range of services. Except internationally, size is of itself not all that important. What the customer wants most is a bank that is efficient and adaptable. The more managements there are to take decisions about innovations, the better the chance that more innovations will in fact be introduced.

So far as competition is concerned, the entry of foreign banks and, initially, of the American banks in particular, greatly increased the degree of inter-bank competition and considerably enriched and enlivened banking arrangements in the City of London. This competition is reflected in market shares. In terms of sterling deposits, the London clearing banks are still dominant, accounting for 45 per cent of the total, followed by Other British Banks (over 22 per cent) and Other Overseas Banks (over 10 per cent). The Accepting Houses and the

Scottish clearing banks each attract over 5 per cent of the total, the American banks 6.5 per cent and the Japanese banks only 2.7 per cent. However, when one turns to other currency deposits, the Japanese (with over 25 per cent of the total) and the American banks (21 per cent) are the most important national groups, with Other Overseas Banks contributing a further 27 per cent. The London clearing banks attract less than 6 per cent and Other British Banks about 11 per cent. The importance of the foreign banks in the 'other currency' field reflects the role of the City of London as an international financial centre and, in particular, the significance of the Euro-currency markets.

Another major source of competition against which the banks have been fighting back (e.g., their own mortgage lending and some return to Saturday morning opening) is the building societies, which are a particularly strong competitor for savings. The sterling deposits of the London clearing banks are about £65 billion (for all banks in the United Kingdom, approaching £145 billion); for the building societies, the total of personal-sector deposits (which is thought to be the appropriate figure) exceeds £70 billion. So far as mortgages are concerned, the building societies remain the main lenders, the banks having come into this field only rather more recently. But competition for savings both between the building societies themselves and with other institutions providing saving facilities has become ever more intense. The building societies have expanded their branches – now about 6,500 compared with about 11,000 for the clearing banks; they operate more flexible opening hours, including Saturday mornings; they offer attractive savings packages (e.g., premium-rate accounts); latterly, some of their savings accounts have been combined with a 'moneylink' package aiming at that 40 per cent of the population that does not have a bank account (providing a minimum deposit is maintained, it will earn normal interest and, with a collaborative non-clearing bank, a current account can be maintained with free banking as long as that account is in credit, and cheques can be cashed at the building-society branches as well as at the bank);[12] and the building societies have become more flexible in their lending arrangements. They have also been spending more on advertising and marketing. Moreover, following the Finance Act 1983, which permitted them to pay interest gross on certificates of deposit, they have had access to the market for certificates of deposit, which is said to have been worth an extra £4 billion to them as an additional source of resources.[13]

Australia

The beginnings of Australian banking were similar to those in England. Local banks were set up in the form of small exclusive partnerships and these issued bank notes that gradually pushed out of existence the highly miscellaneous issues previously made both by storekeepers and, for that matter, by private individuals without trading connections.

The first Australian bank – the Bank of New South Wales – was established in 1817 and it was followed in the 1820s by the setting up of a number of other colonial banks. The next phase was financed mainly by British capital and was associated with the pastoral boom of the 1830s, the only important new colonial bank being the Commercial Banking Company of Sydney (1834) – the colonists preferred the profits to be derived directly from the production of wool rather than an indirect share in the form of high interest rates on loans. Hence, it was British capital that founded the Bank of Australasia (which began operations in 1835), the Union Bank of Australia (1837), and the Bank of South Australia (1837). It was 'only as the boom reached its turbulent crest [that] there was a flurry of colonial bank formations',[14] but they failed to survive the crash of 1843.

The result of these developments was not merely a multiplication of banks. All the banks in the colony had also greatly extended their activities. In place of a few local banking units, depending on their capital for loanable funds, there was now a number of fairly large banks competing fiercely for all available deposits (both domestic and from overseas) and firmly establishing deposit banking as the accepted basis for doing business. Furthermore, the competition for new business as settlement spread to the west, south and north (in ten years effectively occupying 'half a continent' – to quote Butlin) resulted in the early rejection of 'unit banking' in favour of institutions trading through what was to become an expanding network of branches.

The Australian banking system had already begun to take shape during the pastoral expansion of the 1830s, as new banks promoted from England began to compete vigorously with the banks already established in the Colony. 'Competition led to the opening of branches in the larger outposts of settlement, and branch banking on the Scottish lines rather than the unit banks of England [as they then were] and of the United States became characteristic of Australian banking.'[15] The slump of 1841-3 was accompanied by some bank failures, but for most of the banks it was rather a matter of reduced volume of business. 'It continued to be what it had become, a semi-competitive system, accept-ting branch banking as its mode of expansion and otherwise closely modelled on the structure and practice of English banking and, like it, subject only to a minimum of legislative control.[16] Australians had discovered that 'oldfashioned restricted banking through a single office on the basis of shareholders' funds had had its day'.[17]

At the same time, it is essential that one retains one's sense of perspective in this matter and it must be emphasised that prior to 1850 the total number of bank branches in Australia was quite small – about 10 – though thereafter there was a steady growth to about 70 by 1860, 350 by 1870, 800 by 1880, and 1,400 by 1890, after which there was some reduction (following the banking crisis of 1893) to less than 1,200, before the upward trend was resumed at the turn of the century to approach 2,200 by 1914 and over 3,200 by 1929.[18] There was some rationalisation of branches during World War II, but latterly the tendency was again to extend branch networks. As at 30 June 1982, the main trading banks operated 4,780 branches and the other trading banks 384. In addition, the banks had some 1,050 agencies throughout Australia.[19]

Two comments might be made about these early bank branches in Australia. Firstly, none of them was initially profitable and by no means all of them survived. Indeed, some of the early branches had quite a high rate of mortality.[20] Even much later, after the turn of the twentieth century, it was reckoned that it took three years before a new branch made reasonable profits.[21] Secondly, the possibilities of branch expansion were obviously restricted by the difficulty of finding men of experience and integrity. For this latter reason, bank directors 'were cautious of going afar'.[22]

The adoption of branch banking in Australia was supposed by tradition to be due to the predominance of Scots amongst the country's early bankers, but as Butlin has observed, 'all the evidence points to a predominance of Englishmen and to a general reluctance of banks to establish branches as a matter of policy'.[23] Competition for business in an economy that was expanding geographically was the true reason for the opening up of branches. Only in this way could banks retain contact with a rapidly migrating population and attract deposits from the new areas that were being opened up.

Often a bank would put up its sign 'on a small wooden dwelling at dusty crossroads, where lay a forge and store and a few scattered dwellings, and grew slowly with the town'. Often it followed the new lines of railway fanning out from the capital cities and, sometimes, a bank set up its branch 'years ahead of the railway and had a thriving business before the first steam train arrived'.[24]

> The normal pattern was that isolated settlers in an area were content to bank in the metropolis (or not bank at all) until their numbers increased; then they pressed for local facilities and, when these were not forthcoming, set about forming their own local institutions. Threatened with a loss of accounts, the metropolitan bank most directly interested opened a branch. Sometimes this was not done quickly enough to forestall the local proposals. . . More usually the branch killed the plan for a local bank before it was established. . . Even where a 'local' bank commenced operations it soon succumbed, . . . after the middle-thirties no 'local' bank was able to withstand competition, real or threatened, from the branch of an established bank.[25]

By 1840, every major centre of population in the country had at least one branch, though at that time there were admittedly not very many 'major centres of population' in Australia. Furthermore, the expansion in branch banking was by no means uninterrupted. The slump of 1841-3 prompted some second thoughts and a number of branches were actually closed. Indeed, the Commercial Banking Company of Sydney, despite protests, temporarily abolished all its branches and agencies from the end of March 1844. However, the retreat was merely temporary and, during the later 1840s, there was a cautious resumption in opening bank branches. By 1850, even the Bank of New South Wales was at last showing an active interest in branch development,[26] and the advantages of branch banking both from the point of view of metropolitan banks and of their customers in outlying areas seemed by then to be generally accepted.

Although new banks continued to be established from time to time – over 30 new institutions appeared between 1800 and 1888 – successful competition with the existing banks depended on the adoption by the new banks of similar methods of doing business. This included the seeking of deposits by opening branches. At this stage, purchase of another bank, or amalgamation with it, was not regarded as a means of acquiring additional offices. Prior to 1880, only three banks had been taken over by other institutions – one in 1835 by the Bank of Australasia, one in 1840 by the Union Bank of Australia, and one in 1841 again by the Bank of Australasia (though in this case they found that they had scotched the snake not killed it, since a dissenting minority of the shareholders of the bank taken over established a new bank with which to fight back).[27] Indeed, only in the 1880s (when there were seven), in World War I (five), and during the 1920s (six) were amalgamations relatively numerous. In addition, three banks were taken over in the early 1890s and there were several amalgamations at the beginning of the 1930s (including the absorption of the Australian Bank of Commerce by the Bank of New South Wales in 1931). Two major amalgamations also took place in the years following World War II. Again, in 1969, several merger proposals were put forward and there was some further concentration when the Australia and New Zealand Bank (itself the product of the 1951 merger between the Bank of Australasia and the Union Bank of Australia) joined forces with the English, Scottish and Australian Bank.

The emphasis on absorption and amalgamation during the 1880s and early 1890s was undoubtedly due to the growing appreciation that a large bank with a widespread network of branches was likely to secure a better spread of risks than the smaller institutions with a more localised type of business. In addition, one would expect the larger banks to appreciate the advantages of territorial expansion by acquiring other banks, and thereby branches, in areas where previously they had been inadequately represented. Nevertheless, during this first period of active amalgamation, mergers between banks in what were then different colonies seemed to have been a less important means of building up a nationwide branch network than they were to become during the second main period of activity – 1917 to 1927, i.e. after federation in 1900. Nor can this be explained solely on political grounds, since interstate branching had already taken place before 1900 and there were no legislative impediments to the expansion of branches beyond the boundaries of any particular colony.

In the earlier period, the Union Bank of Australia had acquired banks in South Australia and Tasmania (both in 1892) and the Commercial Bank of Australia had taken over a Sydney bank in 1891. (Both the Commercial and the Union were Melbourne banks, the latter with respect to its Australian business, since its head office was in London.) But during the decade 1917 to 1927, the emphasis was much more obviously on inter-state expansion. Thus, in 1917, the Commercial Bank of Australia acquired a bank in Tasmania, the English, Scottish and Australian Bank following suit in 1921. A year later, the National Bank of Australasia took over a bank in Queensland (itself a result of a previous amalgamation in that state); in 1927, the Bank of New South Wales absorbed the Western Australian Bank; and the Commercial of Sydney considerably strengthened its position in Victoria by amalgamating with the Bank of Victoria. In all these cases, business and branches were acquired in states where the larger banks had previously been under-represented. In 1947, the National Bank of Australasia again took steps to increase its hold on banking business in Queensland by amalgamating with the Queensland National Bank[28] and, in 1951 (as indicated above), the Bank of Australasia and the Union Bank of Australia merged to form the Australia and New Zealand Bank, one of the objects being to unite in a single operating unit the business of two institutions that had over the years developed along largely complementary lines.

Thus, by seeking new business through the branches they opened themselves and by amalgamating with other banks with branch networks, most of the major trading banks in Australia (with the partial exception of the Bank of Adelaide, though it had at least one branch in each state) were now represented by offices that extended throughout the country; at the same time, there were still significant variations in the extent to which the several banks were represented in particular States as well as in the character of the business that they did.[29] The only remaining institution with a mainly regional business was the Bank of Adelaide, the activities of which were largely confined to South Australia, though the Commercial Banking Company of Sydney had relatively few branches outside eastern Australia.

Following further amalgamations in 1981, the major trading banks in Australia included the government-owned Commonwealth Trading Bank of Australia (from 1959, part of the Commonwealth Banking Corporation group)[30] and a number of privately-owned trading banks – Westpac Banking Corporation, which formally came into existence on 1 October 1982, following the merger of the Bank of New South Wales (founded in 1817) with The Commercial Bank of Australia Limited, (founded in 1866); National Commercial Banking Corporation of Australia Limited (National Australia Bank), which derived from a merger of The National Bank of Australasia Limited (founded in 1858) and The Commercial Banking Company of Sydney Limited (founded in 1834) effective on 1 October 1981, the two banks integrating their operations under the new name as from 1 January 1983; and the Australia and New Zealand Banking Group Limited, which had acquired The Bank of Adelaide and its wholly-owned subsidiary, Finance Corporation of Australia, in November 1979.[31]

Other trading banks which are incorporated in the statistics for All Trading Banks include Bank of New Zealand, Bank of Queensland Limited, and Banque Nationale de Paris (which initially as the old

Comptoir National d'Escompte de Paris had long been established in Australia) and (since February 1981) the new and quite small Australian Bank Limited.[32] All these banks submit returns under the Banking Act 1959, but also included in the figures are returns voluntarily submitted by State Bank of New South Wales, State Bank of Victoria, State Bank of South Australia, and the Rural and Industries Bank of Western Australia (the Federal Government's powers do not extend to them, hence their voluntary cooperation). All the major trading-bank groups also operate savings banks, finance companies, and other financial subsidiaries and some of the state banks have savings-bank divisions. In addition, in South Australia, The Savings Bank of South Australia has been merged with the State Bank; there are two trustee savings banks in Tasmania – the Savings Bank of Tasmania and the Launceston Bank for Savings. There is also the Commonwealth Savings Bank, part of the Commonwealth Banking Corporation. The major trading banks, which have branch networks throughout Australia, hold about 87 per cent of all trading-bank assets and the State-government-owned trading banks about 11 per cent, with branches confined to their home states.[33] Trading banks remain the largest institutional group in the Australian financial system, but their importance in relation to all financial institutions has declined over the years and, since the early 1960s, has fluctuated around 25 per cent, part of their business having gone to the finance companies and other new financial institutions. Savings banks until the late 1960s held a fairly steady 20 per cent share of total assets of all financial institutions, but latterly in a regulatory climate that did not favour them they have lost ground and have now declined to about 13.5 per cent.

Other banking institutions include the Commonwealth Development Bank (a specialist development bank, until 1976 funded by way of capital subscription, retained earnings, and special borrowing arrangements with the Commonwealth Savings Bank and more recently by open-market borrowings and retained earnings); the Australian Resources Development Bank (jointly owned by the major trading banks and two state-owned trading banks) established in 1967 to facilitate the medium- to long-term financing of large scale projects of national importance; and the Primary Industry Bank of Australia established in 1978 (jointly owned by the Commonwealth government, the major trading banks, and a consortium of four government-owned State banks), whose role is to re-finance long-term loans made by approved lenders to primary producers – its main sources of funds now derive from public issues (like a semi-government authority) and, latterly, its interest rates have tended to be very competitive. A Term Loan Fund and a Farm Development Loan Fund were initially established by releases from special reserve deposits held by trading banks with the Reserve Bank of Australia – the country's central bank – together with other funds lodged by the trading banks; these provided for term lending by major trading banks, but for some years now they have been of no practical significance as they have not been replenished. Loans formerly made out of these funds are now being financed by Australian Resources Development Bank, Primary Industry Bank, or by the bank making the loan. Also, in 1964, the Australian Banks' Export Re-finance Corporation (ABERC) was established by the major trading banks, with the support of the Reserve Bank, to provide greater scope (by re-financing bank loans) for individual trading banks to extend term export finance. But from 1 February 1980, the ABERC became a wholly-owned subsidiary of the Australian Resources Development Bank.[34] The Australian Industry Development Corporation, a statutory corporation owned by the Commonwealth of Australia, provides development funds to Australian industry, particularly mining and manufacture. It began operations in 1971.

Finance companies have already been mentioned; those owned or controlled by Australian banks account for almost half the total assets of finance companies; they supplement bank finance at short- and medium-term to the household and business sectors (one-third of their funds goes to the former and two-thirds to the latter, a substantial part to small business). Recently, the emphasis has been on the provision of lease finance to business, and consumer and personal loans. The larger finance companies obtain their funds predominantly from the household sector by issuing debentures and unsecured notes. They may also resort to money-market funds. Finance companies (and a smaller 'general financiers' group funded by parent and related companies and institutions) hold something like 14 per cent of the total assets of all financial institutions.

Other categories of financial institution include the 'money-market corporations' (merchant banks), which operate principally in the area of short-term wholesale finance (i.e. in large 'chunks' of money), servicing the needs of the larger corporations and public authorities; they also trade in government and public-authority securities and bank and other corporate debt instruments, and provide financial advice and services (e.g., underwriting and placements for semi-government clients); their domestic funds come principally from corporate and institutional sources; their share of financial institutions' assets is about

6 per cent. Another group of importance is the authorised short-term money-market dealers; they fund themselves by accepting large deposits and enjoy lender-of-last-resort facilities at the Reserve Bank. Balance sheet data (less than 1 per cent of financial institutions' assets) do not fully reflect the importance of the authorised dealers, whose trading operations are substantial and also provide the basis of money-market arrangements.

The 'permanent' building societies are similar to building societies in the United Kingdom; they operate primarily to finance the purchase of housing by owner-occupiers, though they also provide a limited amount of finance for commercial residential development. They operate on a State basis (subject to State legislation) and are generally organised as cooperative non-profit institutions – only a small number are established on a conventional corporate basis. In recent years, there have been a considerable number of mergers among these societies, mostly larger societies taking over smaller and less viable societies, but quite a number of large mergers as well. These societies draw the great bulk of their funds from the household sector, but also accept moneys from the small business sector and, in some instances, operate in the money markets. Latterly, they have moved into providing cash management-type facilities. They developed rapidly after the mid-1960s in meeting a largely unsatisfied demand for housing finance. Today they would hold 6-7 per cent of total assets of financial institutions. So-called 'terminating' building societies (granting loans on concessional terms to eligible low-income borrowers, which are funded by borrowing from other intermediaries against a State government guarantee or from a State government agency) are relatively unimportant.

Credit cooperatives (credit unions), although small (1½ per cent of total financial assets), are one of the most rapidly growing financial institutions and have made a significant impact on the personal market, particularly by providing alternative payments services.

Pastoral finance companies deserve a mention, since they provide a range of quasi-banking services mainly to rural business, their financing operations being principally ancillary to their traditional activities as wool brokers, retail traders, and stock and property agents. Finance provided by the pastoral companies is mainly for working capital, including seasonal requirements. For some customers, they also provide a demand order facility similar to a cheque account. They are no longer an important source of rural finance. There are in all about 15 company groups, of which the two largest control about half the total assets and another three (say) a further 25 per cent. Two of the larger companies are wholly foreign-owned; others are partially owned overseas. Some of the larger pastoral finance houses have substantial equity interests in merchant banks and finance companies.

Life-insurance offices have always been important in Australia. By the early 1970s, they held some 15 per cent of the total assets of all financial institutions, but latterly this fell to about 10 per cent. The reasons are complex – high inflation, rising interest rates, and the termination of long-standing tax privileges have reduced the relative attractiveness of life insurance compared with investment (say) in housing and short-term higher-yielding fixed-interest claims. Their significance in Australian financial markets remains their role as mobilisers of long-term household savings traditionally in conjunction with the provision of death cover. The industry is closely associated with the management of private pension and superannuation funds. Life-insurance-administered funds account for about half of all assets controlled by private superannuation funds. Separately constituted superannuation funds, together with public pension and superannuation funds, would account for another 8 per cent of total assets of financial institutions and general insurance for a further 5 per cent, invested primarily in marketable securities and liquid assets.

One of the most striking facts about Australian banking development was the small number of bank failures. In part, this was a function of the relatively small number of banks established. In all, some 60 commercial (or trading) banks have been founded in Australia at various times. Of these, some 40 disappeared as a result of purchase or amalgamation and only 15 actually failed. The fact that more banks were not established is no doubt a reflection partly of the early development of branch banking but also in the country's earlier years of the relatively limited availability of economic resources and the consequently restricted rate of population growth. For example, as compared with the United States, a country of similar size but much greater wealth, there never was the same inducement in Australia to found a large number of local banks and, therefore, less risk that a 'unit-banking' system would long survive, especially in the absence of legislation that might otherwise have encouraged it.

Papua New Guinea

Formerly, Papua New Guinea was an Australian trustee territory; over a period of many years, it had also had strong economic and financial links with the Commonwealth of Australia. Australian trading banks operated in Papua New Guinea, partly to finance the range of Australian business interests that had developed there. The Reserve Bank of Australia was represented in Port Moresby, the territory's capital and, at a relatively early stage, set up a Department under Dr. P. W. E. Curtin at its Head Office in Sydney with a view to exploring the changes that would be necessary following independence.

In March 1971, 'the Select Committee on Constitutional Development of the Papua New Guinea House of Assembly recommended that steps be taken to prepare Papua New Guinea for internal self-government. The Australian Minister for External Territories considered banking an area in which the recommendations of the Select Committee should be applied.' Accordingly, in September 1971, 'the Minister for External Territories in cooperation with the Australian Treasurer established the Committee on Banking in Papua New Guinea with representatives from the Department of External Territories (Chairman), the Commonwealth Treasury, the Reserve Bank of Australia and and Papua New Guinea Administration.'

The Committee's terms of reference were broadly defined. *Inter alia*, it was to:

(i) 'advise on a banking framework appropriate to self-government and independence, giving special attention to the part which Australian, overseas and Papua New Guinean institutions should play';
(ii) 'make recommendations as to the lines along which the Papua New Guinean banking system should be developed over the ensuing few years'; and
(iii) 'make recommendations on the nature and the timing of the various steps for setting up an appropriate banking system in Papua New Guinea'.

The Committee completed its preliminary report in March 1972. Its recommendations were endorsed in principle first by the Australian Government and later by the Government of Papua New Guinea. In particular, it recommended that:

(i) the Papua New Guinean authorities be given the power to license, control and supervise banks and other financial institutions conducting business in Papua New Guinea;

(ii) a Central Bank be established based on the Port Moresby office of the Reserve Bank of Australia;
(iii) the existing private commercial banks be allowed to continue their operations with appropriate changes in structure and procedures, subject to any conditions imposed by the government; and
(iv) the question of allowing the entry of new overseas banks (other than from Australia) into Papua New Guinea be left open.

Almost all the recommendations put forward by the Committee were accepted and subsequently implemented. The Reserve Bank of Australia's Port Moresby office was converted into the nation's central bank on 1 November 1973 and became known as the Bank of Papua New Guinea. In April 1974, the Papua New Guinea Banking Corporation was established and took over most of the Papua New Guinean assets of the Commonwealth Trading Bank of Australia, although the latter continued to operate a small branch in Port Moresby until September 1982. The original capital of the Papua New Guinea Banking Corporation came from an Australian government grant; latterly, it has been supplemented by the building up of reserves. A new Papua New Guinea currency was introduced on 19 April 1975, the currency units being the Kina and Toea. For a period, the country maintained a dual currency system, with the Kina trading at parity to the Australian dollar. On 1 January 1976, Papua New Guinean currency became the only legal tender within the country. Since May 1977, the exchange rate for the Kina has been set daily with reference to a basket of currencies of Papua New Guinea's major trading partners.[35]

Currently, the commercial banks operating in Papua New Guinea are comprised of one nationally-owned enterprise, three Australian-based banks and two new banks, which began operations in 1983 and are 51 per cent owned by local interests each in collaboration with a non-Australian overseas bank. The banks now trading in Papua New Guinea are as follows:

(i) Papua New Guinea Banking Corporation (wholly government-owned);
(ii) Westpac Bank – PNG – Limited (a subsidiary of Westpac Banking Corporation, Sydney, Australia, formerly Bank of New South Wales);
(iii) Bank of South Pacific Limited (a subsidiary of National

Australia Bank Group, Melbourne, Australia);

(iv) Australia and New Zealand Banking Group (PNG) Limited (a subsidiary of ANZ Banking Group Limited, Melbourne, Australia);

(v) Indosuez Niugini Bank Limited (an affiliate of Banque de l'Indochine et de Suez, Paris, France); and

(vi) Niugini-Lloyds International Bank Limited (an affiliate of Lloyds Bank International, London).

The two new Papua New Guinean banks have a 51 per cent local ownership compared with 10-15 per cent among the several Australian banks. It was also thought that these new banks would increase competition, which hopefully would lead to greater efficiency and lower costs. It was felt, too, that the two overseas parents already had extensive and varied experience in developing countries and that this would enable them to introduce new services and procedures. The new arrangements would also add to the country's financial contacts overseas. Both the new banks were required to establish branches outside Port Moresby within three years of their first operations (e.g., at places like Lae, Goroka, or Mount Hagen). Banks must now be licensed.

As it happens, following the Australian tradition, all of the established banks already had developed networks of branches. The Papua New Guinea Banking Corporation took over the branches of the Commonwealth Trading Bank and added to them. It has developed a wider coverage than any of the other banks, partly because it is government-owned and can therefore undertake to open more 'pioneer' offices. It has more sub-branches than the other banks and now has 223 agencies. Westpac also has a good coverage, though fewer sub-branches and agencies. All the main towns are covered, including those on the offshore islands of New Britain, New Ireland and Bougainville. The branches and sub-branches are supplemented by a variety of agencies, the more important of which are bank-staffed, the remainder being special agencies which cater for an installation like a power station, a business unit – like a large plantation company, printing works, or a brewery – or a tertiary educational establishment or schools. As at the end of 1983, there were 57 bank branches, 36 sub-branches, 383 agencies of various kinds all serving the public in Papua New Guinea (see Table 2.1). Central bank permission is necessary to open or close branches.

The usual range of banking business is undertaken by the commercial banks in Papua New Guinea. Deposits are accepted in current

Table 2.1: Bank Branches and Agencies, Papua New Guinea

	Bank	Branches	Sub-Branches	Agencies
December 1983	PNGBC	20	28	223
	BNSW*	16	7	134
	BSP	7	1	17
	ANZ	8	—	9
	ISN	4	–	–
	N-LI	2	–	–
	Total	57	36	383
December 1976	PNGBC	14	13	196
	BNSW	14	2	68
	BSP	6	–	22
	ANZ	6	–	–
	Total	40	15	286

Source: Bank of Papua New Guinea
*now Westpac

account and at term; savings facilities are also offered. Capital ratios exceed what is required. Liquid assets include cash and balances with the Bank of Papua New Guinea (the central bank), Treasury bills,[36] which since September 1981 are auctioned on a monthly basis, and short-dated government securities.[37] There is a minimum liquid-asset requirement, which may be varied by the central bank. Both deposits and bank liquidity tend to be quite variable, because of the country's exposure to sharp swings in its balance of payments stemming, in large part, from variations in world prices for its major exports – gold, copper, coffee, and cocoa. For example, the banking system was very liquid up to 1980 – embarrassingly so in some years from the point of view of the Central Bank. Subsequently, there have been times when the banks have been very much less liquid and operating to a lower liquid-asset requirement. The bulk of the banks' assets consists of loans and advances, much of it by way of overdraft, with limits reviewed at least annually. The Australian-based banks also use the 'fully drawn advance' (as in Australia)[38] for hard-core borrowing. The banks also discount trade bills to a limited extent. Personal loans are likewise made (e.g., to finance the purchase of automobiles, house improvements, or as small business loans).

Another group of institutions which have been in existence for a number of years are the savings and loan societies. They really derive from the situation as it was in 1949, when village economies were swamped with war-reparations money (e.g., in respect of damage to coconut trees) and the government needed to find some means of mopping it up. The legislative basis was the Native Economic Development Act of 1951, which aimed to foster village business. Very wide powers were given to a Registrar; although there was no mention of cooperation at that time, cooperatives began to be set up in the coastal areas, buying copra and establishing trade stores. Cooperative officers were appointed to assist and religious missions also provided honorary advice. District associations of village societies were established (acting as wholesalers – latterly, importing direct from overseas – and bankers). The movement grew apace and arrangements became more complex. Under the same Act, rural progress societies were set up, sponsored by the Department of Agriculture; crops such as peanuts, coffee and cocoa, and rice (in the Sepik area) were encouraged. But the old Act was no longer broad enough and, in 1965, a new Cooperatives Act was passed, incorporating a list of cooperative principles. It was about this time, too, that the Highlands were being opened up and numerous coffee societies were being formed. There was considerable prosperity; some societies became relatively rich and began to diversify. Further legislative adjustments were made (e.g., The Business Groups Act 1974 and a new Division V of the Companies Act in 1976), which made it possible to accommodate customary law. On these bases, the cooperative movement has achieved a degree of stability in recent years. The Societies are now the responsibility of the Registry of Savings and Loan Societies, for which the Bank of Papua New Guinea has assumed responsibility.

At the end of 1983, there were 114 savings and loan societies (there were over 100 in mid-1976), though new societies are occasionally established. Membership has risen from less than 90,000 at the end of 1976 to nearly 107,000 in mid-1983 (and it has been higher). Total assets (made up of cash at bank, loans to members – the largest item[39] – investments, and fixed assets) were K12.7 million at the end of 1976, K58.6 million at the end of June 1983. Members are mostly farmers, traders, public servants (they have their own societies)[40] and the funds derive from their savings, on which interest is paid. Some accounts – possibly 10 per cent of the total – are dormant (no deposits, no withdrawals). Some members are illiterate but operate an account on the basis of a photograph and a key word. To supplement their funds, savings and loan societies may borrow from their own Federation of Savings and Loan Societies; excess deposits may well be held either with their Federation or with a commercial bank. The General Reserve

Fund is invested on a term basis with the Federation.

Several finance companies have also been established – the first in the 1960s and early 1970s. Initially, they were concerned with hire-purchase and instalment-credit business. This has now tended to stabilise. Latterly, the finance companies also entered the field of leasing and this has greatly expanded. At the end of 1983, the net value of total leasing agreements outstanding stood at K25.3 million, whereas the total balance outstanding on all non-leasing loans was only K4.2 million. Unsecured deposits are the major source of funding for finance companies. The majority of these deposits were of a short-term nature. Only one company has engaged in a public debenture issue. As at the end of 1983, there were five finance companies operating in Papua New Guinea, of which three were relatively large.

In order to supplement the lending of the commercial banks – and more particularly to provide loan assistance to Papuan New Guineans – the Papua New Guinea Development Bank was established in 1967, six years before internal self-government in October 1973 (full independence came on 16 September 1975.) It was originally capitalised by a grant from the Australian government to the government of Papua New Guinea (a grant in aid). It has also attracted finance from international organisations like the International Development Association and the Asian Development Bank; the government does the borrowing and the moneys are on-lent to the Bank. Since the Development Bank is 100 per cent government-owned, the government must be prepared to absorb any losses. Lending to customers may be to provide working capital (to pay for labour, seeds, and fertiliser) or for capital equipment (tractors or cultivators), or to purchase pigs and poultry with access to a processing and distribution plant; finance may also be provided to cover contingencies. Some cattle loans have been made. Other ventures that have been financed are oil palm small-holdings grouped around a factory, the purchase of trucks (on a hire-purchase basis), garages, trade stores (both the building and the stock), hotels and property loans (with a mortgage as security) and industrial buildings (again against a mortgage). Even village handicrafts may be financed. Where appropriate, progressive drawings are monitored by the Bank. Since security may not be easy to obtain – much property consists of clan land, when there is no individual ownership – quite a high proportion of loans will be unsecured. Alternatively, a character reference, even a personal guarantee may be given (e.g., by a chief) or a charge may be taken (e.g., over stock) or a mortgage as indicated. Loan commitments for agriculture, forestry and fishing make up approximately

60 per cent of new approvals; transport, storage and communications 12 per cent, manufacturing 9 per cent, and commerce about 7 per cent. Total loans outstanding at the end of September 1983 were K50 million. The Bank operates through a number of branches and agencies throughout the country.

A development of some importance was the establishment of a merchant bank in December 1979. It was felt by the authorities that the existing commercial banks were not able to supply the full range of financial services that business enterprises in Papua New Guinea would increasingly require in the future. The kind of thing that would be needed included advice on corporate investment decisions, feasibility studies for new business undertakings, advice on mergers and acquisitions, the underwriting of new shares, locating equity partners for joint ventures, and advice on offshore and domestic sources of funds. Hence the setting up of the country's first merchant bank – Resources and Investment Finance Limited owned equally by the Hong Kong and Shanghai Banking Corporation, the Commonwealth Trading Bank of Australia, and the Papua New Guinea Banking Corporation. It was designated as an authorised dealer in the short-term money market on 15 August 1980. 'Its main operations are local and offshore lending, project finance, leasing, money market operations, corporate financial services, portfolio investment, equity investment and underwriting.'[41] It has managed issues of shares by the two new banks and it has been authorised as a dealer in government securities. It may accept deposits from the public. These amounted at the end of June 1983 to K11.0 million; loans were then at K6.0 million.

In a developing country such as Papua New Guinea, financial institutions face a number of special problems. Firstly, there is 'localisation' – the progressive employment in the banks of native Papuan New Guineans (nationals). This has been favoured by the banks and (by number of staff) local participation now exceeds 80 per cent. The banks seek out suitably qualified and experienced nationals for appointment as branch managers, but in this respect they have been handicapped by the rather high rate of national staff turnover. Unless they can hold national staff for a sufficient period of time, it will be difficult to 'localise' more senior positions. Secondly, as in many developing countries, the banks tend to be criticised for not lending with sufficient freedom to nationals.[42] Even if such loans are approved, rates of interest may be thought to be relatively high. A key difficulty is security, which may be difficult to obtain if, for example, clan land is involved. Part of the problem may be resolved by subsidising interest rates (government carrying the difference between market rates and the concessionary rate charged to the borrower). The question of security can be partially resolved by the Credit Guarantee Loan Scheme, which has existed in Papua New Guinea since 1976 with a view to assisting Papuan New Guinean nationals.[43] Under this scheme, the Papua New Guinea government guarantees 80 per cent of loans from the commercial banks to local business groups, loans which would not have been available if normal bank-lending criteria had been applied. There is a similar Housing Loan Guarantee Scheme to ensure some housing-loan availability in rural areas, though in fact the major housing problems are in urban centres.[44]

Two other schemes have greatly assisted economic development. The Village Economic Development Fund was established in early 1974, but no longer operates. The scheme basically aimed at providing financing assistance to small-scale and, preferably, village-based rural-development activities with a maximum capital requirement of approximately K125,000. In order to obtain funds under this scheme, a group was required to raise 20 per cent of the total amount required. Another 40 per cent of the funds were granted under this scheme and the remaining 40 per cent borrowed from the Papua New Guinea Development Bank. The National Investors' Scheme has been designed to assist Papua New Guinea business groups wishing to initiate large-scale commercial projects with costs exceeding K125,000. This scheme is operated by the National Investment and Development Authority and assists national investors by providing funds for feasibility studies and by lending for projects on an unsecured basis, thus complementing commercial financing. It also provides technical and financing advice on subjects such as management and how to approach banks for loan finance. Including loans under the several credit-guarantee schemes, the commercial banks were by November 1983 making over 50 per cent of their loans to companies with majority Papua New Guinea ownership.

New Zealand

A country with a rather similar banking history to Australia, though the distances are much shorter, is New Zealand and, indeed, several of the banks that have traded in New Zealand have been Australian in origin. In other ways, too, there are similarities in the institutional developments in the two countries.

Today, New Zealand is served by four trading banks, each with a developed system of branches. The largest of these banks is the Bank of New Zealand, which is wholly government-owned. The remainder are private trading banks – Westpac Banking Corporation, ANZ Banking Group (New Zealand) Ltd, and the National Bank of New Zealand. The first two are partly foreign- and partly domestically-owned,[45] the third being wholly-owned by Lloyds Bank PLC, London. All the trading banks have savings bank subsidiaries,[46] which compete directly with the twelve trustee savings banks (the largest of which are in Auckland and Christchurch) and the Post Office Savings Bank, a subsidiary of the wholly government-owned Post Office, which is not quite as large as all the trustee savings banks put together. The trading banks provide a full range of banking services. However, in the provision of personal-sector facilities, the savings banks are becoming increasingly competitive *vis-à-vis* the trading banks. By 1974, the trustee savings banks and Post Office Savings Bank were permitted to offer personal cheque account services[47] and private savings banks may likewise now offer these services. None the less, the emphasis of savings-bank services is still on personal savings and transactions (e.g., the financing of house purchase), though the trustee savings banks are steadily expanding into commercial business. Some provide loans to farmers and small businesses.[48]

A third major institutional category is the large finance company group, which provides 'near-banking' facilities. Some of them also have subsidiaries which deal in the short-term money market and now have licences to deal in foreign exchange. Altogether, there are about 250 finance companies, of which (say) 24 are large and do 80-90 per cent of the business. Trading banks have interests in some of them. Originally, the emphasis was on hire-purchase finance, but nowdays they do a lot of industrial financing, including leasing. The large finance companies mainly accept deposits on a term basis, but their subsidiaries offer a range of services based on short-term funds and moneys placed at call. Since 1974, the activities of the finance companies have shown rapid growth. As total deposits, debentures, and notes of large finance companies are approximately equal to Post Office Savings Bank deposits, they represent a significant competitive factor.

In the early 1970s, the government allowed certain overseas banks to take up an interest in merchant banks; these are now majority share holdings. The merchant banks were instrumental in extending the commercial bill market, which until early 1978 was effectively closed to the trading banks. The bulk of the bills is accommodation bills, but there are also some trade bills.

Some of these bills are held by money-market houses as well, but in order to encourage the development of the latter the authorities appointed 27 specialised government-securities dealers, including the trading banks and certain money-market dealers. Formerly, they got their supplies of government securities from the Reserve Bank, which sold direct to them and the dealers then sold them on retail, mainly to banks. In 1983, a new tendering system was introduced, whereby financial institutions obtain their holdings of government securities by tendering at six- to eight-week intervals. Specialised dealers have limited continuing direct access to the Reserve Bank, but otherwise obtain their portfolio requirements by tendering for paper or purchasing it on the secondary market. Only a small amount of government securities is held by the non-bank sector – to a limited extent by non-financial corporations,[49] but they are not large holders.

There were two types of building societies in New Zealand: terminating societies, which allocated loans out of subscribed funds on the basis of a ballot (their growth had been steady but not spectacular); and permanent building societies, which accepted deposits and issued debentures, lending these moneys out to finance house purchase. Following a review of building-society legislation in 1980, new business is now effectively based on the permanent-society approach. The top three account for about 75 per cent of total assets and amalgamations have already given some societies a national coverage.

Stock and station agents also provide quasi-banking services for the agricultural sector; however, this business is no longer growing significantly. Although primarily lending for seasonal purposes, such agents can get locked into long-term debt (e.g., due to bad seasons). In recent years, they have been subject to regulations which effectively prevented them from competing for deposits and debentures and this forced them to resort to bank-overdraft facilities to fund activities.

Of the life-insurance offices, some are mutuals; all of them necessarily tend to invest long-term against future commitments. Like the trading banks, the savings banks, and the building societies, a proportion of the life-insurance offices' resources has to be invested in government securities – in the case of life-insurance offices 31 per cent, of which 11 per cent can be held in local-government securities. They are also subject to directives requiring them to invest in housing and farming.

Other groups, which at times may have an important role to play in the transfer of financial surpluses throughout the economy, include solicitors' nominee companies, trustee companies, friendly societies, and credit unions. Solicitors and solicitors' nominee companies, for example, are estimated to provide between 10 and 15 per cent of all housing mortgages registered, through their management of trusts, estates, and clients' finances. The role and significance of these various groups have varied widely over recent times, largely as a reflection of the constraints imposed on the mainstream institutions' ability to compete. Over the early part of the 1970s and again after June 1982, these financial intermediaries on the periphery of New Zealand's financial system provided an increasingly large proportion of loan finance due to interest-rate controls on the mainstream financial institutions, which prevented them from attracting sufficient deposits to match the demand for loan finance that they were then experiencing.

There are in addition a number of government institutions (apart from the Post Office Savings Bank) that provide loan finance for particular sectors of the community. Although on the whole they do not compete directly with the various deposit-accepting institutions already mentioned, the size of their operations clearly has an indirect impact on the private-sector institutions' ability to attract deposits via paper issued on the private market, in order to provide additional funding in excess of that obtained from the Public Account. The most important of the government institutions is the Housing Corporation, but also significant are the Development Finance Corporation (which does obtain funds directly from the New Zealand public and also borrows offshore in its own right), the National Provident Fund, and the Rural Banking and Finance Corporation.[50]

Canada

Another interesting contrast to the 'unit-banking' system that grew up in the United States is the branch-banking system that has been evolved in Canada. Indeed, one might have expected that the northern neighbour of the United States would perhaps have been fairly directly influenced by developments across the border, but in the matter of banking structure such trans-border influence as there has been has if anything run the other way. For example, in States like California, where branch banking has for long been permitted on a State-wide basis, American banks have in the past imported bankers from Canada to teach them how to organise a banking business based on a network of branches.

The reasons for Canada adopting a branch banking system are fourfold. Firstly, their bankers looked, over a period of many years, to

Scottish traditions for their inspiration – even early American influence in the matter of bank charters[51] reflected Scottish and English influence at one remove, since the promoters were themselves guided by British experience.[52] Secondly, there was a geographic factor somewhat similar to that obtaining in Australia – not only were the distances in Canada also quite considerable, but it, too, was thinly populated, with a rate of population growth very much lower than that in the United States, reflecting the greater difficulty of developing the then known economic resources. Branch banking was a means of bringing the capital and facilities of a city institution to remote towns and villages and of lending the surplus financial resources of one area to another where the local provision was less adequate. In addition, it was possible to diversify lending risks and to avoid the difficulties that might arise if a bank was dependent upon business in only one locality. Thirdly, Scottish influence was also responsible for the use of branches to put notes into circulation. It was likewise a means whereby lending activities could be financed in excess of deposits received and without being limited by the amount of specie available:

> The country was only sparsely settled, natural resources were largely undeveloped and, compared with recent times, money was exceedingly scarce. It meant a great deal to all concerned, therefore, that each bank was able to issue notes as required to the extent of its paid-up capital. At comparatively small expense. . . the notes provided till money for branches and enabled the banks to operate a greater number than would otherwise have been possible. It also enabled them to expand their loans to move the crops and to assist in the marketing of other products.[53]

Finally, there were no specific legal restrictions on branch development. Although there was no express provision in the early bank charters in Lower Canada authorising the establishment of branches, neither was there any express prohibition and the banks concerned assumed that the general powers of the directors included authority to establish branches and they acted accordingly. On the other hand, specific authority to establish branches was granted from the beginning in the charter given to the Bank of Upper Canada.

Prior to the 1800s, the only 'banking' business done in British North America was as an extension of the granting of commercial credit by local merchants. The first real bank was established in Montreal in 1817 (the same year as the Bank of New South Wales in Australia). Having failed in their earlier attempts to obtain a charter, the promoters established a private corporation at that time entitled The Montreal Bank. Subsequently, in 1822, an Act was proclaimed by the Province of Lower Canada granting a charter to 'the President, Directors and Company of the Bank of Montreal' and, although the Bank of New Brunswick received its charter in 1820, the Bank of Montreal is in fact accepted as Canada's first bank. Three other banks began operations in 1822 – the Bank of Canada, Montreal; the Quebec Bank, Quebec; and the Bank of Upper Canada, York (afterwards Toronto). In Nova Scotia, after failing to obtain a charter (rejected chiefly because it wanted a monopoly), the Halifax Banking Company was also organised as a private corporation and began to operate in 1825, but, in 1832, a charter was granted to another group which founded the Bank of Nova Scotia.

Subsequent to the granting of these early bank charters and prior to Confederation, a number of other banks received charters from the provincial governments and, in two instances, where most of the shareholders and directors were resident in Great Britain, from the government of the United Kingdom. All these charters followed much the same general pattern, with a usual life of ten years, though as new and renewal charters were granted the opportunity was taken to introduce such changes as experience suggested were necessary to strengthen the banks and to afford better protection to the public. In this matter, pressure was exerted from London, the Provinces being given to understand in 1834 that 'no further Acts relating to banking would receive the royal assent unless they conformed to regulations for colonial bank charters adopted in 1830 by the Committee of the Privy Council for Trade.'[54]

After Confederation under the British North America Act 1867, the Parliament of Canada was given exclusive legislative authority in all matters pertaining to currency and coinage, banking, incorporation of banks, and the issue of paper money. However, in the initial proposals that were put forward as the basis of general banking legislation, it was actually proposed to abandon the system of branch banking and to encourage the establishment of small independent county banks as in the United States. The Toronto banks, in particular, fought this proposal with all the strength they could muster and forced the Government to reconsider the position and, in the Bank Act 1871, the principle of branch banking was accepted, laying the foundations for the spread of networks of bank branches right across the country.[55]

At that time, there were 19 chartered banks in Canada enumerated in a schedule to the new Bank Act and provision was made for other institutions, if they so desired, to apply to the Treasury Board for a charter. The Bank Act was subject to revision every ten years and the charters granted under it also had to be renewed on each such occasion. In 1900, the government of the day offered to make bank charters perpetual but the banks, after a full discussion, preferred to retain the existing system, because they

> believed it to be in the public interest that the whole question of banking should be discussed generally by the banks and the Government at least once in every ten years, in order that a review of the past might be made with a view to improvements for the future, and in order that the system might be made as far as possible continuously suitable to the growing requirements of the country.[56]

At the time of Confederation, there were 28 banks in the Provinces of Canada, New Brunswick, and Nova Scotia.[57] Of these, 19 were in the Province of Canada – nine in Montreal and three in Toronto – and as many as eight in the Maritime Provinces. Indeed, by the early 1870s, some 20 banks were operating in the Maritimes, all but two being 'native' banks.

Until 1885, when the peak number of 41 banks was reached, there was a fairly steady growth in the number of banking corporations in Canada, interrupted only by brief periods of recession. From 1886 onwards, however, there was a steady decline in the number of chartered banks, which reached ten by 1928. A new charter was issued in 1953 – to the Mercantile Bank of Canada – and this temporarily raised the total to 11. Subsequently, in 1955, the Toronto Bank and the Dominion Bank amalgamated,[58] and Barclays (Canada) Limited was taken over by the Imperial Bank of Canada in 1956 (with Barclays group holding an interest in the latter) and, in 1961, the Canadian Bank of Commerce merged with the Imperial to form the Canadian Imperial Bank of Commerce. In September 1963, the First National City Bank of New York bought up a controlling interest in the Mercantile Bank. Despite the advantages of size, there has still been room in the Canadian system for small banks. Thus, in 1968, the Bank of British Columbia was established to serve the interests of western Canada with 35 branches in British Columbia and ten in Alberta. In 1976, charters were also issued to two wholesale banks in Alberta – Northland Bank (based in Calgary) and Canadian Commercial Bank (Edmonton) in order to take advantage of the rapid economic growth of this province based on oil and gas. Meanwhile, there were two banks largely operating in the Province of Quebec and nearby Ontario – the Banque Provinciale du Canada and Banque Canadienne Nationale; they merged to form the National Bank of Canada in 1979; again, size was important (e.g., larger capital, especially important in the Euro-currency markets, and the economies of scale) and there was much scope for rationalisation (closing duplicate branches and cutting staff). Latterly, too, branches have been opened up across the country and the bank is now represented in all ten Provinces and overseas. None the less, the bulk of its branches are still located in the Province of Quebec and to a much lesser extent in Ontario. It is the sixth largest domestically-owned chartered bank in Canada, of which there are now 14, with over 7,000 branches. There are also 58 foreign bank subsidiaries.

In addition to their commercial-banking activities, the chartered banks also operate as savings banks, but the two aspects of their business are fully integrated; no segregation of assets is attempted in relation to current accounts or savings deposits. In Montreal, there is the Montreal City and District Savings Bank incorporated under the Quebec Savings Bank Act.

In Quebec also there is the ***Fédération des Caisses Populaires Desjardins*** (at Lévis), with over 1,500 ***caisses populaires***, themselves formed into ten regional unions, which have been federated; its size, wide spread of its business, which now comprehends most of what a commercial bank can do (including credit cards) and its closely knit organisation give it a unique importance. Elsewhere in Canada, credit unions are quite strong; there are about 2,400 across the country, and at their apex is the Canadian Cooperative Credit Society; their assets amount to about one-fifth of those of the banks, with a sizeable interest in personal loan business (about 15 per cent of the total market and about 10 per cent of mortgage loans).

For many years, foreign banks were not permitted to operate branches in Canada, though a number had representative offices. New regulatory legislation was passed in 1980, which permitted the setting up of subsidiaries. Under the new law, each foreign-owned bank was allotted a so-called 'deemed authorised capital' and its Canadian assets for prudential reasons were not initially to exceed twenty times that amount; Canadian and international assets were not to exceed twenty times each foreign-owned bank's capital and reserves; and collectively foreign-owned banks were initially not permitted to book more than 8 per cent of the domestic business booked by the entire Canadian banking system (since raised to 16 per cent). Subsequently, the 'deemed' capital was increased for some 22 of the 58 foreign banks, including certain of the newcomers. Criteria for any such increase was 'need' as measured by the size of the applicant's portfolio and also the nature of its business. Certain banks also found the initial 8 per cent ceiling too restrictive. In addition, the deductibility of interest charges may be lost if a foreign-owned bank borrows more than a certain amount from its parent abroad. In 1984, countries whose banks operated subsidiaries in Canada included the United States of America (19 banks), Japan (seven), the United Kingdom (six), France (five), Switzerland (three), and West Germany and Israel (two each). There is a feeling among some Canadian bankers that the authorities should be more liberal with regard to foreign banks operating in Canada, given the extent to which Canadian banks themselves operate abroad. For the big foreign banks, the emphasis of much of their business has been wholesale banking, but a number has also sought 'middle-market' business. 'Ethnic banks' (e.g., from countries like Greece, Israel, Italy, Korea, and Hong Kong) have tended to concentrate on retail banking, opening branches among their communities from whom they attract deposits and handle the remittance of funds to the home country.

Another category of deposit-taking institutions that is of importance in Canada is the trust and loan companies. They were originally founded in the second half of the nineteenth century to perform trustee and executor functions and grew into deposit-taking institutions, which with their associated mortgage and loans companies gradually moved into banking activities proper. Latterly, there have been proposals to permit them to make commercial loans and to compete more or less directly with the chartered banks. They have long offered deposit and savings accounts, cheque facilities, and personal loans and some commercial loans on the basis of industrial mortgages. The seven largest companies control about 85 per cent of the trust business and more than 70 per cent of the deposits. Although it is proposed to give them greater flexibility, they are still subject to restrictions that do not apply to banks; on the other hand, banks may not undertake trust business, which has become something of a growth area in contrast to mortgage lending which is declining (as a result of an ageing population and a more restrictive immigration policy).

Of total assets of financial institutions, the chartered banks hold about 45 per cent; trust and mortgage loan companies (excluding those associated with chartered banks) 13 per cent; life-insurance companies, 11.5 per cent; pension funds, over 14 per cent; and sales-finance companies, 4.5 per cent.

At one time or another since Confederation, there have been over 70 banks in existence in Canada – 26 of these disappeared as a result of insolvencies or liquidations (five of the latter were voluntary), the business of two of the banks that failed being taken over by other banks; and 35 were absorbed by other banks and lost their identities by amalgamation. Half of the failures occurred in the 1870s and 1880s – four each in 1879 and 1887. There were only three in the 1890s, but eight between 1905 and 1914, of which three were in 1908.[59] The last failure – Home Bank – was in 1923. There were no failures of Canadian banks during the Great Depression of the 1930s, in striking contrast to the situation across the border in the United States.

On the other hand, amalgamations prior to 1900 were quite few – one in 1868, two in the 1870s, and one in 1883. Between 1900 and 1914, however, 18 banks were absorbed by other banks (13 of these took place between 1905 and 1914, which was also a period with a relatively high incidence of bank failures), and the combined effects of failure and amalgamation, followed by 12 more mergers between 1917 and 1931 (seven of which were in the 1920s) did much to eliminate the remaining weaknesses in the Canadian banking system.

It is not surprising that bank mergers should have been few and far between prior to 1900, since it was impossible to proceed without a special Act of Parliament. However, under the Bank Act 1900, banks could be merged, upon agreement between the banks concerned, with the approval of the Governor-in-Council on the recommendation of the Treasury Board. Under the 1913 revisions of the Bank Act, it was further provided that a bank might not enter into an agreement with another bank to sell its assets until the Minister of Finance had given his consent in writing.

An analysis of the amalgamations that have taken place reveals another interesting fact, namely, how active all the big banks of today were in building up their positions by means of amalgamation. Thus, the Bank of Montreal and the Canadian Bank of Commerce were each concerned in seven of the amalgamations, the Royal Bank of Canada with five, the Bank of Nova Scotia with four, and the Imperial Bank of Canada (which was to absorb Barclays and later to merge with the Canadian Bank of Commerce) with two.

In most cases, these mergers were of a small bank of a more or less local character with a larger one developing country-wide ramifications.

Usually the smaller bank had reached a stage where, if it was to make further progress and be able to retain certain of its larger

> customers, it would be necessary to expand its operations. Rather than incur the risk that this would entail, it preferred to negotiate with a larger bank to which its branch organisation and business would prove desirable acquisitions. In other cases the smaller bank had perhaps run into difficulties and was finding it hard to earn sufficient to make necessary appropriations for losses and maintain its dividend. In still other cases a larger bank was able to make an offer which even a sound and prosperous smaller bank could not very well refuse.[60]

Because of the distribution of population and therefore of banks the bulk of these amalgamations affected institutions in Ontario and Quebec (13 and 7 respectively), but collectively the Maritimes accounted for nineteen, which was itself a reflection of the initiative and enterprise that had been shown there over the years in establishing banking institutions.

The only group of banks that up to 1979 stood outside the main stream of amalgamation were the French-Canadian banks, the interests of which were primarily concentrated in Quebec Province, though in that area they built up a very strong regional business.

Indeed, this was true of most Canadian banks during their earlier years, when they tended to restrict their operations to their own Province. This was not remarkable, since several of them began their careers under provincial charters and only developed wider business connections after Confederation. Furthermore, as we have seen, amalgamation was somewhat difficult prior to the relaxations in the law in 1900. Initially, the banks had sought to build up their business over a wider area by opening branches, first in contiguous districts and, later still, in cities and towns further afield.[61]

Progress was steady but not spectacular and the number of bank branches, which was about 120 at the time of Confederation, had only grown to 400 by 1889, and to just over 700 by 1900. However, Canada's Western boom from 1900 to 1914 provided a considerable impetus and, by 1914, the number of branches had increased to about 3,000. This required a considerable recruitment of manpower. Some of it was found locally, but much of it was imported from Scotland by inviting applications from young employees of banks there.[62]

During World War I, scarcely any new branches were opened by the Canadian banks, but following the Armistice, branch expansion was again resumed and, by 1920, there were 4,676. However, subsequent experience showed that many branches had been opened in places where business was insufficient to justify them. By 1926, the number of branches had been reduced to 3,770. The trend was again reversed to reach 4,081 by the end of 1930, but in 1931, a real effort was made to eliminate unprofitable branches and, by 1939, the figure had been reduced to 3,320. Further reductions were effected during World War II, but, during the post-war years, numbers again expanded and they now stand at over 7,000. In particular, competition was active in extending branches to the suburbs of the main cities in order to attract deposits and to make personal and even mortgage loans. 'Indeed, the banks went out to the shopping centres and the suburbs in an effort both to retain their share of savings deposits, and to participate in the newer and profitable forms of lending to households.'[63]

South Africa

For many years, virtually nowhere else in the world – apart from Soviet-type institutions – was there such a highly concentrated banking system as in South Africa, though this position has become somewhat modified in more recent years as a result of the policy consciously pursued by the authorities in encouraging the growth of the smaller and 'indigenous' banks. Formerly, something like 90 per cent of total liabilities to the public within the Union was held by the two big banks, both with head offices in London. Because of the growth of local banks and other institutions,[64] the dominance of the two big banks – the Standard Bank of South Africa and Barclays Bank D.C.O. (now Barclays National Bank Ltd) – which existed in 1948[65] is now rather less marked and their share of the commercial banks' total liabilities to the public has dropped significantly. None the less, of the 11 commercial banks, four – Barclays, Nedbank, Standard, and Volkskas – hold 90 per cent of total bank deposits and maintain a country-wide network of branches (1336 out of 1660). Through their respective groups, each of them provides a comprehensive range of services.[66]

The first bank to be established in South Africa was the Bank van Leening (or Lombard Bank), which from 1793 to 1837 operated virtually as a government banking monopoly until South Africa's first privately owned bank – the Cape of Good Hope Bank – was set up. Within the next two years, two other private banks had been established and, by 1862, the number had risen to 28. But this emphasis on small-scale local banking was not to last very long. In 1861, the London and South African Bank had been founded and in the following year the Standard Bank of South Africa was established. As a matter of conscious policy, these two so-called 'imperial banks' (and especially the Standard) set out to effect the consolidation of the South African banking system by themselves absorbing the local banks. Not unnaturally, there was local opposition to overcome, but this was directed not so much against the principle of amalgamation as against the 'imperial' character and the external affiliations of the new banks. However, amalgamation and insolvency had by the time of Union (1909) reduced the number of banks to seven and, shortly afterwards, two of these amalgamated with the National Bank of South Africa. In 1917, when the Banks Act came into force, five commercial banks were in operation: African Banking Corporation Ltd; National Bank of South Africa Ltd; Netherlands Bank of South Africa; Standard Bank of South Africa Ltd; and Stellenbosch District Bank Ltd. Of these, the African Banking Corporation amalgamated with the Standard Bank in 1920 and the National Bank merged with Barclays (D.C. & O.) in 1926.[67] But certain other institutions, not originally recognised as commercial banks under the Act, also carried on a banking business. One of these – Volkskas Beperk – began to operate as a commercial bank in 1941 and was registered as a commercial bank under the 1942 Act. There are also several institutions operating either subsidiaries or branches of foreign banks.

It was not doubted that this consolidation of the banking system had assisted it to secure a wider spread of risks and considerably strengthened its ability to withstand financial crises, but whether such a high degree of concentration was a good thing was felt to be a much more open question. Thus, as at 30 September 1947, of the total commercial bank assets in the Union, the Standard Bank 'held 47.5 per cent, Barclays Bank 45.6 per cent, Volkskas 3.5 per cent, the Netherlands Bank 3.2 per cent, and the Stellenbosch District Bank 0.3 per cent. The two big banks between them held about 95 per cent of all demand deposits, about 86 per cent of discounts, about 85 per cent of loans and advances and about 96 per cent of investments.[68]

The main fear seems to have been the extent to which this high degree of concentration would have the effect of restricting competition. Thus, in 1928, Dr E.H.D. Arndt, later to become Registrar of Banks and subsequently Deputy Governor of the Reserve Bank, wrote: 'These banks [i.e. Barclays, the Netherlands and the Standard banks] work in close co-operation with one another in the fixing of discount, exchange and interest rates', though he did add: 'There is no doubt scope for a certain amount of competition in the form of services and credit terms, since the discount rates agreed upon are minimum rates to which only a small percentage of customers are entitled.'[69]

Apart from an increase in the proportion of customers that were by then charged minmum rates on advances, the Social and Economic Planning Council thought these observations still to be valid in 1947. Within the limits imposed by 'agreements and understandings' there was still a good deal of competition, but it was obviously felt that there might be more, so that commercial banking services might be made available to the public on as economical a basis as possible. Furthermore, it seems to have been suspected that 'the concentration of banking business includes also a concentration of financial power such as might conceivably be exercised in a manner detrimental to the national interests'.[70] The authorities themselves seemed to have accepted this view and to the extent that it has been possible to encourage the growth of the smaller institutions and to increase the number of registered commercial banks, they have done so.

As a concomitant of this high degree of concentration, there was also quite a remarkable growth of branch banking. Thus, by 1914, there were already nearly 500 commercial bank branches and agencies in the Union. By 1946, there were over 800, by 1959 about 1,500; in 1983, there were 1,660.

There have been periods when it would seem that the banks have been rather too eager to open new branches and these have been followed by a reduction in the number of offices. For example, between 1921 and 1925, the two largest banks decided to reduce the number of their branches from 876 to 602, partly because of 'the extraordinary losses suffered in some instances'[71] and Dr Arndt argued in favour of the Registrar of Banks (which he was later to become) being given power to regulate both the opening of new branches and the closing of those already in existence. Evidence was also given by Dr M.H. de Kock (the then Deputy Governor of the Reserve Bank) before the Select Committee on Banking Legislation suggesting that about one-third of the branches of the Barclays and Standard banks did not pay.[72] It was appreciated, however, that any such statement must be received with caution, since in a branch-banking system the allocation of costs between branches is of necessity highly arbitrary.

Apart from the commercial banks and the discount houses (which will not be discussed here), other categories of institutions that provide financial services include the 24 'general banks' (already briefly referred to), which comprehend a variety of activities such as savings banks, finance companies, industrial banking (hire-purchase), trust and executor business; the 10 merchant banks (*inter alia* acceptance credits, discounting trade bills, cash advances, factoring, leasing, export/import finance, international issues, underwriting, corporate advice – e.g., on stock exchange listings, mergers and acquisitions – and portfolio management – e.g., for pension funds); they also deal in money- and capital-market instruments and in foreign exchange; insurance companies; and mutual funds (unit trusts). Many of these institutions fall within the control of the main banking groups. Other institutions that are more independent are the building societies and the Land Bank, to which more detailed consideration will now be given.

The first 'permanent' building society was established in South Africa in 1874. After the commercial banks and the long-term insurers, the building-society movement is now the third largest group of financial institutions in South Africa. Eleven building societies operate in South Africa and one in South West Africa. At the end of 1981, total assets amounted to R13.8 billion, compared with total assets of R19.5 billion for the commercial banks, R15.0 billion for long-term insurers, R11.3 billion for private pension and provident funds, and R11.6 billion for general banks. In comparison with other large financial institutions, the building societies had shown the fastest rate of growth between the end of 1946 and the end of 1960, by which time building societies, in terms of total assets, had outgrown the commercial banks and had become the largest single group of financial institutions in South Africa. However, during the subsequent two decades, the building societies lost some ground to the commercial banks and other newly established banking institutions, such as merchant banks and general banks, as well as to contractual savings institutions, such as long-term insurers and private pension and provident funds (see Table 2.2).[73]

The function of the building societies is to mobilise small savings for the purpose of granting mortgage loans against the security of urban residential property. The movement is the source of over 80 per cent of all private residential mortgage finance, the remainder being met mainly by life-insurance companies, pension funds, and employers. The liabilities of the building societies comprise mostly various classes of deposits and shares, while assets consist largely of mortgage loans and prescribed investments (see Table 2.3).[74] In addition to the intake of new funds, capital repayments on existing mortgages are an important source of funds for the building societies.

The building-society movement has experienced considerable difficulty in recent years, because of its inability to attract sufficient deposits in the increasingly competitive savings market at a time when

Table 2.2: Total Assets of Selected Groups of Financial Institutions, South Africa

	1946		1960		1981		Growth rate*
	Rm	%	Rm	%	Rm	%	1960-81
Building societies	331	20.7	1,297	28.1	13,816	18.3	11.9
Commercial banks	712	44.4	1,252	27.1	19,487	25.8	14.0
General banks	46	2.9	253	5.5	11,616	15.4	20.0
Merchant banks	–	–	76	1.6	1,589	2.1	15.6
Government savings schemes†	237	14.8	252	5.5	2,659	3.5	11.9
Long-term insurers	276	17.2	963	20.9	15,031	19.9	14.0
Private pension and provident funds	–	–	521	11.3	11,316	15.0	15.8
Total	1,602	100.0	4,614	100.0	75,514	100.0	14.2

*Compound annual rate
†Post Office Savings Bank, National Savings Certificates and Treasury bonds.

Table 2.3: Asset Structure of Building Societies, South Africa

	1946[1]		1960[2]		1970[2]		1981[2]	
	Rm	%	Rm	%	Rm	%	Rm	%
Cash and deposits	8	2.8	25	1.9	226	7.4	1,124	8.2
Government securities	32	11.3	53	4.1	112	3.6	288	2.1
Other securities[3]	16	5.7	135	10.4	156	5.1	571	4.1
Sub-total	56	19.8	213	16.4	494	16.1	1,983	14.4
Mortgage loans	218	77.3	1,024	79.0	2,397	78.0	11,085	80.2
Loans against shares and deposits	1	0.4	8	0.6	60	2.0	417	3.0
Fixed property[4]	7	2.5	51	3.9	101	3.3	324	2.3
Other assets	–	–	2	0.1	20	0.6	8	0.1
Total assets	282	100.0	1,298	100.0	3,072	100.0	13.817	100.0

Notes: 1. 31 March. 2. 31 December. 3. Mostly semi-gilt-edged securities. 4. Including investment in property development subsidiaries.

the demand for house mortgages has been increasing following a sharp rise in the value of residential property.

Because the mortgage bond rate has been a sensitive issue in South African politics, the building societies have not been able to raise their lending rate fully to compensate for the rising costs of their deposits. Nevertheless, the mortgage bond rate rose to a record level along with the sharp rise in the whole structure of South African interest rates following the monetary authorities' shift to a more market-related monetary policy.

In March 1983, the Minister of Finance announced that following reports of two commissions of inquiry into building society matters[75] the government had agreed that building societies would gradually be subjected to similar disciplines as banking institutions. These disciplines would eventually include the same cash reserve and liquid asset requirements as those for banks. Since building societies have to compete with banks and other financial institutions for deposits, it has also been agreed that building societies will not only be permitted, but also encouraged, to quote market-related borrowing and lending rates. To ensure the effective implementation of these measures the present instruments through which building societies attract deposits will be phased out and replaced with a system by which government will pay a direct interest rate subsidy to mortgagors who qualify for a subsidy.[76]

Finally, a word about the Land and Agricultural Bank (the Land Bank). This was established by statute in 1912. The bank provides various types of farm credit – mortgage loans to assist in the purchase of fixed property, charge loans to finance improvements to property (e.g., irrigation or electricity), and short-term loans to meet seasonal requirements.

By the end of the 1982 harvest season the outstanding loans of commercial banks to the Land Bank amounted to R2,680m and accounted for more than 40 per cent of banks' total liquid assets. Because these loans rank as liquid assets for the commercial banks and therefore increase their overall ability to lend, a high level of borrowing by the Land Bank frustrates the implementation of monetary policy. During 1982 the structure of Land Bank borrowing from the commercial banks was adjusted to take greater account of the higher level of interest rates.[77]

The severe drought of 1982-3 put a great strain on the finances of the agricultural sector and farmers were allowed either to stretch repayments of their carry-over debt with the farming cooperatives over a six-year period or to have that debt consolidated into the bonds over their farms. This option would allow repayment over a period of 20 years.

Republic of Ireland

There are four Associated Banks in the Republic of Ireland, two of which are much larger than the others. The two major banks are Allied Irish Banks Limited and The Governor and Company of the Bank of Ireland (Bank of Ireland); the other two, which are rather smaller, are both based in Northern Ireland – Northern Bank Limited (a subsidiary of Midland Bank from 1965) and Ulster Bank Limited (which since 1917 has been a subsidiary of what eventually became National Westminster). They operate 668 branches throughout the Republic of Ireland, plus 277 sub-offices; in addition, they are represented in Northern Ireland (275 branches) and in two cases – Allied Irish Bank Limited and the Bank of Ireland – by retail branches in Great Britain (35 and 26 respectively). Previously, there were eight Associated Banks as designated in the Central Bank Act 1942, which gave them a special relationship with the Central Bank. Six of them were organised in two domestically-controlled groups, which were amalgamated in 1966 into the two major groups of today. Thus, the Munster and Leinster Bank Limited, the Provincial Bank of Ireland Limited, and the Royal Bank of Ireland Limited amalgamated to form Allied Irish Banks Limited; and the Bank of Ireland purchased the National Bank Limited, having already acquired the Hibernian Bank Limited, in 1958. These amalgamations were followed by a period of tremendous growth and development. In retrospect, too, Ireland's entry into the European Monetary System (EMS) and abandoning the historical parity with sterling were events of similar significance. The latter greatly extended the foreign side of banking business in Ireland with the rapid development of foreign exchange rooms to meet the needs of an economy half of whose trade was conducted in what had now become a foreign currency. There was also the need for forward cover and a related expertise, and foreign borrowings suddenly became big business for the Irish Banks, particularly in Deutschmarks. All the banks suffered the impact of recession and the incidence of bad debts depleted profits. One of the Northern Ireland banks – Northern Bank – which had financed its business in the Republic on the basis of sterling, made heavy foreign-exchange losses. Leasing developed very rapidly and this, and preference-share and tax-sheltered borrowings (called Section 84 after the relevant part of the Corporation Tax Act), became popular with industry because of its mixture of grants and tax incentives.[78]

Until the 1960s, the range of specialist financial facilities available in Ireland was somewhat restricted. Then came a rapid development of the economy and a demand during the 1960s for additional banking services. Apart from the amalgamations referred to above, there was the arrival of the North American banks; the establishment of merchant banking, industrial banking, and a number of other banking subsidiaries by the Associated Banks; the emergence of new financial markets; and a further development of the role of the Central Bank in regulating credit and the banking system.[79]

The non-Associated Banks are comprised of several groups. For the most part, they are located in Dublin and do not have a network of branches throughout the country. They collect deposits both from within the country and quite substantially from foreign sources. They also undertake types of financial activity rather different from that of the Associated Banks. Their current account business is relatively small.

The first group of non-Associated Banks consists of the merchant banks, of which there are now seven. Four are subsidiaries of Associated Banks, three of London merchant banks. Normally, they accept only large deposits (I£50,000 or more). Their loans are tailored to each customer's requirements, sometimes taking the form of a set amount for a given period; sometimes, the loan will be geared to the cash-flow expectations of the customer. Rates of interest charged tend to be related fairly closely to the current marginal cost of funds in the money markets – rather more than in the case of the Associated Banks. Other specialised financial facilities that they offer include advice on methods of financing and on mergers and takeovers; they also manage portfolios on behalf of large investors such as pension funds.[80] For liquidity purposes, they tend to hold short-term assets rather than cash and place their liquid balances in Dublin, thereby assisting greatly in the development of an inter-bank market, from which at times they also borrow quite substantially. The merchant-bank sector has been growing fast. Of this market, the Big Two – Allied Irish Investment Bank Limited and The Investment Bank of Ireland Limited – have a market share of over 60 per cent, with a further 25 per cent going to the investment subsidiaries of the Ulster and Northern Banks.

The second group of these banks consists of the five North American banks. The first of these arrived in 1965. The reasons for these institutions coming to Ireland was either to follow or to anticipate the location in Ireland of corporate customers, many of them branches of

American firms; they also sensed the development that was about to take place in Ireland and a market for the kind of services they could offer. In some respects, their activities are somewhat similar to those of the merchant banks, but they compete more closely than the latter with the Associated Banks in providing a full commercial banking service, somewhat assisted by the occasions when the Associated Banks were closed down by labour disputes.[81] More generally, domestic lending substantially exceeds their domestic resources, the difference being financed externally, resulting in large inflows of capital. Like the merchant banks, the American banks have also been major participants in the development of the Dublin inter-bank market, though more as takers than as suppliers of funds.

The third category consists of eleven industrial banks; they are mainly concerned with instalment credit. Originally, they concentrated on hire-purchase, principally to finance consumer durables. Latterly, the three largest industrial banks which are subsidiaries of Associated Banks, have moved into industrial loans, export/import finance, equipment leasing, finance for industrial building, bridging loans, company finance, block discounting, and the financing of contracts. Nevertheless, a considerable part of their total instalment credit outstanding is to finance consumer items. Substantial funds are attracted from abroad.

Other banks include seven subsidiaries of foreign banks (other than North American banks) out of a total of 16 'other' Irish licensed banks. Some of the 'other banks' are essentially merchant banks.

There is a number of state-owned financial institutions. The Post Office Savings Bank (operating mainly through post offices) has some 1,400 branches throughout the country. The bulk of its business is the provision of time deposit facilities, but withdrawals on demand up to I£50 per day are permitted. A current-account service is provided by the four trustee savings banks. Funds accruing to the Post Office Savings Bank and the Trustee Savings Banks are made available to the Minister for Finance. Then there is the Agricultural Credit Corporation Limited, which provides capital to finance agricultural development. Its liabilities consist mainly of deposits from the public, funds supplied by the exchequer, and borrowing abroad. These funds are lent out as indicated. The Industrial Credit Company Limited operates as an industrial development bank and provides capital for industry by way of medium- and long-term loans, direct share investment, industrial hire-purchase, and leasing facilities. The bulk of the Company's resources comes from the Ministry of Finance either as share investment or repayable advances; it may also accept deposits and resort to some foreign borrowing, with the European Investment Bank funding a growing proportion of its lending.

Building societies are an important part of the financial sector in Ireland. They are the largest single providers of mortgage finance for housing in Ireland, providing approximately three-quarters of what is available. Their assets are primarily long-term, but this is based on short-term liabilities in the form of shares and deposits. Of the 16 building societies, only five are relatively large. The larger societies have branches in most of the bigger urban areas.

In addition, a large number of insurance companies do business in the Republic of Ireland (66 in all, 11 of them Irish-controlled). Twenty-four are life-assurance companies, while the remainder engage in various classes of general insurance. Life-assurance companies are important collectors of savings – premiums normally exceed substantially what must be paid out each year against claims or matured policies. In general insurance, claims and expenses each year more or less equal total receipts. Much of the funds available are invested in Ireland and the assurance companies are of increasing importance in Irish financial markets.

Since the early 1960s, credit unions have grown very rapidly in the Republic of Ireland. The latest official figure (31 December 1983) was 379. As at 31 December 1982, the number of members was estimated to be 446,000. Unofficial estimates put the value of total shares and deposits in the Republic at I£160 million (at 31 December 1982).

Although not licensed banks, hire-purchase finance companies, of which there are approximately 30, in common with the industrial banks extend instalment credit, but in the case of the hire-purchase finance companies this is their main business. Their resources are derived mostly from loans made to them by their own banking affiliates or from the non-Associated Banks; they are prohibited from accepting deposits from the public.

Notes

1. Indeed, it was not until 1946 that this system was formally ended, and the designation of the banks' local representatives was altered from 'agent' to 'manager'.

2. 'Its advantage to the bank lay in the intimate knowledge of the inhabitants and their business which the local man, like the old private banker, might be assumed to possess and the business which he might draw to a newly opened branch. The disadvantages lay in the part-time nature of the agent's services, his lack of knowledge of banking routine, and the discouragement of the staff

recruited as apprentices in the closing to them of many of the higher appointments.' F.S. Taylor, 'Banking in Scotland' being *Scottish Banking Practice no. 1* (Institute of Bankers in Scotland, Edinburgh, 1949), pp. 54-5.

3. However, under the Bank Notes (Scotland) Act 1845, the banks in Scotland lost their previous rights to issue notes without limit.

4. See T.E. Gregory, *The Westminster Bank Through a Century* (London, 1936); vol. 1, pp. 200-14.

5. It was this failure that revealed the grave dangers of unlimited liability. Any squeamishness that remained was relieved by introducing the principle of 'reserved liability', whereby the unpaid portion of bank shares having limited liability was divided into two parts, one being callable at the discretion of the directors and the other only in the event of winding up (see W.F. Crick and J.E. Wadsworth, *A Hundred Years of Joint Stock Banking* (London, 1936) pp. 33-4.) The general adoption of limited liability was also to be an indirect means of accelerating the amalgamation process. With limited liability, it became necessary to publish an annual balance sheet. The unwillingness of certain of the provincial banks to register with limited liability placed them at something of a disadvantage *vis-à-vis* their more progressive rivals, since it was felt that only those who were prepared to demonstrate their strength by publishing a balance sheet could be truly strong. Shares of banks with unlimited liability tended to decline and those institutions that the market deemed to be weaker were steadily forced to surrender their identities by amalgamation with banks that had chosen limited liability and its attendant publicity (ibid., pp. 34 and 310).

6. See T.E. Gregory, *The Westminster Bank*, pp. 190-1.

7. Crick and Wadsworth, *Joint Stock Banking*, p. 41.

8. Ibid. The firm of Fox, Fowler and Co. of Wellington, Somerset was absorbed by Lloyds Bank in 1921.

9. See R.S. Sayers, *Lloyds Bank in the History of English Banking* (Oxford, 1957), p. 274.

10. Williams & Glyn's was formed in 1969 and took over on 25 September 1970 the business of Glyn, Mills & Co., Williams Deacon's Bank and the National Bank. The first two had been subsidiaries of the Royal Bank of Scotland. The National Bank had been a public company until 1966, when it was acquired by National Commercial Bank of Scotland, having first sold its Irish business to the Bank of Ireland. The three banks fell under common ownership when their Scottish parents merged in 1968. The enlarged group was reorganised so that the merged Royal Bank of Sotland and Williams & Glyn's each became a subsidiary of a common holding company, National and Commercial Banking Group (see *The London Clearing Banks*, Evidence by the Committee of London Clearing Bankers to the Committee to Review the Functioning of Financial Institutions, November 1977). For further details relating to some of these mergers, see Maxwell Gaskin, *The Scottish Banks* (London, 1965) pp. 21-46.

11. See *Financial Times*, 31 January 1985.

12. See *The Times*, 18 June 1983.

13. See *The Times*, 4 August 1983.

14. S.J. Butlin, *Foundations of the Australian Monetary System, 1788-1851* (Melbourne, 1953), p. 10.

15. See Geoffrey Blainey, *Gold and Paper – A History of the National Bank of Australasia Limited* (Melbourne, 1958), p. 2.

16. Butlin, *Foundations*, p. 11.

17. Ibid., p. 244.

18. See A.G.L. Mackay, *The Australian Banking and Credit System* (London, 1931), Appendix VIII, pp. 245-6.

19. *Yearbook Australia 1983*, no. 67, p. 565.

20. See Blainey, *Gold and Paper*, pp. 35-7.
21. Ibid., p. 250.
22. Ibid., p. 38.
23. Butlin, *Foundations*, p. 287.
24. Blainey, *Gold and Paper*,p. 94.
25. Butlin, *Foundations*, p. 288.
26. See R.F. Holder, *Bank of New South Wales – A History*, Volume I: 1817-1893 (Sydney, 1970), pp. 189ff. Many of the early branches were associated with the growth of the goldmining industry. For later developments, see pp. 266ff.
27. See Butlin, *Foundations*, p. 396.
28. In 1955, it also took over one of the two remaining small local banks, the Ballarat Banking Company in Victoria.
29. For a discussion of the degree to which the trading banks developed specialised business interests, see H.W. Arndt, *The Australian Trading Banks*, 1st edn (Melbourne, 1957), pp. 18-24.
30. For a summary of its history, see R.F. Holder, 'Australia' in W.F. Crick (ed.), *Commonwealth Banking Systems* (Oxford, 1965). It has now been announced that the Australian government plans to make the Commonwealth Savings Bank a wholly-owned subsidiary of the Commonwealth Trading Bank and to rename the trading bank the Commonwealth Bank of Australia. In addition, the capital position of the new bank will be supplemented by transferring A$75 million in Commonwealth Development Bank reserves to the restructured bank. Presumably, the Commonwealth Development Bank will be continued as a separate entity. (See *Financial Times*, 3 April 1984).
31. In 1976, ANZ Bank had transferred its domicile from England to Australia.
32. For many years, except for a very small number of foreign banks that had been established in Australia long ago, foreign banks were not permitted entry into Australia, though they could operate in a customer-liaison role on behalf of their parent bank through representative offices or subsidiaries (e.g., merchant banks, money-market subsidiaries, and finance companies). Whether there should be greater foreign participation and, in particular, the entry of new foreign banks, was discussed in the course of the Campbell Committee Inquiry (see Committee of Inquiry into the Australian Financial System, *Final Report* (September 1981), pp. 435-50) and was again referred to in the *Report of the Review Group* of the Australian Financial System, December 1983, pp. 66-85; the latter felt that, subject to certain limitations, 'additional foreign participation in banking . . . would be beneficial to the Australian community.' By September 1984 (see *Financial Times*, 11 September 1984), applications were being invited from foreign banks for an unspecified number of new banking licences. It was expected that there would be a significant amount of Australian participation, but, if the potential economic benefits were great enough, foreign ownership might exceed 50 per cent. It was expected that the new licences would be formally granted in early 1985. At the same time, a limited Australian banking licence was granted as a special case to the Bank of China, the Chinese foreign-trade bank.
33. However, State Bank of New South Wales now has a branch in the Australian Capital Territory.
34. As a result, ARDB now funds re-finance loans through ABERC to assist trading banks' provision of extended-term finance for Australian exports of capital goods and services.
35. See Ivan Gutai, 'Recent Developments in Papua New Guinea's Financial System', *Bank of Papua New Guinea Quarterly Economic Bulletin* (June 1983).
36. See E.B. Sukbat: 'Treasury Bills and the Government Securities Market', *Bank of Papua New Guinea Quarterly Economic Bulletin* (September 1980). Note

that the Bank of Papua New Guinea does not participate directly in the auctions but at auction times will subscribe to Treasury bills additional to those put on auction. The Bank acquires these bills at the common auction price and will sell them to the dealers between auctions and thus provide additional bills to the market.

37. Commercial banks and the new merchant bank have been nominated as government-securities dealers 'to encourage the development of an active market in Government Securities'.

38. These are more like a term loan. For details, see Chapter 6, p. 304-5.

39. Loans to members are mostly for building materials and tools, fencing wire, machines (e.g., coffee mills for grinding), buying poultry, debt consolidation, air fares and holidays, medical and funeral expenses, financing the buying of coffee, the purchasing of trade store goods (a big item), or for buying vehicles (another big item). If it is a large loan, security will be taken (e.g., a mortgage over land and buildings, bill of sale for vehicles or machines). Some loans may be for up to five years. Delinquency ratios tend to be high (e.g., 30 per cent), but loss ratios are very much lower.

40. Some of the largest societies are urban-based.

41. *Bank of Papua New Guinea Quarterly Economic Bulletin* (June 1983).

42. However, PNGBC, the largest bank with 50 per cent of all deposits and loans, explicitly discriminates *in favour of* national borrowers. So does the Development Bank, which now lends *only* to PNG nationals.

43. The Papua New Guinea Banking Corporation was in the scheme from the beginning (January 1976); the scheme was only extended to the other local banks in October 1979.

44. See Paul M. Dickie, 'Commercial Banking in Papua New Guinea's Development', *Bank of Papua New Guinea Quarterly Economic Bulletin* (March 1981).

45. The New Zealand operations of Westpac are organised as a branch operation of the Australian parent bank. Some Westpac shares are held by New Zealand interests but not because of any regulatory requirement that a proportion of shares should be made available. The ANZ Bank operation is in the form of a subsidiary-company operation with 25 per cent of the shares held by New Zealand interests.

46. A new Private Savings Banks Act has now been passed. It provides for private savings banks to offer cheque accounts on their own behalf.

47. And from 1979, overdraft facilities to a limited extent.

48. There is also a Public Service Investment Society, which runs retail shops and a savings-bank business; it may also make a range of loans, mainly in the fields of housing and consumer durables.

49. There are a few multinationals in New Zealand, but the bulk of business firms is medium-sized, even small.

50. For a useful survey of the non-bank financial institutions, see 'Non-Bank Financial Institutions – the Market for Long Term Funds', *Reserve Bank of New Zealand Bulletin* (October 1978).

51. The earliest charters granted in Lower Canada were modelled on those largely prepared by Alexander Hamilton for the Bank of New York (1784) and the First Bank of the United States (1791).

52. The first bank to receive a charter in what was to become Canada was in fact the Bank of New Brunswick, the charter of which was not influenced by those drawn up by Hamilton. Banking in New Brunswick developed independently, but 'with strong American influence of its own, particularly from the New England States. Indeed, it could scarcely be otherwise in view of the Loyalist origins of many of the Saint John merchants and legal community, and the many remaining strong family ties with relatives in the States, particularly Massa-

chusetts, which made for much coming and going between the two areas. At the same time, commercial relations were close with Boston and New York and, in the then state of communications, practically non-existent with Montreal.' (See 'Canada's First Chartered Bank', *Bank of Nova Scotia Monthly Review* (May 1956).)

53. A.B. Jamieson, *Chartered Banking in Canada* (Toronto, 1953), pp. 162-3.

54. Ibid., pp. 6-7.

55. See Joseph Schull, *100 Years of Banking in Canada – A History of the Toronto-Dominion Bank* (Toronto, 1958), pp. 34-7.

56. Quoted in Jamieson, *Chartered Banking*, p. 34.

57. Newfoundland, Prince Edward Island, and British Columbia did not enter the Confederation at this time. In Newfoundland and Prince Edward Island, a few banks operated under local charters and, in British Columbia, two banks had been set up under charters granted by the United Kingdom.

58. This was the first amalgamation since 1931 and rather different in kind. Unlike some of the earlier mergers, which had been prompted by weaknesses in the banking system, the Toronto-Dominion Bank merger took place between two strong well-established institutions, in order to take advantage of the complementary character of their businesses and to secure better branch representation than would have been possible without both banks going to the considerable expense of opening up new branches.

59. In the case of most of the earlier failures, the deposits of the banks in question were much lower than the paid-up capital of the shareholders. See Jamieson, *Chartered Banking*, p. 370.

60. Ibid., p. 41.

61. The history of the Bank of Nova Scotia is interesting from this point of view. See *Bank of Nova Scotia Monthly Review* (August-September 1952).

62. In some of the older settlements of the West, private bankers were another source of men, and also provided premises. It was not uncommon for a chartered bank to extend its operations into one of the older settlements by taking over the business of a private banker and installing him as manager of the new branch. (See Jamieson, *Chartered Banking*, p. 36). This again reflected Scottish influence since it was in this way that the Scottish banks had recruited many of their own 'agents' in the early days of their branch expansion.

63. J. Douglas Gibson, 'Banking Since the War – a Story of Restricted Adjustment', *The Canadian Banker*, vol. 74, no. 4 (Winter 1967).

64. The 24 general banks (which include hire-purchase banks and savings banks), 10 merchant banks and 3 discount houses.

65. See Union of South Africa, Social and Economic Planning Council, *Central and Commercial Banking in South Africa*, report no. 12 (Pretoria, 1948), pp. 114-18.

66. For details of the various institutions, see The Registrar of Banks, *Thirty-Seventh Annual Report* (year ended 31 December 1982), Appendix 1.

67. Barclays Bank (Dominion, Colonial & Overseas) had its origins in the Colonial Bank, which was established in 1836 by Royal Charter for the purpose of carrying on banking business in the West Indies. It was re-incorporated with wider powers under the Colonial Bank Act of 1925 and, in the same year, the name was changed to Barclays Bank (Dominion, Colonial, & Overseas) on its acquiring the undertakings of the Anglo-Egyptian Bank Ltd and the National Bank of South Africa Ltd with a head office in London. Subsequently (in 1954), it became Barclays Bank D.C.O. and, in 1971, again changed its name to Barclays National Bank Ltd. See W.T. Newlyn, 'The Colonial Empire' in R.S. Sayers (ed.), *Banking in The British Commonwealth* (Oxford, 1952), p. 436. Furthermore, in 1973, it obtained a listing on the Johannesburg Stock Exchange to become a truly

South African bank, with its head office in Johannesburg. In 1951, the Netherlands Bank of South Africa, which was now to operate as the Nederlandse Bank van Suid-Afrika Beperk (from 1971, as Nedbank Ltd) had moved its head office (formerly in Amsterdam) initially to Pretoria and, from 1960, to Johannesburg. The Standard Bank of South Africa Ltd followed in 1961. The head office of Volkskas Beperk has remained throughout in Pretoria.

68. Social and Economic Planning Council, *Banking in South Africa*, pp. 114 and 232.

69. E.H.D. Arndt, *Banking and Currency Development in South Africa (1652-1927)* (Capetown, 1928), pp. 478-9. Actually, the cartel of South African commercial banks (the so-called Register of Cooperation) was not to be abolished finally until the end of February 1983 'following growing dissatisfaction with its provisions in Government circles, among the public and even among some of the banks themselves'. Termination of the cartel was expected to lead to increasingly fierce competition among the banks. (See *Financial Times*, 11 February 1983).

70. Social and Economic Planning Council, *Banking in South Africa*, p. 115. See also paras. 238-9, pp. 115-18.

71. E.H.D. Arndt, *Banking and Currency Development*, p. 481. Again, in 1941, reference was made to 'the present over-done branch development': see 'The Proposed New Banking Legislation', *South African Journal of Economics* (September 1941), p. 283. South African banking legislation prior to the Banking Act 1942and the content and interpretation of the Act itself is summarised in *First Annual Report of the Registrar of Banks* (period ended 30 June 1946), pp. 1-22.

72. Quoted in Social and Economic Planning Council, *Banking in South Africa*, p. 119.

73. See Second Interim Report of The Commission of Inquiry into the Monetary System and Monetary Policy in South Africa, *The Building Societies, the Financial Markets and Monetary Policy* (1982), Appendix A.

74. In terms of the Building Societies Act, building societies are required to hold a minimum amount of liquid assets and other prescribed investments. Prescribed investments, as defined for building societies, include 'liquid assets' and consist mostly of coin, bank notes, call loans and other deposits, Treasury and Land Bank bills, government stock, Land Bank debentures, and stock of and loans to local authorities and public corporations.

75. The de Kock Commission, which had been reviewing the South African financial system in general and the du Plessis Commission which was more specifically concerned with the work of the societies.

76. *South Africa: An Appraisal*, 2nd edn (The Nedbank Group, 1983), p. 109. For details of the de Kock Commission's recommendations with regard to building societies, see their Second Interim Report, Chapter 6.

77. *South Africa: An Appraisal*, pp. 106-7.

78. Under the provisions of the Finance Act 1984, the tax advantages previously available have been restricted to loans made to 'specified' borrowers (principally those engaged in the manufacture of goods; those trading within Shannon airport; services which are grant-aided under the Industrial Development Act 1981 and subsidiary companies of agricultural or fishery cooperatives). Certain loan obligations concluded prior to 25 January 1984 or then under negotiaation were exempted from this restriction. Similarly, the Finance Act 1984 imposed restrictions on the availability of capital allowances to lessors of machinery or plant.

79. See T.K. Whitaker, 'The Changing Face of Irish Banking', a paper delivered to the Manchester Statistical Society on 30 November 1971.

80. They manage some personal funds as well, since a number of people in

Ireland still have significant holdings of capital.

81. Between 1966 and 1976, labour disputes closed all the clearing banks on three occasions for a total period of nearly a year. The longest time was in 1970, when the dispute lasted six-and-a-half months. On the whole, however, Ireland survived without its large banks, because of the emergence of a 'highly personalised credit system without any definite time horizon for the eventual clearing of debits and credits substituted for the existing instutionalised bank system.' In effect, pubs and shops emerged as a substitute banking system; when the banks are closed for an indefinite period, the cheque is used as a medium of exchange. See Antoin E. Murphy, *Money in an Economy without Banks: the Case of Ireland* (The Manchester School of Economic and Social Studies, vol. 46 March 1978).

3 UNIT BANKING: THE EXPERIENCE OF THE USA

In direct contrast with those banking systems which consist of a relatively small number of commercial banks with widespread networks of branches centrally controlled, there is the so-called 'unit-banking' system of the United States, elements of which are also to be found in a number of other countries. American banking structure is something of a special case and it is therefore proposed to consider in some detail certain of the more important formative influences.

At first glance, it is perhaps rather surprising that bank organisation in the United States should be so very different from that of England. One would expect to find evidence of systems of behaviour imported from England both in matters of law and commercial practice. In some respects, such influences have undoubtedly been present. In the field of banking structure, however, it is not difficult to explain why evidence of direct English influence should be hard to find. First, the United States was already politically independent before the main structural changes in English banking had begun to take place. The Declaration of Independence was made in 1776 and the first commercial bank in the country was established in Philadelphia soon afterwards.[1] It was only in the second half of the nineteenth century that the amalgamation movement really got under way in England and that the banking structure began to assume the characteristics that today are taken for granted.

Secondly, in the United States, by reason of its diverse ethnic origins, British influences in the course of the years were considerably diluted in the wider stream of cultural inheritance. Because of this, it is frequently difficult to isolate the impact effects of any specific national influence. There was rather a ferment of ideas, which only gradually assumed a recognisable shape.

Thirdly, political freedom prompted intellectual freedom and this was evidenced in the banking field by discontinuities in the evolution of American institutions. There was much experiment. Some of these experiments failed; others succeeded. Many were notable for their originality and relative independence of banking traditions elsewhere. It was out of this welter of experience that an American banking system began to evolve.

Fourthly, the United States chose a federal form of government, with a constitution that permitted both federal and state legislatures to pass laws to regulate banking. A banking firm could therefore be subject to banking laws in its own State and to those passed by the Federal Congress. Moreover, in matters of commercial bank structure (e.g., permission to establish branches), the states were able to enforce their wishes, and of itself this cut right across the forces of integration operating on a national basis.

This was a very important factor indeed. The constitutional pattern reflected the dominant political philosophy in the country, but the choice of these constitutional arrangements obviously provided the legal framework that encouraged the establishment and retention of a large number of 'unit banks'. Nevertheless, the choice of federalism as a constitutional form need not have obstructed the working out of factors making for greater concentration of financial power. It was rather the division of powers within the federation that constituted the barrier. Thus, in Australia a federal form of constitution was also adopted (as it happened, modelled very largely on the constitution of the United States), but the federal government was accorded the exclusive power to legislate with respect to 'Banking, other than State banking; also State banking extending beyond the limits of the State concerned, the incorporation of banks, and the issue of paper money'. This permitted the passage of bank legislation of general applicability. In any event, branch banking has been restricted very little in Australia. Indeed, even before federation in 1900, the unifying process was already in evidence. The Australian states were then separate colonies, but their laws, though various in content were uniformly mild in the nature of the restrictions imposed on banking development.

Sufficient has been said to suggest some of the general reasons for the divergence between bank organisation in the United States and the type of structure that evolved in Britain. But how did a 'unit-banking' system come to be established in the United States and why was it retained over a long period without radical modification? In seeking an answer to these two related questions, a variety of factors has to be taken into account. Thus, at the outset, the facts of economic geography determined the general character of the social environment within which banks were established and began to grow. In addition to the economic aspects of environment, there were also, from the first, socio-political factors of at least equal importance.

The development of banking in the United States was moulded, first by the rapid opening up of the country during the nineteenth century, to a large extent by private enterprise, which was itself the product of a strong pioneering spirit; and secondly by a widespread distrust of monopoly and the deep-rooted fear that a 'money trust' might develop.

As the frontiers of settlement were pushed rapidly westwards, the scarcity of capital in relation to profitable opportunities for investment and development became increasingly apparent. There was both a heavy demand for loans and a chronic shortage of cash. The need for banks to supply credit and to issue notes to serve as a medium of exchange was obvious. To satisfy these demands, banks sprang up right across the country in small towns and large. At this stage, too, communications, especially at the frontiers of settlement and between the frontier and the established centres of finance and commerce, were still relatively undeveloped. The great river system that served the heart of the country could do much, but it was not until the railroads were well established that east-west traffic could expand rapidly. Moreover, the steady territorial expansion of the United States quickly converted it into a country of immense distances – almost 3,000 miles from east to west and about 1,600 miles from north to south. In these circumstances, one would expect a large number of banks to be established to serve the diverse and rapidly expanding needs of a growing and constantly migrating population. Furthermore, as long as communications remained imperfect, it was unlikely that banks could build up networks of branches, since effective supervision at a distance would be difficult to maintain.

This much was obvious. What required explanation was the subsequent failure of bank mergers or amalgamations to produce a concerted concentration of financial resources in the hands of larger banking units that served local needs through a network of branches.

The retention of a primarily 'unit-banking' system long after the barriers of distance had been broken down was partly due to constitutional factors – the choice of a federal system of government that left considerable powers in the hands of the states. It was also due in part to an underlying political philosophy that emphasised the virtues of individualism and free competition, while opposing any concentration of economic and financial power (though not always, it must be freely admitted, with any great degree of success). Certain states legislated to prohibit branch banking altogether, while many others considerably restricted its scope. This cut right across the possible evolution of a nationwide system of bank branches or even the development of branch systems on a regional basis.[2]

Nor was it merely a matter of state legislation. Such restrictions also became a feature of federal banking laws. The fact that those restrictions continued to be applied over so wide an area may be traced back to the basic fear of a 'money trust' that has characterised much American thinking over a long period. Indeed, in many parts of the country, this became a dominant political attitude, as witness the political strength of the so-called 'independent bankers'. A relatively recent manifestation of the extent of their influence was the passing of the Bank Holding Company Act of 1956, as amended. Bank mergers also remain a very lively topic of discussion in the United States and are regulated by the federal bank-supervisory agencies under the Bank Merger Acts of 1960 and 1966.

In the financial field, distrust of monopoly probably originated in the fear on the part of pioneering debtors of the entrenched moneyed interests of New York and the North-East generally. The American preferred to deal with his local banker, thereby maintaining (as he imagined) his independence of the large institutions of New York, Boston and Philadelphia. The local banker, though he often leaned heavily on his city correspondent both for out-of-town services and financial assistance, encouraged this belief in the virtues of independence, and state and federal legislatures respected it. Bank legislation was therefore framed to render difficult the growth of large banking units and to restrict somewhat narrowly the possible growth of branch systems. The administration of banking laws had a similar bias. Furthermore, except in those few cases where branches outside the head-office state had already been established, inter-state branch systems were definitely prohibited.

This was also the basis of the 'dual' character of American banking, whereby 'national banks' are chartered by the Federal Comptroller of the Currency (under the National Banking Acts of 1863 and 1864),[3] and state banks by their respective state banking authorities; banks do from time to time change from one type of charter to the other. The 'dual' system was also emphasised when central banking arrangements were set up in 1913. Only the national banks were required to be members of the Federal Reserve System; state banks were and are permitted to join if they so wish. Federal Reserve membership means that both national and state member banks are subject to the supervision of at least two authorities, since the Fed is not concerned merely with credit policy, but has important regulatory functions as well. At the end of 1983, 5,803 banks in the United States were members of the Federal Reserve System. Member banks accounted for 38 per cent of all commercial banks in the United States and for 64 per cent of commercial bank offices. Despite a tendency for membership to fall in the latter part of the 1970s, there has latterly again been a net increase in numbers, and it remains true that the more important banks in the country are all members. The vast majority of American banks – about 99 per cent – were covered by the Federal Deposit Insurance Corporation (FDIC), which insures the first $100,000 of each bank deposit.

The Board of Governors of the Federal Reserve System administers the Bank Holding Company Act, the Bank Merger Act, and the Change in Bank Control Act for state member banks and for all bank holding companies. In doing so, the Federal Reserve acts on a variety of proposals that directly or indirectly affect American banking structure at the local, regional, and national levels. The Board also has primary responsibility for regulating the international operations of domestic banking organisations and the American operations of foreign banks that engage in banking in the United States, either directly through a branch or agency or indirectly through a subsidiary commercial lending company. In addition, the Board has established regulations for the inter-state banking activities of these foreign banks and for foreign banks that control an American subsidiary commercial bank.

For the broad historical reasons outlined above, there are still quite a number of unit banks throughout the country. However, of a total of 59,050 bank offices at end-1983, 43,610 – almost 74 per cent – were branches. In December 1983,[4] there were 15,440 banks in the country. Of these, 393 were mutual savings banks. Of the 15,047 commercial banks and non-deposit trust companies, 5,803 were members of the Federal Reserve System (1,052 of these were state banks) and 8,666 were non-members. Member banks therefore accounted for about 40 per cent of the total. Also, as of December 1983, the domestic offices of member banks held 75 per cent of the assets of all insured domestic banking offices and about 71 per cent of total deposits. States with large numbers of non-member banks included Texas, Illinois, Missouri, Minnesota, Iowa, Wisconsin, and Kansas, but a number of others with fewer banks nevertheless had a high proportion of non-member banks.[5] 'Unit' banks, on the other hand, still numbered 8,034. They were particularly numerous in Texas and Illinois, followed by Minnesota, Kansas, and Colorado.

Most of the commercial banks are relatively small,[6] but some of them are very large indeed (e.g. Citibank of New York and the Bank of America which – despite its name – operates the vast majority of its branches within the state of California). The big banks are, of course, located in the larger financial centres, though many of the medium-sized banks (say $1 billion to $2.5 billion of assets) are located in centres of secondary importance.

Branch Banking

Not only are United States banking arrangements characterised by a large number of banks, but – despite some degree of relaxation over the years – there are still in some states restrictions on branch banking and therefore a large number of 'unit' banks. In addition to the states already listed, unit banks are also numerous in Oklahoma, Wisconsin, Nebraska, Missouri, and Iowa. Even in important branch-banking states like California and New York, unit banks are a significant percentage of the total number (nearly 43 per cent and 48 per cent respectively). It is because of this that one still talks of the existence of unit banking in the United States. However, such an emphasis must not be allowed to obscure both the great diversity of forms of bank organisation that obtains and the degree to which branch banking already exists. Indeed, banks in states which permit either state-wide or limited branching account for about 78 per cent of the nation's total domestic banking assets. The proximate reason for restrictions on branching was a legal one. But behind the legal restrictions there lay the long-standing opposition of powerful groups – such as the so-called 'independent bankers' – to large financial institutions as such. This was a rationalisation of the ingrained fear of monopoly and of money trusts that has permeated American society. One must also take into account the vastness of the country and the great diversity of economic activity. Such diversity is due in part to marked differences between the various regions into which the country is climatically divided, but in addition much variety is to be found even within a particular region. A bank with branches sufficient to span and adequately serve the whole country – or a large part of it – would be a giant indeed.

It is quite impossible to summarise adequately and briefly the vast mass of legislation that has been concerned over the years to regulate branch banking in the 50 states (in this matter, federal statutes defer to the laws of the individual states). Suffice it to say that in a number of states branch banking has been permitted for many years on a state-wide basis (it has also been permitted in the District of Columbia); in some states, it was permitted in limited areas, though there were various differences of definition in this respect; in other states, branches were specifically prohibited, though various ways of evading this prohibition were developed over the years and facilities were established that on some definitions could be regarded as 'branches'. In states where branches were specifically prohibited, but banks possessed branches at the time the laws were introduced, the general procedure was to 'freeze' the position as at that date. In some states, there were no laws relating to branch banking. It should also be noted that the extent of branch banking in a particular State was not determined merely by the restrictiveness (or otherwise) of the relevant laws; it was also influenced most directly by the interpretation of those laws. Furthermore, the authorities – state and, for national banks, the Federal Comptroller of the Currency – had the power to refuse applications for new branches (as well as new banks) if an area was already adequately provided with banking facilities; in order to establish the position, appropriate consultations and procedures were followed. If anything, the authorities tended to err on the side of conservatism and this often had the effect of confirming existing banks in their local monopolies or duopolies. The very measures that were calculated to maintain the competitiveness of banking not infrequently served to encourage the retention of monopolistic elements, confined though these may have been to the appropriate trading area of the banks concerned. However, both because of the liberalisation of the laws in a number of states and as a result of the ingenuity of bankers in developing facilities which evaded the strict letter of the law, itself permitted by a loosening interpretation of the relevant laws, branch banking had steadily spread throughout the United States and today, in terms of official statistics, there is no state that does not have some branches; whether it is a strong 'unit banking' state or not, sometimes the percentage of branches to total offices is quite small (e.g., in Wyoming, 3.5 per cent, in Texas and Colorado, about 16 per cent, in Oklahoma and Nebraska, 21 per cent and 23 per cent respectively); in other cases, the proportion of branches is of rising significance – Kansas 25 per cent, Minnesota 31 per cent, West Virginia 33 per cent, but Missouri 42 per cent, Iowa 45 per cent, and Wisconsin 46 per cent.[7] Over the years, the trend has been progressively upwards.

Also, there has been a steady build-up in the percentage of banks that operate branches – it was only 9.6 per cent at the end of 1950, 18.6 per cent in 1960, 30.4 per cent in 1970, and 47.4 per cent in 1980. The latest figure is for the end of 1983 – 48 per cent. As a concomitant, the number of branches has been increasing decade by decade, the relevant figures being 5,058 at the end of 1950 and 41,902 at the end of 1980 (by 1983, 43,610); in addition, the percentage of bank offices that are branches – 25.7 per cent at the end of 1950, 44.2 per cent by 1960, 61.8 per cent by 1970, and 73.2 per cent by 1980 (by 1983, 73.85 per cent) has been rising steadily. For many states, in absolute terms, the decade showing the most dramatic increases in branches[8] was 1970-80 (some 14 states), with some 12 states showing such growth over the two decades 1960-80. Latterly, in some states – eight in all, but most notably in New York – there has been a fall in the number of branches.[9] Over the years, the greatest number of branches has been in California and New York – California has long had branching state-wide and so, more recently, has New York. Between them, they had 9.5 per cent of total offices in 1950, 12.8 per cent in 1960, and 15.7 per cent in both 1970 and 1980, and 16.3 per cent by 1983. Other states with large numbers of branches are Pennsylvania, Ohio, and Michigan. New Jersey and North Carolina are also important. But only in California and New York is there anything comparable to the position in the United Kingdom. Another feature is that in a number of states – rather more than a dozen – banks operating branches would only average one or two branches per bank. Many of these are the former unit-banking states, including Illinois, Texas, Kansas, Minnesota, Missouri, Oklahoma, and West Virginia; furthermore, many of their 'branches' really remain only a facility attached to a unit bank. Very few branches are situated outside the head-office state, three of them in Portland, Seattle, and Tacoma belonging to a Californian bank, where the arrangements pre-dated the introduction of specific legislative requirements.[10]

The increasing importance of branches reflected to some extent the more liberal legislation in many states with regard to branching (or sometimes the more liberal interpretation of existing laws), but a more important factor was undoubtedly the stimulus given to banking growth some years ago both by the rapidly rising population and high levels of economic activity. In some cases, branch developments in particular parts of the country were encouraged by shifts of population (e.g., to California) and, in the case of the large cities, it became necessary to establish a large number of new offices (by no means all of them branches) in the 'neighbourhoods' or suburbs now increasingly served by shopping centres of their own. Indeed, many of the 'downtown' stores some years ago themselves had to establish branches in the 'dormitory areas' in order to retain business and 'neighbourhood' banks followed them.

Despite much opposition from 'independent' bankers and other defenders of American individualism, there has been a distinct tendency to develop 'multiple-office banking'. This conclusion is reinforced by the extent to which alternatives to branch banking proper were sought in areas where formerly the establishment of branches was either prohibited or restricted. Thus, states such as Arkansas, Iowa and North Dakota did not permit 'branches' as such, but they permitted 'offices', 'agencies', or 'stations' at which moneys might be deposited or cheques cashed. Again, in certain states, the banking authorities permitted banks to open a 'branch' by subterfuge. For example, a bank may have had a parking lot with a 'drive-in' nearby. There were also 'walk-up' windows. All these would be connected by pneumatic tube with the main office. In Missouri, the state banking authorities, supported by an 'opinion' from the Attorney-General, did not consider this to be a branch, because employees in the outside office had no discretion, the items being merely put into tubes and dealt with in the main office. A variation of this consisted of 'drive-in' arrangements which, although across the street, were connected by a tunnel with the main office and were therefore not treated as a branch by state banking authorities. The Federal Reserve, on the other hand, was more open about it and, in all these cases, such offices or facilities were classified as branches in its statistics.

Another alternative which has been employed – particularly, but not exclusively, where branching was prohibited – was 'banking by mail'. Thus, in Chicago, Illinois, where in earlier years the prohibition on branching was strictly enforced, banking by mail became fairly general amongst the larger banks, though it was not done by the very small banks, whose business was restricted to their own communities. The main purpose of banking-by-mail facilities was to attract deposits, competition for these being somewhat prejudiced by the absence of branches. The amount of business handled by mail could be quite considerable. For one Chicago bank, at that time, in terms of number of items, the business that came in by mail amounted to about 20 per cent of the total. Another technique that was employed in Chicago (and elsewhere) to supplement banking facilities was a resort to 'currency exchanges', which undertook much of the mechanical work of cashing cheques and provided a number of other facilities.[11]

In the context of branch banking, much of our concern has been with the views of the authorities, but the attitudes both of bankers and their public have also been highly relevant. Thus, in states where branch banking had either been prohibited or greatly restricted (e.g., Missouri and Illinois), it was clear from the evidence that attitudes were changing. Resort was made to referenda (e.g., in Missouri) and attempts were made to modify by statute the basic banking structure (Missouri) or – unsuccessfully for a time – to secure the passage of legislation which would permit branching (Illinois). The pressure for change built up in the 1960s[12] with a significant increase in branching in both Illinois and Missouri in the decade 1970-80 and, as we have seen, branch banking is generally now much more common than it was, though in 15 or 16 states the number of branches per bank remained quite small.

Group Banking[13]

Over a period of many years, one of the chief ways in which restrictions on branch banking were evaded was by building up banking groups. Group banking was not confined to states which prohibited or restricted branching, but in a large number of cases there could be little doubt that it was employed as a means of evading such prohibitions and restrictions. Latterly, too, it was the only way in which multiple-office banking could spread beyond the confines of a single state.[14]

Hence, a primary reason for the development of the bank holding company form of organisation in the United States was the historical dominance of unit banking. Where banks were denied branching by law, the formation of multibank holding companies provided banks with a means to expand beyond their local banking market. Generally speaking, banks in a group had a much greater degree of autonomy than would a branch, though there was a great deal of variation in this respect and in several instances the smaller group banks were treated almost like branches of a larger bank in the group. But whatever the emphasis in this respect, there were matters which clearly lent themselves to group action and, sometimes, to common policies. Certain of the holding companies felt that the more autonomy they left with the banks in their group, the stronger their management and local boards of directors were likely to be and that this would develop sound, self-reliant institutions. Further, emphasis on local control helped to attract and to retain local business. Where units within a group were scattered over a wide area, autonomy was also likely to be a common-sense approach, since the men on the spot were generally much better qualified to take many of the decisions than those in a central office. In some matters, common policies were certainly advantageous (e.g., salaries, profit sharing, hospitalisation, and pension schemes), though, where a philosophy of relative freedom was subscribed to, the holding company would prefer to implement common action by persuasion rather than by direction. Probably the most general infringement of the autonomy of the individual banks in the group has been the centralised control of the bond account,[15] which was frequently run for the group as a whole by specialists employed in the largest constitutent institution. Sometimes, only the market dealings were centralised, the decisions being made by the individual banks themselves. On other occasions, the group banks might have the right to object to what was done on their behalf. In almost all cases, quite a large number of specialist advisory services were available to banks within the group, though on occasion this type of service was provided more by an exchange of ideas at group conferences or committees. Where specialist services were available, they covered such matters as personnel, bank buildings, operations, auditing, advertising, instalment loans, insurance, mortgage and real-estate problems, and trust business. Where appropriate (e.g. consumer credit and mortgage loans), standard forms would be provided and advice would be made available on matters of procedure. Usually, services were provided by the central organisation on a fee basis. The autonomy of banks within the group has undoubtedly been greatest in the lending field. Each bank in the group would usually have full authority to lend up to its legal limit. Beyond this, it would in any case have to send its customer either to another bank or to an alternative lending institution. Frequently, the country banker would send such an 'overline' to a city correspondent bank. In the case of banks in a group, 'overlines' could be kept within the same organisation. Quite apart from loans in excess of the legal lending limit for the bank in question, certain group organisations required reports to be made to them, sometimes of all loans made, sometimes only of, for example, loans exceeding a specified limit (in these circumstances, the autonomy of the group banks was something of a fiction and their position was not greatly different from that of a branch). In addition, the smaller banks in a group would from time to time seek counsel and advice from senior loan officers at the centre of the organisation.

As a legal device, the holding company form of organisation dates from the 1890s.[16] The formation of bank holding companies in the United States began during the first decade of the twentieth century. In the early part of the century, bank holding companies were concentrated in the North-West (e.g., Minnesota) and some of these earliest companies are still in business. As in the case of branch banking, the development of holding companies was limited by state law and, as a result, the pattern of development was not uniform across the nation.[17]

The first Act dealing expressly with bank holding companies was passed by Congress in 1956. This was the Bank Holding Company Act of 1956.

> The purposes of the Act were to define bank holding companies, to control their future expansion, and to require divestiture of their nonbank affiliates. In the Act, a bank holding company was defined as any company that owned 25 per cent or more of the stock of two or more banks, or otherwise controlled the election of a majority of the directors of two or more banks. The Act made it unlawful for any bank holding company to acquire 5 per cent or more of another bank or for any company to become a multibank holding company without the prior approval of the Board of Governors of the Federal Reserve System. Also, bank holding companies were required to divest themselves of affiliates engaged in nonpermissible activities. In addition, the Act outlined the factors that the Federal Reserve was to consider when processing an application – the convenience, needs, and welfare of the applicant's community, along with limits on bank holding companies organisation consistent with adequate and sound banking, the public interest, and the preservation of competition in banking.[18]

One-bank holding companies (i.e. with only a single bank in the group, though it might comprehend other non-bank affiliates) did not come under the jurisdiction of the 1956 Act. But this called in question the effectiveness of holding-company regulation, especially as the number of one-bank holding companies grew very rapidly in the 1960s. Hence, in order to bring one-bank holding companies under federal regulation, amendments to the Act were passed by Congress in 1970.

> Under the amended Act, one-bank and multibank holding companies were subjected to the same regulations, and the Federal Reserve was given the responsibility of determining permissible activities for all bank holding companies. An important result of the 1970 amendments was the elimination of much of the uncertainty that had accompanied the creation of bank holding companies before 1970. With permissible activities explicitly set out, bank holding company formation proceeded without fear of legal obstacles.[19]

Although bank holding companies had existed in the United States since the early part of the twentieth century, until the latter part of the 1960s they were relatively unimportant in the banking industry. By 1965, there were only 53 multibank holding companies and they controlled only about 8 per cent of all commercial bank deposits. An estimated 550 one-bank holding companies existed in 1965, controlling 4.5 per cent of total deposits. Thus, by 1965, holding companies controlled slightly less than 13 per cent of commercial-bank deposits. In the last half of the 1960s, however, growth was very rapid. The number of multibank holding companies more than doubled, increasing from 53 in 1965 to 121 in 1970. The relative importance of multibank holding companies also increased as the percentage of deposits controlled by these organisations rose from about 8 per cent in 1965 to about 16 per cent in 1970. One-bank holding companies also grew rapidly in the 1965-70 period, increasing in number from 550 in 1965 to 895 in 1970. In terms of relative importance, one-bank holding companies which were not subject to activity restrictions under the Bank Holding Company Act of 1956, grew even more rapidly than multibank holding companies. Between 1965 and 1970, one-bank holding companies increased their control of total deposits from 4.5 per cent to 33 per cent. One-bank and multibank holding companies together controlled just under 50 per cent of the nation's commercial bank deposits by 1970.

Much of the 1965-70 growth in one-bank holding companies occurred in 1968 and 1969. Thus, during the last four months of 1968, seven one-bank holding companies were formed and an additional 76 banking organisations announced plans to form one-bank holding companies. Of these 76 banks, seven were among the twelve largest banks in the United States. This increase in the formation of holding companies was precipitated by the possibility that federal legislation would be enacted to regulate the activities of one-bank holding companies. In the belief that Congress would 'grandfather' some of the activities of existing organisations, many banks established holding companies before the anticipated legislation could come into effect.

Multibank holding companies continued to grow rapidly in the early 1970s, both in numbers and in relative importance. By 1975, these organisations controlled about 38 per cent of total deposits, an increase from just over 16 per cent in 1970. By way of contrast, while the number of one-bank holding companies rose in the early 1970s, their relative importance declined. The percentage of deposits controlled by one-bank organisations fell from 33 per cent in 1970 to about 29 per cent in 1975. The decline in relative importance of one-bank holding companies in the early 1970s was more than offset by the increase in the importance of multibank organisations. Thus, the percentage of deposits held by all bank holding companies rose from just under 50 per cent in 1970 to 67 per cent in 1975. In the latter part of the 1970s, the number of both one-bank and multibank holding companies continued to increase rapidly. However, while the importance of one-bank holding companies declined and that of multibank companies rose in the early 1970s, the situation was reversed in the late 1970s. To some extent, the relatively rapid growth in one-bank holding companies in the late 1970s was due to a change in the state banking laws, particularly in New York. In 1975, that state enacted legislation allowing state-wide branching. As a result, a number of multibank holding companies in that state changed to one-bank companies through the merger of bank subsidiaries into the 'lead' bank. By 1980, 361 multibank holding companies controlled about 35 per cent of total deposits, a decrease from just under 38 per cent in 1975. There were 2,544 one-bank holding companies in 1980 that accounted for about 41 per cent of total deposits, a sharp increase from the 29 per cent held in 1975. Altogether, the percentage of deposits held by holding companies rose from 67 per cent in 1975 to just under 77 per cent in 1980.[20] Moreover, year by year, more and more holding companies are being established, though a proportion of the applications is always denied.[21]

Thus, during the 15-year period from 1965 to 1980, the bank holding company form of organisation, which had only been of modest importance in American banking, had become the dominant form of banking organisation. While only about one-third of the commercial banks in the United States are part of either a one-bank or multibank holding company, almost all of the larger banks are members of such companies. Many of the nation's larger banks are 'lead' banks in multibank organisations. In 1980 there were 2,410 commercial banks in the 361 multibank holding company groups, or about an average of seven banks for each group. The relative importance of multibank and one-bank holding companies varies among the different states, depending mainly on state laws concerning branching and holding companies. By 1984, state-wide branch banking was permissible in 21 states and the District of Columbia. Limited branch banking was allowed in 21 states. All of the staes that allowed limited branching also allowed multibank companies, but in eight of these states, the multibank form of organisation was prohibited or otherwise restricted. The laws of eight states prohibited branch banking of any kind. In seven of the unit-banking states, multibank companies were allowed. As one would expect, one-bank holding companies are more important in the states that allow state-wide branching, while multibank holding companies are more important in those with limited branching or unit banking and which allow multibank organisations. The greater importance of multibank holding companies in unit-banking and limited-branching states reflects the fact that, in these states, banking organisations that wish to expand resort to the multibank method because the branching alternative is limited or not available. On the other hand, in those states that allow branching, expansion can occur without use of the multibank method.

It is appropriate to conclude this section with an outline of regulatory procedures. Under the Banking Act 1933 and the Bank Holding Company Act 1956, as amended in 1970, the Board of Governors of the Federal Reserve System is responsible for regulating bank holding companies. The regulatory policies of the Federal Reserve System are calculated to influence the internal affairs of a holding company with a view to promoting sound banking practices; they are also concerned to influence the structure of the banking industry in order to ensure that competitive market conditions are maintained. This is achieved in two main ways: first all proposals to form a bank holding company or to acquire an additional bank or non-bank subsidiary are subject to the prior approval of the Federal Reserve; and, secondly, compliance with regulations is secured through ongoing supervision of the activities of the holding company.

> When a company formally applies to become a bank holding company, or when a bank holding company proposes to acquire an additional bank or nonbank subsidiary, the Federal Reserve is directed by the Bank Holding Company Act to consider the effect of the proposal on banking, competition, and factors relating to convenience and needs. Where a proposal has . . . [a substantially] adverse effect upon any of these elements it will be denied if there are no counterbalancing considerations. However, a proposal to acquire a nonbank subsidiary will be approved only where there is a positive public effect.
>
> In the case where the proposed acquisition is a bank, banking factors include an evaluation of the financial and managerial aspects of the proposal. With regard to the financial aspects of the proposal, the Federal Reserve is interested mainly in the ability of the holding company to retire any debt incurred in the acquisition of the bank and the ability of the holding company to maintain adequate capital in the bank. In short, the Board of Governors wants to ensure that

the holding company is a source of financial strength for the bank. Regarding managerial considerations, the Federal Reserve evaluates the managerial expertise of both the holding company and the bank by reviewing examination reports for violations of banking laws or regulations.

The Federal Reserve also assesses the probable competitive impact of a holding company proposal in order to prevent any acquisition that would tend either to create a monopoly or to cause a substantial lessening of competition. . . . Generally, the level of concentration in total deposits and the market shares in total deposits of the two firms are estimated in the relevant geographic market. Although the Federal Reserve is not bound by the merger guidelines of the US Department of Justice, the guidelines are used to detect a possible anticompetitive effect.

Finally, the Federal Reserve evaluates the impact of the proposed acquisition on the convenience and needs of the community to be served. Here, the concern is whether or not the proposal will result in improved banking services. Although the application requests information on any proposed changes in banking services, the Federal Reserve also reviews prior examinations of the applicant and the target bank to check for compliance with consumer laws and regulations and with the Community Reinvestment Act. In short, the aim is to ensure that the applicant and the bank are meeting the credit needs of their communities and doing so in a responsible manner.

With regard to an application to acquire a nonbank subsidiary, the Federal Reserve is empowered to determine the activities in which it is permissible for holding companies to engage. This 'laundry list' includes activities closely related to banking or to managing or controlling banks. These include trust operations, investment or financial advising, certain leasing and insurance activities, and several other activities.[22] The purpose of the review procedure is to guarantee that the activites of the nonbank subsidiary do not pose a potential threat to the financial stability of any bank subsidiary. The competitive impact of the acquisition is assessed and, in addition, the Federal Reserve determines whether the acquisition would result in an undue concentration of resources in an activity closely related to banking. Finally, public benefits[23] of the acquisition are reviewed to determine if the proposal will result in greater convenience to the public, gains in efficiency, or lower charges for services.[24]

Mergers[25]

Opposition to excessive concentrations of financial and economic power have long been a cherished part of the American way of life. It is reflected in the fear of monopoly and belief in competition almost as an end in itself. In the banking field, competition has often been equated with the continued existence of a large number of banks each in active competition with the others. Hence, the absorption of small banks by big banks, or the combination of big banks into bigger banks, has been the occasion for concern whenever it has been accompanied by a decline in total numbers.

Yet significant changes in the structure of the American economy have over the years put an increasing premium on size in banking. It is appropriate, therefore, briefly to consider some of the relevant factors. Thus, and especially in the 1950s and 1960s, production and population were both growing at a rapid rate. This produced a related growth in the demand for banking services. Moreover, the volume of business was growing faster than the number of businesses. To the extent that industrial growth encouraged the further expansion of the larger business empires, the major banks had to expand in order to meet the demands of their bigger customers, which themselves had often become even bigger as a result of mergers. In addition, the upward trends in production and in population were accompanied by some geographic redistribution and there was a tendency to shift away from the established centres. These shifts occurred at two levels. Over a period of years, more and more people – and the stores that served them – were moving out of the cities to the suburbs. Industry, too moved from the centre to the periphery of many cities. Also, for the country as a whole, there was a much faster rate of growth on the West Coast and in the South-West, latterly, too, in the South-East, with a relative decline in the North-East. The rise of new industrial centres and the decline of old ones obviously required an adjustment in the provision of banking services. Banks must follow their customers if they are to retain their share of the business. Again, there were changes in the distribution of income, with an emphasis on the growth of the middle incomes. It was this middle group which had become an important source of bank deposits, offsetting in part the relative decline in the deposits of business firms which began to hold a substantial part of their idle funds in the form of short-term securities that could readily be sold as required on the money and capital markets. Moreover, the middle-income group not only became an important source of deposits; it also emerged as a major borrowing group. Finally, the foreign trade of the United States has grown dramatically during the post-war years and its financing has made additional demands on banking services.

The first of the major changes that occurred in the economic environment was quantitative. There was a tremendous growth in the volume of business and an increase in the size of the business unit. This, it was argued, required bigger banking units, because larger businesses needed larger loans and banks could only make these if their lending limits could be raised. Under American banking laws, lending limits are related to capital and surplus – e.g., over a long period and subject to certain exceptions, the maximum amount a national bank could lend to any single borrower was restricted to 10 per cent of its capital and unimpaired surplus; from 1982, this was raised to 15 per cent plus an additional 10 per cent for loans secured by readily marketable collateral; these limitations were also applied to loans made to foreign governments and their agencies. It was true even in the earlier years that the average bank now had a capital and surplus many times what it was in the 1920s. Furthermore, alternatives to bank finance were often resorted to – ploughing back profits or borrowing from institutions other than banks. For many concerns, it was also customary to borrow from and use the services of more than one bank. Moreover, competition prompted a desire for larger capital resources and therefore higher lending limits. A bank would not be able to attract borrowing business from a large concern unless it had a reasonably high lending limit. It might even lose a proportion of medium-sized loans by having to send 'overlines' elsewhere. Lending limits were not likely to worry the true giants, which might not wish to lend up to their maximum, but for the medium-sized and smaller banks, limitation on the amounts they could lend were often a problem. Moreover, it could be difficult to raise bank capital by public issues, and retention of profits was too slow a process of capital accumulation. Such banks therefore tended to improve their competitive position by consolidating with other banks of somewhat similar size. Again, one such move in a particular city was generally followed by other consolidations – for competitive reasons. Where mergers took place between two banks with branch systems, competition likewise encouraged similar moves by other institutions in the same area, though in this case a large city bank might (where it was possible) achieve its objective by absorbing small banks at some distance from the 'downtown' area, or in the suburbs. Prestige and empire-building also played their part. This depended more on personalities and it is less easy to generalise. Nevertheless, the quest for bigness proved to be a contagious disease and it is a factor that cannot be overlooked. Moreover, growth was just as important as size. When there was growth, there was a ferment of ideas, which gave a bank life and brought out the best it had to offer. Often, this could be achieved by obtaining through merger the services of able and go-ahead personnel in another institution.

There were also qualitative changes taking place in the economic environment. Reference has already been made to the changing distribution of income, with greater emphasis on the middle-income groups. A mass market developed for banking services as for everything else. This was accompanied by a much more widely spread sophistication in financial matters. More people now had chequing and savings accounts; more people carried life insurance or held savings bonds; more people were purchasing houses on an instalment basis, also the things that go inside and outside them. With high levels of employment and greater social security, the public was prepared to carry a higher ratio of private debt to income. All this forced the banks in their search for more business and their fight to maintain if not improve their relative position to provide an increasing range of services and to offer the 'department-store' or 'retail' types of banking facility. On the one hand, banks that were expansion-minded sought to secure a foothold in other areas of the economy. On the other, institutions that had held overlong to the view that the greatest margin of profit lay in lending 'big chunks' of money to big borrowers began to suffer a relative decline through neglecting the mass demand of the smaller borrowers, which made up in volume what it might have lacked in margin of profit. The latter type of institution had then to decide, before it was too late, to seek a merger with a bank already in the retail field. Again, a bank with a strong capital position and anxious to expand its loans could take a short cut in this direction by merging with an aggressive lending bank less adequately supplied with capital. Such unions were usually marriages of convenience, especially when a primarily retail bank found it impossible to obtain coveted wholesale accounts in any other way. In addition, successful retail banking almost inevitably required branches, which could often be got more simply by merger or absorption than by opening them *de novo*. The attraction of deposits from small savers was greatly facilitated by a network of branches. So, too, was an aggressive instalment-lending programme which could tap the business offered by the mass of consumers over as wide an area as possible (the purchase of dealer paper could only be a partial substitute for active competition in the field).

The drive to build up branches in outlying areas, often most easily and rapidly effected by absorbing either another bank with existing branches or a number of 'neighbourhood' banks that could be converted into branches, was considerably reinforced by another structural change that was taking place, namely, the shifting of industry and population from 'downtown' areas to the suburbs. Quite some years ago, in many leading American cities, signs of decay at the centre became apparent, with the growth areas tending to locate themselves further out, in this way avoiding both the high costs of city sites and the congestion occasioned by overloaded transport facilities. In other instances, there was a locational shift of business in the city proper – e.g., in the 1950s in Houston, the shopping and financial centres of the town 'moved up eight blocks' in a city where the banks were then all roughly of the same size and highly competitive in their business. The banks were forced to follow their customers and to build new premises uptown. Another city in which certain of the banks found it difficult to keep abreast of the changing whims of the local population was Los Angeles, California. Moreover, bankers there were for some time not sure what the future locational pattern would be and some of them frankly pursued a policy of 'wait and see'.[26] Los Angeles also experienced a phenomenally rapid suburban growth, so rapid that there was ample business to be had both by the expanding branch networks of established institutions and by newly-formed banks serving the 'neighbourhoods'.

Quite apart from structural changes in the economy as a whole, there were often 'domestic' reasons prompting bank mergers. These related to the problems of profitability and internal bank organisation. Thus, there were a number of cases of banks that were under-or overcapitalised and mergers could be a convenient way of establishing a more appropriate relation between capital and deposits. Some banks could produce a better earnings record (on the basis of yield and dividend history) if they could build up deposits in relation to capital; others could expand their business if only they had a wider capital base. For either of these reasons, mergers might be sought and, sometimes, both types of desiderata could be satisfied in one and the same union. Again, the effort to reduce costs was also an important factor in inducing resort to mergers. Over the years, there had tended to be an increase in overheads. Banks felt the need to employ more experts and specialists in order to cope with the growing complexity of banker-customer relationships. This tended to be associated with a contemporaneous rise in salary scales and there was therefore every inducement to economise by using the available expertise to maximum effect. Another important domestic reason for mergers was sometimes the difficulty of staff and management recruitment. This most obviously affected the smaller institutions, where management succession could be a major problem. A local banker approaching the age of retirement might find that he had made no adequate provision for his eventual succession. Without the possibility of merger, the market for such a bank could be unduly narrow. The problem of management succession has probably been the most important single reason why smaller banks have been tempted to merge, but many a large bank, too, has sought to obtain high-grade and experienced officers by merging with an institution more generously supplied with such material than its own. Furthermore, the attraction of competent staff, even by medium-sized banks, may well be prejudiced by limited opportunities for promotion, which may seem to be better in a larger institution. A large bank may also offer better pension and social-security arrangements.

It is against this background that the attempts to regulate bank mergers must be viewed. When Congress passed the Bank Merger Act in 1960, the intention was 'to provide safequards against mergers and consolidations of banks which might lessen competition unduly or tend unduly to create a monopoly in the field of banking'. Bank mergers and consolidations were already subject to some regulation and control, but there were many gaps. State-insured banks wishing to merge were required to obtain prior written approval from either the Federal Reserve Board or, in certain cases, the Federal Deposit Insurance Corporation. Under separate legislation, the Federal Comptroller of the Currency (in the case of national banks or District of Columbia banks) also found that the control he could in fact exercise was rather indirect. Likewise, the provisions of the Clayton Act could easily be evaded by effecting mergers through acquisitions of assets, while the Sherman Anti-Trust Act was general rather than specific in prohibiting activities 'in restraint of interstate or foreign trade or commerce' and made it 'illegal to monopolise . . . any part of such trade or commerce'.

The new legislation amended the relevant section of the Federal Deposit Insurance Act and prohibited mergers or consolidations of all federally-insured banks (95 per cent of total number, holding over 97 per cent of total assets of all banks) unless 'prior written consent' had been obtained from the appropriate federal bank-supervisory agency. In acting on any merger application, the agency with jurisdiction was required to consider a number of factors, including the financial history and condition of each of the banks involved, the adequacy of its capital structure, its future earnings prospects, the general character of its management, the convenience and needs of the community to be served, the effect of the transaction on competition and any tendency towards monopoly. Even so, approval would not be given unless, after considering all these factors, the transaction was also found to be in the public interest. Both Houses of Congress, through their Banking and Currency Committees, were concerned to ensure the maintenance of vigorous competition between 'strong, aggressive and sound banks'. At the same time they recognised that there were economic forces at work that encouraged an increasing resort to bank mergers. During the hearings which preceded the passage of the 1960 legislation it was emphasised that some bank mergers might 'increase and strengthen competition', while others were 'in the public interest, even though they lessen competition'.

It was appreciated – by the Senate Committee – that one could not require unrestricted competition in the field of banking; 'it would be impossible to subject banks to the rules applicable to ordinary industrial and commercial concerns, not subject to regulation and not vested with a public interest'. It was precisely because of this that there was at times so much difficulty. Not only must the authorities weigh banking and economic factors and the public interest; the final decision must also be consistent with (or seem to be consistent with) the laws of the land; fulfilment of the latter requirement was often a matter of interpretation and the occasion for much argument. Hence, the basis of regulation was quite as much political and legal as economic.[27]

This, too, was recognised by Congress. Both the Senate and House Committees recommended that the appropriate bank-supervisory agency (in all but certain emergency cases) be required to seek the views of the Attorney-General as to the 'competitive factors' involved in a proposed merger. This represented a significant change from the optional consultation provided for in earlier Bills. It was included because of the Attorney-General's statutory responsibility for the overall enforcement of the anti-trust laws. At the same time, the House Committee emphasised that the report from the Attorney-General was to be 'purely advisory' and responsibility to approve or disapprove lay with the banking agency concerned. Meanwhile, the Senate Committee had indicated that the competiive factors were 'only one element of several to be considered' and that 'the various banking factors in any particular case may be held to outweigh the competitive factors'; the latter 'are not, in and of themselves, controlling on the decision. And, of course, the banking agencies are not bound in their consideration of the competitive factors by the report of the Attorney-General.' However, this advisory role represented much less than the Department of Justice had wanted – and this helps to explain subsequent developments. The Department of Justice felt that the bank-merger laws were not being enforced with the necessary degree of vigour and enthusiasm. It cited as evidence the great wave of large bank mergers that had recently taken place and argued that the regulatory agencies were failing to maintain an adequate degree of competition. It therefore sought the means of taking more positive action by applying the provisions of the Clayton and Sherman Anti-Trust Acts.[28]

By February 1961, with Robert Kennedy as Attorney-General, the Department had already moved to block the merger of the two large banks in Philadelphia, thereby seeking to apply anti-trust doctrine to a completely new area. This was followed in March by an unsuccessful court action to prevent the merger of two of the largest banks in Lexington, Kentucky. The Department of Justice then moved against Bank Stock Corporation in Milwaukee, which already controlled the second largest bank in the city and which was seeking to acquire two more. Subsequently, in September, the Department applied for a restraining order to block a merger between two banks in Chicago. This was refused. Later that month the Department again failed in its bid to block a major bank merger after it had been approved by a federal bank-regulatory agency. This was between Manufacturers' Trust and Hanover in New York.

Nor were the competent authorities inactive in these matters. Although the Federal Reserve Board had undoubtedly approved a large number of mergers, it had also on occasion denied applications to merge or consolidate with, or to acquire the assets of, another bank. Moreover, each case was looked at on its merits and all the several factors were carefully weighed – banking considerations, the convenience and needs of the community, and the impact on competition. Each decision was supported by a published statement, with any dissenting statement(s) appended. Whether one agreed with a Board decision or not, it was clear that every effort was made to be as objective and fair as was humanly possible. Within their own jurisdictions, the FDIC and the Comptroller of the Currency also approved consolidations, mergers and cash absorptions. All these authorities have over the years been assisted by highly competent staffs, possessed of the appropriate expertise. This has not always been true of the courts, which have sometimes been surprised to learn of matters that are common knowledge to banking experts.[29]

However, the specific reason for concern was not so much the new line of attack favoured by the Attorney-General as his challenging through the courts decisions on mergers that had already been approved by a competent authority. The concern increased when it was announced that there now existed a new understanding as to procedure. Henceforth, if the Comptroller of the Currency saw no grounds for withholding his approval from a bank merger but after consultations with the Department of Justice the latter felt obliged to oppose it and to bring suit to enjoin the proposed action by the banks as a violation of the anti-trust laws, the Comptroller would defer his final official approval of the banks' proposal until a decision resolving the relevant legal issues had been reached in the courts. This understanding was not to be binding on the successors to the parties making it and, in any event, was subject to review and subsequently ceased to have effect. But for some time it did result in the holding up of several important decisions. Latterly, the backlog of applications to merge pending before the banking agencies was virtually eliminated.

Substantially the same arguments were put forward by the Department of Justice in each of the suits it filed in opposition to the merging of banks – that existing and potential competition in commercial banking was likely to be substantially and unreasonably lessened (e.g., in the important case relating to the proposed merger of the Philadelphia National Bank and the Girard Trust Corn Exchange Bank). There is no need to recapitulate all the arguments. After a full trial, the court agreed completely with the conclusions of the Comptroller of the Currency, who had approved this merger 'as not involving undue concentration of banking power, not tending toward a monopoly, not destructive of competition in the commercial banking field, and definitely in the public interest'. Accordingly, the court dismissed the complaint in its entirety, though because of its importance the case went on appeal to the Supreme Court, before which it was argued on 20-21 February 1963.

The opinion of the Supreme Court was delivered by Mr Justice Brennan on 17 June 1963. Somewhat surprisingly, with Mr Justice Harlan and Mr Justice Stewart Dissenting, the judgement of the District Court was reversed. The Majority of the Supreme Court held that 'the merger of appellees is forbidden by Section 7 of the Clayton Act and so must be enjoined; we need not, and therefore do not, reach the further question of alleged violation of Section 1 of the Sherman Act'. The case was remanded with direction to enter judgement enjoining the proposed merger.

It was stated in the opinion that:

Section 7 does not mandate cut-throat competition in the banking industry, and does not exclude defenses based on dangers to liquidity or solvency, if to avert them a merger is necessary. It does require, however, that the forces of competition be allowed to operate within the broad framework of governmental regulation of the industry. The fact that banking is a highly regulated industry critical to the Nation's welfare makes the play of competition not less important but more so . . . we note that if the businessman is denied credit because his banking alternatives have been eliminated by mergers, the whole edifice of an entrepreneurial system is threatened; if the costs of banking services and credit are allowed to become excessive by the absence of competitive pressures, virtually all costs, in our credit economy, will be affected; and unless competition is allowed to fulfil its role as an economic regulator in the banking industry, the result may well be even more governmental regulation. Subject to narrow qualifications, it is surely the case that competition is our fundamental national economic policy, offering as it does the only alternative to the cartelization or governmental regimentation of large portions of the economy.

The activities of the Department of Justice and the way in which these tended to undermine the whole structure of bank regulation and supervision served to focus attention on the desirability of rationalising existing regulatory procedures. It was even suggested that there might be one single authority to assume sole responsibility for the several supervisory functions currently divided between the Federal Reserve Board, the Comptroller of the Currency (who is located in the Treasury) and the Federal Deposit Insurance Corporation.[30] However, in place of this more drastic solution, steps were taken to amend the Bank Merger Act of 1960.

According to Gerald C. Fischer,[31] 'the history of the Bank Merger Act shows beyond any reasonable doubt that the law makers did not expect that under any circumstances bank acquisitions would be judged solely on the basis of the factors considered by the Supreme Court in the *Philadelphia* and *Lexington* cases'. It was therefore clear that a new law was required, which would spell out more carefully the intentions of Federal legislators in these matters. Accordingly, early in 1966, Congress amended the Bank Merger Act with the intention of stating more clearly its position on this issue.

From the point of view of any bank facing anti-trust litigation, the provisions of the 1966 Amendment to the Bank Merger Act were partly favourable and partly unfavourable. Some of its more important paragraphs were as follows:

(5) The responsible agency shall not approve

(A) any proposed merger transactions which would result in a monopoly, or which would be in furtherance of any combination or conspiracy to monopolize or to attempt to monopolize the business of banking in any part of the United States, or

(B) any other proposed merger transaction whose effect in any section of the country may be substantially to lessen competition, or to tend to create a monopoly, or which in any other manner would be in restraint of trade, unless it finds that the anticompetitive effects of the proposed transaction are clearly outweighed in the public interest by the probable effect of the transaction in meeting the convenience and needs of the community to be served. In every case, the responsible agency shall take into consideration the financial and managerial resources and future prospects of the existing and proposed institutions, and the convenience and needs of the community to be served.

(6) The responsible agency shall immediately notify the Attorney General of any approval by it pursuant to this subsection of a proposed merger transaction. If the agency has found that it must act immediately to prevent the probable failure of one of the banks involved and reports on the competitive factors have been dispensed with, the transaction may be consummated immediately upon approval by the agency. If the agency has advised the Attorney General and the other two banking agencies of the existence of an emergency requiring expeditious action and has requested reports on the competitive factors within ten days, the transaction may not be consummated before the fifth calendar day after the date of approval by the agency. In all other cases, the transaction may not be consummated before the thirtieth calendar day after the date of approval by the agency.

(7) (A) Any action brought under the antitrust laws arising out of a merger transaction shall be commenced prior to the earliest time under paragraph (6) at which a merger trans-

action approved under paragraph (5) might be consummated. The commencement of such an action shall stay the effectiveness of the agency's approval unless the court shall otherwise specifically order. In any such action, the court shall review de novo the issues presented.

(B) In any judicial proceeding attacking a merger transaction approved under paragraph (5) on the ground that the merger transaction alone and of itself constituted a violation of any antitrust laws other than section 2 of the Act of July 2, 1890 (section 2 of the Sherman Antitrust Act, 15 U.S.C. 2), the standards applied by the court shall be identical with those that the banking agencies are directed to apply under paragraph (5).

(C) Upon the consummation of a merger transaction in compliance with this subsection and after the termination of any antitrust litigation commenced within the period prescribed in this paragraph, or upon the termination of such period if no such litigation is commenced therein, the transaction may not thereafter be attacked in any judicial proceeding on the ground that it alone and of itself constituted a violation of any antitrust laws other than section 2 of the Act of July 2, 1890 (section 2 of the Sherman Antitrust Act, 15 U.S.C. 2), but nothing in this subsection shall exempt any bank resulting from a merger transaction from complying with the antitrust laws after the consummation of such transaction.

(D) In any action brought under the antitrust laws arising out of a merger transaction approved by a Federal supervisory agency pursuant to this subsection, such agency and any State banking supervisory agency having jurisdiction within the State involved, may appear as a party of its own motion and as of right, and be represented by its counsel.

(8) For the purposes of this subsection, the term 'antitrust laws' means the Act of July 2, 1890 (the Sherman Antitrust Act, 15 U.S.C 1-7), the Act of October 15, 1914 (the Clayton Act, 15 U.S.C. 12-27), and any other Acts in pari materia.

In Fischer's words:

Considering the high degree of regulation in banking, the service nature of this industry, and the technical problems encountered in this area, it is very doubtful that a purely competitive standard could possibly have been completely satisfactory as the only test of the legality of all bank mergers. Surely in at least some instances more than a concentration ratio or the fact that the banks involved may have been 'major competitors' in a market would have to be weighed in determining the lawfulness of a merger, if 'the convenience and needs of the community were to be served'. With this in mind the Congress in drafting the 1966 amendment to the Bank Merger Act (hereafter termed simply 'the 1966 amendment') directed the courts to consider both 'banking factors' and competitive factors in determining the legality of a merger, no doubt assuming that in a very limited number of cases a bank merger would still be in the public interest, although competition might be significantly reduced.

It was also hoped to eliminate much of the confusion that had developed as a result of the different standards applied in implementing the Bank Merger Act 1960 and the anti-trust laws. Under the new legislation, the courts were directed to employ the same criteria as those used by the banking agencies themselves. But as Fischer has observed, and contrary to what is frequently believed, the amendment could increase the importance attached to competition in a given market. In the original Bank Merger Act, the banking agencies had been directed to consider competition but only as one of the several factors to be weighed in deciding whether a merger should be approved. Now, however, a banking agency 'must make a substantive antitrust judgement, and where it finds a substantial lessening of competition may occur the merger is to be approved only if this factor is clearly outweighed by the positive benefits which are expected to accrue to the community, assuming the merger is authorized'.[32]

More positively, from the point of view of the banks, the 1966 amendment eliminated retroactive application of Section 1 of the Sherman Act or Section 7 of the Clayton Act to any merger involving an insured bank. This removed any uncertainty regarding the validity of a large number of past bank mergers. This was accepted, but a bitter controversy developed with respect to those cases where the parties had already been found to violate the anti-trust laws. Two mergers which had been enjoined by the courts – Lexington and Manufacturers Hanover – 'were held to be conclusively presumed to have not been in violation of Section 1 of the Sherman Act and Section 7 of the Clayton Act, along with the still pending *Continental Illinois* merger. In addition any unchallenged bank merger consummated between 16 June 1963 and 21 February 1966 . . . could not now be attacked in any judicial proceeding on the ground that it alone and of itself constituted a violation of the antitrust laws other than Section 2 of the Sherman Act.'[33] Ironically, the Philadelphia banks which had never merged but which waited until the issues had been clarified in the courts were not now permitted to merge.

Although the 1966 amendment contained a number of provisions of which the Anti-trust Division of the Department of Justice did not approve, it did include other provisions that the Department of Justice had long desired. Thus, under the new legislation, the Department of Justice was to receive pre-merger notification in much the same way as it did under the original Bank Merger Act of 1960, but the Attorney-General had now been given the additional power to enjoin a merger merely by commencing an action against it. Previously, under the 1960 legislation, the Department of Justice had to seek an injunction in the courts to stop a bank acquisition; now the injunction was to become 'automatic' and could only be removed if the courts issued a specific order to permit the consummation of the merger. As the Supreme Court observed:

> A stay is not mandatory under any and all circumstances. But absent a frivolous complaint by the United States, which we presume will be infrequent, a stay is essential until the judicial remedies have been exhausted. The legislative history is replete with references to the difficulty of unscrambling two or more banks *after* their merger. The normal procedure therefore should be maintenance of the *status quo* until the antitrust litigation has run its course, lest consummation take place and the unscrambling process that Congress abhorred *in the case of banks* be necessary.[34]

Unfortunately, in a number of instances,[35] the new legislation (and this was also true of the 1966 amendments to the Bank Holding Company Act) tended to introduce a degree of confusion rather than clarification. In other words, the amendments included 'new, untested standards whose significance cannot even be estimated until a body of case law develops'.[36]

'From the view point of the merged or merging bank, it would seem that the major gain from this legislation stems from the provisions preventing attack upon past mergers under Section 1 of the Sherman Act and Section 7 of the Clayton Act or upon present mergers after a 30-day waiting period. The major loss on the other hand, results from the "automatic injunction" now available to Justice and . . . from the increased emphasis which the banking agencies are expected to give to antitrust factors in considering merger applications.'[37]

Latterly, in May 1968, the Department of Justice issued comprehensive guidelines outlining its standards for determining whether to challenge corporate acquisitions or mergers. These were significantly revised in 1982[38] and further refined in 1984. Its objective was to 'acquaint the business community, the legal profession, and other interested groups and individuals' with the Department's policy of enforcing Section 7 of the Clayton Act. At the time of their release, Attorney-General Ramsey Clark expressed the hope that

> the guidelines would provide the basis for a continuing dialogue between government and private industry concerning the role and scope of antimerger enforcement under the Clayton Act. The guidelines specifically stated that they might be amended from time to time to reflect any relevant public comments, court rulings, or Department reevaluations.

The preamble to the guidelines stated that 'the primary role of Section 7 enforcement is to preserve and promote market structure conducive to competition'. In these circumstances, it was not surprising that the guidelines were phrased exclusively in terms of market-structure data. In defending its reliance on such criteria, the Justice Department noted that the conduct of individual firms in a market tends to be primarily controlled by their relative size in the market, the total number of competitors and degree of concentration in the market, and the ease or difficulty with which new firms can enter the market.[39] 'Moreover, these indicators of market structure are vastly easier to obtain and analyze than information on market conduct or performance. However, the Department realized that in certain circumstances structural factors alone would not be conclusive and it therefore preserved the option of conducting a more complex review.'

Under these guidelines, the concentration of a market was measured by the percentage of total sales generated by the market's largest participants, usually the four largest firms. When the four-firm concentration ratio exceeded 75 per cent, the market was considered to be highly concentrated. Also, if a market exhibited 'a significant trend toward increased concentration' over the previous five to ten years, the

Justice Department proposed to challenge the merger of any of the market's larger firms with any firm controlling a market share of approximately 2 per cent or more.

However, depending on the 'unique circumstances' of each case, the Justice Department

> reserved the right to challenge certain mergers which might not violate the guidelines, and not to challenge other mergers which might exceed the guidelines. Considerations which would outweigh simple market share data might include rapid technological change in an industry or the existence of small but unusually 'disruptive' competitors in the market . . . In the absence of any mitigating or aggravating circumstances, however, any merger would be subject to challenge simply by exceeding the market share limits established in the guidelines.

At this stage, the Justice Department specifically recommended that total deposits should be used to determine the market share of commercial banking organisations, clearly implying that the guidelines, which were designed to apply to a wide range of industries, also applied to commercial banking. Although the Federal Reserve Board did not specifically endorse these guidelines for general use in analysing commercial bank affiliations, it did quote them from time to time in support of its rulings and the Board's decisions have generally been consistent with them.[40]

Although over the years there had been a widespread acceptance of the original guidelines by regulators and the courts, the Reagan administration decided to undertake a major re-evaluation of the federal government's anti-trust policy. The new philosophy was succinctly stated by Attorney-General William French Smith: 'bigness is not necessarily badness'. The new policies were relatively more concerned with market concentration and 'the likelihood of successful collusion among firms in that market' than with the overall size of the merger partners. Because of the new philosophy's emphasis on market concentration, the revised merger guidelines continued to be phrased exclusively in terms of market-structure criteria. However, instead of using the four-firm concentration ratio, the guidelines now employed the Herfindahl index of concentration, defined as the sum of the squares of the market shares of the firms in a particular market.[41] In the view of Joseph E. Gagnon, the revised guidelines take a slightly more lenient stance towards mergers between competing firms, but the changes are likely to have less of an impact on merger policy for commercial banking than for other industries.

As we have seen, the Bank Merger Act requires that all proposed bank mergers receive the prior approval of the appropriate federal bank-regulatory agency. If the bank surviving the merger is a state member bank, the Federal Reserve has primary jurisdiction. Before approving a bank merger, the Federal Reserve considers the community's convenience and needs, the financial and managerial resources and prospects of the existing and proposed institutions, and the competitive effects of the proposal; also, the Board must consider the views of certain other agencies on the competitive factors involved in the transaction. When the Comptroller of the Currency or the Federal Deposit Insurance Corporation has jurisdiction over a merger, the Board is asked to comment on the competitive factors to assure comparable enforcement of the anti-monopoly provisions of the Act. Both the Board and these agencies have now adopted standard terminology for assessing competitive factors in bank merger cases, thereby assuring consistency in the administration of the Bank Merger Act.

Correspondent Banking

In addition to the political attitudes that underlie the retention of unit banking in the United States, important sociological factors also seem to have contributed to this preference. Long ago, Walter Bagehot described the appeal of the private banker – who was also a local banker – as follows:

> A man of known wealth, known integrity, and known ability is largely entrusted with the money of his neighbours. The confidence is strictly personal. His neighbours know him, and trust him because they know him. They see daily his manner of life, and judge from it that their confidence is deserved. In rural districts . . . it was difficult for a man to ruin himself except at the place in which he lived; for the most part he spent his money there, and speculated there if he speculated at all. Those who lived there also would soon see if he was acting in a manner to shake their confidence. Even in large cities, as cities then were, it was possible for most persons to ascertain with fair certainty the real position of conspicuous persons and to learn all that was material in fixing their credit.[42]

Although those words applied to a system which in England had largely disappeared even in Bagehot's time, they still describe fairly accurately the position in many parts of the United States, especially in the rural areas. The preference for the local banker would also seem to be intimately related to what one might describe as the American 'service complex' – the desire for the best possible service and, linked with this, the desire for personal attention from a man one feels one knows and knows one can trust.

The small banker can without doubt provide his customer with a more 'personalised' service than can the large institution, the branches of which (where they exist) are controlled from a head office more or less distant from the actual scene of operations. The local banker can also give his customer the benefit of a quick decision and consideration of applications will generally be subject to less formality. Whether one can assume that more personal attention necessarily amounts to better service is, however, a more open question. The small bank, even when it draws on the facilities of a city correspondent and – within its own organisation – employs all the modern electronic aids available, is unlikely to be able to provide the same range of services that will be offered to the customers of a large bank. For example, there is less opportunity in a small institution to employ experts in fields like instalment credit, mortgage business, and the financing of agriculture and, where such persons are added to the staff, it is less likely that the volume of business undertaken will be sufficient to absorb completely the related addition to overheads. In the circumstances, the customer will probably find that the provision of personal attention is more expensive. If, therefore, he insists on getting personal attention, he will have to pay more for it.

The demand for 'personalised' service undoubtedly has economic implications, but insofar as this demand appears to be stronger in some countries than in others, it would seem to derive primarily from differences in social attitudes. A factor more directly economic in character is the common assertion of local bankers and their customers that a banker with local connections will almost certainly possess greater knowledge of local trades and industries. The local banker will also have a greater personal knowledge of his customers and their affairs. On both these grounds, he is therefore able to accept classes of business which to the larger institution, without an intimate knowledge of the locality, may seem to be too risky and beyond its province. In this way, the local banker is able, at least in part, to offset the advantage held by the larger institution in securing a wider spread of risks – both territorially and as between industries, whether the larger banks effect this by means of branch networks or through the agency of a large number of correspondents.

The one big advantage that the local banker enjoys is flexibility – he can adjust his policies readily to meet current needs. Because of this, specifically local needs are likely to be accommodated more completely and expeditiously. There is much truth in this argument, but in satisfying these needs, the local banker is obviously limited by the resources available to him. He may be able to supplement these resources to some extent by borrowing from a city correspondent, or placing a part of the loan with him, but there will generally be restrictions on the extent to which this is possible and the placing of loans elsewhere will often be subject to the satisfaction of conditions not greatly different from those that would apply to a branch manager. Hence, the advantages enjoyed by the local banker in the matter of loans may well be much less than would at first sight appear to be the case.

This is not to deny that a developed network of correspondent relationships can in fact achieve a great deal. In the author's view, however, it is still likely to produce a second-best solution of the problem of how to integrate a large number of banks into a 'system', but there are many who disagree, especially in the United States, where, over a long period, correspondent banks have given yeoman service. Indeed, without general resort to this institution, American retention of 'unit banking', even on a reduced scale, would never have been possible.

It is pertinent, therefore, to attempt an outline of the range of services offered by city correspondents and to evaluate the degree of their responsibility for the efficient operation of American banking arrangements. Correspondent banking is resorted to in a large number of countries – in some form or other, in all countries – but nowhere is it more highly developed than in the United States.

The scope for correspondent banking is greatest in those parts of the United States (e.g., Texas, Illinois, Minnesota and Kansas), where branching is still extremely restricted and there is a large number of small country banks, and/or where many of them are not members of the Federal Reserve System (as in these same states). The services provided by the city correspondents are many and various, but obviously the system could not operate if it were not mutually advantageous. Both aspects of the relationship must therefore be discussed.

What is the range of services offered by the larger banks that act as city correspondents? First, there is the clearance of cheques and the collection of proceeds (e.g., of coupons, or the proceeds of a sale of securities). Member banks in the cities would normally clear their cheques through a Federal Reserve Bank, but country banks would often tend to employ a city correspondent for this purpose, even when they are members of the Federal Reserve System. This is so, because many city banks offer special clearance facilities (e.g., at airports) that are more expeditious than those offered by the Fed. Thus, they may have special arrangements at the airport to receive and despatch cheques, thereby avoiding the loss of time involved in bringing cheques into a city office for processing. A number of city banks work three shifts right round the clock to clear the cheques from their correspondents and many others work two shifts for this purpose. In addition, items on non-par banks (banks which make an 'exchange' charge for the clearance of cheques) will be accepted, foreign items handled, immediate credit granted on all cash items, out-of-town clearings can be microfilmed, and so on.

Secondly, city banks customarily hold in safe custody their correspondent banks' securities, pledging them against loans from themselves as and when necessary. On the whole, inter-bank lending may take the form of a repurchase agreement or a federal funds transaction. In either case, the current rate on federal funds would be the key rate for pricing purposes.

Thirdly, in most instances, the city banks offer advice, when it is sought, on the buying and selling of securities by their correspondent banks and often assist them with the detailed management of their investment portfolios, which are scrutinised at regular intervals. In addition, the city bank will buy and sell securities on behalf of correspondents, sometimes keeping a trading account for the purpose. By no means all of the country banks use these services and many are surprisingly independent, preferring to seek outside advice from an investment counsel and to put their business through their own broker. In some cases, country banks employ both sets of facilities, especially in the matter of investment advice.

Fourthly, all banks are subject to lending limits laid down either by state or federal laws. In the case of a national bank, for example, and subject to a number of exemptions for certain types of business, not more than 15 per cent of unimpaired capital and surplus may now be lent to any one borrower, plus an additional 10 per cent for loans secured by readily marketable collateral; these limitations are also now applied to loans made to foreign governments and their agencies. Hence, the smaller banks frequently find it difficult to accomodate within their own lending limit the credit needs of their larger customers. In these circumstances, it is not uncommon for the country bank to sell a 'participation' in such loans to his city correspondent for whom he will often continue to 'service' the loan (i.e. ensure that interest is paid on due dates, that the lender's margin of security is maintained, and that repayment is effected as agreed, for which the country bank may be allowed ½ per cent per annum on the amount taken over by the city correspondent). Loans beyond a bank's lending limit which are placed with another bank are described as 'overlines' but the same technique is employed whenever it is desired to 'lay off' loans in this way. Thus, lending limits aside, loans may have to be passed on to city correspondents to accommodate peak seasonal demands.[43] This is the general rule in the cattle areas, where banks in centres like St Louis, Kansas City and Omaha regularly relieve the seasonal pressure in this way. Again, the Memphis banks, at the height of the cotton-buying season, send on to New York banks many of the loans that are made to the local cotton brokers (in this case some of the Memphis banks virtually act as agents of the New York banks). In Dallas, the city banks take in participations in cattle and oil loans from country correspondents. On cattle and agricultural loans, the city bank leaves the fixing of the rate to the country correspondent, but on oil loans (which are in any case somewhat tricky) the city bank fixes the rate and the country bank gets ½ per cent for servicing the loan. The Dallas banks, which are big in the oil-loans business, themselves sell off participations in their loans to banks in New York and Chicago, as well as in other centres.

However, city correspondents will not always accept 'overlines' from country banks and, on occasion (and not always because they are themselves 'lent up'), they have been very selective indeed. In other cases they complain about the poor quality of the 'overlines' they are obliged to accept in virtue of the strength of local competition for correspondent accounts. On the other hand, certain country banks are most unwilling to send in participations in their own loans to city banks, mainly because they fear that the latter will try to steal their larger accounts. Where a local banker is himself a wealthy man, he may make such loans on a personal basis. Alternatively, a man of substance (or a group of such men) may have controlling interests in several banks and large loans can be divided among the banks in the group. At times, too, local bankers will join forces in order to keep a large loan within their own community and, not infrequently, the reason for this will be no more than a vague suspicion of outsiders.

At certain times of the year, for seasonal reasons, country banks may run short of loans and wish to fill out their loan portfolio in order to keep their funds fully employed. To this end, though less so in more recent years, banks in some areas followed the practice of buying either 'commercial paper' (short-term unsecured notes placed on the market by leading corporations through the agency of brokers) or 'finance paper', as it was then called (similar notes placed directly by the leading finance companies like General Motors Acceptance Corporation and Commercial Investment Trust Finance Corporation (CIT).[44] Where there was a regular local demand for such paper, city correspondents would both advise country banks on 'names' and also purchase such paper on their behalf. Indeed, some city banks carried an inventory of such paper, which they appraised themselves on the basis of an analysis of the financial statements of the issuing firms. They also checked with their 'line' banks on the other borrowings of such firms, in order to make sure than their market paper was covered by unused credit lines. Frequently, the country banks' commercial paper was kept in safe custody by the city correspondent, which collected it for them when it fell due.

The demand for paper to offset the seasonal low in the loan portfolio came mainly from the smaller banks and there were certain areas where the buying of commercial paper was almost traditional. For example, the Cape Cod banks in Massachusetts and some of the banks in Maine which depended for much of their business on vacation spending in the summer months bought commercial paper during the off-season as a means of investing their funds, taking in maturities which would fit in with their pay-outs over succeeding months. To some extent, the degree of seasonality in certain of these areas was greatly reduced as they developed a winter trade as well. Another area in which commercial paper was held by country banks (to counter the seasonal decline in agricultural loans) occurred in the Federal Reserve District of Minneapolis. Here banks bought the paper of the large milling firms and of finance companies. Again, banks in Kentucky absorbed funds in this way during the 'dead season' following the liquidation of the tobacco loans, the paper maturing about the time the growers would again be coming into the banks for finance. There was a 'between-seasons' demand for commercial paper from country banks in Nebraska, where loans were high to finance grain-growing in the summer and cattle-feeding in the winter. In between seasons, some of the banks went into commercial paper to absorb their funds, but the majority appeared at that time to use Treasury bills for this purpose. In California, too, one of the leading San Francisco banks purchased short-term commercial paper notes for its country bank correspondents, which in some cases were heavily involved in the finance of seasonal speciality crops, e.g., lettuces. (This used to be much more common in California than it is now. With the further development of branching, banks tended to achieve a greater degree of balance in their loan portfolio and this considerably reduced the seasonal fluctuation in loan demand.) Where it occurred, the chief reason for bank purchase of commercial paper was undoubtedly the seasonal character of local business. Use of commercial paper for this purpose is now much rarer, but the problem remains; latterly, a major outlet for surplus resources has been the federal-funds market. Banks do in fact still buy commercial paper (frequently now through brokers) sometimes still for their own account, but the largest proportion of it would now be for their trust departments.

In several parts of the country city correspondents have long sold participations in their own loans to country banks in their area. In former times and in some parts of the country, this was frowned upon as bad practice. Latterly, the buying of loans from other institutions has become an accepted banking procedure, though there are risks, which may affect both small banks (e.g., the REIT loans of the 1970s) and large banks (e.g., the Penn Square episode of the 1980s).

Over the years, some banks, of course, when the seasonal demand for loans was low, preferred to place funds temporarily either in Treasury bills or other short-dated securities. Again, normal procedure would be to buy such securities through city correspondents, selling out as and when necessary. But, as already indicated, even small banks now use the federal funds market quite extensively for this purpose.

Fifthly, the majority of member banks receive their supplies of notes and coin direct from the Fed, though in some areas where the Fed is not represented the shipping of currency is handled by a city correspondent (e.g., in Wisconsin, a commercial bank in Milwaukee supplies the bulk of these needs). Non-member banks have no option and must obtain their currency supplies from their correspondents.

Finally, city correspondents also provide quite a variety of ancillary services. Thus, they will assist other banks with credit information. This is the general rule in the United States, where there is a very frank interchange of credit information between banks that are otherwise in keen competition with each other, but country correspondents are

Table 3.1: Typical Correspondent Services

Service	Most important correspondent service in terms of balances maintained as payment* (per cent)
Cash letter (cheque collection)	80
Federal funds trading	36
Wire transfer	27
Securities safekeeping	52
Coupon collection	15
Securities clearance	27
Government securities trading	8
Investment advisory service for bank's bond portfolio	na
Short-term money market investments	5
Foreign-exchange service	7
Municipal securities trading	6
Data-processing services	na
Computerised cash balance reporting service	1
Account reconciliation plan	na
Overline facility	23
Domestic loan participation	18
Financial forecasting and planning assistance	3
Commercial letter of credit	3
Domestic credit investigations	1

*Percentage of all surveyed banks indicating the services that were responsible for the largest portion of their correspondent balances.
na. data not available.
Based on 1978 research publised in part in *Correspondent Banking 1980*, Greenwich Research Associates, Inc. Greenwich, CT, 1980 and reproduced in *Federal Reserve Bank of Boston New England Economic Review*, (September/October 1981).

frequently accorded even more detailed reports than are customary. In this way, a country banker is, in effect, able to draw on the very complete files kept by the leading city banks and to secure the benefit of records that it would be quite impossible for him to keep himself. Some city banks regularly offer expert advice to country banks on operational techniques (e.g., instalment credit and mortgage loans) accounting methods, data processing and computerisation. They may also assist them with advice on advertising techniques, on remodelling their offices, safe custody installations, etc. In a number of cases they will marry transactions in the buying and selling of country banks[45] (for which the market is somewhat narrow) and may lend money to assist purchase. They may help country banks to fill executive posts by acting as a clearing house for bank appointments. Again, a leading city bank will often make available to its country correspondents its direct wire facilities, which permits rapid and efficient communication with all the important banks in the United States. Further, many city banks provide a range of services through their foreign banking division, though the completeness of the services offered naturally varies with the importance of the centre in which the city correspondent operates. However, country banks would usually only require letters of credit, travellers' cheques, or the making of a foreign remittance. There is also the multitude of personal services that city correspondents habitually provide – the securing of hotel accommodation, travel bookings, baseball and theatre tickets, etc. Some city banks even run conferences for the benefit of their country correspondents, inviting leading persons to them for the purpose of imparting their expertise on a wide range of topics.

When account is taken of the vast range of services, which the city correspondent is called upon to provide, one can scarcely not be impressed by its costliness, especially as competition for this business for a long time precluded the levying of specific service charges. Yet there were few of the leading city correspondent banks that did not feel that it was well worthwhile. Correspondent balances were and are an important element in total deposits (and in this respect it should be remembered that banks in the more important financial centres draw correspondent balances from all over the country and, indeed, from abroad as well); 'overline' business is a useful supplement to a city correspondent's own lending[46] (on occasion it has been regarded, somewhat unscrupulously, as a means of securing access to additional lending outlets – this is one reason, as has been mentioned, why a number of country banks are a little loath to send their 'overlines' into a city bank);[47] both of a large number of correspondent-bank accounts and the related higher level of deposits have long been important in building up and maintaining size and prestige, which in a highly competitive world cannot be underestimated. In order to attract big business one has to have a big bank.

In recent years, specific fees for particular correspondent services have been increasingly adopted. This is in addition to the minimum-balance system of remuneration.

> Services especially suitable for the assessment of specific charges include: domestic collections, foreign collections, non-par cheque clearance, despatch of securities, provision of amortization schedules, providing letters of credit, remittances, arrangement of

> export-import credits, provision of foreign drafts, safekeeping of securities, provision of wire and cable services, foreign-exchange transactions, data-processing services, handling collateral on brokers' day loans, advice on systems of operation or control of expenditure, advice on service charges, handling securities transactions, posting, foreign transactions, employee training and acting as trustee for retirement fund.[48]

It is true that over more recent years, payment by fee for correspondent services rendered has become relatively more important, but payment in terms of balances is still the predominant method of reimbursing a bank for the provision of correspondent bank services. 'In 1979 income from correspondent balances averaged 81.6 percent of banks' total income from correspondent services and fees generated only 18.4 percent.'[49] As a matter of interest, in one useful study, 'the revenues from selling correspondent services are estimated for each bank by multiplying the deposits its respondents hold with it (the correspondent's 'due to' balances) by the three-month Treasury Bill rate. These revenues are equal to the costs of producing correspondent services plus profit plus the reserve requirement tax passed on to the respondent.'[50]

On a balance of considerations, correspondence business still seems to be profitable and many city banks cost their services regularly to make sure that it is. There are also the indirect benefits, such as access to new accounts. Moreover, for every country bank that is inclined to abuse the range of services offered, there are many others that hold good balances and are very little trouble. However, when account is taken of the vast duplication of service facilities implied by a highly developed correspondent network, it would seem that these arrangements could be provided much more economically through the wider spread of branch banking.

International Banking

In order to trace the international banking activities of United States institutions back to their beginnings, one ought to start with the 1919 amendment to the Federal Reserve Act initiated by Senator Walter Edge, which enabled American banks to establish subsidiary corporations outside their home state. However, these Edge Act corporations were only permitted to finance foreign trade or to undertake business abroad. For many years, there were relatively few Edge Act corporations (Edges) – in 1960, there were 15 throughout the United States. But over the next 15 years, the number increased to 117, the most rapid expansion being throughout the 1960s and early 1970s. By July 1984, there were 142 Edges (34 majority-owned by foreign banks), plus 118 domestic and 23 foreign branch offices of these corporations, and 5 Agreement corporations. For the most part, they have been established by the multi-billion-dollar banks located in major port cities or in a major money centre like New York, Chicago, or San Francisco. When it comes to regional banks, only the largest and best located regionals have opened Edges (or foreign branches). Thus, on a national basis, there were only three banks in 1980 with less than $1 billion in total assets that had opened Edges.[51] The reason has been the cost. Edges must have a capital of at least $2 million (and which may not constitute more than 10 per cent of the parent's capital and surplus); they need to be staffed with a full complement of calling officers and operations personnel which is costly to train; and real estate is expensive in places like New York or Florida, which is another popular location (not so much perhaps in a Caribbean context as for Latin America). Hence, in order to be profitable, a large volume of international business is required. On the other hand, there is much good business to be done in money-market and international trade centres. Setting up an Edge in such a location permitted local customers to finance their international trade with a local bank and in a convenient location in which to conduct international business. Some big banks (e.g., in New York, but also elsewhere) have more than one Edge and in different locations. Many Edges confine their operations to financing exports and imports, the latter primarily on a short-term basis. But this can be extended to financing operations related to foreign trade (e.g., financing the purchase of second-hand eqipment, where there is an intention to export after reconditioning). Funding derives from overseas depositors and banks overseas – time deposits (including certificates of deposits), savings and chequing accounts. Customers include both individuals and corporations – e.g., an importer in Latin America, or an American exporter provided he is using the account for foreign trade. Some accommodation is made available on the basis of Euro-currency borrowings. Edges also act for customers of small banks – letters of credit, foreign exchange, etc. In Florida, too, tourism is an invisible export and requires to be financed. In addition to American Edges, under the International Banking Act 1978, foreign banks could now open Edge Act corporations, which could also accept deposits and make loans so long as these were directly related to international transactions.

Agreement corporations can also be located outside a bank's home state. Unlike Edges, which are chartered by the Federal Reserve System and are not subject to state corporate and banking laws, Agreement corporations are chartered under state laws. There are no restrictions on their capitalisation (as with Edges), but Agreements can only engage in international banking; other foreign financial operations are not permitted. Both can engage in domestic business only if it is incidental to international trade. In recent years, Edges have been far more popular than Agreements and following passage of the International Banking Act of 1978 have been allowed to establish domestic branch offices. Many American banks have restructured their domestic Edge corporations into branch systems.

Where American banks have wished to undertake banking or quasi-banking operations abroad, they could establish either a 'shell' branch or a representative office. A 'shell' branch was the easiest and cheapest way of gaining access to the Euro-currency markets (see below), whether for domestic funding or as a reserve-free location from which to issue foreign loans. 'Shells are booking offices located abroad which have no contact with their local market. The shell's actual banking activities take place at the U.S. head office. Most were originally located in the Bahamas because it offered a stable government and did not tax the income of the shells. Recently, most shells have been opened in the Grand Cayman Islands for the same reasons.'[52] They are a reserve-free source of funds for foreign lending activities. Shells proved to be popular both with large money-centre banks and also with regional banks.

Where a country prohibits direct foreign-bank entry, or the potential business available is too small to warrant the setting up of a full foreign branch, a bank may choose to open a representative office. Such offices may be described as 'foreign loan production offices', with the processing of the loans being done at home base; usually, they have a small staff to search out local business and to handle the local aspects of on-going business. They may not accept deposits and provide a full range of services, but – given reasonable rents – they are a relatively inexpensive way of establishing a local presence.

Where the amount of business warrants it – or is expected to warrant it – a full-service foreign branch offers many advantages and a direct foreign banking presence. It is a legal extension of the bank and does not require separate capitalisation. Since a branch is an integral part of its bank, it has the same status in the international market (e.g., in a borrowing situation) as the bank of which it is a part. It is also the most flexible foreign-banking vehicle available to an American bank. For example, it is in a position to attract new business and to maintain old relationships by continuing to service abroad domestic customers themselves with branches or subsidiaries abroad. It can also be used to gather foreign credit information. And, if in a leading money-market centre (e.g., London), it will give ready access to the Euro-currency markets with ready transfer of funds (Euro-currency or other) either way between head office and branch. Its most obvious disadvantage is expense and clearly the amount of business attracted must more than cover this. The provision and retention of experienced staff may also be a problem. Furthermore, it is unlikely to develop an adequate deposit base and will therefore require ready access to inter-bank and similar markets from which to supplement its resources. The emphasis of its business will tend to be on the wholesale side. Its local income may be heavily taxed. In a number of cases, the choice of a branch location may be restricted by national laws.

As already indicated, one important reason for establishing an international facility has been access to the Euro-currency markets. These have grown rapidly since their inception in the late 1950s. Transactions take place between banks that issue and accept deposits in currencies other than those of the country in which the bank is located. The market is wholesale in character and almost totally exempt from national regulation, though this has been considered from time to time. If a bank has no immediate use for an incoming Euro-currency deposit, it may lend that deposit in the inter-bank market. It operates on a name basis and, since loans are unsecured, banks normally impose credit limits on other bank participants. The markets are intensely competitive. Many customers prefer to hold their deposits outside their own country in Euro-currency markets (e.g., for the purpose of trade payments). Companies can also hold deposits at interest for even the shortest periods. Governments likewise may decide to hold reserves in 'hard' Western currencies and in countries where risk of seizure is minimal. For banks, although rates may be higher than similar United States deposit rates, it can be an easy and reliable source of funds (e.g., for funding Euro-currency loans or syndicated participations). Most Euro-currency loans and syndications carry floating rates, adjusted every three or six months and related to the London Inter-Bank Offered Rate (LIBOR), plus a fixed spread.

Finally, in early December 1981, 'international banking facilities' (the so-called IBFs) were introduced in the United States.[53] In fact, they are merely a separate set of books within an existing banking institution – a US-chartered depository institution, a US branch or agency of a foreign bank, or a US office of an Edge Act corporation.

They can only take deposits from and make loans to nonresidents of the United States, other IBFs and their establishing entities. Moreover, IBFs are not subject to the regulations that apply to domestic banking activity; they avoid reserve requirements, interest rate ceilings and deposit insurance assessment. In effect, they are accorded the advantages of many offshore banking centers without the need to be physically offshore.[54]

The regulatory and legislative changes that permitted and encouraged the establishment and growth of IBFs were as follows: first, the Federal Reserve Board changed its regulations in 1981 to allow their establishment; secondly, federal legislation enacted late in 1981 exempted IBFs from the insurance coverage and assessments imposed by the FDIC; and thirdly, several states granted special tax status to the operating profits from IBFs, or reduced restrictions to encourage their establishment. In Florida, IBFs are entirely exempt from local taxes. But there are a number of restrictions designed to ensure separation from domestic money markets.

While IBFs may transact banking business with U.S. nonresidents on more or less the same terms as banks located offshore, they may not deal with U.S. residents at all, apart from their parent institution or other IBFs. Funds borrowed by a parent from its own IBF are subject to eurocurrency reserve requirements just as funds borrowed from an offshore branch would be.

Four other restrictions on IBFs are designed to ensure their separation from domestic money markets. First, the initial maturity of deposits taken from nonbank foreign customers must be at least two working days. Overnight deposits, however, may be offered to overseas banks, other IBFs and the parent bank. This restriction ensures that IBFs do not create a close substitute for checking accounts.

Second, the minimum transaction with an IBF by a nonbank customer is $100,000, except to withdraw interest or close an account. This effectively limits the activity of IBFs to the 'wholesale' money market, in which the customers are likely to be governments, major corporations or other international banks. There is no restriction on the size of interbank transactions.

> Third, IBFs are not permitted to issue negotiable instruments, such as certificates of deposit (CDs), because such instruments would be easily marketable in U.S. money markets, thereby breaking down the intended separation between IBFs and the domestic money market.
>
> Finally, deposits and loans of IBFs must not be related to a non-resident customer's activities in the United States. This regulation prevents IBFs from competing directly with domestic credit sources for finance related to domestic economic activity.[55]

IBFs are located mainly in the major financial centres. Just under half of the 477 IBFs are in New York (208). California (84), Florida (79), and Illinois (30) have the bulk of the remainder. In terms of value of liabilities, however,

> the distribution is even more skewed. Of IBFs reporting monthly to the Federal Reserve (those with assets or liabilities in excess of $300 million), 77 percent of total liabilities were in New York, with California (12 percent) and Illinois (7.5 percent) a long way behind. It is notable that Florida, which has 16.5 percent of the IBFs, has only 2 percent of the liabilities of reporting banks.[56]

It seems that the establishment of IBFs in the United States only represents a change in the geographical pattern of international banking. It has facilitated the conduct in the United States of some business that was previously done offshore. It has also increased the ease with which foreign banks can operate branches in the United States. But the creation of IBFs does not seem to have increased the total volume of international banking business done in the country.

Deregulation and Financial Innovation

It should be clear from our survey so far that there has been an evolution in the pattern of American banking going back quite some years. This evolution probably became more apparent from the early 1970s onwards. In recent years, the quickening pace of change has become even more obvious. Unregulated financial institutions (even some non-financial institutions) have moved into certain traditional banking activities, able to operate without the restrictions imposed by regulation on banks. At the same time, depository institutions have been broadening the scope of their activities and themselves offering a fuller range of financial services.

One of the chief competitors to emerge and to attract significant sums of money away from the banks was the money-market mutual fund, which provides access to individuals and businesses with relatively small amounts of funds to open-market investments, which in the past were only available to large corporations. These funds were first offered to the public in 1972, but they increased rapidly in importance – in terms of growth in number of shareholders and balances in shareholder accounts – only after 1974, and especially after 1977. By August 1984, there were about 340 money-market mutual funds in existence, holding about $190 billion in assets. Many of these funds pay a market rate of return and also offer the facility of writing cheques (e.g., in minimum amounts of $500). Moreover, they were seen to be at least partial substitutes for demand deposits. Like savings accounts, they offered high liquidity, since fund shares could be purchased or sold on any business day without a sales charge, and, indeed, they appeared to have more in common with savings accounts (e.g., similarity in turnover rates) than with demand-deposit accounts. The aggregate volume of these money-market mutual funds had reached a peak of about $240 billion late in 1982, but subsequently declined after American commercial banks and thrifts obtained the power to offer a competitive investment vehicle. Securities firms, insurance companies, and other non-depository institutions also moved aggressively into providing a range of liquid financial instruments.

In addition, large manufacturing and retail firms moved into the commercial and retail lending businesses. For example, Sears, Roebuck and Company owns a savings and loan association and in 1981 acquired a major securities-brokerage house and the nation's largest independent broker and real estate dealer. General Electric operates a broad range of financial services, including commercial and retail lending and insurance. Recently, it also purchased an industrial-loan company which takes in savings deposits. Manufacturing firms have also moved directly into the consumer-banking business. Gulf and Western acquired a federally chartered commercial bank in 1980. The bank was not covered by the Bank Holding Company Act because it did not make commercial loans. In 1981, a steel-manufacturing company became the owner of one of the largest federal savings and loan associations in the country. Citizen's Federal Savings and Loan Association, San Francisco, merged West Side Federal Savings and Loan of New York and Washington Savings and Loan Association in Miami Beach, forming a nationwide $7 billion financial institution. Citizen's was owned by National Steel Corporation. The resulting holding company is now called First Nationwide Financial Corporation and its savings and loan subsidiary is First Nationwide Savings (formerly Citizen's).

Meanwhile, depository institutions had developed a number of new services. One of the most notable was the Negotiated Order of Withdrawal (NOW) account. NOW accounts were similar to savings accounts but subject to a 'negotiated order of withdrawal'; negotiable drafts could be written on savings accounts at banks, mutual savings banks, and savings and loan associations; in effect, they provided a near-substitute for chequing facilities. Hence, NOW accounts became a readily transferable means of payment. Over the period 1972 to 1980, NOW accounts spread in piecemeal fashion throughout New England, New York, and New Jersey. In parts of New England, mutual savings banks had also been offering NOWs over a period of some years,[57] while depository institutions of all types had after 1976 been able to offer NOWs in all six New England states. Subsequently, they were authorised on a nationwide basis.

> One of the most prominent features of the New England NOW experiment has been the wide diversity of experience, both across states and among different types of institutions. In particular the penetration of NOWs among consumers and the rate at which personal checking balances converted to NOWs differed among states, while commercial banks and thrift institutions differed in the terms they imposed and the average balance and market share they attracted. This wide diversity of outcomes indicates that the impact of NOWs is the result of a complex interaction of factors such as the local banking structure, the competitive environment, and the pricing schemes and promotional strategies adopted by each bank.[58]

Share drafts at credit unions also became a means of payment.

> NOW accounts and share drafts, however, differ from demand deposits at commercial banks in that they bear interest. Hence, for the first time since 1933, when interest on demand deposits was prohibited by law, what amounts to interest-bearing demand deposits comprises part of the nation's payments medium. Moreover, since November 1, 1978 commercial banks have been allowed to cover their customers' overdrafts by automatically transferring funds from savings to checking accounts. This too allows the use of interest-

bearing deposits for making payments.[59]

In New England, commercial banks were able to attract NOW balances that exceeded those of the thrift institutions; as a result, they acquired a market share of balances that exceeded their market share of accounts. The commercial-bank strategy was to require substantial minimum balances to limit loss of NOW balances to thrift institutions, but this was likely to be less effective in the long run, when ability to compete would depend on the bank's attracting new accounts. In fact, whether due to the more stringent minimum-balance requirements or the decline in the relative number of offices, commercial banks in most of the New England states experienced after 1976 a slow but significant erosion of their NOW market share.[60]

Reference has already been made to automatic transfer services (ATS). In this case, depositors were allowed after November 1978 to arrange with their banks for the automatic transfer of funds from an interest-bearing savings account to a chequing account; they are the functional equivalent of NOW accounts and share drafts. ATS are a direct substitute for traditional chequing balances and have been authorised on a nationwide basis for all commercial banks.[61]

Some innovations go back a long time – commercial banks have been important suppliers of corporate cash-management services (including cash-flow forecasting and internal accounting control systems) over much of the post-World War II period; the large negotiable certificate of deposit specifically designed to attract corporate funds, and for which a secondary market soon developed, was introduced in February 1961; savings accounts for state and local governments and businesses, on the one hand, and telephone transfers from savings accounts, on the other, were both undertaken by federal savings and loan associations in the 1960s, and by commercial banks in the mid-1970s; similarly with pre-authorised third-party transfers from savings accounts for recurring transactions – for savings and loan associations beginning in 1970, for the banks again the mid-1970s; savings and loan remote service units – machines that allow a customer to make deposits to, and withdrawals from, his savings account at stores and other places away from the institution maintaining the account – were first authorised in early 1974; and re-purchase agreements in 1969; the last were for the most part short-term contracts, whereby a bank purchased immediately available funds against the collateral of securities, which securities were re-purchased by the bank at the end of the contract; there are no reserve requirements on re-purchase agreements secured by US government or government-guaranteed securities, though a marginal reserve requirement on 'managed liabilities', including such re-purchase agreements, was in force between October 1979 and July 1980. Latterly, retail re-purchase agreements (e.g., for individuals and medium-sized firms) have been developed.[62]

The rapid pace of financial innovation of recent years is due largely to three major factors. The first of these was the serious inflation the economy had suffered after 1965 and especially after 1973. The second was the rapid development of computer and communications technology. The third was a change in the regulatory environment dating from the early 1960s.

Inflation accelerated the pace of financial innovation through its impact on interest rates. Inflation has become an important determinant of the level of interest rates, because the level of interest rates reflects anticipations of future inflation and anticipations more or less follow recent experience with inflation. In this environment, lenders sought higher interest rates as compensation for the depreciating purchasing power of their savings and borrowers competing for funds have been willing to pay higher interest rates because they could expect corresponding increases in income from investments financed through borrowings. Consequently, rising rates of inflation led to higher interest rates. High interest rates increase the opportunity cost of holding non-interest-bearing assets and encourage the economising of such assets.

An example of how this leads to innovation is seen in the case of commercial banks, which are required by law to hold reserves in the form of non-interest-bearing assets. The interest forgone on these reserves, and hence the cost of holding them, rises with the level of market interest rates. In a period of high rates, banks try harder to reduce the amount of reserves required by law. Commercial banks can achieve these results in a variety of ways. Their efforts to do so have resulted in a significant diversification of bank liabilities, hence in the claims on banks held by bank customers. The liabilities side of bank balance sheets now include, in much larger proportion than in the 1960s, RPs, federal funds purchases, negotiable and non-negotiable CDs, consumer-type CDs, and in the case of large banks, Euro-dollar borrowings and other liabilities to foreign branches. These liabilities all involve lower legal reserve requirements than demand deposits and have been the principal means by which banks manage their liabilities to support asset levels not otherwise possible through the normal accretion of customer deposits. These liability-management operations, of course, involve added risk to the bank in question – e.g., increased interest expenses and the potential volatility of the funds purchased.

High interest rates provide incentives for individuals and businesses to shift out of demand deposits and into new types of bank liabilities. Hence, commercial banks and other financial institutions find a ready market for new interest-bearing liquid substitutes for demand deposits that their ingenuity can devise.

The rapid development of computer and communications technology has given individual institutions the capacity to process massive amounts of data and to make transfers rapidly and efficiently. In many instances, sophisticated new equipment has resulted in sizeable amounts of excess capacity, thereby creating incentives for expanding existing services and offering new kinds of services. In short, the revolution in computer and communications technology has played an important role in recent financial innovation.

Between the early 1930s and the 1960s, bank-regulatory philosophy was dominated by a preoccupation with the soundness of individual institutions. Competition in banking was viewed as a double-edged sword, incorporating notable disadvantages as well as some generally accepted advantages in improving the quality of banking services to the public. Indeed, some bank regulations, such as the prohibition of the payment of interest on demand deposits and the limitation on interest payable on savings deposits, were designed explicitly to discourage competition.

In the early and mid-1960s, major changes were made in federal and state laws and regulations; most of these tended to encourage competition not only among banks but also between commercial banks and other financial institutions. With the introduction of the negotiable CD in 1961, large commercial banks found a way to compete for money-market funds. Shortly afterwards, both large and small banks, which until the 1960s had shown relatively little interest in consumer-type savings deposits, began moving vigorously into this market. These moves ushered in an era of ever-sharpening competition within the commercial-banking community and between commercial banks and other financial intermediaries. Subsequent changes in bank holding-company law, liberalisation of regulations for thrift institutions, and a more competitive international banking climate reinforced this move towards more intensive competition. In any case, there was in the period after 1961 a more or less steady relaxation of regulatory constraints and a significant increase in competition among all types of financial institutions.[63]

But the steady relaxation of regulatory constraints did not always result from an initiative taken by the regulators themselves. A simple illustration of this is the NOW account case.

> The secular rise in interest rates in the late 1960's was especially troublesome for mutual savings banks. As legal ceilings on the interest they could pay became increasingly restrictive, their ability to compete for funds deteriorated and their deposit growth slowed. Federal law prohibited payment of interest on checking accounts, but the prohibition did not extend to mutual savings banks that were not insured by the FDIC.

In 1970, in its search for deposits, a state-insured Massachusetts mutual savings bank sought authority from the state commissioner of banking to offer NOW accounts. This was refused, but overturned on appeal to the State Supreme Court, on grounds that state law provided no restrictions on the form in which deposits could be drawn. Federal law then authorised the issue of NOW accounts by commercial banks and thrift institutions, first in Massachusetts and New Hampshire, then in all New England states, followed by New York and New Jersey; finally, their issue became nationwide, effective 31 December 1980. To preserve competitive equity nationally, commercial banks were allowed to offer automatic transfer services from November 1978.[64]

Throughout these years, there had been much discussion and an input of considerable effort by members of Congress, all the regulatory agencies and the financial industry itself and this culminated in the passage of the Depository Institutions Deregulation and Monetary Control Act of 1980, signed by President Carter on 31 March of that year. The object was to change some of the rules under which American financial institutions had operated for nearly half a century. In many respects, these rules had become obsolete as a result of changes in the economy, the functioning of credit markets, the advance of technology, the consumer demand for new financial services, and the competitive environment.

A number of studies including the Report of the Commission on Money and Credit in 1961 and the Report of the President's Commission on Financial Structure and Regulation (Hunt Commission) of 1971 had recommended many of the reforms finally adopted in the Act and, in more recent years, the Federal Reserve Board had given strong support, firstly, to phasing out deposit-interest ceilings coupled with broader investment powers for thrift institutions, and secondly, to the broader and more uniform application of reserve requirements. In adopting the new law, Congress either dealt with, or at least touched on, most of the major issues that had been the subject of controversy over the years. Inevitably, what emerged was a rather untidy piece of legislation, the product of much compromise. Some were inclined to regard it as the most significant piece of financial legislation since the 1930s[65] but that was probably going too far.

There were several factors which interacted finally to precipitate legislative action on a massive set of reform measures. Above all, there was the high level of inflation and interest rates that exacerbated what had been recognised as problems under the old regulations; this convinced all parties that a piecemeal approach would be unworkable. The erosion of Federal Reserve membership quickened as high investment yields increased the penalty imposed on member banks by the requirement that they hold non-interest bearing reserve deposits at the Federal Reserve; also small savers were heavily disadvantaged when their returns were compared with those available to large investors; again, disintermediation hurt the housing market as savers withdrew funds from mortgage-lending institutions and invested them in high-yielding money-market mutual funds and other market instruments; furthermore, the viability of thrift institutions was seriously threatened by the imbalance between cost of funds and their returns on long-term mortgage portfolios;[66] and, at times, usury laws in some states effectively cut off credit to small businesses, farmers and households. Other factors included the promise of better customer service as a result of new technology (e.g., electronic devices for funds transfer) and the growing availability of payments services from depository institutions other than commercial banks. In addition, it was felt that Federal Reserve credit should be available as an ultimate source of liquidity to all such institutions. Finally, there was increased emphasis on monetary aggregates as intermediate targets of monetary policy and this focused attention on the need for changes that would permit better measurement and control of these aggregates.

The principal objectives of the Act included attempts, firstly, to improve monetary control and to equalise more nearly its cost among depository institutions; secondly, to remove impediments to competition for funds by depository institutions, at the same time allowing small savers a market rate of return; and thirdly, to expand the availability of financial services to the public and to reduce competitive inequalities between financial institutions offering them.

The major changes[67] made by the new Act were as follows:

1. The imposition of uniform Federal Reserve requirements on

similar classes of reservable liabilities being transactions accounts at all depository institutions; these included commercial banks, savings and loan associations, mutual savings banks, and credit unions. Transactions accounts comprehended demand deposits, NOW accounts, telephone transfers, automatic transfers, and share drafts. The relevant institutions now had to maintain reserves in the ratio of 3 per cent for that portion of their transactions accounts below $25 million and initially 12 per cent (the Board can vary this between 8 and 14 per cent) for the portion above $25 million. They also had to maintain reserves initially of 3 per cent (or within the range of 0 to 9 per cent) against their non-personal time deposits and had to report (directly or indirectly) their liabilities and assets to the Federal Reserve. The Act provided for an eight-year phasing-in of reserve requirements for depository institutions which were not members of the Federal Reserve and a four-year phasing-down of previous reserve requirements for member banks. Member banks could no longer avoid the cost of holding sterile reserves by simply withdrawing from membership in the Federal Reserve System. Banks that withdraw must now hold the same amount of reserves as member banks. The Act permits the Federal Reserve Board, in 'extraordinary circumstances', to impose an additional reserve requirement on any depository institution of up to 4 per cent of its transactions accounts. If it were imposed, this supplemental reserve would earn interest.

2. Authorisation for the collection of data necessary for the monitoring and control of the money and credit aggregates. Accurate and timely information on the monetary and credit aggregates is essential to the effective discharge of the Federal Reserve's monetary policy responsibilities. Previous data estimates relied heavily on reports submitted by member banks of the Federal Reserve System. In the past, however, it was often necessary to make large revisions when non-member institution data, such as for quarterly 'benchmark' dates, became available. Some improvement in the quality and timeliness of monetary and credit aggregates data had been made possible by voluntary reporting of certain non-member institutions, as when the monetary aggregates were redefined in early 1980. But even with these improvements, current data estimates were imprecise and subject to revision as additional data became available, often with a significant time lag.

In order to remedy these deficiencies, the new law authorised the Board to require all depository institutions to submit reports of their assets and liabilities as needed or desirable for monetary policy purposes. However, the Board's authority to require data reporting was not to be used indiscriminately and the new law stipulated that every effort should be made to avoid imposing unnecessary burdens and duplicate reporting requirements on depository institutions.

3. Access to the discount window at Federal Reserve Banks was widened. Any depository institution issuing transactions accounts or non-personal time deposits now had the same discount and borrowing privilege at the Federal Reserve as member banks; this was effective immediately.

4. There was a requirement that the Federal Reserve price its services and grant all depository institutions access to such services. The Fed was now required to establish fees for services such as currency and coin services, cheque clearing and collection, wire transfers, and automated clearing house services. The fees were to take effect by 1 October 1981 and the Board had to publish a proposed fee schedule by 1 October 1980.

5. As a result of its deliberations, Congress had declared that interest-rate ceilings on deposits (e.g., the old Regulation Q) discouraged saving and created inequities for depositors, especially for savers of modest amounts. The Act therefore set up machinery to phase out interest-rate ceilings on deposits over a six-year period.[68]

6. An attempt was made to grasp the nettle of the state usury laws. Thus, state usury ceilings on first residential mortgage loans were eliminated (as of 31 March 1980) unless a state adopted a new ceiling before 1 April 1983. Credit unions could increase their loan-rate ceiling from 12 per cent to 15 per cent and might raise the ceiling higher for periods of up to 18 months. The Act also pre-empted (or overrode) state usury ceilings on business and agricultural loans above $25,000 and permitted an interest rate of not more than 5 per cent above the Federal Reserve discount rate, including any surcharge, on 90-day commercial paper. This provision would expire on 1 April 1983 or earlier if the state reinstituted its ceiling.[69] The problems with usury laws were fairly straightforward. First, the costs and risks of lending small amounts to poor credit risks made such lending unremunerative at the statutory levels. Consequently, such borrowers would not be accommodated at all at the statutory rate. Secondly, the profit opportunities inherent in lending to such borrowers at an unrestricted rate gave rise to a variety of devices, legal and illegal, to circumvent the ceilings. Exceptions to the usury ceilings had proliferated, 'making a tangled web of the statutes governing lending in many states'. Finally, even usury ceilings that had appeared reasonable in normal times, in

the sense of allowing lenders a modest but competitive rate of return, had become wholly unrealistic as market interest rates had risen sharply over recent years.

7. NOW accounts were now to be authorised on a nationwide basis, as were certain interest-bearing balances at both banks and thrift institutions capable of being used for transactions purposes. After 31 December 1980, all depository institutions could offer NOW accounts (interest-earning chequing accounts) to individuals and non-profit organisations. The Act also allowed banks to provide automatic transfer services from savings to chequing accounts, permitted savings and loan associations to use remote service units, and authorised all federally insured credit unions to offer share-draft accounts, effective immediately.

8. The permissible activities of thrift institutions were broadened considerably. For example, the Act gave federal savings and loan associations greater lending flexibility and higher loan ceilings, expanded their investing authority, permitted them to issue credit cards, and provided them with trust powers.[70] Most states subsequently enacted similar expansions of powers not previously available to their thrift institutions. One of the most significant new powers for federal savings banks was commercial lending and related demand deposits for businesses.

9. The Act increased federal deposit insurance at commercial banks, savings banks, savings and loan associations, and credit unions from $40,000 to $100,000, effective immediately.

10. Finally, the new Act simplified 'Truth in Lending' disclosures and financial regulations to make it easier for creditors to comply with its disclosure provisions. The Federal Reserve was required to publish model disclosure forms; it exempted agricultural credit from coverage by Truth in Lending, and permitted lenders greater tolerance (1/8 of 1 per cent) in disclosing the annual percentage rate. The Act also authorised the enforcing agency to require reimbursements in cases where the annual percentage rate or finance charge was inaccurately disclosed, but released creditors from civil liability for unintentional violations resulting from bona-fide errors.[71] This was a very necessary reform. While there was much to be said for the extensive regulation of consumer financial services – by both the federal government and the individual states – there had tended to be a proliferation over the years that had become distinctly oppressive. Traditionally, the states had occupied this field – setting usury limits, establishing permissible contract provisions, and providing other consumer protections; latterly, the

federal government had become increasingly involved by regulating areas like credit disclosures, billing practices, consumer leasing transactions, electronic fund transfers, mortgage rates, and mortgage instruments.[72] In these circumstances, small banks in particular were at risk as a result of rising costs (since much time had to be spent and the services of senior personnel deployed in making sure the regulations were being observed), and frivolous but costly actions were not unknown. As one president of a small bank put it to the author: 'There is not much fun in banking any more.'

Latterly, under the Act, the transition to pricing of the Federal Reserve's payments services to depository institutions was essentially completed during 1983. With regard to the deregulation of interest-rate ceilings, the regulations are now all in place. For 'IRA' and 'KEOGH' depositors (special tax-sheltered accounts for individuals and small business firms), the $2,500 minimum deposit was removed on 1 December 1983 for money-market deposit accounts, Super-NOW accounts, and seven- to 31-day accounts. For other depositors, these minima were reduced to $1,000 on 1 January 1985 and were to be removed on 1 January 1986.

Subsequently, new legislation permitted depository institutions to offer money-market deposit accounts free of interest-rate restrictions. This became possible under the Garn-St Germain Depository Institutions Act of 1982.[73] The new account was required to be 'directly equivalent to and competitive with money market mutual funds'. The accounts had no minimum maturity and were permitted up to three pre-authorised or automatic transfers and three transfers to third parties (cheques) per month. In addition to authorising this account as from 14 December 1982, the Depository Institutions Deregulation Committee issued regulations (as from 5 January 1983) to permit a Super-NOW Account subject to no interest rates ceilings but with unlimited chequing facilities (or third-party transfers) to individuals willing to maintain a minimum balance of $2,500 in a chequing account; the same minimum applied to money-market deposit accounts (MMDAs). The primary difference between them was that Super-NOW accounts permitted an unlimited number of cheques and were treated as transactions accounts for reserve-requirement purposes, while money-market deposit accounts had limited chequing facilities and were not classified as transactions accounts. Hence, as personal accounts, the latter carried no required reserves, and non-personal accounts a 3 per cent reserve requirement.

These innovations, together with the earlier introduction of money-market mutual funds, savings deposits with automatic transfer services, and the NOW accounts, raised important questions about their effects on the measurement of the monetary aggregates used as a basis for policy. 'Serious concern has been expressed about the continued reliability of monetary aggregates as economic indicators and their usefulness for monetary policy.' Some analysts concluded that M1 would be subject to large and unpredictable changes that would adversely affect its relationships with spending and inflation, while M2 would remain unaffected. As a result, it was suggested that the Federal Reserve should focus more attention on M2 in the conduct of monetary policy'[74]

To summarise the conclusions of a useful study by the Federal Reserve Bank of St. Louis:

> Strong concern has been expressed that newly authorized financial instruments at depository institutions will substantially alter M1, thus reducing its usefulness as a target for conducting monetary policy. In particular, the current concern is that M1 will be either pushed upward by additions of idle or non-transaction balances to meet the higher minimum for Super-NOW accounts, or pushed downward by shifts of idle or non-transaction balances from demand and NOW deposits to MMDAs. Since such shifting is primarily between assets within the M2 measure, it has been widely asserted that the shifts do not affect the measure of M2 and, by implication, will not distort its meaning or usefulness for the conduct of monetary policy.
>
> A broader view of the money supply process reaches the opposite conclusions. The newly created money market deposit accounts are non-reservable deposits with limited transaction services and are quite similar, in practice as well as in legislative intent, to money market mutual funds. The principal differences are federal insurance and geographic convenience. Similarly, Super-NOW accounts are virtually identical to NOW accounts, except that a $2,500 minimum balance is required by law and the instrument is free of rate regulation.
>
> Money market mutual fund-type assets, like money market deposit accounts, have no effect on M1 or its velocity. Increases in such assets do tend to raise M2, however, and to reduce its velocity. Super-NOWs are similar to other checkable deposits and are unlikely to affect M1 or M2 measures or their relationships to spending. In principle, the higher yields on Super-NOWs compared with other transaction balances could lower currency demand relative to total

transaction deposits, thereby increasing both the demand for M1 and its multiplier. The evidence from the introduction of ATS and, later, NOW accounts provides no support for this conjecture, however.

Finally, it does not appear that M2 is likely to be superior to M1 as a target for conducting monetary policy. The conventional view that the M2-GNP relationship is both statistically significant and stable has not been supported by the experience over the past several years.[75]

The Future

Within the financial services industry, the functions of institutions have become significantly broader over the past two decades; product and geographic markets have become much more integrated. Institutions that once looked quite different from each other now offer similar products and offer them in much broader geographic markets. Initially, it may have been a case of non-depository institutions intruding into what had been regarded as the domain of banks and thrift institutions (e.g., the invasion by companies like Sears, Merrill Lynch, American Express, and Prudential). Latterly, banks and thrifts have also 'hurried to diversify', greatly assisted in the case of the thrifts by the Garn-St. Germain Depository Institutions Act of 1982, which permitted federally chartered savings and loan associations and savings banks for the first time to make overdraft loans; to invest in the accounts of other insured institutions; and more importantly, to make commercial loans. The Act also increased their powers to invest in state and local-government obligations; to make residential and non-residential real-estate loans; and to make consumer and educational loans.

> Commercial banks and their holding companies have moved into credit cards, discount brokerage, leasing, operating finance companies and many other activities. . . Thrift institutions, though slow to diversify until the 1980s, have received broad new powers from the Monetary Control Act of 1980 and the more recent Garn-St Germain Act. They may now offer a wide range of products to consumers and businesses where before they were limited to individual savings and mortgage markets. Considerable evidence from financial reports and advertisements indicates that an important segment of the thrift industry is using its new powers.

In what was once called the non-depository sector,

> firms of all sorts have been crossing institutional boundaries with abandon . . . Insurance companies have pushed diversification into securities, consumer finance and even banking and thrift industries. Prudential is probably the best known of these firms with its acquisition of Bache, its money fund and its nonbank bank – a chartered and insured bank that, because it is owned by a nonbank company, is not subject to the restrictions of the Bank Holding Company Act. American General, with money market funds, more traditional mutual funds and its billion-dollar finance company, may have gone further in decreasing its concentration on insurance alone. Travelers has embarked on an entirely different strategy of expanding into a broader variety of businesses, providing financial services at the wholesale level to financial firms of all types. (Travelers also has a nonbank bank.)
>
> Among securities firms, Merrill Lynch is the quintessential diversified financial corporation, but others have accomplished much the same sort of diversification.

Others have ventured *inter alia* into insurance underwriting and sales, commercial lending, and non-bank banks.[76] Firms that were once consumer-finance companies have also diversified. Household International, for example, is hardly an old-style finance company any more. It owns a non-bank bank, a group of thrifts and a life-insurance company. A competitor, Beneficial Corporation, also has a non-bank bank and insurance companies and has expanded into commercial finance, leasing and sales finance. Household is also engaged in pilot programmes that make insurance, ATMs, equity lines of credit and safe-deposit boxes available at its consumer-finance offices. Such offices could become the one-stop financial centre for a substantial portion of the population.

> The diversification of other institutions into banking functions has been motivated by a pull from the market for bank products and a push from the markets in which the other institutions operated. Banks have been, in many ways, the most diversified segment of the financial services industry. Their diversification and the markets in which they are diversified have provided them with good, steady earnings growth and, just as important, excellent earnings stability. Through the financial turmoil of the last 25 years, banks in the

> aggregate have suffered just one year of earnings decline – 1959. Their compound earnings growth rate over that period has been 9.1 percent – well above the inflation rate for the period. In addition, bank earnings have been quite stable, around 0.75 percent return on assets . . . Other segments of the industry have not fared so well.

The thrift industry, for example, faced problems over a period of several years (mainly due to a past emphasis on fixed-rate lending on mortgages). Even before the sharp rise in interest rates on their liabilities, their earnings had been quite cyclical, with a much greater year-to-year variation than applied to the commercial banks. Security dealers 'suffered a shake-out', partly due to the commission deregulation of the early and mid-1970s. Although their health improved, earnings remained quite volatile. In the life-insurance sector, there was much competition from group insurance and many customers allowed their ordinary life policies to lapse. The emergence of many new types of savings instruments caused insurance firms 'to reassess their positions and products'.

However, the financial performance of the banks, which reflected the value of their markets, created problems for them by attracting 'a multitude of competitors'. 'Commercial banks' share of the financial assets held by all private financial institutions dropped sharply after 1975, as did their share of consumer credit. . . The banks' share of business credit began declining earlier, in the 1960s, and has declined further in recent years.' Banks lost market share not only because their managements failed to keep pace with those diversifying into their markets. Regulatory limitations also prevented them from meeting many challenges with proper pricing or product. 'As it became obvious how much impact these limits were having on commercial banks' market shares and thrifts' earnings during the high-interest period of the early 1980s, some of the restrictions were lifted by the government.' Thus, interest-rate limits were removed gradually to permit unlimited competition for funds. As a result, the time and savings deposits of both banks and thrifts recovered. The activities allowed to banks and thrifts were increased. Although questioning some submissions, the Federal Reserve added 'credit insurance underwriting and sales, finance and mortgage company operations, leasing, discount brokerages, financial advice and several other businesses to the activities permitted bank holding companies . . . At the same time, Congress and the Federal Home Loan Bank Board have greatly extended permissible activities for thrifts.'[77] In many states, too, geographic barriers are being removed (by April 1984, some 17 states had already passed some kind of limited inter-state banking legislation[78] and several more were considering such laws);[79] sometimes, the barriers were reduced by federal regulators when 'responding to emergencies' (e.g., savings and loan associations have been acquired in inter-state emergency mergers).

The effect of this continuing elimination of barriers has been to deny the usefulness of referring to different financial sectors such as banks, thrifts, insurance, finance and securities companies. All such institutions can now offer products that substantially overlap.

> Integration of product and geographic markets means there are few protected markets left. Protective limits are gone; entering new markets is relatively easy. Economies of scale are of minor importance in the production of many services, so many potential entrants are moving into most markets. Where economies of scale exist, service corporations that can exploit them can wholesale their advantage to many small institutions acting as agents. In such situations, products tend to become commodities. Differentiation is more difficult when most products can be copied and produced easily and when price is an important dimension.

This has given rise to a series of new challenges to management – likewise for regulators.[80]

> A situation is developing in which the financial industry is becoming like most others. There is no clear protection; getting into banking does not guarantee a business that is somewhat proprietary, that provides a monopolistic right. With this easier entry, sharp profit squeezes are likely in the future and more and more bank products are going to be commodities rather than unique services. A major skill required of future senior management will be to design products that are unique or at least a bit different from those offered by the competition.
>
> Success in providing financial services is going to be similar to succeeding in any other business. The major focus will be on finding out what customers want and really working to supply those needs.[81]

What customers seem to want is high quality of existing products and a consistent and quality service, and attention to customer needs will be the most crucial factor in the success of financial institutions over the coming years.

Deregulation Outside North America

Shifting patterns in financial markets have also become a feature of recent developments in the United Kingdom with the clearing banks (and others) extending their interests in other financial institutions, including stock-exchange firms; more generally, there has been an interest in building up in London a number of financial-services conglomerates, though clearly it will be necessary to guard against possible conflicts of interest. In West Germany, though subject to detailed prudential supervision, banking is already deregulated – even a foreign bank or broker can secure ready entry – and a high degree of competition obtains. Countries that are now proceeding with financial deregulation include Australia, Canada, France, Italy, Spain, Sweden and Japan.

Notes

1. This was the Bank of North America incorporated in 1781.
2. The story of branch banking in California, which is a large state and was therefore something of an exception, deserves some attention. Originally, California also was served by unit banks. None the less, branch banking was permitted and, when Mr A.P. Giannini began to expand the business of the Bank of Italy (later to become Bank of America) in serving the needs of immigrant communities (beginning in 1909) he chose the path initially of bank acquisitions and conversion into branches. It should also be remembered that the state was endowed with good land and a good climate, which fostered a diversified agriculture. Given a man of vision like Giannini, it was ripe for development. Expansion was also encouraged by the booms of World War 1 and the 1920s. The bank grew both as a result of 'natural' growth and 'purchased' growth. Indeed, during World War 1, about 60 per cent of the Bank of Italy's enormous increase in deposits came from banks bought 'in the course of the surge through the agricultural valleys'. See Marquis and Bessie Rowland James, *Biography of a Bank: The Story of Bank of America* (New York, 1954), especially Chapters IV, V, VI, VII, XIII, and XVIII.
3. See Charles R. Whittlesey, Arthur M. Freedman and Edward S. Herman, *Money and Banking: Analysis and Policy* (New York, 1963), pp. 207ff.
4. See FDIC, *1983 Statistics on Banking*, Table 103.
5. Some of the reasons non-member banks give for remaining outside the Federal Reserve System include the desire 'to follow their own pattern' free from restriction; the less rigorous examinations procedure of the state authorities and/or of the Federal Deposit Insurance Corporation; the more elastic application of reserve requirements usually provided for under state laws, permitting them to tie up less of their cash reserves (frequently state laws permit part of the reserve to be held in securities); the advantages in terms of services provided when cash

balances are held with correspondent banks rather than with the Federal Reserve Bank; and the fact that they do not have to hold Federal Reserve Bank stock. In general terms, they are inclined to sum up their attitude in the form of a question: what can the Federal Reserve give us that we haven't got already?

Of 15,182 commercial banks for which information was available at the end of 1983, 12,641 had assets of less than $100 million. Only 56 (of which six were mutual savings banks) had assets of $5 billion or more, or 34.9 per cent of the total and less than 1.35 per cent of the banks (295) had 56.96 per cent of total assets. See FDIC, *1983 Statistics on Banking*, Table 104.

7. See FDIC, *1983 Statistics on Banking*.

8. Most conspicuously in Florida as a result of changes in the law effective 1 January 1977 (county-wide branching) and 1 July 1980 (state-wide branching by merger). Formerly, Florida was a unit-banking state, but the law permitted state-wide holding companies.

9. In the earlier years, commercial banks in the United States were disinclined to recognise the value of offering banking services to consumers. Indeed, in the matter of consumer deposits, in much of the period immediately after World War II, savings and loan associations, savings banks, and credit unions were gaining significantly at the expense of commercial banks. As indicated, and with variations of degree, branch expansion took place mainly in the period 1960-80. Latterly, there have been clear signs of a decline in the role of branches as a means of delivering banking services. During the period when deposit ceilings were binding, banks offered non-rate compensation to depositors. This compensation included free services (such as chequing accounts) and also a proliferation of convenient office locations. With the rationalisation of interest payments, numerous branches became redundant and branches subsequently became even less necessary as a result of a resort to the use of remote funds-transfer services (such as the telephone) and by easily accessible automated teller machines. Furthermore, the increases of service charges on deposit accounts have encouraged use of non-paper (hence non-branch) funds-transfer services.

10. Much of this analysis has been based on statistics published by the FDIC in its *Annual Reports*, latterly in *Statistics on Banking*.

11. See J.S.G. Wilson, 'America's Changing Banking Scene, the Structure as a Whole', *The Banker* (March 1957).

12. Supported by an inquiry financed by the Chicago Association of Commerce and Industry. See Irving Schweiger and John S. McGee, 'Chicago Banking', *Journal of Business of the University of Chicago* (July 1961), pp. 203-366. This trend in the formation of opinion was reflected also in the Report of the United States Commission on Money and Credit published in 1961. Although the evidence was not conclusive, the Commission felt that 'competition among branches of several large institutions and with unit banks will produce more adequate banking facilities in a community than competition among several small independent institutions'. On the whole, the Commission's recommendations were constructive; it endeavoured to lead public opinion rather than follow it.

13 Group banking, it should be emphasised, was formally different from 'chain banking', which will not be separately considered, in that banks in a 'group' were controlled by a holding company whereas control over banks in a 'chain' was exercised through ownership by an individual (or a small number of individuals) of a controlling interest in each of the independently incorporated banks in the 'chain'. However, there was only one really big chain-banking organisation in the country, the so-called Florida National group of banks. The banks in this chain comprised part of the DuPont estate, which as a trust estate was in any event exempt from the type of regulation that could be applied to a holding company. (See *Control of Bank Holding Companies*, Senate Hearings 84th Con-

gress, First Session, as printed pp. 72-3).

14. Originally, the Bank Holding Company Act of 1956 precluded inter-state banking, except for companies that were accorded grandfather rights, but did not preclude multibank holding companies from offering 'closely related' financial services through non-bank subsidiaries anywhere in the United States. These non-banking powers were broadened by the 1970 amendments for both one-bank and multibank holding companies and the rules made applicable to both (formerly, one-bank holding companies were not subject to activity restrictions). More recently, inter-state acquisitions of depository institutions were permitted in cases of failing banks or thrift institutions. The 'non-bank bank' (an entity which had divested either its commercial loan or demand deposit activity to avoid coming under the Bank Holding Company Act definition of a bank) was another way in which inter-state banking could be conducted under another name.

15. Another reason for the development of the holding company – which affected the other side of the balance sheet – was the issue of ceiling-free debt instruments for the purpose of funding their assets.

16. Before holding companies were legalised, it was a violation of the common law for one corporation to own another. New Jersey was the first state to pass laws legalising the holding company form, but other states followed soon after.

17. For bank holding-company development before 1960, see Gerald C. Fischer, *Bank Holding Companies* (New York, 1961).

18. See Thomas G. Watkins and Robert Craig West, 'Bank Holding Companies: Development and Regulation', *Federal Reserve Bank of Kansas City Economic Review* (June 1982), pp. 4-5. In large measure, the 1956 Act was aimed at Transamerica Corporation, which had embarked on an aggressive acquisition campaign in Western States in the early 1950s.

19. Ibid., p. 5.

20. See ibid., pp. 7-8.

21. See section on 'Regulation of U.S. Banking Structure' and relevant Table in Board of Governors of the Federal Reserve System *Annual Reports*.

22. For example, consumer finance, mortgage banking, credit cards, factoring, and operating an industrial bank.

23. The full 'public-benefits test' in Section 4(c) (8) of the Bank Holding Company Act states 'the Board shall consider whether performance [of a non-banking activity] by an affiliate of a holding company can reasonably be expected to produce benefits to the public, such as greater convenience, increased competition, or gains in efficiency, that outweigh possible adverse effects, such as undue concentration of resources, decreased or unfair competition, conflicts of interest, or unsound banking practices'.

24. See Watkins and West, 'Bank Holding Companies', pp. 5-6. In this same article there is a survey of holding companies' experience in the tenth district (Kansas City Fed). For a more detailed study in Texas, see Charles J. Smaistrla and David M. Cordell, 'Expansion and Performance of Multibank Holding Companies in Texas', *Voice of the Federal Reserve Bank of Dallas*, (April 1979). Another interesting study – Norman N. Bowsher, 'Have Multibank Holding Companies Affected Commercial Bank Performance?', *Federal Reserve Bank of St Louis Review* (April 1978) – concluded that 'the net effects of the holding company movement have been favorable for the general public' and that, on balance, multibank holding companies 'have offered a slightly wider range of banking services and have increased credit extended to consumers and small businesses over what otherwise would have been likely'. Affiliates of such companies are 'not as well capitalised as their independent counterparts, but risk is reduced through greater diversification. Independent banks do not seem to have been harmed by the introduction of a holding company operation in their

market area, having grown at roughly the same rate' as similar-sized holding companies. Reference might also be made to Stephen A. Rhoades and Roger D. Rutz, 'Impact of Bank Holding Companies on Competition and Performance in Banking Markets', Staff Studies no. 107 of the Board of Governors of the Federal Reserve System (1979) and Donald M. Brown, 'The Effect of State Banking Laws on Holding Company Banks', *Federal Reserve Bank of St. Louis Review* (August/September 1983).

25. See also Paul M. Horwitz, 'The Role of Mergers in Fostering a Viable Banking System' in Harry L. Johnson and Ernest W. Walker (eds.), *Monetary Issues of the 1960s* (Bureau of Business Research, University of Texas at Austin, 1968). It should be noted in the present section 'merger' is used as a generic term, which in addition to mergers proper may be employed to include consolidations, absorptions and purchases. In the present context, we are interested in the movement from the point of view of economic effects. There are, however, important legal differences in the several methods that may be employed.

26. Some believed that Los Angeles was so much of an 'automobile town' that location was a matter of secondary importance.

27. In this context, it has been pointed out to the author that changes in regulation have frequently taken place after the evolution of market developments that had already resulted in a significant shift of market shares. In other words, it seems to be the general rule that both the US Congress and the US regulators react to events. But so far as politicians are concerned – probably regulators also – that tends to be generally true.

28. In addition to action taken against mergers and consolidations, the Department of Justice twice attacked rate-fixing by banks and brought anti-trust actions against them – in Clinton, New Jersey (where the case was settled by consent decree, whereby the defendants were enjoined from continuing to agree upon service charges) and, later, in Minneapolis (where a grand jury returned three separate indictments charging eighteen banks, a bank holding company and a clearing-house association with fixing interest rates on loans and time deposits as well as service charges).

29. For example, in the PNB-Girard case: 'It was very surprising to learn . . . that not only New York banks solicit and receive substantial business from customers within the four-county area, but also large banks from all the larger cities in the nation do likewise.'

30. See J.S.G. Wilson, *Monetary Policy and the Development of Money Markets* (London, 1966), p. 215: 'when the tasks of bank supervision and regulation are divided not only between the States and Washington but also at the centre between several agencies, then even with the best will in the world cross-reference and consultation will produce delays. In addition, there will tend to be departures from the canons of consistency and overlapping jurisdictions are likely to lead to conflicting policies and inefficient administration. Some would argue that the time has come when Federal bank supervision should be concentrated in the hands of one central agency, competently staffed by men with specialist knowledge of the banking system. It is also important that the authority selected should be given some measure of independence.' See also ibid., pp. 215-7. This matter has been most recently reconsidered by the Task Group on Regulation of Financial Services (the Bush Task Group), which on 31 January 1984 'unanimously endorsed a proposal to substantially reorganise the federal agencies which regulate commercial banks'.

31. G.C. Fisher, *American Banking Structure* (New York, 1968), p. 311.

32. Ibid., p. 314.

33. Ibid., p. 315. In addition, according to Horwitz, 'The Role of Mergers', p. 58, 'the Lexington merger had to be relitigated on Sherman Act Section 2 grounds and other pending suits were to remain in the courts to be decided on

the basis of the new legislation.'

34. See *U.S. v. First City National Bank of Houston* and *U.S. v. Provident National Bank*, 386 U.S. 361 (1967), 18 L. ed. 2d 151, 158 (1967).

35. See, for example, Fischer, *American Banking Structure*, pp. 317-18.

36. Ibid., p. 164.

37. Ibid., p. 325.

38. See Joseph E. Gagnon, 'The New Merger Guidelines: Implications for New England Banking Markets', *Federal Reserve Bank of Boston New England Economic Review* (July/August 1982).

39. Numerous studies have been published citing the relationship of market concentration and barriers to entry with the conduct and profitability of firms in an industry. For a summary of those studies that relate to commercial banking, see Stephen Rhoades, *Structure-Performance Studies in Banking: A Summary and Evaluation*, Staff Economic Studies no. 92 (Board of Governors of the Federal Reserve System, December 1977).

40. The Comptroller of the Currency and the Federal Deposit Insurance Corporation have not quoted the guidelines in their merger decisions, but have instead relied somewhat more on the comments of the Federal Reserve Board and the Department of Justice concerning the competitive factors in each application.

41. A market was now considered 'least concentrated' if the Herfindahl index was between 0 and 1,000. A market was moderately concentrated if the index fell between 1,000 and 1,800, and highly concentrated if the index was above 1,800. For purposes of the revised guidelines, it was the market's concentration after the merger that was used to classify it as least, moderately or highly concentrated. Unlike the old guidelines, the new guidelines did not apply a significantly different and tougher standard towards mergers in markets that exhibited a trend towards increasing concentration. Instead, any trend towards increasing or decreasing concentration in the market would be considered along with other unusual factors in the case, such as very high or low barriers to entry. See Joseph E. Gagnon, 'The New Merger Guidelines: Implications for New England Banking Markets', *New England Economic Review* (July/August 1982).

42. W. Bagehot, *Lombard Street: a Description of the Money Market*, new and revised edition (London, 1900), pp. 269-70.

43. To a certain extent, too, country banks may share in loans originated by their city correspondents (e.g., where a large borrower has a local plant or factory in the area concerned).

44. Today, one refers only to 'commercial paper' – finance paper has disappeared as a separate category.

45. Outside New York, this seems to be the general rule. In New York itself, there is a small number of brokers specialising in bank stocks. They assemble lists of banks that want to sell out and they seek out buyers for these banks. Sometimes, too, they will be approached by a large bank looking for small banks to absorb.

46. Personal enquiry by the author at various times suggested that 'overlines' did not in fact represent a very significant proportion of total loans, but at their seasonal maximum 'overlines' might sometimes represent as much as 20 per cent of the relevant bank's loan portfolio and, in other cases, 10 per cent was quoted.

47. This is one of the conflicts inherent in correspondent banking and is most obvious when the city correspondent maintains branches in centres where some of his country correspondents are located. In such circumstances, the city correspondent must attempt to maintain a nice balance between his desire for country-bank deposits and the aggressiveness of his competition for loan business

in these areas.

48. Ira O. Scott Jr.,'"Correspondent" Banking in the U.S.A.', *The Banker* (August 1965).

49. *American Bankers Association Banking Journal* (November 1979), p. 56.

50. Constance Dunham, 'Commercial Bank Costs and Correspondent Banking', *New England Economic Review*, (September/October 1981), see especially pp. 29-33 on 'The Costs of Correspondent Services'.

51. See Richard K. Abrams, 'Regional Banks and International Banking', *Federal Reserve Bank of Kansas City Economic Review* (November 1980).

52. Ibid., p. 10.

53. See Sydney J. Key, 'Activities of International Banking Facilities: the Early Experience', *The Federal Reserve Bank of Chicago Economic Perspectives* (Autumn 1982).

54. See K.A. Chrystal, 'International Banking Facilities', *Federal Reserve Bank of St. Louis Review* (April 1984). As at 28 September 1983, there were 477 IBFs – 144 related to American chartered banks, 264 to agencies and branches of foreign banks, and 69 to Edge Act corporations.

55. Ibid.

56. Ibid., and see Table 1 on p. 7.

57. These could be cleared through normal cheque-clearing channels and are paid by the commercial bank with which the issuing thrift institution maintains a correspondent relationship.

58. See Richard C. Kimball, 'Variations in the New England NOW Account Experiment', *New England Economic Review* (November/December 1980), p. 23.

59. See Marvin Goodfriend, James Parthemos and Bruce Summers, 'Recent Financial Innovations: Causes, Consequences for the Payments System, and Implications for Monetary Control', *Federal Reserve Bank of Richmond Economic Review* (March/April 1980), p. 15.

60. Kimball, 'The New England NOW Account Experiment', p. 39.

61. Automatic transfer services were priced more conservatively by banks than were NOW accounts as originally offered in New England. It should also be noted that banks, but not thrift institutions, were authorised to offer ATS. These two factors were important in determining the growth of ATS accounts, which expanded rapidly when first introduced but which have subsequently grown much more slowly. In fact, ATS has had only a marginal initial impact on traditional payments arrangements. See Goodfriend *et al.*, 'Recent Financial Innovations', p. 21.

62. For a good summary of the position, see ibid., pp. 14-27.

63. An exception to this steady relaxation of regulatory constraints is the Interest Adjustment Act of 1966, which extended coverage of deposit-rate ceilings to the thrift industry and established a differential between maximum rates that banks and thrifts could pay on deposits. This action was a direct result of the heightened competition for consumer deposits occurring in the early and mid-1960s. See ibid., p. 17.

64. Ibid., pp. 15-17.

65. It was, according to Senator William A. Proxmire, 'the most significant banking legislation before the Congress since the passage of the Federal Reserve Act in 1913', and according to Representative Henry S. Reuss, 'the most significant package of financial legislation since the 1930s'. See 'The Depository Institutions Deregulation and Monetary Control Act of 1980 – Landmark financial legislation for the eighties', *Economic Perspectives* (September/October 1980).

66. See Bronwyn Brock, 'Mortgages with Adjustable Interest Rates Improve

Viability of Thrift Industry', *Voice* (February 1981) and Daniel J. Vrabac, 'Savings and Loan Associations: An Analysis of the Recent Decline in Profitability', *Federal Reserve Bank of Kansas City Economic Review* (July/August 1982).

67. Discussed in detail in *Economic Perspectives* (September/October 1980), with a useful summary in *Federal Reserve Bank of Atlanta Economic Review* (March/April 1980).

68. See *Economic Perspectives* (September/October 1980), pp. 12-16.

69. See ibid., pp. 16-18.

70. See ibid., pp. 18-22.

71. Additional matters of less importance are summarised in ibid., pp. 22-3.

72. Note, in this context there is a Doctrine of Preemption. Federal preemption means that, by operation of constitutional law, federal law overrides state law in a given field. The override may take one of two forms: the federal law may nullify the state law for all purposes, or it may render the state law inapplicable under limited circumstances (*Federal Reserve Bulletin* (November 1983), p. 823).

73. For details, see *Economic Perspectives* (March/April 1983), pp. 7-9.

74. See John A. Tatom, 'Money Market Deposit Accounts, Super-NOWs and Monetary Policy', *Federal Reserve Bank of St Louis Review*, (March 1983), p. 5.

75. Ibid., p. 16. Note that M1 is the measure of money narrowly defined to include coin and currency in circulation outside the banking system and private demand deposits adjusted. A broader measure M2 includes, as well as M1, time and savings deposits at commercial banks except for large-denomination negotiable certificates of deposit. See also Goodfriend *et al.*, 'Recent Financial Innovations', especially pp. 24-27; and Bryon Higgins & Jon Faust, NOW's and Super NOW's: Implications For Defining and Measuring Money', *Federal Reserve Bank of Kansas City Economic Review* (January 1983).

76. The non-bank bank is a strange word and a strange concept growing out of the Bank Holding Company Act's definition of a bank. The Act says that to be considered and regulated as a bank holding company a company must own an institution that offers both demand deposits and commercial loans. Non-bank firms have been acquiring bank charters and using them to operate insured depository institutions without demand deposits or without commercial loans in order to avoid the limits of the Bank Holding Company Act.

77. For much of this discussion, see Donald L. Koch, 'The Emerging Financial Services Industry: Challenge and Innovation', *Federal Reserve Bank of Atlanta Economic Review* (April 1984). See also *inter alia* Constance Dunham, 'Mutual Savings Banks: Are They Now or Will They Ever Be Commercial Banks?', *New England Economic Review* (May/June 1982); Joseph Gagnon and Steve Yokas, 'Recent Developments in Federal and New England Banking Laws', *New England Economic Review* (January/February 1983); Constance Dunham and Margaret Guerin-Calvert, 'How Quickly Can Thrifts Move into Commercial Lending?', *New England Economic Review* (November/December 1983).

78. For some discussion of this important topic see the following articles in *Federal Reserve Bank of Atlanta Economic Review*: David D. Whitehead, 'Positioning for Interstate Banking: More Evidence from the Sixth District' (January 1983); Whitehead, 'Interstate Banking: Taking Inventory' (May 1983); Whitehead and Jan Luytjes, 'Can Interstate Banking Increase Competitive Market Performance? An Empirical Test' (January 1984). See also Richard F. Syron, 'The "New England Experiment" in Interstate Banking', *New England Economic Review* (March/April 1984); Constance Dunham and Richard F. Syron, 'Interstate Banking: The Drive to Consolidate', *New England Economic Review* (May/June 1984).

'Interstate banking is prohibited by federal law, but banking organizations throughout the nation are providing financial services across state lines and have been for many years. Commercial banks commonly accept demand deposits and savings deposits from consumers in other states. Many banks aggressively market large certificates of deposit, credit cards and cash management services nationwide. Some banking organizations have calling officers who solicit banking customers nationwide. Loan production offices, electronic funds transfers and loan participations are among the wide array of other financial services provided by banking organizations on an interstate basis . . .

'Although banks may not establish banking offices across state lines, they may establish offices of nonbank subsidiaries capable of offering financial services similar to those provided by banks. Legally, a commercial bank is an entity that both offers demand deposits and makes commercial loans. . . . By simply separating the lending and deposit functions, banking organizations may circumvent interstate restrictions and provide financial services on an interstate basis.

'One way to accomplish this is through the creation or acquisition of nonbank subsidiaries by bank holding companies. Nonbank subsidiaries offer a more limited array of financial services than commercial banks and do not offer both demand deposits and commercial loans. The nonbank subsidiary would not, therefore, constitute a commercial bank and, hence would be free to open offices on an interstate basis. This in turn allows the bank holding company to establish its name, its expertise and contacts in geographic areas prohibited to its banking subsidiaries. Besides the profit and risk diversification motives, the establishment of nonbank subsidiaries across state lines is a good indication that a given holding company may be more likely to move to interstate banking if or when the law permits' (*Federal Reserve Bank of Atlanta Economic Review* (January 1983).

79. Latterly, States like Georgia, South Carolina, and Florida have enacted reciprocal banking laws, which have paved the way for a regional inter-state banking system. Such legislation will permit banks in South-Eastern States that pass similar laws to acquire or merge with local banks and already major mergers are being announced (e.g., Sun Banks of Florida and Trust Company of Georgia). These moves are defensive and are 'inspired, in part, by fears that smaller regional banks could be swamped by big-city money-centre banks if and when federal restrictions on interstate banking are eased'. See *Financial Times*, 24 May 1984 and 3 July 1984.

80. For one point of view, see Roger Guffey, 'After Deregulation: The Regulatory Role of the Federal Reserve', *Federal Reserve Bank of Kansas City Economic Review* (June 1983).

81. Donald L. Koch, 'The Emerging Financial Services Industry', pp. 28-9.

4 HYBRID BANKING SYSTEMS

Attention has already been drawn to a type of banking structure which appears to fall between a 'unit-banking' system (such as we have had over a period of years at least in some parts of the USA, though as we have seen it has latterly been greatly modified) and a developed system of branch banking (such as grew up in the United Kingdom and which has generally been followed in a number of Commonwealth countries, though again over more recent years subject to change and modification). The third type of banking structure has been called, for want of a better term, a 'hybrid' system. The classical examples of a 'hybrid' banking structure have been France and India, which despite their very different cultures and circumstances – both social and economic – have banking systems which in many ways are strikingly similar. Thus, France has long had – and substantial nationalisation of the constituent banks has not altered this – a system in which there are large banks with nationwide networks of branches, a number of regional banks of importance, though very few independent of Paris, and still a relatively large number of local bankers. In India, there have long been large banks – likewise now nationalised – with nationwide networks of branches; truly regional commercial banks have now all but disappeared, though for a number of years India also boasted a number of these (e.g., in Bengal, the Punjab and in the South of India) and, latterly, there has been some move back towards regionalism through the regional rural banks sponsored by the large commercial banks; and, so far as local banks were concerned, the so-called indigenous bankers and the moneylenders (though perhaps now rather less important) have supplied local needs, supplemented by the cooperative banks. What is surprising is that a structure that was well established in both these countries over half a century ago should have changed – in structural terms – comparatively little, though there have of course been some modifications, which it will be our purpose to delineate. Other examples of hybrid systems may be less clear-cut – mostly they have been drawn from the countries of Western Europe and Japan – but in one form or another they evidence this combination of large banks with nationwide branch networks and varying degrees of regional and local representation, especially if one includes institutions like savings banks and the variety of quasi-banking bodies that has grown up in recent years. What is more, with the continued invasion of foreign banks and the establishment of new types of financial institution, there is a sense in which 'hybridisation' has tended to increase rather than diminish. Also, in our case studies, we shall need to look for the obstacles which have operated to impede integration and the concentration of financial services in the hands of a small number of large banks with nationwide networks of branches. One would expect the precise character of these impediments to vary from country to country, but there also likely to be certain similarities and it is hoped that our case studies will offer sufficient unity of experience to enable us to establish that 'hybrid' banking systems in the sense of our definition do in fact exist and may even claim to have some degree of stability.

France

Following the banking legislation of 1945 and for many years thereafter, the French banking system consisted of three main groups of banks: (a) deposit banks (formerly divided into the three large nationalised banks, a relatively large number of Parisian deposit banks, regional and local deposit banks, and the *maisons de réescompte*, together with the French banks with head offices in *départements* or territories overseas, and foreign banks); (b) *banques d'affaires*, some subject to French control with their head offices in France and others under foreign control with head offices either in France or in Monaco; and (c) the *banques de crédit à long et moyen terme*, divided in a similar way.

Latterly (under Law No. 82-155 of 11 February 1982), the remaining large and medium-sized banks (36 in all plus two financial holding companies – Indosuez and Paribas) were nationalised and, on 24 January 1984, a new Law – no. 84-46 – was promulgated; this defined *établissements de crédit* and the banking operations that they would undertake. The old divisions between the several categories of banks disappeared and all *établissements de crédit* now became subject to the law. *Etablissements de crédit* were defined as institutions that engaged in banking operations – the receipt of deposits from the public, credit operations (including loans), and the provision of means of payment. Competition will now be encouraged between each of a wide range of institutions and the intention will be to move cautiously towards a system of 'universal banking'. Thus, the new Law was applied not merely to banks as such but also to the *Caisse Nationale de Crédit*

Agricole, the *Chambre Syndicale* of the *banques populaires, la Confédération National du Crédit Mutuel*, the *Caisse Centrale* of the *crédit cooperatif, la fédération centrale du crédit mutuel agricole et rural* and the *centre national* of the savings banks; the new law will also apply to the *Crédit Foncier* and the *Crédit National*, but not to the *Caisse des Dépôts et Consignations*, or to the *Banque de France* (and similar institutions for overseas French possessions), the Treasury, and the financial services of the Post Office. By controlling the central organisations, influence can be exerted on all the institutions affiliated with them. The new legislation will continue in existence the *Conseil National du Crédit* (National Credit Council), but with an extension of its powers. Two committees were set up with members drawn from the CNC – the *comité de la réglementation bancaire* and the *comité des etablissements de crédit* – and these will report to it annually. The competence of the *Commission de Contrôle des Banques* has been greatly extended and a *commission bancaire* with wide powers will now exercise control and supervision over all the *établissements de crédit* approved by the *comité des établissements de crédit* with a framework laid down by the *comité de la réglementation bancaire*. It will also be responsible for *compagnies financières* set up as holding companies to manage *établissements de crédit* as a group, of which at least one must be a bank. Government commissioners were to be nominated to represent the State on the several central financial organisations to which the Law applies.

Moreover, it should be remembered that these semi-public and cooperative institutions – whether comprehended by the new Law or not – constitute an important part of the banking sector in France. It should also be remembered that statutes that specifically relate to them are still part of the law. Of these institutions, the *Crédit Agricole* (*Caisse Nationale* and *Caisses Régionales*) is a very large organisation indeed. Other important institutions include the *Crédit Mutuel* and the *banques populaires* (mutual organisations, which enjoy certain fiscal privileges and which can offer subsidised loans). In addition, the *Caisse des Dépôts et Consignations*, to which the new Law does not apply and which concentrates in its hands the bulk of the country's savings bank deposits, is likewise a central element in the French financial system.

For the most part, retention of a hybrid banking system in France can be explained in terms of social attitudes. In the first place, it has to be emphasised that the Frenchman is above all an individualist. This is something still very deeply rooted in French character. Until a few years ago, it was reflected in the large number of small business units in the country, a phenomenon that was also to be found in the banking field. The Frenchman did not willingly surrender his independence and he often preferred a lower income in order to remain his own master. That situation is now changing and banking structure with it, but historically it has been important. Secondly, there is still some evidence in both Paris and the provinces of a continuing demand for the smaller banking unit, though this also is less true than it was. Certain classes in French society with aristocratic or bourgeois traditions tended for a long time to remain loyal to the established family concern with which their own families may have banked for generations. These classes are now in decline and the institutions that served them are having to change their character. But the reason they survived for so long on the old basis is again to be found in the French character. Many French men and women demanded personal service and preferred the institutions that could provide it. A large number of bank customers liked to feel that their bankers took a special interest in their financial affairs. They preferred a banker who was willing and able to give them the benefit of his own personal knowledge and attention. This was why the private and local banker for so long enjoyed the patronage of a specific and usually select clientele, without which his prolonged existence would not have been possible. To a certain extent, he still does. Thirdly, one has to take into account the strength of French particularism, which manifested itself (then as now) in strong local patriotisms, sometimes amounting almost to parochialism. Indeed, it was to exploit these local patriotisms, while at the same time providing the benefits of a wider connection, that one of the large Paris banks – the Crédit Industrial et Commercial – built up the group of regional banks that was associated with it, rivalling the large banks with nationwide networks of branches in the territorial distribution of its own branches. A fourth factor that has been of some historical importance was the decision of several of the large banks in the early days of branch development to build up a network of branches by establishing new offices in competition with existing local institutions. They preferred to do this rather than to absorb local banks and convert these into branches. Because of the strength of local loyalties, many of the branches established *de novo* experienced a long uphill struggle for business, in some cases reflected to this day in their share of local accounts. There were, of course, a number of absorptions over the years, but on the whole this tended to be a secondary line of development and the chief emphasis for a long time was on setting up a branch in a new area and seeking local business in competition with the banks already established locally.[1]

As we have seen, banking institutions in France were classified after World War II into three main groups: deposit banks, *banques d'affaires* (or investment banks), and institutions that were rather specialised or operated mainly outside France. New banking legislation in 1966 greatly reduced the importance of the distinction between deposit banks and *banques d'affaires*; the main distinction was now between commercial banks, on the one hand, and a range of other banking and financial institutions, on the other. Along with this there was (a) a further concentration of banking resources, as a result of several large mergers and also of greater financial integration through share-exchange agreements and interlocking directorates, and (b) the conversion of a number of *banques d'affaires* into deposit banks, which hived off their investment interests into separate investment or holding companies. Also, they either opened important deposit departments to undertake deposit-banking business, or they took up interests in the medium-sized and smaller deposit banks, which were absorbed into a group.

The main reason for this development was the relative superfluity of deposit bank funds, along with a scarcity of funds at the disposal of the *banques d'affaires*. There had always been a bigger demand for capital than the *banques d'affaires* themselves were able to provide, but, so long as a high proportion of medium-term commercial notes were rediscountable at semi-public institutions or at the Bank of France, the *banques d'affaires* could turn over their funds fairly frequently by rediscounting; this was now no longer possible on the same scale. In consequence, the *banques d'affaires* had to seek deposits more actively. Meanwhile, the deposit banks had begun to attract an increasing proportion of their funds from private individuals (who were making much less use of notes), and these banks sought to hold such business by expanding their retail-banking facilities (e.g., personal loans and mortgage lending). But they were also permitted to carry more time deposits and these funds were now used to finance their medium-term lending; hence, they had less need to rediscount.

What emerged from these changes was five major banking groups – the big three nationalised deposit banks (Banque Nationale de Paris, Crédit Lyonnais, and Société Générale pour favoriser le développement du commerce et de l'industrie en France) with holdings in a number of other banks and financial institutions, and two large holding companies – Paribas, the core institution of which was the Banque de Paris et des Pays-Bas, formerly a *banque d'affaires*, but latterly a deposit bank, and Indosuez, which derived from a marriage between the Compagnie

Financière de Suez and the old Banque de l'Indochine, the core bank that emerged as a *banque d'affaires* being the Banque de l'Indochine et de Suez (now called the Banque Indosuez). In addition, there were two other non-nationalised banks of importance – the Crédit Commercial de France and the Crédit Industriel et Commercial, the latter of which headed a group of regional banks as already indicated. Both were deposit banks, the former being represented by large branches in most of the important provincial towns of France with interests also in a number of local banks. Furthermore, there was a large regional bank – the Crédit du Nord – of similar size; although still classified as a regional bank, it had already expanded well beyond its region.

On 1 January 1984 there were 289 banks operating in France. Of these, 78 were based in Paris, including the three biggest banks; 19 were regional banks and 49 were local banks. In addition, there were in Paris seven *maisons de réescompte*. Other deposit banks included banks with head offices in *départements* overseas (six), head offices in territories overseas (six), in Monaco (five), and foreign banks (119, of which 58 were branches and 61 based in France). *Banques d'affaires* numbered 39 (19 French with head offices in France, 17 under foreign control but with head offices in France, and 3 with head offices in Monaco); of the *banques d'affaires*, one (Banque Indosuez) is large and three are medium-sized; the remainder are small.

Of the regional banks, ten were associated by way of stockholdings and common directors[2] with the Crédit Industriel et Commercial in Paris and others with the Big Three – the Société Générale, the Crédit Lyonnais, and the Banque Nationale de Paris. The vast majority of the local banks are also owned by one or other of the big banks[3] and there are probably only about ten completely independent local banks left in France. Hence, despite the structure that exists, the French banking system is really quite highly concentrated. All the regional banks and some of the local banks have networks of branches, though some of these networks are quite small. Latterly, there has been some tidying up in the structure. This derived from a reform programme presented by the Minister of Finance (Jacques Delors) in February 1983. The objective of the regrouping was to merge some of the smaller banks, to increase competition among the larger institutions, and to strengthen regional banking, which has for many years been a feature of French banking arrangements, partly because of the balanced character of many of the regional economies which have provided them with a good spread of risks. In several areas (e.g., Alsace-Lorraine, Rhône-Alpes, the North of France, and the Midi, less obviously perhaps in Brittany), these banks serve not only a prosperous agriculture but also a number of local industries. At the same time, as we have seen, all *établissements de crédit* would now come under one supervisory umbrella. In particular, this would bring into the same regulatory structure the Caisse Nationale de Crédit Agricole, the giant semi-public farmers' cooperative bank, and encourage it to develop further its industrial lending, though its main function would remain financing agriculture. The Crédit Industriel et Commercial will retain its majority shares and control in running the ten regional banks, which were grouped together with it before nationalisation, and the shareholding of the Compagnie Financière de Suez in CIC – achieved some years ago after a bitter struggle with Paribas and only resolved after the intervention of the Bank of France – has now been reduced to a substantial minority holding in favour of a direct holding by the State itself; the Banque de l'Union Européenne, formerly owned by the Empain-Schneider group, was absorbed into the CIC group, for which it would now undertake international business. Banque Worms, the fourth largest French *banque d'affaires*, was eventually taken over by the largest nationalised insurance group in France – the Union des Assurances de Paris – and the Suez group took up a majority interest in Banque Vernes. The Suez group also acquired an interest in the Banque Parisienne de Crédit. The former Rothschild bank – now L'Européenne de Banque – sold their industrial participations to the Compagnie Financière de Suez and is now associated with the Crédit Commercial de France (which itself owns a number of local banks), as is the Union de Banques à Paris.

It was feared that the further bank nationalisation in France might lead to political dictation of policy, particularly in a period of recession, when many major industries had been making heavy losses and were in deep trouble; also, as a matter of policy, the government favoured increased lending at subsidised interest rates to small and medium-sized industries. But the new heads of the nationalised banks have in fact been able to retain a high degree of independence largely as a result of the gradualist approach of the then Minister of Finance, who initially held regular sessions with the top men in the banks in order to convey his views on developments that might be considered in the future. In addition, the prudence for which the French banks have always been known has continued and they were supported in this by the Banking Control Commission. Despite the considerable development of their international banking interests, the exposure of the French banks has been less in the field of foreign lending than was the case with the American and German banks. None the less, bad and doubtful debt provisions had to be made, also for loans to French companies badly affected by the recession and this reduced profits. It likewise highlighted the capital position of the French banks, which particularly for the big banks had never been strong. They have maintained their high credit ratings because it was thought that the French government in some sense stood behind them. But now that there are 39 nationalised banks, questions of capital adequacy have assumed problem proportions. Most of the medium-sized banks are adequately capitalised, but perhaps eight to ten banks are not. Also, with lower profits, there has been less to plough back. Certain of the large institutions (e.g., the Caisse Nationale de Crédit Agricole and the Crédit National) have resorted to subordinated debt by approaching the international bond markets (e.g., on the basis of floating-rate notes). Further assistance has been provided in two ways: by the introduction of the *titres participatifs*, which represent non-voting loan stock, somewhere between a bond and a share. Firstly, these can be issued by the large nationalised industrial companies and public utilities (e.g., Saint Gobain, Rhône-Poulenc, Thomson-Brandt, Compagnie Générale d'Electricité and Renault – in order to raise funds both to plug losses and to finance new investment, thereby reducing the demands made by these concerns on the nationalised banks; and, secondly, issues of these securities can be made by the big nationalised banks in order to supplement their capital resources and thereby improve capital adequacy. In effect, the *titres participatifs* provide a form of permanent capital somewhat akin to equity, but without involving any dilution of government shareholdings. Yields are based partly on an interest portion (possibly with a floating rate) and partly on a measure of the company's financial performance. On the whole, these issues seem to have been a success.

India

Over quite a long period of years, the structure of banking in India was not very different from that of France, since it had a large number of banks, of which only a relatively few were national in importance. Some could be described as being mainly regional in character, while the interests of the smaller banks were distinctly local. Latterly, the reduction in the number of small banks was rapid. For example, the total number of reporting banks in India in 1952 was 517. This had fallen to 154 by 1964, to 109 in 1965, to 99 in 1966, and to 90 in

1967. Subsequently, there has been an increase due to the setting up of regional rural banks (see below). By the end of June 1983, in terms of 'scheduled banks' (i.e. banks included in the second schedule of the Reserve Bank of India Act and having paid-up capital and reserves of not less than Rs 5 lakhs or Rs 500,000), 222 were included in the schedule and 4 were non-scheduled.

Of the 222 scheduled banks at the end of June 1983, 28 were public-sector banks,[4] 142 regional rural banks (which are also regarded as being in the public sector), 52 were private sector banks, of which 18 were private sector foreign banks. There were 4 non-scheduled banks, or 226 in all. The 28 public sector banks included the 14 large commercial banks nationalised in 1969, the State Bank of India and its 7 subsidiaries, and the 6 additional banks nationalised on 15 April 1980. These accounted for over 90 per cent of aggregate deposits of all commercial banks in India. Hence, the remaining banks must have been very small.

The regional rural banks were set up following promulgation of the Regional Bank Ordinance 1975 'to provide institutional credit to rural people'; they are mostly sponsored by one or other of the nationalised commercial banks and have increased rapidly in number over recent years. In particular, they have served to increase the flow of credit to smaller borrowers in the rural areas. They have a specified area of operations – usually limited to one or more districts; staff are recruited locally. Their lending operations are directed towards assisting specified weaker sections of the community – small and marginal farmers, landless labourers, artisans and small entrepreneurs. They have access to liberal re-finance facilities from the National Bank for Agriculture and Rural Development and each of the banks sponsoring a regional rural bank. They also undertake a certain amount of other commercial banking business in contrast to the 28 large banks in the public sector, which transact all types of banking business. As at the end of June 1983, there were 142 regional rural banks functioning in 249 districts in 21 states, with a total network of 6,812 branches.

In addition, the community was served by a network of cooperative banks – in June 1982, 27 state cooperative banks (of which 17 were scheduled banks), 338 central cooperative banks, 1,258 primary cooperative banks (urban cooperative banks), 9 industrial cooperative banks, 94,628 primary agricultural credit societies and over 20,350 primary non-agricultural credit societies. These institutions mainly provide short-term credit. The medium- and long-term credit institutions in the cooperative sector comprise 19 central land development banks and 896 primary land development banks. The membership of the co-operative movement exceeded 60.7 million. These banks are supplemented – particularly in South India – (a) by chit funds, which accept and pay interest on monthly deposits against which it is only possible to draw by way of loan; money can also be borrowed against fixed assets; and (b) by nidhis, which are mutual loan societies that have developed into semi-banking institutions, but which deal only with their member shareholders.[5]

In India, there is also a still large but unknown number of indigenous bankers and money-lenders, who particularly in the rural parts of India, continue to provide a significant part of the available banking and quasi-banking services. However, under new arrangements, first, in the form of the 'social control' of banking and, more recently, following the nationalisation of the 14 largest private Indian banks in 1969, the commercial banks accelerated the opening of more branches in rural and semi-rural areas in order to complement the facilities already offered by the State Bank of India (and subsidiaries) and by the co-operatives.

The authorities have long favoured the progressive expansion of the number of branches, though not their continued concentration in the larger cities and towns. In other words, both the government and the Reserve Bank have been less concerned with the number of branches in existence than with their appropriate location from the point of view of serving to the maximum advantage the needs of the community as a whole. In particular, they have been concerned to provide the rural areas with adequate facilities. For a number of years, the former Imperial Bank of India was under an obligation to open 'pioneering' branches and its successor, the State Bank of India, has likewise been required actively to continue this programme. More recently, this policy was reinforced, first, by 'social controls' and, latterly, by the nationalisation of the largest private Indian banks. All the commercial banks wishing to expand their business were now required to open rural branches that more than matched in number their expansion in the towns.

Effective from 1 January 1977, the Reserve Bank of India modified the entitlement formula for the opening of new bank offices so as to give more weight to opening offices in unbanked rural centres. According to the revised formula, a bank can now open one office each in a metropolitan or port town and a banked centre for every four offices in unbanked rural centres; earlier the ratio was 1:2 in the case of banks having more than 60 per cent of their offices in rural and semi-urban areas and 1:3 in all other cases. In September 1978, the Reserve Bank of India issued a comprehensive Branch Expansion Policy according to which about 6,500 new offices would be opened during the period 1979-81 in rural and semi-urban areas of districts, where the average population per bank office was higher than the national average. It was also proposed to cover every unbanked community development block headquarters in the country with a bank office before the end of June 1979. Expansion in urban/metropolitan/port town centres was to be allowed only on a highly selective basis. The aim of the new branch licensing policy for the April 1982-March 1985 period was to achieve by the end of March 1985 a banking coverage on average of one office per 17,000 population on the basis of the 1981 population census in the rural and urban areas. Accordingly, about 8,000 new offices were to be opened in rural and urban areas over the period 1982-5.

This process was greatly quickened, first, by the nationalisation of the 14 largest private Indian banks in July 1969 (all the Indian private banks with deposits of Rs 50 crores[6] or more) and then by the nationalisation of a further 6 commercial banks in April 1980. None of the foreign banks was nationalised. Much more direct pressure could now be exerted in the matter of opening a large number of new branches and a positive programme was introduced designating 'lead' banks especially in the under-banked districts of India. The responsibilities of a 'lead' bank were to draw up 'district credit plans' and – as a first among equals – to coordinate the activities of all banks in fulfilling these plans. It was an 'area approach', the purpose of which was to evolve plans and programmes for the development of an adequate banking and credit structure in the rural areas. Thus, the 'lead' bank was to act as a consortium leader for coordinating the efforts of all credit institutions in each of the allotted districts, for the expansion of branch-banking facilities and for meeting the credit needs of the rural economy. To enable banks to assume their lead role in an effective and systematic manner, all districts in the country (excepting the metropolitan cities of Bombay, Calcutta and Madras and urban areas of the Union Territories of Delhi and Chandigarh) were allotted among public-sector banks and a few private-sector banks. The planning has now gone down to the level of 'community development blocks', since sometimes a district is too large and the various regions in a district too heterogeneous to be dealt with optimally in a single plan or by a single set of priorities.

In the first decade after the nationalisation of the 14 major commercial banks, over 21,900 new bank offices were opened throughout the country, raising the total number of functioning offices from 8,262 in June 1969 to 30,202 at the end of June 1979. By the end of June 1983, there were 42,016 commercial bank offices in India. Of the new offices, over 60 per cent were opened in centres where there had previously been no commercial bank office. The number of rural offices increased from 1,833 to 22,678 during the period 1969-83 and their share in the total network of commercial bank offices in the country went up from 22 per cent to 54 per cent. The average population per bank office declined from 65,000 in June 1969 to 16,000 in June 1983. This remarkable progress notwithstanding, deficiencies in the availability of banking infrastructure persist in some areas. Hence, the policy of concentrating on relatively under-banked areas like Bihar, Uttar Pradesh, Orissa, West Bengal, Tripura, and Madhya Pradesh.

Although both mergers and branch development served to hasten the integration of the Indian banking system and its concentration into fewer banking units, the process of change was for a long time relatively slow. It is to the impediments to change therefore that we must now turn, since some of these were until recently still operative.

At the outset, attention should be focused on what has been one of the main characteristics of the Indian economy. India has long been primarily an agricultural country with an economic and social life based to a large extent on village communities. Moreover, India is a big country and distances are often accentuated because of the fact that, over large areas, communications still leave much room for improvement, especially once one gets off the main trunk roads. This means that at times many village communities are still physically difficult to reach and, until communications are more generally improved, the full and effective integration of modern India and the life in the villages must remain incomplete. Moreover, the rural branches of a city bank are expensive to run and branch development beyond towns and villages of moderate size – if these branches are to cover their costs within a reasonable period of time – must depend on the extension of more efficient communications and the effective development of wider customer contacts.

Secondly, there is a number of social factors that continue to hamper radical change. There is, for example, much evidence of local particularism and, in some cases, this is reinforced by inadequate communications with the rest of the economy. The bulk of the Indian population is comprised of peasant agriculturists and the peasant in any country is notoriously conservative. In many cases, he remains suspicious of change. In addition, there have been the great barriers of ignorance and illiteracy, which have considerably impeded the spread of new ideas and new institutions to rural India, especially when they came to the village through the agency of someone outside. This is now changing. Massive efforts have been made to eradicate illiteracy and these are now beginning to bear fruit. Furthermore, there are the remarkable developments of recent years as a result of the 'green revolution' based on better seeds, the use of fertilisers, improved husbandry, and so on. Even so, the progress has been somewhat patchy and is much more apparent in some parts of the country than in others.

Some degree of literacy is important if a person is to operate a bank account, though deposit and also loan accounts may be opened in the names of illiterate farmer customers. In addition to the photograph of an illiterate farmer customer, his left thumb impression, witnessed by two individuals known to the bank, is recorded at the lending bank for the purpose of identification. All operations on the loan account can be conducted only by the account holder in person. For these reasons alone, it has taken time to foster the development of the banking habit in the villages. Moreover, so far as habits of thrift were concerned, there could be little basis in many cases for much saving until living standards could be lifted to levels sufficient to provide the margin of income that could be so applied. This is now beginning to happen, though progress can be greatly interrupted by major disasters like cyclones and floods, or by the incidence of drought.

There are also the barriers of language and caste. It is probable that caste will gradually become a less obvious obstacle to social integration, though it still remains a problem, but the language barrier has shown many signs of becoming more strongly entrenched (as witness the agitations there have been for new states, based on linguistic differences, and the uncertainty that exists with regard to the general acceptance of a language common to the country as a whole). For this reason, banks are now also endeavouring to do business in regional languages. There are other factors of a social character as well – such as the complications of joint family ownership (again less common that it was), which may render difficult the provision of acceptable security for a loan. These kinds of social impediment will no doubt gradually disappear. But it would seem that in India they are likely to hold up further integration of the economy and of the financial structure for some time yet.

However, Indian bankers are inclined to take a more optimistic view. With the adoption of regional languages as a basis for business, the banks no longer worry very much about the language problem. It is said that caste, whatever its socio-political influence, has not affected the functioning of banks. The incidence of joint family ownership is declining – there is now a ceiling on land holdings in many states. Even in the case of joint ownership, banks are now evolving suitable procedures to ensure that this does not stand in the way of lending. More significantly in terms of lending criteria, banks now regard security as less important than the viability of the project. Some would maintain that there is now 'no evidence of social impediments holding up the integration of the financial structure at least so far as organised banking is concerned'.

Thirdly, there were institutional impediments to change in the banking field itself. The village communities were not entirely without banking facilities of a kind, and indigenous institutions already provided a wide range of services. These have existed for centuries. But sheer inertia and an ingrained conservatism encouraged the belief that the processes of modification and integration would be slow to operate, as indeed for a time they were. Moreover, the villager – even many of the townsmen – often preferred the type of services these institutions had on offer.

For example, there was the indigenous banker who supplemented his resources by accepting deposits and thus provided a repository for surplus funds. He also made loans and, by means of several different kinds of hundi (an indigenous credit instrument in the form of a bill of exchange), he financed a large part of India's internal trade, besides providing remittance facilities on quite a developed scale. Indeed, in many an up-country centre, the indigenous banker was the only institution available for the transmission of funds, moneys being remitted through the agency of indigenous bankers elsewhere. From the point of view of the customer, it was advantageous to deal with an indigenous banker, because of the absence of formality and because of his ability to give a speedy decision. The indigenous banker was always accessible and his methods were flexible. He might run greater risks, but these were offset by his close personal knowledge of the customer and in part by his higher charges. Today, in up-country centres, he is still of some importance, though the remittance side of his business is now being taken over more and more by the rural and semi-rural branches of the larger banks.

Another indigenous source of finance of considerable importance was the petty money-lender, who generally traded on his own capital or borrowed from other money-lenders. Despite numerous attempts to control his activities – attempts that sometimes drove him underground – he has continued to survive because of the pressure of demand. His interest charges are often exorbitant and his methods more than a little doubtful, but the risks of lending are also high and the fault is not always on his side.

The authorities for a long time would have liked to see the indigenous lending institutions largely supplanted by a system of credit cooperatives and they did much to encourage their growth, but the expansion of cooperative banking supplemented rather than replaced the indigenous lenders. When the All-India Rural Credit Survey was undertaken in 1954, only about 3 per cent of total loans to agriculturalists were actually made by cooperative banks. It was the private money-lender who then dominated the scene (professional money-lenders providing about 44 per cent of the total and the agricultural money-lender roughly 25 per cent). Recently, the growth of cooperatives has been more vigorous – though still a little patchy – and, latterly, the facilities of the cooperatives have been supplemented both by the regional rural banks and by the increasing number of rural branches opened up by the commercial banks. Now it would seem that these are going to be the main bases of policy. In this way, the institutional impediments to change will eventually be removed.

If now we can summarise the more recent developments in branch expansion policy, following the failure of the cooperatives to make very much headway in catering for agricultural finance, there was a decision to encourage commercial banks to open branches in rural and semi-rural areas. First, the old Imperial Bank of India pioneered branching; second, after the nationalisation of the Imperial Bank in 1955, the new State Bank accelerated the process; third, after nationalisation of the 14 large private banks in 1969 (the remaining large banks have since been nationalised), all large commercial banks began to open rural and semi-urban branches. The objective was to extend banking facilities to each and every village in the country – through the agency of the lead bank scheme. But there are an estimated 575,000 villages in India. Hence the immensity of the task that is being undertaken.

A number of problems face both the banks and the authorities. First, there is the problem of staffing – the necessity to train managers and supporting staff on a vast scale; all the banks have good staff-training facilities largely using seconded staff with appropriate experience. Secondly, there is the viability of rural and semi-urban branches: it takes at least five years before a branch can be expected to become viable – at worst, some branches will never be viable; social considerations have tended to be more important to the authorities than profitability. Thirdly, there has been the need to provide sufficient incentives to persuade staff to serve in the more out-of-the-way places – sometimes cut off at certain times of the year by bad roads, floods, snow and ice; to some extent the problem has been met by offering discomfort allowances and assistance with medical and educational services; usually staff are left there for two to three years. Fourthly, since they are on a higher salary scale than the local community, managers and staff are often very much outsiders in the village concerned and are regarded as being out of touch with the village. Finally, there has been a decline in standards of customer service.[7]

Because of this last factor and the inability of banks always to provide funds for lending (partly as a result of 'priority' loans), Indian businessmen have long been accustomed to attracting deposits from the public and resort to this source seems to be increasing, much of this business being done through brokers. This also affects the banks in another way, since companies are taking investible funds that would otherwise have gone into the banks as deposits and on which companies are permitted to pay much higher rates.

There was a move away from regional banking after 1969 when the newly nationalised banks that previously had been regional in character were encouraged to open branches right across the country. The problem was the size of India and, because it was impossible quickly to develop a national coverage, these banks necessarily still retained some of their regional concentrations – e.g., the Calcutta banks tended still to have more branches in the eastern part of the country, the Punjab National still had more branches in the north, whereas the Tamil Nadu and Karnataka banks tended to be represented more heavily in the south. It should be noted that the very large State Bank of India, which operates on the basis of regional zones or 'circles' (13 in all) has in this way also operated on a regional basis, which business would exceed in size the local business of banks that were originally regional in character. On the agricultural front, there has been a move back through the regional rural banks sponsored by the large commercial banks towards more regional banking once again. The advantage for the regional rural banks is that business is done in local languages and also salaries have been kept at a level more in line with those of the local people.

With regard to some of the indigenous institutions, one had hoped years ago to see the development of a linkage between the Multani shroff[8] and the Reserve Bank of India through the rediscounting of Multani paper with the Reserve Bank. But the Multanis never came to accept the divestment of their non-banking business (which would have been required by the Reserve Bank of India) and, far from the linkage being established, the facilities of Multani hundi discounts were reduced rather than increased. As a result, there has been a gradual squeezing out of the Multani shroff in Bombay (and elsewhere); the limits for the rediscounting of hundis are no longer available from some banks and at other banks have been greatly reduced (certainly in real terms). As bankers, the Multanis will gradually die out as their sons go into the professions or other forms of business.

Again, there has been an erosion of the business done by the indigenous bankers, who it should be noted are true bankers – accepting deposits and making loans – and not to be confused with money-lenders. But, as commercial-bank branches increasingly invade the indigenous bankers' former up-country strongholds, the business done by them will be further eroded and their share of total banking activity will continue to shrink.

With greater direction from the authorities so far as location of branches is concerned and the increasing emphasis on priority lending (as well as the captive market for government securities) – not just because of the nationalisation of 20 banks plus the State Bank and its subsidiaries, which do over 90 per cent of the business of the banking system as a whole – there is an edging away from a market-oriented banking system towards something that has been integrated into a National Plan.

However, not everyone would agree with this judgement and an Indian banker may prefer to put matters differently. To quote one such view:

> While there is governmental control to the extent of over 90 per cent of the organised banking business in the country, all the banks in the public sector compete with one another for deposit as well as advances business. While banks are persuaded to extend credit according to developmental priorities, there are no compulsions on banks in financing customers or on customers in choosing the banks, provided there is no unhealthy competition. Market-orientation of banks cannot thus be said to have declined. The endeavour in India is to utilise banking as an instrument of social change and rapid economic development of the country and, therefore, there is no incompatibility between market orientation and the banks' functioning within the overall framework of the national plan.

It should be noted, too, that in India the bank trade unions are very strong and militant; they have been so successful in forcing up salaries that they are amongst the best-paid sectors in the economy. For a time, this militancy also went with a high degree of labour indiscipline and a lack of cooperation with management – e.g., their refusal to accept mechanisation and computerisation to improve the efficiency of banking services, which were primarily still carried out by hand. Obviously, the reason for his was their fear of redundancy. But clearly the industry was expanding at such a pace that it would go on creating additional employment and, latterly, employee trade unions have increasingly accepted mechanisation and computerisation and certain agreements have now been signed at the national level permitting the introduction of computers for banking transactions.

Another matter that deserves attention is the position of the foreign banks. Their branching is limited by the authorities. They concentrate on the financing of foreign trade and on foreign exchange business, the latter of which is very profitable. They tend also to attract large accounts. Rates of taxation are higher than those on domestic banks, though the foreign banks presumably still feel that it is worthwhile staying in business and, indeed, there are more foreign banks still seeking entry. It should be noted that salaries in foreign banks are higher than those in the nationalised banks, but the advantage is largely lost because of high taxation, the only remaining advantage being the pension rights of their employees.

Finally, it can be argued that there is a case for the merger of some of the nationalised banks, especially to get better spreads of branching across the country. Nevertheless, one would like to see the retention of (say) a minimum of ten banks which it is believed are necessary in order to maintain an effective degree of competition.

West Germany

An even more direct conflict between the forces favouring concentration and those that operate against them is probably to be found in West Germany. Formerly, Germany was comprised of a large number of separate states. Modern Germany was the creation of the nineteenth century both in political and in economic terms. Prior to 1848, the year in which the first joint-stock bank was established, there was little evidence of the highly developed industrial economy that was to emerge. Indeed, the two were to develop together, because a number of the banks that were established after 1848 were from the beginning specifically linked with the promotion of industrial enterprises. For this reason, the banks were inclined to rely mainly on their own capital resources in assisting industry and did not at first favour the attraction of deposits from the public. Indeed, it was not until after 1874 that there was any major departure from this policy, when the Deutsche Bank began to seek deposits through offices specially opened for the purpose. This was done to provide cheap finance for traders, with deposits being invested in mercantile bills which were regarded as both safe and liquid.

This was an important period in the evolution of German banking,[9] because it was at this time that the attempt was begun to fuse the principles of deposit banking on the British model with long-term financing that was favoured by the French *banques d'affaires*. Once the decision had been taken to supplement the available resources by attracting deposits, the way was open to the building up of a widespread network of branch offices. These also became the means of establishing and maintaining industrial contacts throughout the country. Such developments were greatly assisted by the unification of Germany, which removed the political obstacles to the emergence of a more integrated banking system and the selection of Berlin as the capital ensured its choice as the country's financial centre. When the Empire was proclaimed in 1871, four of the largest German banks were already established in Berlin and the new Reichsbank was set up there in 1876. Furthermore, the Berlin stock exchange rapidly displaced Frankfurt am Main as the country's leading securities market and this assured Berlin of its pre-eminence as an outlet for short-term funds.

Integration of the German banking system proceeded on two fronts. First, the larger and more enterprising provincial banks were now attracted to the capital. Initially, a provincial institution would open a branch office there, soon to become a coordinate head office that rivalled in importance the bank's original head office, the provincial bank by now being virtually a Berlin bank. It was in this way that the number of *Berliner Grossbanken* grew from four to nine. By then, there was little purpose in the opening of Berlin branches by the remaining provincial banks, which maintained contact with the money market in the capital through the agency of one of the leading Berlin banks as correspondent.

This prepared the ground for the second stage, whereby the Berlin banks began to extend their influence throughout the provinces. Initially, this was done by developing correspondent relationships. Both parties stood to gain from the correspondent relationship – the provincial bank by being able to rediscount its bills and employing the city correspondent to buy and sell securities; and the Berlin bank by attracting temporarily surplus funds from provincial sources as well as a certain amount of business that the provincial banks were either unable or unwilling to handle themselves. In addition, the Berlin banks were anxious to extend and to diversify their contacts with German industry, with a view to widening the spread of their investment business – and the related risks – both geographically and in terms of the industries catered for, as well as to enlarge the area from which they could reliably expect to draw funds for investment in industry.

Subsequently, the links between the Berlin bank and its provincial correspondent would usually become rather closer, with the former taking up a capital participation in the provincial institution and being accorded a representative on the latter's Board of Supervisors. Sometimes, the provincial bank might also acquire a capital holding in and secure a seat on the Board of the Berlin bank, but almost invariably it was the provincial bank that stood to lose some of its independence. It was in this way that each of the big D-banks – the Deutsche Bank, the Discontogesellschaft, the Darmstädter Bank, and the Dresdner Bank – came to be surrounded by a group of provincial banks more or less under the control of the Berlin institution.

At the same time, both the Berlin banks and the provincial banks associated with them were expanding directly the scope of their organisations by means of branches, usually as a result of absorbing a private banking business, sometimes by buying up the assets of a provincial bank that had been forced into liquidation. By now, competition for banking business had become quite fierce, both among the credit banks and between the latter and the private bankers, among whose ranks there were many failures in the years 1888-90. Many of the rest decided to sell their businesses to the credit banks before they were taken from them. Only some of the largest (usually those with an established position in the Berlin money market) were able to survive.

The elimination of many of the smaller institutions and the consequent consolidation of the banking system, aided perhaps by the regulation of competition that was beginning to emerge (by means of cartels),[10] does seem to have been associated with an absence of serious bank failures during the decade or so preceding World War I. Even the banks that fell in 1910 illustrated the moral, the two most important being independent provincial banks that had each become over-committed to a single large local borrower. Small local banks, too, periodically got into difficulties and either had to go into liquidation or sell out to a Berlin bank, but these casualties only served to emphasise the better distribution of risks that greater concentration afforded.

As one would expect, World War I (with its emphasis on centralised control) and the disturbances of the early post-war years culminating in hyper-inflation did little but weaken the smaller members of the German banking system and the Berlin banks were able to strengthen their position further. By 1917, the process of absorbing some of the provincial members of existing bank groups had begun, the offices of the banks now acquired being converted into branches of the institution at the head of the group. Indeed, between 1913 and 1918 the proportion of total bank deposits held by the big Berlin banks had risen from 53.4 per cent to 65.6 per cent.[11]

A third phase, in which the emphasis was to be on amalgamation, was about to begin. What had started during the later years of the war accelerated in the years following, particularly during 1920-2. It was not merely a matter of amalgamations between the Berlin banks and those in provincial centres, but now between the big Berlin banks as well, reducing their numbers to seven. Hence, in addition to the tendency to substitute for the earlier 'group' organisation a network of branches under single control, there was now also a shift towards much larger branch systems.

However, by no means all of the factors in operation made for greater concentration of banking resources in the hands of the large Berlin banks. Thus, quite apart from the setting up of the specialised industrial banks and the increasing importance of publicly-owned banking institutions (e.g., the communal savings banks), there were certain provincial banks (e.g., in Leipzig and Munich) which developed their own defensive alliances by establishing a 'community of interest' between themselves and exchanging directors; again, in seeking to extend their influence, the Berlin banks found themselves competing with some of the leading industrialists for control of provincial banks; and, finally, the effects of the amalgamations were partially offset by the appearance of a number of new banks, mainly in Berlin (and including private banking firms), in response to both the large profits being made and the volume of business offering.

This economic honeymoon could not be expected to last for ever. The depreciation in the value of money consequent upon inflation, the speculations (e.g., on the foreign exchanges) into which banks were tempted and the losses that were eventually revealed led to a new crop of failures and, in the more important cases, to the taking over of their business connections (including branches) by their stronger brethren. But the further consolidation of the German banking system during these years of 'stabilisation' was as nothing compared with the impact of the financial crisis of 1931 and the Great Depression that followed it. This story has been told too often to warrant its repetition.[12] Suffice it is say that failures and liquidations occasioned further consolidation of the private banking sector, resulting in the emergence of a Big Three – the Deutsche Bank, the Dresdner Bank, and the Commerzbank; that the period of reconstruction would have been much more difficult had it not been for the assistance of the State; that, despite the temptation to nationalise the German credit banks, the authorities decided to limit their reforms to a far-reaching system of control, the banking system – under the Nazi regime – itself becoming little more than an instrument of totalitarian economy. In addition, the publicly-owned banks (mainly the savings banks) now came to hold virtually three-quarters of all deposits.

After World War II, the Allies imposed on Germany a programme of de-concentration, to be applied both to the banks and to the big industrial combines and this set the pattern for the structural changes made in the German commercial-banking system over the ensuing years. No commercial bank in West Germany was now permitted to operate branches in more than one *land* or province. The remaining big banks – the Deutsche Bank, the Dresdner Bank and the Commerzbank – ceased to exist as trading units, their business being taken over by 30 'successor' banks. This had several consequences – it increased the demand for bank cash and other liquid assets, since smaller banks felt the need for a larger margin of safety; senior bank management now had to be allocated to each of the successor institutions, which meant that it had to be spread around much more thinly, a circumstance that could only be partially overcome by informal and unofficial consultations between the former members of a large bank board; it was felt that working efficency had been impaired and that the banks had thereby lost goodwill; it was expected that the smaller banks would also have to charge higher rates of interest and this would drive up borrowing costs.

These were some of the considerations that lay behind the proposals to reconvert the banks into units large enough to be viable. Legislation to permit this came into operation in March 1952, when West Germany was divided into three banking districts, with the requirement that no bank might operate branches in more than one of those three districts. This made it possible for the former three large banks each to regroup its 'successor' institutions into three regional banks, one to operate in the northern, one in the western, and one in the southern district. This was effected by September 1952. At the same time, the three large banks were permitted to continue in existence, ostensibly for the purpose of winding up their affairs, though in reality they were biding their time until full German sovereignty could be restored and the former banking empires could be completely reunited under the old management.

This step was taken during the early months of 1957 after enabling legislation had been passed by the Bundestag at the beginning of the year. The three banks in the Deutsche Bank group agreed to merge in April 1957. The same procedure was followed in May by the Dresdner Bank group. In both cases, the pre-war names were also readopted. But the three banks in the Commerzbank group for a time preferred a looser form of organisation. Nevertheless, the strong position held by the Commerzbank in Düsseldorf enabled it to acquire a large block of the share capital of each of the Frankfurt and Hamburg banks so that in fact it could exercise effective control, and the relationship was virtually one between a parent company and its subsidiaries. Subsequently (in 1958), the Commerzebank likewise opted for a much more centralised organisation and the Big Three were outwardly restored to their old position.

If now we look at the figures (December 1983), the structure of West German banking is much less highly concentrated than one might think. As at the end of December 1983, there were 234 commercial banks and 592 savings banks, together with their 12 central giro institutions, which have themselves become large 'universal' banks like the Big Three. In relation to all banking institutions, these groups accounted for about 63 per cent of total deposits and borrowings from non-banks and, with a somewhat different distribution, 60 per cent of total lending to domestic and foreign non-banks, including Treasury bill credits and security holdings. However, for the six big banks, which comprise the Big Three 'universal' banks[13] and their Berlin subsidiaries, with balance sheet totals exceeding DM 225 billion, the relevant figures were 10.1 per cent (total deposits) and 8.3 per cent (total lending and securities); meanwhile, the 12 central giro institutions had shares of 6.0 per cent and 16.4 per cent respectively, and the savings banks for which they act as central institutions 36.2 per cent (of which well over half was savings deposits) and 22.7 per cent respectively. Collectively, the 3,754 credit cooperatives were also important (and growing fast) with figures of 18.7 per cent and 11.6 per cent; figures for the mortgage

Table 4.1: West German Banking Groups, December 1983

Group	Number	Total deposits and borrowing from non-banks	Total lending and securities incl. Treasury bills
		%	%
Commercial banks	234	20.9	21.1
Big banks*	6	(10.1)	(8.3)
Regional banks and other commercial banks	94	(9.0)	(10.3)
Branches of foreign banks	58	(0.5)	(1.2)
Private bankers	76	(1.3)	(1.2)
Central giro institutions (incl. Deutsche Girozentrale)	12	6.0	16.4
Savings banks	592	36.2	22.7
Central institutions of credit cooperatives (incl. Deutsche Genossenschaftsbank)	9	0.9	1.7
Credit cooperatives	2,250	18.7	11.6
Mortgage banks	37	7.7	18.5
Private	25	(3.1)	(11.8)
Public	12	(4.6)	(6.7)
Instalment sales financing institutions	101	0.9	1.5
Banks with special functions	16	5.7	5.3
Postal giro and postal savings-bank offices	15	3.1	1.2

(There were also 32 building and loan associations – 19 private and 13 public)[14]
*Deutsche Bank AG. Dresdner Bank AG, Commerzbank AG and their Berlin subsidiaries
Source: *Deutsche Bundesbank Monthly Report*

banks were 7.7 per cent and 18.5 per cent (see Table 4.1). Of the several types of banks, the largest in order of size were:

Deutsche Bank
Dresdner Bank
Westdeutsche Landesbank Girozentrale
Commerzbank
Bayerische Vereinsbank
Bayerische Landesbank
Bayerische Hypotheken- und Wechsel-Bank
Deutsche Genossenschaftsbank
Norddeutsche Landesbank Girozentrale
Hessische Landesbank Girozentrale.

For all types of banking institutions at the end of 1983, there were 44,669 bank offices, of which 39,821 were branches.

These statistics reflect the fact that the savings banks, which go back to the seventeenth century, are very important and have over a long period offered a wide range of facilities in direct competition with the commercial banks and, indeed, a number of them – together with their *Girozentralen* or central institutions – are to all intents and purposes 'universal' banks like the Big Three and the larger regional banks. Moreover, the story goes back a long way, since it was in 1909 that the savings banks were first permitted to have cheques drawn on them and they have also had a giro clearing since the 1920s. In terms of their competitiveness and their share of total business, the savings banks were well established during the inter-war period. Savings virtually disappeared during the war and post-war inflations and, even after the currency reform, they made little progress until after the re-stocking boom had run its course. From then onwards, however, the savings bank expansion was cumulative and received an added impetus when the distribution of income began to shift towards the wage-earning and middle classes.

Moreover, from a situation in which the savings banks only provided a limited range of services – initially, they only granted secured credits – many of them now offer virtually the whole range of facilities, including unsecured credits. But their great strength was that they served persons in the lower-income groups and those with smaller businesses. This was the traditional structure, with the commercial banks concentrating more on big business and wealthy individuals. There was a division of labour between the retail banking done largely by the savings banks and the wholesale-banking facilities offered by the large commercial banks. Hence, when there was a big post-war expansion in the demand for retail-banking services, the savings banks were strategically placed to meet it – not only in the savings field, but in opening up current accounts to which salary payments could be credited and which could be operated upon either by cheque or giro transfer, and making loans for a variety of purposes at short-, medium-, and long-term. Latterly, some of the savings banks (and especially their central institutions – the *Girozentralen*) moved into the wholesale-banking field as well. In other words, the savings banks developed a more balanced clientele and the larger ones rapidly became 'universal' banks just like the big commercial banks. Only in stock-exchange and foreign-banking business did the big banks remain largely unchallenged and, in this context, one would include the *Girozentralen* and other central institutions like the Deutsche Genossenschaftsbank (for the cooperative banks) as big banks.

Without doubt, this is a remarkable situation and its development has been possible because of the high degree of competition that obtains in banking matters in West Germany. Even a foreign bank or broker can secure ready entry and, subject to detailed prudential supervisions,[15] enjoy freedom to conduct any banking business open to the domestic banks. In these circumstances, it may seem a little surprising that the Big Three should fail to hold their own. Admittedly, they moved late into the retail-banking field in competition with the savings banks. Having discovered the public demand for savings accounts and retail-banking facilities, there was something of a scramble to open a large number of *de novo* branches.[16] New services were offered and it became necessary to ensure that specialist expertise was available within the bank concerned and at the contact points with customers. Moreover, some services were likely to be more profitable than others – e.g., investment banking (the selling of securities and offering investment advice) – and more emphasis may well have been placed on these. There may also have been a case for greater decentralisation in the disposition of senior management so that more decisions could be taken at local level.

In addition, the banks found themselves exposed to a profit squeeze. Firstly, there was the changing structure of their liabilities with a greater emphasis on savings deposits on which it was necessary to pay interest. None the less, savings deposits were a relatively inexpensive source of funding. Secondly, with the abolition of the Interest Rates Order with effect from 1 April 1967, there was complete freedom to compete for deposits by paying higher rates of interest (now also being paid on a higher volume of deposits).[17] Third, on the basis of the increase in their savings deposits, the banks had locked themselves into long-term loans at fixed rates of interest. Indeed, the pressure on earnings during a period of high interest rates was largely the result of a disproportionately high level of fixed-rate loans.

Another sector that deserves to be mentioned are the private bankers, of which there were still 76 at the end of 1983, only ten being of medium-size. Nor was it very difficult to establish why these banks were able to survive, since this is always possible where one can specialise. The bigger private banks are important in the fields of investment and wholesale banking and the smaller men can always do well in stock-exchange centres like Frankfurt and Dusseldorf and in the rather less important centres like Hamburg and Munich, because of the dealing business to be found there. And that is the point – a number of the smaller men are not really bankers in the full sense, existing mainly on stock-exchange dealing, investment advice, portfolio management, insurance and mortgage broking.

As the statistics indicate, this is clearly a 'hybrid' system, with three big banks (and their Berlin subsidiaries), a number of sizeable regional banks, an important savings-bank sector (with large central institutions, and some large individual savings banks), the private bankers, the co-operative movement, the hire-purchase banks, and mortgage and other specialist banks. To explain this situation – not just the survival of small banks – it needs to be emphasised that because of its origins as a collection of separate states Germany has always been a rather decentralised kind of country – this was true even when Berlin was the capital. There have always been a number of provincial cities of importance – Frankfurt, Cologne, Dusseldorf, Hamburg, Hanover, and Munich – and both economic and cultural life is dispersed. As in France, there is still evidence of particularism and strong regional banks survive (e.g., in Bavaria) for similar reasons (cf. Alsace, the North of France, and Marseilles). What also makes it possible is the strength of the competitive philosophy (and the amount of profitable business available with a minimum of regulation); to some extent, the enforced decentralisation of the early post-war years may also have left its mark. On the other hand, the economic influence of the Big Three is rather more important than the figures might indicate and this is true also beyond the areas of investment and foreign banking. Various regional and private banks are within the area of influence of the big banks. In some cases, the latter hold participations in other banks. In other instances, they own them. In addition, the Big Three have shares in certain of the private mortgage banks. Hence, in these several ways, there exists much more integration than appears on the surface. Finally, the trends that are evident elsewhere obtrude here as well. Major mergers have taken place between two of the large *Girozentralen* and between sizeable banks in Frankfurt – Frankfurter Bank and Berliner Handelgesellschaft – and mergers between the regional banks are certainly the object of conversation. Private banks have merged and others are planning to merge. Alternatively, cross-participations may be taken up. In the savings-bank field, too, there is the possibility of further mergers not merely between individual savings banks but between *Girozentralen* as well. The same is true with the cooperatives, where numbers have dropped significantly over the past twenty years. The banking system in West Germany remains a hybrid system but the trend towards greater concentration is clearly in evidence and may be expected to continue, though possibly at a slower pace.

Austria

To an important extent, the economy of Austria is linked – as is its exchange rate – to that of Western Germany and there are respects, too, in which Austrian banking arrangements are somewhat similar to those in Western Germany. For example, almost all the Austrian banks are 'universal' commercial banks – in Austrian terms, 'all-purpose' banks. In this context, several of the central institutions (e.g., for the savings banks and the rural cooperatives) and the big savings banks are large institutions and compete as 'all-purpose' banks with the large commercial banks and one or two of the larger specialist institutions; this tends to cut across financial sectors, which include the commercial banks proper (big joint-stock banks, the regional banks, private banking houses,[18] certain special credit institutions,[19] and foreign banks), the savings banks and their *Girozentralen*, the provincial mortgage banks, the rural cooperatives (*Raiffeisen* banks) and their central institution (the Genossenschaftliche Zentralbank AG), the *Volksbanken* (catering particularly for small business and the professions, i.e. for small and medium-sized borrowers), and the building societies.[20]

All credit institutions, including for most purposes the Postal Savings Bank and the savings banks (subject to the special provisions of the Savings Bank Act – the *Sparkassengesetz*) are subject to the Banking Act 1979 (the *Kreditwesengesetz*), which requires all banks to be licensed and sets out a comprehensive framework for prudential supervision. It excludes the Central Bank, building societies, and insurance companies. A third Act of importance to the banking system is the Federal Act regulating the issue of debentures (the *Wertpaper-Emissionsgesetz*), which requires that the issue of debentures (with minor exceptions) be subject to a written authorisation by the Federal Ministry of Finance. Banks and bankers are members of the Association of Austrian Banks and Bankers (59 members).[21] This is a 'statutory interest group'. There are also the Austrian Savings Bank Association, the Association of Raiffeisen Banks, and the Association of Volksbanken. These are all free associations, but act as the 'statutory interest group' for the *Fachverband*. In addition, there is a non-statutory Free Association of Provincial Mortgage Banks. These associations safeguard and promote common professional interests of members; they also promote economic and cultural institutions. They are consulted on the content of relevant parliamentary bills and maintain contact with the monetary authorities, ministries, and the media. They also ensure cooperation in matters such as the organisation of banking business and wage agreements. Finally, the Banking Act envisages the participation of the 'statutory interest groups' in the conclusion of deposit-rate agreements and also in binding agreements on credit ceilings, as and when necessary, and, more generally, in arrangements commonly referred to as 'gentlemen's agreements'.

Of the 34 joint-stock banks, one – the Creditanstalt – is much larger than the rest and another (the Oesterreichische Länderbank) quite large, though rivalled by a specialist institution (the Kontrollbank) and a large savings bank (the Zentralsparkasse), but second in size between these two groups is the Girozentrale und Bank der Oesterreichischen Sparkassen AG, the central institution for the 133 savings banks and their wholly-owned subsidiary (see Table 4.2).

Table 4.2: Austria's Nine Largest Credit Institutions, end-of-year balance-sheet totals (AS billion)

	1981	1982	1983
Creditanstalt-Bankverein	243.0	277.1	300.9
Girozentrale[1]	176.7	195.5	213.2
Oesterreichische Kontrollbank[2]	140.9	145.4	153.1
Oesterreichische Länderbank	133.1	144.3	160.1
Zentralsparkasse, Vienna[3]	122.2	131.4	149.0
PO Savings Bank	94.5	109.4	126.3
Genossenschaftliche Zentralbank[4]	95.4	108.8	123.4
Bank für Arbeit und Wirtschaft	89.2	102.8	123.5
Erste Oesterreichische Spar-Casse[3]	84.9	94.6	103.6

Notes: 1. Wholesale bank and umbrella bank for savings banks. 2. Vehicle for export credit guarantee system. 3. Savings bank. 4. Wholesale bank and umbrella bank for rural cooperatives.
Source: Girozentrale, Vienna (Quoted in *Financial Times*, World Banking Supplement, 9 May 1983).

Of the eight regional banks, three are in the Creditanstalt group and one belongs to the Länderbank group, while several financial institutions have capital holdings in other regional banks. Despite marked differences with regard to volume of business and networks of branches, the regional banks constitute a relatively homogeneous group. They tend to concentrate their operations in one or two federal provinces and, in contrast to other banks, they have strong regional ties as well as a relatively high proportion of savings deposits. They provide finance for regional industries and medium- and small-sized enterprises.

In 1946, three of the large Austrian commercial banks were nationalised – Creditanstalt-Bankverein, Oesterreichische Länderbank AG, Oesterreichische Creditinstitut AG – and the first two partially denationalised in 1956. The Creditinstitut was taken over in stages by the Länderbank. This was completed in 1975. The 'all-purpose' or 'universal' commercial banks offer the full range of banking services. They make loans to large, medium-sized and small industrial and commercial enterprises; they have a developed foreign-exchange and Eurocurrency business; and they undertake security transactions both for customers and for their own portfolio. All this business is based on deposits attracted from a range of business enterprises and from private individuals, also on moneys borrowed from other banks. Latterly (since the 1960s), there has been a considerable growth of retail banking – small personal loans, savings deposits, salary and pension accounts. However, loans to manufacturing industry, trade and commerce, and foreign borrowers (excluding banks) account for just over 70 per cent of commercial bank loans, wage and salary earners together with public authorities to only 12 per cent. Finally, and partly for historical reasons, a number of joint-stock banks, especially the large ones, have significant holdings in industrial enterprises.

Over more recent years, almost all categories of Austrian banks have experienced a considerable expansion of business; this included the major instalment credit institutions and these were authorised by the Federal Ministry of Finance in December 1977 to offer a full range of banking services and have become fully licensed banks.

Although the private bankers – or 'banking houses' – do less than 2 per cent of total banking business, many of them carry famous banking names. Formerly, they were owned exclusively by partners who were personally liable; some are now joint-stock institutions. Since for all banking institutions with balance sheet totals exceeding AS 300 million it is necessary to publish annual accounts, the larger private banking houses publish their balance sheets. On the whole, these bankers provide tailor-made facilities for private customers; others specialise in making facilities available to certain customer groups or specific types of business.

There is a total of 12 foreign banks, some with links with the Communist countries – e.g., the Soviet Union, Hungary, Poland, and Yugoslavia; there are also American, French, and Brazilian interests. In addition, ten foreign credit institutions maintain representative offices in

Austria. For the most part, these banks either finance trade and business with the Eastern bloc countries (which Austria is ideally placed to do), or they provide facilities for multinationals and finance foreign trade. Much of their lending is in foreign currencies and, because they lack a developed local deposit base, a significant proportion of their resources derives from the inter-bank market (for domestic funds) or the Euro-currency markets.

A number of specialist institutions have been set up. The largest is the Oesterreichische Kontrollbank, founded in 1946 by a number of Austrian banks and now owned jointly by the two largest commercial banks and a number of others, including several regional banks; it acts as the sole agent for the Republic in the field of export guarantees and provides refinancing facilities to Austrian banks for export credits they have extended; since 1965, it has also acted as a central depository and clearing agency for securities. It is a leading dealer in the Austrian money market and has an important role in the capital market (e.g., in organising syndicates for domestic bond issues). Another institution – Oesterreichische Investitionskredit AG (Investkredit), founded in 1957 as a subsidiary of the Kontrollbank – provides medium- and long-term credit to industry on the basis of the issue of medium- and long-term bonds, placed for the most part with the investing public. Oesterreichische Kommunalkredit-AG (1958) provides long-term loans for industry through local authorities. Another specialist institution – Oesterreichischer Exportfonds Gesellschaft mbH (1950) – provides export finance, especially for smaller and medium-sized concerns. The Bürgschaftsfonds (1954) provides either guarantees or interest-rate subsidies for investment loans particularly to small industrial enterprises and another – Finanzierungsgarantie-Gesellschaft mit beschränkter Haftung (1969) – offers guarantees to encourage long-term borrowing for investment projects of manuacturing enterprises and the tourist and transport industries. Its activities were further extended by the Guarantee Act of 1977, as amended (e.g., to facilitate structural adjustments and thereby assist enterprises to regain sound financial health).

An important group of institutions in Austria is the 133 savings banks (two[22] of them very large),[23] together with their central institution – Girozentrale und Bank der Oesterreichischen Sparkassen AG, which ranks as the second largest credit institution in the country; it is also a universal bank and offers a full range of services. Its share capital is wholly owned by the savings banks. As the central institution for the savings-bank movement, the Girozentrale holds the required liquidity reserves of the savings banks (only the largest of which may deposit unlimited funds with banks other than the Austrian National Bank and the Girozentrale); the Girozentrale may also provide finance as necessary to the smaller individual savings banks as well as a range of services (e.g., in syndicating loans or underwriting bond issues as well as handling their foreign business). In addition, it operates as a wholesale bank with an emphasis on large-scale financing and on capital market transactions both at home and abroad. All these institutions come under the Banking Act 1979 and also a special Savings Bank Act 1979.[24] Under the latter, the savings banks were accorded the same status as all other banking institutions and the way was upon for the larger banks to become 'all-purpose' or 'universal' banks and for all savings banks to undertake a general banking business. Former restrictions on the scope of their business were repealed. The legislation was also followed by a number of mergers, which greatly strengthened the successor institutions and increased their ability to compete. Both the two largest savings banks sought to develop quite intensively their commercial business by lending to industry, whether enterprises were large, or small and medium-sized; both also expanded strongly their international activities. Savings deposits nevertheless remain a highly important ingredient in their liabilities. Formerly, the smaller savings banks lent heavily in the inter-bank money market through the Girozentrale. Latterly, these savings banks have tended to absorb their funds in lending to individuals (personal or consumer credit) and to small and medium-sized businesses. The Girozentrale and the large savings banks have for quite some time now been borrowers in this market as well as lenders; it depends – as it does for the other large banks – on the current liquidity position.

The nine provincial mortgage banks, although they operate as real-estate credit institutions, also offer a full range of banking services. Each of the Austrian provinces has its own provincial mortgage bank, raising the funds necessary to their operations (largely loans eligible for mortgage bond cover) by the issue of bonds (mortgage and communal bonds). Each province acts as guarantor for the liabilities assumed by its own mortgage bank.

The *Raiffeisen* agricultural credit cooperatives, of which there were 2,790 individual cooperatives in 1980, are federated on the basis of provincial centres, with a central institution – the Genossenschaftliche Zentralbank AG, which is a large credit institution. The individual credit institutions tend to be small. Deposits amount to about 21 per cent of the total for all Austrian banking institutions and loans to about 16.5 per cent. Financing activities are concentrated on agriculture and forestry, tourism, and loans to small and medium-sized industrial enterprises. Over the past 20 years or so, there have been many mergers and this process has latterly tended to accelerate, affecting particularly the small cooperatives.

On the urban front, there are small business cooperatives called *Volksbanken* (134 independent *Volksbanken* at the end of 1979, as well as 'civil servants banks' and employees credit cooperatives). There is a central institution called Oesterreichische Volksbanken AG (OEVAG), which is authorised to conduct all types of banking business at home and abroad, except the issue of mortgage and communal bonds. Its specific tasks are (a) to manage and invest the funds provided by the small business credit cooperatives (especially their liquidity reserves); (b) to grant loans, credit aid and temporary liquidity aid, and to facilitate money and business transactions within the sector and *vis-à-vis* third parties; (c) to carry out, foster, develop and promote cashless payments, transactions and other banking services; and (d) to issue funded bonds. On the whole, *Volksbanken* are relatively small institutions, though on average larger than the *Raiffeisen* banks.

In Austria, there are also four building societies – one is associated with the Girozentrale and serves the savings-bank sector, and one each the *Volksbanken* and *Raiffeisen* sectors. These are domiciled in Vienna; a fourth is domiciled in Salzburg. Loans are granted exclusively to building society savers to finance the acquisition or improvement of dwellings, or for the redemption of payments previously incurred for that purpose.

There are three factoring companies, a business which has been growing fast, particularly non-recourse factoring, which besides its financing function comprises the management of receivables and offers a guarantee for actual payment. They are subsidiaries of other institutions. Leasing, it should be noted, is not considered a banking business in Austria, but some is undertaken by non-banks.

Finally, there is the Austrian Postal Savings Bank (Postsparkasse) founded in 1883. Until its reorganisation in the mid-1920s, the Austrian Postal Savings Bank was under the authority of the Ministry of Commerce. In 1926, the bank for the first time gained an independent organisational status and was established as an economic entity with its own responsibilities. Austria's annexation by the German Reich (1938) put an end to the bank's independent status. After World War II, the bank was placed under the control of the Federal Ministry of Finance and only acquired its independence in 1970 (Postal Savings Bank Act 1969), when it was placed under an obligation to conduct its business in accordance with commercial principles. There were two amendments to the Austrian Postal Savings Bank Act: firstly, in 1981, legislation came into effect to widen the role of the bank; under the amended law, it was accorded the right to issue bonds and to assume guarantees for third parties within certain limits; it might now engage in all types of banking business, except commercial and personal (consumer) credits; secondly, the bank was authorised in 1982 to grant short-term overdraft facilities on cheque accounts. Certain restrictions are also imposed on the use of deposits; the State acts as guarantor for all liabilities of PSK. Business activities are mainly concentrated on postal cheque and postal savings transactions. Approximately 2,300 post offices throughout Austria operate on behalf of the Postal Savings Bank. One of PSK's specific functions is its participation in the management of the public debt through the Committee for the Administration of the Public Debt, which regularly studies the conditions and trends in the money and capital markets. Furthermore, PSK maintains an office booth for the State lottery and betting pools.

One might note, too, that in 1982 legislation came into effect to enable banks to set up equity finance companies funded by public subscription, and to authorise their involvement in the provision of home-improvement and urban-renewal loans at assisted rates.[25]

An indication of changes in market share is given in Table 4.3 from which it will be seen that, after a fall in the middle of the period 1960-82, the joint-stock banks have more or less recovered to something over 30 per cent; the savings banks have lost relatively; *Raiffeisen* banks have increased in importance and the *Volksbanken* have suffered a fall. Building societies have latterly become much more important – due largely to the tax privileges granted to building society savers.

Over the years the density of branches has increased considerably (see table 4.4). Based on branches for all types of institutions, there is now one branch for every 1,450 inhabitants. At the same time, the number of independent institutions declined by 860 – from 2,169 to 1,309. Mostly this affected the agricultural credit cooperatives, also the savings banks and the *Volksbanken*. The number of commercial banks increased by 26.

The other important point to note is the increasing degree of concentration of the Austrian banking system. Clearly, it remains a 'hybrid' system, but (a) in the savings-bank, *Raiffeisen* and *Volksbanken* sectors, there have been many mergers and amalgamations; and (b) in the

Table 4.3: Market Shares of Credit Institutions, Austria

	End of 1960 Balance-sheet totals		End of 1970 Balance-sheet totals		End of 1982 Balance-sheet totals	
	in AS billion	in % of aggregate balance sheet total	in AS billion	in % of aggregate balance sheet total	in AS billion	in % of aggregate balance sheet total
Joint stock banks[1]	30.4	31.3	94.2	26.8	716.2	30.4
Banking Houses[2]	2.4	2.4	9.5	2.7	37.9	1.6
Special credit institutions[3]	11.6	11.9	30.0	8.5	312.2	13.2
Provincial mortgage banks	5.8	6.0	23.2	6.6	113.2	4.8
Banks in the wider sense	50.2	51.6	156.9	44.6	1,179.5	50.0
Savings banks[4]	26.1	26.9	94.7	26.9	570.3	24.2
Raiffeisen banks[5]	13.5	13.9	63.6	18.1	400.2	17.0
Volksbanken[6]	6.0	6.2	22.6	6.4	111.1	4.7
Building societies	1.4	1.4	14.1	4.0	96.4	4.1
Total	97.2	100.0	351.9	100.0	2,357.5	100.0

Notes: 1. Including former instalment-credit institutions. 2. Some banking houses have been converted into joint-stock banks.
3. Oesterreichische Kontrollbank AG; Postal Savings Bank; Oesterreichische Investitionskredit AG; CENTRO Internationale Handelsbank AG; Oesterreichische Exportfondsgesellschaft mbH; Oesterreichische Kommunalkredit AG; Allgemeine Finanz- und Waren-Treuhand AG; Hotel- und Fremdenverkehrs- Treuhandgesellschaft mbH; and the factoring banks are the chief institutions in this group.
4. Including Girozentrale und Bank der Oesterreichischischen Sparkassen AG. 5. Including Genossenschaftliche Zentralbank AG.
6. Including Oesterreichische Volksbanken AG.
Source: Diwok, *The Austrian Banking System.*

Table 4.4: Main Offices and Branches, Austria (1960-82)

	Main offices	Branches	Outlets	Main offices	Branches	Outlets	Main offices	Branches	Outlets	Change in number of outlets 1960-82
		End of 1960			End of 1970			End of 1982		
Joint-stock banks	30	192	222	34	294	328	40	708	748	+ 526
Banking houses	18	19	37	16	25	41	10	39	49	+ 12
Special credit institutions	9	23	32	13	28	41	33	28	61	+ 29
Provincial mortgage banks	10	10	20	10	15	25	10	79	89	+ 69
Banks in the wider sense	67	244	311	73	362	435	93	854	947	+ 636
Savings banks	177	269	446	172	398	570	133	1,105	1,238	+ 792
Raiffeisen banks	1,764	75	1,839	1,614	295	1,909	960	1,470	2,430	+ 591
Volksbanken	157	68	225	161	139	300	119	370	489	+ 264
Building societies	4	4	8	4	43	47	4	35	39	+ 31
Total	2,169	660	2,829	2,024	1,237	3,261	1,309	3,834	5,143	+ 2,314

Source: Diwok, *The Austrian Banking System.*

banking sector proper, there has been the emergence of two large banking groups – the Creditanstalt group and the Länderbank group (in each case, a large bank with a number of subsidiaries). Excluding holdings in special-purpose credit institutions, their aggregate balance sheet figures are now rather more than 60 per cent of those for the joint-stock banks as a whole, with the Creditanstalt group almost twice as large as the Länderbank group.

Belgium

Prior to 1914, and with the notable exception of the Société Générale, whose group of affiliated banks included about 60 offices, nearly all the banks in Belgium were 'unit banks'. Superimposed on this structure came the considerable banking expansion of the 1920s, largely nurtured by inflation and the illusion of great prosperity.

Two main factors[26] contributed to 'rationalisation' and the concentration of control in fewer hands: the tendency of the Belgian banks to commit too large a proportion of their resources to investment in industrial equities, and the large number of banks and bank offices competing for what in a small country – even with rising money incomes – was a relatively limited amount of retail-banking business. It is certain that during the 1920s the Belgian banks made many mistakes in their choice of investments; also that by 1929-30 there was a great number of localities in Belgium that were over-banked. Malinvestment led to heavy losses (particularly when depression supervened in the early 1930s), while the excessively large number of branches resulted in an increase in costs.

The movement towards greater concentration was already under way towards the end of the 1920s, but it was greatly accelerated once the advent of depression had revealed the extent of the banks' investment losses. Finally, in common with experience in other countries, the competition of the leading Belgian banks for a larger share both of the available business and of deposits was another important factor behind the movement towards greater concentration, with networks of branches under the control of larger institutions. This was already evident in the 1920s, but as the struggle for influence between the Société Générale and the Banque de Bruxelles became more intense in the 1930s, the pace perceptibly quickened. By the early 1930s, the large banking groups were themselves converted into monolithic institutions, the main offices and branches of the former affiliates becoming branches of the absorbing parent bank, control being effectively concentrated either in head office or – in some matters– in the main regional offices. It was about this time, too, that another group of banks merged to form the Kredietbank, which is rather smaller than the other two, but which also has a developed network of branches. There was a further increase in the number of bank branches following World War II, largely prompted by the intensive competition for deposits.[27]

The mergers in the 1930s were also used as a means of writing off the losses revealed by economic depression, since in the process of merging it was possible to employ reserves for this purpose without attracting too much attention. Subsequently, in 1935, the attempt was made to 'reform' the Belgian banking system, by 'hiving off' the banks' industrial investment business. Each concern was split into two distinct corporations – one with banking functions and the other for the purpose of conducting 'financial' activities, which included the business of industrial investment and subscribing the capital for the newly separated banking business. The change was clearly much less than was intended. Furthermore, when a bank is not only substantially owned by an industrial finance corporation, but is also obliged to lend large sums to it, the links between commercial banking and industrial finance obviously remain quite close.[28] That the 1935 'reforms' had had only a qualified success was underlined by the action taken in 1956, when the Banking Commission exercised its moral authority to secure 'a wider distribution of bank shares', involving 'the unloading of the greater part of the holdings of these shares in the portfolios of the major investment companies'.[29] It was in this way that the Commission sought to ensure that henceforth both the spirit and the letter of the 1935 reform would be observed.

The basic regulatory framework in Belgium is still provided by the Banking Law of 1935 (Arrêté Royal no. 185 of 9 July 1935). Under that Law, a bank is defined as an institution whose usual business is to collect deposits repayable at call or a maximum term of two years, with a view to using them for its own account for the purpose of banking, lending and investment operations. Since this general definition is very broad, the banks have been left with considerable freedom to develop their business activities as they wish; also, because of this, different banks may conduct their business in very different ways and (as we shall see) fundamental differences can emerge.

Three bodies are responsible for the regulation of banking operations in Belgium. These are the Banking Commission, the National Bank, and the Institut Belgo-Luxembourgeois du Change (IBLC). Although these three institutions have distinct functions, which are defined in their respective statutes, they do in fact work closely together and there is much liaison. At the same time, the Banking Commission is the agency responsible for supervising all banks in Belgium, latterly the savings banks as well, and it ensures that the banks comply with the banking laws. In addition to its responsibilities for the supervision of the commerical-banking sector and the savings banks, the Banking Commission is also responsible for the supervision of investment holding companies, unit trusts, and advises on admissions to listing on the Belgian Stock Exchange. Indeed, on the capital market, they exercise a moral authority and any major financial operation or reorganisation of companies would be submitted to them for their judgement and advice.

The criteria on the basis of which the Commission (and its agents) operate are of a prudential character. Thus, the Commission is concerned with questions of solvability, liquidity, profitability, and the expertise of the management. There are rules relating to capital adequacy, also to liquidity (again, these are prudential in character and may be varied from time to time). Even when liquidity ratios are not being applied, the Commission supervises bank liquidity in a general way. Capital adequacy of banks is becoming a problem in Belgium as capital ratios tend to decline. Hence, a greater emphasis on subordinated debt. Banks seem to be less profitable than formerly and at times it has been difficult to issue equity on the capital market. However, in 1982 and 1983, there were a number of increases in bank capital by means of new share issues stimulated by fiscal measures to encourage the provision of more risk capital. Subordinated debt may be included in the capital ratio, but only up to a certain limit. The Commission (and its agents) are concerned, too, with the risk structures of the loan portfolios of the banks and the Commission receives reports on all borrowers whose aggregate borrowings exceed 20 per cent of a bank's own resources. Foreign banks come under the same regime of regulation as the domestic banks. There is also an investigation whenever a foreign bank wishes to set up a branch or a subsidiary in Belgium, but once a foreign bank has obtained entry it is free to establish further branches if it so desires. Subsequently, the foreign bank becomes subject to the same rules as the domestic banks. But in regulating the banking system, there is a lot of emphasis on the Commission's moral authority and on persuasion. Regulation tends to be informal and pragmatic. Nevertheless, everybody is aware that there are statutory powers in the background. Ultimately, the Commission could withdraw a bank's licence, when all activities would cease. More generally, if the circumstances warranted it, the Commission might suggest the restructuring of a bank, perhaps its merger with a larger bank.

The National Bank of Belgium, which is owned 50 per cent by the State, has the sole right of note issue in Belgium; as central bank, it is the banker's bank and is banker to the government. It is a source of rediscount finance and is responsible for coordinating the clearance and collection of cheques and credit transfers between financial institutions. To this end, a clearing centre for the Belgian financial system was set up.

In Belgium, there are three main groups of financial institutions, which are concerned with the attraction of funds from the public and on-lending or investing these funds in a variety of ways. These are the banks, the private savings banks and the public-sector financial institutions, which have their own statutes. Although these several institutions offer broadly similar services, there are none the less significant differences in the provision of credit. For example, the commercial banks for the most part lend to the productive private sector; in particular, they provide short-term loans to commerce and industry and international financing. In conjunction with the Postal Cheque Office, they are responsible for the system of domestic and international payments. The private savings banks, on the other hand, specialise more particularly in housing loans and some of them in agricultural credit, and this is also one of the most important activities of certain of the public financial institutions. Other public financial institutions specialise in medium- and long-term loans to industry and commerce. In terms of source of funds employed, the commercial banks usually rely more heavily on deposits, while the public financial institutions depend more on issuing bonds and medium-term notes. Private savings banks occupy an intermediate position. In round figures, the commercial banks are responsible for 42 per cent of total deposits; the public credit insitutions likewise for 42 per cent; and the private savings banks for about 15 per cent, but in terms of total balance-sheet figures the banks represent two-thirds. The tendency has been for the share of the banks to increase and for that of the public credit institutions to diminish. There has been a slight increase in the share of private savings banks.

The public-sector financial institutions include the Caisse Générale d'Epargne et de Retraite (CGER), which is the government-owned savings bank mainly engaged in private house financing and some industrial and commercial real-estate financing; since 1980, the CGER has also been able to conduct all types of banking transactions permitted for commercial banks and it is subject to the same type of regulations and controls relating to these operations; of major financial institutions, its balance sheet is fourth in size; next there are three major medium- and long-term financial institutions – the Société Nationale de Crédit à l'Industrie (SNCI) designed to finance industrial growth on the basis of the issue of loan stock; a substantial part of its credits are government-subsidised loans granted in conjunction with commercial banks; the Caisse National de Crédit Professionel (CNCP), which grants similar credits to retail and small business enterprises; and the Société Nationale d'Investissement (SNI), which undertakes a significant amount of long-term financing for Belgian industry – this body, the constitution of which was revised by the law of 4 August 1978, is a public holding company having two primary objectives: firstly, the stimulation and development of productive industry normally through equity or convertible debenture investment; and secondly, assistance to new productive and distributive industries and the establishment of whatever means of investment or financing are appropriate for the business concerned. There is aso the Crédit Communal de Belgique, which provides banking and financial services for the local authorities; in size of balance sheet it is third after the two big commercial banks. In the field of agricultural credit, there is a *Raiffeisen* cooperatives organisation called the Boerenbond. In addition, there is the Institut de Réescompte et de Garantie (IRG), which assists the central bank in the regulation of liquidity by acting essentially as a broker for commercial bills. Only banks and financial institutions have access to this market. The IRG also acts as a discount house for selected bankers' acceptances and plays an important role in Credit-Export – the pool formed by SNCI, IRG, CGER and a number of other banks to finance exports and, under certain conditions, to re-finance medium- and long-term capital-goods projects. In addition, the IRG supervises and administers the convention signed by all banks and private savings banks established under Belgian law to form a depositor protection pool for use in the event of a bank failure. It is run by a Board of Directors composed of representatives of the private credit sector and the central bank. It is also subject to the oversight of a government commissioner. Finally, there is the postal giro system, which accepts non-interest-bearing sight deposits which are chiefly important for the settlement of small accounts and small payments by government and public institutions. Accounts cannot be overdrawn.

In 1982, there were 81 banking institutions in Belgium – about the same as there were at the end of 1960. Of these, 56 are registered under

Belgian law (some are foreign affiliates) and 25 banks under foreign law, the latter being merely Belgian-based branches of major foreign banks, with no legal status other than being such branches. Since 1960, there have been big changes, with a considerable increase in both bank branches and bank accounts, though the number of bank branches has now stabilised. In Belgium, there is now about one branch per 2,700 inhabitants and about 80 bank accounts (demand and time deposit accounts and bank books) per 100 inhabitants. In addition, there are the public credit institutions, the private savings banks, and the Postal Cheque Service, which also have a large number of branches and accounts, but for which accurate data are not available. As well as the growth of domestic business, there is of course the considerable expansion in international banking activity and foreign-exchange business, especially associated with the growth of the Euro-currency market – by the end of 1983, more than 60 per cent of the funds of the Belgian banking sector (including inter-bank accounts) came from abroad. In another context, too, there is a significant foreign interest in Belgian banking. More than half of the banks operating under Belgian law – 31 in fact – are over 50 per cent owned by one or more foreign groups – for the most part by large foreign banks. Hence, there are only 26 banks in which Belgian shareholders hold a majority stake, though even here there are foreign controlling stakes in some of them. Whether through a branch or a subsidiary, in terms of numbers, Japanese and American interests have the greatest representation; other countries which are relatively well represented include France (large in terms of balance-sheet figures), the Netherlands, the United Kingdom, and Spain. A few foreign banks have been active in Belgium for a long time – some for more than a century – but the majority came in the 1970s.

This invasion by foreign banks is part of the progressive internationalisation of banking over past decades. It is associated with the internationalisation of business life in general and the emergence of multinational enterprises in particular. Hence, it became increasingly necessary for banks to have their own physical representation abroad in order to remain competitive; also, it gave them the opportunity of gaining business from local enterprises and access to local money and capital markets. Nor should one underestimate the importance of an emerging Euro-currency market in inducing many American and Japan-Japanese banks to open up in Europe. But why in Belgium? For a number of reasons – its favourable geographic location, its well-developed financial infrastructure, and the presence of the EEC Commission. Equally important was the fact that the Belgian monetary authorities and the Banking Commission in particular favour a liberal policy in the context of foreign bank representation and have not generally required reciprocity in the treatment of Belgian banks abroad. Without doubt, the presence of foreign banks has intensified inter-bank competition, especially for corporate business based on the borrowing of money-market funds by way of large short-term deposits and their on-lending short-term to large businesses.

Such developments were not without their impact on the domestic banks. Since the end of 1960, 42 banks with a Belgian majority shareholding have disappeared, largely as a result of mergers and takeovers.

> In most cases, smaller, local banks were concerned, for which enlargement of scale was the appropriate if not the only way of survival in a climate of increasing competition, both among banks themselves and from the private savings banks and public credit institutions, which in the course of years have been increasingly encroaching on the traditional province of the banks. Keen competition has led to the erosion or abolition of most agreements on prices and interest rates. For an even greater part of banking activity, market conditions became the price-determining factor.[30]

Now we have a situation where in terms of numbers (not in volume of business) two-thirds of the Belgian banks are foreign-owned.

As one would expect with a relatively large number of banks, there are considerable differences in size. There is also quite a high degree of concentration. By far the largest are the Société Générale de Banque, the Banque Bruxelles Lambert,[31] and the Kredietbank (with a subsidiary in Wallonia, the French-speaking part of Belgium; this is called the Crédit Général S.A. de Banque). As already indicated, there are also two large public-sector financial institutions. These are followed in gradually reducing size by a number of medium-sized banks[32] (mostly foreign-owned) and a rather large number of smaller institutions[33] (see Table 4.5). But in recent years there has been some decrease in the degree of concentration in the banking sector, mainly as a result of the growing competition of foreign banks, and between 1975 and 1982, the market share of the three big banks fell by about 6 per cent. By 1983, their share within the banking sector was 46 per cent but, when account is taken of the competition of the private savings banks and certain of the public credit institutions (and others engaged in the collection of deposits and/or granting credit), their share would only be

Table 4.5: Belgian Banks by Size and Market Share

1982 financial year	Number of banks*	Market share (%)
Banks classified by balance sheet total		
Over BFr 500 billion	3	46
From BFr 100 billion to BFr 500 billion	11	33
From BFr 25 billion to BFr 100 billion	20	14
From BFr 10 billion to BFr 25 billion	19	5
Under BFr 10 billion	28	2
Total	81	100
Banks classified by customers' deposits (BFr + foreign exchange)		
Over BFr 100 billion	3	73
From BFr 20 billion to BFr 100 billion	7	11
From BFr 10 billion to BFr 20 billion	10	7
Under BFr 10 billion	61	9
Total	81	100
Banks classified by volume of credit to the private sector		
Over BFr 100 billion	3	53
From BFr 20 billion to BFr 100 billion	16	29
From BFr 10 billion to BFr 20 billion	12	10
Under BFr 10 billion	50	8
Total	81	100

*Excluding Banque Belge pour l'Etranger, which operates only abroad.
Source: 'The Belgian Banking Sector in Profile', *Kredietbank Weekly Bulletin* (22 April 1983).

about 30 per cent of the total.

One should perhaps add a word about the 31 private savings banks, some of which are quite large institutions and which are now competing much more directly with the commercial banks, especially in attracting deposits with a wide range of packages (savings accounts are also repayable virtually on demand), less so on the lending side and in foreign-exchange business, though these are now being developed. They tend to be most active in providing consumer finance and as always in financing house purchase and construction against a mortgage, an area into which the commercial banks themselves are moving. But the savings banks have begun to lend to small business and are now competing more actively with the commercial banks in this field.

So far as the commercial banks are concerned, the three big Belgian banks – the Société Générale de Banque, the Banque Bruxelles Lambert, and the Kredietbank – all command a broad deposit base, which derives from an extensive branch network. They are active in both the retail and corporate markets. Credit to the public sector is also relatively significant for these banks, as is their international-banking and foreign-exchange business. But of the other universal or 'diversified' banks, some are wholesale banks, which tend to lend large chunks of money to corporate businesses rather than to private persons. They have a less developed network of branches and, of their total loan portfolios, less is lent to the public sector. Almost all of these wholesale banks are controlled by foreign groups, whereas the three big banks are wholly or predominantly Belgian-owned. Both groups are net takers on the inter-bank market.

Another group of banks has been described as 'money-market' banks.[34] Generally speaking, these banks have one or only a few branches. They finance themselves mainly by means of bankers' deposits, though they also attract a limited proportion of their working funds as deposits from (mostly large) enterprises. Typically, too, these banks have an important international-banking business (in the sense of operations with foreign centres) and are also important in foreign-exchange business (foreign currency transactions). Within this group, however, a further distinction can be made – between banks with a relatively important lending activity and those which engage primarily in inter-bank deposit business and which specialise mainly in foreign-exchange arbitrage. Nearly all money-market banks are branches or affiliates of foreign banks.

A third group of commercial banks consists of small and medium-sized 'customer banks'.[35] In this case, transactions with other banks are relatively less important, banking business being centred mainly on households and enterprises. Compared with their loan portfolio, they tend to have an ample deposit base, part of which is reinvested in the inter-bank market. Among most of these banks, many of which are Belgian-owned, international-banking and foreign-exchange business is relatively insignificant. Customer banks can be broken down further, depending on whether they obtain their deposits chiefly from corporate sources or from private customers. Most banks in the latter group have a definite retail character, as well as a local or regional network of branches. The loans they provide are mainly to small and medium-sized enterprises and to private persons. About five of these institutions specialise in consumer loans; among the others the granting of corporate loans is preponderant.

Of the 30 private savings banks that belong to the Association of Private Savings Banks,[36] five are large and nine medium-sized; the remaining 16 are quite small. There is also one medium-sized savings bank outside the Association. Beginning in the 1960s, the business of the private savings banks – and especially of the larger ones – has become increasing de-specialised. Formerly, the savings banks merely accepted savings deposits and issued *bons de caisse* against which they invested a proportion in government bonds and government-guaranteed securities, the remainder going to finance house purchase on the basis of mortgages[37] or into construction loans. Latterly, the savings banks moved into the financing of small and medium-sized businesses, on the one hand, and the granting of personal loans and credits for consumption purposes, on the other. But there is a lot of variation between the several savings banks and it is the larger savings banks rather than the medium-sized and smaller ones that have moved closer to the types of business done by the commercial banks, including the undertaking of some foreign business. As already indicated, the savings banks are also now subject to the Banking Commission. In practice, the Commission applies much the same regulations to the savings banks as it does to the commercial banks. Before 1976, the savings banks had their own regulatory body, but this was merged with the Banking Commission as from 1 May 1976.

Although technically the interest rates on mortgages are free, the savings banks consult informally with each other and collectively they are the price leaders for mortgage rates; for deposits, the commercial banks tend to be the price leaders, and for *bons de caisse*, the public institutions. Subject to a maximum laid down by the law, the savings banks tend to follow the lead of the commercial banks with regard to the rates on personal loans.

Finally, in what sense is this a 'hybrid' system? It is true that there is a relatively high degree of concentration – three banks account for about 46 per cent of total banking business and 10 medium-sized banks for about a further 31 per cent (some of these are regional banks related to the Big Three; others are independent) – but the remainder is spread between some 68 other banks of which 31 are more than 50 per cent foreign-owned and 25 are foreign-bank branches. In addition, there are the 31 private savings banks (five large, nine medium-sized), many of which compete with the commercial banks, not to mention the public-sector institutions, which rival the commercial banks as a whole in size of deposits. More than that – there is the breakdown into quite different kinds of banks – the large 'universal' banks active in both the retail and corporate markets, with developed networks of branches; wholesale banks with relatively few branches and mainly foreign-controlled that make big loans to corporate businesses; again, there are the 'money-market' banks financed mainly by bankers' deposits, some with a relatively important lending activity (including international business), others that engage primarily in inter-bank deposit business and foreign-exchange arbitrage; and lastly, the small and medium-sized 'customer banks' mainly catering for households and the smaller enterprises (those that have a retail character would tend to have a local or regional network of branches). This would seem to be essentially a hybrid system.

The Netherlands

The Netherlands has one of the oldest banking systems in the world and a tradition going back at least to the early seventeenth century. There are in the Netherlands some 89 registered commercial banks but, although a number of smaller institutions continue to survive, the system is dominated by two large commercial banks, which themselves own smaller banks – Algemene Bank Nederland (ABN) and Amsterdam-Rotterdam Bank (AMRO Bank) – and by Rabobank Nederland, heading a cooperative bank organisation (Coöperatieve Rabobank) of about the same size as the other two; the Nederlandsche Middenstandsbank is rather smaller – about half the size of the other three. The ABN was the result of a merger in 1964 between Nederlandsche Handel-Maatschappij (founded in 1824 and, despite its overseas connections (e.g., in what became Indonesia) always with an important domestic business as well) and the Twentsche Bank (founded in 1861). Then, in 1968, the Algemene Bank Nederland and the Hollandsche Bank-Unie (which had been formed in 1933 by merging two other banks and which was largely concerned with overseas business) joined forces. AMRO Bank was also the result of a major merger – likewise in 1964 – between the Amsterdamsche Bank (established in 1871 and which had absorbed the business of the Incasso-Bank – established in 1891 – and with which it had had a 'cooperation agreement' since 1948) and the Rotterdamsche Bank (established in 1863 and itself the product of many mergers and amalgamations). The Nederlandsche Middenstandsbank, which was set up to serve the so-called 'middle classes', i.e. the smaller craftsmen, shopkeepers and professional men, was established in 1927. The fifth largest bank is the Nederlandse Credietbank, very much smaller than the others and really medium-sized; it is now wholly owned by Chase Manhattan Overseas Banking Corporation.[38] Rabobank Nederland was the product of a merger in

1972 of two central institutions originally established in 1898 to serve the cooperative movement. These were the Coöperatieve Centrale Boerenleenbank with a head office at Eindhoven and the Coöperatieve Centrale Raiffeisen Bank based in Utrecht, which in due course also became the head office of Rabobank, with which is linked some 952 cooperative banks.[39] The official name of the present central institution is Coöperatieve Centrale Raiffeisen Boerenleenbank.

Formerly, there were several independent medium-sized banks. One of these came on the scene when in 1962 R. Mees & Zoonen decided to link their business interests with Hope and Company. Subsequently, they merged and, in March 1969, took over the Nederlandse Overzee Bank to trade under the name of Bank Mees & Hope. In 1975, this bank was taken over by ABN. Another private bank – Pierson, Heldring & Pierson – was bought by AMRO Bank. Both banks still operate very independently; Pierson, Heldring & Pierson tends to specialise in merchant banking. A bank that still sustains a family interest, though partly owned by Rabobank (40 per cent) and by National Westminster Bank (30 per cent) is F. van Lanschot Bankiers of 's-Hertogenbosch – it has a balance sheet of approximately 5 per cent of the size of the large banks. About twice this size was another former private bank – N.V. Slavenburg's Bank of Rotterdam – in which Crédit Lyonnais had a major interest; financial scandals gave rise to serious difficulties in the first half of 1983 and it re-emerged in June 1983 under the new name Crédit Lyonnais Bank Nederland. The only foreign bank to develop into a medium-sized Dutch bank was the Banque de Paris et des Pays-Bas. It is represented in Amsterdam and in many of the provincial towns of the Netherlands. It is owned by Paribas International (88 per cent) and Paribas-Warburg (12 per cent), both in Paris. Altogether, there are 44 foreign banks, of which 19 are branches and the remainder subsidiaries (owned 50 per cent or more by foreign banks). In addition, there are 17 representative offices.

A very specialised commercial bank is the Kas-Associatie. It provides clearing facilities for security transactions as well as accepting both demand and time deposits and making loans against collateral (e.g., to stock-exchange staff). Mention might also be made of the Nationale Investeringsbank, over 50 per cent State-owned (established as Herstelbank in 1945 to finance reconstruction); the Nederlandse Participatie Maatschappij (1948), to provide risk capital to small and medium-sized firms; and the Export-Financiering-Maatschappij (1951) to finance the export of capital goods. There is also the Bank voor Nederlandsche Gemeenten (Bank for Netherlands Municipalities), 50 per cent State-owned, which finances short-term borrowings of local government authorities and also makes long-term loans mainly to municipalities, as well as to provinces, public utilities, and housing-construction corporations. The emphasis tends to be on its long-term business. The local authorities keep their temporarily surplus funds on deposit with it and effect their transfer payments through it. It issues bonds on the capital market and is also interested in private placements, which are its main sources of finance; these are then on-lent to the municipalities and other public bodies.

It should be noted that the big banks in the Netherlands are not owned by holding companies. In effect, there are banking groups, but the main bank in the group itself owns shares in subsidiaries as direct investments. Subsidiaries include finance companies, sometimes a mortgage bank. Independent mortgage banks[40] normally issue mortgage-bank bonds over the counter. Neither the banks themselves, nor the authorities, would wish to see any further mergers between the big commercial banks and it would seem that the position has now stabilised. But further amalgamations between smaller institutions (e.g., cooperatives and savings banks) are likely to be encouraged.

The legislation to which the banks are subject for purposes of regulation is the Act on the Supervision of the Credit System (which was originally passed in 1952 and revised in 1956 and 1978); it is implemented in detail by regulations.[41] But in the background an agreement will have been reached between the Netherlands Bank and the banking community on the basis of which to implement the regulation of liquidity and of solvency. It is the normal circumstance that, after due discussion, the parties always come to agree and, indeed, here as elsewhere it is important that there should be at all times a high degree of cooperation between the Central Bank and its banking community, because only thus will the system work. The Act also provides for a licensing system and the registration of banks and other credit institutions.

Although in absolute terms the savings banks have experienced an exceptionally strong growth, they have lagged somewhat in relation to the universal banks. Partly this has been due to the interest-rate structure. When the yield curve was inverse, their market shares declined, because they were not permitted to grant short-term credits and were therefore not interested in attracting deposits at money-market rates. But their share of private savings increased somewhat after the inverse-yield structure came to an end at the beginning of 1982. They also suffered because of their small size in relation to the commercial banks and the lower return on their investments due to the limits laid down by investment regulations. They invest in public bonds, in private placements, and in house-purchase mortgages and they still have a significant share of total savings (at the end of 1983 about 18 per cent). Subject to being of a minimum size and having a developed credit department and administrative structure, they may now grant business credits at variable rates. So far, the savings banks have not moved very much into consumer finance, though borrowing against a mortgage does sometimes have a consumer aspect. As has already been indicated, there has been some movement towards further concentration and this is encouraged by the Netherlands Bank.

Another small and minor group are the 17 'security credit institutions'. They act as dealers on the stock exchange and grant credits to customers to assist in stock-exchange purchases. Their numbers have decreased and their balance sheets are small. Some are owned by the commercial banks themselves.

Finance companies are not covered by the banking legislation. A lot of their funding is either from their own resources (which derive from institutional investors) or by borrowing from the banks. They lend by way of consumer financing. A distinction should be made between *financieringsmaatschappijen* (finance companies), which finance instalment credit transactions, and *voorschotbanken* (credit banks), which grant loans to private individuals, generally for purchases of consumer goods. The supervision of finance companies is exercised by the Ministry of Economic Affairs (Instalment Credit Sales Act 1961), whereas that of credit banks is the responsibility of the Ministry of Welfare, Public Health and Culture (Consumer Credit Act 1972).

There has been a proposal to establish a Postal Bank based on the 2,850 postal offices throughout the country. In a bill presented to the Second Chamber of Parliament in April 1984, the government set forth its intention to pursue the integration of the Post Office Savings Bank and the postal cheque and giro services in the form of a public limited company to be set up for that purpose. The resulting institution would be somewhat smaller than the Nederlandsche Middenstandsbank.

In 1979, the Post Giro took over the Municipal Giro in Amsterdam (which however still operates under its own name). These provide quite serious competition for the commercial banks, especially in the matter of private demand deposits. The postal giro system effects small payments on quite a large scale. In addition, there is a bank giro, which comprehends all the commercial banks, the savings banks, and the cooperative banks. In fact, most transfers take place through one giro or the other.[42] Cheques are very seldom used in the Netherlands.

Italy

Originally, the large Italian banks were established to operate as 'mixed banks' as in a number of other European countries. Following the crisis of the early 1930s, however, it was decided to separate short-term from the various types of medium- and long-term banking business and this was implemented under the terms of the Banking Law of 1936, a statute which reserved each kind of business specifically for a separate type of organisation. As a result, Italian arrangements contrasted strongly with the West German concept of a 'universal' bank, the tendency in Italy being to specialise, though the distinction has been somewhat blurred in recent years as credit terms have tended to lengthen out and the ordinary banks have begun to expand their security portfolios. A better basis for the distinction might now be between retail and wholesale banking.

On the whole, the big banks tended to operate on a national scale and to do business mostly with the large and medium-sized firms. Likewise their branches tended to be limited to the capital towns of the provinces and to the busy centres of industry and commerce. Traditionally, the medium-sized and smaller banks accommodated the credit demands of the medium-sized and smaller customers. But, as indicated, there have been changes over recent years and the big banks, stimulated partly by the growth in middle-range incomes, latterly began to develop a retail-banking business, especially in the field of personal loans, and certain of the medium-sized banks (also some of the savings banks) have grown in size and importance and now attract business even from the very large concerns. Although short- and long-term lending to agriculture is generally granted by special credit institutions, the big banks now also operate in fields like short-term agricultural credit, which require a network of branches and they have had to extend their branching arrangements accordingly (sometimes by taking over smaller banks in the regions).

Although there is a degree of concentration of banking resources, there is still evidence of much decentralisation in Italian banking. This dates back to the time before unification when Italy was made up of a number of separate states and kingdoms and, indeed, to some extent, regionalism is still evident. Only in northern and central Italy is there strong evidence of integration in the banking field, though as the South is developed economically a better balance will emerge and this will provide the basis for a more highly integrated system. Also, there has been more concentration than there might seem, as large banks began taking over majority control of smaller banks without proceeding to a merger. This was partly due to fiscal advantages (e.g., avoiding the highest rates of progressive tax on profits). Thus, a number of banks that appeared to be independent were in fact part of the same management group.

At first glance, the structure of banking in Italy appears to be rather complicated, but there are certain main banking sectors into which the several groups of institutions can be divided and this makes the task of description rather easier. A basic feature of the Italian banking system is a clear-cut division between commercial banks, granting almost exclusively short-term loans, and special-credit institutions, operating in the medium- and long-term sectors. The Italian commercial banks (*aziende di credito*), which for all categories numbered 1,092 at the end of 1983, with 12,918 offices, virtually fall into seven categrories.[43] Firstly, the public law banks (*istituti di credito di diritto pubblico*), six in all, of which the largest are the Banca Nazionale del Lavoro, Istituto Bancario S. Paolo di Torino, and Banco di Napoli; these banks are either fully owned by the State or owned by foundations; at the end of 1983, they had 1,766 offices; they themselves own and control a network of special-credit institutions called 'sections', which operate in specialised fields of credit (e.g., industry, real estate, foreign trade, etc.), but which in effect are merged with the bank itself. Secondly, the banks of 'national interest' (*banche d'interesse nazionale*), of which there are three – Banca Commerciale Italiana, Credito Italiano, and Banco di Roma (917 offices) – and which are controlled by the Istituto per la Ricostruzione Industriale (IRI), the major industrial State-owned holding company. Thirdly, ordinary-credit banks (*banche di credito ordinario*), of which there are 155 (3,004 offices) and which are privately-owned joint-stock companies, or otherwise incorporated institutions; these tend to be rather smaller institutions; the most important are the Banca Nazionale dell' Agricoltura, the Banco di S. Spirito, and the Istituto Bancario Italiano. Fourthly, and included in the ordinary credit-bank figure are the 33 foreign banks (54 offices), the opening of branches being regulated by the Bank of Italy; such branches are restricted in number (indeed, they are mostly unit banks) and this means that their deposit base is limited and they therefore have to fund their operations with wholesale money; otherwise, there is no discrimination against foreign banks. Foreign banks may also have a number of para-banking operations as do the Italian banks themselves – e.g., a finance company (for consumer credit), leasing and factoring companies, and merchant banking. Fifthly, savings banks and first-class pledge banks (*casse di risparmio e monti di credito su pegno di 1° categoria*) – 87 in all with 3,623 offices – are also important in Italy; several are large and have spread out beyond their own geographic area; they are mainly devoted to the collection of small savings, but now the larger ones also engage in general banking business and operate at the national level; nevertheless, there is still an emphasis on long-term lending partly based on the issue of bonds through their medium- and long-term credit sections – mortgages, loans to agriculture and public-works loans; they have a central clearing house called Istituto di Credito delle Casse di Risparmio Italiane (ICCRI)[44] and an Association (Associazione fra le Casse di Risparmio Italiane). In total, savings banks attract about a quarter of Italian deposits. The cooperative institutions form the final two categories; on the one hand, there are the people's banks (*banche popolari cooperative*), of which there are 148, with 2,408 offices, and which come under a special law (there are special national and special individual statutes); these are in effect commercial banks; and, on the other hand, there are 686 rural and artisan banks (*casse rurali e artigiane e monti di credito su pegno di 2° categoria*) with 1,162 offices, inspired by the *Raiffeisen* idea – cooperative societies set up to cater for groups of small agriculturalists and artisans as common members of each *cassa*, with a central credit institute in Rome called *Istituto di Credito delle Casse Rurali e Artigiane* (ICCREA). There are also a number of special-credit institutions, which can both borrow and lend at medium-term and long-term – e.g., for building and construction, shipbuilding, the development of tourism, lending to companies at medium-term, lending to finance the purchase of equipment, etc. Like the special-credit sections of the public law banks and the savings banks, they borrow by issuing bonds or special certificates of deposit (minimum maturity of 18 months).

Although the leading institute remains the Istituto Mobiliare Italiano (IMI), a public body founded in 1931, there was a growing need after World War II for industrial finance in Italy, both to provide the capital to support the growth of the economy and, as part of this process, to finance the introduction of modern technologies and the development of new industrial ventures. It was the latter that made necessary the provision of new financing channels. There were two phases in the process of this development – initially, it had a sectoral character, and this merged into a second phase where there was a more geographical orientation.

> During the first phase new institutions were set up by the different categories of banks (banks of national interest, public law institutes, people's banks, and so on). During the second phase numerous regional institutes were created, on the initiative of the State and with the participation of the local banks. Because, too, of the limited amount of autonomous resources at the disposal of these new bodies, a financing institute (*Mediocredito Centrale*) was set up in 1952, the task of which was to refinance those bodies and reduce the cost of financing the medium-size and small firms and, subsequently, of the export credits. At the same time the *Artigiancassa* was given tasks similar to those set for the *Mediocredito Centrale* relating to transactions effected in favour of artisan enterprises by the banks empowered to do so.
>
> The funds of the refinancing institutes are provided by the Italian Treasury; owing to the paucity of its endowment fund, the intervention of the refinancing institute has mainly taken the form of interest subsidies, granted as an alternative to or in conjunction with rediscounting. In more recent years the *Mediocredito Centrale* has raised funds on the market by means of bond issues, the proceeds of which have been advanced to the regional institutes; it has thus become the financing centre of these institutes.[45]

In addition, *Mediocredito Centrale* obtains loans from the European Investment Bank. Nowadays, several of the regional institutes (*Mediocrediti regionali*) also issue bonds directly through the market.

The major banks concentrate almost entirely on commercial banking, foreign banking and securities business. They have subsidiaries that provide industrial credit and real-estate financing. They also offer a wide variety of services and therefore attract a larger share of the business.

For some years after World War II, the continued survival of small institutions appeared to have the support of the authorities and there was some attempt to limit the movement towards further banking concentration and the absorption of small units.[46] In the late 1960s, however, there was a change in the official attitude towards bank mergers and it was accepted that there was a need to proceed along the path of rationalisation and automation, as well as to spread risks more widely. In the result, the authorities began to encourage the merging of smaller banks into larger units.

The market shares of total deposits of the several categories of bank at the end of 1983 are given in Table 4.6.

Table 4.6: Market Shares of Italian Banks, by Category (%)

Public law banks	19.2
Banks of 'national interest'	11.6
Ordinary credit banks	24.2
People's banks and rural and other artisan banks	16.4
Savings banks and first-class pledge banks	28.6
	100.0

Switzerland[47]

In the commercial-banking sector in Switzerland, there are three large 'universal' banks – the Union Bank of Switzerland, the Swiss Bank Corporation, and Crédit Suisse – which together with the much smaller Swiss Volksbank and Bank Leu accounted for over 37 per cent (1983) of total domestic bank deposits; they have 922 branches and a number of banking, finance and other subsidiaries both in Switzerland and abroad. The second important group is comprised of the cantonal banks, of which there are 29, with 1,316 branches. Nine of the 29 cantonal banks were established between 1834 (Berne) and 1916 (Valais). Jura, as a newly created canton, opened its bank in 1979. They accounted for 33.4 per cent of total domestic deposit business in 1983. Of the cantons, which go to make up the Swiss Federation, the majority have one cantonal bank each, while the cantons of Berne, Geneva, and Vaud each have two. These banks are primarily responsible for meeting the banking needs of their cantons both in terms of financial facilities for government and for industry and commerce, where the bulk of their customers is small and medium-sized; they also have a sizeable mortgage business, which is, however, hived off in a second institution in those cantons that have two banks. Both the cantonal banks of Zürich and Berne are authorised by their respective laws to undertake foreign business, and the Zürcher Kantonalbank is very active in this field. Since there is no regulation forbidding it, a number of others are also interested. Where business tends to overlap, two or three cantonal banks may well arrange syndicated loans shared between them; they may also be members of larger syndicates. Except for four banks, which are limited-liability companies, the capital of these banks is subscribed by the relevant canton and they are classified as public law institutions. For the most part, their liabilities are guaranteed by their canton. A third group is the 25 private banks, most of which are based in Geneva (including two that are relatively large – Lombard Odier and Pictet). The two big private banks in Zürich – Vontobel Holdings and Julius Baer – are now incorporated as joint-stock companies. In terms of deposits the private banks' share of total banking business is very small. Private banks have been primarily concerned with portfolio management, although the larger ones have diversified quite considerably – e.g., by expanding their institutional activity in Switzerland, the USA, Britain, and the Middle East, also by participating in international joint ventures. Other banks include 178 heterogenous institutions (Swiss banks and institutions; also foreign-controlled banks in Switzerland) with 6.4 per cent (1983) of total domestic deposits and 17 branches of foreign banks (less than 1 per cent of total deposits). Of the Swiss banks, some are commercial banks, others specialise in stock-exchange transactions, and some in personal loans; others, though registered in Switzerland, are really foreign-owned. Although by no means homogeneous, this foreign-owned group tends to cater for a foreign clientele and is concerned to effect mainly international banking transactions.

The regional and savings banks (217 institutions, with 1,086 offices) derive from institutions that formerly comprised *crédit fonciers*, local or regional banks, or savings banks. Collectively, as at 1983, they attracted almost 16 per cent of total deposits. But many of them are now moving in the direction of becoming universal banks. At the same time, this trend is more obvious in the case of regional banks than for the savings banks, where mortgage lending is still the most important part of their business, as is their relative dependence on savings deposits; likewise, own funds often derive from reserves. In attempting to generalise, one might say that the regional banks and the savings banks now undertake a business that is quite similar to that of the cantonal banks.

There are also the Swiss Union of *Raiffeisen* cooperatives and the Federation in Vaud of the *caisses de crédit mutuel*. There are two central institutions and the organisations between them have 1,245 offices. The constituent *caisses* cater for members only and on a very local basis. Security for their loans usually takes the form of a guarantee or a pledge. Altogether, these *caisses* and their two central institutions account for 6.0 per cent (1983) of total domestic banking and banking-type business in Switzerland.

Finance companies, of which there are 100, though with quite a small share of the market (0.4 per cent of total domestic loans), are of two main kinds: first, those which undertake a kind of banking business based on the attraction of deposits from the public, though their operations tend to be for longer terms than would apply in the case of the banks proper (for example, they would make financial resources available to their customers, which would be mainly enterprises and not individuals, by way of placements of capital and the taking up of participations as well as the granting of credits, such financial assistance being spread around a number of enterprises); and secondly, those which financially assist enterprises within the same business group and which therefore do not have a banking characteristic.

The remaining elements in the Swiss financial structure include the Postal Cheque System, which accepts deposits against which cheques can be drawn, pays no interest, and only lends to the federal government (there is no Postal Savings Bank in Switzerland); insurance companies and pension funds, which are active in both the money and capital markets and also important in lending against mortgages (their share of this market is about 11 per cent); factoring companies, which are often banking subsidiaries, or, where independent, still have a direct relationship with a particular bank; and investment trusts, which after a rapid growth in the early 1970s have now tended to level out in financial terms.

All banks in Switzerland are subject to prudential supervision, which is provided by the Federal Banking Commission[48] based in Berne. It operates under a Banking Law going back to November 1934, which seeks to protect both creditors and depositors. It came into operation on 1 March 1935 and was amended in1971; a revised Banking Law is being framed. A Banking Ordinance of 1972 was amended in 1976 and 1981. The present Banking Law applies to all financial institutions that accept deposits (universal banks, cantonal banks, private bankers, savings banks, and finance companies). Investment trusts are subject to the Federal Law Relating to Investment Trusts. Each of these institutions (including branches of foreign banks,[49] but excepting the cantonal banks) must be licensed and observe certain ratios relating to liquidity, own resources (capital) and the distribution of risks. Accounts must be maintained in proper form and are subject to audit by firms approved by the Federal Banking Commission. Any failure to meet the necessary conditions can result in the withdrawal of the licence and the bank could be forced into liquidation.

The regulation of credit, on the other hand, is the responsibility of the Swiss National Bank, which is in charge of monetary policy. Its

Table 4.7: Swiss Banks and Finance Companies, 1978-83

	Number of banks or finance companies (total number of offices in brackets)[1]					
	1978	1979	1980	1981	1982	1983
Cantonal banks	28	29	29	29	29	29
	(1,272)	(1,275)	(1,274)	(1,294)	(1,308)	(1,316)
Big banks	5	5	5	5	5	5
	(752)	(777)	(799)	(873)	(903)	(922)
Regional and savings banks	223	220	220	219	218	217
	(1,119)	(1,102)	(1,097)	(1,097)	(1,096)	(1,086)
Loan and *Raiffeisen* Bank Associations[2]	2	2	2	2	2	2
	(1,220)	(1,225)	(1,231)	(1,238)	(1,244)	(1,245)
Private banks	25	25	25	25	25	25
	(27)	(26)	(26)	(26)	(27)	(27)
Branches of foreign banks	14	15	16	16	17	17
	(25)	(27)	(27)	(26)	(30)	(29)
Other banks	181	178	176	178	181	178
	(405)	(409)	(416)	(420)	(435)	(436)
Finance companies	73	80	84	90	95	100
	(76)	(84)	(88)	(95)	(98)	(106)

Notes: 1. Including headquarters operations and foreign branches of Swiss banks.
2. Two associations with a total of 1,227 member banks at end of 1983.
Source: Swiss National Bank.

role is so to regulate the money supply that it is maintained at levels that remain between the broad limits usually projected on an annual basis. It is primarily concerned with the medium-term, though will intervene from time to time to offset short-term fluctuations when that seems to be desirable. The main objectives are to avoid or reduce inflation and to moderate the extent to which the Swiss franc is used as an international currency. This cannot wholly be avoided since the big Swiss banks already have an important international business. Switzerland is also a country with a high savings ratio and, on this basis, it exports medium- and long-term capital, though this is subject to official regulation. The Swiss National Bank is empowered to vary discount rate and the slightly higher Lombard rate, though when the Swiss banks are very liquid such variations are not likely to be very influential. The central bank may also undertake open-market operations, and it has done so. Likewise, since 1979, it has had the power to vary cash and liquidity requirements with a view to influencing credit policy. Basically, under the Swiss Federal Banking Law dating from 1934, the Banking Commission has exercised a prudential control and, indeed, cash and liquidity requirements are still largely prudential in character.

Japan

In Japan, the structure of banking that has emerged presents an interesting study of the combined effects of local environment and of imported ideas. Much of what emerged owes its origins to the forces of history and the best way to approach Japanese banking structure, therefore, is first to examine the historical background.

Although the House of Tokugawa ruled the country as *shogun* (or military governor) from 1603 to 1868 (with the Emperor holding aloof from the administration) and controlled the central government, the effective government of the several regions was in the hands of lords (or *daimyo*), some of the more important of whom enjoyed a considerable measure of independence. In fact, Japanese society of this period still retained many characteristics inherited from its earlier purely feudal organisation. Thus, each *daimyo* claimed the allegiance of large numbers of retainers (or *samurai*) and, although this latter class was military in origin, many of those who now exercised important administrative functions were recruited from it. In theory, the other classes in the community – the merchants, artisans and peasants – were wholly subservient to the privileged groups and did not share in government.

By the middle of the nineteenth century, the socio-political bases of this structure were well on the way to breaking up, as a result of economic changes that had virtually destroyed the foundations of the older society and because of the financial difficulties and factional disputes that threatened the stability of the central government. Except for the few that held important administrative posts, the *samurai* were impoverished, while many of the merchants – a supposedly inferior class – had become wealthy men, partly as a result of their activities as financial agents of the *daimyo*.

Hence, the times were ripe for change and the old regime was overthrown. However, it is not with these political developments that we are primarily concerned. Suffice it to say that the economic bases on which to build were already in existence. Internal commerce was well developed and there was an efficient organisation for the transport of commodities by sea. Certain of the merchant firms that financed the *daimyo* and looked after the disposal of their rice revenues had by now come to operate on quite a large scale, with branches in different parts of the country, through which facilities could be made available for the remittance of funds. The merchants collected dues and taxes (which were then paid in rice), sold a proportion of this produce in commercial centres like Osaka, and transferred the receipts to the feudal treasuries. They accepted deposits, made loans both to officials and to local governments, issued notes against their reserves, and at regular intervals transmitted funds from the provinces to the capital in order to cover the costs of *sankin-kotai* – 'alternate attendance' – which imposed an obligation on the *daimyo* to reside initially every other year and later for half a year in Yedo (Tokyo). Various types of credit instrument were also in use and these likewise were to assist in the development of banking arrangements. The only major obstacle to further progress was the confused state of the currency, which consisted of a miscellaneous variety of coins (often debased) circulated by the central government, *hansatu* (the illegal issues of the *daimyo*), the 'wrapped money'[50] of private exchange houses, and latterly (in the ports trading with the outside world) Mexican dollars imported for purposes of trade by foreign merchants, and the difficulties of establishing appropriate rates of exchange between these several issues were by no means resolved by the agreement signed with the foreign powers in 1859. Initially, this did little more than provide foreigners with golden opportunities to make handsome profits[51] and it was in fact some years before a semblance of order was imposed.

Following the Restoration in 1868, the government began its attempts to modernise the country's monetary institutions, though for a long time it continued to be plagued with currency difficulties and little progress could be expected until these were resolved. For the most part, the troubles were budgetary in origin, greatly intensified by the central government's assumption of additional responsibilities (e.g., for the administration of local territories and the compensation of the displayed *daimyo* and *samurai* when the *han* or feudal territories of the *daimyo* were abolished in 1871).[52]

Yet it was these same difficulties that prompted the early experiments in banking reform, when the attempt was made in 1872 to establish a modern banking system modelled on the American 'national banks'.[53] These new Japanese banks were empowered to issue notes convertible into gold, but they soon found themselves unable to maintain this convertibility. In 1876, therefore, the National Banks Ordinance was revised and the national banks were now permitted to issue notes against the deposit with the Treasury of government bonds equal to 80 per cent of their capital. In place of a reserve of specie, they could now hold government paper money. By this means, it was hoped not only to stimulate banking activity, but also to prevent the further depreciation of bonds that had been issued when the hereditary pensions of the *samurai* (for which the central government had accepted responsibility when the feudal system was formally abolished in 1871) had been commuted. After 1876, about 150 new national banks were established, with the result that a large issue of inconvertible bank notes was added to the government's own issues of paper money.

Indeed, over this period, Japan experienced considerable currency difficulties. Prior to 1871, there had been a kind of *de facto* bimetallism and, although the gold standard was formally adopted in 1871 (under the New Coins Ordinance), the currency was almost immediately declared inconvertible and the continued expansion in paper money inevitably resulted in the depreciation of paper in terms of silver specie as of gold. All the symptoms of a serious inflation were present when the government regained control of the situation by introducing disinflationary tax increases. Furthermore, the Bank of Japan was established in 1882 to reorganise the currency. The national banks were deprived of their privilege of note issue, which was granted exclusively to the Bank of Japan and both the inconvertible government paper and the national bank notes were rapidly retired, the Bank of Japan beginning specie payments (in silver) against its own notes in 1886. This put Japan on to a silver standard and this continued until 1897, when the gold standard was finally adopted.

With the object of regulating the activities of those banks and other financial institutions which were not covered by the Ordinance relating to national banks, the government promulgated the Ordinary Banks Ordinance of 1890 and this was enforced in 1893. Further, as the terms of their respective charters expired, most of the national banks continued their business as 'ordinary' banks, subject to the general banking law.

Meanwhile, one of Japan's great Finance Ministers – Count Matsukata –had begun to apply a policy based on his belief that a sound banking system should include banks with specialised functions. Because of the shortage of available capital, the Japanese banks, in addition to granting short-term commercial credits, had become accustomed to make credit available to agriculturalists on the security of real estate, and to provide long-term finance to industrial enterprises mainly by granting advances against government paper but also against real estate. In Japan, it was maintained that the banks were able to lend long-term mainly because of the high proportion of their total resources raised in the form of time deposits. Nevertheless, on a number of occasions, the banks found themselves in a highly illiquid condition and the Bank of Japan was forced to come to their rescue by lending to them against loans that had become frozen. It was partly to meet this difficulty that Count Matsukata sought to establish institutions that could specialise in long-term lending. But he carried the principle further than that and believed that the several branches of banking business should each be done by an institution specifically set up for the purpose. These functions included not only the provision of long-term loans for industry and agriculture, but the handling of foreign-exchange transactions, domestic commercial business, and the collection of the savings of the poorer classes.

It was in this way that specialised banks like the Yokohama Specie Bank came to be established with the support and under the partial control of the government. Founded in 1880, this institution was at that time the only Japanese foreign-exchange bank in the country, in competition with the foreign banks that had previously monopolised this class of business. Other specialised institutions that were set up in accordance with the Matsukata policy included the Mortgage Bank of Japan (1897) to make long-term loans to agriculture, the fishing industry, and against the mortgage of real estate in urban areas, and the Industrial Bank of Japan (1902) to lend long-term to industrial concerns, both of these obtaining the resources necessary for long-term operations largely by issuing debentures. In addition, there were special banks to assist in financing colonial expansion such as the Bank of Taiwan (1899), which was both the central bank for Formosa and the agency for financing trade with that island and the South Seas; the Chosen Bank[54] (1911); and the Oriental Development Company (1908) to finance the industrial development of Manchuria. The capital of all these banks was partially subscribed by the Japanese government and they were subject to official supervision.

The modernisation and expansion of Japan's economy was associated also with the rapid development of commercial banking by private enterprise. Some of these banks grew out of the exchange houses of pre-Restoration times,[55] while others were originally established as national banks during the 1870s. Many of them were small and their business remained local in character, though by the early 1900s a few of them had already become large institutions with a developed network of branches. These included the Mitsui, Mitsubishi, Sumitomo, and Yasuda banks. However, at that stage, the number of small banks was still very large. Indeed, in 1920, prior to the successive banking crises that culminated in the panic of 1927, there were 2,036 separate banks in Japan (of which 1,322 were ordinary banks),[56] but these were reduced either by bankruptcy or by amalgamation to 895 by 1930 (of which 779 were ordinary banks). After the crisis of 1927, which forced the government to declare a general moritorium and obliged the Bank of Japan to come once again to the rescue, the concentration of bank activities into fewer and larger institutions became a matter of public policy and the contraction in numbers proceeded. There were 369 by 1940 (289 ordinary banks) and only 69 by 1945. Since then, there has been a small increase, due partly to the establishment of new banks and partly to the conversion into 'ordinary' banks of other categories of banks.

In effecting this degree of concentration, the *Zaibatsu* played a major part. *Zaibatsu* means 'property groups' or 'plutocracy' and is a term commonly used to describe the great business houses of Japan, notably Mitsui, Mitsubishi, Sumitomo, and Yasuda (but there were others), all of which in the years prior to World War II developed an immense range of interests. Japan had established a number of important consumer-goods industries by the end of World War I and had built up a considerable business in shipping, with a financial system well equipped to satisfy the varying and growing requirements of her economy. This period also witnessed an increase in agricultural production and a general improvement in standards of living, progress that was greatly assisted by assimilating foreign technologies and by importing foreign capital.

During the years between the wars, there was an acceleration in the rate of economic growth, which was accompanied by a diversification of the Japanese industrial structure, based in part on the development of dependent areas as new sources of raw materials. This period was also characterised by further concentration of financial, industrial, and commercial interests, which after 1937 facilitated the emergence of a toalitarian economy geared to the demands of war.

Prior to World War II, there had been seven big banks in Japan, all of which, except the Sanwa Bank, were controlled by large *Zaibatsu* groups. By mid-1941, these seven banks held 58 per cent of the deposits, 66 per cent of the discounts, loans and advances, and 47 per cent of the security holdings of the 245 'ordinary' banks then in existence. During the war, the share of the big banks became even larger, partly because of their absorption of many of the smaller institutions, but also because they were in a favoured position when it came to financing war production. By the end of 1945, loans to munitions industries ranged from 30 to 50 per cent of the outstanding loans and investments of the big banks and their share in the total of loans, discounts and advances for all 'ordinary' banks had risen to 83 per cent (their security holdings meanwhile had fallen to 38 per cent of the total). Moreover, a large part of this wartime financing by the big banks had itself been based on loans obtained from the Bank of Japan, more than half of which consisted of 'special' loans, i.e. loans not backed by the normally required collateral. For the other 'ordinary' banks, only 18 per cent of Central Bank loans were made on a 'special' basis.

After World War II, the Allied authorities brought pressure to bear on the Japanese government with a view to de-concentrating the old *Zaibatsu* economic and financial empires. The *Zaibatsu* in the sense of family groups were liquidated in 1947. Yet, for a variety of reasons, it was not proposed to inflict on Japan as drastic a policy as had been imposed on Germany. It was recognised, for example, that, if the large financial institutions were broken up, this would greatly retard the post-war reconstruction of the Japanese economy. Nevertheless, the attempt was made to sever some of the ties that linked the big banks with the industrial, commercial and other financial interests of the *Zaibatsu*. These included

> the removal of officers who had exercised power on behalf of the Zaibatsu, the elimination of Zaibatsu ownership of bank stocks, the limitation of the amount of stock which one individual or company could hold in a financial institution, the elimination of interlocking directorates between financial institutions and other juridical persons, and the termination of contractual service arrangements or other alliances between financial institutions and industrial and commercial organisations.[57]

It is highly doubtful whether any of these measures wholly achieved their intended purpose. Despite a change of names, the institutions and companies that formerly belonged to the *Zaibatsu* retained much of their importance and in a general way retained many of the old links. Moreover, the big banks continued to lend mainly to the larger concerns. Although in terms of the number of employees small enterprises accounted for more than half of Japan's industry, their demand for funds from the banks was not in proportion. In any event, the credit needs of small enterprises were met in part by specialised financial institutions.

Following the restoration of full Japanese sovereignty in mid-1952, measures adopted during the Allied occupation were gradually eliminated – in banking as in other fields. In particular, the de-concentration programme was reversed. So far as the banks were concerned, this was facilitated by the liberalisation in 1954 of the rules governing eligibility for bank directorships and by the elimination of restrictions on bank holdings of securities. The way was thereby cleared for the re-concentration of financial holdings in the hands of the former *Zaibatsu* groups. In any event, the post-war redistribution of security holdings, as a result of the activities of the Securities Co-ordinating Liquidation Commission set up in June 1947, probably only achieved a partial break-up of former *Zaibatsu* interests. When it completed its work in July 1951, the Co-ordinating Commission had disposed of securities worth 14.3 billion yen – almost one-half by auction sales to the public and the remainder by sales to employees of the respective companies and by marketing them through securities dealers.

> It is impossible to appraise the effects of these operations from the standpoint of the deconcentration objective. According to a study made by the Securities and Exchange Commission, between 1945 and the end of 1949 the number of shares increased nearly fivefold and the number of shareholders rose approximately from one and one half million to four million, the increase being entirely accounted for by individual holders. On the other hand, dealers registered the largest gain in percentage distribution of the aggregate value of the securities by groups of holders. The increasing interest taken by individuals in stock may be attributed in part to specific factors – such as the special efforts made to dispose of shares among companies' employees, and the revaluation of companies' assets with resulting expectation of large dividends – and in part to the general inflationary boom prevailing in the economy. It is not improbable, however, that a significant portion of the redistributed shares were bought by firms and individuals acting for the account of former Zaibatsu families.[58]

In recognition that the change had been less than it seemed, former *Zaibatsu* banks, which had altered their names at the government's request, now, with one exception, changed them back to the old style.

As at the end of 1983, there were 76 ordinary banks which undertook commercial banking business in Japan. Of these, 13 were city banks, generally based in the large cities and operating on a national scale through a network of branch offices – the average number of domestic offices per bank at that time was 225. The city banks included the Dai-Ichi Kangyo Bank, the Fuji Bank, the Sumitomo Bank, the Sanwa Bank, the Mitsubishi Bank, the Tokai Bank, the Taiyo Kobe Bank, the Mitsui Bank, the Daiwa Bank, the Kyowa Bank, the Saitama Bank, the Hokkaido Takushoku Bank, and the Bank of Tokyo, a specialised foreign-exchange bank. The first five banks were markedly larger than the rest. At the end of 1983, city banks accounted for about 25 per cent of the financial resources of all financial institutions and about 52 per cent of the resources of all banks. The remaining 63 were regional banks, based on a prefecture, though some extend their operations into neighbouring prefectures. In this way, they service localised and regional communities throughout the country. Regional banks have also expanded their operations into big cities like Tokyo and Osaka; at that time, the average number of their domestic offices was 100. City banks deal mainly with the big enterprises, but also with smaller enterprises and individuals, and the regional banks, some of which are large, mainly with regional enterprises and public corporations, though loans extended to large business enterprises may account for about 20 per cent of the total amount. In average size, they are about one-ninth of the average for the city banks. All these banks are subject to the Bank Law of 1981. On a reciprocal basis, Japan has also permitted the establishment of some 75 foreign banks, with a total of 103 branch offices at the end of 1983. In addition, there are about 100 representative offices. There are three long-term credit banks – the Industrial Bank of Japan, the Long-Term Credit Bank of Japan, and the Nippon Credit Bank – established under the Long-Term Credit Bank Law of 1952. These institutions have a restricted right to accept deposits (solely from qualified customers), but issue debentures to ensure a supply of adequate resources (up to 30 times capital and reserves); so, too, does the Bank of Tokyo, though to a much more limited extent; indeed, about 70 per cent of its resources still derives from deposits; it also resorts to money-market funds. As their name suggests, the expertise of the long-term credit banks is the raising of finance for long-term lending. However, to the extent that self-financing becomes more common in Japanese industry, the long-term credit banks may find it more difficult to lend and, in these circumstances, may wish to seek diversification in their business. However, they only have some 56 branches (as at the end of 1983) and it would not therefore be easy to compete for ordinary-banking business with either the city or regional banks. On the other hand, they are important in the capital market as trustees or agents for the issuance of public and corporate bonds; also, it is probable that they are relatively more important than the ordinary banks in the field of international banking business. There are seven trust banks, which are permitted concurrently to engage in trust business and this is more important than their banking; 71 *sogo* (mutual) banks, and at the end of 1983, 456 credit associations (*shinyo-kinko* abbreviated to *shinkin*) and 468 credit cooperatives (*shinyo-kumiai*), which are regional financial institutions that cater mainly for smaller enterprises. There is also a Shoko Chukin Bank (the Central Bank for Commercial and Industrial Cooperatives) and financial institutions for agriculture, forestry, and fisheries. At the level of the prefecture, the latter form federations of agricultural credit cooperatives, while at national level there is the Norinchukin Bank (the Central Cooperative Bank for Agriculture and Forestry), which evens out the surpluses and deficits of member institutions. In addition, there are insurance companies – life and non-life – and securities companies. Banking and securities business were formerly separated in Japan, though under the Banking Act 1982 the banks are now allowed to underwrite private-company bonds and, subject to certain conditions, to deal on the capital market in national, government-guaranteed and local government bonds. Of the 217 securities companies in Japan, most of which are small, the Big Four – Nomura Securities, Nikko Securities, Daiwa Securities and Yamaichi Securities – do the bulk of the business (in the underwriting, buying and selling of securities their share exceeds 70 per cent; in the buying and selling of equity shares, it would be about 50 per cent). Finally, there are a number of government financial institutions – two banks (the Japan Development Bank and the Export-Import Bank of Japan) and ten finance corporations (*koko*), which supplement the activities of the private financial institutions in a variety of fields – e.g., regional development finance, the finance of housing, and the financing of smaller enterprises.

In essence, therefore, banking business in Japan is largely concentrated in the hands of the big institutions, with the city banks accounting for over 50 per cent of total banking business. Then there are the regional banks, some of which are also large; they account for almost 30 per cent of total banking business, followed by the long-term credit banks (11.7 per cent) and the trust banks (6.6 per cent). Within the regional banking sector (63 banks) quite a number are relatively small and – even if we exclude the *sogo* (mutual) banks, *shinkin*, and the credit cooperatives – the banking structure in Japan is essentially 'hybrid' in character.

As one would expect in such a system, the regional and local banks have need of city correspondents not only for the purpose of holding surplus balances but also for assistance in investing their funds, especially in the call-money market. In addition, the city banks may introduce certain of their large customers to a regional or local bank (e.g., where the customer is a big company with a local factory) with a view to a loan from the smaller bank to the customer concerned (it is usual for the big companies in Japan to employ from 5 to 10 bankers at any one time),[59] but city correspondents in Japan do not provide the wide range of ancillary services that is common in the United States.

The framework of prudential regulation is laid down by the Ministry of Finance, which has a Banking Bureau divided into a number of divisions – for coordination, commercial banks, special banks, 'small finance', research, life and non-life insurance, and the examination departments of both the administrative and inspection divisions. In addition, there are bureaux for securities, international finance, and loan finance. Supervision is exercised by way of 'administrative guidance' based on a number of notifications by the Director-General of the Banking Bureau. For example, in order to establish and maintain sound bank management, the Ministry of Finance has requested the maintenance of a number of specified financial ratios: the ratio of average lending to deposits, which should be below 80 per cent (since 1957); the ratio of current assets to the average of deposits, which should be 30 per cent or more (since 1959); the ratio of real-estate assets (office buildings and land) to net worth, which should be under 50 per cent – it must now be kept below 40 per cent (from 1968); and the ratio of net worth to the outstanding amount of deposits should exceed 10 per cent (actually, the published capital ratios are quite low, but all banks carry very substantial hidden reserves based on highly conservative valuations of both securities and real estate assets). There are also certain rules that have to be followed in preparing bank accounts; only a certain proportion of a bank's net worth can be committed by way of a loan to any single customer (20 per cent for ordinary banks, 30 per cent for long-term credit banks, and 40 per cent for the Bank of Tokyo); regulations apply to the opening and closing of branches, also changes of location; the setting up of affiliated companies is regulated – e.g., it is permitted to set up affiliated companies for credit-guarantee business, credit-card business, and leasing or computer services, but not for less related activities such as real-estate brokerage, golf courses, and travel agencies; and compensatory and compulsory deposits are either to be reduced or (hopefully) completely removed.

In addition to prudential controls, the central bank – the Bank of Japan – regulates monetary and credit conditions throughout the economy. It can influence the amount of credit granted by the commercial banks by varying their cash reserves and also by adjusting the ease or difficulty with which they are able to obtain additional cash. The basic instruments of monetary policy are variation of cash-reserve requirements, alteration of the official discount rate, open-market operations, and supplementary measures such as 'window guidance'.

Notes

1. For a fuller discussion, especially of the historical background, see J.S.G. Wilson, *French Banking Structure and Credit Policy* (London, 1957); see also J.S.G. Wilson, 'France' in R.S. Sayers (ed.), *Banking in Western Europe* (Oxford, 1962), pp. 1-52.

2. Even as between nationalised banks, it is still possible for a nationalised bank to hold shares in another bank. Where the other bank was already nationalised the State sells shares back to the larger nationalised bank, which now holds shares in the second bank. It is really something of a bookkeeping transaction.

3. Local banks retain their old family names because a local name still matters in retaining local loyalties.

4. Strictly speaking, the State Bank of India is not a wholly nationalised bank – as much as 7 per cent of its shares are held by private individuals. In the case of the seven subsidiaries of the State Bank of India, three of them are fully owned by the State Bank, while the remaining four also have individual shareholders.

5. See also J.S.G. Wilson 'The Business of Banking in India' in R.S. Sayers (ed.), *Banking in the British Commonwealth* (Oxford, 1952), pp. 199-201.

6. One crore equals 10 million.

7. But see Reserve Bank of India, *Report on Trend and Progress of Banking in India 1982-83*, p. 96.

8. For a detailed account of his activities, see J.S.G. Wilson, 'The Business of Banking in India', pp. 169-71.

9. All who write in this field are necessarily indebted to the late Professor P. Barrett Whale, who drew together much of the material relating to these formative years. See his *Joint Stock Banking in Germany* (London, 1930).

10. See ibid., pp. 178-80.

11. Ibid., p. 208.

12. The crisis – and more particularly the measures it gave rise to in Germany – is well summarised by L.J.H. Dark in A.M. Allen *et al.*, *Commercial Banking Legislation and Control* (London, 1938), pp. 193-224.

13. Their business is not limited to commercial or investment banking or brokerage activities. They are in a position to provide all banking services; loans, traditional banking services, investment banking, trading in securities for own or customer's account, as well as cross-border transactions through their own

branches abroad or banking correspondents.

14. See *Deutsche Bundesbank Monthly Report* (April 1983), pp. 25-33.

15. See the Banking Act of the Federal Republic of Germany (*Gesetz über das Kreditwesen*) of 10 July 1961, as amended in 1976 and 1985.

16. This was possible following the three judgements of the Federal Supreme Administrative Court of 10 July 1958. 'The Court laid down that to require proof of need in connection with the licensing of credit institutions and their branches conflicts with the principle of free choice of occupation, and is therefore irreconcilable with the Basic Law of the Federal Republic of Germany, and inadmissible. According to these Judgements the Bank Supervisory Authorities can refuse permission for establishment of new credit institutions only in the very seldom cases where the persons conducting the business are not respectable, or not technically trained, or where the required resources are not available within the country. The consequence has been that the number of new branches of credit institutions establsihed has rapidly risen.' *Deutsche Bundesbank Monthly Report* (October 1959), p. 56). In the nine months following these judgements, the number of bank branches increased by 1,350 compared with 441 for the nine months before the judgements.

17. See 'First Results of the Enquiry on Bank Interest Rates', *Deutsche Bundesbank Monthly Report* (October 1967), p. 45-50. Indeed, because of these trends, even the savings banks were somewhat unwilling to see their deposits rise further.

18. Some banking houses have been converted into joint-stock banks.

19. Oesterreichische Kontrollbank AG; Postal Savings Bank; Oesterreichische Investitionskredit AG; CENTRO Internationale Handelsbank AG; Oesterreichische Exportfondsgesellschaft mbH; Oesterreichische Kommunalkredit AG; Allgemeine Finanz- und Waren-Treuhand AG; Hotel-und Fremdenverkehrs-Treuhandgesellschaft mbH, and the factoring banks are the chief institutes in this group.

20. For a very useful survey, see Fritz Diwok, *The Austrian Banking System* (Creditanstalt, Vienna, 1983).

21. Thirty-four of these are joint-stock banks (including the foreign banks and the regional banks), ten are private banks, six are banks with limited liability, and nine are rural mortgage banks.

22. The Zentralsparkasse und Kommerzialbank, Vienna (formerly, the Zentralsparkasse der Gemeinde Wien; the name was changed in June 1979) and the Erste Oesterreichische Spar-Casse (First Austrian Bank). Other medium-sized savings banks are regionally based – some with branches elsewhere in Austria.

23. Several of the regional savings banks are also quite large.

24. See Diwok, *the Austrian Banking System*, pp. 112ff.

25. Austrian National Bank, *Annual Report* (1982), p. 13.

26. See B.S. Chlepner, *Belgian Banking and Banking Theory* (Washington, 1943), pp. 57-69.

27. The post-war drive for deposits by opening more branches has analogies in the United States. Just as the American banks (where it was possible) opened branches in the 'neighbourhoods' in order to attract deposits and personal loan business, so too, did the Belgian banks, their objective being the attraction of those members of the public who had so far preferred to use the very cheap services of the postal cheque system, or who perhaps refused to use any kind of banking institution. By bringing bank services (including instalment credit)to his very doorstep, the Belgian banks sought – with some success – the deposits and business of the smaller businessman, as well as the accounts of private individuals of modest means. This expansion into 'retail banking' was most marked in the growing suburbs of the larger cities and towns.

28. See Chlepner, *Belgian Banking*, pp. 115-17. But note that Almanij, the holding company of Kredietbank, only holds participations in financial institutions

and companies engaged in related activities.

29. See Gavin Gordon, 'Banking Reform in Belgium', *The Banker* (November 1956), pp. 707-11.

30. 'The Belgian Banking Sector in Profile', *Kredietbank Weekly Bulletin* (22 April 1983).

31. Which resulted from a merger of the Banque de Bruxelles and Banque Lambert dating from 30 June 1975.

32. One of these – the Banque de Paris et des Pays-Bas – is incorporated in Belgium and, unlike other foreign banks, is strong in retail business.

33. Some of these would be regional banks related to the Big Three; others – say, five or six – would be independent; others again are very small local banks, often being concerned only with *gestion des fortunes*, though some would also be active commercially.

34. See 'The Belgian Banking Sector in Profile'.

35. Ibid.

36. One member, which is also the largest, is the Centrale des Caisses Rurales, which is the central institution for the *Raiffeisen* Cooperatives. The Centrale is the eighth largest banking institution in Belgium.

37. On average for 15-20 years, with the emphasis on 20-year mortgages. Some low cost mortgages are for 25 years. On average, the term of a mortgage is 10-12 years. It used to be shorter (7-8 years). The reasons for the change are higher interest rates, lower real income and therefore less opportunity to save, smaller families.

38. Some of the past history is summarised in J.S.G. Wilson, 'The Netherlands' in Sayers (ed.), *Banking in Western Europe*, pp. 199-203.

39. For the background, see ibid., pp. 210-16.

40. Their number diminished greatly following a worsening of the real-estate market.

41. For the details, see Netherlands Bank, *The Revised Act on the Supervision of the Credit System* (March 1979); and Netherlands Bank, *Solvency and Liquidity Directives* (June 1983); and Chapter 5 each year of Netherlands Bank, *Annual Reports*.

42. It is intended to integrate these several payments systems into one national payments circuit to be partially operational by 1985.

43. In accordance with Article 5 of the Banking Law 1936, the Bank of Italy is responsible for the regulation of public-law banks, banks of national interest, ordinary credit banks and branches of foreign banks, as well as savings banks, people's banks and rural and artisan banks. All these different categories of *aziende di credito*, even though they differ in their historical origins, statutory aims and legal form, are all regarded as 'commercial banks'.

44. This is the most important of the five *istituti di categoria*, group institutions that act as central clearing houses.

45. Vincenzo Pontolillo, 'Medium- and Long-term Credit in Italy', *Banca Nazionale del Lavoro Quarterly Review* (September 1972), p. 299.

46. See L. Ceriani, 'Italy – I. The Commercial Banks and Financial Institutions' in Sayers (ed.), *Banking in Western Europe*, p. 125.

47. Unless otherwise stated, the figures for deposits and loans relate to domestic business in Swiss francs.

48. There are seven part-time members and a secretariat (a total of 27 staff members.)

49. Supplementary conditions must be met before a licence is granted to a foreign bank –e.g., reciprocity in the country concerned, choice of a company name that does not imply that the bank is Swiss in character, and an agreement to adhere to Swiss credit and monetary policies.

50. 'Wrapped money' consisted of gold or silver coins wrapped in paper and sealed by the exchange houses that issued it, the value being marked on the paper wrapper.

51. For an outline of the currency position in Japan at this time, see G.C. Allen and Audrey G. Donnithorne, *Western Enterprise in Far Eastern Economic Development – China and Japan* (London, 1954), pp. 199-200.

52. Ibid., p. 212.

53. The United States National Banking Act had been passed in 1863, though revised in important particulars the following year.

54. Originally, the Dai-Ichii Bank had a branch in Korea (established in 1878), which issued legal tender notes. Latterly, a Bank of Korea was also established. These were amalgamated to form the new Bank of Korea in 1906, which changed its named to the Chosen Bank in 1911, after Korea had officially become a Japanese colony.

55. The concept of modern banking was in fact imported into Japan but in a number of cases persons who had run exchange houses subsequently began to undertake banking business.

56. The remainder were savings or special banks.

57. See E.E. Ehrlich and F.M. Tamagna, 'Japan' in B.H. Beckhart (ed.) *Banking Systems* (New York, 1954), p. 539.

58. See ibid., p. 561.

59. Some of the very big enterprises might use as many as 25-30 banks.

5 THE NORDIC COUNTRIES: BANKING STRUCTURES

There is a case for taking the Nordic countries together. Climatically, they are similar and, since in the case of Norway it has been argued that geography and climate have at least in the past been factors that have directly influenced banking structure, it was appropriate to look elsewhere in these countries to see whether geographic factors in particular had had other results. Moreover, whatever the relevance of geography, there does seem to be evidence of a more socio-economic kind to suggest that past social attitudes have been a more direct influence than geography in helping to form the banking structures that grew up in this part of the world. Yet even in this context – if we ignore the geographic infuences in Norway (see below) – one might argue that climatic factors might well have been the main reason – especially in the past – for relative physical isolation, which in many instances is itself likely to have been the background to an emphasis on provincialism, even parochialism. Let us therefore briefly consider the evidence.

Norway

Norway provides perhaps the most obvious example of the possible effects on banking structure of the facts of geography. In Norway, with a population of 4.1 million, there were, at the end of 1952, 83 joint-stock commercial banks. By 1983, the number of commercial banks in Norway had fallen from 83 to 22,[1] the three largest of which account for two-thirds of aggregate total assets, the remainder being regional or local banks. Three have developed branch networks, though mainly in the southern part of the country. These are: Den norske Creditbank, Kreditkasse/Fiskernes Bank (the result of a merger between Christiania Bank og Kreditkasse and Fiskernes Bank in 1984), and Bergen Bank. In addition, there were 253 savings banks,[2] with the jointly-owned Fellesbanken that has its head office in Oslo. Three of the savings banks – Oslo & Akershus in Oslo, Rogaland in Stavanger, and Sparebanken Vest in Bergen – are relatively large. Now Oslo & Akershus has merged with Fellesbanken to form the fourth largest bank in Norway. The other important group of banking institutions is the 11 State banks, of which the State Housing Bank and the Municipal Bank are the largest. Others service Industry, Fishing, and Agriculture. Only in the Industry Bank is a proportion of the capital in private hands. There is also a Post Office Savings Bank and a Loan Fund for Education. The last two are also in effect State banks. In relative importance, on the basis of 1983 figures, the commercial banks accounted for about 16 per cent of the country's domestic credit supply to the private sector and municipalities, the savings banks 15 per cent, and the State banks (including the Bank of Norway) 18 per cent (38 per cent in 1980). Loan associations,[3] etc., account for 15 per cent, and the bond market 8 per cent. Finance companies are small. For many years, there were no foreign banks in Norway, but 4 foreign banks had representative offices there.[4] The Bank of Norway is the central bank and there is also a Bank Inspectorate.

However, it is not sufficient to look only at the Norwegian banking system as it exists today. It is important to see how this system has been derived. As has been indicated, Norway has steadily reduced the numbers of both its commercial banks and of its savings banks. It now has three large banks, but only one – Kreditkasse/Fiskernes Bank – has a nationwide spread of branches. This structure has an obvious geographical explanation. Apart from a relatively cultivable coastal area running round to the south from Oslo to Bergen, with something of a plateau behind, this being where the bulk of the bank branches are, Norway is very mountainous with heavy snowfall for much of the year. Even with the development of air services to supplement the railways (which link Oslo with important towns like Bergen, Trondheim and Stavanger) and the road system, overland transport during the winter months is somewhat limited. For the rest, Norway has a long and highly indented coastline with the mountains rising steeply behind stretching up from Bergen past Trondheim and Tromsø (the 'capital of the Arctic') beyond the North Cape to Kirkenes on the Soviet border. For year-round transport and communication only the Coastal Express (with ships of from about 2,190 to 4,200 tons) keeps a continuing contact with the numerous small towns, villages, and settlements that are strung out along a narrow shore. Even aircraft cannot always get through. And this is where most of the remainder of the bank branches are to be found, as well as the regional and local banks and many of the savings banks.

In the past and still to some extent today, in addition to the big banks' branches, Norway was also served by a relatively large number of regional and local banks, except in northern Norway, where (for the fishing industry) the Bank of Norway itself offered facilities through its branches; these facilities have virtually now been withdrawn as no longer necessary. At that time, one of the big Oslo banks – Christiania Bank og Kreditkasse – confined its offices to the Oslo area,[5] but also acted as banker for many local banks. Latterly, beginning in the early 1960s, it began to build up a branch system outside Oslo and eventually over much of the populated areas of the country. None the less, the number of branches outside Oslo is still only about one-third of its total, whereas for the other two big banks very approximately the reverse would be true (for Bergen Bank, Bergen will obviously be its main urban concentration, though it is also quite well represented in Oslo). As at November 1984, the three large banks had the following numbers of branches – Den norske Creditbank (125), Christiania Bank og Kreditkasse/Fiskernes Bank, as it has become (155), and Bergen Bank (109). Norwegian banks also have a number of subsidiaries (e.g., in leasing and factoring).

The number of regional and local commercial banks (with head offices outside Oslo) has now been reduced to 15 (in 1983). Sometimes local banks amalgamated into district banks; latterly, there were instances of a small or medium-sized bank being absorbed by one of the the big banks. Apart from the Big Three (and the Fellesbanken), the joint-stock banks are comparatively small. Some of these smaller banks have branches, but apart in a number of cases from an office in Oslo – the main capital market – these are confined to the area adjacent to the town in which the bank has its head office.

Hence, over a period of years, when inter-regional contacts were rather restricted, a banking system with elements of 'unit banking' was the obvious result. Furthermore, geographic and climatic obstacles tended to reinforce strong local patriotisms and these operated to perpetuate the independence of the local banker. Also, for a time, even banking experts appeared to favour some decentralisation in Norway. Elements of 'unit banking' have given way to a 'hybrid' system (as already defined). Under both heads, there are those who would argue that these forms of organisation have had their origins in Norway in the facts of geography.[6] Norwegian bankers would maintain that this view is an exaggeration. In their judgement, local communities are rarely cut off from the rest of the world and the desire for a local bank merely reflected local loyalties. It is felt, too, that as a result of improvements in communications – and especially in telecommunications – Norway has developed into a much more integrated society, though local loyalties undoubtedly still exist. Yet there seems to be a certain logic about a basic geographic/climatic explanation and certainly the facts of geography condition the distribution both of population and related banking facilities, whether these be provided by bank branches or by regional or local banks.

One must remember, too, that the banking system in Norway has never been as decentralised as the number of banks would seem to indicate and there has long been a considerable concentration of resources in the hands of the major banks. The three largest banks hold two-thirds of aggregate banking assets. Inter-bank deposits are relatively large and the more important joint-stock banks have long cooperated with the smaller banks in making loans on what are called a 'joint-account' basis. More generally, as in the United States, correspondent-bank relationships are important. Moreover, the savings banks have their own joint-stock bank – the Fellesbanken – in Oslo and are thereby able to share some of the advantages that would accrue to a bank with a wide spread of branches.

Over the years, many progressive Norwegian bankers have increasingly favoured a more integrated banking system, as have Committees on Banking Structure.

> In the recommendations by The Banking Committee of 1960 (The Committee on Banking Structure) it was emphasized, inter alia, that in areas where there is a suitable basis for local bank mergers, strong regional banks should be developed. This was considered desirable as a counterbalance to the concentration around a few large commercial banks in the country's two largest cities.
>
> In a statement to the Storting in February 1968 on this question, the Ministry of Finance declared it desirable to continue to work towards the goal recommended by the Committee of a balanced banking system based on regional banks and branches of the major banks. The Ministry emphasized the importance of implementing structural rationalization as soon as possible.
>
> The Ministry saw no reason for maintaining the practice of recent years of postponing the consideration of applications from the large banks concerning the establishment of branches in districts where mergers are desirable. The development of the network of branches should take place in such a manner that the districts are given the possibility of choice and that necessary competition be assured . . .
>
> The Ministry indicates that the banking institutions themselves must decide how to solve the actual structural problems. Prior contact with the authorities in cases of mergers and the establishment of

> branches is considered desirable by the Ministry. Such contact is particularly important in areas where alternative solutions are possible.[7]

The recommendations of the Committee on Banking Structure were confirmed in the Report of the Storting (no. 35, 1967-8) and the Finance Committee of the Storting agreed that the structural rationalisation of the commercial banking system should continue to be founded on a balanced banking system 'based on regional banks and branches of larger banks'.[8] And with regard to the savings banks,The Regional Committee of the Association of Norwegian Savings Banks reported in July 1967 that

> the savings banks should not lose their characteristics as regional district banks and they should maintain their local ties in their organizational structure. Even though the optimal size of a bank will increase steadily, the committee considered the county to be the largest geographical unit.[9]

Nevertheless, it was contemplated in the Report that the number of savings banks might over time be reduced from well over 500 possibly to something under 100.

More recently, a working group has again assessed the banking structure in Norway. It presented its recommendations in December 1982.[10] The working group considered that the trend towards larger banking units should continue. This applied particularly in the savings-banks sector. However, a majority recommended that the authorities should not permit mergers between the three largest commercial banks (Den norske Creditbank, Kreditkassen and Bergen Bank) and other banks. The working group further recommended that banks should be free to set up branches in their home county. The rules on setting up branches outside the home county should also be relaxed. However, applications to set up such branches should continue to be subject to approval by the authorities. The working group also advocated that a small number of foreign banks should be allowed to establish operations in Norway and that this should be in the form of subsidiaries, subject to the same credit and foreign-exchange policy constraints as Norwegian banks. This has been agreed – see p. 219, note 4. Foreign bank branching should, however, be restricted.

The report of the working group was circulated for comment among

> a number of bodies. Relaxation of the concession rules governing the establishment of branches received widespread support. Most of the commenting bodies also endorsed the view that the authorities should be empowered to prevent bank mergers which are not in keeping with key banking structure goals, e.g., mergers which would entail further concentration around the three largest commercial banks. None of the commenting bodies directly opposed the idea that foreign banks be allowed entry to Norway.[11]

It was agreed that mergers between banks should normally be approved; applications for mergers involving Den norske Creditbank, Bergen Bank, and Christiania Bank og Kreditkasse should be dealt with very restrictively; in mergers between commercial banks and savings banks, the parties involved should decide the organisational form of the merged unit. With regard to the last, the government coalition parties amended the proposals such that 'units resulting from mergers between commercial banks and savings banks should as a rule be organized as savings banks, and that savings banks which may be characterized as regional banks should be permitted to establish subsidiaries in Oslo'.[12]

Sweden

Altogether, there are 15 commercial banks in Sweden, mergers having reduced them from 84 at the beginning of the century. Of these, four are major banks – Post- och Kreditbanken (PKbanken), which is partially owned by the State, the Skandinaviska Enskilda Banken, the Svenska Handelsbanken, and the rather smaller Götabanken. In addition, there are six regional banks, with head offices in the provinces, though they are also represented in Stockholm and Gothenburg. Except for Uplandsbanken, Wermlandsbanken and Sundsvallsbanken and the small Jämtlands Folkbank (a local bank), which serve central Sweden, the other regional banks and local bank are in the South. Only in Stockholm and Gothenburg do they compete with each other, but in their regions they have of course to compete with those banks that have a nationwide business and also with the local savings bank and the cooperatives. In agricultural areas, the cooperatives can be very strong and very competitive. The Sparbankernas Bank and the Föreningsbankernas Bank function both as commercial banks and as clearing banks within the savings-bank and cooperative-bank movements respectively. There are 155 savings banks (with about 1,400 branches) and 395 cooperative banks (with 696 branches). There are no foreign banks in Sweden,[13] though there are some 30 representative offices. Swedish banks may not have branches abroad, though they can operate subsidiaries abroad, or have minority shares in banks in other countries, as well as representative offices. The present banking structure is thought to be relatively stable. No more mergers are expected between the commercial banks. Only further mergers between savings banks are likely to be encouraged in the immediate future.

Finance companies are also very active in Sweden, with a rapid growth in business over recent years. There are about 160 in the country as a whole, though some of the largest operate as holding companies with four or five subsidiaries. Eighty-five per cent of the business is done by ten companies, most of which are owned by banks. Primarily, the biggest companies are concerned with factoring and leasing, but consumer credits (including the re-financing of instalment paper) is important and directly or indirectly they also do credit-card business. There are, too, credit companies that finance the business and export sectors.

There are also a number of large insurance companies in Sweden, a National Pension Insurance Fund, which invests large sums of money, and a number of mortgage societies, which issue housing bonds. Although not a credit institution, there is a Housing Board, which is a government authority that administers funds that derive from the budget.

As in a number of other countries, Sweden has also set up a range of specialised financial institutions, the lending of which is directed towards a particular sector of the economy. These institutions raise funds by borrowing against bonds or promissory notes, the bonds being purchased mainly by insurance companies, the National Pension Insurance Fund and the banks. Certain of the specialised financial institutions have a semi-official status, since the government provided the original capital and continues to exercise an influence over the composition of their boards of directors. Credits are granted against the security of mortgages in the agricultural, housing and shipping sectors. In this context, the mortgage societies occupy a prominent position lending long-term against residential buildings, as well as business and office buildings. The long-term loans replace construction credits from banks when the buildings are completed. In the rural sector, the General Mortgage Bank raises funds by issuing bonds; it has ten affiliated rural mortgage societies (each covering one or more counties). Loans are made to farmers who are members of these societies. Lantbrukskredit AB is an institution entrusted with helping finance companies that process or distribute agricultural or forest products. Long-term credits to small and medium-sized firms are provided by AB Industrikredit. This institution grants long-term loans at fixed rates of interest to small and medium-sized companies. These loans normally run for 15 years. Another institution – Företagskapital AB – provides risk capital for small and medium-sized companies by acquiring minority shareholdings or debentures. There is also the Swedish Investment Bank, entirely owned by the government; it also borrows (largely on the international capital market) and provides credits and guarantees to relatively large, risky projects in the business sector and it finances exports. Long-term credits (usually for five to ten years) in international trade are provided by AB Svensk Exportkredit and there is a Swedish Export Credits Guarantee Board to cover the risks connected with the granting of export credits. Finally, two credit institutions have the special function of providing loans to the local authorities. Kommunlåneinstituet AB is owned jointly by the commercial and the cooperative banks; Kommunkredit AB is affiliated with the savings banks.

As elsewhere, the prudential controls of the Bank Inspection Board and the credit restrictions imposed by the Central Bank (the Riksbank) provide the framework within which the commercial banks and other financial institutions must operate.[14]

Sweden, with a population of 8.3 million, has a very different geography from Norway – only in the North is it truly mountainous[15] and not nearly as high as in Norway. Along the Gulf of Bothnia, too, there is much relatively flat and low-lying land, which is readily habitable. Elsewhere also communications are much less impeded than in Norway and in Sweden therefore we find a much more integrated banking system. The big banks all have virtually nationwide distributions of branches (as a result of numerous bank mergers in the past), determined for the system as a whole by the distribution of population. PKbanken has fewer branches (130 at the end of 1983) than Skandinaviska Enskilda Banken (356) and Svenska Handelsbanken (454), but it also operates through some 1,800 post-office outlets. Götabanken is rather smaller than the other three; it had 169 branches (end of 1983) but not as complete a national coverage with gaps in the northern part of its branch system. One might add that in 1982 Sveabanken was licensed and began operations in 1983; it was established to serve small and medium-sized companies.

In addition, there are six regional banks (341 branches) and three local banks (12 branches). The savings banks, too, are regional and local in character. As already indicated, the regional and local banks are mainly located in the southern third of the country (i.e. on the plains), where most of the population is. Three regional banks and a local bank (together of course with a number of savings banks) cater for the central area; the North is serviced by branches of the three largest banks. Hence, Sweden – like Norway – has a 'hybrid' type of banking system. Clearly, there are no really geographic reasons to explain the retention of regional and local banks – climatic reasons perhaps, which in the past might have resulted in a degree of physical isolation. More probably, the regional banks derived as much in the past from local patriotisms that – as in Norway – are part of the Scandinavian make-up. Also, over the centuries, there must have been to some extent a shared cultural outlook, since at various times and in different combinations all the Scandinavian countries have been with some other Scandinavian country part of the same kingdom.

Finland

Finland, with a population of 4.8 million, offers another contrast to Norway. Although it is a land of many lakes and virtually a Continental type of climate, there is an absence of mountain barriers and communications are not generally difficult. Of the total area, 8 per cent is cultivated, 9 per cent is water, and 65 per cent is covered by forests. Apart from a few towns like Oulu, which is on the coast near the northern end of the Gulf of Bothnia, the main population centres are in the southern third of the country.

The number of joint-stock banks has never been large. At present, there are ten (including three foreign subsidiaries). Three have always operated a large number of branches. The savings banks and the cooperative banks operate in loose alliances and some have many branches. It is therefore clearly a branch-banking system.

Thus, the structure of banking in Finland is relatively simple. Excluding the foreign subsidiaries, Finland has seven commercial banks,[16] of which two are much larger than the rest; these are Kansallis-Osake-Pankki (443 branches and 193 service points in 1983) and the Union Bank of Finland (346 branches and 214 service points) and, together with the Bank of Helsinki (114 branches and 24 service points), they each have a nationwide network of branches. Total branches for the 7 commercial banks numbered 924 in 1983. The commercial banks provide about 27 per cent of the 'credit stock' (Finnmark and foreign-currency-denominated loans); Postipankki is State-owned and, as a deposit bank with post-giro facilities, provides 6.3 per cent of the credit stock; it also holds government balances; it had 40 branches in 1983 and, through the Bank of Finland's 12 branch offices and post-office service points (3,211 in 1983), it operates a large number of other service points for certain purposes. In 1983, there were 270 savings banks[17] (with 1,052 branches) and 371 cooperative banks (845 branches), each of which groups has a central institution – Skopbank and Okobank respectively. The cooperative banks traditionally financed mainly agriculture and forestry, but they have diversified as people have moved into the towns and both the savings banks and the cooperative banks finance housing and lend to business enterprises as well.[18] Both of their central institutions operate as normal commercial banks; they also provide foreign exchange and other services to their associated institutions. One of the commercial banks – The Bank of Åland – is a regional bank that services the Åland islands; it also has a branch in Helsinki. There are four mortgage credit banks, which issue their own bonds and grant industrial and commercial mortgage loans (it is the banks which primarily lend to finance house purchase, which is also catered for by the central government and the municipalities). Some of the mortgage credit banks are associated with commercial banks and one with the Bank of Finland, which is the Central Bank. The commercial banks, Postipankki, Skopbank and Okobank and (in some respects) the largest savings bank – Finnish Workers' Savings Bank – are all 'universal banks' and provide a wide range of financial services, including stockbroking. The large savings and cooperative banks provide stockbroking services through their central institutions. There are a number of special-credit institutions which include the Industrialisation Fund of Finland, Finnish Export Credit, the State Investment Fund, and the Regional Development Fund. Finally, there are a number of insurance companies (which tend to be large), and finance companies (usually subsidiaries of commercial banks), which undertake hire-purchase financing, factoring and leasing operations; they also arrange finance on the basis of special contracts. The respective shares of the several banking sectors are set out in Table 5.1.

Under new bank legislation which came into force in 1979, the scope for foreign bank participation in Finland's financial markets has been increased. Previously, they could only operate representative offices. Now foreign banks may set up subsidiaries in Finland and engage in the full range of banking business. Because the Finnish banks are already well established in retail-banking business and it would be

Table 5.1: Finnmark Deposits and Credits

	Deposits		Credits	
	1970	1983	1970	1983
	%	%	%	%
Commercial banks	41	35	47	39
Savings banks	28	29	26	26
Co-operative banks	20	24	20	24
Postipankki	11	12	7	11

Source: Union Bank of Finland

expensive to set up a network of branches to compete with them, foreign banks concentrate on wholesale-banking business and service corporate customers. The first such subsidiary was established in March 1982 and, by mid-1983, there were three foreign-owned banks' subsidiaries in Helsinki – the parents being Chase Manhattan, Citibank, and Indosuez (with Postipankki, which has a 15 per cent stake). Hambros Bank and Skandinaviska Enskilda Banken maintain representative offices. Also, under the 1979 legislation, it is possible, subject to approval by the Ministry of Finance, for foreigners to own shares in Finnish banks, provided the total share ownership by foreigners does not exceed 20 per cent of the bank's equity. In addition, foreign credit institutions (with the permission of the Council of State and a licence from the Bank of Finland to permit the import of capital into the country for the purpose of purchasing the shares) can be authorised to acquire more than a 20 per cent stake in a Finnish commercial bank, mortgage bank, or credit company and to establish subsidiaries in Finland.[19]

There is a range of legislation that applies to credit institutions operating on the Finnish financial markets. There is a separate law for each deposit-bank group, laws which were standardised when bank legislation was reformed in 1969. Special laws apply to the mortgage-credit banks and the special-credit institutions. Various aspects of general economic legislation are also relevant and there are several specific laws (e.g. that relate to cheques and bills, bond and debenture loans, and foreign-capital movements).

The Parliamentary Banking Committee and sometimes the Parliamentary Finance Committee consider bills concerning the financial markets which the government has placed before Parliament. As a rule, the Bank Acts are prepared by the Ministry of Finance which is the highest body supervising banking activity. The Ministry of Finance's permission is also required to establish a bank. The Bank Inspectorate, which is subordinate to the Ministry of Finance, supervises banks and credit institutions and ensures that they operate in accordance with the law. In addition, the Bank Inspectorate collects data concerning the banks' activities, financial standing and ownership. They may also examine any documents they deem necessary. Furthermore, the Bank Inspectorate supervises the banks' lending activity, their service forms and approves types of account. The activity of the Inspectorate is prescribed by law.

As the country's central bank, the Bank of Finland is responsible for the country's monetary policy which plays a central role in economic policy. Monetary policy has traditionally been directed towards the commercial banks, including the central institutions of the savings banks and of the cooperative banks. By controlling the net liquidity position of the banks *vis-à-vis* the central bank and by influencing interest rates, the Bank of Finland can affect bank operations and consequently economic activity and developments.

Denmark

There are no particular geographic features relevant to banking structure in Denmark. It is a substantially flat country of good agricultural land and a more moderate climate than the rest of the Nordic countries; it is ideal country – one would have thought – for a branch-banking system and, in a sense (as we shall see), there is a considerable emphasis on branching. Yet, unlike Finland, Denmark has a 'hybrid' system (by our definition), with a small number of big banks and a relatively large total number of banks of all sizes to serve a population of only 5.1 million. Hence, if geography fails us, we shall have to look elsewhere for the explanation of 'hybridity' in the banking structure. Most simply, it probably derives from entrenched local loyalties, which seem to have been a feature of most of these Nordic countries – Finland being largely an exception – due to their many cultural links and much common history.

Again, as we shall find, the structure of the Danish banking system is very simple – there are 5 large banks, including the Big Three in Copenhagen – the Kjøbenhavns Handelsbank (367 branches in 1983), Den Danske Bank (288), and Privatbanken (226); Den Danske Provinsbank (144 branches)with its head office in Aarhus; and Andelsbanken in Copenhagen (238); in addition, there are 13 medium-sized banks (with over 520 branches) and 59 smaller banks (averaging 5 or 6 branches each), or 77 banks in all. Virtually all banks, including regional and local banks, have branches. The total number of branches was 2,164 at the end of 1983. Over the years, there have been a number of mergers. Competition is strong between the big banks, the regional banks, and the larger local banks; substantially, the competition of the small and medium-sized banks is based on local loyalties. Again, the regional and larger local banks are probably more flexible in their operations and large enough to employ specialist expertise. There are also about 150 savings banks (with over 1,300 branches), of which two SDS and BIKUBEN – are large (with about 60 per cent of savings-bank business); since 1975, the savings banks, which are mutuals, have also undertaken a commercial-banking business, though their deposits are less than half those of the commercial banks. They have a central institution –the Fællesbanken, which provides centralised services for the smaller savings banks (e.g., foreign-exchange dealing) and in reality operates as a commercial bank. The commercial banks likewise compete for savings. After Denmark joined the European Economic Community, several foreign banks – three American, one British, one Dutch, and one Islamic – began to operate in Denmark as branches of their parent banks (in addition, there is one subsidiary of a foreign bank). Other financial institutions in Denmark, which play a relevant role, are mortgage-credit associations, cooperative banks, a Post Office Giro, insurance companies, and pension funds. There are also a number of specialised financial institutions.

As elsewhere, the banks in Denmark work within the framework of prudential regulation imposed in this instance by the Bank Inspectorate (which itself comes under the Ministry of Industry); the central bank is the Danmarks Nationalbank.

In general, the similarities in Nordic banking would appear to derive from their past historical connections and common cultural influences – not so much from the facts of geography, even of climate (though these would appear to have been formative elements in the Norwegian situation). Moreover, there is today still much cooperation and consultation between Nordic countries. For example, there is quite a measure of consultation between the several central banks in the Nordic countries with a tendency to exchange ideas with each other. Again, there is cooperation in the form of the famous SAS airline. Formerly, several of the commercial banks in these countries owned a London-based consortium bank – Nordic Bank – and the buying-out of its three other shareholding partners by Den norske Creditbank[20] was less a desire to split up the ownership than the fact that the era of consortium banking was coming to a close. Most individual banks with international interests now favoured setting up and operating their own overseas banks both to tighten up control and to avoid conflicts of interest. Subsequently, Scandinavian Bank's two Danish partners withdrew in favour of the Skandinaviska Enskilda Banken, with the possibility that the latter would at some time in the future concentrate its London business therein. The trend seems to be for the big banks to go it alone in London, but some of the not-so-big banks are still interested in joint ventures.[21]

Notes

1. In 1919 there were 195 banks, and 104 in 1939.
2. Latterly, these have been subject to many mergers.
3. Loan associations issue bonds and finance house purchase against mortgages, business investments, shipbuilding and exports.
4. However, power existed under the Act relating to Commercial Banks to permit the entry of foreign banks and the matter had been discussed by an advisory body called the Commission on Foreign Establishments (see Morten Carlsen, 'Establishment of Foreign Banks in Norway', *Bank of Norway Economic Bulletin*, 4 (1982), pp. 271ff; and 'Foreign Banks in Norway?', *Norwegian Commercial Banks, Financial Review*, 4 (1982), pp. 4-6). In June 1984 the Norwegian Parliament approved legislation to permit the establishment by 'first class, internationally recognised' foreign banks of bank subsidiaries in Norway, not branches. Only up to a third of board members may be foreigners; chairmen must be Norwegian citizens resident in Norway. (See also *The Norwegian Bankers' Association Financial Review*, 3 (1984), pp. 3-4)
5. In 1984, a new bank was established in Oslo called Oslobanken.
6. See, for example, R.S. Sayers, *Banking in Western Europe* (Oxford, 1962), pp. 299-300.
7. Bank of Norway, *Annual Report* (1967), pp. 95-6.
8. Bank of Norway, *Annual Report* (1968), p. 72.
9. Bank of Norway, *Annual Report* (1967), p. 96.
10. See *Bank of Norway Economic Bulletin*, 1 (1984).
11. Ibid., p. 53.
12. Ibid., p. 54.
13. But this will change, probably by 1986. The Swedish government is planning to legislate to permit foreign banks to set up foreign operations in Sweden. See *Financial Times*, 7 September 1984.
14. The Bank Inspection Board is responsible for the savings banks and the cooperatives as well as the commercial banks.
15. In this part of Sweden, as in Norway, bank offices tend to be on the coast.
16. In 1920 there were 24, 10 in 1940, seven from 1960 onwards.
17. 457 in 1920 449 in 1940, 390 in 1960.

18. The savings banks also lend heavily to agriculture.
19. *Bank of Finland Monthly Bulletin* (April 1982), p. 32.
20. See *Financial Times*, 23 August 1983.
21. See 'Banking Abroad: the End of an Era' in 'Nordic Countries Banking, Finance and Investment', *Financial Times*, 29 November 1983.

6 THE BUSINESS OF BANKING

In its fundamentals, banking business is very similar the world over. Yet there are some significant differences, and the attempt to explain the reasons for these variations in emphasis (or, it may be, departures from principle) therefore warrants our attention.

A banker is a dealer in money and credit. The business of banking consists of borrowing and lending. As in other businesses, it is necessary to base one's trading on capital, but it is sometimes surprising, in those countries where banking is accepted as commonplace and taken for granted, how little of their own capital banks do in fact employ in relation to the total volume of their transactions.

The bulk of the resources employed by a modern banker consists of borrowed moneys – largely deposits – which are lent out as profitably as is consistent with safety. Bankers are not in the business for the good of their health and they are therefore anxious to make as large a profit as they can. At the same time, they must never forget that the bulk of their resources consists of deposits, that a large proportion of these is repayable on demand, and the remainder often at short notice. They must in consequence hold part of their assets in cash in order to meet claims for payment on demand, and a proportion of the rest of their assets in forms that can be quickly converted, without significant loss, into cash.

For the rest, practice varies a little. British bankers have long maintained that for the most part loans should be short-term in character and, in theory, repayable on demand, as is much of the money which the bankers themselves have borrowed, though admittedly this principle is often more honoured in the breach than in the observance and a proportion of their loans has long been at least medium-term in character. Latterly, this fact has been recognised by defining such accommodation as 'term loans'. In other countries, lending has at times been surprisingly long-term and it will be our purpose to examine the origins of this rather different attitude to bank lending and the ways in which it is possible to pursue such a policy, while still retaining the main link with the canons of orthodox banking.

In an attempt to compare the business of banking as it is pursued in a number of different countries, it is necessary to have some standard of reference. It is proposed therefore to base the discussion on a simple bank balance sheet, the main ingredients of which will be common to banks in all countries. Within this framework, reference will be made to two banking traditions, which appear to have been particularly influential in determining business practice, namely, the British and the Continental European traditions. One might perhaps claim that the United States represents a third, but it is more probable that traditions there derive in fact from a cross-fertilisation of ideas imported from a number of countries across the Atlantic. The reference balance sheet may be set out as follows:

Liabilities	**Assets**
1. Capital and Reserves Subordinated Debt	1. Cash & Deposits with other Banks
2. Deposits: Other Banks Current (Demand) Savings Time, 'Fixed', or Term	2. Liquid Assets: Call Money Short-Term Government Paper Commercial Bills
3. Wholesale or 'Bought' Money	3. Investments: Medium- and Long-Term Government Paper (including where appropriate local governments) Industrial Securities (where appropriate)
	4. Advances and Loans
	5. Premises

Contingent Liabilities offset by contra-entries.
Acceptance or *Aval*.
These may or may not be included in the main Balance Sheet

This is as complete a statement of the general position as is consistent with simplification. The main categories on the liabilities side are capital, deposits, and 'bought' money; and, on the assets side, cash, liquid assets, investments (or securities), and loans.

Liabilities

Capital and Reserves

Capital and Reserves are usually a small proportion of total liabilities (even as low as 1 or 2 per cent). It is sometimes less easy nowadays for banks to make new issues of capital, though in the years after World War II the impact of inflation in many countries resulted in a number of new issues and, from time to time, banks have latterly also taken action to bring their capital structure more in line with the volume of business done. Often, additional capital has been accumulated by building up reserves derived from undistributed profits and, on occasion, such funds may be formally capitalised (as in Italy).

At one time, a bank's capital was the main basis of its operations, but with the development of deposit banking and the carrying on of banking business on the basis of borrowed money, capital and reserves have tended to become the ultimate cover against losses (e.g., on loans and investments) and, in the event of disaster, the last resort of depositors. This is admittedly a simplification but under modern banking conditions it contains more than an element of truth. That the trading functions of capital are still of some moment is evidenced by certain of the exceptions to the general statement that has just been made. Thus, recurrent inflation prompted many of the French banks in the earlier post-war years to increase the absolute amount of capital employed, in order to restore a more appropriate capital/deposit ratio; in a developing economy like Australia, certain of the trading banks also saw fit after World War II to increase their capital; and in the United States, the capital account has for long been important as the statutory basis of bank lending limits, though the American banks have usually sought to raise their capital to higher levels not so much by new issues as by ploughing back profits or by means of mergers and consolidations. Nevertheless, they have also resorted in a number of cases to 'rights issues' as a means of raising their lending limits. Again, in a number of countries, banks – both large and small – have over the years issued new share capital as a means of improving their capital/deposit ratios and broadening their resources base and, at times, this has gone hand in hand with quite a vigorous mergers programme.

Whatever the stated reasons, when increases in bank capital have been made, this has usually been due to a feeling that capital and reserves should not be allowed to shrink below some conventional proportion of deposits, and the reserve character of these items is probably still a paramount consideration in the minds of bankers brought up in the British tradition. On the other hand, for bankers educated in the Continental European tradition, the trading functions of capital have sometimes seemed to be more important. Where at least a proportion of loans and investments is likely to be long-term, the maintenance of an adequate capital structure has been regarded as no more than ordinary business prudence. This, in their heyday, the capital and reserves of the French *banques d'affaires* as a percentage of the total balance sheet figure were significantly higher than for the deposit banks.[1]

None the less, when one considers the figures, certain banks would seem to be under-capitalised and the authorities in a number of countries have over a period of years been greatly concerned with questions of capital adequacy. For example, in some countries – e.g., Italy, Portugal, India, and, to a lesser extent, Belgium, the Netherlands and, for the larger banks, France – capital ratios are low – sometimes of the order of 2 per cent or even lower (capital and reserves in relation to total liabilities). Sometimes, this is due to the combined effects of inflation (with the related fast growth in deposits) and the fact that the larger banks are nationalised as in France, India, Italy and, in Australia, the Commonwealth Trading Bank; in these instances, the State is often loath to provide additional capital, though in some sense there is thought to be a kind of State guarantee, i.e. it is believed that such banks would in no circumstances be allowed to fail.[2] On the other hand, a large number of banks throughout the world, including those in the United Kingdom, the United States, the Scandinavian countries, Australia, New Zealand and Japan (if one includes the hidden reserves) enjoy capital ratios of (say) 5-7 per cent, in the United Kingdom even higher. In other countries – e.g., Switzerand and Austria – the authorities lay down guidelines and monitor the situation carefully, as indeed do many regulators elsewhere.

Further consideration may be given to the situation in the United States, where certain of the largest banks (e.g., Bank of America, Chemical, Citicorp, and Manufacturers Hanover) are thought to have capital ratios that are too low (between 5 and 5.5 per cent) in the light of the authorities' guidelines (i.e. as indicated by the Fed, the FDIC and the Comptroller of the Currency) requiring a minimum primary capital to assets ratio of 5.5 per cent and a minimum capital to assets ratio of 6 per cent. Indeed, according to the FDIC, about 700 American banks currently fall below the proposed new ratios and the authorities were expected to exert pressure on banks and bank holding companies to improve their capital ratios either by trimming assets or by raising new capital.[3]

As a result of more extensive prudential supervision, a number of countries now require a minimum-capital provision for banks, though it is often so low as not to be of any real significance. But in addition, whether formally or not, the authorities, as in the United States, frequently exert pressure in an upwards direction in order to improve the capital position of banks in the country concerned. Thus, in Italy, where the capital ratios of banks are a little over 2 per cent, the Bank of Italy is trying to move them in the direction of 3 per cent; in Sweden, where the ratios are good (say, 6 to 7 per cent), the authorities encourage the banks to make rights issues in order to maintain adequate capital; in Norway, there is a required minimum of 6.5 per cent, subject to exclusions (actually, it is of the order of 5 per cent); Denmark aims at 8 per cent of total liabilities (subject to some exclusions); and in Japan, the authorities feel that net worth/deposit liabilities should exceed 10 per cent (including hidden reserves), though published ratios are quite low. In Australia and New Zealand, capital adequacy is thought 'not to be a problem'. Foreign banks, too, may be required to maintain a local capital base in order to cover the operations of their branches – this may be done by way of a guarantee given by the parent bank to the central bank of the country concerned.

There are various ways in which a bank can attempt to maintain the adequacy of its capital provision. Banks always plough back a proportion of their profits and transfer them to general reserves (after making specific provision for bad and doubtful debts or for anticipated losses). How much they can retain in this way depends on the level of profits; also on policy with respect to dividends. But rarely are these provisions adequate to offset inflationary erosion and to provide the basis for further expansion. New issues of capital (often by way of rights issues to existing shareholders) are the obvious way of building up capital account, though resort to this source of capital funds will obviously depend on a bank's own profit record and the state of the equity market. Over the years, there have been many new issues of shares by banks around the world. Sometimes, the authorities have actively encouraged banks to expand their capital in this way (e.g, in Sweden); alternatively, tax measures have been introduced to encourage resort to risk capital (e.g., in Belgium as a result of which a number of new issues were made by banks in 1982 and 1983).

Another option is subordinated debt, subordinated in the sense that the claims of other creditors of the bank would have to be met first, though holders of subordinated debt would rank before shareholders. Interest paid on subordinated debt would of course rank as a business expense. The rate of interest may be fixed, or it may be a floatin rate. The relevant debt may be in the form of bonds (or debentures) or notes,[4] but it will often be issued at medium to long term[5] – possibly out to 20 years; maturities of (say) seven to 12 years are quite common. In other words, it is different in kind from buying 'wholesale money' on the short-term money markets. The issue of such debt may be subject to a ceiling applied by the regulatory authorities (e.g., the central bank), though rarely are such ceilings approached. Again, subject to a ceiling, the bank may be required to repay a proportion of the debt each year. Usually, such debt is included as part of the capital structure of the bank (e.g., for purposes of calculating a capital ratio) at least until it is approaching maturity. Sometimes, all such debt may be included in the capital ratio, on other occasions only a proportion. An interesting variant of this type of capital raising was the introduction of *titres participatifs* in France; these securities represent non-voting loan stock, somewhere between a bond and a share (see p. 141).[6]

Reference has already been made to hidden reserves. In some countries, which require full disclosure, these are forbidden (e.g., in the United Kingdom and in Italy); in others, they are not only permitted but may represent a significant part of bank capital (e.g., in Japan, where the published capital ratios are low). They are achieved by conservative valuation of assets (e.g., securities – particularly equities – and real estate). Also, where capital ratios are really low (e.g., in India), hidden reserves may be capitalised (e.g., banks can add to published reserves amounts that they transfer from existing hidden reserves), but clearly this cannot be done indefinitely.

Deposits

The banker's other main liability consists of deposits. These are borrowed moneys which, in so far as they provide the banker with additional cash, constitute an important supplement to loanable resources. For the banking system as a whole, it is true that an increase in loans will itself result in a related addition to notes in circulation (which means an immediate loss of cash) or to deposits (which involves an increase in the potential liability to pay out cash). Further, to the extent that the amounts lent to a bank customer pass into the hands of another customer of the same bank, this will again be true. However, individual commercial banks can generally expect that an increase in deposits will result in some net acquisition of cash or in a corresponding claim for receipt of cash from a third party. This is most obvious when the growth in deposits is attributable to an increase in government expenditure financed by government borrowing from the central bank. It is in this sense that an accretion to deposits provides the basis for further bank lending.

From the point of view of balance sheet structure, there are two significant questions to be asked about deposits. First, what are the sources of deposits other than the creation of central bank credit? Second, what degree of 'inertia' can they be expected to display? To a certain extent, the two questions are interrelated.

Two lines of division can be offered when considering source. Deposits may be drawn from other bankers (being in the nature of clearing or correspondent balances), or from the public at large – private individuals and business firms. One would expect – and one does find – that banking systems of the 'unit' or 'hybrid' type hold a higher proportion of correspondent balances than systems in which banking business is concentrated in a few hands and which are more fully integrated. In the latter type of system, bankers' deposits are likely to be held for the most part with the central bank. Alternatively, deposits may be derived either from within the domestic economy or from abroad. Indeed, there have been times when banks in certain countries have been obliged to depend on foreign or overseas deposits for a significant proportion of their resources. For example, for some years prior to the banking crisis of 1893, the Australian trading banks attracted moneys by way of deposit from the United Kingdom, and the withdrawal of large sums when crisis supervened was one of the proximate reasons for the difficulties that faced these banks throughout the 1890s.[7] The German credit banks were similarly dependent on foreign deposits during the 1920s and the loss of these deposits after 1929 did much to undermine the position of these banks during the crisis of the early 1930s.[8] More recently (since World War II), the West German monetary authorities have again at times been considerably embarrassed by a heavy inflow of foreign money placed on deposit with German banks and greatly adding to their liquidity. Nor will one forget very quickly the failure of Intra Bank in the Lebanon in October 1966, when large amounts of Middle Eastern deposits were withdrawn.

Though the degree of dependence has been less, there have also been occasions when foreign deposits have been a significant supplementary source of funds in countries like the United Kingdom, the United States, Switzerland, and the Netherlands.

Foreign deposits are at all times likely to be more volatile than home deposits, since rumours from a distance frequently prompt more precipitate action than in cases where it is possible to judge a situation on the spot. It is this that lies at the root of the phenomenon of 'hot money'. In addition, there is always the danger that the foreign depositors' funds may become frozen, because of exchange difficulties or political changes.

What, next, can one say about the inertia displayed by deposits? Deposits are of different kinds, quite apart from differences of origin. Most simply, deposits may be repayable either on demand, or only after the expiration of a fixed term or when due notice has been given. Bankers frequently attach considerable importance to this distinction. Legally, it is only demand deposits that represent an immediate threat to their cash position. Where it has been agreed between banker and customer that the deposit is only repayable after stated notice or the expiration of a fixed term, the liability to repay can legally be deferred and the banker may gain valuable time in which to mobilise his resources against heavy demands for repayment. Yet, although legally, the banker may insist on the observance of these provisions, it is quite common for him to waive such rights when so requested in consideration of a reduction in the interest payable.[9] The banker is disposed to release moneys in this way in order to retain goodwill and, indeed, to maintain confidence. Alternatively, he will be prepared to lend against the security of such fixed deposits and the interest penalty will then take the form of a difference between the rates charged and allowed.[10]

There are also more fundamental reasons for this attitude. The banker knows that the basis of credit is confidence and that an effort on his part to enforce his rights of deferred payment may so damage the confidence of the public in the banking system that he will be obliged to pay virtually on demand. Nevertheless, the 'fixed' or term deposit may impart some degree of inertia to the deposit structure, since many people who have placed their money on deposit for a stated term will feel bound to observe their contract. Further, there is the deterrent of at least a partial loss of interest. Only when subjected to financial pressure will they seek variation of the contract and request earlier repayment. Even then, a banker can usually rely on a breathing space within which to mobilise his assets against an anticipated 'run' and, if his position is so insecure that he feels he must insist on his rights, then virtually nothing can save him.

In England, moneys held on deposit account have at various times been subject to notice of from seven to 21 days, though seven days' notice has been usual. If no notice is given, the deposit 'runs on'. Latterly, there have been in addition a variety of deposit packages, including a range of longer-term deposits and high-interest accounts with some chequing facilities. In Scotland, moneys have long been placed on deposit account, a receipt being issued to a customer in respect of an interest-bearing deposit. Interest is calculated on a day-to-day basis and is payable when the receipt is encashed, provided the funds lie for at least 30 days (which incidentally allows the customer to decide into which tax year he wishes the interest to fall). These facilities are much used (eg., by the legal profession) by those who wish to keep parcels of funds separate or who wish to hold large sums for short periods. One of the Scottish banks – the Royal Bank of Scotland – however has replaced this by a savings account, for which depositors are issued with a passbook; apart from withdrawing without notice at their own branch, there are limited withdrawal facilities at other branches; interest is calculated on the minimum monthly balance and paid annually. But the big innovation by the Royal was the introduction of 'Cashline deposit accounts', to which may be credited direct salary or wages and on which interest is paid in the same way as on savings accounts; they do not carry cheque-book facilities but are linked to the bank's extensive network of Cashline machines and teller terminals. With Cashline card withdrawals can be made without notice to the extent of the credit balance at one's own branch, with more limited facilities at other pay-out points. No overdrafts are permitted on these accounts, which have increased progressively in popularity. The Scottish banks likewise now offer a range of other deposit packages such as solicitors' special deposit accounts, investment accounts, high interest deposits, etc. In West Germany, the arrangements are quite elaborate, the customer having the option of lodging moneys either at sight or for a variety of maturities up to and exceeding four years, or on a similar basis for fixed periods, or as savings deposits (which over more recent years have become very important), and bank savings bonds. A low rate of interest is paid on sight deposits. Again, in Australia, over a period of many years, deposits have been fixed – for a long time for periods of up to 24 months, but over more recent years for longer periods as well, with appropriate variations in the interest rate payable. Savings-bank business in Australia is conducted by separate institutions, but after 1956 the trading banks, as commercial banks are called in Australia, also set up savings-bank subsidiaries to undertake this business in competition with the Commonwealth Savings Bank, the several State banks (e.g., New South Wales, Victoria, South Australia, and Western Australia) and the two trustee savings banks in Tasmania. The same legislation applies to all savings-bank institutions. Over recent years, the savings banks have offered a whole range of deposit products, or packages including investment accounts, which represent about 50 per cent of total savings-bank deposits.

Likewise, there are different ways of providing the customer with evidence of deposit. In Scotland (as we have seen) and in Australia, the banks issue non-negotiable deposit receipts in acknowledgement of moneys placed on deposit or fixed-deposit account. There is less formality in England. It is merely necessary to fill in a deposit account slip (together with a specimen signature, if it is a new account) and the item is entered in a deposit account under the customer's name. There is no longer a deposit-account book. Statements are issued as required. A receipt would only be issued if requested (e.g., by solicitors).

Over the years, in France, the deposit structure has taken various forms, but basically the division has been between current accounts (demand deposits) – originally *comptes de chèques* (the smaller part) – and *comptes courants*, with time deposits (*bons et comptes à échéance fixe*) much less important. Subsequently, *comptes spéciaux* were introduced; they were offered to individuals and were subject to a maximum rate and a limit on the amount that might be so lodged; they were replaced by *comptes sur livrets* as a result of the banking reforms of 1965-6.[11] They were withdrawable at sight but only on the basis of a passbook. By 1970, the division was between *comptes à vue* (demand deposits) and *comptes à échéance* (time deposits), and – for private individuals – *comptes d'épargne à régime spécial* (a special savings account), plus *bons de caisse* (savings bonds). Latterly, in the 1980s, the main divisions of the deposit structure in France had been between *comptes ordinaires* (demand deposits) – on 3 January 1984, 12.4 per cent of the balance sheet for the *banques inscrites* – and *comptes à terme* (time deposits) – as at the same date, 6.9 per cent – with *comptes d'épargne à régime spécial* (5.0 per cent) shown separately and now rather more important, as are *bons de caisse* (3.2 per cent). *Comptes à terme* are fixed for a predetermined period and when such an account is opened the customer must stipulate in a formal letter for how long he proposes to leave his deposit untouched. The agreement is binding and the depositor cannot make any withdrawals from his account during the term of the deposit. However, the customer may borrow against the security of the time deposit. Like time deposits, *bons de caisse* have a fixed maturity but unlike time deposits they may be transferable (when made repayable to bearer). Otherwise, they may not be cashed before maturity, though they may be borrowed against. In the case both of time deposits and *bons de caisse* higher rates apply on the longer maturities. It should be noted, however, that 34.5 per cent of the total liabilities of the French banks (*banques inscrites*) was now 'bought money' – borrowings and time deposits of banks and other financial institutions (see below), so that in France – as elsewhere – there had been a considerable shift of emphasis over the years.[12] However, these figures relate to the banks registered with the Banking Control Commission. Although comparable figures do not seem to exist for other banking sectors, it is important to note that, in addition to the *banques inscrites*, the Crédit Agricole and the PTT (*Centre de chèques postaux*) are important and other sectors (like the *banques populaires* and the *crédit mutuel*) are significant. Thus, at the end of 1983, the Crédit Agricole attracted 18.0 per cent of total demand deposits (compared with 53.9 per cent by the *banques inscrites*, 14.9 per cent by the PTT, 6.1 per cent by the *banques populaires*, and 2.5 per cent by the *crédit mutuel*). The remaining components of the banking sector are very small.[13] One should note, too, that demand deposits may be held either in French francs or in foreign currencies – for residents, French francs account for 95.8 per cent of the total (for non-residents 1.3 per cent); residents hold 1.25 per cent of the total in foreign currencies (non-residents 1.6 per cent).[14] For passbook deposits, term deposits, bonds, etc., the *banques inscrites* accounted for 27.9 per cent, the Crédit Agricole for 15.6 per cent, the savings banks (*caisses d'épargne*) for 43.8 per cent, the *banques populaires* for 3.0 per cent, and the *crédit mutuel* for 5.3 per cent.[15] Other holdings were very small. Of the total figures, passbook deposits (*livrets* of all kinds) accounted for 56.7 per cent, term deposits for 17.5 per cent, bonds for 17.3 per cent, and *plans d'épargne-logement* for 8.5 per cent.[16]

In the United States, time deposits are an important source of bank funds (on average for all banks at the end of 1983, 44 per cent of total deposits). Savings deposits are also important – 32 per cent as at the same date. The banks have every inducement to attract funds in this way, since the minimum reserves that have to be held against time and savings deposits are much lower than those required against demand deposits. Nevertheless, the relative importance of time deposits varies somewhat from one part of the country to another. The rates paid may also vary across the country, though where banks of similar size operate in the same area competition usually obliges them to pay much the same, formerly sometimes forcing them hard against the ceiling imposed by Regulation Q. In states where branching is extensive, some of the larger banks pay a uniform rate on time deposits at all their branches, but on occasion even the relatively large banks may be forced by local competition to pay different rates at different branches. Sometimes, the actual rate payable is camouflaged by complicated methods of calculating interest. Nevertheless, some banks maintain that established banker-customer relationships and the convenience of transacting savings and personal-borrowing business with the same institution are more important as a means of attracting time deposits than the rate as such, which need not therefore be fully competitive with those paid by other types of institutions.

For the city banks in Japan, a very substantial part of their resources derives from deposits and certificates of deposit. There are several different categories of deposit – current accounts, on which no interest is payable; ordinary deposits (which are like savings deposits, on which a low rate of interest is payable and which for the city banks at the end of 1983 represented about 12.5 per cent of total deposits and for the regional banks 18 per cent); deposits at 7 days' notice (at a slightly higher rate of interest), about 9.8 per cent of the total for the city banks; and time deposits[17] (at appropriate higher rates of interest for the longer maturities) which represent about 61 per cent of the total for the city banks and 63 per cent for the regional banks. For the long-term credit banks (for which deposits are less important) time deposits are about 33 per cent of the total.[18] Interest rates on deposits are the same for all the city banks and tend to be determined in accordance with Bank of Japan guidelines. Time deposits as a proportion of total deposits have over many years been very significant in Japan and have long represented over 50 per cent of total deposits. However, it is possible that this will gradually change, since the public is beginning to invest moneys in government bonds and in overseas securities (like United States Treasury bills), foreign-currency deposits, also the new CDs (see below), even in equities. The current account deposits are definitely in decline as a proportion of total deposits and show a steady shrinkage over recent years. This has been due mainly to more sophisticated fund management by corporations, which tend to invest surplus moneys in CDs, the Gensaki market (see pp. 247-8), or in bonds. Meanwhile, the Ministry of Finance had requested that 'compensatory' or 'compulsory' deposits be reduced or completely abandoned when corporations were arranging a loan from their bankers.[19] In Japan, these deposits were usually for seven days or time deposits. Nevertheless, if good balances are kept by the customer, he can usually obtain accommodation at a lower interest rate; he might also be able to obtain a loan during a period of tight money.

Wholesale or 'Bought' Money

In many countries – but more particularly in those with sophisticated money markets like the United Kingdom (London) and the United States – wholesale or 'bought' money is today a significant element in most bank balance sheets. The process of buying money in large amounts really started with the introduction of the certificate of deposit (CD) in the United States, a development that was greatly assisted in the 1960s when such CDs became 'negotiable' and a secondary market began to develop. These certificates were employed in the United States as a means of trapping the funds of business corporations, which had previously been inclined to choose other forms of financial investment such as Treasury bills. Certificates of deposit had in fact been issued for many years by banks in the United States as paper evidence of the lodgement of time money, but these were largely non-marketable and, as such, had no special value as a monetary instrument. What now made them attractive was their conversion into instruments that could be sold and bought on a secondary market. This new feature was introduced in February 1961, when the First National City Bank of New York (as it then was) introduced its so-called 'negotiable' time certificate of deposit, offered to corporate customers and intended to appeal especially to them by reason of its marketability. The other major money-market banks in New York and elsewhere soon followed suit, some with more enthusiasm than others.

Before 1961, and for many years following the Great Depression of the 1930s, the major money-market banks had restricted the use of time deposits to foreign institutions, state and municipal funds, and charitable organisations. They had been reluctant to offer these facilities to corporate customers, because of the fear that balances would be switched away from demand to time deposits. But after World War II, corporation treasurers with sharp pencils began increasingly to invest their temporarily excess balances in various money-market instruments, including United States and foreign Treasury bills. Time deposits with an American bank had no great appeal for corporation treasurers, because normally they could not be realised before maturity and were therefore illiquid.

Hence, if CDs were to attract corporation treasurers and assist the banks in their fight to retain more of the business deposits available, it was necessary, firstly, to enable the banks to pay interest rates that would be competitive with those paid on near-substitute investment paper (this was assured by a raising of the interest ceilings under Regulation Q) and, secondly, to encourage the development of a secondary market in such certificates. This development became the responsibility primarily of the Discount Corporation in New York (originally formed after World War I to develop a similar market in bankers' acceptances), though subsequently a number of other dealers in New York also began to trade in CDs. If a corporation treasurer had need of his money before the date on which his certificate matured, he could sell it on the market to a dealer at market rates (i.e. subject to any changes that may have taken place in the market since the original contract was entered into) and the dealer in turn would look for another party (usually another corporation) with funds to invest, the dealer making his profit from a market spread of about five basis points (i.e. 0.05 per cent). Normally, the dealer would carry an inventory but he might also have to go out looking for a supply. The names traded were mostly those of the major money-market banks. In addition, there were normally limits placed on the amounts that a treasurer might put under any one name as well as on the total amount he might hold in CDs. But in aggregate a significant and continuing demand soon developed for this new credit instrument, which quickly established itself as a permanent feature of the market scene.

At the same time, the rate initially allowed on a CD remained subject to the ceiling under Regulation Q and the continuing tightness of money towards the end of 1968 encouraged large commercial banks that had set up holding companies to move into the commercial paper market as a means of seeking additional funds. Although not possible for the original bank, its holding company as a commercial concern could issue this kind of paper. The first corporation to make such an issue was Chemical Bank N.Y. Corporation and it was subsequently imitated by Bankers Trust N.Y. Corporation and Conill Corporation (the holding company of Continental Illinois Bank of Chicago). Although not at that time encouraged by the authorities, this market greatly expanded the funds to which the banks had access (as was evidenced by the expansion in commercial and finance company paper to new high levels then totalling in excess of $20 billion).

Despite some lifting of the ceilings from time to time, as long as Regulation Q (which also applied to CDs) remained in place. American banks were prevented from competing as actively as they would have liked for deposits in the United States. Hence, the interest of the American banks in the Euro-dollar market. These operations derived from the acceptance of dollar-claim deposits – created by the United States balance-of-payments deficit and largely foreign-owned – by banks (mostly in Europe) and the lending of these claims to other customers usually for short periods. The development of this market (then largely based in London) was stimulated by the non-resident convertibility of sterling which came at the end of 1958 (non-residents could now exchange European currencies without restriction into dollars).[20] It was also encouraged by the relatively wide spread between borrowing and lending rates in the United States market. Although the United States authorities (as was only natural) initially did all they could to discourage such transactions, United States banks (usually through their overseas branches) borrowed heavily in Euro-dollars as a means of repatriating funds for lending in the United States. It was also a means of financing the operations of United States subsidiaries abroad and avoiding the necessity of transferring funds from the United States.

But the American banks buy wholesale money in other ways besides CDs and Euro-currencies. Over the years (going back to 1921, but only developing into a national market in the 1950s) the buying and selling of federal funds (originally entitlements to balances with a Federal Reserve Bank, of which there are 12 forming with the Federal Reserve Board of Governors the central banking system of the United States) increased progressively in importance both geographically, in the number of banks prepared to act as dealers, and latterly in the range of banks (both large and small) that participated in this market.[21] Based originally on the temporarily surplus balances of member banks of the System with the several Federal Reserve Banks, the federal-funds market has latterly been extended to include virtually all depository institutions (comprehending, for example, not only banks and savings banks, but also savings and loan associations and credit unions), since all these institutions were under the 1980 legislation now required to hold reserves with the Federal Reserve System, not just the member banks as was formerly the case.

Another means of buying (and also selling) money is by means of a re-purchase agreement. This had long been a favoured means of financing dealer portfolios – the dealer selling securities for immediate cash subject to an agreement to repurchase them at a later date. The advantage of this system to the lender was that there was no risk of price fluctuations (as there would have been had he bought securities outright); also he could choose the maturity date he required. The dealer for his part knew that he had the funds for a specified period. Since there were both bank and non-bank government-security dealers, banks also resorted to RPs – first the dealer banks and latterly an increasingly wider range of banks. Such RPs can be done both with other financial institutions and non-financial corporations, also with state and city authorities – indeed, with anybody with a reasonable amount of temporarily surplus funds available for short-term investment.

It is difficult to establish from banking statistics and individual bank balance sheets precisely to what extent banks depend on 'bought' money in the United States, and it does vary over the course of time, but on the basis of Federal Reserve figures,[22] for all large weekly-reporting banks, about 18 per cent of total liabilities derived from federal funds purchased and securities sold under agreements to repurchase; for large weekly-reporting banks in the city of New York, the figure was about 25 per cent in early 1984. This does not take into account CDs, but for banks that provide such data in their annual reports, the total figure would certainly be of the order of 30 to 35 per cent, in some cases up to 50 per cent. This compares with the results of field work over all the Federal Reserve Districts during the second half of 1979, when the author found that a large number of banks were raising a significant proportion of their resources in the form of 'bought' money – federal funds, Repos, large negotiable CDs, and Euro-dollars – the concentration being very much in the area of 30 to 40 per cent of total liabilities, with some as high as 70 to 80 per cent (the latter figures seem to be dangerously high to the author and there is reason to believe that such banks subsequently adopted more conservative policies in the matter of 'bought' money).

Although somewhat different in kind, refernce should also be made here to the financial-futures markets, the most important in the USA being that in Chicago (based on the activities of its famous Commodity Exchange and experience with commodity futures); latterly, New York has also provided these facilities. In Chicago, this type of transaction dates back to about the mid-1970s. Briefly, a futures contract specifies that the seller of the contract will deliver whatever item the contract is for to the buyer at some future date at some fixed price. In the United States, futures contracts are standardised agreements made and traded on exchanges that are chartered, designated, and licensed to serve as a trading arena in specific futures contacts. By way of contrast with forward contracts, delivery is rarely made in connection with futures contracts. Instead a buyer of a futures contract will typically close out his position before the contract matures by making an offsetting sale of the same contract, a seller by making an offsetting purchase, the reason being that people enter into futures contracts either to offset risk on a long or short position in a 'commodity', i.e. to hedge that position by taking an equal and offsetting position in futures, or to speculate on a change in the price of the 'commodity' or a change in price spreads.[23] The users of financial futures include money- and bond-market dealers (which would involve a number of the big banks), arbitrageurs and speculators ('without the liquidity they give the market, there would be no market').

> Dealers, particularly of long bonds, quickly saw that the sale of futures contracts was an attractive alternative to short sales as a hedging device. The use of futures to hedge has increased dealers' ability to bid for and position securities during difficult markets, and that in turn, has contributed to liquidity in the cash market.[24]

Some of the more common items dealt in include United States Treasury bonds and bills, certificates of deposit, three-month Eurodollars, GNMA (Ginnie Maes), and a number of major foreign-currency contracts (including sterling). The contract that really took off was that in bill futures, the volume of which rose 'rapidly and dramatically'; in fact, 'the market in bill futures came to be used more widely and more rapidly than any futures market ever had been'.[25]

In the early 1960s, the English banks, whose competition for deposits had been subject to a gentlemen's agreement limiting the interest rates that could be offered, began to expand (or in some cases to initiate) flexible back-door competition for deposits (through subsidiaries at rates higher than were permitted under the gentlemen's agreement that bound their London principals).[26] Subsequently, negotiable certificates of deposit denominated in sterling were also launched in London. The scheme had been in preparation for some time and was introduced on 28 October 1968, following the successful development of a market in dollar certificates of deposit, which were introduced in the United Kingdom in May 1966. The new CDs were issued for a minimum amount of £50,000 and at that time could run up in multiples of £10,000 to a maximum of £250,000. (By the early 1980s, the effective minimum size had become £250,000, the average about £500,000 and, for marketing reasons, £1 million was the maximum.) The primary market consisted of the issuers of the certificates and these included the deposit-taking subsidiaries of the clearing banks, the overseas and merchant banks. The minimum period for which a certificate was issued in the primary market was three months and this was in fact the most popular term. Once they had been issued, the CDs could be sold in the secondary market which was serviced by the discount houses. They not only bought CDs (often from the banks themselves) but held them in portfolios.[27] selling them off to banks and others in response to demand. In a situation in which bills had been in short supply, this enabled the market (including the banks) to obtain paper at virtually any maturity up to three months. Usually, the CDs were only held by the dealers for a very short time, so that in effect the discount market was in this context also performing its traditional function as a broker.

By the time the London clearing banks submitted their evidence to the Wilson Committee, there were about 140 banks in London which had been given permission to issue them. Largely because of their ready marketability, CDs could be issued with longer maturities than most other wholesale deposits, which was an important consideration in view of the growth that had by then begun in the banks' term lending. The value of sterling CDs expanded rapidly after the introduction of the new policy of Competition and Credit Control by the Bank of England in September 1971 and quickly outpaced that of London issues of dollar CDs, though sterling CDs declined heavily after November 1973; this was due to a fall in the demand for bank credit, which led to less reliance on CDs and inter-bank funds, which was the other major source of wholesale money.[28]

The inter-bank market went back to the mid-1950s,[29] but by the early 1970s it had grown considerably and was used by a widening range of institutions (including the London clearing banks and the Scottish banks).[30] Money is lent through brokers[31] on an unsecured basis both overnight and for various periods up to one year. Because moneys traded in are unsecured, arrangements are less formal, though the attendant risks are higher and banks impose limits on their transactions in order to reduce the degree of exposure by operating over a wider spread. This is also true in the Euro-currency markets,[32] which also became an important source of wholesale money.

The proportion of total liabilities attracted by the banks in the form of wholesale money increased rapidly until by 1973 – for the London clearing bank groups – it was over 45 per cent of total sterling deposits; latterly, there was a fall in the proportion to 39 per cent (1975) and 41.5 per cent (1976) due to a fall in the demand for lending.[33] In recent years, the figures have built up again – 44 per cent in 1980, 48 per cent (1981), 57 per cent (1982), and almost 60 per cent in 1983. Latterly, CDs have represented between 5 and 6 per cent of total sterling deposits.[34] In fact, the figures fluctuate not only between years – and vary for different times of the year – but also will differ between the several large banks, depending on the pattern of their business. All banks, too, tend to experience seasonal fluctuations in their deposits. Thus, in most years, deposits tend to increase from March to May, when loans tend to fall. On the other hand, loans are likely to be high in November, when there would tend to be a need for more wholesale money. Another factor in determining the level of deposits is the competition from building societies and also from National Savings as well as the interest rates being paid. On the whole, the big banks seem to feel that the resources that derive from current accounts and deposit accounts (seven days' notice) are relatively stable. The special deposit packages introduced some years ago (largely in an effort to meet building-society competition)[35] only seem to have contributed in a small way. Hence, when there is need of more money, the wholesale markets will be tapped.

However, in interpreting the figures, the definition of wholesale money is also of relevance. For example, wholesale branch deposits are for all the big banks an important source of funds. On amounts of £10,000 and over (£25,000 in one large bank) market-related rates are paid[36] and a large part of a bank's funding comes in from the branches in this way (sometimes such branch money may amount to almost 50 per cent of the total wholesale money of a bank). In this respect, one might compare the position in the United Kingdom with that of Canada, where the large banks also have a highly developed branch system. For the rest, sterling wholesale money would derive from CDs (the smaller part)[37] and the inter-bank market. Even when banks do not really have need of money, they may well issue a CD in order to meet a customer's requirement. And by no means always are the big banks borrowers in the inter-bank market. One bank may at times be a net lender of funds; another a net borrower; but all would tend regularly to be in and out on one side or the other, depending on whether they are experiencing a temporary surplus of funds or a shortage. For the most part, the banks would use the services of a money broker, but deals may also be done direct.

The estimates of a bank's position on which money management is based can be made difficult by sudden movements of large deposits whether in or out); hence early advice of such movements is sought; alternatively, when rates move, customers may suddenly draw down their overdrafts (possibly to arbitrage) and this could result in a sudden loss of deposits; there may be hold-ups in the clearing, which could be embarrassing, though banks tend to know which customers are likely to be a problem and therefore keep an eye on them; and, finally, it is not unknown for errors to throw a spanner in the works.

During periods of interest-rate uncertainty, the average maturity of wholesale money has tended to shorten, but the banks will do anything at a price and if a customer really wanted a six-month CD, a bank will quote, though usually banks issue CDs to a discount house, which sells them on. If they are interested, the big companies buy CDs in the secondary market. In the matter of the maturity of CDs, another factor that deserves mention is the way in which the majority of term loans is 'rolled over'. Clearly, if the loan demand is increasing beyond what can be handled on the basis of branch originating resources, the wholesale-money markets must be approached. But, in addition, for term loans it has become common to undertake a certain amount of 'matching' (virtually always, if it is a Euro-currency loan) such that money is bought at a certain rate for either three or six months and a related rate is charged over the equivalent period on the term loan, which is 'rolled over' from period to period subject to a rate adjustment. In this way, interest-rate exposure is eliminated.[38] Hence, there will be some demand for three-and six month money.

Another basis of adjustment in which the banks have become interested is the financial-futures market in London, where the 'commodities' dealt in are either an interest-rate or a currency contract. Interest-rate contracts include a 20-year 12% notional gilt (in effect, a package of gilts to yield 12%) and an 8% US Treasury Bond. There are contracts in three-month Euro-dollars and three-month sterling deposits and currency contracts in sterling, Deutsch marks, Swiss francs, and Japanese yen. Customers themselves can also hedge in this market. The parties that participate are the hedger, on the one hand, and the trader (speculator) on the other. The discount houses are partly hedgers, partly speculators. For a deal to be accommodated, there need to be equal and opposite views.

After the Scottish banks entered the hire-purchase field in the late 1950s in competition with the finance companies, they began to seek funds for fixed periods usually at a higher rate of interest as a basis for extending their medium-term lending. Hire-purchase companies were already advertising extensively for longer-term funds, which suited the nature of their lending and on which they were prepared to pay higher rates. Once the Scottish banks had their own hire-purchase interests, they could offer these higher rates to their customers, while still keeping the funds within the group. In the early 1960s – unable to compete in the wholesale markets themselves because of restrictive agreements – most of the Scottish banks set up 'bidding subsidiaries' to do so. Latterly, following the introduction of Competition and Credit Control in 1971, the banks themselves began to offer higher rates for larger sums for fixed periods, but while in total the amounts were substantial (term deposits of Scottish clearing banks and their banking subsidiaries amounted to over £480 million by November 1976), they still only represented a modest proportion of the overall figures. The inter-bank market, on the other hand, which enabled surplus funds in the hands of one bank to be borrowed unsecured to offset a shortage elsewhere in the banking system, remained a relatively small source for Scottish clearing banks' funds; more often than not, the net position indicated that the Scottish banks were lenders to this market. That was also true – from 1974 to 1976 – of the use made of the London market in negotiable sterling certificates of deposit. However, since 1980, the Scottish clearing bank groups seemed to have resorted to CDs rather more than in the past and the proportion of total sterling deposits raised by way of CDs, which was something less than 4 per cent in 1978 and 1979, rose to about 7.5 per cent in 1980 and 1981, falling to just over 5 per cent in 1983. Time deposits meanwhile increased from 55 per cent in 1978 to 67 per cent in 1982 and 1983.[39] Where the Scottish banks had become rather more active was in attracting foreign-currency deposits. This began about 1971 and became by far the fastest growing sector of their business, with the equivalent of £621 million outstanding in November 1976. This grew steadily (and particularly in 1981 and 1982) to reach the equivalent of £2,682 million by 1983, of which nearly 82 per cent were time deposits.

Scottish banks have always had a high proportion of interest-bearing deposit accounts, but current accounts have also tended to hold up rather more than for the English banks. On the whole, the deposit base of the banks in Scotland seems to have remained fairly stable. Indeed, the bulk of their 'wholesale' money also comes from their own customers through their branches, large deposits attracting interest rates related to money-market rates. With the introduction of mortgage lending against house properties, a bank might sometimes find loans running away with them making it necessary to go into the market (inter-bank market or by issuing CDs). Subsidiaries of the Scottish banks (e.g., the merchant-banking arms and/or finance houses) have also been funded at least in part from the market. However, the Scottish banks tend to use the inter-bank market less than the English banks, though at times they can be significant placers of funds and, of course, the inter-bank market will be used from time to time as an overnight borrower for purposes of short-term adjustment. Inter-bank transactions are mostly done through brokers and in London (as are issues of CDs). As in England, big term loans tend to be matched – particularly Euro-currency loans – with a rate adjustment every three or six months, though formal term lending has probably not increased as much in Scotland as in England.

Because of its proximity to the United States, one would expect the Canadians to follow something like American practice in their funding arrangements. But there is a big structural difference in banking arrangements between the two countries, namely, the importance of retail banking in Canada on the basis of what are usually nationwide networks of branches. Some of the 'retail' money, i.e. money coming in through the branches, is in relatively large amounts on which market rates are paid. In effect, it is 'semi-wholesale money', whereas wholesale money proper would be in really big chunks (e.g., $500,000 or $1 million). It is also relevant to observe that for the big banks with nationwide networks of branches management of their day-to-day money positions is never likely to be easy even if the required cash reserves can be averaged out over a period of approximately two weeks. By advising large cash movements (whether in or out) from the branches, everything is done to take these into account, though in fact the major changes in available resources tend to result from movements on the international side of the banks' business.

Wholesale or bought money in Canada is of several kinds. Some use is made of an instrument that is somewhat similar to the negotiable CD in New York. This is the bearer discount note (BDN), which is bearer in form, sold at a discount, and negotiable. They have varying maturities of up to one year. The banks tend to sell them to dealers as a means of getting money fast. There is also a reasonably active secondary market, where holders can liquidate them. CDs are not nearly as important as they are in the United States. Few are negotiable and the secondary market is not very active. Non-negotiable CDs can be encashed prior to maturity, but subject to a sacrifice of interest. None the less, when interest rates rise, it is not unusual to encash outstanding certificates and to reinvest the moneys at a higher rate. For some banks, resort to the inter-bank call money market is quite significant, though more particularly towards the end of the period over which cash reserves may be averaged. Sometimes, it is used as an adjustment instrument in connection with the management of a bank's cash position as an alternative to selling Treasury bills or commercial paper held in portfolio. Also, when the banks become short of money, they may buy US dollar deposits which are then swapped into Canadian dollars in order to support Canadian asset demands. In short, there is generally a lot of rolling over of bank liabilities. The resort to swaps is interesting, because the banks secure money from 90 days to six months on the basis of a northbound swap, whereas corporations not infrequently put out their temporarily surplus moneys in the form of southbound swaps. Indirectly, therefore, the Canadian banks may often be borrowing from their own corporation customers. These moneys are now subject to required reserves under the Bank Act 1980. This is not the same thing as attracting Euro-dollar deposits, which is often done through branches outside Canada, and used specifically to fund international loans also in Euro-dollars. Business done in US dollars is quite large.

On the funding side, Canadian banks have become very much more wholesale institutions than they used to be. For one of the bigger banks, bought money might represent about 40 per cent of total resources. It depends, of course, on how one defines it and, if one is thinking only of wholesale money proper – bought in big chunks, the figure might come down to 30 per cent. For one of the largest banks, bought money may amount to 25 per cent of the total, but almost 45 per cent if semi-bought money (e.g., coming in from branches) is included, whereas for another of the largest banks it would be no more than 20 per cent. This should be contrasted with the experience of some of the newer small banks, which operate a wholesale business on both sides of the balance sheet; wholesale money (bought through investment dealers from municipalities, banks and corporations) constitutes the bulk of their available funds. Such moneys would be purchased against the issue of non-transferable CDs and (negotiable) BDNs. The bulk of such bank lending is in the form of term loans, with foreign lending financed by Euro-deposits. The call money market is used to put out any temporary surpluses (e.g., if a customer elects to prepay a loan).

Over the years since 1969, several countries have introduced certificates of deposit – Australia (1969), Spain (1969), New Zealand (1977), Japan (1979), Sweden (1980), and Italy (1983). Their possible introduction has been discussed in Austria, Norway, Finland, and latterly in France. It is proposed to consider these countries first in the context of wholesale money, reserving the latter part of our discussion for countries that depend on other kinds of technique.

As has been indicated, negotiable CDs go back to 1969 in Australia, but their original introduction proved to be only moderately successful, mainly because of the ceiling on interest rates. Negotiable CDs were also liable to stamp duty. Subsequently, this was abolished in certain states (initially, Victoria and New South Wales) to be replaced by a broader financial-transactions tax. CDs were freed from all interest-rate controls in September 1973. For a time, the amounts attracted against the issue of CDs were small and their significance was really only marginal, the banks resorting to them mainly when their liquidity was threatened and they needed an urgent addition to their funds. In other words, issues of CDs (minimum size of A$100,000) were then used mainly for 'topping up' a bank's liquidity. Latterly (mid-1983), CDs outstanding, subject to some variation from month to month, have exceeded A$4,000 million (compared with over A$20,000 million for the fixed deposits of all trading banks and over A$12,000 million in current accounts). Some banks still regard CDs as a basis of marginal adjustment; others consider them as a means of sustaining a desired level of lending. Resort to CDs is also likely to become increasingly important with the establishment of a relatively active secondary market. Another source of money (no longer subject to a maximum interest rate) are large market-orientated deposits (in amounts of over A$50,000), where rates are negotiable, though less volatile than on CDs. 'Big' deposits may be accepted for terms of 14 days to four years. It remains true that time deposits provide a more stable pool of money than CDs.

In New Zealand, authority for trading banks to issue transferable certificates of deposit (TCDs) was given in November 1971. TCDs are registered in a name, but can be transferred from holder to holder. Initially, the minimum term was two years. This was reduced to six months in November 1973 and to 30 days in March 1978. Latterly, the most popular maturity has been 90-180 days. Amounts at issue vary, but by 1983 a total of NZ$945 million had been exceeded. For negotiable CDs, authority to introduce which was given to the trading banks in late 1977, holdings have been small, never exceeding NZ$7 million and more recently they have at times disappeared. NCDs are bearer instruments, but carry stamp duty. Savings banks do not issue TCDs or NCDs, but they usually hold them in order to protect their liquidity. For the trading banks, the attraction of wholesale deposits mostly against the issue of TCDs is the most important element in trading bank management of short-term funds; they may be held as well as being issued. In other words, they can be used to absorb funds as well as to attract them and may therefore be used as a liquid-funds management instrument on either side of the balance sheet. For obvious reasons, however, banks are not permitted to hold their own

CDs.

Of the additional countries to experiment in introducing CDs, Spain was one of the earliest. When CDs were first permitted in 1969, only the industrial banks (which were rather like the French *banques d'affaires*) could issue CDs and they remained relatively important as issuers. After 1974, all banks might do so. They were issued in multiples of Pta. 1 million (about £5,000), which was also the minimum size. Since this was really very small, issues of Pta. 5 million soon became more common. They are subject to a small stamp tax (levied in relation to nominal value). Interest rates were free of regulation for CDs of over six months and there was therefore an incentive to issue them for a period of one day more than six months. CDs could be redeemed before maturity subject to a 4 per cent penalty (introduced by the authorities in January 1981), but it was also possible for a customer to sell his CD to another customer of the bank. Indeed, something of a secondary market began to develop on the basis of bank branches advising the Madrid office (or the head office elsewhere) of CDs that customers wished to sell, or alternatively of bids for CDs that might come up for sale, when the two sets of transactions could be paired. But it was usually a matter of several days before deals could be consummated. In a true secondary market, the significance of which is that a holder of a CD can disinvest easily and quickly, the transaction would be effected within the day. After they were originally authorised, total issues of CDs only increased slowly; then they began to grow rather more rapidly (the interest rate was relatively high) until they constituted something like 15 per cent of total bank funds (excluding capital), where they tended to stabilise.

Another source of finance – largely pioneered by the foreign banks but also used by the Spanish domestic banks – is the commercial bill or bankers acceptance, which can subsequently be sold on (hence its interest to the foreign banks, which lack a developed deposit base) through the stock exchange. The bank will draw a bill against the firm to which it is lending and which accepts it. Formerly, this bill would have gone into the bank's portfolio to be held until maturity. Now the bank sells this bill on the market to somebody who wants to invest his moneys for the relevant period with full recourse against the bank. Formerly, transactions were effected through stockbrokers who charged a small commission and a bill once traded was kept for a small fee with the stock exchange as a depository.[40] When the bill matures, the bank makes provision for payment and recovers the money from the firm in question to which it has lent. This market in commercial bills was started in 1980 and has been growing fairly rapidly, though it is still only a marginal activity.

Certificates of deposit were introduced by the Swedish commercial banks in March 1980. They were intended for the short-term investment of fairly large sums, with a minimum of SKr 1 million and, in principle, multiples thereof. In a sense, they were a substitute for deposits on 'special conditions' (see below). The size traded in is usually SKr 10 million, but there are a lot of SKr 1,2 and 3 million CDs on issue, though these are not normally traded. They tend to be held. There is no stamp duty on CDs. The certificates are made out to bearer and show the date of maturity and nominal amount (including interest). Terms vary between 30 and 360 days. The certificate can be sold at any time prior to maturity for immediate cash and without any fee. The rates of interest, and thus the prices of the certificates, depends on the general level of interest rates which in turn reflect the supply of and demand for liquid funds in banks and companies. Rates of interest for different remaining terms are quoted daily on the stock exchange. CDs provide an alternative to deposits on 'special conditions' and by December 1980 for all commercial banks amounted to 7.5 per cent of total deposits plus CDs; the figure had declined to 6.4 per cent by the end of 1981 but had risen to 7.7 per cent by the end of 1982. CDs are issued by the banks primarily to the insurance companies, large business corporations, and local authorities, and these are the prime traders in the secondary market, though the banks may also hold another bank's CDs.[41] The large banks will buy the CDs of the smaller regional banks if they pay well, though they know they will not be able to re-sell them on the secondary market. The Central Bank for Savings also holds other banks' CDs. Banks may buy back their own CDs from time to time.[42] But as the secondary market develops this will become less necessary. Finance companies may *not* issue CDs, but they may buy them on the secondary market to hold in their own portfolios. It is a telephone market at the rates quoted on the stock exchange and there are no brokers. CDs are not issued with a maturity of less than a month and may be issued with a maturity of up to 12 months. Typically, maturities are 1-3 months. The banks will tend to do swaps or RPs (in government securities or in CDs) to absorb funds for less than a month – commonly, say, for 2, 3, or 5 days (e.g., for window-dressing at month-ends). Money can also be obtained for short periods on 'special conditions' (see below). But there can be little doubt that CDs have given greater stability to funds management.

Formerly, the banks[43] offered deposits on 'special conditions' (introduced in the 1960s) and they still do – as a basis of competing for the big money of business corporations, especially when they are highly liquid.[44] Rates are negotiable, but tend to vary with the penalty rate of the Riksbank, also the rate on CDs. Formerly, it was by no means a perfect market, since deals tended to be bilateral in character and a knowledge of what was going on elsewhere in the market was not always complete. Now with the issue of CDs and the market for 'wholesale' money, the market in special deposits has become much more sophisticated. Such deposits may be accepted for seven or 15 days or for three months.[45] There is the possibility of prepayment – this also is negotiable. Regional banks have a lot of special deposits, but some of these have now gone into CDs, which they also issue. These they guarantee to buy back at market price, if necessary. Both the savings banks and the Central Bank for Savings also do special deposit deals.

The attraction of moneys by issuing negotiable CDs was introduced in Japan in May 1979. The amount of CDs outstanding increased rapidly, especially after the third quarter of 1981. Some banks use this instrument more than others. The minimum size for a CD is Y500 million. By early 1984, banks could issue up to 75 per cent of their capital account by way of CDs (it had been raised in steps from 25 per cent). Foreign banks can also issue CDs up to a limit set by the Ministry of Finance. The maturity of CDs must be between three and six months. Six-months' maturity is the absolute limit for domestic CDs. Interest rates are freely determined and slightly higher than on ordinary deposits. Tanshi houses act as brokers in the secondary market,[46] as also banks and their affiliated companies for other banks' CDs. Banks may hold other banks' CDs and do so from time to time, but mainly for the purpose of re-selling these CDs to their corporate customers, which buy them for the purpose of absorbing their temporarily surplus funds. It is through this secondary market, too, that a holder of a CD can sell his instrument at the current market price and thereby disinvest. However, CDs were initially 'registered' in Japan and not payable to bearer. Hence, when a purchaser sold a CD, the consent of the issuer's bank was required – the 'registered claim transfer formula'. But it was the intention that Japan would change to a payable-to-order or bearer system.

Another market in Japan that has become relevant to CDs is the Gensaki market, which is primarily used by banks to place funds with securities houses, the transaction being effected by way of a re-purchase agreement, or buy-back. This market goes back to the beginning of the 1950s.[47] Although used by banks, much of Gensaki business is carried out by parties other than banks (e.g. by parties that can not resort to the inter-bank market). Once the growth in the issue of CDs accelerated after the third quarter of 1981, Gensaki trading (swap transactions) was introduced to the CD market as well.

In a number of other countries, however, the issue of negotiable CDs has not been favoured as a means of attracting wholesale money. Thus, in West Germany, in order to achieve greater equilibrium in their deposit structure, which for the biggest banks largely depends on retail deposits now less stable than they perhaps once were, the banks are accustomed to attract from customers 'wholesale money' or large deposits for which the market is very flexible and very competitive. This is a relatively new development – it was the foreign banks that began to buy wholesale moneys for short periods – and relates to large sums of money bought from customers for three, four or five days, whereas the minimum period for a time deposit is 30 days. An obvious question is why CDs were not introduced for the purpose and some bankers would prefer CDs, though the authorities are not keen; other bankers maintain that they can already raise all the deposits they require without resorting to CDs.

Large deposits are also sought after by all the banks in Austria, but the source of such deposits is less likely to be the large corporations (which can usually employ the moneys to better purpose in their own businesses and in any case prefer term deposits) as wealthy individuals and professional people (like doctors and lawyers). Many of these deposits are for short periods only. Interest rates would relate to money-market rates and are negotiable. These deposits tend not to be nearly as large as savings deposits, but for the banks constitute a useful additional resource. It has not been increasing in recent years, though it does fluctuate from time to time. No doubt, the banks could attract a lot more if they were prepared to compete for it – it is a question of profitability. Also, although the big depositors shop around, rates tend to come into line, as a result of competition; in any case, the package of services provided is often as important as the rate.

One might note that the possibility of introducing certificates of deposit to meet this kind of demand has been discussed in Austria, but rates on large deposits are comparable to what CDs might attract and, in any case, the Austrian market is probably too small to permit the development of a proper secondary market, so that the holder of a CD could withdraw his funds by sale if he wished. In any event, the Austrian banks will usually allow withdrawal of a deposit prior to maturity.

As we have seen, in France, about one-third of total liabilities has been bought money (34.5 per cent on 3 January 1984). This derives from borrowings and time deposits of banks and other financial institutions, There is much borrowing and lending inter-bank. The vast majority of these transactions are done *en pension*,[48] though a few are *en blanc* or unsecured. Another source of bought money would be currency 'swaps' (in Euro-currencies – primarily Euro-dollars), usually for three to six months but up to 12 months, with forward cover.

Another country where the buying of large deposits is important is Italy and this is reflected in interest rates. One should note, too, that the difference between savings and current accounts has all but disappeared in Italy so far as the rate of interest is concerned. People are tending to move their moneys from savings accounts into current accounts – they are paid much the same rate of interest and receive in addition a wider range of services. None the less, one still gets marked differences between the deposit structures of different commercial banks – in some, savings accounts are relatively small; in others, still fairly important. But the really attractive rates are paid on large deposits of the order of L1 billion and upwards – these would be, say, 2 per cent higher than on a deposit of L500,000. Smaller banks may pay 3 per cent more. In fact, it is a somewhat imperfect market and rates are negotiable.[49]

One means of raising both large amounts and money at longer term is by means of the 'private placements' employed in the Netherlands.[50] These may be arranged with pension funds and insurance companies through brokers and would be for at least five to seven years. They may go up to 25-30 years. In the early 1980s, the limit was about 20 years.

In Belgium, wholesale money derives from large deposits purchased from business corporations, which deposits are often short-term and on which market-related rates are paid. On the inter-bank market, also, the sums lent and borrowed can be quite significant. Such borrowings are normally unsecured, but are subject to internal limits set by the banks themselves.

The Nordic countries (apart from Sweden, which has already been discussed) operate in a somewhat similar way – by attracting wholesale money (in Norway and Denmark as 'special deposits'). In Norway, special deposits are usually for large amounts and would run for between seven days and three months, with a preference on average for three months; occasionally, they could go out to 12 months. Only one of the big banks habitually uses a broker (when both buyer and seller each pay $\frac{1}{8}$ per cent per annum as commission). Local and district banks use this market a great deal and a significant part of the market relates to banks outside Oslo – commercial and savings banks. The lenders are mostly industrial and commercial companies (including shipping companies). It is said that the market is rather unsophisticated and somewhat imperfect. On the whole, the banks prefer to do direct deals. Normally, transactions are in amounts of Kr1 million to Kr10 million. It is a telephone market and transactions take place between 9 a.m. and noon, since all transactions must go through the Bank of Norway by noon. Usually, it is the banks that are looking for money and the corporations that are seeking an outlet for short-term investment. 'Special deposits' in Denmark are often lodged for one month – about 50 per cent would be for this period – but they are also accepted for short periods, especially when they are large amounts (e.g., over a weekend for a big customer). The market for special deposits is imperfect and subject to negotiated deals – e.g., on rates. They represent a varying amount of total domestic deposits, depending both on the liquidity position of the bank and of its customers. The position in Finland is slightly different. Some wholesale money is borrowed by banks for short periods from big customers and from municipalities; this is sometimes done on the basis of a re-purchase agreement. The rate of interest tends to be quite high and there is a minimum amount. This type of activity has existed for some time and already contributes to the banks' funds management. Deals are done on the telephone and are based on confidence in the other parties, though a receipt is also sent.

A separate word might be said about resort to the Euro-currency markets, on which all these countries depend at least to some extent. Quite apart from the British and American banks, it is also important for banks in a number of other countries – West Germany, France, Italy,[51] the Netherlands, Belgium, Switzerland, and Spain. Japan perhaps more than other countries resorts to both the Euro-dollar and the Asian dollar markets. The Nordic countries, too, borrow considerably from abroad, a proportion of it in Euro-currencies. On the other hand, Euro-currencies as a source of funds are rather less important in Austria than in some other countries. The general pattern is for banks to borrow in Euro-currencies for on-lending to domestic borrowers in the same Euro-currency; in due course, the loan must be repaid in the relevant Euro-currency; the borrowing customer carries the exchange risk, though he may cover himself by buying forward. Euro-currency funding usually relates to Euro-currency lending; likewise when the borrowing and lending is off shore. Sometimes, there is funding from a combination of domestic sources and Euro-currencies. Also, if there is a shortage of Euro-currency and a surplus of domestic money, there may be a transfer of resources to foreign branches (e.g., by banks in West Germany, France, the Netherlands, and Switzerland), though this would depend on relative interest rates. From time to time, swap operations may be undertaken (e.g., by banks in West Germany, France, and Belgium).

What then are the essential determinants of the 'inertia' of deposits? In general terms, the willingness of the public to leave the balance of their moneys whether on current or deposit account with a bank for either a fixed or indefinite period will depend (i) on the confidence of the public both in the individual institution and in the stability of the banking system itself; (ii) on the strength of the banking habit (itself a function of the degree of confidence); and (iii) on variations in the demand for cash and in liquidity preference.

Relative inertia in deposit balances generally (and not merely in time deposits) is most obviously a function of confidence in the banking system. On current accounts, the public will withdraw and re-deposit continuously, the balance left on deposit with their bankers representing their surplus cash holdings. It is only when they fear possible collapse of the banks, or of the currency, that they move out of bank deposits into cash (i.e. notes and coin), gold, other currencies, or other commodities that may serve as stores of value.

Confidence in the banks and a developed banking habit go together, though the banking habit may be further encouraged by education, propaganda and advertisement. Indeed, the main reason for the introduction of new banking services is often to foster the extension of the banking habit to a wider range of customers (and if possible to attract somebody else's customers to one's own institution).

The third factor relates both to the transactions demand for money and to the demand for money to hold. Fluctuations in the transactions demand for cash due to seasonal influences are a common experience. The Christmas and summer holiday efflux of notes is a well-known phenomenon. There may also be seasonal demands to finance the movement of crops and exports, as in India, Pakistan, Sri Lanka and Australia. Variations in the degree of liquidity preference, however, are more difficult to forecast. In general terms, the demand for liquidity is a function of uncertainty. The most radical changes occur during times of considerable monetary disturbance. Thus, in the event of a threat of war, or of political instability, or of persistent inflation, the proportion of total deposits which are fixed, or subject to some kind of notice, has generally declined. People have preferred to have money available on demand just in case it should be required urgently. In extreme cases, they will withdraw their money altogether and prefer hard cash to bank deposits. Indeed, in such circumstances, they may not be satisfied even with cash. On the other hand, once war has broken out and a war economy has been established, the imposition of physical controls together with the creation of new money to finance the war effort will usually result in a marked increase in holdings of liquid resources, whether the public actively desires it or not. Immediately after a war, however, the necessity of re-stocking the economy provides an inducement to remain temporarily liquid in anticipation of the related expenditures. Inflation that can be more or less effectively suppressed will always result in an increase in total liquidity, which may then be run down fairly gradually as controls are relaxed; but 'open' inflation with rapidly rising prices will act as a deterrent to the holding of idle money, since the public will attempt to convert their money into goods before prices rise still further (as in Japan in 1946-8 and the United Kingdom in 1967-9). Conversely, deflation and a sagging price level will encourage the holding of idle balances. If prices are expected to fall further, there is little inducement to spend.

In the judgement of some authorities,[52] neither the theoretical mobility of the current-account deposit nor the proportion of total deposits held in deposit account are of great significance under English conditions. Indeed, if it were not possible to assume that the total of demand deposits would remain relatively stable – at least in the short period – the business of deposit banking as we know it would not be a practicable proposition. All the larger payments transactions in a modern society (and many of the smaller ones) are settled simply by transferring these deposits from one owner to another. For such purposes, virtually all businesses and a large number of private persons find it essential to hold deposits, on which they can draw on demand. From the point of view of the banks, these arrangements have the advantage that deposits can be attracted without paying interest on them (none the less, the costs of operating cheque accounts are not insignificant), and, further, the maintenance of large total balances, broadly related to the money value of the national income, can in fact always be relied upon. 'Individual balances go up and down, depositors come and depositors go, but the total on current account goes on for ever.'[53]

From the point of view of the individual bank, the attribute of these deposits that is most frequently stressed is the obligation to repay them on demand,

> from which an inference commonly drawn is that the banker should be especially cautious in his 'use' of these deposits. This theoretical mobility of the current account deposit has at times been invoked in support of the practice of making overdrafts formally repayable on demand and of the policy of confining bank lending to highly liquid purposes. This consideration has, no doubt, great force when banks are small and insecure, but firmly established banks as large as the present English banks can . . . safely regard their demand liabilities in total as containing a hard core of permanent resources.[54]

It should also be added that, these days, there is a central bank in the background willing to act as a lender of last resort and to provide the ultimate safeguard.

Under English conditions, too, moneys received on 'deposit account' (usually repayable at seven days' notice and on which interest is paid) have characteristics not greatly different from those held in current account. Although moneys on deposit account are not directly subject to cheque, there is in practice little objection to the occasional transfer of moneys from deposit account to current account for the purposes of enabling a cheque to be met, or (subject to a sacrifice of interest) to encashment on demand. Furthermore, it is not an uncommon experience for a rise in interest rates to be followed by transfers of funds from current account to deposit account, the increase in the latter continuing only so long as the higher level of deposit rates is maintained, with the probability of a transfer in the opposite direction when rates on deposit account fall back to their former level. Although such shifts between demand and time deposits (or vice versa) may on occasion be quite sizeable, it is unlikely that the degree of inertia (or volatility, as the case may be) will vary by as much as the changed relation between the two categories of deposit.

From the depositor's point of view, a balance on deposit account has almost as much 'moneyness' as one in current account. Moreover, bankers, 'although they may sometimes speak of deposit accounts as more stable than current accounts, nevertheless in practice appear to lump all their deposit liabilities together, and to treat them as in effect repayable on demand.'[55] Nevertheless, the Radcliffe Committee agreed that the 'differential nature of the deposit account' (or time deposit) is 'more important in other countries where the periods of notice are longer than the seven days which has become standard (in England), and where indeed the terms on which these deposits are taken vary over a wide range both of periods and of interest rates'. They implied that even an effective minimum period of one month (as in Scotland) was sufficient to justify a more traditional attitude.

So far as the behaviour of demand deposits is concerned, the means of measurement most commonly employed relates to their rate of turnover, or velocity of circulation. Even if their total volume remained much the same, their rate of turnover might fluctuate quite markedly and, indeed, inversely to movements in volume. Such estimates are based on the figures for bank clearings and the average of demand deposits over a related period. But there are many pitfalls. Obviously, rates of deposit turnover will reflect whatever in a particular instance are the specific institutional arrangements on which payments are based. Furthermore, the limitations of the underlying statistical data are bound to reflect in estimates of rates of deposit turnover.[56]

Another aspect of deposits that deserves some attention relates to their 'protection'. In countries that have at various times been subject to panic withdrawals of deposits and associated bank crises, deposit insurance has sometimes been favoured as a means of inspiring the necessary degree of confidence in the banking system. In the United States, for example, the Federal Deposit Insurance Corporation was established in 1933 and, through its agency, the deposits of all insured banks and financial institutions (which now include the vast majority of the commercial banks in the United States accounting for over 99 per cent of all commercial-bank deposits, savings banks, savings and loan associations, and credit unions) are fully insured against loss up to an amount of $100,000 for each depositor.[57] In the event of failure, the FDIC makes insured deposits immediately available to the parties concerned usually in the form of deposits with some other bank in the vicinity. At the same time, the Corporation is primarily concerned to prevent failures (e.g., by examination and, where necessary, by suggesting a merger with a stronger bank of any banks in a weakened condition) rather than to assist depositors after failure.

Subsequently (in January 1962), India established a Deposit Insurance Corporation (latterly to become – with wider powers – the Deposit Insurance and Credit Guarantee Corporation). This was prompted by the experience of 1960, when there had been sporadic runs on one or two large banks following the failure of two medium-sized banks. All operating commercial banks in India were registered with the Corporation as insured banks and all banks that might be established in the future would also have to be so registered. Because the average deposit is relatively small and often below the figure of Rs 30,000 which is covered per account, a significant proportion of total deposits in India is in fact covered by deposit insurance. Deposits of governments and of banking companies were not eligible for insurance. Because of the close association of the Reserve Bank with the Corporation (the Governor of the Reserve Bank is Chairman of the Board of Directors of the Corporation), it is possible readily to coordinate the functions of supervising the banking system in the general interest, thereby avoiding overlap and additional expenditures. Although all the larger banks are now nationalised, India has retained its deposit-insurance arrangements and, at the end of June 1983, the scheme covered 83 commercial banks, 140 regional rural banks, and 1,495 cooperative banks.[58]

Following the Intra Bank crisis in the Lebanon in October 1966, when Intra Bank had to suspend payments and the operations of the whole banking structure in the Lebanon, as well as Intra Bank subsidiaries elsewhere, were severely disrupted, the Central Council of the Bank of Lebanon recommended *inter alia* the setting up of an institution of deposit insurance and, under a law passed in 1967 (28/67), a Deposit Insurance Institution was established in association with the Ministry of Finance, the Bank of Lebanon, and the Association of Banks (four of its seven directors were to be elected by the banks and three appointed by the government).

For many years – even during the 1930s – it was felt that the large British banks were so solid that disaster was never likely to afflict them. During the earlier years after World War II, much the same view prevailed. It came as a great shock therefore when the secondary banking crisis of 1973-5 supervened[59] and a 'lifeboat' had to be launched by the Bank of England and the big London clearing banks. Subsequently, the Scottish clearing banks and Williams & Glyn's Bank were also invited to participate. In retrospect, the crisis of December 1973 may be seen as

> the culmination of a fifteen-year period of rapid change in the City of London's banking and financial mechanisms. In 1958 new influences, partly political and partly economic, began to make for an environment which was more hospitable than before to new money enterprises.
>
> After nearly twenty years of wartime and post-war restriction

> the Conservative Government sought to return the economy to something like peacetime normality by sweeping away certain curbs on financial activity.[60]

Many new financial concerns were established in the late 1950s and early 1960s; subsequently, as 'fringe' institutions – some sooner than later – these were to be driven out of business, often leaving a pile of bad debts. A Protection of Depositors Act was passed in 1963 to limit the freedom of companies to advertise without making available certain stipulated information about themselves, though banks were exempt from the requirement. But this was only a small step on the way towards official regulation on behalf of savers and depositors. The story relating to subsequent developments has already been well told by Margaret Reid and there is no point in reiteration. Suffice it to say that much attention was now given to the organisation of effective bank supervision,[61] including the publication of a White Paper in August 1976.[62] *Inter alia*, it proposed to institute 'a mandatory deposit protection fund' to provide the public with an additional safeguard against the loss of deposits. This suggestion was not universally welcomed, especially by the big banks. Their argument was that they would be putting money into the fund to underwrite 'fringe' institutions, which would be able to raise their deposit rates and attract customers away from the clearing banks. These customers could seek out the highest rates available secure in the knowledge that they would be rescued if their bank collapsed.[63] In the end, legislation was introduced and the Banking Act 1979 received the Royal Assent on 4 April 1979 and for the most part its provisions were implemented as from 1 October 1979.[64]

The deposit-protection scheme in the United Kingdom came into operation in February 1982. Under the scheme it was provided that a depositor with balances of up to £10,000 in the approximately 600 recognised banks and deposit takers would get back 75 per cent (i.e. £7,500) of his/her money in the event of failure of the institution concerned. There was provision for the £10,000 limit to be raised if this became necessary. The fund is financed by a levy on all recognised banks and licensed deposit-takers based on a percentage of their deposit base. The minimum call was initially £2,500 and the maximum £300,000 and the size of the fund at that time was between £5 million and £6 million. Subsequently, further contributions had to be sought. The scheme is being administered by the Deposit Protection Board, under the chairmanship of the Governor of the Bank of England. Also on the Board are the Deputy Governor and the Chief Cashier of the Bank, together with an unspecified number of other members, of which three are representatives of the contributory institutions.

In May 1982, the building societies introduced a voluntary scheme of their own – the Building Societies Protection Fund; in this context, investors could expect a minimum of 75 per cent cover (for non-contributing societies) and a maximum of 90 per cent (for contributor societies). The maximum contribution of any society is 0.3 per cent of assets; no loss greater than £400 million would be covered. (£400 million would, however, represent fraud or mismanagement on a scale not seen since the days of the Liberator Building Society.)

Argentina, on the other hand, adopted a different technique; under a law introduced in March 1946, deposits, but not the banks, were 'nationalised'. Deposits might be made with any bank – private or public – but the recipient bank acted in this connection merely as the agent of a central bank owned and controlled by the State. Nor were the deposits that were received by a particular bank as agent of the State necessarily available as a basis for lending by that bank. Apart from capital and reserves, all commercial banks were dependent on rediscounts with the central bank for their loanable funds and, in this way, a strict control over their lending operations was maintained. In origin, the system may have been inspired by the desire to 'protect' depositors, but quite clearly it could also be used as an engine of central bank control of a more general character.

This system was retained for more than ten years. Its repeal was recommended by Dr Prebisch in January 1956 and on October 24 1957 Señor Vasena, as Treasury Minister, announced that with effect from 1 December 1957 commercial banks in Argentina would no longer be required to act as central bank agents in respect of deposits. These would be re-transferred to the commercial banks by the central bank. At the same time, the commercial banks were permitted to resume full responsibility for their loan business. However, in the case of certain banks that were holding deposits for the account of the central bank greatly in excess of their loan business, the changeover from one system to the other had to be effected gradually, in order to counter any related inflationary pressures. It was also proposed to fund the huge volume of government indebtedness held by the official banks.[65]

Finally, as a means of protecting bank depositors against the evils of inflation, Finland's interesting experiment of 'index-tied' deposits deserves attention. Despite its remarkable recovery from the economic consequences of war,[66] inflation persisted in Finland throughout much of the post-war period and twice threatened to get out of control. It was against the background of inflation that Professor Suviranta published calculations[67] indicating that the 'real' rate of interest paid on commercial-bank deposits in Finland (i.e. the nominal rate adjusted for changes in the index of wholesale prices) had been negative for every year (exept 1949) from 1938 to 1951. In 1949, the wholesale-price index rose by only 3.1 per cent. But between January and September 1951, when the nominal interest rate on deposits was 7 per cent, wholesale prices rose by 33.1 per cent, so that the 'real' interest rate was minus 19.6 per cent. Similarly, the 'real' interest rates charged by the commercial banks on their loans had been negative, except in 1944 and 1949. Between January and September 1951, the nominal maximum rate was 10 per cent, but the equivalent 'real' rate was minus 17.4 per cent.

Total commercial-bank deposits at the end of September 1951 were Fmk 41.9 billion, or 460 per cent more than at the end of 1938. Yet the real value of these deposits, as measured by the change in the cost-of-living index number, was only 51 per cent of their value at the end of 1938, and only 33 per cent of 1938 values, if changes in the wholesale-price index were used as the basis of comparison. Naturally, a negative rate (in real terms) on loans tended to increase the demand for credit and monetary institutions were obliged to resort to credit rationing, though this could provide no more than a partial solution.

As a result of this experience, the commercial banks in Finland decided in 1952 to investigate the possibility of tying interest rates on both their deposits and their business loans to the cost-of-living index. If the index rose above the level at a specified date, the banks would apply a surcharge to the ordinary interest rate charged to their borrowers and would grant their depositors appropriate compensation in the form of a higher rate of interest. However the scheme was not actually introduced until early in 1955 and, effectively, only then by the provincial savings banks and cooperative credit societies. Initially, the commercial banks were half-hearted. When the scheme was first introduced, the Finnish public showed little interest in it, largely because at that time prices were showing signs of achieving some degree of stability. In these circumstances, the commercial banks decided that no useful purpose would be served by continuing the experiment and agreed between themselves not to open any more index-tied accounts. The Helskinki savings banks took similar action. But the faith of the other savings banks and the cooperatives was rewarded and the total placed in the new type of deposit began to increase quite markedly.

It was for this reason that the commercial banks decided to reintroduce index-tied deposits as from 1 January 1957. It was stipulated that these deposits must be made for a period of at least 12 months and for a minimum amount of Fmk 30,000. Deposits in an 'index account A' were to be subject to adjustment in proportion to any increase in the cost-of-living index of not less than a full 1 per cent and were subject to ordinary taxation. Deposits in an 'index account B' were to be adjusted to the extent of only 50 per cent of any increase in the cost-of-living index but were tax exempt. A fall in the cost-of-living index would not entail any reduction in a deposit. In order to provide the funds necessary to pay this 'compensation' to depositors, the commercial banks' borrowers were levied with a surcharge on amounts borrowed in addition to the regular interest charge. This merely served to offset what in real terms was the borrowers' diminished liability to repay. So popular did this scheme become with bank depositors that, by October 1957, about one-fifth of all deposits was held in index-linked accounts. This proportion rose to one-quarter by mid-1958.

Then with the worldwide return to something like monetary stability, the index-tied deposits began to lose their appeal, since – in the absence of rising prices – index-tied deposits offered a return one per cent below that paid on ordinary accounts. Nevertheless, the index-tied deposits had served their purpose by helping to maintain the level of savings in Finland during a period of rising prices.

It has frequently been stated that the habit of using cheques is much less highly developed on the Continent of Europe than in Britain and the United States, and certainly the holding of ordinary private banking accounts is more common in these latter countries. Nevertheless, the use made on the Continent of the postal cheque and giro systems[68] must not be overlooked. In the past, it was difficult in Europe to persuade the man in the street to keep a bank account merely for making personal payments, but the use made of these postal cheque and giro systems is almost universal. They are convenient, relatively cheap and well understood. In these circumstances, there has been little incentive to use the ordinary cheque for private transactions. But this has entailed a very serious competition for deposits and, despite attempts by banks to extend their facilities, the growth of bank resources in Continental European countries has thereby been considerably restricted. The total deposits of postal cheque or giro systems represent the equivalent of a large commercial bank and the consequentially more active competition for deposits, involving the payment of higher rates of interest than might otherwise have been necessary, has tended to force up the general level of bank charges. Latterly, commercial banks (e.g., in France and West Germany) began to compete much more actively for deposits (especially for savings deposits), but the *cheques postaux* and giro were so well established that the impact on their business was only marginal. One might compare this experience with that in Britain where a Post Office giro – the National Giro – was introduced in October 1968.[69] Its success was initially very limited and this was no doubt mainly due to the alternative services that were already available from the joint-stock banks (including their own credit-transfer system). At the same time, the establishment of the National Giro helped to create a much more competitive atmosphere and latterly its facilities have been employed quite extensively.

Assets

In an important sense, a bank's liabilities – deposits and capital funds – constitute its resources and, on any accounting criteria, in order to ensure solvency, liabilities must be matched by assets. But much can also be learned from the way in which a bank distributes the funds available to it among the several types of assets that it might hold and, in particular, between its stock-in-trade, which is cash, and the various types of financial investment, the earnings on which provide it with its income.

Cash and Liquidity

The essence of the banker-customer relationship is an undertaking on the part of the bank to provide customers with cash on demand, or in the case of 'fixed' or time deposits, with cash after a stated interval varying with the terms of the agreement. Hence the necessity to hold a cash reserve and to maintain a certain ratio between cash and deposits. Just what, under given circumstances, will be regarded as a 'safe' ratio has varied from time to time and from country to country. Generally speaking, it has been experience that dictated the ratio chosen as appropriate and, in origin, this has been the basis of the 'conventional' ratios adopted in a number of countries. In systems where for various reasons the authorities have felt that conventions were less than adequate, the maintenance of minimum ratios has been required by legislative enactment and penalties have been imposed in the event of their non-observance. Nevertheless, the basis of authoritarian decision has again usually been past experience, if not in the country concerned then in some other country whose habits it is desired to emulate. In modern banking systems, not all 'cash' need be kept either in the till or in the vaults. Indeed, the greater part of it may be held on deposit with another bank, usually the central bank, though in countries where correspondent relationships are important (e.g., the United States and certain European countries) balances may also be held at other commercial banks and, on occasion, the authorities have permitted the inclusion of such balances as part of the regular cash reserve.

One of the first bankers to publicise the importance of maintaining an adequate proportion of deposits in the form of cash and other liquid assets was George Rae[70] (during the latter part of the nineteenth century in England). By insisting on the maintenance of appropriate ratios, Rae was able effectively to raise the standard of liquidity in his own bank (the North and South Wales Bank) and, by precept and example, in other institutions also. Thus, in 1875, he began to submit to his Board of Directors

> weekly financial statements setting out the ratios for the various items over which the bank's funds were distributed. Until that time loans and bills had almost invariably exceeded deposits, but thereafter the relative weight of advances was reduced, and the proportion of bank funds invested in gilt-edged securities increased. Following the events of 1878 the distribution of bank funds was altered once again and came to approach much more nearly the ratios current in present-day banking.[71]

Yet this was only a beginning. Following the Baring Crisis of 1890, banking reserves in England became a subject for widespread and critical comment. As a consequence of the ensuing discussion, the several large joint-stock banks began the publication of

> monthly statements of account representing the position at the close of business on a particular day in each month. Thus the proportion between cash and deposit liabilities was brought into prominence and the banks began to become effectively 'ratio conscious' . . . and the conception of a regular cash ratio used as a practical guide in banking operations was steadily evolved.[72]

For a long time, the banks in the United Kingdom worked to a minimum cash ratio of something like 10 per cent of deposits to which level it had been gradually reduced by the end of the 1920s,[73] but because the individual banks 'made up' on different days of the week, 'window-dressing' was possible and commonly practised, published ratios being likely to present a rather more favourable picture than in fact obtained.[74] Officially, 'window-dressing' was abolished in 1946 and a fixed cash ratio of 8 per cent was introduced. In fact, the banks worked very closely to this figure and, with some official assistance, attempted to manage their money positions accordingly – 'the small elasticity allowed in practice is the minimum required if the rule is not to be an intolerable nuisance'.[75]

It is rare that an attempt is made to maintain a more or less fixed cash ratio as became the practice in England (until 1971) and English banks must have been virtually unique in so doing. Even if one is rather less ambitious and only aims at a degree of stability in the cash ratio, however, that is only possible where there is a considerable degree of elasticity in the available supply of liquid assets other than cash, an elasticity that in England has been provided through the agency of the discount market and either the Treasury bill or commercial bills (with Bank of England support).

Some degree of variation in the ratio of cash to deposits is much more general. Thus, the 8 per cent rule to which the English banks were subject was not applied in Scotland, where the banks were left entirely free in deciding on their cash reserves, which probably included, in the case of at least some of the Scottish banks, some part of the balances they held with London clearing banks.[76] It should be emphasised, however, that Scottish arrangements were rather special. As the Radcliffe Committee pointed out in its Report:

> Bank of England notes held by a Scottish bank can simultaneously serve two purposes: as till-money in the ordinary way, as cover for the banks own notes in circulation. Also, the fact that unissued notes – notes printed but lying in the bank's own tills and vaults – do not require cover, makes it possible to provide small branches with adequate till-money (including unissued notes) at very little cost. For these reasons, and because they can safely operate with relatively lower working balances than the London clearing banks need to hold, it would not be appropriate to apply to the Scottish banks a rule identical with the requirement of 8 per cent cash in a London clearing bank; and no such rule is imposed.[77]

Even when reserve requirements are fixed within the terms of a banking statute (as they are in a large number of countries), such provisions relate to required minima and effective cash reserves are usually somewhat higher and, sometimes, much higher. Moreover, for seasonal reasons, movements in cash reserves are often quite marked. Thus, over a long period of years, the cash (and other liquidity) ratios of the Australian trading banks were very variable,[78] though latterly this was only true at very low levels, since a proportion of trading-bank funds was frozen during World War II and the earlier post-war years under special account procedures.[79] Then, in January 1960, minimum cash-reserve requirements were introduced. Much the same has been true of the New Zealand banks[80] and it is significant that, since the introduction to New Zealand in 1952 of variable minimum cash reserves fixed by the central bank, the requirements have at times been subject to frequent adjustments largely as a result of the necessity to accommodate seasonal factors.[81]

Whether there are cash requirements or not (which are not properly part of a bank's available liquidity), it will be apparent from even the most cursory examination of a bank balance sheet that whatever cash provision were made (short of 100 per cent cover at least with respect to demand deposits), no bank would be able to meet in their entirety the claims of its depositors, that is, if a bank's customers suddenly elected to exercise fully their rights to demand cash. Indeed, if that were a common phenomenon, banking as a business based on deposits would be virtually impossible. Rather is it the general experience that for the most part people are prepared to leave their surplus cash on deposit with their bankers, confident that when they want it their money will be available on demand. Such behaviour is obviously fundamental to the continued existence of deposit banking. Nevertheless, times of emergency may recur and, when confidence is at a low ebb, demands for cash tend to exceed what might reasonably have been anticipated. A banker must be prepared to meet such a situation and the rest of his assets might be thought of as ranged in lines of defence against the possibility of attack by the bank's creditors, i.e. by its depositors.

> A run does not usually advertize its advent a month or so beforehand, and some of our worst panics have come upon us without much previous warning. You cannot pull your resources together in a few days, or a few weeks, if they are widely spread, and difficult of realization. The normal position of a banker is like that of a general in the field, with an enemy in front of him, against whose assault he must be armed at all points, if he would not find himself assailed

some day, and suffer loss and discomfiture.[82]

In other words, a banker must be in a position to convert at least a proportion of his assets more or less quickly into cash either by sale, or by borrowing against them. In theory, even his less liquid assets should be self-liquidating within a reasonable period of time. In effect, there is a 'defence in depth'. (That these considerations are still relevant is evidenced by the experience of 'runs' on a number of occasions since World War II, as for example in Hong Kong, India, Malaysia, the Lebanon, and the United States).

There are three main ways in which assets may be mobilised for this purpose: loans may be 'callable', i.e. repayment may be demanded from debtors either immediately or at short notice; securities may be marketable, the proceeds being realised by sale on a recognised and organised market such as a stock exchange or a bill market; or the paper representing loans or investments may be submitted as security for an advance from the central bank, in which case its acceptance will make it 'eligible'. All bank assets, other than premises, can be so divided.

However in the event of a sudden and imperious demand for cash by bank depositors, the sudden calling in of loans would disrupt the delicate nexus of debtor-creditor relationships and exaggerate the loss of confidence that had presumably been the occasion for the initial run on the banks. Again, heavy selling on the markets would mean a sharp fall in prices and heavy losses on marketable assets would have further repercussions on the state of confidence. Ready cash may only be obtainable at a high price.

Hence the need for certain conventions which will permit the system to work under pressure. Either the banks must keep their cash reserves and truly liquid assets at a very high level, or there must exist a 'lender of last resort' (usually a central bank) that will provide cash when required, subject only to the observance of certain well-understood conditions. In either event, 'liquid assets' – assets which can readily be converted into cash without risk of substantial loss – are an essential ingredient in a bank balance sheet.

'Call money' (really overnight money) is the most liquid of assets other than cash. The lender has the right virtually to demand immediate repayment. Ordinarily, call money markets serve the purpose of ensuring employment for temporarily surplus cash and, in the banking system as a whole, there will usually exist a 'revolving fund' of such cash, much of which is borrowed one day, repaid the next, and often then reborrowed. It may be employed in a discount market as in

London; it may be lent out to the stock exchange against marketable security (as was formerly done to quite a considerable extent in New York and on certain of the European security markets); or money may be lent at call on an inter-bank basis and provide the means of re-distributing the flow of cash between the various commercial banks operating in a particular centre (leading examples include the 'call money markets' of Bombay and Calcutta, Singapore and Hong Kong, Tokyo and Osaka, and in a number of West European countries). The federal-funds market in the United States serves a similar purpose.

Even so, the 'callability' of money would not automatically ensure liquidity, unless there were a lender of last resort in the background ready to relieve any excessive tightness that might develop in the money market. The classic example of such an arrangement is the London discount market, where the resources employed by the discount houses consist largely of money borrowed, for the most part at call, from the clearing banks and other lenders. In the event of heavy calling, these houses may apply, subject to well-understood conditions, for assistance from the Bank of England. Such assistance depends on the 'eligibility' of the types of assets held by such institutions either for outright purchase by the central bank or as the basis for short-term loans from it. Indeed, in a modern money market, the eligibility of specified assets at the central bank is the essential basis of liquidity, since this ensures that accommodation will, if necessary, and at a price, always be made available.

These arrangements provide the framework within which liquid assets are held and the basis on which they may be converted into cash. But what amounts of liquid assets are usually considered to be adequate? In England, a '30 per cent rule' came to be accorded wide, if not universal, acceptance. Although by no means rigidly adhered to, there seemed to be evidence of some attachment to a 30 per cent liquid-assets/deposits ratio prior to World War II.[83] In the post-war years, the 30 per cent liquid-assets ratio gradually became a virtual minimum. An important step towards a uniform and explicit minimum liquidity ratio for the London clearing banks was taken in 1951 when the Governor of the Bank of England indicated to the banks that a liquidity ratio of from 32-28 per cent would be regarded as normal but that it would be undesirable for the ratio to be allowed to fall below 25 per cent as an extreme limit. By 1957, a 30 per cent minimum had become more rigid (and was reduced to 28 per cent in 1963).[84] This lasted until 1971, when – under Competition and Credit Control – a new 12½ per cent minimum reserve ratio (excluding till cash) was introduced. This related to 'eligible liabilities' (primarily sterling deposits of up to 2 years maturity, including sterling certificates of deposit). When called upon to do so, the banks could also be required to place special deposits with the Bank of England. These arrangements were replaced in August 1981 by (i) a voluntary holding of operational funds with the Bank of England by the London clearing banks ('for clearing purposes'); (ii) a uniform requirement of ½ per cent of an institution's eligible liabilities that would be applied to all banks and licensed deposit-takers with eligible liabilities averaging more than £10 million; this was the non-operational requirement and was to be set twice a year in relation to average eligible liabilities in the previous six months.[85] In calculating eligible liabilities, inter-bank loans and secured call money placed with discount houses, money brokers, and gilt-edged jobbers in the stock exchange were treated as an offset. Window-dressing was to be avoided, since it would be 'contrary to the objective of these agreed arrangements for any institution to reduce its eligible liabilities deliberately or artificially on reporting dates'. The Bank of England accordingly reserved the right to make spot checks. Also, as from 20 August 1981, the date when the new changes came in, all banks that were eligible acceptors were normally required to hold an average equivalent to 6 per cent of their eligible liabilities either as secured money with discount houses or as secured call money with money brokers and gilt-edged jobbers, but the amount held in the form of secured money with a discount house was not normally to fall below 4 per cent of eligible liabilities. This was to be monitored by the Bank of England, to which banks would make monthly returns of daily figures. This money became known as 'club money'.[86]

A requirement analogous to the maintenance of a minimum liquid-assets ratio on the English model was the *plancher* or 'floor' that was applied to the French banks (in conjunction with the imposition of ceilings or *plafonds* on the amounts of commercial paper they could rediscount with the Bank of France). As from 1 October 1948, all banks were required to hold in Treasury paper a minimum equal to 95 per cent of their holdings on 30 September 1948. In the event of any increase in deposit liabilities beyond the level as at that date, holdings of Treasury paper were to be increased to the extent of 20 per cent of the rise in these liabilities. If there should be a fall in deposits, holdings of Treasury paper might be reduced in sympathy to the extent of 80 per cent of the decrease. These arrangements were introduced in order to prevent the banks from selling government securities for the purpose of obtaining resources with which to expand credit to commerce and industry, a practice that had occasioned the authorities considerable anxiety during 1946 and 1947 and which had only been partially curbed by gentlemen's agreements not to reduce existing holdings of Treasury paper except when there was a net withdrawal of deposits. Nevertheless, the *plancher* requirements could effect no net reduction in bank credit, unless the funds transferred to the Treasury in this way were used to repay its advances from the Bank of France, or were applied in some other way in reduction of State debt. Nor was there any provision in the regulations requiring that the additional holdings of government paper in consequence of a rise in deposits should be acquired from the Treasury direct and it was therefore possible to obtain such paper from non-bank investors, thus releasing funds for expenditure in the private sector. Initially, it was only necessary for the banks to observe the *plancher* at month-ends, but in October 1951 the regulations were tightened up and the banks had to maintain the *plancher* on a daily basis. In this way, it was hoped to eliminate the lag between the growth in deposits and their absorption in holdings of Treasury paper.

There was a further tightening up of the *plancher* requirements in mid-1956, when the stipulated ratio of short-dated Treasury paper was raised to 25 per cent of total deposits. In the event of a bank's *plancher* requirements as calculated on the 1948 basis being in excess of 25 per cent of its deposit liabilities when the change in formula was introduced it was obliged to maintain its portfolio with the higher level as a minimum. At that time, however, the holdings of the majority of the banks did not exceed 21 per cent of total deposits. The immediate effect of the new requirements on loans to commerce and industry was limited as the banks met the new *plancher* largely by rediscounting medium-term paper. There were also grounds for believing that the new measure was rather more likely to provide the Treasury with badly-needed funds, than to operate as an effective restriction of bank credit.

In addition, in February 1948, the authorities in France had instituted a liquid-assets ratio of 60 per cent of short-term liabilities (with power to raise it to 70 per cent for particular banks), but this was not intended to operate as a credit control. It was imposed by the Banking Control Commission as a means of guaranteeing bank solvency and as a protection to depositors. Nor was the maintenance of this ratio particularly onerous and liquid assets were defined most liberally.

For the banks in Australia, the main techniques of control have been the regulation of trading-bank liquidity by a combination of variations in the statutory reserve deposits (SRDs) held by trading banks with the

Reserve Bank and an agreement to maintain the liquid-assets and government-securities (LGS) convention. The range of SRD ratios, which replaced special accounts in 1960, has been 3 per cent to 16.5 per cent (after early 1981, it was set at 7 per cent). It must be uniform for trading banks other than prescribed banks,[87] for which it may be lower. A low rate of interest is paid on SRD accounts (e.g., 5 per cent per annum in 1983). Under the LGS convention, which was agreed in 1956, each major trading bank undertakes to so direct its policy that its LGS ratio to deposits[88] does not fall below the agreed minimum which is determined from time to time. If necessary, a bank is expected to borrow at short-term from the Reserve Bank in order to at least maintain the minimum ratio while it adjusts its balance sheet. The rate on such loans is fixed at the discretion of the Reserve Bank and is not known to a bank in advance of the loan being obtained. In practice, the trading banks have made little use of this facility. The Reserve Bank may also make loans to the banks outside the LGS arrangement (e.g., as in October 1974, to increase the liquidity of the banking system and the economy generally). The minimum LGS ratio has not been changed very often. At the outset, it was established at 14 per cent. Since then it has been increased – by agreement with the banks – to 16 per cent in 1960 and 18 per cent in 1962; in February 1976, it was temporarily increased to 23 per cent but reverted to 18 per cent in March 1977. Although the prescribed banks are not a party to the LGS convention, understandings have been agreed regarding minimum holdings of selected liquid assets. It appears that the range of assets involved is a little wider then that applicable under the LGS convention; some additional private sector assets are involved.

If a central bank can depend on observation by the commercial banks of an established convention with respect to cash and/or other liquidity ratios, its influence over credit conditions will obviously be greatly strengthened, since it will know that when pressure is brought to bear on the banks' liquid resources (e.g., by open-market operations), there will be a definite reaction point. Once the banks' liquid assets have been forced down to that minimum, they will be compelled to take appropriate action in order not to fall below it. Nevertheless, such a convention may take longer to establish than the authorities are prepared to wait. Hence, several of the central banks established in the 1950s were specifically empowered to impose liquidity requirements. Thus, the Bank of Ghana,[89] the Central Bank of Nigeria,[90] and the Central Bank of Malaya[91] (which became Bank Negara Malaysia) were empowered in very similar terms to prescribe an amount of specified liquid assets that must be held by each bank carrying on business in their territory. Alternatively, as in the banking laws of the former Central African Federation and of Jamaica, specific minimum ratios may be laid down in the legislation itself –thus, in the Federation of Rhodesia and Nyasaland, the Act prescribed that 'commercial banks shall maintain, as a minimum, liquid assets equal to 25 per cent of their liabilities to the public in the Federation'[92] and in Jamaica, the banks were required to maintain a cash reserve of not less than 5 per cent of a bank's deposit liabilities and a liquid assets ratio of 15 per cent.[93]

The situation was somewhat different in the United States, where for all banks that were members of the Federal Reserve System minimum reserves had to be maintained with a Federal Reserve Bank.[94] For this purpose, after July 1966, member banks were classified[95] either as 'reserve city banks' or as 'country banks'. In the former case, the minimum reserve that might be required was 10 per cent of net demand deposits with a maximum of 22 per cent; in the latter, the relevant percentages were 7 and 14. For time deposits (for all classes of banks), the percentages were 3 and 10 (savings deposits were also included). Within these limits, the ratios might be varied from time to time and the authorities might also discriminate between deposits that were under or over $5 million.[96] State laws, which related to non-member banks, were various, but basically similar principles applied.

The required minimum reserves held with the Fed had to be maintained on the basis of a weekly average. Reserve city banks had to furnish a return at the close of business each Wednesday; country banks reported twice a month. Net demand deposits were calculated for every day of the statement week (including holidays), the banks being permitted to deduct from gross demand deposits cash items in process of collection, and reciprocal inter-bank demand deposits with banks in the United States (with the exception of private banks and American branches of foreign banks) might be shown net. Time deposits also had to be reported. Member banks that showed a deficiency in reserves when averaged over the week might be permitted – at the discretion of the relevant Federal Reserve Bank – to offset any deficiency in one statement week by an excess of reserves in the immediately following period, provided the deficiency did not exceed 2 per cent of that bank's required reserves. If there was a deficiency not accommodated by this concession, a penalty would be applied, the amount of the fine being determined by multiplying the average deficiency by a rate 2 per cent above the Federal Reserve Bank's discount rate. Fines appear to have been rare and, when the sanction was applied, it was not so much the amount involved that hurt as the indignity of being arraigned.

Unless they were prepared to carry a high level of excess reserves – and few of the larger banks followed this practice – the banks had to watch their money position from day to day in order to provide for their ordinary business needs and to meet statutory requirements. Since on any one day banks were free to draw on their balances at the Fed, the basis of the money adjustment had to be the maintenance of their reserve requirements as averaged over the week. In other words, the daily adjustment had to be viewed in the light of the accumulated weekly position.[97] If a bank's current cash position was short, it had to judge whether this was likely to be temporary or not. If it was necessary to take corrective action, it might choose one or other of several methods, the technique of adjustment selected depending on relative money rates and yields, partly on convenience and partly on the size of the bank.

Techniques that were employed included the buying and selling of federal funds (which were then simply entitlements to balances with a Federal Reserve Bank). Resort to this market developed as an alternative to operations in government securities; or a bank might resort to re-purchase agreements against government securities (RPs), whereby securities could be sold to another institution subject to an agreement to re-purchase (in reverse, it could be used as a means of investing temporarily surplus funds); or the cash balance might be adjusted by buying or selling government paper, such as Treasury bills or bonds (in the earlier days, for the smaller banks, operations in Treasury bills would be the most usual means of adjustment; today, even small banks tend to use federal funds). As a last resort, member banks could borrow at a Federal Reserve Bank.

However, as we have seen (pp. 116-17), the Depository Institutions Deregulation and Monetary Act of 1980 now specifies that any reserve requirements (for details, see the appropriate Table in *Federal Reserve Bulletins*) – whether on net transactions accounts, non-personal time deposits or Euro-currency liabilities – will now be uniformly applied to all transactions accounts at all depository institutions; under the Act, these included commercial banks, mutual savings banks, savings and loan associations, credit unions, agencies and branches of foreign banks, and Edge Act Corporations. In addition, any depository institution issuing transactions accounts or non-personal time deposits now had the same discount and borrowing privileges at the Federal Reserve as the member banks themselves.

For other countries, there is no need to provide a detailed account of their somewhat similar arrangements; in this context these are not markedly different – for example, in Canada, Australia (as already mentioned), New Zealand, India and Pakistan, Sri Lanka, a number of countries in Western Europe (including France and West Germany) and Japan. There are variations of detail, but in general there is much similarity and the objectives of the authorities are essentially the same.

Security Portfolios

For the most part, the security portfolio of a bank (referred to as 'investments' by banks in the United Kingdom) consist of government securities of various kinds, though banks in certain countries may also hold some industrial securities and 'participations' in industrial and commercial businesses; they may likewise operate a trading portfolio.

In managing its portfolio of securities, a bank would be influenced by certain criteria. The most important of these would be liquidity, yield, and interest-rate expectations. Obviously, liquidity (in the sense of being able to sell the securities at short notice and without risk of substantial loss) is important, since all deposit banks are liable to repay a proportion of their deposits on demand or at short notice. Liquidity depends on marketability, which tends to increase as securities approach maturity; hence, there will tend to be some emphasis on short-term holdings. Clearly, too, yield (or the rate of return) will be important, since – subject to meeting liquidity desiderata – a bank will wish to maximise its earnings. However, the degree of risk is also relevant and few banks would aim at very high yields (except perhaps on a small proportion of their portfolio) if such yields were associated with a high degree of risk. Hence, in this context, a bank's concern with interest-rate expectations, since if rates are likely to rise the market prices of securities will tend to fall, whereas if rates are likely to fall, such prices will tend to rise. Even so, when rates are high, a bank will not infrequently acquire a block of securities with no intention of re-sale in order to enjoy a high return on a proportion of its portfolio. Of more particular interest to a bank are the probable future movements of interest rates and a bank may 'take a position' (i.e. speculate) with regard to what is likely to happen. If, for example, it buys in anticipation of a fall in interest rates (with a resultant rise in the prices of securities) it hopes to make a capital gain; it will also usually buy at least medium-term securities, possibly some longs as well. If it is wrong, there may only be a running yield, or even a capital loss. If, on the other hand, a bank expects rates to rise (and prices therefore to fall), it will tend for the time being to stay short, with the intention of buying later at lower prices for a higher yield; it will also seek to avoid capital losses. Also, at times of great uncertainty with regard to movements in interest rates, banks tend to stay short in their portfolios, continuing to reinvest at short-term as securities mature.

Not always, however, are the banks free to decide when to buy. It may be a 'captive' market in the country concerned, where the authorities require banks (and others) to hold a certain percentage of their assets in the form of government securities, though usually it is still possible to do switches and they can therefore vary their maturity distributions. Nevertheless, official policy determines the quantum that must be held.

Much the same principles as apply to liquid assets also apply to the security portfolio, though there are significant differences of degree. It was common practice (and it is still done by some banks today) for banks to hold a 'spread' of maturities, such that a proportion of their security holdings were regularly approaching redemption,[98] being replaced at the other end of the portfolio by longer-dated securities, which in due course themselves became increasingly shorter-dated. However, because of the limited availability of dates, portfolios might become 'lumpy' from time to time. In many cases, it was normal banking policy to hold these securities to redemption, though realisation prior to redemption was always a possibility and might be undertaken for a variety of reasons. For example, if the price was right, it might be desired to reshuffle the portfolio in order to vary the spread of maturities (e.g., to reduce the degree of 'lumpiness'); or to avoid the risk of depreciation; or in order to take 'tax losses'. At other times, it might be necessary to sell securities (possibly at a loss) to restore a bank's liquidity, or to expand loans.

In a developed money-market centre, 'mobilisation' of securities for any of these purposes would be effected by sale on the stock exchange at current market prices (though the authorities may – and do – have to come in when transactions are large). Because market conditions will be variable and there is less opportunity to avoid loss by holding securities to maturity, these assets must be regarded as rather less liquid than money-market assets proper, such as call money, Treasury bills, and commercial bills.

It is true that there may also be losses on sales of Treasury bills and similar paper (due to changes in the central bank's discount rate and related price changes affecting the bills themselves) but the risks will be less because of their shorter maturities[99] and there is also the possibility of so arranging the schedule of maturities that a succession of repayments at par can be achieved without great difficulty.

The variability of market conditions also explains the banks' policy of valuing their securities conservatively, when drawing up their balance sheets. For much the same reason, the banks feel it is necessary to hold a portfolio of securities most of which is short to medium in term and part of which is always approaching maturity, since, for securities close to maturity, market price (if they have to be sold) is unlikely to diverge greatly from nominal value. Thus, although the detailed practice varies from one bank to another, the clearing banks in England hold a portfolio of government securities that is 'laddered' with as regular a run-off of maturities as it is possible to achieve given the availability of securities with appropriate dates, the impact of market conditions, and any past sales that might have been forced on the bank in order to accommodate an increasing demand for loans. Normally, in England, the banks aimed to hold the greater part of their portfolio in bonds with less than ten years to run to maturity and usually

> total holdings of Government and Government-guaranteed securities have been more or less evenly divided between bonds with less than five years and bonds with more than five years to run to final maturity date. The emphasis on short bonds is due to the banks' preference for bonds that can be marketed at any time without great capital loss, a safeguard that is maximised by holding a portfolio with a range of maturities extending year by year over the immediately following years, so that each year a substantial sum is available from maturities on which there is no question of any capital loss at all.[100]

In more recent years (e.g., the early 1980s), because of interest-rate uncertainties, the banks in the United Kingdom (on the basis of banks that publish this information) have shortened their portfolios with the majority of their holdings maturing within four or five years and an average maturity that is much shorter. Hence, it is clear that at least some laddering of the portfolio is still favoured.

Over the years in England and Wales, and in order to meet an expanding loan demand, the ratio of 'investments' to deposits has fallen – it was 19.5 per cent in 1960; after 1965, it was between 12 and 14 per cent. Latterly, it fell to quite low levels and, although it varies between banks, for the London clearing banks in the early 1980s, it could vary from a low of 1 per cent of total assets to about 3.5 per cent. (For the London clearing banks and their subsidiaries in the banking sector, all groups aggregate balance sheet for mid-November, it was of the order of 3.5 to 4.0 per cent (1981-3), which is a little higher than one finds in any of the annual balance sheets for the individual banks themselves). As already indicated, this has been accompanied by a shortening of average maturities and the bulk would now have no more than 5 years to run. As those securities mature, at least a proportion of the funds so released will be reinvested at the longer end, but because of the limited availability of dates, portfolios inevitably become 'lumpy' from time to time and this may force sales that involve losses. On other occasions, if the prices are right, a bank will go into the market to buy required maturities and in that way attempt to reduce the degree of 'lumpiness'.

Because of their greater emphasis on the attraction of 'savings deposits', the Scottish banks were inclined to commit themselves 'more deeply in their investment portfolios; these have formed a larger proportion of their total assets and they have been willing to hold longer bonds than some English banks would have thought suitable'.[101] Latterly, however, there was again a tendency to shorten the average life of their portfolios, the maturities of which now became very similar to those of the English clearing banks. Also, although at the time of the Radcliffe Committee Report they still maintained over 20 per cent of total deposits in 'investments', which was much higher than the English experience, their figures have likewise come down to levels comparable with the English clearing banks – 3.8 per cent (1981), 2.8 per cent (1982), and 4.2 per cent (1983) of total assets compared with 3.5-4.0 per cent for the English clearing banks.

The situation is somewhat different in the United States, where a good deal of paper (like Treasury bills) that in the United Kingdom would be classified under liquid assets appears as part of the portfolio of United States government securities (state and municipal obligations,[102] which are often very important and also on average at longer term, are shown separately). Banks in the United States still hold a higher proportion of total assets in their securities portfolios (also referred to as 'investment securities') than do the British banks – for all commercial banks, about 20 per cent for the calendar years 1981, 1982, and 1983, compared with 23.9 per cent in 1975. However, the ratios are lower for the big banks, especially for the large reporting commercial banks in the city of New York, where it is about 10 per cent (US government securities over these year-ends being 3.3 per cent, 3.7 per cent, and 3.8 per cent). For the large New York banks, these figures exclude their trading accounts, data for which are not available for reasons of confidentiality.[103]

In both the United States government securities and 'municipals' portfolios, the banks were accustomed to ladder their maturities so that they got both a good spread and if possible, a regular run-off of cash, which could either be used for reinvestment at the long end of the portfolio or to feed a rising loan demand. Then, in the later 1960s and early 1970s, the so-called 'dumb-bell' distribution seems to have become popular in the United States, also in Canada, and one still finds instances of it. In these cases, banks hold a significant proportion of the total portfolio in long-dated maturities with a high yield, a small proportion in the middle ranges, and another significant proportion in short-dated maturities. In order to maintain such a distribution, in addition to the reinvestment of moneys as securities mature, some switching will be necessary from time to time. On the basis of field work conducted by the author in all the Federal Reserve districts in 1979, it was established that some banks still ladder their US government securities portfolios and this means of arranging a spread of maturities remains the general rule with municipals, though sometimes these are described as being only 'loosely laddered'[104] and some distributions are more 'lumpy' than others. Also, during periods of great uncertainty with regard to the probable movement of interest rates (e.g., 1978-9), a new type of maturity distribution seems to have become common; this might be called a T-distribution – a wide band of shorts at the top, with smaller amounts of medium to longer maturities in support; some banks however did no more than shorten their maturities somewhat and a true T-distribution was by no means universal.

As one would expect, the views of individual banks on the appropriate average maturity and spread of holdings vary considerably, but statistical surveys demonstrate that at any particular time there tends to be a concentration of average maturities within a certain period of years.[105] Thus, in 1955-6, in a survey of banks in all the Federal Reserve Districts, the author found that in terms of the average maturities of commercial-bank security portfolios there was a concentration within the three- to five-year range; by 1962 (on the basis of a more limited survey taking in about three-quarters of the Federal Reserve Districts), the concentration was in the range of one to three years. More recently (1979), again on the basis of field work in all the Federal Reserve Districts, the concentration for the US government securities portfolio was again in the one- to three-year range, though flanked by a significant number of instances both of under one year and of three to four years. For municipals, the concentration was from five to nine years, with nothing shorter than five years, but with odd instances out beyond ten years (usually with an average maturity of no more than 13 years, though one was over 17 years). Practice with regard to agencies was various – on average, as many portfolios were short (the majority averaging two to three years, but some shorter) as were medium to long (with instances ranging from five to 13 years, one with an average of over 18 years). For small banks, with consequently small holdings of securities, sometimes with just a few issues, whether of US governments, agencies or municipals, averages of maturities were virtually meaningless. However, the content of many bank portfolios is subject to almost continuous change either in consequence of adjustments to the cash position (which might itself be prompted by tight money, or a higher demand for loans) or – particularly at banks in the highest corporation-tax bracket – because of the taking of 'tax losses'.

Another interesting type of maturity distribution related to bank security portfolios in India, where the author undertook field work in 1980. In a number of cases (though not in all) either as an ideal or as a rough approximation to practice, Indian banks then favoured two versions of what might be described as a 'flask-shaped' distribution. In the first version, there were some short-dated securities held for liquidity; this was followed by a bulge in the middle of the distribution, which was held for yield (medium-dated paper, with a limited risk of depreciation if interest rates rose); and a smaller holding of long-dated paper, which was kept down in size because of the strong risk of depreciation if and when interest rates rose. The second version of the 'flask' was based on increasing holdings of securities as one moved out from the short-dated into the medium-dated and ultimately into the longer-dated securities. Here the banks were clearly going for yield and did not worry unduly about the depreciation of their longer-dated securities if and when interest rates rose. The apparent intention was to hold the securities until maturity and to hold them meanwhile to fulfil their statutory liquidity requirement. (In fact, the author also found one or two cases of the dumb-bell distribution. Nevertheless, in one such case, the bank regarded a 'flask-shaped' distribution as its 'ideal').) Sometimes the banks moved from the first type of 'flask shape' to the second in search of yield.

In the context of maturity distributions, one might add a qualification or two. In India, what is short, medium, or long tends to be much longer than (say) in the United Kingdom or the United States. Also, in India, even when the intention is to hold securities to maturity, the banks undertake switches from time to time in order to adjust their maturity distributions, often looking for an even higher yield. Sometimes these transactions go through the stock exchange; sometimes through the Reserve Bank of India. It might be noted that the Indian banks only resort to Treasury bills when they have unexpected and/or large temporary surpluses of liquidity. Putting funds into Treasury bills is used solely as a temporary measure, since the rate is too low to do otherwise.

The essential difference between 'money-market assets' and 'investments' in a bank balance sheet is that the 'liquidity' of the latter depends primarily on marketability and not in part on eligibility at the central bank (even though in support of government securities the authorties do come into the market from time to time and help to 'make' it). The true test of whether an asset is liquid or not is the ease with which it can be converted into cash without loss, or at any rate without appreciable loss. On this criterion, only the shortest-dated bonds would qualify without serious objection, since the rest would be much more subject to the vagaries of day-to-day market conditions. Nevertheless, there have been times (for example in the United States) when stable prices in the bond market have been 'guaranteed' almost completely by the authorities and, in this context, 'investments' have become virtually as liquid as money-market assets proper.[106] Similarly, in the United Kingdom, when a policy of 'cheap money' has been favoured.[107]

Nevertheless, investments and money-market assets merge into each other. The dividing line is arbitrary, though as we have seen there is a difference. The liquidity of investments depends primarily on marketability (though sometimes it also depends on the readiness of the government or its agent to exchange its own securities for cash). The liquidity of money-market assets, on the other hand, depends partly on marketability but mainly on the willingness of the central bank to purchase them or accept them as collateral for a loan. This is why money-market assets are more liquid than investments.

When interest rates are low, there is an incentive to borrow though this may be offset by a lack of confidence. Despite modest rates, lenders will almost certainly desire to lend, since normally there is a greater margin of profit on loans as compared with 'investments', especially when the latter are comprised mainly of government securities. On the other hand, the profitability of lending tends to be even greater when interest rates are high. There also then tends to be an increasing pressure to borrow and, to the extent that the authorities permit this to be satisfied, the banks will expand their loans in order to accommodate the rise in the demand for loanable funds. In large part, this will be met by running down holdings of government securities, which will have to be absorbed by other investors and, in some measure, almost certainly by the authorities (usually by the central bank). At other times, when the level of lending is low, bank funds will be absorbed by investing them in securities. Hence, 'investments' tend to be a residual – only what is left over after the loan demand has been satisfied will be available for investment in securities.

So far, it has been implied that bank investments consist almost solely of government or semi-government securities of one kind or another. Nothing has been said about bank holdings of industrial stocks and bonds. As we shall see in Chapter 7, bank holdings of industrial securities are much more common on the Continent of Europe than elsewhere. Japanese arrangements are somewhat similar. In Britain, however, exept for holdings in what are primarily financial subsidiaries usually within the group, the clearing banks do not hold in portfolio either industrial shares or industrial bonds or debentures. Nor do they as do banks in certain other countries – e.g., the Netherlands, West Germany, France, Switzerland, Finland and Japan – operate a trading account in order to provide stock-exchange facilities direct to customers, although latterly they have begun to acquire interests in separate stock-exchange firms.

Loans, Discounts and Advances

Amongst the assets in a bank balance sheet, it is the loans and advances that constitute the core of a bank's earning assets. It is this group of assets that is usually the most profitable. In theory, most bankers would regard their advances either as primarily short-term in character or – especially in more recent years and sometimes to a significant extent – as medium-term.

But banking theory and banking practice have not always been identical. Overdrafts, which are the common means of bank lending in the United Kingdom, in certain Commonwealth countries, and in a number of Continental European countries, are in theory repayable on demand (and in fact repayable only after due and reasonable notice has been given),[108] but in practice they run on sometimes for quite long periods, though always subject to review (usually annually). Again, discountable paper of various kinds, which was the more usual way of granting accommodation in certain Continental European countries (as, indeed, it was in England until well into the nineteenth century) is in theory also self-liquidating as it comes to maturity. In practice, such accommodation may be renewed a number of times before finally being paid off. In those Continental European countries that favoured it, finance by way of discountable paper virtually performed the same function as the overdraft in the United Kingdom, but from the point of view of liquidity the position was complicated by the fact that on the Continent such paper would often be eligible for rediscount at the central bank (e.g. in France and Germany). What would otherwise have been as illiquid an asset as a bank overdraft in the United Kingdom had thereby been transformed (within the limits that might be prescribed from time to time) into an almost completely liquid asset, simply because it could be rediscounted at the central bank

For many years in the United Kingdom, the purpose of bank loans was regarded for the most part as the provision of working capital and it was felt that the longer-term needs of industry and agriculture[109] should be satisfied either through the capital market, or through the agency of specialist investment institutions, to the capital resources of which the clearing banks (and to some extent the Bank of England and other financial institutions) contributed (e.g., the Industrial and Commercial Finance Corporation and the Finance Corporation for Industry – now both grouped under Investors in Industry; the Agricultural Mortgage Corporation; the Ship Mortgage Finance Company; Tanker Finance Limited; and – for Commonwealth countries – the Commonwealth Development Finance Company). Latterly, a significant proportion of medium-term lending, also to a lesser extent personal loans (consumer lending) has been provided. (Term lending will be considered separately.) The same basic philosophy underlay the preference of banks in the United Kingdom (under Scottish leadership) for taking up a capital interest in hire-purchase finance (i.e. instalment credit) companies rather than going into this form of business direct.[110] Similarly, with the special banking subsidiaries of the clearing banks, which have been more concerned with medium-term and specialist lending. By this means, it was argued, specialised forms of lending were concentrated in the hands of institutions that, because they specialised, were able to develop the appropriate techniques and expertise. In addition, the banks' total commitments in such fields were more precisely determined and they could not therefore become over-extended in a line of business that may have been unfamiliar to them. On the other hand, banks in Continental European countries (see pp. 333ff.) have in the past tended to ally themselves much more directly with industrial groups, financing their development by holding the relevant securities until these could be marketed, though – as in England – much lip-service has often also been paid to the importance of loans of a 'self-liquidating' character. United States banking appears to represent a sort of half-way house between British and Continental European practice and, in the United States, the 'term loan' has long been an accepted lending technique. When the term loan was first introduced in the United States (i.e. before it became more general), it was possible in these circumstances to establish with greater certainty than was the case in Britain or on the Continent of Europe the extent to which a banker had committed himself over the longer term and to judge rather more quickly the degree to which his funds were in fact tied up. Subsequently, term-loan lending became quite common in an increasingly large number of countries.

Although attitudes are changing, bankers in the United Kingdom for a long time retained a strong preference for short-term lending of the self-liquidating type. It is only latterly that there has been a tendency – where appropriate – to offer a combination of loan packages that will serve a range of purposes. This earlier preference was firmly rooted in past history and stemmed from an

> awareness of the risk to which a small bank exposed itself if it could not turn its assets quickly into cash to meet sudden demands from its depositors; but the preference still has some sound basis in that it limits the range of judgement required in the lending banker. The great majority of overdraft agreements made by the banks must be based, at least in part, on the judgement of branch managers, and these managers may reasonably be expected to assess the capacity of a borrower to repay in a short time, though they could have no assurance in estimating long-term profitability. English bankers have therefore traditionally regarded . . . themselves as properly engaged in financing working capital, particularly of the 'seed-time to harvest' kind, 'bridging transactions', and (within cautious limits) the temporary financing of fixed capital development pending the raising of long-term finance through other channels.[111]

Broadly speaking, British bankers sought to avoid more than the minimum of formal long-term commitments. Nevertheless, there was a good deal of lending even by way of overdraft that might reasonably have been described as medium-term. If such loans nevertheless turned out to be long-term in character, that could almost certainly be ascribed to errors of judgement on the part of the bankers concerned. It was not likely to be due to conscious policy. This emphasis in theory and, for the most part, in practice on loans that were self-liquidating was not merely a matter of bankers' preference. It could also be traced back to two characteristics of early industrial financing in Britain: the extent to which industrialists (more particularly in England) were dependent for their long-term needs either on self-financing[112] or on help from wealthy friends; and the early and, for a time, very considerable use made in England of the inland bill of exchange in order to meet the business demand for working capital, though these bills were not infrequently allowed to run on by way of renewal. In other words, there was a less obvious need than in countries like Germany and Belgium for institutions that would provide long-term finance to industry and the banks became accustomed therefore to making 'self-liquidating' loans in a convenient form.

In Scotland, the bill of exchange seems to have been largely superseded by an alternative lending technique, when – after 1728 – the Royal Bank of Scotland devised the cash credit bond, whereby a customer was allowed to overdraw his account up to the amount of the bond, which was in effect a guarantee of the borrower's worth by two or more men of substance. Interest was paid only on the amount actually borrowed and the 'cash credit' (a term that was also to be used for many years in India and Pakistan, where it was brought in by Scottish bankers) was undoubtedly one of the precursors of the modern overdraft.

Meanwhile, in England, the bill remained virtually supreme and, indeed, through the agency of the bill brokers, was for a long time an indispensable adjunct to English banking, since it provided the means of distributing loanable funds throughout the country, making them available where they were most needed. Not until after the 1857 crisis, as a result of the falling off in regular country-bank discounting, did the internal bill begin to decline in importance and the process was not at all marked until the 1870s. It was in fact the bank-amalgamation movement and the associated development of branch banking that enabled the banks to perform within their own organisations the function of making loanable funds available wherever these were most urgently required. It now became a matter of indifference to the banks, whether they financed their customers by discounting bills, or by granting loans and advances, and soon it was the latter technique that came to predominate.[113]

However, in England, bank accommodation was not for some time to be granted generally by way of overdraft. At a relatively early stage, the overdraft seems to have become a conventional lending technique in country areas, but in London the loan-account method continued to be used for many years.[114] The differences were not unimportant. Cheques could not be drawn against a loan account, though a separate current account could, of course, be maintained and operated. At that time, loan accounts attracted interest at lower rates than overdrafts, since interest had to be paid on the whole amount borrowed. To the customer, however, the flexibility of an advance by way of overdraft had definite attractions and, in many trades, the internal bill of exchange was gradually replaced by what was then known as the 'open-credit' system. This was in effect the modern overdraft and it proved to be a much more convenient means of borrowing. A bill had a fixed date of repayment, whereas an overdraft was usually allowed to run on. It was true that a bill might be renewed but at times it was difficult to do so, and this offset its relative cheapness on other occasions. Flexibility was an attraction to the banker as well, since the mere continuation of overdraft facilities could be employed for the purpose of financing the medium-term needs of industry whenever particular circumstances might warrant it. This is not to say that the self-liquidating character of an advance was overlooked and, even after an overdraft limit had been granted, it remained subject to periodic review.

It has long been the practice of British bankers to examine closely all applications for an advance by way of overdraft with a view either to ensuring its repayment within a more or less definite period or its regular fluctuation (i.e. from debit into credit and again into debit, or about some recognised mean). In the latter case, where an overdraft limit (and often it may be large) had been sanctioned as a fluctuating requirement, borrowings usually showed a large monthly or quarterly swing and, under normal conditions, a bank would expect to continue such a facility indefinitely (subject only to an annual review). In other words, there was a semi-permanent provision of working capital which ran on. For good accounts, there could be no question of a bank's requiring repayment. In no sense was there a rigid rule that required repayment within three, six or 12 months. The arrangement depended essentially on the character of the business so financed, though no banker would willingly become involved in truly long-term lending on this basis – the fluctuating requirement was regarded as virtually a succession of short-term loans. In all cases, other than the fluctuating requirement, the banker sought to work out with his customer a realistic programme of repayment over a reasonable period of time. This applied as much to loan accounts as to overdrafts.

When an overdraft was being arranged, the terms might be confirmed by an exchange of letters. The most important details related to the limit up to which the customer might overdraw his account and the rate of interest to be charged. On other occasions, the arrangement was made by word of mouth, though the details would be noted by the manager on a customer's information card or as a memorandum of interview that was placed on the file. Only in the case of large borrowings (especially when the application had to be referred to head office) would there usually be a confirmation by letter,[115] but many loans were made without reference to head office, since all managers enjoyed lending limits up to which they might lend at their own discretion. As already indicated, usually accounts were subject to an annual review (in the case of big companies sometimes six-monthly), unless a shorter period had been agreed in the case of a specific project. For overdrafts, similar arrangements still apply. Factors that are relevant when an account is being reviewed include the state of trade, the position of the firm itself as indicated by its cash-flow statement and the audited accounts, the state of the bank account (whether it is turning over regularly), and the content of the balance sheet, which would be looked at carefully every year (e.g., to see whether the firm was under-capitalised or carrying too large a proportion of debtors). Latterly, some of the English banks began moving in the direction of more formal credit analysis and the study of ratios has become more common. But none of them goes to the lengths of the American banks in this respect.

Although all overdrafts that go beyond the agreed limit would be reported either to head office or to a regional controller, banks tended to leave matters very much in the hands of their managers. In the event of an account beginning to go bad, every attempt would be made by the banker (by persuasion and, if necessary, by stern warnings) to restore a healthy position. In the event of continued difficulty, the banker would seek to work out an arrangement (such as a scheme of reduction) that would in due course restore his customer's affairs to a more healthy condition. Indeed, not infrequently, a banker had to nurse his customer along and help as much with advice as with finance. Very rarely would a banker wish to close an account and, if it became necessary to do so, he would certainly have to give a reasonable amount of notice. But such a step would probably be only a preliminary to a winding-up petition or a bankruptcy.

Quite a significant proportion of a bank's lending would normally be unsecured. On the whole, these would be the big companies (also persons of substance) and all unsecured loans would necessarily be regarded as prime risks. Where security is taken, practice varies somewhat between the banks, but the most common types of security include the mortgage of deeds of property (long leaseholds and freeholds, and including fixed assets); assignment of life-assurance policies (acceptable security up to surrender value); marketable stocks, shares, and debentures (often under a memorandum of deposit, but with the right to exercise a legal mortgage, if necessary); a floating charge[116] ('mortgage and charge' over land and premises, machinery, fixtures, and chattels present and future); (in some cases) a mortgage debenture[117] (which covers freehold and leasehold property, fixed plant and machinery, securities, book debts, and so on, with power to put in a receiver if necessary);[118] if stocks (or inventories) and debtors are the main assets, a floating charge over the assets of the company, or an 'all-moneys debenture'; and (with hire-purchase finance companies) a charge over their hire-purchase agreements. Other types of security include a guarantee by one party of the present or future debt of a second party in the form of a promise to the principal debtor; in some circumstances, a pledge or hypothecation of goods; and the mortgage of ships. For private borrowers – 'personal and professional' – when security is taken[119] a mortgage over property (usually a first mortgage, rarely a second) is quite common; and so, too, is the assignment of a life policy or lodgement of stocks and shares (under a memorandum of deposit, as above), or a guarantee[120] (usually this is given by an individual but it could be a company guarantee).[121]

For the most part, if a borrowing customer is in trouble, the banker will assist him to find his feet. In many cases, he has no option, since he is already committed and the only way to save his money may be to lend more, though under the strictest possible control. So far as big companies are concerned, if they are going to die they will die slowly and the banker has time in which to adjust his position. It is the smaller and medium-sized companies – sometimes the private borrower – that may create difficulties. But, as has been indicated, the banker will already have made every effort to secure a working arrangement and, if he has failed, making a demand for repayment is really only a preliminary to winding up or bankruptcy, or to getting rid of the account. Sometimes, it is another creditor who petitions for liquidation. If a banker is unsecured, he will have nothing to realise and must take his chance as an ordinary unsecured creditor. But if he is secured (e.g., by a mortgage over fixed assets), he will take steps to realise his security and apply the proceeds to repayment of the loan.

Reference has already been made to the loan-account technique, where the whole amount of the loan is debited to loan account, interest being paid on the full amount outstanding. Types of accommodation that were customarily made by way of loan account included house purchase; 'produce loans' to dealers to finance the holding of produce; loans to commodity brokers; in some cases, loans to timber merchants, because these loans tended to be longer in term due to the need to finance the seasoning period; loans for farm purchase, when permitted; finance to assist the purchase of a capital item like a machine tool or to pay for the extension of a factory,[122] it being regarded as desirable to keep this separate from the provision of working capital by way of overdraft; and, more generally, in the United Kingdom in advance of resort to formal term lending. In addition, the loan-account technique was resorted to on occasion as a means of increasing the degree of discipline that could be applied and was adopted therefore where the bank desired to exercise a greater measure of control with regard to the operation of the account (e.g., the transfer of 'hard-core' lending to loan account, particularly in agriculture).[123] This is true of salary earners quite as much as of small and medium-sized businesses, since in both cases it is desirable to ensure that the advance is regularly reduced. Partly because the loan account is employed when the bank wishes to watch things more carefully and supervision is therefore likely to be close, banks now charge a higher rate on loan account than on overdraft.

Personal-loan schemes were also launched by several of the English banks in September 1958 (with the Midland Bank as the pioneer) to assist in the financing of the purchase of cars and other durable consumer goods, along lines made familiar by a large number of American banks. Under the English arrangements, advances were offered, without security, for sums initially up to £500 and repayable with interest, calculated at a rate based on the amount of the original loan. Since these loans were repayable in equal monthly instalments over a period of up to two years,[124] the effective rate was much higher than that on an overdraft. One advantage offered by some banks under this scheme was the cancellation of any part of the debt that might be outstanding on the death of the borrower. In addition, until the 1969 Budget modified the concession, interest payments on all such loans ranked for income-tax relief, whereas hire-purchase charges did not. Personal loans – in the United Kingdom as elsewhere – are now an established means of bank lending to finance consumer items.

United States banking practice is nearer the Continental European than the British. One of the most striking features of bank-lending arrangements in the United States is the formality of the techniques adopted. In the United Kingdom, for many years (as we have seen) the vast majority of bank loans were made available in the form of an overdraft, which is a relatively informal way of lending. Overdrafts in the United States are very much the exception and when they occur they are often accidental (i.e. not pre-arranged), though latterly they have been introduced in some areas as part of a 'personal-service' package. Much of American bank lending – as in other countries – is of a short-term character in order to meet the working-capital requirements of business. The American banks also lend sizeable amounts in the form of term loans, much of it for the purpose of financing industrial expansion. This will be considered separately.

On the basis of Wednesday figures for April-May 1984,[125] for all banks, commercial and industrial loans are the most important single item – about 37 per cent of total loans and leases. For the large banks, the figure approaches 40 per cent and, for the large New York City banks, it is about 47 per cent. The other important ingredient in the overall portfolio is real-estate loans – for all banks, over 29 per cent, for large banks, nearly 25 per cent, but for the large New York City banks, just over 16 per cent. There is a similar pattern for personal loans, the respective figures being 19.6 per cent, 16.2 per cent, and 10.9 per cent. Areas in which the figures of the large New York City banks are relatively high – as one would expect – are loans to depository and financial institutions (a total of 9.5 per cent), for purchasing and carrying securities (5.9 per cent), and to municipal bodies (5.0 per cent). For all banks, lending to agriculture is small (3.3 per cent of total loans) – even smaller for the big banks and very small for the large New York City banks.

The larger banks and especially those operating from leading financial centres attract loan business from all parts of the country either through their correspondents or loan-production offices and their 'new-business' and 'contact' men. Hence, their portfolios tend to be highly diversified with no marked emphasis in one industrial category rather than another. However, the loan portfolios of local banks, even when these institutions are relatively large, do tend to reflect the major emphases of the local economy and they will be seasonally high in the related loan categories. Thus, grain loans are a common ingredient in the portfolios of banks in the Minneapolis and Kansas City Federal Reserve Districts and, in the latter case, cattle loans also. The banks in Memphis are heavily committed in the season to financing the movement of cotton and, in the cotton-growing areas, production loans will obviously be prominent. Oil loans are large in the books of the Dallas banks; tobacco and whiskey loans in Louisville; and timber loans in

Seattle. These are given merely as examples and banks in other areas (particularly in cities like New York and Chicago) are also frequently interested in these types of loans either directly or on a participating basis. However, all of them require special knowledge and, in some instances, the lending techniques themselves are somewhat specific. It would be quite impossible in the space available to go into these matters in any detail, but it is important to emphasise the degree to which the content of the loan portfolio may vary from one bank (and area) to another.

As already indicated, one of the most striking features of lending arrangements in the United States is the formality of the techniques adopted by the banks. In almost all cases, the banker will insist on his customer's signing a promissory note of a duly specified maturity. In this way, the banker is able to define both the amount and the term of loans actually made, though it is not uncommon for such loans to be made within the terms of an agreed line of credit (normally reviewed once a year) and, indeed, for notes to be renewed when they mature. Promissory notes may take several different forms. The ordinary note is a simple promise to pay, but sometimes the customer may be asked to sign a note with an 'accelerator clause', whereby in the event of a change in the customer's borrowing status the bank may at its option require immediate repayment of the loan. Where there is more than one borrower, a more elaborate statement of conditions may be incorporated in the note. Again, the customer may be asked to sign a 'collateral note', on which are listed the securities taken in to cover the loan and which empowers the bank, if necessary, to 'negotiate' the collateral. But the most typical form of borrowing from banks in the United States is on the basis of an unsecured note usually at three months, though some banks prefer a demand note. Formerly, it was usual to require 'compensating balances' – normally 10 per cent of the line of credit, plus 10 per cent of the usage. These have become progressively more difficult to obtain and, in New York, where competition is intense, have been 'greatly eroded', being largely replaced by 'all-in pricing'. If balances are maintained, a lower rate of interest will tend to be charged; if balances are difficult to obtain, the rate will be higher and, in addition, a commitment fee will usually be charged.

Although large in absolute terms ($79.5 billion in May 1984, or 6.7 per cent of total loans and leases of all commercial banks), bankers' acceptances have never become a truly important lending instrument in the United States. The authorities first gave active support to their development in the 1920s, but dealings in them never became a major activity. A significant quantum of the acceptances relates to the finance of imports and exports – over 40 per cent – but acceptances to finance goods stored in or shipped between foreign countries is even larger – well over 50 per cent. Acceptances to finance domestic shipments and storage are small, but at times have been relatively important. They relate to marketable staples, particularly cotton. Dollar exchange bills, which are intended to alleviate temporary shortages of dollars for payment of external obligations of certain nations, particularly those in Central and South America and the Caribbean area and not therefore associated with the movement or storage of specific merchandise, are small and at times disappear from the statistics altogether. Well over half of the acceptances are held in New York; San Francisco is next in importance (about one-fifth), with Chicago and Cleveland at over 5 per cent each of bills held by accepting banks. A significant proportion of the acceptances is discounted by the acceptors themselves and does not come on to the market, where much of the activity is in any case confined to 'swap' transactions between accepting banks.

Banks quite commonly lend against 'accounts receivable', i.e. sundry debtors, and thereby enable businesses to anticipate the payment of moneys owing to them. Usually, the bank will lend only up to a specified proportion of accounts receivable, over which it would normally take a general assignment. As a rule, this is a relatively expensive way for firms to raise working capital. In addition to interest, there is frequently a collection charge on each item. A number of banks also have factoring divisions which 'buy' accounts receivable. The debtor's credit is thoroughly investigated before the shipment of the goods and the account receivable is assigned to the bank against immediate payment to the creditor, the bank itself making the collection from the debtor in due course. This system facilitates the granting of credit to their customers by small companies which cannot themselves maintain the staff necessary to make the relevant enquiries. Since the factor actually purchases the account receivable, he bears the whole credit risk and retains no rights of recourse against the shipper, though he might claim for 'adjustments' if the shipment were faulty or the goods were damaged. In effect, the factor guarantees the debt and for this service he charges a commission. In addition, over the period for which the debt is outstanding, the shipper pays interest on the value of the accounts receivable sold, since he has immediate use of this money in advance of collection.

After 1946, one of the more significant developments in American bank lending was the increase in loans against real estate. A substantial proportion of these loans was made to mortgage companies to assist them to carry inventories of residential mortgages against a firm commitment made by an insurance company or mutual savings bank to take over the mortgages as a permanent investment as soon as they had accumulated sufficient funds. This was known as the 'warehousing' of mortgages. It was also done occasionally for insurance companies, when they had agreed to take up more mortgages than for the time being they could conveniently carry. In addition, many banks make mortgage loans of their own. These may take the form of the so-called 'conventional' mortgage, when the bank bears the full risk. For the most part, these have maturities of from 25 to 30 years, with an average life of between (say) six and nine-and-a-half years, and an average of seven to eight years (due to prepayment and customers' taking out a new mortgage after moving to a new location); experience varies a little from one bank to another, and from one part of the country to another. The bulk of these loans is usually made against house property, but money may also be lent against commercial and industrial properties, even on the security of a farm mortgage, though many banks actively dislike the latter. Alternatively, the banks may hold mortgages guaranteed either by the Federal Housing Administration or by the Veterans' Administration. These loans have usually been made for 20 to 25 years, but they can be sold if necessary and, in the event of the loan 'going bad', they are virtually underwritten by the federal government. This expansion in mortgage lending combined with the increase in construction loans (usually for between 18 months and three years) reflected the high level of building activity that developed during the years post-World War II.

The banks in the United States have also become heavily committed in the instalment credit field. This reflected an important structural change in American bank lending. In the years after World War II, the banks began looking for greater diversification in their loan portfolios. The bigger banks sought to supplement their 'wholesale' banking (the lending of 'large chunks' of money) by expanding their 'retail' loans. Although the net return in the latter sector tended to be lower even when relatively high rates were charged, it was a form of lending that could be highly profitable provided the business was done in sufficient volume and the rate of turnover was maintained at high levels by an aggressive lending policy. In attracting this class of business, a developed branch system proved to be a decided advantage, but even where branching was either prohibited or greatly restricted this limitation could be partly overcome by purchasing the paper of dealers from a number of points within the bank's trading area. Sometimes, the bank accepted such paper subject to the right of recourse in the event of the borrower's default, but usually it was acquired on a 'hold-back' basis, i.e. the bank withheld a proportion of the moneys that accrued as paper matured (e.g., 5 per cent) against the possibility of default on paper still outstanding. The amount held back constituted a reserve fund against possible losses and was only paid over to the dealer when the account was wound up. In addition to buying the paper relating to the instalment loans made by dealers to their purchasing customers, banks frequently financed the dealers' acquisition of stock from the manufacturers (e.g., in the case of automobiles and, sometimes, of farm machinery). This was known as 'floor planting' and such loans were usually very short-term, being replaced by dealer paper representing sales on credit.

Although they varied from time to time depending on the state of the economy, by careful selection of credit risks in respect both of direct loans and of dealer paper, delinquency and loss ratios were usually kept at low levels, delinquency ratios being defined as the amount of delinquent loans expressed as a percentage of the total number of loans outstanding at the end of a month multiplied by the number of days delinquent. Loss ratios were not generally available but were much lower and, although experience varied from time to time, have been described by individual banks as 'quite nominal'. It is only fair to point out that all banks in this field have a special staff working on 'recoveries' with developed 'follow-up' techniques. These have been the bases on which business has been developed over the years. In the majority of cases, the main ingredient in the bank's instalment-loan portfolios is automobile paper, usually with maturities of up to three years (even four years) on new cars, though two years is more generally regarded as the more appropriate term, with shorter terms for used cars. Automobile paper may amount to 50 per cent or more of total instalment credits, which are themselves often a significant proportion of the loan portfolio as a whole. In addition, a proportion of the 'personal loans' granted by banks (usually unsecured for a term of 12 or 18 months) are also used to purchase automobiles, though more generally such accommodation is intended to provide the funds to meet personal items such as expenditure on medical services or vacations, the loan being paid off in regular instalments. For the rest, the making of home-improvement loans, whether guaranteed by the FHA or not, appears to be very common, but in the past many banks seem to have been much less keen to lend for the purpose of financing the purchase of home appliances (such as refrigerators) or of furniture. Yet though often loath to make the loans themselves, the banks might nevertheless buy the relevant contracts from the stores selling these items. Finally, some banks finance the purchase of heavy-duty equipment on an instalment basis, the repayment sometimes being spread over three to five years. Farm equipment may also be financed in this way. However, these are strictly speaking business rather than consumer loans.

The usual procedure in making an instalment loan is to discount a single note, on which is stipulated the term of the loan and repayment provisions (usually equal monthly instalments). Most banks regard the character and earning status of the borrower as of prime importance and are much less concerned about the nature of the collateral. Indeed, many loans are in fact made on an unsecured basis, in which case it is usual to insure the life of the borrower. Frequently, a bank will also insist on the signature of the borrower's wife to the note and, where the application is regarded as somewhat marginal, the signature of a co-maker or guarantor may be required. For the most part, the customers who borrow in this way come from the lower end of the middle-income groups and a prime test is the amount of the monthly payment in relation to income and existing commitments. In many cases, too, instalment credit is resorted to by persons who hold liquid assets that sometimes exceed their indebtedness.

In addition to direct instalment lending, the banks make accommodation available to the sales-finance companies, which are in competition with them. The sales-finance companies customarily borrow from the commercial banks a proportion of the funds they employ in this business, the banks lending to them up to an agreed limit against an unsecured promissory note. The finance companies borrow in rotation from a number of banks, so that their indebtedness to any one is redeemed at regular intervals. The bulk of these loans goes to the large finance companies, but many banks also accommodate in this way certain of the smaller companies as well. It is usual for the banks to insist on the maintenance of minimum balances related to the line of credit that is accorded.

Although for the banks as a whole the amounts lent to agriculture are small, mention must also be made of the farm loans of the commercial banks, which are of course important for banks in agricultural areas. The majority of these loans are either for seasonal purposes or to finance 'intermediate-term investments'. The banks are very much less interested in financing the purchase of farm real estate. Seasonal loans tended to be of greatest relative importance in the Southern and Western Federal Reserve Districts. Chattel mortgages (or conditional sales contracts) are the most common form of security for farm loans. Renewals are common.

The minimum rate charged by the commercial banks in the United States on loans to creditworthy borrowers is referred to as the Prime Rate. It is related to, but does not necessarily change at the same time as, the Federal Reserve Banks' rediscount rates. Moreover, it is regarded as a true minimum rate and even the most creditworthy borrower will not usually be accommodated below it. However, there have been times when interest-rate competition has become acute and banks have admitted to breaking the Prime Rate. In general, the actual rates charged tend to vary with the size and the financial strength of the borrower. Excluding the instalment credit and personal loans, the higher rates tend to be paid by borrowers in the construction and 'service' industries, and in retail trade, categories in which the smaller and less well-established businesses predominate and the individual loan is usually small to medium in size. On instalment loans, rates tend to run at about double those on medium-sized business loans. This is because the quoted rate is usually much the same as that on business loans of similar amount, but it is applied on either a discount or an 'add-on' basis, which means that the effective rate of interest is roughly twice that quoted.

For similar types of business, regional differences are not marked, though rates do seem to be slightly higher (especially on instalment credit) on the West Coast and (on commercial loans) in Texas. Country banks with a smaller average size of loan typically charge rather higher rates and also tend to adopt a much more rigid rate structure. Indeed, during a visit to the United States in the 1950s, the author found that some of them charged 6 per cent whatever the level of the Fed's discount rate. As one of them reported to the author: 'Our customers would think there was something wrong if we didn't charge 6 per cent.' Even in a state with developed branch systems like California, where one would expect the financial structure to be much more highly integrated than in a state dominated by unit banks, branches in country areas (e.g., 'up the valleys') have in the past charged higher rates than the city branches for purely historical reasons, i.e. because rates have always been higher there. It is a phenomenon that cannot wholly be explained by the presence or absence of local competition.

An aspect of American bank lending that must be emphasised is the attention paid to credit analysis. This has been developed almost into a fine art. Bank credit files contain a full coverage of current information on all borrowing customers, together with a history of the firm's business and credit experience. This information, which is recorded on 'spread sheets' for a period of years, is based both on balance sheets and interim financial statements and on enquiries from other banks and the firm's own customers and competitors. Nowadays, this information would often be stored on computers – even by small banks. Frank and detailed enquiry in all possible quarters is accepted practice. The American businessman has no privacy whatsoever and he expects none. Indeed, bankers in the United States have little patience with the discreet and cryptic comments made by British bankers in response to enquiries about the creditworthiness of their customers, and between themselves they exchange information most freely. This may seem odd in as competitive a society as that of the United States, but on the whole the ethics of bank credit men are good; answers to credit enquiries should never be used as a means of competing away another bank's business. Only on this basis could information about customers be exchanged as freely as it is with the consequent advantage of greatly reducing the risks inherent in multiple borrowing arrangements. Nevertheless, in the final analysis, there can be no substitute for the banker's judgement of the character and ability of the borrower and this is as well appreciated in the United States as elsewhere.

Competition between banks in the United States for both loans and deposits has tended to be much more aggressive than it has ever been in the United Kingdom. Indeed, at times and in some parts of the country, it can almost be described as 'cut-throat'. Advertising tends to be more strident and a wider range of media is employed, one of the most imporant being the bank building. Throughout the length and breadth of the country, over the years, buildings have been modernised with competition as the sole objective. In small country towns, quite as much as in the big cities, modernisation of the bank on one corner has been quickly matched by radical alterations across the street. The larger banks (at which level the competition is national as well as local) also have teams of 'new-business' or 'contact' men, who perform the role of commercial travellers in banking services, visiting regularly both correspondent banks and large borrower and deposit accounts from coast to coast. Every effort is made to convince the public that one's own bank can offer the best available service and facilities and the whole emphasis is on building up an attractive bank 'personality'.

As has been indicated, size has been an increasingly important factor in competition both for loans and correspondent business. This was one reason for the spate of mergers. Branch expansion (where the law permitted) has been another means of competing for deposits and for small-loan and consumer-credit business. Over a period of years now, this has given rise to quite active inter-bank competition for convenient locations.

For the most part, competition in lending rates has tended to be rare and banks have preferred to attract loan business by streamlining their lending departments in order to give a quick decision. Most banks would argue that it is only when a new customer is coming on to the market that rate is important. Nevertheless, there have been cases of rate-cutting (see above)and 'breaking the rate' has sometimes been the means of attracting the business of the big national corporation accounts. In competing for deposits, the basis chosen is sometimes the services not charged for. Occasionally, however, the competition becomes so fierce that subsequently the banks get together informally and bring their charges into line. The provision of free services and the pursuit of a 'flexible' policy is one means by which a newly-established bank gets a footing in a town. Later, when it has built up a following, it will begin to impose charges at least on the more expensive types of services. But, on the whole, price competition has tended to be the exception and the provision of a wide range of well-advertised services has been regarded as the major weapon.

Term Loans

For many years, American bank lending was formally much heavier in the medium- and longer-term categories than was the case in the United Kingdom. In addition to extensive instalment lending, many banks in the United States had been making term loans since the 1930s, when they were introduced in an attempt to offset the poor levels of the loan demand at that time. It was a period, too, when the stock markets were unfavourable for new issues and the banks tried to expand their loans by offering finance for a period of years. Such loans were greatly expanded after World War II. Often such loans were too large for any one bank to handle and were shared between a group of institutions, the participating arrangements being made by a 'lead' bank, a practice by no means confined to term loans. Typically, a syndicate might be (for New York and Chicago banks) between five and ten banks, with the giant corporations using perhaps over 100 banks. The effective maximum maturity for such loans seems still to be about ten years, though occasionally this limit is exceeded. A limit of seven to eight years is more usual with a modal concentration within three to five years, but with quite a number within the five-to seven-years range. Formerly, loans in excess of ten years would be referred to the insurance companies, which at times did quite a large amount of lending to business. Indeed, many banks would not lend for more than five years and sometimes an arrangement was entered into whereby banks would take the first five years and the insurance companies the remainder. In some cases, banks established close connections with particular insurance companies, with which they shared much of their longer-term business. This is not nearly as prevalent as it was, but reference of the larger part of a term loan to an insurance company is still sometimes done.

Term loans are usually subject to a formal loan agreement, which sets out not only the amount of the loan, the rate of interest, and the terms of repayment, but also various covenants and warranties (i.e. in respect of legal capacity, the maintenance of a satisfactory financial position, provision of all necessary information, and the avoidance of action prejudicial to the interests of the lender). It is the smaller institutions that may dispense with a formal agreement. As the loan is taken up, the borrower's indebtedness will be evidenced in the usual way by a series of notes with maturities related to the repayment provisions. A commitment fee may be required on that part of the credit that is for the time being unused. Arrangements for repayment vary from one loan agreement to another. The loan may be amortised by means of equal annual, or biannual, instalments; or there may be no repayments during the first year or two, and annual amortisation payments thereafter; or there may possibly be a 'balloon' at the end with respect to a proportion of the loan, which may be paid off in a lump sum, or perhaps refinanced. Balloons tend now to be infrequent. If it is a 'bullet' loan, the whole amount would be paid off in one lump sum at the end. As a rule, a penalty is stipulated to discourage prepayment, but generally it would be applied only if the borrower intended to re-finance elsewhere. The rates of interest are higher than on short-term lending – from ¼-½ per cent to 1½-2 per cent higher though occasionally in highly competitive conditions the rate even on a term loan may be driven down to Prime.

The extent to which banks in the United States are prepared to make term loans to industry has meant that in many ways the overall financial requirements of business corporations have over a long period been more adequately catered for by the commercial banks there than has been the case in the United Kingdom, where for a long time much more conservative traditions prevailed. Even fairly small American banks make term loans to enable local business to expand. Some indication of their importance can be gleaned from a survey made by the author for all the Federal Reserve Districts in 1979, when as a proportion of the commercial and industrial loan portfolio (which, except for banks in agricultural areas, tends to be an important part of the total loan portfolio) about two-thirds of the banks quoted 20-40 per cent, and the remainder 50 per cent or more. A small number – usually the small banks in the survey – had 10 per cent or less.

As one might expect, Canadian lending arrangements evidence a degree of similarity to practice in the United States. The bulk of the loans proper[126] – particularly when short-term – are made on the basis of a promissory note within a line of credit. The overdraft has all but disappeared. Term loans (where a promissory note may also be employed, but subject to a formal term-loan agreement) are often quite important, though accurate figures are difficult to obtain.[127] Finally, because the Canadian chartered banks are all large retail banks, loans to individuals whether in the form of personal loans, consumer instalment loans, mortgage loans (largely to finance house purchase), and credit cards[128] are a very important element in the total loan portfolio. Loans in overseas currency[129] are often very important indeed and are funded by borrowings in the money market, Euro-credits, and on the basis of local deposits, where banks operate retail branches abroad (as in the Caribbean). Furthermore, because Canadian corporations resort to a significant extent to issues of commercial paper (through dealers) banks are now offering bankers' acceptance notes as alternative accommodation. Leasing must be undertaken through subsidiaries, as is much new mortgage lending since it is thereby possible to avoid reserve requirements.

Two factors seem to have been behind the introduction of the formal term loan by the banks in the United Kingdom: a growing awareness of the extent to which this form of lending had expanded in the United States; and the influence of the Radcliffe Committee Report[130] which favoured term-loan facilities. But the big breakthrough came after the introduction of Competition and Credit Control in 1971.

As already indicated, the Radcliffe Committee favoured term-loan facilities, within reasonable limits and having regard to the banks' liquidity requirements, 'as an alternative to a running overdraft for creditworthy industrial and commercial customers'. Likewise for creditworthy farming customers. This suggestion was first taken up by the Midland Bank, which announced plans to make long-term loans to farmers and 'term loans' for the finance of small businesses. The former were to be made for capital purposes, subject to repayment by annual reductions over a period (up to 20 years against a farm mortgage) and subject to recall on demand if there was a serious deterioration in the farmer's business situation. The latter type of loan was to be made for the purchase and improvement of capital assets, such as plant, equipment, and business premises. Normally, the limit was to be £10,000, with terms of between three and five years for plant and equipment and for up to ten years for the acquisition of business premises. Security requirements were subject to the same considerations as for normal bank lending. The rate of interest was 1 per cent above the usual rate for overdrafts with a minimun of 6 per cent. Repayments were by equal six-monthly instalments, when interest would also be debited. These loans only became repayable on demand if the instalments fell into arrears.

The other banks either introduced similar schemes or offered alternative facilities, though the degree of formality was usually less. The operation of the Midland Bank scheme to finance farm purchase was discontinued in November 1964, as a result of credit restrictions, although a number of these loans remained on their books. Moreover, although no formal arrangements now existed for this type of lending, the several clearing banks (including the Midland Bank) continued to be prepared to consider transactions involving facilities for relatively long periods on the understanding that these would be repayable, if required, over a period of (say) ten to 12 years. For its term loans to small businesses, though not for agriculture, the Midland Bank required a formal application; other banks did not, or were content to set out the terms in an exchange of letters. Term loans to small businesses were introduced at a time when there was a temporary easing of the credit squeeze (1958-9). Subsequently, restrictions were reimposed and, if anything, became progressively more stringent. In these circumstances, after a short period of expansion both farm loans and term loans to small businesses began to decline (loans to agriculture fared rather better because this was regarded as a priority sector, both by the authorities and the banks). Indeed, for industry generally, during the 1960s the development of contractual medium-term lending facilities was largely in the hands of the clearing banks' subsidiaries, which were in a position to buy money at higher rates than permitted by the cartel and for longer terms. Nevertheless, the figures remained fairly modest, except for shipbuilding loans and the long-term finance for exports provided by the banks themselves, which grew rapidly and were, indeed, cause for some concern. Terms began to lengthen, the finance was made available at a fixed rate (determined by the authorities) and, despite various refinancing facilities provided by the Bank of England, these loans were thought not to conform to the 'traditional principles of bank lending'.

Meanwhile, in the agricultural field, the Westminster Bank (as it then was) in 1966 introduced a Farm Development Loan Scheme. These loans were made available to 'sound, practical farmers for such purposes as the purchase of stock, machinery and plant, and farm improvements'. The loans were available originally for amounts of up to £5,000, later increased in stages to £20,000, and interest was charged at the rate of 6½ per cent per annum on the full amount for the full term (so that the true rate came out at about 12 per cent per annum and the rate was fixed for the duration of the term).[131] The loan and interest were repayable in equal monthly instalments up to a maximum period of five to seven years, though the term might be extended to avoid hardship. The big advantage to the farmer was that under normal circumstances these loans could not be called in. Admittedly, this finance was more expensive than that provided by overdraft, but these loans were intended to provide a facility that came somewhere between proposals suitable for overdraft and proposals where hire-purchase or leasing arrangements might be more appropriate. Although the demand from farmers for these loans was not at first very large, latterly it had been increasing.[132] But the big breakthrough in clearing bank term lending came in 1971. This was associated with the greater freedom stemming from the introduction of Competition and Credit Control adumbrated in May 1971 and formally launched in September. So far as term lending was concerned, both Barclays Bank and Lloyds Bank made the move in August 1971. In both cases, loans might be provided for any productive purpose; they were for a set term (Lloyds favoured terms that were relatively short, i.e. between three and five years) and subject to a planned repayment programme. It was expected that the loans would be covered by tangible security, and the rate charged would generally be somewhat above that paid by the customer for an overdraft. About the same time, the National Westminster introduced its Business Development Loan. Later, the Midland Bank also introduced a term loan proper and made special arrangemens for agriculture. This was agreed around the end of October 1971, but not effectively launched until December that year.[133]

Term loans granted by the clearing banks began to build up steadily. They were now regarded as the appropriate form of financing for investment projects likely to extend up to between five and seven years. Such loans were contractual and subject to a formal term-loan agreement (this replaced the exchange of letters usually resorted to in the early days of term ending).[134] These agreements which are generally employed incorporate details relating to the purpose of the loan, the period of the term, the programme for repayment, and the basis on which interest is to be charged. Although the term of such loans is usually for up to between five and seven years, longer terms may be agreed in exceptional cases. Repayment arrangements are negotiable and tailored to the particular requirements of the borrower, often with a moratorium during the earlier part of the loan, where the project being financed has a 'development phase'. Interest-rate arrangements are also flexible. Following the introduction of Competition and Credit Control, interest rates tended to be linked to the London Inter-Bank Offered Rate (LIBOR) with adjustments to the rate usually at six-monthly intervals. Latterly, loans have been available at rates linked to LIBOR or to market related bank Base Rates.[135] Prior to 1971, interest rates on medium-term loans were linked to Bank rate. After the substitution of Base Rate for Bank rate in October 1971, the former (which was market related) became the basis of the calculation. (The merchant-banking subsidiaries of the clearing banks resorted to LIBOR rates even before the clearers themselves.) Alternatively, loans have been made available at agreed fixed interest rates, though there have been times when this was not popular.[136] All term-loan agreements contain a set of conditions. For example, the whole of the loan outstanding may become immediately repayable if the borrower defaults in any way, or becomes insolvent, or applies a substantial part of the loan to other than an agreed purpose. Finally, where term loans are large, commitments may be syndicated between groups of banks.

Moreover, term lending has been related to term borrowing and the expansion that has taken place in medium-term lending by the clearing banks would scarcely have been possible at least on this scale if it had not been for the attraction of 'wholesale' deposits, or the buying of large blocks of money. Previously, the clearing banks relied almost exclusively on branch deposits for their funds. Part of these was held on deposit account, usually at seven days' notice[137] and these funds had tended to grow at a faster rate than interest-free current accounts. It was during the 1960s that a market in wholesale deposits developed – these deposits were available for varying periods and at interest rates usually higher than that paid by the clearing banks for money at seven days' notice. The subsidiary companies of the clearing banks obtained their funds mainly from this wholesale market. After September 1971, the clearing banks were also free to resort to this market. Thus, they could borrow from other banks in the inter-bank market and they could issue to large depositors certificates of deposit, for which there was a secondary market where these instruments could be bought and sold. Likewise, the clearing banks could lend in these markets, including amounts of over £10,000 for customers.

It has not been policy to attempt to match term loans precisely with term deposits, though there may have been occasional elements of it, but the evidence does point to a high degree of matching over certain periods between the figures for term loans and those for wholesale deposits. Moreover, although the bulk of the sterling deposits is at short-term, these moneys are rolled over regularly, market conditions being reflected in movements in interest rates, with adjustments to the rate at three- or six-monthly intervals. There may also be a commitment fee or non-utilisation fee. For the most part, the rates on medium-term loans will be adjusted in sympathy. Where loans are made at fixed rates, expected changes in interest rates will of course have been taken into account. Where term loans are large, commitments may be syndicated between a grouping of banks.

In order to give some idea of the degree of build-up in term lending by the London clearing banks (and their subsidiaries), for non-personal borrowers only, the percentage of contractual (term) lending and special export schemes in relation to total lending was 35.6 in 1973 and 44.2 and 47.4 respectively in 1975 and 1976.[138] Similar figures for 1981 and 1983 (29.4 per cent and 32.7 per cent) suggest there has latterly been some decline.[139] Special export schemes included ship-building loans and the finance of other capital goods, much of it assisted by Export Credit Guarantee Department (ECGD) facilities, including the topping up of the interest rate for cheap fixed-rate loans; there were also re-financing arrangements at the Bank of England, subsequently taken over by the ECGD or the Department of Industry as appropriate.[140] Financing North Sea oil was another important activity.[141]

For the Scottish banks, by November 1976, total term lending to the non-personal sectors amounted to 35.5 per cent of non-personal lending compared with 24.3 per cent in 1973. If special export schemes (as above) are included (net of re-finance) this increases to 39.4 per cent. Adding back re-finance, raises the figure to 45.8 per cent. By 1982 and 1983 (mid-November), the non-personal term lending (more than one year) to United Kingdom residents by the Scottish clearing banks and their subsidiaries (including lending under the Department of Industry special scheme for shipbuilding) was 18.1 per cent and 17.0

per cent respectively of total United Kingdom non-personal lending.[142] Hence, there is also evidence of some decline in Scotland.

It should be remembered, too, that in addition to these term commitments, there was – and still is – throughout the United Kingdom an element of hard-core lending on overdraft, which can in practice be even longer-term than loans specifically defined as term loans. This was even more true in the past.

Both the London and Scottish clearing banks felt[143] that any further large rise in their medium-term lending 'could be imprudent'. Their deposits – including those raised in the wholesale-money markets – are mostly short-term. While they can protect themselves against interest-rate fluctuations by resorting to variable-rate loans, they still 'attach importance to the traditional argument about matching the maturity of assets and liabilities: it is unwise to borrow short and lend long'. If therefore there was to be any further increase in term lending in response to industry's demand for it, they argued that there could be a case for a re-financing facility at the Bank of England in order to 'overcome the banks' prudential constraints', or – as the Treasury put it – to 'overcome the problem of a mismatch of maturities'. Indeed, it was the latter consideration that led to the introduction in 1970 of facilities for the re-financing by the government of export credit and shipbuilding loans.

At one time during the post-war period, the commercial banks in West Germany were disinclined to make formal medium- to long-term loans. In order to avoid showing such loans in their balance sheets, they lent formally for maturities of up to 3 years 11 months, though such loans might well be renegotiated and extended further – in effect beyond the four years. Indeed, although there was never a contractual arrangement, such a possibility may well have been contemplated from the outset in some kind of understanding between banker and customer. Latterly, the banks came to accept much more frankly that a significant proportion of their lending was at medium- and long term. Long-term loans were defined as loans for four years or more. The terms of the loan are set out and accepted (usually) in an exchange of letters, which will also contain reference to a number of standard conditions, though sometimes there will in fact be a formal loan agreement between the parties. So far as the rate is concerned, the banks have always attempted to avoid a rate that is fixed for the duration of the loan, though at times competition for loan business has obliged them to offer a fixed rate. More usually, if a rate is fixed, it is for a period shorter than the maturity of the loan, with the possibility of renegotiation. Or an 'agreed' rate will operate until further notice. Alternatively, the rate may fluctuate with the Bundesbank discount rate, usually being 3½ per cent but sometimes 4-4½ per cent above. Long-term loans to domestic borrowers may be made for up to ten years (in the 1960s, the maximum term was about twelve years). Actual maturities have been of the order of four to six years (again shorter than in the 1960s when six to eight years was common).

In this context, one might note that the *Girozentralen* (which operate as central institutions for the savings banks, but which themselves undertake a wide range of commercial banking business), partly because of their origins, seem to lend at longer term than the Big Three commercial banks. On their medium-term loans (averaging, say, five years), too, they appear to lend more often at fixed rates than do the Big Three. They also lend at ten to fifteen years, but with an adjustment to the interest rate over the course of the loan. Some of their long-term credits will be on a revolving basis. Another reason why the *Girozentralen* are more interested in the longer end of the maturity spectrum is their ability to raise finance by the issue of bonds, which makes possible some matching of long-term lending with long-term borrowing. But the differences between the Big Three commercial banks and the *Girozentralen* have tended to diminish over the years, with the Big Three rather more willing to lend at long term and the *Girozentralen* moving from longer-term lending towards more lending at the shorter end to industrial customers.

Prepayment of long-term loans may be permitted, but only after a minimum period. It is not usual for term loans to be renewed, but it can happen. More commonly, a new loan may be negotiated for a related purpose. On the whole, the German banks prefer not to lend too long and generally send really long-term lending on to a mortgage-bank subsidiary (a number of these were set up towards the end of 1971). Only in the foreign field (e.g., to finance the purchase of export goods) would the banks lend for up to fifteen years,[144] but such loans would generally be guaranteed by public institutions and might well be arranged on a roll-over basis using Euro-money raised through a Luxembourg subsidiary.

As already indicated, in the earlier post-war years, the German commercial banks were rather reluctant to lend at long term (certainly to show such loans in their balance sheets), mainly because of the large volume of short-term deposits on which their lending was then primarily based. Latterly, the saving ratios of private households increased dramatically – it doubled between 1960 and 1975, when it approximated 15 per cent – and the Big Three commercial banks began actively to seek savings deposits (one of them now describes itself as the 'largest savings bank' in the Federal Republic). Meanwhile, there had been a reduction in the ability of German industrial companies to generate their own finance and the need for outside finance increased both in absolute and in relative terms. The commercial banks were now more willing to lend at longer term, relating this type of business directly – and as a conscious act of policy – to the considerable growth in their savings deposits (formerly long-term loans were made largely from public funds,[145] but these were now much less important than in earlier years). At the same time, there is no actual matching between term loans and term deposits and in fact savings and time deposits still exceed long-term credits.

In considering term lending in Japan, it is first necessary to outline the structure of the loan portfolio itself. For the city and regional banks, this is comprised of bills discounted, loans against promissory notes (PNs), loans against deeds, and overdrafts. For the end of 1983, the breakdown was as in Table 6.1. As can be seen, for both the city banks and the regional banks, loans against PNs are the most important

Table 6.1: Bank Lending in Japan – Structure of Loan Portfolio (per cent)

Type of accommodation	City Banks	Regional Banks	Long-Term Credit Banks
Bills discounted	16.8	17.8	1.7
Loans against PNs	45.0	43.0	23.9
Loans against deeds	34.7	36.7	73.9
Overdrafts	3.5	2.5	0.5

Source: Bank of Japan, *Economic Statistics Annual* (1983)

category, followed by loans against deeds. For both, bills discounted represented about 17 per cent of the total, being slightly higher for the regional banks (for both, it was 20 per cent or more in 1981). But for the long-term credit banks, loans against deeds are the overwhelmingly important item. In all cases, overdrafts are small (though latterly slightly up) and for the long-term credits banks negligible.

It is loans against deeds that relate to term lending. These are for over 12 months – on average (say) for three to five years, but they could go up to seven years, or occasionally longer (e.g., ten years, when there may be a moratorium of one to three years). Some housing loans are made by the city and regional banks (they would be classified as loans against deeds, being secured by a mortgage) and would run for up to 20 years. Personal loans would be resorted to to finance the purchase of durable consumer goods like automobiles, white goods, home improvements, even holidays. Personal loans would be for up to 24 months and are usually referred to a bank by a dealer. Term loans (which come under loans against deeds) are of course secured. Usually, the moneys are lent in order to finance capital expenditure and there is a formal term-loan agreement; the 'deed' will be a mortgage or debenture over land, buildings, and equipment. Long-term credit banks lend against a floating debenture and this covers land, buildings, and equipment; only for companies with a very high credit standing would goods in process and raw materials be included, when the bank would lend against total assets.

Traditionally, the overdraft was the most favoured means of lending in Australia, the limit being reviewed once every 12 months (sometimes, every six months), or whenever a new application was made. Latterly, in order to reduce costs, overdraft limits have sometimes been looked at less frequently and some banks are content to review those of their larger clients every two to four years. Smaller companies would be reviewed more frequently, subject to reductions; professional borrowers likewise. Overdrafts are still important in the rural sector and in the commercial/industrial sector, when the borrowers' requirements fluctuate. Utilisation of limits varies, but tends to exceed 70 per cent. It is quite usual for a trading bank to charge either a line-of-credit fee or an unused-limit fee on overdrafts.[146] Advances are usually secured. The ratio of overdrafts to total lending varies between the trading banks and at different times of the year, but in all cases is important. Nevertheless, over a period of some 15 years, there has been an accelerating shift in lending towards the fully-drawn advance, which now also represents a significant figure for the larger trading banks. In this case, it is expected that the customer will draw down the relevant moneys immediately or perhaps in several tranches, any temporary excess being transferred to a current account. Such advances are subject to a loan agreement. Usually, the bank will build into the financial provision a margin to provide flexibility and the balance can be transferred to an operating account (as above), though no set-off (of interest) would be allowed as may be the case with an overdraft. Fully-drawn advances primarily provide for capital funding – e.g., for plant and equipment.[147] Smaller men would be accommodated by way of a personal loan, which is also the technique employed to finance consumer expenditure (though much of this business would pass to a subsidiary finance company). Flat rates have been charged on personal loans (which makes them expensive), though this may now be subject to review. The majority of these loans is still on a secured basis. Consumer finance would comprehend automobiles, white goods and travel, with a pay-out period of 12 to 60 months. Bankcard is another form of consumer credit that is made available and is much used.

An alternative to the overdraft that is employed in Australia is bill finance. In 1965, banks were authorised to undertake additional commercial bill activity in order to test and explore the real demand for this form of financing. Simultaneously, authorised dealers in the official short-term money market were granted permission to deal in commercial bills, which had been accepted or endorsed by a trading bank, and to hold a proportion of their portfolios in bills of this type.[148] For middle-sized to larger companies, an integrated financial package may be arranged with the several parts of a corporation's requirements being met by overdraft, a fully-drawn advance, and bills (bank acceptances or an acceptance discount line)[149] with terms (usances) of three and six months. In addition, merchant banks make accommodation available to large corporations in the form of bank-endorsed bills against a roll-over facility. Banks are also increasingly involved in the development of a letter-of-credit market and in underwriting of promissory-note issues by larger companies and various statutory authorities.

In 1962, a Term-Loan Fund was established for major trading banks (initially funded by releases from special reserve deposits held by trading banks with the Reserve Bank of Australia – the country's central bank – together with other funds lodged by the trading banks); these provided for term lending by major trading banks, and enabled them to enter fixed term lending – usually for from three to eight years or a little longer – for capital expenditure in the rural, industrial, commercial and export sectors. The term of these loans was subsequently extended to ten years, or slightly more. Term loans are subject to a formal term-loan agreement and a commitment fee is charged. Rates are reviewed biannually. A little later (in 1966), a Farm Development Loan Fund (funded in a similar way) was also set up for major trading banks to provide fixed-term lending (initially for periods of up to 15 years and at concessional rates of interest) to rural producers for farm-development purposes. The scope of the Fund's lending activities was widened in 1972 to include finance for such purposes as farm purchase. This method of funding term lending was phased out from 1978, with funds from these sources running out in October 1979 (for farm-development loans) and January 1980 (for term loans). Since then, term lending has been funded on the same basis as all other forms of lending. Loans formerly made out of these funds are now being financed by the Australian Resources Development Bank, the Primary Industry Bank, or by the bank making the loan.

Since 1967, trading banks have been permitted to provide 'bridging' finance at 'reasonable' interest rates (subject to consultation with the Reserve Bank) but above the maximum overdraft rate. A year later (1968), approval was granted to the trading banks to engage in lease financing on a modest scale at rates determined in consultation with the Reserve Bank, but again above the maximum overdraft rate. Leasing is still relatively small, but growing strongly.

The percentage breakdown of trading bank lending in its several forms in March 1979 is compared with more recent dates (July 1982 and June 1984 respectively) in Table 6.2. Separate figures are not published for fully-drawn advances, but in a survey carried out by the Australian Bankers' Association in May 1979, the proportion of fully-drawn advances to total overdraft balances was shown to be 42 per cent. Since that time, it has probably grown further.

Table 6.2: Major Trading Bank Loans, Advances and Bills Discounted, Australia (per cent)

	Total Lending		
Type of loan	March 1979	July 1982	June 1984
Term loans	10.5	10.5	12.0
Farm-development loans	3.6	4.3	3.8
Temporary advances to woolbuyers[1]	1.2	1.1	—
Bills discounted	3.4	1.7	1.7
Bankcard outstandings	4.1	6.0	7.3
Personal instalment loans	13.0	16.6	17.6
All other advances[2]	64.2	—	—
Other overdrafts	—	55.5	54.1[3]
Lease finance	—	4.3	3.5
Total	100	100	100

Notes: 1. Short-term overdraft lending facilities covering pre-shipment and post-shipment finance for woolbuyers. 2. Includes overdrafts, fully-drawn advances, leasing and bridging finance. 3. Includes temporary advances to woolbuyers.
Source: *Reserve Bank of Australia Bulletins*

In New Zealand, it is said that the quantitative growth in loans tends to be mostly a function of deposit growth, with each bank focussing primarily on its deposit share. Consequently, it may be said that the New Zealand banking system is driven mainly from the liabilities side, lending strategy being determined as the residual in the equation after allowance has been made for the reserve requirements imposed by the monetary authorities.

In the past, the bulk of bank lending in New Zealand was done by way of overdraft up to a limit which would normally be reviewed once a year, discounts being more particularly linked to export or import finance. For many years, also, advances were subject to limitations on the rate of interest that could be charged. Hence, when trading banks were permitted after March 1963 to make term loans at higher rates they began to shift out of overdrafts into term loans for appropriate types of business (e.g., for what was likely to be longer-term lending) and the advantage remained even after the freeing of interest rates in March 1976. On term loans, too, the banks may charge a commitment fee if the loan is not taken up immediately. The trend away from overdraft lending towards term loans has continued, mainly, it is said, because of the greater ease of management. Such loans would tend to have a maximum term of five years, but this may be exceeded (typically being extended to seven years). However, many term loans would be shorter than this – the average is probably three years. They are normally subject to a fairly simple term-loan agreement. Term loans now represent an average of around 43 per cent of total advances, loans, and discounts, though the figure varies somewhat between the several trading banks, some of which are heavier in term loans than others. There has also been an extension of commercial bill discount lines; the banks have likewise moved significantly into leasing. Personal loans are also of some importance to the trading banks and are tending to increase; alternative finance can be secured at the finance companies.

The amount of bill finance fluctuates from time to time, but it has tended to increase and (by March 1984) total bills outstanding had exceeded NZ$1,288 million. Bills may be classified as trade bills or as accommodation bills. A trade bill derives from an ordinary trading transaction involving a deferred payment for actual goods received. An accommodation bill is a bill drawn under an acceptance facility extended by a bill dealer or a discount line granted by a trading bank, where there is normally no directly-related trading transaction involved; it is purely and simply a finance bill. Trade bills proper vary in importance from time to time. Thus, in 1982 their importance fluctuated between 37 per cent of the total and less than 10 per cent (and there have been marked fluctuations in other recent years). However, they have tended over recent years always to have been much less important than accommodation bills. Banks may discount bills and hold them in portfolio or buy bills from the market (in order to absorb liquidity). When they buy from the market, they will impose limits and not buy more than a certain amount of bills in a particular name (or names). In addition to bills held by banks, bills are held by dealers and also by investors other than dealers or banks. The last would include bills in which a dealer or a bank has only acted as broker between one client and another.

For many years in France, the most important single ingredient in the banks' asset structure was its *portefeuille-effets* – in the first decade or so after World War II it varied for the nationalised banks between 55 and 65 per cent of total assets; for the regional banks, it was even higher (from 60 to 70 per cent). By the end of 1969, when this item was last shown in *Bilans des Banques*, for the nationalized banks it was still well over 50 per cent. *Avances* were shown separately. Then, in 1970, the *portefeuille* was divided between credits at short, medium and long term, remaining in total for the nationalised banks at about 35 per cent of total assets, a further loan item (*comptes débiteurs*) being about 13 per cent. By the beginning of 1984, for the three largest nationalised banks, credits to customers were divided into *créances commerciales*, other short-term credits, and credits at medium and long term, in total amounting to about 38 per cent of total assets.

Portefeuille-effets was an omnibus item and included Treasury bills and similar paper with short maturities; the 'acceptances' of the *Crédit National* (medium-term paper rendered liquid by its ultimate eligibility for rediscount at the Bank of France); and commercial paper which was also eligible for rediscount. By far the larger part of *portefeuille-effets* held by the banks was included under *autres effets* (i.e. discountable paper other than Treasury bills and similar items), much of it representing the finance of business which in England would be accommodated by way of overdraft, though *avances* were also resorted to at that time in France. Nevertheless, French practice was to lend primarily for this purpose on the basis of discountable paper. After World War II, more was lent in this way than in 1938 and the ratio settled down both for the nationalised and regional banks to something less than half of total assets – a very significant figure.[150]

Over more recent years, there has been a tendency for medium-term and long-term credits to increase as a percentage of total credits – in

1970, they represented about 35 per cent of the total *portefeuille* of the three large nationalised banks; in early 1984, 41 per cent (for the deposit banks as a whole, over 57 per cent). Short-term credits are usually made on the basis of a *billet à ordre* (similar to a promissory note), and a proportion of these *effets privés* (up to 90 days maturity and with three signatures) is eligible for rediscount at the Bank of France. These would fall within the *créances commerciales* item in the balance sheet and this represented 17.6 per cent of total credits for the deposit banks in early 1984 (18 per cent for the three big nationalized banks).

Again, one should note (as was done for the various categories of deposits) that there are other banking sectors besides the *banques inscrites*. Thus, as at the end of 1983, of total bank credits to the French economy, the *banques inscrites* which include the large commercial banks referred to above) accounted for 63.6 per cent, the Crédit Agricole for a further 19.6 per cent, the *établissements financiers* for 7.6 per cent, the *banques populaires* for 3.6 per cent, the *crédit mutuel* for 3.0 per cent, and the Banque Française du Commerce Extérieur for 2.6 per cent. Total credits to the economy amounted to FFr 3,261.5 milliards; of these FFr 3,261.5 milliards; were bank credits and FFr 1,154.9 milliards non-bank credits, provided mainly by the semi-public financial institutions, of which the most important were the Caisse des Dépôts et Consignations (together with the *caisses d'épargne*) 38.2 per cent, the Caisse de prêts aux HLM (18.8 per cent), the Crédit Foncier de France 13.1 per cent), and the Crédit National (6.5 per cent); credits to finance energy and telecommunications are the most important of the remainder. The *sociétés de développement régional* furnished 1.8 per cent of the total. Of total credits, over 90 per cent were granted in French francs, the remainder in foreign currencies. Of the franc credits, 22.0 per cent were short-term, 6.2 per cent 'mobilisable' medium-term credits, and 69.7 per cent 'non-mobilisable' or long-term credits. Just over 2.0 per cent had no precise term.[151]

For many years, discounted bills was the main lending instrument in Spain also. By 1981, however, this was no longer so. Credit accounts and loans now accounted for about 60 per cent of the total bank-credit portfolio. But in Portugal bill finance (discounted promissory notes) is still important.

West Germany was another major country where there was a significant emphasis on discount paper on the basis of *Wechsel*. These are bills of exchange drawn to finance the movement of goods (exports and imports, but domestically as well), and have long been rediscountable with the Bundesbank up to specified quotas. They become eligible once they have a maturity of no more than three months. If a bank has already exhausted its quota, it will have to go to the money market for its additional discounts or obtain accommodation from the central bank on the basis of a Lombard loan,[152] i.e. borrow against government securities lodged in safe custody with the Bundesbank. In this context, they may also include good trade bills as security. It should be noted, however, that Lombard loans have not always been available. So far as the customer is concerned, *Wechsel* are discounted at market rates up to an agreed line of credit, which is reconsidered every three or six months. A line of credit is also laid down for use as a current account or cash credit. This is noted in the bank's books and the customer can draw up to that amount. He will usually be charged a commission or commitment fee on the amount of the line of credit that remains unused. (This is not done in the case of *Wechsel*.) The terms of the loan which will usually be for six or 12 months, will be set out in a letter to the customer. Sometimes, these loans are allowed to run on and they may on occasion be formally converted into medium-term loans.

Nowadays and for some years past, *Wechsel* have been much less important. As far back as 1973, *Wechsel* (or bills discounted) only represented 4 per cent of total lending to non-banks; loans of up to one year were then 18.8 per cent of the total. For July 1984, the relevant figures were 3.2 per cent and 14.6 per cent.

As already indicated, in Japan, bills discounted have latterly represented about 17 per cent of the total loan portfolio of the city banks, slightly higher for the regional banks. Bills discounted are almost all domestic bills with only a very small amount of bank acceptances. All represent an underlying business transaction – there are no finance bills. For the most part, maturities are of less than three months.[153] The bills are 'clean', i.e. there are no documents attached. Loans against PNs are primarily short-term – the PNs are for three months, but the loans are rolled over. Sometimes, a facility is offered which will run on for longer than a year; this would be done on the basis of an understanding. For short-term loans, a borrower may have a credit line which is secured and then roll over his borrowings against that line. A loan contract may also apply, though for domestic loans the conventions are rather loose – there may only be an understanding based on discussions with the customer. However, often a security agreement is entered into.

In a number of West European countries, the overdraft, or something very similar to it, is used as a major lending technique. Thus, for a long time in The Netherlands, short-term lending to commerce and industry has been mostly by way of overdraft, limits normally being reviewed once a year, or when a new application is made. Customers operate on such accounts by means of a giro transfer, not by cheque.

Medium-term lending, which probably represents 30-35 per cent of total loans to private companies, is normally for three to seven years, with an average term of five years. For medium-term loans, there is an attempt to match[154] lending with resources at least for the period during which interest rates remain fixed (interest rates tend to be reviewed every one to five years and thereafter be fixed until the next review). Term loans tend to be secured often by means of a mortgage. As with other bank loans, they are always subject to a formal term-loan agreement. Some overdrafts will also be secured by a mortgage or guarantee. In addition, there is something like a floating charge in the Netherlands (covering, for example, raw materials, goods in process, and receivables). For the big banks with a large market share, fluctuations in the use made of overdrafts tend to offset each other, though such fluctuations may create some difficulty for the small banks.

Bill finance is used only for export financing. Bills are under certain conditions eligible for rediscount at the Netherlands Bank. Medium-term financing of exported capital goods is for terms of five to seven years, but this may be done on the basis of the special export finance arrangements (EFA) between the Netherlands Bank and the other banks. EFA bills can be used by banks as security for borrowing from the Netherlands Bank.

Apart from trade bill accommodation, the normal way of lending in Belgium is by way of overdraft[155] (the limit is reviewed normally every 12 months, by one big bank semi-annually), but there has in recent years been a considerable growth, too, in 'straight loans', where the banks lend a fixed amount for a short period, mostly for one to three months, with 12 months as the maximum. The minimum maturity would be three days. These loans, which tend to be taken up by big customers, are financed from money-market funds and the rate relates to the inter-bank money-market rate. The rate is fixed for the period of the straight loan and very often the loan is matched by one- to three-months borrowing. The rate charged on overdraft is variable – it depends on the cost of money (e.g., what they have to pay on deposits, but it also relates to inter-bank market rates). There is a base rate (which is not published)[156] to which a margin may be added. There may also be a commitment fee or a non-utilisation fee. Term loans, which tend to be matched by long-term deposits (*bons de caisse* and a proportion of savings deposits) are also made by the banks – for five, seven, even 10-15 years). Normally, the banks look for repayment in five to ten years. These loans are subject to a formal term-loan agreement and are usually secured. Personal loans relate to private customers (for consumer credit) and lending to small firms. The big banks also lend to finance house purchase against a mortgage (with a pay-out period of 25 years, though the effective period would be 10-11 years, formerly seven years). All the big banks have an important guarantee business; often the guarantee is given by way of an *aval*. The security taken for a loan is often a mortgage or a guarantee/*aval*.

In Switzerland, the main way of lending at short term is current-account lending (similar to the overdraft) both unsecured and secured (a significant proportion against a mortgage), with a line of credit that is reviewed at least every 12 months; it is subject to a loan contract. Bankers prefer customers to use only one bank, but in fact many borrowers use more than one[157] (they may have their overdraft with one of the Big Five and a mortgage loan from a cantonal bank). For the very large borrowers, loans would be syndicated. As we have noted, some loans are secured by a mortgage; other forms of security include bonds and shares taken as collateral, guarantees and *avals*, and (exceptionally) warehouse receipts. No use is made of the floating charge in Switzerland. Term or 'time' loans, which may represent almost twice the amount of short-term lending, are made in fixed amounts over a certain period of time, which varies with the project being financed. There is a time-loan agreement, but the loan can be called in if there is a significant change in the circumstances surrounding the loan. Usually, the loans are amortised. Time loans are by no means always secured, but each loan is subject to detailed credit analysis. Time loans might be for as long as (say) five or six years, but often for between three months and 12 months at fixed rates. The rate of interest is higher than on an overdraft (say, ¾ per cent higher whether secured or not), but with a time loan there is no additional commission; on an unsecured overdraft, interest is charged plus ¼ per cent commission per quarter. Rates on loans, which are subject to an agreement as to minimum rates, are not fixed and may be negotiated. Rates on mortgages (primarily to finance house purchase) tend to be lower – for socio-political reasons. The banks also undertake industrial mortgages, which are more profitable and are amortised on a proper basis. The cantonal banks lend more particularly to small and medium-sized businesses and on the basis of mortgages, part of the latter being financed from their savings deposits, on which however the rates tend to be low (being linked to the relatively low mortgage rate). There has therefore been a shift into time deposits in order to get a higher rate. But in absolute terms the big banks also do quite a sizeable mortgage business and it is by no means any more the prerogative of the cantonal and savings banks. Except for the cantonal banks in Zurich and Berne (and only up to low restrictive limits), the cantonal banks do not undertake foreign business.

When corporations are borrowing in Austria, they first approach a bank (and most corporations would use the services of more than one banker)[158] and seek to obtain a 'promise' or commitment to lend from that bank. In consideration of this commitment, a fee will be paid. Very frequently, the bank will enter into a commitment to lend first and then go out and look for the relevant moneys to lend – in other words, there seems to be quite a large amount of matching. When the loan is drawn, the relevant moneys would then be transferred to a current account, but there is an ultimate limit up to which the customer can draw. Usually, customers use up to 60 to 70 per cent of their line; if they borrow right up to the limit, it may have to be increased. The commitment (or limit) is reviewed (say) quarterly, even monthly; working capital loans tend to run on, even to increase over time. The security taken is usually a mortgage or a guarantee; for commercial loans, a blank bill of exchange (duly signed) might also be taken as security. There is no floating charge, or the pledging of invoices, debtors, or book debts in Austria. Some loans, when the amounts are large, would be syndicated. Term loans may be granted for periods of up to ten years (on average for about five years) with annual or semi-annual repayments. These loans would be subject to a term-loan agreement though for short-term borrowing also a loan contract would be drawn up and this would include security arrangements. Private customers might be allowed to overdraw up to (say) twice their salary. This is what is usually called an overdraft in Austria. Dossiers would be kept for each customer and, where relevant, information about customers is exchanged between banks. All the banks make personal loans (consumer credit) to private customers at a higher rate; they also make mortgage loans to finance house purchase (such loans are still a more significant element in the savings banks' loan portfolios than for the commercial banks, but the latter have in recent years developed a much greater interest than formerly. They also lend against a mortgage of industrial and commercial properties).

Bill finance probably represents the most manageable means of lending and the large banks sometimes therefore favour resort to the *Wechsel*, for which a three-month maturity is common, though bill finance could run out to five years (e.g., for investment purposes, when a series of bills would be employed). When such bills are based on a genuine trading transaction (i.e. value has been received), are for a maturity of no more than three months, and carry a minimum of three good signatures, they are eligible for rediscount at the National Bank. *Wechsel* tend to be only a small percentage of the total loan portfolio.

In Norway a significant amount of lending is done by way of overdraft (also referred to as a 'cash credit'). Lines of credit are made available to industry and commerce (by the savings banks also to agriculture to meet seasonal needs). Generally, the overdraft is allowed to run on; usually, the line of credit is reviewed annually. Overdrafts may or may not be secured but the tendency has latterly been for more loans to be secured. Mortgages of all kinds are popular as security and now Norwegian banks may also hold a general charge over the assets of a business[159] (debtors/receivables, stocks of raw materials and semi-finished goods). Overdrafts are less common in shipping, which is mostly financed in foreign currencies. Personal overdrafts are quite small, instalment loans being preferred. Although it varies between the banks, the largest item on the lending side tends to be the formal loan. Almost all of these are term loans – typically for three to five years, sometimes for seven years – repayment being on the basis of semi-annual instalments. There may possibly be a prepayment with no penalty, but, since it is often difficult to secure bank accommodation in Norway, there tends to be very little prepayment. Such loans tend to be secured often by a mortgage. They would be subject to a formal term-loan agreement and a small commitment fee would be charged. Term loans may be used to finance the purchase of buildings (say, loans for six to ten years), or for the installation of plant and equipment. Big firms would tend to use more than one bank. They would also in case of need be able to issue their own bonds, or borrow from a long-term lender, who issues bonds on the market to finance such loans. In addition, banks make construction loans (for a shorter period – say, 12 to 18 months, when the long-term lender takes over) and to finance house purchase (normally for 12 to 15 years). Housing loans may be made by the State Housing Bank, by savings banks, and also by the commercial banks and insurance companies. This would include home-improvement loans. Savings and commercial banks likewise lend to municipalities –

e.g., to build schools – and to small and medium-sized businesses both by way of overdraft and medium-term investment loans. Instalment credit – mainly to finance the purchase of private cars and trucks – is quite small. Accommodation made available on the basis of the discount of a bill of exchange is small. Mostly this is 90-day paper and is usually partially renewed at least once. It is a means of extending the credit of the companies concerned. Bill finance is tending to decrease in importance – in absolute terms it is much the same, but tending to fall in both relative and real terms. But bills are still used traditionally in wholesale markets and in the timber trade.

Foreign-currency may be financed on a matched basis by foreign-currency borrowing. Norwegian banks borrow on a direct basis from foreign banks. Either they borrow foreign exchange or they may do a swap – in this context, they may obtain kroner against borrowed dollars, which they sell to whomever needs them;[160] they may also cover themselves forward, or the swap may be done with the same party (rather like a sale-and-re-purchase agreement). The banks do not use brokers for foreign-exchange transactions – they do it all themselves.

For the most part, bank lending in Sweden is in the form of a short-term loan, often at six months' notice, though they may be rolled over. There is a formal letter of agreement. Even term loans are formally at six or 12 months' notice, but they are subject to an agreement (e.g., on repayments) which may run for an average of seven years, exceptionally for as long as ten years. In terms of the prudential requirements, loans should be secured, banks being permitted to lend unsecured only up to 10 per cent of their balance sheet and, indeed, a proportion of their loans is unsecured. Loans would amount to up to 60 per cent of total bank lending in Swedish kroner, though it would vary somewhat between banks. Building construction credits are next in order of importance – something less than 20 per cent. The bulk of these is to finance the building of houses; these credits are subject to an agreement with the authorities (each bank has a quota which has to be met) and are priority loans. Banks also lend for commercial and industrial building on a non-priority basis, but in the same form. Formally, building credits are a 12-months loan, but this may be extended and on average they run for 18 months. Overdrafts are also employed; they would amount to at least 10 per cent of the portfolio and for some banks are rather higher. Accounts may be overdrawn up to a limit, which is formally reviewed once a year. These 'current-account credits' (as they are sometimes called) are often used for personal purposes (e.g., for consumer credit), but also to provide working capital for corporations, though in that context the banks would prefer a loan. Utilisation of an overdraft is normally about 45 per cent. Again, within the terms of the prudential requirements, the overdraft would usually be wholly or partly secured and subject to an agreement. Overdrafts may be used to finance house purchase, when they may run on for ten years, even longer. Home-improvement loans would be for a much shorter period. Bill finance is small and is tending to diminish. Bills may be used to provide short-term credits to farmers, or to finance stock-in-trade, also to hire-purchase dealers (overdrafts are also employed for this). For car purchase, banks may resort to revolving credits secured by bills. Some may be finance bills – drawn on one company by another for the sole purpose of raising finance. On the whole, bill finance has been taken over by the overdraft, or by short loans. However, all banks would have outstanding a small quantum of documentary credits. Bank lending has from time to time been subject to credit ceilings, which the banks dislike, preferring the liquidity requirements. Only foreign-currency loans are outside the ceiling; in this case, the banks borrow foreign currency for on-lending to Swedish firms in foreign currency, the borrower bearing the exchange risk, though he may cover forward. The importance of these loans varies between banks, but for the largest they can be very significant (on average, say, 30 per cent of total lending).

The savings banks have a central institution and in their case loans may be made by a local savings bank in collaboration with the Central Bank for Savings; in addition, savings banks may borrow from the CBS and on-lend in their own name. There are also syndicated loans with the CBS as the lead bank, the syndicate being made up of a number of the larger savings banks; in this way they can cater for the needs of the large corporations. The CBS would also borrow in foreign currencies for on-lending to Swedish borrowers.

The most important way of advancing money to customers resorted to by the banks in Finland is by way of loan – for the large banks, it represents about two-thirds of total domestic lending; for the two largest banks, credits in foreign currency – financed by foreign-currency borrowings – would be 20 per cent or more.[161] Loans are made against a signed promissory note, or on the basis of a loan agreement or letter of agreement. It may provide for the loan to be repaid in monthly or six-monthly instalments over a period of (say) four years, with a floating rate of interest, but loans may be for longer periods, an average term being four to five years. (Personal loans for house purchase usually do not exceed 15 years, but are normally shorter; for durable consumer goods, two years, with a maximum of five years for a car, but in practice two to three years). Interest rates vary with the Bank of Finland's base rate. The Bank of Finland imposes a ceiling, which can be exceeded if loans are overdue. The Bank of Finland also requires that a bank's average lending rate does not exceed a certain level. Industry and commerce also resort to bill finance and overdrafts for the provision of working capital. The use made of overdrafts[162] varies from time to time, though in the total figures it is small. There is a limit up to which the customer may overdraw,[163] which is usually reviewed annually, or when a new application for an advance is lodged; more commonly, if additional finance is required, it would be made available in the form of bill finance or a loan. Bill finance, the use of which is declining,[164] is primarily used for financing stocks (e.g., by wholesalers and retailers) on a seasonal basis; it can also be used for the purchase of raw materials by producers, especially where sales are seasonal. Usually, it is 90-day paper, which may be renewed, but there are also six- and sometimes 12-months bills. Other items in the loan portfolio include loans with an interest rate subsidy – e.g., housing loans, student loans, and agricultural loans.

In Denmark, the two big lending items are overdrafts and 'other loans' (which excludes bills of exchange, building and mortgage loans) – together accounting for about 90 per cent of the total, divided almost equally between the two. At the same time, there has been a tendency for the overdraft[165] to decline in importance. Industry has been loath to borrow and to invest.[166] In addition, during periods of tight money, the banks would prefer to expand their term loans, which are subject to a more rigorous repayment programme than overdrafts, which tend to run on, even to increase, but industry is not very interested in term loans. Term loans would be for not longer than ten years, usually for four to eight years. They are subject to a formal loan agreement. Usually, the loan is linked to a floating rate, tied to the National Bank's discount rate. Building loans, which are small, are usually for from six to 12 months, when a permanent lender like a mortgage-credit association takes over the mortgage, though the banks make some mortgage loans as well. In the automobile field, banks tend to finance the intermediate dealer, who can discount finance paper up to limits. For other durable consumer goods, the banks discount paper for the large suppliers. Personal loans to individual buyers are also resorted to. The last reflects the importance of households in total bank business. Danish banks are not themselves permitted to borrow abroad. But Danish firms may borrow abroad against a guarantee from a Danish bank.[167] Indeed, guarantees are important and, in total, amount approximately to the same figure as overdraft facilities.

It will already have become apparent that in the United States customers frequently employ the services of more than one banker. Possibly, in small towns, a local bank will have something of a monopoly, but even in small towns a loan of any size will normally (if only because of statutory restrictions on size of loan to a single customer) have to be shared as an 'overline' with a city correspondent bank. And for the medium-sized and large corporations alike, it has long been necessary for them to use a number of bankers – ranging from several for a medium-sized firm to many for the truly big corporations, which would use the services of banks throughout the United States. Furthermore, it will have become clear that in most countries – these days – industrial and commercial customers (even quite frequently private customers) normally resort to a number of bankers both for borrowing facilities and a widening range of services.

But this was not always so, especially in Britain, or in countries which tended to follow the British banking tradition. Thus, except for the largest customers, it was formerly the case in Britain for most customers – whether manufacturers, traders, farmers, or private persons – to employ the services of one bank (except perhaps for a savings-bank account), or more generally, one main banker to meet the bulk of their banking needs. This was associated with what might be called the 'all-or-nothing' principle in British bank lending, though latterly this applied most obviously to the smaller customers. When a proposal was submitted to a banker in the United Kingdom, one of the questions he would ask himself was whether sufficient finance was being sought. Borrowers sometimes asked for less than they would need, though the opposite was more usual and frequently proposals had to be pared down to more modest proportions. Although it was not in the interests of the bank that excess accommodation be provided, it was equally unsatisfactory if a venture was inadequately financed. If it was a good proposition (and acceptable on other grounds – e.g., was consistent with the Bank of England directives then current), the bank would wish to see it through in its entirety. Furthermore, the banker would want to establish in advance the size of his eventual commitment. There was a dislike for supplementary loan applications from customers, due to an initial estimate of needs that turned out to be too modest. (Separate ventures would be in a different category.)

Under these circumstances, a banker in the United Kingdom was likely to lend 'all or nothing'. Except when it was a question of an excessive estimate of requirements, he was unlikely to offer a proportion only of the funds sought. He would rather reject the whole proposition. Nor did this generally mean that great hardship was imposed on bank borrowers. Unless there was an obvious clash with the policy of the monetary authorities as laid down from time to time, all reasonable credit requirements were in fact likely to be met. The banker was as anxious as his customer to attract good business.

This began to change as banking became more competitive in the United Kingdom. Use of a number of bankers has long been the rule for the big corporations, though they might still regard one of the clearing banks as their main banker; this was true because the borrowing requirements of a very large customer may at times (e.g., from a risk point of view) seem to be large even for a big bank. But in the 1960s – as the banking situation became increasingly competitive – even medium-sized businesses began to resort to more than one institution. There were also instances of customers becoming less than satisfied with their existing bankers and transferring their business to another bank. Doubtless, this always went on to some extent, but it now tended to increase. It also served to emphasise that a minimum number of banking institutions was necessary in order to preserve a sufficient degree of competition. More generally, there was now an increasing tendency for bank customers to use two or more banks instead of depending on a single banker. One would have expected large companies to use more than one banker, but the medium-sized borrowers also began to do so. Moreover, the latter group were less influenced than the large companies in their multiple-borrowing policies by the maintenance of traditional connections inherited as a result of industrial mergers.[168] Probably, this tendency to use more than one bank, which in any event the bankers believed was most common with large companies, was rather less in evidence when money conditions were very tight. During a time of squeeze, customers tended to stay with the bankers that knew them. But there was little doubt that where companies were big enough they would not hesitate to play one bank off against another (even different branches of the same bank). For similar reasons, bank customers now tended to hold with their bankers balances lower than was formerly the case. Nevertheless, there were factors also operating against multiple borrowing, such as 'the desire to minimise working balances or borrowings by concentrating a company's funds or the need to concentrate in order to make the most effective use of computers'.[169] Also, if only one banker were employed, one could set off loans against balances in the calculation of interest. This was certainly a significant consideration when interest rates were high. Latterly, the practice of multiple borrowings continued to increase and has become comparable with the position in the United States, the Continent of Europe, and Japan. One might therefore have expected that in the United Kingdom there would develop a much franker and more complete exchange of risk information (with an inevitable loss of privacy, if the American model were followed, or, as in France and elsewhere, the authorities may have decided to establish a *service central des risques*, where information relating to the borrowings from the several banks would be centralised and it would be possible to compare what a customer had borrowed from one's own bank with the total figure of his borrowings from all banks).[170] That is not in fact what has happened. So far as the big 'blue-chip' companies are concerned, information about their economic and financial situation is public knowledge; the current position can be ascertained from interim or 'management accounts'; and in any case there is so much competition for good lending business that the banks would generally be willing lenders. Some – perhaps many – medium-sized companies would still employ one main banker. For others, the leading clearing banks could depend on their research departments for information about the relevant economic sector; interim or 'management accounts' would still be required in order to indicate the current situation; and, in general, the bank would depend on analysis of the firm's balance-sheet position and information (e.g., about borrowings from other banks) requested direct from the customer. Finally, except where a customer's position was known to be very strong and the bank was prepared to lend unsecured, the bank would be able to look to its security, which in any event many bankers would take where available at the outset of the banker-customer relationship, thereafter checking from time to time on the extent of the cover.

International Lending

A field in which banks throughout the world have greatly expanded their interests over more recent years has been international lending, much of it – as we have seen – on the basis of the Euro-currency markets. They have also added to their capital resources, often by issuing subordinated debt (see pp. 225-6). The international lending by banks has been partly to corporations and partly by way of 'sovereign loans', i.e. to foreign governments and government instrumentalities, much of it to the Third World. As experience in the United States and elsewhere has indicated, severe losses can be made from time to time in domestic lending. There is no need to list the casualties – suffice it to recall the recent trauma of Continental Illinois (and there were a number of other instances in the United States in the early 1980s and especially in 1983); energy-related and property loans seem to have been the chief culprits (also loans to the agricultural sector). But the exposure to potential losses on the domestic front has been as nothing compared with the debt crisis in the Third World, greatly exacerbated by high levels of interest rates. Even where losses have not actually been incurred, provisions for possible losses have made heavy inroads into bank profits and the excessive borrowings of Third World countries have given rise to an international debt crisis of some magnitude. In the search for profit, banks have made many dubious loans; they have also become greatly over-extended in specific areas (particularly in Latin America and especially Brazil, Mexico, and Argentina, but also in Africa, the Comecon countries, and elsewhere). Moreover, it could be argued that they have not only made a number of bad loans, but by their willingness to offer accommodation they have themselves lent some of their Third World borrowers into great trouble, which it will take years of loan rescheduling and probably some reduction in interest rates to reduce to manageable proportions. Currently, even the servicing of outstanding debt is a matter of great difficulty.

It is pertinent therefore to consider what are generally regarded as the appropriate criteria for 'sovereign loan risk'. In addition, the more obvious loan considerations will apply – the creditworthiness of the borrower, ability to fund the loan, the possibility that interest rates may move against the lender, and (in the international field) the risk of adverse movements in the foreign exchanges. But above all it is 'country risk' that is specific to international lending.

Country risk relates to the degree of probability that a country will not in fact be able to generate enough foreign-exchange earnings (by way of exports of all kinds) to service (pay interest on and repay principal) its foreign-currency loans in accordance with the terms laid down in the original loan agreement. There may, too, be an element of political risk – the possible unwillingness of a foreign government to honour its external debt obligations. It is this that is sometimes referred to specifically as 'sovereign risk'. Subsidiary to sovereign risk is the risk associated with the project, where the offshore portion of the finance would be used to acquire machinery, equipment and expertise requiring payment in US dollars or other hard currencies and where the maturity of the Euro-financing would be related to the cash-flow of the asset; since the product is usually exported, it is anticipated that foreign currency will be earned with which to service the debt. Where development of the infrastructure is the objective, project and sovereign risk will overlap.

In attempting to assess sovereign risk, a bank may, on the basis of country reports, firstly, analyse economic indicators relating to a country's domestic economy, such as Gross National Product and its components, external debt levels and service payments. Ratios that the banks would be interested in could include the debt service ratio, GNP per capita, the proportion of investment to GNP, the size of the agricultural and/or mining sectors, since these are the kinds of things that assist in assessing performance or development potential. Secondly, the bank may establish projections based on time series – e.g., relating to the balance of payments and its component parts on the basis of which to project export/import growths, also the growth path for official reserves; the future growth of GNP and its components; employment prospects; and the rate of inflation. These projections can then be compared with the growth of external debt and its maturity profile with a view to establishing whether and how much to lend to each country. *Inter alia*, country reports will assemble statistics on the borrowing countries' general economic and financial situation, the political background, the current political scene and future political prospects, with particular reference to social stability, and above all the size and composition of a country's external indebtedness. There will also be a regular annual or biannual reappraisal, especially where a bank is exposed. Such countries will be ranked as to degrees of risk in order to establish exposure limits and the bank's priorities in international lending.

This summarises the basic approach but some banks will pursue more sophisticated methods than others. For example, they may employ an econometric model based on 'discriminant analysis' in assessing country risk – e.g., historical precedents can be scrutinised in the expectation that countries that have defaulted in the past will show different characteristics from those which have not; or debt service ratios and the maturity structures of debt can be utilised in order to forecast the probability of rescheduling, always looking for a best combination of variables (in one such study[17] these were found to be the public-sector debt service ratio, the rate of growth of exports, the index of export volatility, 'non-compressible' imports as a proportion of total imports, per capita income, amortisation as a proportion of total outstanding debt, ratio of imports to GNP, and the ratio of imports to reserves). One of the advantages of the econometric approach is an ability to identify statistically significant variables on the basis of which to assign weights in a check list (which many banks employ) in that way attempting to reduce the degree of subjectivity. But a major disadvantage is any implicit assumption that factors contributing to the rescheduling of debt remain the same from one period to another. Structural change is bound to take place and to differ from one country to another.

Time series can also be subjected to sophisticated analysis – e.g., the so-called 'spectral analysis' for the descriptive element (trend or long-term component; functions relating to cyclical or oscillatory behaviour; and identification of random components). Linear or multivariate analysis can then be used to provide an explanation of the variation. What banks require, however, is a forecast of future behaviour and what they are likely to depend on here is a 'moving average' – the calculation of running means. This would show whether there is any tendency to a long-term increasing or decreasing trend, or if there is a tendency to periodic fluctuations (this could be useful for detecting the future price level for a commodity on which a country's export earnings depends). None the less – whatever the statistical techniques that are employed – a bank will need to resort to a systematic approach to country-risk evaluation, involving for each country a thorough analysis of economic, political, social and external factors, some of the evaluation of which will be subjective. In other words, in the final analysis – like all banking operations – a sound decision must be based on judgement.

Experience suggests, however, that none of the methods employed is all that reliable and the banks that have been most successful in avoiding or limiting losses are those which were cautious in granting 'sovereign loans', concentrating rather in the international field on corporate lending. The other lesson that should have been learnt by now is not to lend excessively to Third World countries, many of which have quite frankly been lent into trouble by banks seeking what appeared to be very profitable deals, the position having been greatly exacerbated by the emergence of high levels of interest rates.

Notes

1. See J.S.G. Wilson, *French Banking Structure and Credit Policy* (London, 1957), p. 110.

2. On this basis, most – if not all – of these banks are able to maintain quite a good credit rating which is important when borrowing and also when sharing syndicated loans.

3. See *Financial Times*, 24 July 1984.

4. In this context, funds are often raised on the Euro-markets.

5. Partly as a result of the effluxion of time but also as a result of a policy of rolling over their debt, the English clearing banks tend to have a spread of maturities (some of it quite short) in the loan capital they have issued.

6. In August 1984, the Société Générale announced that it would attempt to tap private sector funds by issuing non-voting *certificats d'investissement* in order to strengthen its capital resources. This would be more like equity funding than the *titres participatifs*; they would have all the advantages of shares, except the right to vote, which would remain 100 per cent in State hands. See *Financial Times*, 17 August 1984.

7. See Edward Shann, *An Economic History of Australia* (Cambridge, 1930), pp. 328ff. S.J. Butlin *Australia and New Zealand Bank – The Bank of Australasia and the Union Bank of Australia Limited, 1828-1951* (1961), pp. 306-7, takes a somewhat different view, but the existence and – in certain cases – the importance of British deposits must have exerted some influence on the minds of Australian bankers. Further evidence on temperamental British depositors is offered by Geoffrey Blainey, *Gold and Paper – A History of the National Bank of Australasia Limited* (Melbourne, 1958), pp. 141ff.

8. See Committee on Finance and Industry (Macmillan Committee, 1931), *Evidence*, Vol. II, p. 152.

9. Formerly, both in England and Scotland, interest was paid – as it still is in some countries – on demand deposits as well as on those subject to notice, or fixed for a term. Because of rising costs, the Scottish banks ceased payment of interest on current accounts in 1892, but the English banks – even in London (where it was first abandoned) – paid interest on current accounts until very much later. Indeed, on occasion, interest-rate competition for deposits could be quite fierce (see, for example, R.S. Sayers, *Lloyds Bank in the History of English Banking* (Oxford, 1957), pp. 161-5); but eventually (in 1946) the payment of interest on current accounts was abandoned altogether and, on deposit accounts (until 1971), it became subject to agreement. Competition for deposits now took the form of the services offered by the bank to current account customers, including 'safe custody, investment facilities, financial advice and, more importantly, the possibility of borrowing upon occasion; but above all the bankers' service consists of the cheque service. It is the moneyness of the bank balance that is the basic attraction to the depositor, and the more perfect his service in this direction the more readily will the banker find his resources growing.' (*Report of the Commitee on the Working of the Monetary System*, Cmnd. 827 (1959) (hereinafter referred to as the Radcliffe Committee Report), para. 133, p. 44.) Latterly, in a number of countries, because of competition, payment of interest on demand deposits has begun to creep back.

10. The Radcliffe Committee, reporting on the United Kingdom, were inclined to discount the importance of this distinction between demand and time (or fixed) deposits. See 252-4 for further discussion.

11. In December 1965, the deposit banks were given authority to open savings accounts on the same terms as the savings banks themselves. Previously, the commercial banks in France had not been permitted to offer rates as favourable as those being offered by the savings banks, but by December 1965 the commercial banks were at last authorised to offer the facility of *comptes sur livrets* (savings-book accounts) on exactly the same terms as the savings banks themselves.

12. See Commission de Contrôle des Banques, *Rapport* (1983), p. 79.

13. See *Conseil National du Crédit, Rapport Annuel* (1983), p. 193.

14. Ibid., p. 195.

15. Ibid., p. 205.

16. Ibid., p. 201.

17 Time deposits of 12 months seem to be the most popular – for all banks 59.3 per cent of ordinary time deposits are for 12 months – because of the higher rate and their relative liquidity. For small savers time deposits may be for up to three years.

18. For details, see The Bank of Japan, Research and Statistics Department, *Economic Statistics Annual* (1983).

19. Compare the 'compensating balances' required by American banks up to 20 per cent of a line of credit when a customer is borrowing, though American banks are less able to insist on these now as compared with formerly.

20. Similar operations also came to be carried out in claims to other currencies.

21. See J.S.G. Wilson, 'Money Markets in the United States of America', *Banca Nazionale del Lavoro Quarterly Review* (December 1970).

22. See *Federal Reserve Bulletins*, Tables 1.26, 1.28, and 1.13.

23. See Marcia Stigum, *The Money Market*, newly revised edition, (Homewood, Illinois, 1983), p. 470. For a detailed account of financial futures in the United States, see pp. 471-523.

24. Ibid., p. 511.

25. See ibid., pp. 471 and 472.

26. See 'Competing Through the Backdoor', *The Banker* (February 1965), pp. 84ff.

27. Internal limits would be applied to the certificates of deposit of the individual banks, though for the best names these were not likely to affect the position significantly.

28. See *Evidence* of the London Committee of Clearing Bankers to the Committee to Review the Functioning of Financial Institutions (Wilson Committee) (November 1977), pp. 49-50.

29. See J.S.G. Wilson, *The London Money Markets* (SUERF, 1976), pp. 49-52.

30. See 'Sterling Certificates of Deposit and the Inter-bank Market', *Bank of England Quarterly Bulletin* (September 1983).

31. Other large deposits may be placed directly by the institution concerned or through money brokers.

32. See Wilson, *The London Money Markets*, pp. 45-6.

33. See *Evidence* of Committee of London Clearing Bankers to Wilson Committee, Table 54, p. 273.

34. See Committee of London Clearing Bankers, Statistical Unit, *Abstract of Banking Statistics* (April 1984), Table 1.22. It should be noted that in November 1981 the 'banking sector' was replaced by the 'monetary sector', which for all practical purposes comprises all recognised banks and licensed deposit-taking institutions located in the United Kingdom, plus National Girobank, trustee savings banks, and the Banking Department of the Bank of England. Hence, figures after 1981 are not directly comparable with those before 1981.

35. Lending against mortgages on house property was another means of 'fighting back'.

36. For a fine market rate, the minimum size of deposit would be £100,000 and clearly the size of the deposit is important. The maturity of the deposit has also to be taken into account as well as the banker/customer relationship. Some big companies frequently put money out by way of time deposits (in amounts of £500,000 to get the best rates and for periods of two weeks to three months); others may use the inter-bank market.

37. CDs are popular with building societies of all sizes; they tend to 'lock them up' as part of their liquidity, but they are of course available for sale if they need money.

38. There is still a limited amount of fixed-rate lending (e.g., to small companies in amounts of £250,000 to £500,000), but the rates would be carefully calculated. For large amounts lending would tend to be fully matched.

39. See *Abstract of Banking Statistics*, Table 2.22.

40. This bill was endorsed in blank to the Stock Exchange Committee. What the stock exchange sold was the receipt. It continued to hold the bills until maturity.

41. However, from January 1983, it was no longer permitted to include other banks' CDs in the liquidity ratio.

42. Certain banks have guaranteed that they will do so.

43. Including the savings banks and the Central Bank for Savings, the cooperative banks and the Central Bank for Cooperative Banks; also the finance companies.

44. The National Pension Insurance Fund also puts temporarily surplus money on special deposit with the banks for 14 days.

45. The period that is popular at any time depends on interest-rate expectations.

46. Tanshi houses are estimated to handle about 80 per cent of the business in the CD secondary market.

47. But not finally accepted by the Bank of Japan until 1976. Before that, it was regarded as an 'unofficial' market.

48. An *en pension* transaction, usually done through a broker – of which there are 30 in Paris – is where paper is sold, say, for one or two days, or one month, or even for three to six months, sometimes 12 months, subject to an agreement at the end of that period to repurchase, the rates paid being money-market rates.

49. More recently, Italy has also introduced CDs.

50. Non-financial companies, banks, as well as the central government raise money by way of private placements.

51. So far as possible, banks in Italy must match Euro-currency borrowings with Euro-currency lendings; they may take a position in a particular currency, but in aggregate they must balance their currency books.

52. For example, the Radcliffe Committee Report, pp. 43-4.

53. Ibid., p. 43.

54. Ibid.

55. Ibid., p. 44.

56. See, for example, George Garvy, *Deposit Velocity and its Significance* (Federal Reserve Bank of New York, 1959). Over the years, a number of attempts have been made to improve the United States deposit turnover series.

57. Under the Depository Institutions Deregulation and Monetary Control Act of 1980.

58. See *Reserve Bank of India Annual Report* (1982-83), p. 47.

59. See Margaret Reid, *The Secondary Banking Crisis, 1973-75 – Its Causes and Course* (London, 1982)

60. Ibid., p. 23.

61. See J.S.G. Wilson, 'Supervision of the United Kingdom Banking System', *Banca Nazionale del Lavoro Quarterly Review* (March 1977) for an outline of the story.

62. *The Licensing and Supervision of Deposit-Taking Institutions* (Cmnd. 6584).

63. See *The Times*, 4 August 1976. Cf. R.S. Deane, P.W.E. Nicholl, and R.G. Smith (eds.), *Monetary Policy and the New Zealand Financial System*,

2nd edn (Wellington, 1983), p. 371.

64. For a useful commentary on the Act as a whole, see Ian Morison, Paul Tillett, and Jane Welch, *Banking Act 1979* (London, 1979) and, for the Deposit Protection Scheme, Chapter 4 at pp. 74 ff.

65. For details of the original announcement, see *The Financial Times*, 25 October 1957.

66. See J. William Frederickson, 'The Economic Recovery of Finland since World War II', *The Journal of Political Economy* (February 1960), pp. 17-36.

67. See *Unitas* (Helsinki, November 1951).

68. For an outline of these arrangements, see J.S.G. Wilson, *French Banking Structure*, pp. 97-102.

69. See Glyn Davies, *National Giro: Modern Money Transfer* (London, 1973).

70. See George Rae, *The Country Banker* (London, 1885); also J.E. Wadsworth, 'Banking Ratios, Past and Present', in C.R. Whittlesey and J.S.G. Wilson (eds.), *Essays in Money and Banking in Honour of R.S. Sayers* (Oxford, 1968), pp. 229 ff. For the Scottish experience as compared with England, see J.S.G. Wilson 'An Experiment in Competition and Credit Control', *Geld en Onderneming* (Leiden, 1976), p. 134 (n).

71. W.F. Crick and J.E. Wadsworth: *A Hundred Years of Joint Stock Banking* (London, 1936), p. 190. See also Sayers, *Lloyds Bank in the History of English Banking*, pp. 179-80.

72. Ibid., p. 39.

73. See *Report of the Committee on Finance and Industry* (Macmillan Report), Cmd. 3897. (1931), pp. 35-6. For the ratios that obtained in the 1930s, see T. Balogh, *Studies in Financial Organisation* (Cambridge, 1947), p. 36.

74. R.S. Sayers speaks of a minimum cash reserve ratio of 9 per cent as representing the usual position prior to World War II – See Sayers, *Modern Banking*, reprint of first edition (Oxford, 1941), p. 34. This is consistent with the Macmillan Committee's own statement of the position: 'It is evident . . . that the clearing banks do not maintain from day to day so high a proportion of cash as is shown by the monthly statements, and although we have not available all the data required to make an exact calculation, it seems probable . . . that the total cash reserve kept (apart from balances with other banks and items in transit), is over all about 9½ per cent against the published figure of nearly 11 per cent.' (para. 79, p. 36).

75. Radcliffe Committee Report, para. 505, p.180.

76. Ibid.

77. Ibid.

78. See H.W. Arndt, *The Australian Trading Banks* (Melbourne, 1957), p. 56; H.W. Arndt and C.P. Harris, *The Australian Trading Banks*, 3rd edn (Melbourne, 1965), pp. 74-5. For detailed statistics refer to Commonwealth Bureau of Census and Statistics, *Monthly Bulletin of Banking Statistics*.

79. These are discussed in detail in Chapter 11.

80. See *Monetary and Fiscal Policy in New Zealand* (Submission to the Royal Commission on Monetary, Banking and Credit Systems, 1955 by Reserve Bank of New Zealand, Associated Banks in New Zealand and New Zealand Treasury) (Wellington, 1955), pp. 65 and 69; see also R.S. Deane, P.W.E. Nicholl and R.G. Smith, *Monetary Policy and the New Zealand Financial System* (Wellington, 1983).

81. Although the authorities announced in 1969 that ratios 'will in future be altered less frequently and, in all normal circumstances, will be set at a relatively stable and moderate level' (see 'Monetary Policy', *Reserve Bank of New Zealand Bulletin* (July 1969), p. 145), this has by no means always been true. For the statistics, see relevant Table in *Reserve Bank of New Zealand Bulletins*.

82. George Rae, *The Country Banker*, pp. 203-4.

83. Credit for this can probably again be traced back to George Rae, who recommended 'immediately available resources – your financial reserve – be one-third the amount of your liabilities to the public' (ibid., p. 204).

84. It is also important to remember that these ratios were minimum ratios and that over much of the year the banks maintained balances in excess of the required minima.

85. 'The purpose of the cash ratio scheme is to provide resources and income to the Bank; it is of no relevance to the day-to-day management of the money market since the deposits placed with the Bank are fixed for some months at a time (the period will be six months when the scheme is fully established).' (*Bank of England Quarterly Bulletin* (March 1982), p. 89.)

86. The 'club-money' pool was of the order of £3,000 million; market holdings were (say) £5,500 million. Much of the balance came from secured bank loans to the discount houses over and above the 6 per cent 'club money', as well as from commercial corporations.

87. Bank of New Zealand, Bank of Queensland and Banque Nationale de Paris.

88. LGS assets are defined as notes and coin, cash with the Reserve Bank, Treasury bills and notes and other Commonwealth securities. They do not include deposits with the official short-term money market, commercial bills or other short-term private paper.

89. See The Bank of Ghana Ordinance 1957, Section 41.

90. See Central Bank of Nigeria Ordinance 1958, Section 40 and The Banking Ordinance 1958, Section 8.

91. See The Central Bank of Malaya Ordinance 1958, Section 36.

92. Federal Government Notice No. 229 of 1959, (2 September 1959), in Supplement to *Federal Government Gazette* (Salisbury, Federation of Rhodesia and Nyasaland), 4 September 1959.

93. See The Banking Law 1960, Sections 11 and 12.

94. From 21 June 1917 until December 1959, all required reserves had to be held on deposit with the Federal Reserve Bank. From December 1959 until November 1960 member banks were permitted to count part of their currency and coin as reserves; as from 24 November 1960, they were allowed to count as reserves all the currency and coin held.

95. Until 14 July 1966, there were three classifications – central reserve city banks (New York and Chicago), reserve city banks, and country banks.

96. In August 1969, the Fed brought in a new regulation requiring a 10 per cent reserve on all Euro-dollar borrowings by American banks that were above the average for the base period (the four weeks ending 28 May 1969). The new regulation was to apply as from 16 October in respect of the four weeks to 2 October 1969.

97. Where a bank had a developed network of branches, the calculation of the money position was slightly more complicated, since branch movements both in deposits and in cash had to be taken into account. If the branches were confined to a relatively small area, the necessary information could be sent in easily enough by post or telephone and be brought into the initial calculations of the overall position. But where the area covered by the branch system was large and branches numerous (as on the West Coast) the arrangements were necessarily more complex. Mail to and from many branches took two days. Within the branches, the business of one day was passed through the books on the following day. Because of these factors, in Bank of America, for example, the financial figures took about five days to emerge and the bank had to work very largely on estimates and trends in estabishing what would be the required minimum

reserves and the money position they should aim to achieve in order to cover them.

98. Some banks try to arrange their regular run-off of maturities so that these occur at times in the calendar year when a cushion is required to absorb the impact of customers' tax payments.

99. Usually, Treasury bills are issued with maturities of three months, but sometimes they are issued for longer periods.

100. Radcliffe Committee Report, para. 144, p. 51.

101. Ibid., para. 153, p. 55.

102. A large number of banks in the higher-income ranges like to hold a proportion of their investments in tax-exempt state and municipal securities. The degree of favour with which these were regarded – and the proportion held – used to vary a good deal. In more recent years, they seem to have increased in popularity and in a large number of cases banks hold more in 'municipals' than they do in United States government securities. But because of the rather restricted marketability of 'municipals', banks usually reckon to hold them to maturity, in which case laddering becomes even more important so that relatively even amounts will mature each year, the funds normally being reinvested at the long end. Many of the larger banks are prepared to invest in high-grade municipals (a term that includes the securities of state governments) right across the country, but others prefer a seelction of higher yielding local issues. Many banks also hold local securities in order to support their own communities.

103. See *Federal Reserve Bulletins*, Tables A17, A18, and A19.

104. Alternatively, the municipals may not have been laddered, but 'weighted' with reference to the yield curve.

105. See J.S.G. Wilson, *Monetary Policy and the Development of Money Markets* (London, 1966), pp. 151 and 191 (n).

106. For United States experience, see J.S. Fforde, *The Federal Reserve System, 1945-1949* (Oxford, 1954), pp. 17-19, 25-6, 182-3, 210-17, 274-7, and 282-3

107. In the United Kingdom, the technique of 'cheap money' was developed during the war years; see R.S. Sayers, *Financial Policy, 1939-45* (London, 1956), pp. 146-52, 159 and 162. However, it was Hugh Dalton's attempt to depress and hold the long-term rate at 2½ per cent that has attracted most attention. For a study of 'cheap money' in 1946-7, see R.S. Sayers, *Modern Banking*, 3rd edn (Oxford, 1951), pp. 203-20; also W. Manning Dacey, *The British Banking Mechanism* (London, 1951), pp. 145-80. For a study of pre-war British experience (1931-9), see Edwin Nevin, *The Mechanism of Cheap Money* (Cardiff, 1955).

108. '. . . the period of notice must be long enough to enable the customer, having regard to all the surrounding circumstances, to make alternative arrangements'. See J. Milnes Holden, *The Law and Practice of Banking: Vol. 1 – Banker and Customer*, third edition (London, 1982), p. 89.

109. For a detailed survey of agricultural requirements, see J.S.G. Wilson, *Availability of Capital and Credit to United Kingdom Agriculture* (HMSO, 1973); for the role of the banks, see Chapter 8.

110. This began in 1958. The extent of the interest taken up by individual banks varied from acquisition of the whole of the share capital of a finance company to a holding of less than one half of the equity.

111. Radcliffe Committee Report, para. 136, p. 46.

112. See T.S. Ashton, *An Economic History of England – the 18th Century* (London, 1955), p.128. This is not to suggest that self-finance was the only way in which long-term finance was raised. Thus, as L.S. Pressnell has pointed out in his *Country Banking in the Industrial Revolution* (Oxford, 1956), many banks were set up 'to mobilize capital from the public to finance the business of the

partners and many sound industrial-bankers and trader-bankers . . . borrowed, often heavily, from their own banks' (p. 292). Although many industrialists entered banking primarily to provide means of payment for workers and raw materials and in some cases this was the limit of their banking activities, 'protracted short-term borrowing by the issue of token coins, bank-notes,etc., added up in time to long-term borrowing; where deposits were received from the public, their employment in the banker's own business resulted in a useful compromise between the limitations of the contemporary law of partnership and the advantages, in the mobilization of capital, of the modern joint stock company' (p. 322). Nevertheless, the financing 'by industrial bankers of mining and metal business other than their own appears to have been primarily on a short-term basis. Large and numerous advances on long-term . . . were clearly ruled out by considerations of liquidity and the size of country banks' resources, or were ruled out by bankruptcy if the importance of liquidity were too lightly regarded. The main forms of finance were therefore by the discount of bills and temporary advances, mainly by overdraft.' (p. 326).

113. See Crick and Wadsworth, *Joint Stock Banking*, pp. 336-7.

114. See J.W. Gilbart, *A Practical Treatise on Banking*, (London, 1865), Volume I, p. 35; Pressnell, *Country Banking*, Chapters 9-13, but especially p. 294.

115. Companies likewise often required a letter.

116. Sometimes, there is a combination of floating charge and fixed charge.

117. Where it covers the whole undertaking of the company, it may be called an 'unlimited debenture'.

118. Alternatively, the bank may decide to put an accountant on the company's board.

119. A high proportion – by value – is often unsecured, but these would only be the accounts of persons of substance.

120. With small and medium-sized companies, where directors have private means (such as a large house with a reasonable equity), a bank may seek a director's guarantee.

121. For an extended treatment, see J. Milnes Holden, *The Law and Practice of Banking: Vol. 2 – Securities for Bankers' Advances*, sixth edition (London, 1980), p. 459-77. Scottish law is different from English law. For an outline of Scottish arrangements, see J.J. Gordon and W.A. Mitchell, *Scottish Banking Practice – Securities for Advances*, third edition, revised (Edinburgh, 1968), pp. 95-77.

122. This type of loan might well have been spread over three years with repayment at six-monthly intervals.

123. See J.S.G. Wilson, *Capital and Credit to U.K. Agriculture*, pp. 92-5.

124. In the case of Westminster Bank (as it then was), up to three years. Westminster also introduced a Personal Budget Account.

125. See *Federal Reserve Bulletins*.

126. I.e., excluding corporation bond holdings (which tend to be small) and the rather more important income debentures and floating-rate shares (which are regarded as loan substitution securities).

127. The only figure available based on the author's field work in 1979 was about 20 per cent of the total loan portfolio for one of the large banks. Another bank merely said it was 'very big in term lending'. For all chartered banks, it was said to have averaged about one-third of total business lending over recent years.

128. At present fairly small, but growing rapidly.

129. Usually financed in Euro-dollars often on a matched basis, with limits on the unmatched position, many of them being term loans.

130. Radcliffe Committee Report, paras, 922 and 942.

131. This rate, which is fixed for the full term as stated, may be varied from time to time for new loans.

132. For further details, see J.S.G. Wilson, *Capital and Credit to U.K. Agriculture*, pp. 96-7.

133. For details, see ibid., pp. 97-8.

134. Nevertheless, sometimes the agreement is still in the form of a facility letter.

135. There may also be a commitment fee, or a non-utilisation fee.

136. Occasionally with term loans the banks seek a return additional to the interest charges – e.g., a share of the profits. This would usually be arranged through the clearing banks' merchant-banking subsidiaries, which may take an option that could lead to an equity interest in the firm concerned. It is a difficult area, since the criteria that apply in the case of a bank loan are likely to be different from those that relate to the taking up of an equity interest – in the latter case, the risks will tend to be higher – and there is a case therefore for reference to a subsidiary that employs the relevant specialist expertise.

137. This notice may be waived, subject to an adjustment of interest payments.

138. *Evidence* of Committee of London Clearing Bankers to Wilson Committee, p. 276.

139. *Abstract of Banking Statistics* (April, 1984).

140. See J.S.G. Wilson, *Industrial Banking* (SUERF, 1978) pp. 47-56.

141. See ibid., pp. 56-62.

142. Ibid.

143. Wilson Committee Progress Report, pp. 46ff.

144. Normally, they would not lend for periods exceeding, say, seven years.

145. Loans of 10-12 years are also made by specialist lenders like the Industrielkreditbank; long-term loans are made out of its own resources by the Kreditanstalt für Wiederaufbau.

146. Note that some large customers occasionally resort to the unused part of their limit in order to 'arbitrage', i.e. they borrow against the overdraft limit to on-lend into the money market. This is part of the justification for the unused limit fee and also for instituting the fully drawn advance.

147. 'It is very well suited for borrowings where the funds are required for a specific purpose and where the required loan can be accurately forecast.' See Australian Bankers' Association Submission to *The Committee of Inquiry into the Australian Financial System*, (1979), para. 2.2.35.

148. For much of what follows, see ibid., para. 2.2.27.

149. Against which a customer can draw bills and discount them in the market.

150. For greater detail, see J.S.G. Wilson, *French Banking Structure* pp. 70ff.

151. See *Conseil National du Crédit*, *Rapport Annuel* (1983), pp. 237 and 241.

152. The Lombard may only be done for a limited time (usually one to two days – the maximum is a week) and at a rate above the discount rate. The advantage of a Lombard is that the bank does not have to sell the bills or securities; it may also only want to borrow for two days; or it may expect rates to change and therefore not wish to rediscount. However, banks are reluctant to use the Lombard and only do so for purposes of technical adjustment or in an emergency.

153. In the manufacturing industries, they may run for 120 days.

154. For example, on the basis of a private placement. Banks also depend on the long-term savings-account market.

155. Also referred to as 'current-account lending' or 'cash credits'.

156. Through the Bankers' Association, the banks agree an upper and lower limit on the rates to be charged on overdrafts, trade bills and acceptances; the

individual bank then fixes its rate within these limits. If new limits need fixing, the banks will meet together for further discussions. For the big banks, the rates are not always the same, but competition keeps them more or less in line. Base rates of the several banks are advised to the Bankers' Association, which circulates the information to member banks. (It should be noted that business customers often use more than one banker.)

157. For this reason, there is a regular exchange of credit information in Switzerland.

158. A minimum of two, very often three.

159. As calculated in Norwegian kroner.

160. Foreign-currency deposits relate in part to the provision for the tax payments of the oil companies. The oil companies sell dollars and buy kroner forward to provide for tax payments. Meanwhile, the banks are borrowing dollars and selling them in the market – the Bank of Norway may itself buy these dollars and give them kroner in exchange. And these amounts have become very large figures and increase the liquidity of the banking system.

161. Foreign currency may be on-lent (e.g., to importers – say, for three months) in foreign currency, but more usually the foreign currency is converted into Finnmarks before being on-lent, repayment being in Finnmarks but with the borrowing customer accepting the foreign-exchange risk; sometimes, he will cover himself forward. This is the field in which the foreign banks now compete.

162. With Postipankki, it is a giro-account overdraft and the other banks may offer overdrafts on their bank giro accounts (i.e. their cheque accounts).

163. For arranging this, a commission is charged and, again, there will be a loan agreement, or an exchange of letters.

164. The banks no longer rediscount bills at the Bank of Finland; also, there is more labour involved in bill finance.

165. The limit is normally reviewed once a year and the overdraft is subject to a contract usually in the form of an agreement; really big customers may receive a less formal letter.

166. Instead of investing in plant and equipment, industrialists are tending to buy government securities, which were yielding close to 20 per cent per annum gross.

167. The big corporations (which are relatively small in number in Denmark) would normally use more than one bank (including the international banks).

168. See Monopolies Commission, *Barclays Bank Limited, Lloyds Bank Limited, and Martins Bank Limited – A Report on the Proposed Merger* (July 1968), Appendices 7 and 8 (pp. 70-4, also p. 21).

169. Ibid., p. 21.

170. See J.S.G. Wilson, *French Banking Structure*, pp. 85-7 and *passim*.

171. See C.R. Frank and W.R. Cline, 'Measurement of Debt Capacity: An application of Discriminant Analysis', *Journal of International Economics* (1971), pp. 331-2.

7 INDUSTRIAL BANKING[1]

Over a number of years, there developed quite a sharp contrast between what might be regarded as the British tradition of self-liquidating loans, primarily short-term in character, and Continental European practice, which in the past has favoured much more intimate and longer-term financial relations with industry than were to be found in the United Kingdom. To some extent, these differences have in recent years become rather less obvious. Nevertheless, there remain significant variations in attitudes that call for both comment and analysis. Examples could be drawn from a number of European countries, but it will be sufficient to concentrate largely on experience in France and Germany. Japan has also developed somewhat similar arrangements and can therefore be included in the same category.

British arrangements represent something of a contrast. In the United Kingdom, for example (and a similar pattern has generally been favoured in other Commonwealth countries), the long-term provision of industrial finance has usually been the function of specialist institutions, with the commercial banks providing part of the necessary institutional capital. Thus, in the United Kingdom, there are the Agricutural Mortgage Corporation (established in 1928), the Finance Corporation for Industry and the Industrial and Commercial Finance Corporation (both established in 1945, later amalgamated to form Finance for Industry and, with a Ventures Division to specialise in high-technology businesses, now called Investors in Industry), and (from early 177) Equity Capital for Industry, which provides equity finance for unquoted and small quoted companies. For some years, a National Enterprise Board (established in 1975) disposed of large funds under the Industry Act, with the duty to establish, maintain or to develop industrial undertakings; promote the reorganisation or development of industries; extend public ownership into profitable areas of manufacturing and promote industrial democracy within the undertakings it controls; and to take over and manage public-owned securities and other property.

In addition, there are a number of other relatively small institutions; among these are the Charterhouse Industrial Development Company, the Scottish Agricultural Securities Corporation (which is somewhat similar to the AMC but confines its operations to Scotland), the Ship

Mortgage Finance Company, Tanker Finance Limited, and the Insurance Export Company.

On the Continent of Europe, France led the way with the establishment of special investment banks (the *banques d'affaires*). Although set up more specifically to cater for the needs of industry – just like the deposit banks, which themselves often became involved in long-term lending to industry – the *banques d'affaires* in their early years tended to mix their long-term business with deposit banking proper. For this reason, it was sometimes extremely difficult at that time to distinguish between the French deposit banks and the *banques d'affaires*. Gradually, however, there tended to develop a separation of function and this was subsequently formalised by legislation in December 1945. Latterly, there has been a partial reversion to earlier arrangements, but these developments will be considered at a later stage. It is necessary first to identify the special contribution that was made by the *banques d'affaires*.

Banques d'affaires were now defined as institutions whose principal activities were to take up and administer 'participations' in existing concerns, to assist in the formation of new ventures, and to open credits (subject to no specific limitation as to term) for public and private enterprises, which had benefited or which stood to benefit from such participations. For these purposes, they might employ in addition to their own funds deposits accepted from their own staff; or from concerns in which the *banque d'affaires* already held a participation, or which were about to be assisted by way of a credit or participation; or from mercantile houses for the purposes of their business; or for the account of persons who were shareholders in companies in which the *banque d'affaires* itself was interested and subject to the bank managing the investment account (*compte-titres*) of such persons. Hence, their deposit-banking business, though not a major activity, was important. On the basis of these deposits (and especially those drawn from mercantile houses), the *banques d'affaires* granted a wide range of short-term credits, but for the most part this business was linked more or less directly with their primary function of providing investment finance. This was also true of the export credits granted by the *banques d'affaires* and quite often these were directly connected with the finance of development projects abroad.

In providing for the long-term needs of industry, the initial finance might well be supplied by means of an interim credit, which would be converted at an appropriate stage into a 'participation' in the company concerned. Sometimes, a *banque d'affaires* might be obliged to hold such participations for long periods, since it was one of its functions to 'nurse' investments until the venture in question was established. Then, if, in the judgement of the bank, market conditions were favourable, steps would be taken to convert the original investment into marketable securities and an issue of shares would be made with a view to inviting the public to subscribe. As a prior condition, the shares had to be introduced to the stock exchange. This involved an investigation and a favourable report upon the affairs of the company concerned by the stock exchange authorities. In addition, it was necessary (if it was a bond issue) to secure official approval for its inclusion in the 'calendar', a system which ensured that issues were brought to the market in an 'orderly' fashion, though in fact it tended to favour those made by the government and its agencies. In most cases, only a proportion of a bank's investments would be floated off in either of these ways and ordinarily a *banque d'affaires* would retain an interest in the company sufficient to assure ultimate control of its policy (frequently a holding of not more than 30 per cent was found to be enough). Often a *banque d'affaires* would provide investment finance in conjunction with other banks and associates, and consortia and syndicates organised by a *chef de file* were very common. Furthermore, it was the usual practice to include in the syndicate at least one of the large deposit banks which have long played an important part in the 'placing' of new issues. In this way, the group as a whole could employ the services of a nationwide network of bank branches and could tap the mass market.

Business of this character was much less routine than deposit banking as such and in *banque d'affaires* business a higher proportion of the staff was engaged on investigations and research of various kinds. In one form or another, all these banks built up an industrial-intelligence department, to which were attached a number of engineers and other technical experts, who provided the basic reports when a new venture was being considered. It was not usual to employ outside industrial consultants, though some of the private *banques d'affaires* (i.e. those not incorporated as public companies), with their rather smaller personnel, used on occasion to go outside for advice usually from associates with a first-hand knowledge of the industry or process in question. The larger *banques d'affaires* also drew on the experience of their boards of directors.Thus, there was ample opportunity to weigh carefully the separate reports of the specialist enquiries and to vet thoroughly the proposals that came before them. Finally, once a *banque d'affaires* was committed to the finance of a project, the assistance of its technical experts was always available to the firm concerned. Later,[2] a number of developments took place, new legislation was introduced, and the old distinctions were abandoned with all *établissements de crédit* being brought under the same umbrella, the tendency being for all the big banking groups to become more similar and quite highly integrated.

Germany came rather late into the industrial field and the amount of assistance given by the German banks to industry was largely due to the country's efforts to force the pace of industrialisation and to make up for lost time. Germany's late start may be explained in part by the economic losses imposed by the Thirty Years' War (1618-48). In part, it was also due to political particularism and the consequently large number of German states. Mainly as a result of the operation of these two factors, there was a great dearth of available capital. Capital no doubt existed, but adequate facilities to direct the stream of savings into the finance of industry were lacking.

Something of a revival began about 1848 and, in the next decade or so, a number of important banks were founded in various parts of the country. From the very start, these new institutions were linked with the promotion of industrial development and they provided the capital necessary for many of the newly-established companies. Initially, this seems to have been their chief activity, though the provision of short-term finance was not thereby completely excluded. At the same time, it was not intended that these banks should hold permanently the shares of the companies they had helped to found and the objective was to pass the shares on – in due course – to the investing public. It was appreciated that bank resources should not be allowed to become frozen, especially in those cases where funds had been borrowed from the public. In any event, during the early years, the banks did not in fact encourage the lodgement of deposits to any great extent. It was their intention to rely primarily on their own resources and it was therefore their own capital that for the most part they risked in these long-term loans. Indeed, it was not until after 1874 that there was any clear departure from this policy. They then chose to develop along lines that became a combination of British deposit-banking techniques and the longer-term industrial financing associated with a French *banque d'affaires*.

A good deal of bank business was concerned with the transformation into company form of already existing private businesses (as was also the case in Belgium). Associated with this was the attempt to raise additional capital for such firms and it was quite typical for the initial provision of finance to be made as an advance on current account, this being repaid later from the proceeds of an issue of securities. Provided these securities could be disposed of easily, no serious difficulties were likely to arise. But there were times when the original advance developed first into a long-term loan and, later, as a result of a debt-funding operation, such loans were converted into a participation. Indeed, this was one of the most important means by which German banks became closely associated with industrial companies. In the event of a completely new undertaking being established, the commercial banks frequently delegated the task to specialised banking subsidiaries.

The success of the German banks in the field of industrial finance depended on two factors: the maintenance of a high ratio between capital resources and total liabilities – it was only when this 'golden rule' was ignored that the banks courted real trouble; and the effective distribution of risks – by spreading business over as large a number of industries as possible. Indeed, it was in order to extend the area of operation and to diversify their risks geographically, as well as to widen the area from which they attracted surplus funds for investment purposes, that the Berlin banks began to extend their branches to the provinces and to enter into close associations with provincial banks. For the rest, the banks were also represented on the boards of the companies in which they were interested and this enabled them to keep in close touch with industrial and economic developments over a wide field.

This system worked fairly well during the period prior to World War I. The difficulty was that the theory was not by any means always observed in practice and the period of greatest trial came during the 1930s, when most of these banks found themselves in a highly illiquid position and had to be reconstructed with the assistance of the State. This was the prelude to the Nazi era. Then came World War II and the currency reform of June 1948. But, although the emphasis on long-term lending was greatly modified, the Germans remained persuaded that their methods were essentially sound. During the early days following the currency reform, the German banks were not able to lend long-term, since they had lost much of their capital and, so far as new issues were concerned, there was at that time virtually no capital market through the agency of which to float off issues to the public. During these years, therefore, German industry was forced to a very large extent to depend on self-finance.

Yet, in German financial circles, there was still a widespread acceptance of the tradition that the commercial banks should provide long-term finance to industry and support for this view was based on the argument that there was a substantial hard core even of demand and short-term deposits that was not likely to be withdrawn on any scale and could therefore be used to some extent to provide medium- and longer-term industrial finance without jeopardising the interests of depositors. In addition, a significant percentage of the commercial banks' time deposits was fixed for a year or more and, latterly, there had been active competition for savings deposits to which much of the term lending was now related. In any event, it is unlikely that the central-bank authorities in West Germany will ever again allow the position to get out of hand and adequate facilities (e.g., by way of re-discount) now exist to protect bank liquidity and thereby the interests of depositors.

Term lending by the West German banks has been discussed elsewhere (see pp. 301-3), but in addition it is common practice for West German banks to assist in raising permanent capital for industry by arranging new issues. Thus, after providing a certain amount of pre-financing, it is quite usual to organise a syndicate headed by a 'lead' bank for the launching of an issue, the objective being to float off these shares into the hands of institutional investors and the general public. It is argued by German bankers that the 'universal' bank, which as a single institution offers a very wide range of services to the public, is in a particularly good position to cater conveniently and economically both for 'account saving' and the more permanent investment of customer moneys in industrial securities. Such securities may derive either from new issues or from a trading portfolio maintained by the bank concerned for this purpose and containing no doubt the remnants of past issues which were not fully taken up at the time, but which can then be peddled out as opportunities present themselves. It is further argued that the bank can also assist his customer by way of financial counselling, security analysis, and management of his portfolio and, moreover, that it can do this more efficiently than a stockbroker, especially in a situation where the securities market is comparatively modest in size. In this context, it is particularly the small saver that the banks have in mind, the type of saver that in the United Kingdom is largely catered for by the unit-trust movement. But whatever the mechanism, it is clearly a means of transforming short-term money capital into longer-term investment capital for use by industry as well as securing a wide spread of equity ownership throughout the community.

It should be noted, too, that the private bankers in Germany in particular are very interested in helping medium-sized firms to go public, though many of these firms are very shy about this, since partners in a business are often most anxious to retain control. Quite apart from that, it is expensive to make an issue of shares. An alternative is for the private banker to provide a participation for a certain period (sharing both the risks and the profits), or in certain cases to help in arranging a merger (the latter is said to be a very difficult business but often highly profitable). Other houses merely operate to bring the parties together, i.e. those who have need of participations and those who have funds to lend. Much the same is sometimes true of mergers.

The banks also arrange and underwrite bond issues. These are usually issued by public-sector bodies, occasionally by industrial firms. They have a life of not more than ten years. Normally, they would be redeemed in one sum upon maturity. Again, the banks are interested in placing and selling industrial bonds, but as a matter of policy they 'prefer' not to hold them, because of the need to maintain a high degree of liquidity. Nevertheless, because they underwrite bond issues, they may from time to time have to hold them (e.g., when prices deteriorate following a rise in interest rates). Also, to a certain extent, the bond portfolio represents a residual. If the banks have difficulty in absorbing all their available funds in loans, they will tend to go into bonds to take up the slack. If, at a later stage, the banks require additional funds for lending, they may sell their bonds to feed the loan demand. Because of this contingency, the banks attempt to maintain an appropriate spread of maturities, so that there is always some 'run-off' available for alternative investment. In fact, there have been times when the bond portfolio has been quite an important ingredient in the asset structure.

In addition to these activities, banks in West Germany also hold industrial securities as an investment and this is quite different in kind from the participations held in other financial institutions operating in specialised fields. At the same time, there is a limitation, since the bank's permanent investments in land, buildings, furniture and equipment, ships and participations (at book values), and investments in other companies, may not in aggregate exceed the bank's 'liable capital'. Because industrial securities are generally held as a financial investment, yield is important; they also add to the diversification of a bank's earning portfolio taken as a whole. Some of these shares may have been acquired when a customer was in difficulty; or a big shareholder may sell shares to the bank in order to avoid depressing the market; or to evade an outside bid or a foreign acquisition; the bank would then attempt to locate a buyer or buyers and sell the shares off gradually. As a matter of policy, banks do not usually buy industrial securities with a view to holding them indefinitely and, over the years, there will generally have been quite a significant turnover in their share portfolio.

It is maintained that, even when a significant proportion of a company's shares are held by a bank, such shares are retained on the basis of broad investment considerations and not with a view to influencing the management of the company concerned. The banks will be represented on the company's supervisory board, which nominates the executive management, but this power is divided (there may be several competing banks represented) and bank members, who are likely to be very much in a minority, are regarded as being primarily present as financial experts.

Even where a non-bank shareholder, who is a customer of a bank represented on the board, authorises a bank to vote by proxy on his behalf, the bank is obliged to inform such a shareholder of the details of the agenda, any related proposals that may have been submitted by the management, any counter-proposals submitted by other shareholders, and also the bank's own voting proposals, which the shareholder is in no way bound to accept. Indeed, the shareholder can always authorise his bank to vote at the annual general meeting only in accordance with his instructions and not infrequently does so. Moreover, where the power to exercise proxy voting has been delegated to a bank, such delegation is limited to a period of fifteen months. On these bases, it is argued, shareholders' interests are fully protected.

In Austria, which in banking matters tends to have much in common with West Germany, the large banks (and particularly the Creditanstalt) also have interests in a range of industrial companies; this is mainly an inheritance from the past. Although the large banks have portfolio holdings of stocks and shares for use as a trading account, these are very small. The Postal Savings Bank does not have a trading account at all, but it will buy stocks and shares for customers on a commission basis.

Banks in The Netherlands are involved in the business of new issues and in stockbroking. Indeed, about 80 per cent of the turnover of the stock exchange derives from their transactions. In The Netherlands, this is a traditional activity, banking business having for long been combined with stock-exchange operations.

Another country in Europe, where banks act as stockbrokers is Finland – banks there operate a trading portfolio in bonds, stocks, and shares, on the basis of which they buy and sell for customers' accounts as well as for themselves. In Denmark, the banks buy and sell bonds both for themselves and also for customers, though they do not operate separate trading accounts. What they have not got in portfolio, they can buy on the stock exchange, where they have seats, though they are not members and must therefore deal through brokers. Occasionally, they may be able to marry transactions themselves, where parties are willing to buy and sell for the same amount.

In Belgium, prior to the banking reforms of 1934-5,[3] the links between the banks and their industrial customers were extremely close, the banks frequently holding either shares or bonds of business concerns, on whose boards of directors they were also represented. This was referred to as 'mixed banking'[4] and the great danger was that the banks might get frozen in. Matters came to a head during the Great Depression of the 1930s and, by a Decree of 22 August 1934, banks were prohibited from retaining or holding shares or bonds issued by any industrial, commercial, or agricultural corporation. Under a subsequent decree in 1935, it was made unlawful for any banking corporation to own stocks or bonds issued by other corporations, but an exception was made in the case of securities issued by other banking corporations. Under the first Decree, the prohibition had extended to private bankers and partnerships; this was not done under the second, though subseqently the Banking Commission ruled that private bankers and partnerships could only invest in corporate securities to the extent of their own capital and reserves plus funds originating as long-term deposits.

As a result of these reforms it was necessary to hive off the industrial investment business formerly done by the mixed banks and the relevant securities were transferred to holding companies, which also held shares in an associated bank now constituted as a deposit bank, the deposits formerly held by the mixed banks being transferred to the new banks together with a related amount of assets. However, although not permitted to hold a permanent interest in a non-financial corporation, the Belgian banks were allowed to arrange issues of securities and to hold any securities not sold to the public for a period of up to six months. This rule was supplemented by a second Decree of 9 July 1935 which permitted the holding of securities for up to two years, when such securities had been taken over by a bank in reimbursement of a frozen or doubtful debt. Despite these restrictions, the Belgian banks continued sucessfully to market a number of new issues and also maintained their dealing business in shares and bonds. Dring the post-war years, the position was somewhat liberalised. Under a Law of 3 May 1967, banks were now allowed to hold corporate bonds in portfolio. Furthermore, the period for which banks were allowed to hold newly-issued securities not yet sold to the public was extended to 12 months and, subject to approval by the Banking Commission, this term could be extended by a further year. Again, under a Law of 30 June 1975 banks may acquire shares in one or more trading companies, subject to certain limits fixed by Royal Decree and issued on the advice of the Banking Commission. In addition, the banks hold securities in safe custody for customers, collect dividends for them, and offer investment advice, a range of services calculated to encourage regular purchase of the securities that the bank has on sale.

In Switzerland, securities in portfolio consist of federal government, cantonal and municipal paper; the bonds of other banks and industrial corporations; domestic mortgage bonds; Swiss shares (banks, investment companies and industrial corporations), plus substantial holdings of foreign bonds (including those of public corporations) and some foreign shares. But the big banks, which are also members of the stock exchange, maintain in addition a trading portfolio of securities on the basis of which to sell to, or buy from, bank customers.

Much use is made by overseas borrowers of the Swiss bond market, especially when rates in other markets (e.g., in the USA) have been volatile. Borrowers include foreign governments, supranational organisations (like the World Bank and the Inter-American Development Bank), foreign banks and industrial names. Many of these issues are then passed on to the Swiss domestic investor, who frequently relies on the research done by the Swiss bank. The bulk of these issues would be made by Swiss bank syndicates, with one of the big banks acting as the lead bank.

Private placements have become much more popular in recent years following the lifting of the ceiling by the Swiss National Bank in 1976. Placements need to be notified to the National Bank; they are not usually syndicated, but sold to the underwriting bank's own customers. The borrower must expect to pay slightly more than might be the case with a public issue, but saves in fees that would otherwise be charged. The potential disadvantage to the investor of private placements is that there exists only a limited secondary market for these notes. Typically, they are sold in high denominations (a minimum of SFrs 50,000) and therefore tend to be popular with wealthy private customers and institutional investors.

So far as the public bond market is concerned, many of the Swiss banks, including the Big Five, belong to the Big Syndicate, whose members have traditionally handled about three-quarters of the public bond issues. Foreign bank subsidiaries can also act as lead managers and, since November 1982, have been allowed to act as sub-underwriters, or members of a selling group, in this way helping the market to absorb the paper (e.g., Japanese banks have assisted in marketing the large quantum of Japanese issues).

As in certain European countries, Japan likewise was handicapped in her industrialisation by shortage of available capital and, again, industrial development was financed partly by the commercial banks (which in Japan sought to employ their time deposits in long-term loans), but partly also by setting up specialist institutions, which were permitted to supplement their own capital resources by raising funds against the issue of debentures.

Traditionally, a large proportion of Japanese bank deposits is held at fixed terms, with maturities of three months or more. Time deposits as a proportion of total deposits have over many years been very significant in Japan and have long represented over 50 per cent of total deposits. Over a long period, though this is now changing, rather than invest in securities in Japan, the Japanese preferred to entrust their savings to banks or to other financial institutions, which in turn made direct loans to industry or invested in corporate debentures and government bonds. This had two results: the retarded development of a broadly-based securities market in Japan, where this form of activity tended to be largely in the hands of the banks and other financial institutions; and the relative overdependence of industrial concerns on institutional lenders for the supply of much of their long-term capital, a significant proportion of which took the form of accommodation by way of loans and discounts from private financial institutions.

The risks associated with such lending are high and, in the past, the banks have suffered grievous losses. This was one of the main causes of the high incidence of bank failures and absorptions in the 1920s. Even after the banking structure had been strengthened by amalgamations and the cutting away of much of the dead wood, the pressure on the banks remained considerable and – at least until the 1960s – the large city banks were consistently obliged to borrow quite heavily from the central bank. Latterly, the liquidity position of the city banks improved considerably and gradually the city banks became less dependent on the Bank of Japan.

After some vacillation, a new Long-Term Credit Bank Law was promulgated in June 1952. On the basis of this law specialist institutions were established (based in part on the former semi-governmental 'special banks' that had operated in the industrial field)[5] to provide long-term credits to the several sectors of the economy, on the basis of capital provided mainly by other financial institutions (including the insurance companies) and by the big manufacturing concerns. There are three long-term credit banks – the Industrial Bank of Japan (going back to 1902), the Long-Term Credit Bank of Japan (established in 1952) and the Nippon Credit Bank (established in 1957 and, prior to 1 October 1977, known as the Nippon Fudosan Bank). All these banks for the most part served big business but the last assists the smaller and medium-sized enterprises as well. Funds may be derived from a wide range of sources (including the issue of debentures,[6] which are taken up to an important extent by the commercial banks, and the acceptance of deposits from corporate customers, debenture holders, and government bodies; the acceptance of deposits from the general public is prohibited). In addition, the long-term credit banks hold as securities corporate bonds (some of these would be government-guaranteed public utilities) and shares (often in firms that are bank customers). In other words, these banks (and for that matter, the commercial banks as well, since they are also purchasers of industrial bonds) to some extent play the role of institutional investors.

So far as investment in securities by banks in Japan is concerned, the main item is national government bonds, but a significant quantum of funds is also invested in municipal bonds and industrial bonds. Stocks and shares more often than not are held in trading account – for the convenience of customers – more than as an investment. Banks also hold shares in companies where they are trying to establish a special relationship. In a sense, it is an alternative to lending to them. Industrial bonds with maturities up to 12 years are bought through securities houses and are readily marketable, as are stocks and shares. If it was decided to sell a holding of a particular stock, the relevant corporation would be advised of the bank's intention.

Japan represents the type of problem that many of these countries have had to face – the scarcity of available long-term capital and the formation of a capital market appropriate to the high level of industrialisation that has been evolved. There are two aspects to this problem: the degree to which a high proportion of savings is being ploughed back into existing industrial enterprises by self-financing (especially in the form of depreciation allowances), without being subject to the test of the market place – it is possible that funds are not always being applied in the most profitable manner; the apparent conservatism of the Japanese public with respect to investment in securities – as has been seen, there has for long been a strong preference for time deposits, though there is now some evidence of the development of a greater degree of diversification in private asset holdings. This needs to be encouraged, so that a greater volume of savings will be made available through the market for direct investment in industry.

Notes

1. For further details, see J.S.G. Wilson, *Industrial Banking: A Comparative Survey* (SUERF, 1978), being evidence submitted to the Committee to Review the Functioning of Financial Institutions (the Wilson Committee).

2. See pp. 135-6 and 139-40.

3. See B.S. Chlepner, *Belgian Banking and Banking Theory* (Washington, 1943), pp. 89ff and 115ff.

4. Its historical origins are sketched in ibid., pp. 7ff.

5. The first of these – the Industrial Bank of Japan – was established in 1902 and supplied long-term finance to leading industrial companies.

6. Debentures may be issued up to 20 times the combined total of the bank's capital and reserves. They are of two kinds: coupon debentures issued for 5 years at face value and discount debentures issued at a discount with a currency of one year.

8 ASSETS AND LIABILITIES MANAGEMENT

In the 1960s, bankers referred only to 'liabilities management'; nowadays, it has become 'assets *and* liabilities management', which stresses the fact that the two sides of the balance sheet are intimately interrelated, though sometimes in response to an existing and specific loan demand a bank may go into the money markets to look for funding, whereas on other occasions a bank may go actively – even aggressively – into the money markets seeking out funds at appropriate prices and then try to absorb them by making a range of new loans and/or investments. Sometimes, transactions have been deliberately matched both as to term, amount and currency; on other occasions (and, in more recent years, probably increasingly), there has been deliberate mismatching with a transformation of shorter-dated moneys into loans for longer periods, though with regular adjustments to interest rates in order to keep them in line with the current costs of money.

Hence, assets and liabilities management could be described as comprising a series of techniques whereby, on the one hand, holdings of remunerative assets (loans, advances and investments of various kinds) are funded (or financed) by related (but not necessarily matched) liabiities and, on the other, liabilities may be accepted in advance of commitments and these liabilities subsequently deployed in the acquisition of remunerative assets. Such management may apply both to domestic and to foreign-currency assets and liabilities. Sometimes, the 'management' is sophisticated and all-embracing (where the banker as it were 'runs a book' that comprehends the balance sheet as a whole); at other times, 'management' tends to relate only to marginal adjustments. Moreover, the interrelationship between the assets and liabilities relates to both international funding and lending – funding may derive from either domestic sources or Euro-currency markets; lending likewise may relate to the domestic economy or take the form of international loans, in both cases sometimes being financed partly from domestic sources and partly through the Euro-currency markets.

Necessarily, management of assets and liabilities must operate within the framework of the prudential controls and monetary policy as laid down from time to time by the authorities of the country concerned.

Monetary policy is dealt with in Chapters 9 and 10, but brief reference may be made here to prudential controls. Basically, these are concerned with solvency (and capital adequacy) and liquidity, matters already referred to earlier (see pp. 222-6 and 261-71). But apart from these general considerations, the authorities in a number of countries also impose various more specific requirements. In many countries, banks (and sometimes other institutions) have to be licensed, or registered in some way or other. An authority (not necessarily the central bank; it may be, for example, a Banking Control Commission, or some similar body) will be given the responsibility of monitoring the solvency and liquidity of the relevant institutions, as well as related matters like profitability and the expertise (and succession) of managements. Solvency will relate to own resources (capital) available in relation to the volume and nature of risk-bearing operations (sometimes specified ratios will be required and usually there will be some minimum capital stipulation whether in absolute terms or expressed as a ratio). There may also be a limit (expressed in relation to capital) on the amount that may be lent to a single borrower. Loans to directors and to staff may be restricted, as also may be investments in subsidiaries. On the liquidity front, there will often be minimum cash-reserve requirements and/or a more comprehensive liquidity requirement for banks and similar institutions. Even where specific requirements are minimal, the authorities – e.g., the central bank – will monitor more or less continuously the operational behaviour of banks and similar institutions.[1]

Having attempted to define assets and liabilities management, how did it emerge in the first place? In the development of assets and liabilities management, three major factors seem to have been significant, with variations of degree in different countries: First, there was the increase in rates of inflation, which had been the common situation in a number of countries since the early 1970s with a consequent rise in nominal rates of interest. This fundamentally altered the market conditions within which banks operated – it was no longer sufficient merely to on-lend deposits at a higher rate – and there was an increasing sophistication on the part of market participants (including the banks and their customers) with a growing emphasis on exploiting the relative returns available on alternative assets and also the relative costs of different ways of raising money. Then, towards the end of the 1970s and the early 1980s, there was an increased volatility in interest-rate movements and this had the effect of highlighting the need for flexibility in bank (and other) balance-sheet structures; furthermore, it clearly demonstrated the need for a high level of sophistication in assets and liabilities management. Finally, a trend began to develop from the mid-1960s onwards which favoured deregulation, with increased reliance being placed on market forces as an integral part of the mechanisms of control with rather less emphasis on administered controls. Thus, much of the activity in the financial markets was deregulated so far as interest rates were concerned; there was also an increase in competition partly due to a greater pressure on margins, and both of these had a marked impact on the ways in which assets and liabilities management developed.

In fact, 'liabilities management', as it was then called, had begun rather earlier. Probably beginning in the 1950s, there had been a tendency in the USA for corporation treasurers with temporarily surplus funds available either to transfer these funds to interest-bearing categories within the banks' deposit structure, or themselves to employ these funds actively in the money markets. The issue of negotiable certificates of deposit (commencing in the USA in 1961) was really the beginning of this process and this was accompanied in all countries by a tendency for corporations to run down temporarily surplus funds (previously held on current account as demand deposits) and, in the USA, by a reduced willingness by corporations to accede to the banks' request for 'compensating balances', whereby bank customers had to hold unutilised part of the moneys that had been borrowed. On the other hand, the disinclination of corporations to continue to hold with their bankers significant amounts of interest-free deposits had to be taken into account in the pricing of loans and the charging of fees for specific services. In addition, because the hard core of demand deposits was being eroded, banks had now to look for other sources of funds by issuing negotiable certificates of deposit, or buying money in 'wholesale' markets like the federal-funds market in the USA, or the inter-bank markets in London and elsewhere.

In the UK, where, up to the 1950s, British banking had remained relatively uncompetitive, interest rates both on deposits and on loans and advances had been subject to a cartel. However, even with a change of attitudes and the development of a more competitive spirit in the late 1950s, competition could not be given full rein because for much of the 1960s bank lending was subject to ceilings. The full flowering of competition – perhaps an over-flowering – had to wait until the introduction of Competition and Credit Control in September 1971. Nevertheless, greater flexibility in interest rates had emerged and, later, a higher level of rates had encouraged the clearing banks to become more sensitive to interest rates in the management of their liabilities. Before 1971, because of the cartel, competing for money at higher rates was done through wholly-owned subsidiaries that were outside the cartel. After 1971, the banks could go into the wholesale markets direct. Probably, too, there was now some emulation of techniques already well established across the Atlantic in North America. Also, the emergence of new instruments and new markets (and especially the increasing importance of the Euro-currency markets and the related dollar certificates of deposit, but also for a time, including the sterling CD, a forward market in CDs, and the expansion of the inter-bank market) provided a wider framework within which to operate. In addition to the shifting away from retail deposits to wholesale money, which was entirely interest-bearing and therefore added considerably to total interest costs, there was also a significant development of term lending, with a steady build-up in term loans, especially for financing investment projects likely to extend up to five to seven years, with interest rates linked to the London Inter-Bank Offered Rate (LIBOR), which allowed for adjustments to be made to the rate at three- or six-month intervals. In part, this increase in term lending replaced resort to the debenture market. Although there was at times an apparent relationship between wholesale borrowings and term lending, bankers tended to think in terms of finance for the whole book and they accordingly began to seek out the relevant funds wherever they were likely to be most readily available. Meanwhile, during the 1960s and 1970s, there had been a change in the deposit structure – a decline in the percentage of current-account deposits and a related rise in wholesale deposits, seven-day notice deposits at branches fluctuating somewhat with changes in interest rates. Included in the wholesale deposits were Euro-currency deposits – for most UK banks, all Euro-currency funding is wholesale – and, although the bulk of total deposits was at short term, the moneys were rolled over regularly with market conditions being reflected in movements in interest rates on loans.

Another factor that was operative in these earlier years and which deserves attention was the tendency of monetary authorities when restricting credit to concentrate primarily on the commercial banks (because of their capacity to 'create' credit). This had the result of curbing the rate of growth of commercial-bank assets, while permitting (at least for a time) the business of non-bank financial intermediaries (like building societies or savings and loan associations, also savings banks) to grow much more rapidly; there was also often much mushrooming of new non-bank financial institutions (e.g., of finance companies and credit unions). As a consequence, the share of the commercial banks in the collection of deposits, in the making of loans, even in the provision of transmission services (in this context, note particularly the competition of the Giros) tended to fall significantly.

Nor should we neglect the restraining effect on commercial-bank development of the ceilings on interest rates that could be paid on deposits by commercial banks (sometimes by other types of financial institutions as well). Examples include Regulation Q in the USA and ceilings on interest rates in Australia in respect of both deposits and loans. Either institutions to which the ceilings did not apply were able to compete actively for the public's savings by offering rates higher than the ceilings permitted, or if ceilings were progressively extended, corporation funds in particular might be forced right outside the financial system with the development of an active inter-company market for funds, more or less by-passing altogether the traditional financial system (including the commercial banks). Sometimes, too, as with the building societies and the trustee savings banks in the UK, and the mutual savings banks and savings and loan associations in the USA, the thrift institutions enjoyed tax concessions which gave them a further competitive edge. (Latterly, the thrift institutions themselves had their troubles in the USA, where they held substantial portfolios of fixed-rate loans over a protracted period of high and rising interest rates). It is relevant also to mention that the interest of the American commercial banks in the Euro-dollar markets was due at least in part to the fact that the American banks found funds in these markets more easily available than those that could be obtained at home, where they were subject to Regulation Q ceilings on the rates they could offer for domestic deposits.

What happened with regard to the deposit structures of banks was that there had been a move away from non-interest-bearing demand deposits into interest-bearing time deposits, and a move away from the lower-rate interest-bearing deposits (e.g., savings deposits and the shorter-term time deposits) into higher yielding deposits (e.g., longer-term time deposits and large deposits), certificates of deposit, or even competing instruments like the six-month money-market certificates and the money-market mutual funds in the USA. Both individuals and non-financial corporations have become increasingly interest-rate sensitive in recent years. This has been due to the obvious reason that when interest rates rise corporations certainly (individuals probably to a lesser extent because of a degree of inertia) take advantage of the situation to earn some 'keep' on their temporarily surplus balances. Alternatively, one could say that the opportunity cost of leaving such balances idle increases significantly as interest rates rise and the same result follows. Subsequently, during the later 1970s and early 1980s, with increases in the rate of inflation in almost all countries, interest rates rose dramatically and, quite apart from the arguments already advanced, there was a realisation that many real rates of interest were now negative and, if corporations (and individuals) were even to attempt to offset inflationary erosion, it was imperative to seek the highest interest rates available. Probably, this would affect individuals more than corporations, since the latter, if business prospects were at all reasonable, could expect to make more money in the normal course of business (whether they operated in manufacturing industry or in commerce) though temporarily surplus funds (beyond the immediate needs of the business) would necessarily be invested at short term at the maximum rate obtainable for such moneys. One should note, too, that the rates to be obtained would depend on interest-rate expectations – if future rates were expected to be lower, investors would be faced by a reverse-yield curve with rates lower on the longer maturities than on those for shorter periods.

Another phenomenon that in an inflationary situation calls for comment is the propensity (particularly of individuals) to go on saving, even to increase the levels of personal savings (despite sharp rises in prices and the consequent fall in the value of money), though latterly the relevant moneys have increasingly been placed in non-bank accounts – e.g., in the UK with building societies and in certain forms of National Savings, both of which enjoyed fiscal advantages; in the United States also there were non-bank alternatives – e.g. money-market mutual funds. There seemed to be three main reasons for the relatively high propensity to save: (i) a desire to maintain a certain proportion of income in cash or near-cash balances, such that the absolute amount of such balances tends to be increased as the value of money falls; this is due to a desire to maintain the real value of existing asset stocks; (ii) in an uncertain world (with a possibility of redundancy and unemployment), there is an even greater need to build up and maintain precautionary balances, which can be drawn on in the event of subsequent misfortune; (iii) the substitution effect of high interest rates on the spending/saving decision. Again, one would emphasise that this will probably apply more to individuals than to non-financial corporations. The latter would probably like to do it, but due to inflationary pressures, difficulties with cash-flow, and the escalating costs of maintaining inventories (stocks), few of them are likely to be able to maintain such balances. Indeed, the reverse is likely to be true – borrowing from the banks would probably increase and, at high rates of interest, borrowing even to pay the interest on the moneys originally borrowed has not been unknown. Many corporations subsequently sold off assets or raised additional capital in order to reduce outstanding debt.

Two effects follow: firstly, and to the extent that the banks are having to 'buy' a higher proportion of their money at high or relatively high rates of interest, their interest costs will tend to rise quite significantly; but, secondly, borrowings from the banks will also tend to increase. In a situation of high rates of interest (despite some narrowing of margins), there may be some increase in gross bank profits, offset (as below) by increased risks and the necessity to make substantial provisions. It is pertinent to note, too, the increased cost to the banks of carrying current accounts; in the UK, it is estimated that demand deposits now cost the equivalent of 8-10 per cent in imputed interest and the costs are still rising. If they are wise, the banks ought to be considering the risk situation and whether borrowing corporations can really afford to pay such high rates of interest, also whether it is prudent for them to be borrowing so heavily, especially when to the stresses of inflation are added the impact effects and losses of recession.

In recent years, too, the banks' capital-assets ratios have operated as a constraint and, as a result, there has been something of a shift back from liabilities management to asset management, where the latter may consist of substituting high-yield assets (e.g., advances) for lower-yielding assets (e.g., government securities); alternatively, there may be occasions when a bank may shift into low-risk assets (government securities) in place of high-risk assets (such as advances to Third World countries).

Greater liquidity and flexibility in the management of bank assets has also become possible by resorting to floating-rate notes (which go back to 1970)[2] and for which a secondary market of some depth has now developed. The size of issues and length of maturities available to borrowers (many of them international) have also increased. There has been a significant increase, too, in the demand for floating-rate notes as a marketable investment, especially by banks, which not only issue them but also buy them for matching against their short-term liabilities. There has also been a growth in the use of a slightly different and more recently developed floating-rate instrument – the note-issuance, or revolving underwriting, facility.[3] This blends characteristics of capital-market paper and bank credits in an attempt to match lenders' preference for liquidity with borrowers' demand for medium-term funds. Its recent popularity appears to constitute further evidence of a desire by banks to hold assets in a more liquid form.[4]

One of the consequences of recent developments has been the increasing concern of banks (and similar institutions) with interest-rate sensitivity. It becomes imperative, for example, to monitor the speed at which assets and liabilities change in their composition as rates of interest in the money markets change. Some assets and liabilities are rate insensitive (fixed-rate loans, demand and savings deposits); others, like variable-rate loans and federal funds or inter-bank rates, may be very volatile and change quite rapidly – they are therefore interest-rate sensitive. In other cases, rate sensitivity may relate to the maturity distribution of a portfolio – on the loan side, a fixed-rate portfolio that is on the point of maturity can be expected in a high-rate situation soon to become interest-rate sensitive as loans are moved over to a variable rate; and in the context of securities portfolios, interest-rate expectations will play a leading role in determining maturity distributions (e.g., in a situation where there is a great uncertainty about future rates, banks will tend to stay short; also if rates are likely to rise they will tend to run down, or switch out of, their longer-dated securities because of the risk of capital depreciation).

A consequence of the increased interest of banks (and others) in assets and liabilities management has been the development of new markets or the further growth of old ones in which the banks can 'buy' wholesale money. In the USA, for example, the federal-funds market has expanded considerably over the years and like the discount windows of the Federal Reserve Banks following the Monetary Control Act of 1980 are now used by a number of depository institutions besides the banks; there has also been an increasing resort to 'Repos', or sale and repurchase agreements (largely as a means of funding the securities portfolios and providing outlets for customers with funds temporarily available for lending for what in effect is on a secured basis); in London, as we have seen, the inter-bank market grew up and expanded and the Euro-dollar and Euro-currency markets were established and developed rapidly. Moreover, bought money (as above) is an important source of funds in both the United States and the United Kingdom (often, say, 30-40 per cent or more of total resources, excluding capital). And in both countries, this has been related to term lending.

A further development in sophistication in the United States (and later introduced in the United Kingdom) was the resort to interest-rate futures as a tool of assets and liabilities management. The purpose of futures contracts in bank management is to hedge mismatches (or part of the mismatches) in assets and liabilities maturities. For example, if interest-sensitive liabilities exceed interest-sensitive assets, a banker may hedge against rising interest rates by selling futures contracts in securities of similar maturity to those liabilities he is hedging. Of course, most bankers would not choose to be perfectly hedged in terms of exactly matching asset and liability maturities, since to do so would eliminate significant potential profits from taking a position on the yield curve.

So much for sophisticated assets and liabilities management as evidenced in the United States and the United Kingdom. In a number of other countries, following the earlier experience with 'liabilities' management in North America, the emphasis tended to be at first on the liabilities side of the balance sheet and was rather in the nature of 'funds management', though as term-lending became increasingly common, there was also a change in structure on the assets side. But basically what bankers in these countries were looking for was an adjustment at the margin on the liabilities side, which would accommodate mainly quantitative changes on the assets side. If there was an increasing demand for loans to be met, more funds would have to be sought; if there tended to be funds in excess of immediate lending requirements, management would require that the funds be absorbed elsewhere, often by way of short-term investment in the money markets, or in a money-market-type instrument, such that funds could again be made available (e.g., by sale in a secondary market) if and when loan demand picked up. An alternative that could still be employed was to treat the investment or securities portfolio as a residual, used as necessary to absorb such funds as were not required for lending purposes.

Where a marginal adjustment was required, it might be made in a number of different ways and employ several different kinds of instruments; sometimes, a combination of instruments. The most important included resort to an inter-bank market, the issue (or alternatively, the purchase) of CDs, similar transactions in near-CDs (e.g., bearer discount notes in Canada or transferable certificates of deposit in New Zealand), the attraction of large deposits (similarly, with private placements in the Netherlands), resort to bill markets (as in Spain and Australia) or to Euro-currency markets (especially by banks in Switzerland, the Netherlands, Japan and France), also swaps (Canada and France), and – for the temporary absorption of surplus funds – Treasury bills or Exchequer bills. Nor should one overlook the intervention of central banks by way of discounts and open-market operations.

On the whole, moneys sought by way of a marginal adjustment –

or put out in the money markets, or through secondary markets (e.g., for CDs) – constitute 'wholesale money', but, where banks have a wide spread of branches (as in the UK also), even the attraction of large deposits through such branches is semi-retail/semi-wholesale in character. It also depends on how one defines a 'large' deposit. In addition, not all 'wholesale money' need be obtained through the money markets; some of it can be raised direct from customers, just as it is by no means necessary to go through a broker in arranging deals in the inter-bank money markets. These markets are important in France – primarily on an *en pension* basis (through discount houses) – and in West Germany, the Netherlands and in Ireland.

One of the most useful instruments to be employed both in sophisticated and less sophisticated environments has been the CD, originally developed as a money market instrument in the United States and the United Kingdom. Other countries that have introduced CDs are Australia and Spain (both in 1969), New Zealand (1977), Japan (1979) and Sweden (1980); Italy is the most recent recruit (early 1983).[5] In Australia, after a slow start, they have become an important and regular source of funds, though still somewhat marginal in character. Spain also issued CDs from 1969 onwards; after a slow start, they grew to become a useful supplementary source of bank funds. Much later, Sweden entered the field, CDs becoming a substitute for large deposits on 'special conditions'; they remain a marginal source of funds, though they have given greater stability to funds management. A secondary market is developing. The story is somewhat similar in Japan, where CDs were introduced in May 1979, growth being rapid after the third quarter of 1981, with a secondary market soon developing. Swaps can be arranged through the Gensaki market (pp. 247-8). There has also been a small secondary market in CDs in Ireland going back to about 1970.

Countries in which the direct attraction of large sums of money – i.e. wholesale money – has been the usual form of securing additional funds (instead of issuing CDs) include West Germany and Austria, Italy, Belgium, Norway and Denmark, where such deposits are known as 'special' deposits'. Resort to large deposits has also become significant in Australia – despite CDs, increasing in relative importance as current-account balances have been eroded. Likewise in New Zealand, where wholesale deposits (mostly from large corporations) are in fact the most important instrument in the management of short-term funds and one of the main means of marginal adjustment. Despite a small market in CDs, corporations in Ireland are still quite happy to place wholesale deposits with a bank there (including the foreign banks) at rates related to the inter-bank market.

Another instrument on which marginal adjustments may be based is the bill of exchange – as in Spain, Australia and New Zealand. In Spain, a bank may draw a bill against a firm to which it is lending and which accepts it. The bank then endorses the acceptance. Instead of passing the bill into the bank's portfolio to be held until maturity, the bank may now sell it on the market to a party who wishes to invest moneys for the relevant period with full recourse against the bank. When the bill matures, the bank makes provision for payment. Liabilities or funds management in Australia has been assisted in recent years by the rapid development of a futures market in bank-accepted bills.

> Interest rates on bills and large term deposits are usually closely related because they are close substitutes for many investors. There are, however, occasions where the relationship may change, sometimes significantly. The bank can use the futures market to take advantage of these circumstances and relationships. For example, the bank can take a large, long term deposit, simultaneously buying bill futures contracts of the same value to cover the term of the deposit and invest in a short asset. This so-called 'swap' transaction ensures that whatever the interest rate earned on each 'roll' of the short asset, the futures contracts build in a margin above the cost of the deposit. If interest rates fall, the profit made on the futures contracts offsets the lower earnings made on each roll of the short asset. Conversely, if rates rise, the higher earnings on each roll of the asset more than outweigh the losses made on the futures contracts.[6]

Resort to the Euro-currency markets has already been described; this was in terms of the funding of loans (with on-lending of borrowings and very often a matching of loans against funds borrowed, with the customer bearing the exchange risk), but in addition in certain countries (e.g., Switzerland, the Netherlands, Japan and France, in the last case mainly by way of swaps) the Euro-currency markets are regularly employed quite specifically for effecting a marginal adjustment in the overall management of a bank's liabilities.

On the assets side of the balance sheet, the main changes over recent years in these countries have been in the structure of the loan portfolio, where there has been a general increase in term lending (mostly for up to 5-7 years) with implications for its funding. Almost all countries have gone in for term lending, but in one – Australia – this trend has been supplemented by the conversion of a proportion of bank overdrafts into the 'fully-drawn advance'.[7] Formerly, much lending by way of overdraft was really medium-term in character, with the overdraft 'running on'; hence, term lending and/or the fully-drawn advance was one means of formalising the situation. On the other hand, a fluctuating overdraft (within an agreed limit) lent itself to 'overdraft arbitrage', especially since interest rates could not usually be adjusted quickly enough to keep in step with changes in money-market rates. Thus, in Australia (and to an even greater extent in London):

> On days when money market rates are high, overdraft limits are drawn and lent overnight to the professional cash market. This outflow of funds drains bank liquidity. Up to a point, banks can run down their most liquid securities to meet these outflows (or borrow on the interbank market if possible). However, if the drain is exceptionally large or appears likely to be sustained, banks must compete in the market for deposits . . . This aggressive bank behaviour pushes rates up further, encouraging more overdraft arbitrage.
>
> In this context, it is possible that trading banks buy back their own loan funds at a rate above their lending rates to cover the use of the overdraft facility.[8]

In Belgium, an alternative to the overdraft has been the 'straight loan', where the banks lend a fixed amount for a short period (mostly for one to three months, with 12 months as a maximum).

Except in France, where the amount of discountable paper is still significant, Portugal, where the bulk of bank lending is by way of discounted promissory notes, and Japan, bill finance is much less important than it used to be. West Germany still employs the *Wechsel*, but it is used less than it was; likewise in Austria. In the Netherlands, bill finance is used only for export financing; in Belgium, there is a certain amount of trade-bill accommodation; likewise in Australia as an alternative to the overdraft and, although it fluctuates from time to time, total bills outstanding in New Zealand has tended to increase. In Sweden, bill finance has been mostly taken over by the overdraft. Bill finance is also declining in Finland.

Finally, it is necessary to consider the several ways in which banks in countries that are primarily concerned with funds management on the liabilities side seek to make their marginal adjustments. In virtually all the countries we have surveyed, there is a resort either to an interbank or call money market – in France, the transactions are done mainly *en pension* – or to an official or unofficial money market (as in Australia and formerly New Zealand). In West Germany and Austria, use of the inter-bank market provides the main means of marginal adjustment; this is also the case in Spain, Portugal and Sweden. The issue of CDs (TCDs in New Zealand) is also a popular means of adjustment wherever this instrument is employed, being important in this context in Australia for 'topping up' (in conjunction with large deposits), and in New Zealand and Japan. Apart from Australia, where large deposits are an important source of funds, such deposits are likewise a significant means of adjustment in Belgium and Finland; and in Norway, Sweden and Denmark, 'special deposits', which are similar, are also important. Sometimes use is made of bills of exchange, which can be bought or sold for purposes of adjustment. In one way or another, this is done in Australia, New Zealand, Japan (where they are usually sold in order to attract funds) and Spain.

On the international front, as we have seen, the Euro-currency markets may be employed as an important means of adjustment and this has been particularly true of Switzerland and the Netherlands.

It should perhaps be emphasised that it is not always the case that a bank needs to attract additional funds; it may have a temporary surplus to invest and to this end a variety of markets and instruments can be employed – the inter-bank and (where appropriate) Euro-currency markets, the Gensaki market in Japan, or Treasury bills or (as in Ireland) Exchequer bills can be bought.

In quite a number of countries, resort to the central bank may be part of the final adjustment, as, for example, in Norway, or Finland, where at times the Bank of Finland has indeed been the lender of first resort and, through its agency, a range of other supplementary facilities have from time to time been made available. Indeed, in Finland, the central bank in one way or another has provided the main means of adjustment. Central-bank accommodation is also used in both Sweden and Denmark. Other countries where it is usual to provide central bank help include the Netherlands and Belgium, Switzerland, Spain (where the Bank of Spain auctions its money), Austria and Ireland; in West Germany, discount quotas have long been available as a means of supplementary accommodation. In addition, over the years, a number of central banks in this group of countries have come to undertake open-market operations on a regular basis – e.g. in France and West Germany, in Australia and New Zealand, and – less regularly perhaps – in Japan.

However, from the point of view of the development of assets and liabilities management, what is interesting is that in an increasing number of countries, banks are now employing usually a combination of techniques in making their marginal adjustments. Nor is it merely a matter of securing access to additional funds – it is necessary sometimes to put funds out when they are surplus to current requirements and to invest them temporarily, often in an inter-bank market, or in short-term securities like Treasury bills. Clearly, in the countries surveyed (in addition to the United States and the United Kingdom) assets and liabilities management is already becoming much more sophisticated and an established means of bank operations.

Notes

1. For an outline of prudential supervision in a number of countries, see Jane Welch (ed.), *The Regulation of Banks in the Member States of the EEC*, second edition (London, 1981).

2. The aim was to bridge the gap between the demand for, and supply of, medium- and long-term funds by paying investors an interest rate which changed in line with short-term money-market interest rates. It was a logical counterpart in the bond market to the development of 'roll-over' bank credits and was a means of adapting readily to varying rates of inflation.

3. NIFs (or note-issuance facilities) is an umbrella term for the general concept of a back-up facility for the sale of short-term Euro-notes or CDs. It is in effect a medium-term loan, which is funded by selling short-term paper, typically of three or six months' maturity. A group of underwriting banks guarantees the availability of funds to the borrower by purchasing any unsold notes at each roll-over date, or by providing a stand-by credit. Revolving underwriting facilities, which was the earlier form, are known as RUFs.

4. See 'The International Market for Floating-Rate Instruments' in *Bank of England Quarterly Bulletin* (September 1984).

5. Towards the end of 1984 (see *Financial Times*, 7 December 1984), the French Ministry of Finance put forward proposals to banks with a view to introducing negotiable certificates of deposit denominated either in French francs or in foreign currencies (initially US dollars or ECUS). This surprise announcement precipitated heavy selling of shares in money-market funds and a crisis in the bond market, since French company treasurers – because of excess corporate liquidity – had been investing large amounts in short-term mutual-fund paper. It was feared that these placements might be diverted suddenly to CDs. In terms of the Treasury's initial proposals, the CDs would be issued in minimum amounts of FFr 10 million with maturities of between six months and two years. This would exclude small participants and thereby discourage the emergence of a speculative market. It was thought that the volume of issues was unlikely to build up to more than about FFr 40 billion, which is relatively small when compared with the FFr 150 billion outstanding in short-term unit trusts and mutual funds, in which company treasurers are understood to have significant holdings (see *Financial Times*, 21 January 1985).

6. Graham Hand, 'Developments in Bank Portfolio Management', *Commonwealth Banking Corporation Economic Newsletter Supplement* (March 1983).

7. In New Zealand, overdrafts were in many cases converted directly into term loans.

8. Hand, 'Developments in Bank Portfolio Management'.

9 THE ROLE OF A MONEY MARKET

A money market may be defined as a centre in which financial institutions congregate for the purpose of dealing impersonally in monetary assets. This serves to emphasise three essential characteristics of such markets. Firstly, the group of markets, collectively described as a 'money market', is concerned to deal in a particular type of asset, the chief characteristic of which is its relative liquidity (the readiness with which it can be converted into cash without risk of substantial loss). Secondly, such activities tend to be concentrated in some centre (or centres) which serves (or serve) a region or area; the width of such areas may vary considerably – some 'money markets' (like London and New York) have become world financial centres, or at least international in their scope; the direct influence of others may be restricted to part only of a national economy (e.g, Chicago or San Francisco in the United States, though these may have links more or less strongly developed with other centres in the same economy. In one or two instances, there may be a situation which can almost be described as a 'condominium' (e.g., Sydney and Melbourne in Australia; Bombay and Calcutta in India; Toronto and Montreal in Canada), though ultimately it is the general experience that one or the other will establish primacy. Thirdly, on a very strict definition, the relationships that characterise the money market must be impersonal in character and competition will be relatively pure (dealings between the parties concerned should not be governed or influenced wholly or in part by personal considerations); this ideal is probably more nearly approximated in New York than elsewhere, though relationships are now rather more impersonal in London than used to be the case, with a consequent increase in competitiveness.

Perhaps the last condition can best be emphasised by offering a contrasting example. In a true money market, strictly defined, price differentials for assets of similar type and maturity will tend to be eliminted by the interplay of the conditions of supply and demand. Some differentials will no doubt continue to exist at any one point in time, because in a dynamic situation the system of prices will be caught moving towards whatever, under current conditions, is the 'equilibrium' price. Nevertheless, such differentials as remain will not generally be of any great consequence. When credit relations become 'personal', on the other hand, there may be favoured customers who are accorded special rates, because of the size and continuity of the business offered, or because the borrowing customer and his business are well and favourably known to the lender. Sometimes, a loan may be granted at low rates because of mere friendship between the two parties, but that is the ultimate extreme. Moreover, the reverse experience is also possible – high rates charged to borrowers who offer small and occasional business and who may not be very well known to the lender.

It may be argued, however, that as a description of the real world this is much too 'pure' a view. Even where money markets in the real world are highly competitive, it is not unreasonable to expect that regularity of business, the amount of business, and trust in the individuals with whom one is dealing may give rise to a certain amount of discrimination in the matter of interest-rate structures. A slightly higher interest rate charged to borrowers may well be justified in terms of cost of information and an allowance for risk.

There are certain other pre-conditions that relate to the kind of economy that a money market can be expected to serve. These will already exist in countries in which a money market has grown up over the years and is now well developed, though not all 'developed' countries necessarily enjoy the services of a sophisticated money market. Hence, in countries that have only more recently sought to establish money-market institutions, these same pre-conditions must obtain.

Thus, there are certain questions that need to be asked: the first relates to the nature of the economy within which one can expect a money market to operate. For example, if it is an economy that depends for its prosperity to a large extent on exports – possibly on only one main export commodity, or at most on a small group of commodities – it is likely that the country will be very much at the mercy of its 'terms of trade' (the movement of export prices in terms of import prices); if, further, there are likely to be marked annual variations in external earnings, it may well be difficult to produce a regularly revolving fund of cash and to make available to the economy a quantum of other liquid assets on the basis of which to organise such a money market. This is so much easier to ensure if an economy is already reasonably well diversified and not subject to wide seasonal swings, though holdings of foreign exchange and regulation of their expenditure by the central bank could be one means of providing a cushion against violent fluctuations in export incomes.

Secondly, there will need to be a minimum institutional development already present – an accepted rule of law, relative political stability, and a reasonably well-developed banking and financial system. It is not only important that the managements should be experienced and already subscribe to accepted conventions of sound banking practice; the institutions on which a money market is to be based must also be known for their integrity. Where dealings are to be primarily in short-dated assets, and many must necessarily be based on agreements that are entered into orally, integrity is a *sine qua non.*

This does not mean that the existence of doubtful institutions will necessarily preclude the development of a money market, but it must impede the complete integration into a single system of the several types of banking and other monetary institutions that exist. Alternatively, as in India, the practices of certain institutions (in this case of the indigenous banker) may be unacceptable to the central bank and this may bar the path to fuller integration. Furthermore, if in these circumstances a money market is to exist at all, the central 'organised' sector based on a well-developed commercial banking system and related institutions must be large enough to provide sufficient demand for the types of services that can be supplied in a 'money market' (again, India provides an appropriate example). Yet, even where there existed a minimum number of sizeable banks of unquestioned integrity (e.g., in South Africa) but there were no suitable indigenous institutions on which to build, the introduction of 'money-market' institutions such as discount houses obviously required the provision of specialist expertise.

Thirdly, it is reasonable to ask what useful purpose a 'money market' can be expected to serve. From the point of view of the commercial banks, it should be able to provide an investment outlet for any temporarily surplus funds they may have available. If the several banks operate rather dissimilar types of business, they may well be able to accommodate each other by organising a 'call loan market'; but if their business is liable to be affected by similar seasonal influences, money will be easy or tight for each of them at about the same time, and the problem then becomes one that can most easily be resolved by the provision of special facilities at the central bank. Alternatively, the government may decide to mop up seasonal surpluses (e.g., by issuing Treasury bills for the purpose). For this system to be attractive to the commercial banks, however, there must also be a willingness to release funds during the period of seasonal stringency, either by central bank rediscount of Treasury bills at market rates or by means of a government switch to ways-and-means advances from the central bank (substituting an overdraft at the central bank for government borrowing on the basis of a Treasury bill issue).

Hence, for a money market of some kind to exist, there must be a supply of temporarily idle cash that is seeking short-term investment in an earning asset. There must also exist a demand for temporarily available cash either by banks (and other financial institutions) for the purpose of adjusting their liquidity positions, or by the government, when it chooses to finance itself by adding to the floating debt or by issuing short-dated bonds. If the banks and similar institutions are to employ such short-term borrowed funds with any degree of confidence, however, they must expect the supply of these funds to be reasonably regular (as must governments that borrow against short-dated securities, such as Treasury bills and bonds). In other words, there must in some sense be a revolving fund of cash. Otherwise, financial institutions in particular dare not become dependent on outside sources and must maintain their own internal liquid reserves, necessitating a rather higher cash ratio than they would otherwise need.

Whether such a revolving fund is likely to exist depends on the extent to which we are dealing with an export economy, and on the degree of diversification in its exports, since a seasonally balanced distribution of exports will produce a continuous inflow of external earnings and of bank cash to offset the demands for cash that relate to financing the movement to the ports of the original exports and the subsequent further financing of the imports that ultimately have to be paid for from the proceeds of these exports. But sometimes even economies with quite a high degree of seasonality can nevertheless produce a sufficiently large revolving fund of cash, on which to base money-market development. Thus, it was somewhat surprising to find in Australia that from the beginning there were in fact moneys available to feed into a developing money market and the position has been further strengthened in more recent years by the continuing diversification of the Australian economy, where seasonality is rather less than it once was; similarly in New Zealand. In Canada, on the other hand, funds were released for use in the money market by replacing the traditional 10 per cent (and legal 5 per cent) cash ratio of the chartered banks with a legal 8 per cent minimum based on monthly averaging.

This made it easier for the banks to adjust their cash positions and also freed a large volume of reserves for lending to dealers on a day-to-day basis, in amounts and at rates that enable the latter to carry inventory at a profit. From the banks' point of view, day-to-day loans were a highly liquid earning asset, which facilitated the fullest

> possible employment of their funds, since they were committed for no more than a day at a time.[1]

And, in South Africa, the purpose of setting up the National Finance Corporation was to provide an outlet for some of the large current-account balances (e.g. those of the big corporations) that appeared to be available but which were not being invested in Treasury bills or other government stocks, balances which previously had tended to be invested by the banks in the London money market and which were by this means in effect repatriated to South Africa. If, however, an economy was relatively self-sufficient, and depended for its prosperity to only a minor extent on exports, the cash-flows would be influenced for the most part by internal considerations and the stringencies caused by lags in payments need nót create any embarrassment. That is to say, if it is only the domestic economy that requires finance, the funds that accrue from borrowing and selling must remain available somewhere in the economy, even when they are passed on by spending or lending. In this context, a 'money market' has an obvious task to perform: to seek out the funds wherever they may be and to channel them into the hands of the institutions that require them.

The difficulty is that the market houses that could perform this function may not yet exist. There may be temporarily surplus funds in existence (e.g., in the hands of big industrial and commercial enterprises) but there may be no institutional mechanism to make available such funds for employment elsewhere in the economy and also to ensure that the funds can be recalled as and when required, to be replaced by other temporarily surplus funds from similar sources. There is as yet no means of ensuring that these funds will 'revolve'.

Hence, if the prospect of making a profit out of this situation fails to attract private enterprise, then there may well be a case for a public authority to take the initiative and, by setting up a suitable institution (as when the National Finance Corporation was set up in South Africa in 1949),[2] to provide an earning outlet for such funds as well as facilities for their withdrawal as and when required. Once the necessary stimulus has been provided, private enterprise may well follow the lead given by the authorities. On other occasions (e.g., in Canada)[3] it has been possible to encourage private enterprise itself to supply the desired facilities, while at other times (e.g., in Australia) it was private enterprise that forced the pace and the authorities were ultimately obliged to recognise the existence of a market and to provide it with the lender-of-last-resort facilities without which such a market cannot approach its full potential.

Defined in a narrow sense, the term 'money market' can be applied to that group of related markets which deals in assets of relative liquidity – such as call money, federal funds, Treasury bills or notes, bills of exchange (or other 'commercial paper'), and short-dated government bonds. In some centres, the term has been applied very narrowly indeed, as used to be the case in London where the money market was regarded as deriving primarily from the market relationships between the discount houses and the commercial banks. Nevertheless, such an emphasis where it occurs must not blind us to the fact that the term is not infrequently also applied in a wider and looser context. In its broader connotations, the term encompasses the whole complex of financial institutions, which in varying degrees act together to satisfy the monetary needs of a community and, sometimes, such institutions are scattered spatially over a wide area.

Whatever type of definition one attempts, money-market structure shows a wide diversity of form and it would serve no useful purpose to impose a classification by categories. In this field, probably more than in any other, it is extremely difficult to find any precise lines of division between one 'type' and another. Over recent years, it is true, economists have increasingly attempted to draw a distinction between 'developed'and 'undeveloped' money markets, but the forms of organisation are so various that the line of demarcation becomes decidedly blurred. It is surely all a matter of degree. Yet some 'standard of reference' there must be.

On many occasions, an attempt has been made to resolve this dilemma by employing as a standard of reference a model based on a market already considered to be 'developed' or 'mature'. Over many years, the London money market was so regarded. Latterly, an increasing amount of attention focussed on United States arrangements centred on New York. There are no doubt historical reasons to explain this tendency to refer to experience elsewhere, but when attempts have been made to translate these models to an environment quite different from that in which the relevant model was evolved the results have not always been particularly happy. At the same time, the efficiency of the London and New York institutions in particular in catering for the demands not merely of a complex industrial economy, but also for the needs of that much wider area, which used sterling (in the past) or nowdays resorts to the US dollar as one of its basic currencies, has prompted an intensive study of the mechanism as a means of discovering just what a money market can be expected to do. While this in no way justifies the application of a similar model or blueprint to the rest of the world, there is, nevertheless, some purpose in using the example of a 'mature' money market as a standard of reference. Environments may differ, but the essential characteristics, as distinct from the precise institutional forms, have a generality of possible application much wider than may at first be conceded.

Mature financial centres appear to be distinguished by the satisfaction of the following main sets of conditions: (i) there is in existence an integrated structure of markets and institutions, grouped about a central bank capable and willing to act as a true 'lender of last resort'; (ii) the commercial banks have come to employ their cash reserves more economically, this being evidenced either by the emergence of more or less stable behaviour patterns with regard to cash ratios, the necessary adjustments being effected by movements into and out of other (earning) liquid assets, or by the acceptance of lower cash ratios, in which case there is an obvious economy in the holding of cash (on occasion, there is evidence of both developments); (iii) to the extent that the proportion of deposits held in the form of bank cash has ceased to fluctuate significantly, other liquid assets have assumed the function of providing a cushion and, though the liquid-assets ratio itself may remain highly variable, there is likely to be an increasing emphasis on the desirability of observing an effective minimum; (iv) there is a high degree of specialisation of function.

For a money market of some kind to exist not all of these conditions need be satisfied. The order of arrangement is deliberate. No money market could exist without satisfaction of the first condition, though in developing an appropriate degree of integration elements of (ii), (iii) and (iv) are also likely to emerge.

Integration of structure has two aspects: it may relate to the central money market itself; and it may apply more generally to the overall structure of a country's financial institutions. Complete integration would presuppose both types of condition, but it is possible for one to exist without the other. Thus, in the two main money-market centres of India – Bombay and Calcutta – there was already at quite an early stage a high degree of integration of institutions operating in the central markets, but there was not yet any overall integration in the system as a whole, where firmer links remained to be forged between the so-called 'organised' sector and the indigenous lenders, such as the Multani and Marwari bankers. Latterly, the 'organised' sector has expanded to cover virtually the whole country, and the indigenous lenders (although still in existence) have come to play a relatively less important part. A more or less reverse situation formerly obtained in Australia. There the banking system as such demonstrated a high degree of integration, based on a small number of trading banks, each with developed branch-banking systems. What was rather slow to emerge was a central market concerned with dealings in short-dated paper. At the same time, this situation would scarcely have persisted for so long had the Australian monetary authorities not been so cautious in waiting upon a natural growth of appropriate institutions and techniques. In the result, a sizeable 'unofficial' market was already in existence by the time the authorities finally agreed to accept responsibility and to provide lender-of-last-resort facilities at the central bank.[4]

An integrated structure is significant in that the influences operating in one market, or affecting one particular institution in a group, will tend under these conditions to be transmitted fairly readily to other related markets or institutions and consistency will be maintained in the relationships between the several prices for money and money substitutes. In a central money market, in which money loans are made available in several forms and with a variety of maturities, it will be possible to speak of a truly integrated structure only if continuous relationships are maintained between the relevant markets. Each market will have its own price for the type of money or money substitute in which it deals (e.g., the markets for Treasury bills and other short-dated government securities in London; for commercial bills, local authority paper and certificates of deposit; in New York, Treasury bills and other federal government paper – including Agencies; federal funds – the surplus balances of banks and other depository institutions – bankers' acceptances, commercial paper and negotiable certificates of deposit; in addition to the activity in London, there has also been the external extension of the New York market into Euro-dollars and Euro-currencies generally). For integration to exist, there must be links between these several markets and their respective prices. And this is clearly the case in both London and New York. If one price ceases to be consistent with other related prices, adjustments will tend to take place such that consistency is restored. Borrowers will move out of a market where prices are high in relation to other prices into other markets where prices are more attractive. Similar possibilities must exist for lenders, such that they can move their funds to markets offering them a relatively higher rate of return. In this way, funds will tend to 'spill over' from one market into another. Absolute equality of price need not be – and rarely would be – the final result, but when due account has been taken of considerations of liquidity and maturity (and the several markets' attitudes in such matters), the prices which obtain should be consistent. In order that funds might move in the required directions, channels of communication must run between the several markets. This is a prior condition of effective integration.

The necessary links will be provided by those institutions (e.g. banks of all kinds, dealers, large business corporations, local authorities and insurance companies) which habitually operate either as lenders or borrowers in more than one market. Within limits set either by self-imposed rules (themselves derived from experience) or by the requirements of the monetary authorities, these institutions will usually reshuffle their portfolios from time to time, some of them more or less continuously. They may do this in order to secure the sequence of maturities they desire, to secure capital gains, or more generally as a means of maintaining their profits.

Nevertheless, it is unlikely that perfect shiftability will be possible and a number of 'frictions' will ordinarily operate to impede the free movement of funds from one market to another. The costs of shifting may include brokerages and commissions, taxes and the costs of investigating the placement of funds. In addition, there are the subjective costs associated with the inconvenience and bother of frequent movements into and out of markets. Risk and uncertainty will also operate as a barrier to the free movement of funds. In particular, there is the risk of depreciaton in capital values, which is likely to be influential especially in situations of highly volatile interest rates and where it is not intended to hold securities to maturity. (This is not always as big a deterrent as one might suppose. For example, losses may be treated as a deduction for tax purposes in one year, the proceeds of the sale of the securities that occasioned the loss being reinvested in a similar issue at currently low prices. If these securities should rise in price, they may be sold during the following tax year at a profit, which may then be taxed as a capital gain at a lower rate. Hence, the character of relevant tax arrangements must be taken into account when 'shifting' is being considered and the tax laws may not infrequently be a major influence in determining investment decisions.)

At the same time, frequency of operation will tend to bring its own economies and the deterrent effects of risk and uncertainty are also likely to be weakened as continuous experience of market conditions produces a more informed basis for expectations and for action prompted by them. Indeed, ignorance can operate as the biggest barrier of all.

Thus, where practices vary considerably between markets (as happened between the 'organised' and bazaar markets in India) and there is no common code of conduct, full integration is not possible. There must be mutual trust and an understanding of the relevant techniques and practices, if the risks of shifting are not to loom too large and virtually to forbid movement between dissimilar markets. The situation in India was a rather exceptional case, overlaid by a high degree of integration in the 'organised' sector, but it serves to illustrate the general principle. Once there develops a continuous and significant movement of funds from one market to another, and from one sector to another, the forces making for integration cannot long be denied.

In considering the broader concept, namely, integration as applied to the overall structure of a country's financial institutions, it will be found that similar conditions must be satisfied. For a country's banking system to be integrated, it is implied that funds can be moved without difficulty from one institution to another and from one point in the economy to another. The opposite of an integrated system in this sense would be one in which there were a large number of institutions, whose standing and methods of doing business were so different that each tended to have its own special group of customers, the rates charged being such as might be agreed upon in bilateral deals, very largely in ignorance of what might be charged or offered elsewhere in the economy. This is an extreme unlikely to be met with in precisely that form in any modern country. Improved communications and the forces of competition both operate to preclude the possibility. Nevertheless, approximations to it can still be found (e.g. the operations of the indigenous money-lenders in parts of Asia and Africa, where such relationships are not uncommon).

Complete integration of the domestic banking system will also be difficult to achieve where a country is served to a significant extent by banks owned abroad, though over more recent years such banks have either adopted a measure of local participation and/or become subject to the local authorities (in terms both of prudential requirements and policy). In the past, reserves were often held outside the economy to be drawn on as required and, in the absence of specific measures invoked to limit freedom of action, such banks could remain largely independent of local controls and able to reduce to a minimum their relations with local institutions. Formerly, this was a not unjust description of British exchange banks operating in Asian countries and of the so-called expatriate banks with business connections in Africa. Latterly, both these groups of banks have in a number of instances been obliged by local laws to hold specified proportions of their assets within the areas in which they trade. In addition, they tended to become much less exclusive and began to establish closer relations with indigenous intitutions. There was much assimilation of practice and outlook, with a breaking down of the barriers of ignorance on both sides.

So far little has been said about the mechanical arrangements for effecting integration. A fundamental requirement is the free movement of money and of monetary assets, so that temporarily surplus funds can be absorbed at points in the system where – at current prices – there is a demand for them. Thus, within a money-market centre, there may be a call loan market to assist in ensuring the fullest possible employment of available cash. Leading examples of these arrangements are the call money markets of several West European countries and of Bombay, Calcutta, Karachi, Singapore, Hong Kong, and Tokyo. The commodity dealt in is not strictly 'cash' as such but 'near cash'. This is true both of call money markets and of the similar type of market in federal funds that exists in the United States, based in New York, and which facilitates dealings in the excess balances of depository institutions. The demand comes from other institutions that need to command such balances in order to adjust their reserve positions to accord with statutory or business requirements.

In most of these markets, a proportion of the resources dealt in is placed by brokers. In London, an important group of intermediaries – the discount houses – act as principals and borrow from the banks largely at call in order to carry portfolios of bills and other short-dated securities. When money is called by one bank, it can usually be reborrowed from another (which may, however, be the central bank – see below) and a circulating fund is thereby kept in constant employment. Indeed, because of the compactness of this market, there has probably long been a higher degree of integration at the centre than exists anywhere else in the world. Not only is the market for call money concentrated in the hands of a few specialists, but the same houses that provide the arrangement for evening out the supply of cash as between the commercial banks also serve as retailers of bills and other securities of the required maturities, so that the banks can adjust their secondary reserves of short-dated paper as and when necessary. On the other hand, there have been times (as in recent years in the United Kingdom) when the role of the government in determining cash-flows has become highly significant. In practice, the banking system has found itself with a regular (and growing) daily cash shortage *vis-à-vis* the authorities. In these circumstances, money called by one bank is likely to be the result of an expected drain of cash from that bank to the government, when the discount market would have to look for cash from the Bank of England rather than from another commercial bank. Clearly, for the system to work smoothly, intervention by the Bank of England will be necessary virtually on a continuing basis, latterly largely by absorbing eligible bank bills, i.e. bankers' acceptances issued by accepting houses, the clearing banks, some Commonwealth banks, and (from August 1981) certain foreign banks[5] (when putting funds out), or selling Treasury bills when 'mopping up'. The bulk of the transactions is done direct with intermediaries – the discount houses – but at times the 'indirect route' (via the clearing banks) may also be used.[6]

In Paris, there have also long been discount houses (*maisons de réescompte*), which borrowed from the banks and other financial institutions for the purpose of carrying a portfolio of *bons du Trésor* and other government paper, as well as of commercial paper and, on this basis, assisting the banks to adjust their liquid-assets positions to accord with current requirements. Much of the money market's activity in Paris over a long period of years has related to *en pension* arrangements, whereby short-term accommodation is provided by way of a sale of bonds or bills, subject to an agreement to repurchase (in all essentials similar to the repurchase agreements or 'buy-backs' resorted to elsewhere). The most important single influence in the money market in Paris is the Bank of France and its open-market operations have become increasingly important. These are carried out through the agency of the *maisons de réescompte.*

In the United States,[7] New York is the most important banking and financial centre and it is there that money-market transactions are effectively centralised, though there are subsidiary markets in other centres, of which the most important is Chicago. These markets supplement the facilities offered in New York, but it is the rates and yields established there that provide the basis for dealings in the country at large. Activity in the various centres is fused into a national market in three ways: (i) banks throughout the United States are linked by a widespread network of correspondent relationships both with New York and with other leading centres; (ii) the various dealers in securities likewise have connections across the country as well as branch offices at key points; by these means, surplus funds can be invested in a variety of short-dated assets, which can readily be sold, thereby facilitating the day-to-day adjustment by banks and others of their cash and liquid balances; (iii) the transfer facilities made available by the Federal Reserve System greatly assist the free movement of money around the country. The two groups of institutions that constitute the most important elements in the New York money market – apart from the Federal Reserve authorities themselves – are the larger commercial banks, many of which are themselves dealers in government securities, and the non-bank government securities dealers. The principal assets in which they operate are government securities, securities of federal agencies, and federal funds, the markets in which represent the core of the national money market. There are also subsidiary markets, such as those in commercial paper, bankers' acceptances and negotiable certificates of deposit, besides the extension of United States banks as major operators into the international market for Euro-dollars and Euro-currencies generally, which is centred for the most part in Europe. Portfolios of these several instruments are carried both by dealer banks and non-bank government-securities dealers on the basis of re-purchase agreements mostly against short-dated government securities with banks right across the country, also with state and local authority treasurers, and with large business corporations. These RPs or 'buy-backs' closely resemble the French *en pension* arrangements. The same purpose is served and rates will be consistent with those that currently obtain for federal funds; likewise, with rates in the other markets like bankers' acceptances and commercial paper. The intervention of the United States authorities for the purpose of credit or monetary control is likewise concentrated mainly in the highly developed government-securities market and includes the provision of short-term accommodation to dealers by way of RPs with the Federal Reserve Bank of New York or – for mopping-up purposes – by means of reverse RPs (The Bank of England also now uses sale and re-purchase agreements, or Repos, as and when necessary).[8] In the United States, these operations in turn have an immediate impact on the supply of federal funds and this latter market therefore provides an important initial means of spreading the effects of official monetary action throughout the banking system and the economy.

If there is to be complete integration, the possibility of monetary adjustment must also exist for the system as a whole, so that funds can be moved from points in the economy where they are in surplus to those where – at current prices – there is a deficiency in supply. In a country which possesses a small group of banks doing similar types of business, each with a developed system of branches, funds can be transmitted easily both from one point to another within a particular branch network and, where necessary, between the institutions concerned. Yet the existence of developed branch systems is not an overriding prerequisite of integration in this sense. A unit-banking system can also demonstrate a high degree of integration, provided adequate arrangements exist for the movement of funds between widely separated points in the economy.

The billbrokers supplied such facilities in nineteenth-century England, thereby enabling local banks either to supplement local resources by borrowing on bills or to lend locally surplus funds by buying bills drawn outside their town or district. In the United States, correspondent relationships have enabled 'unit banks' very largely to overcome the disadvantage of restricted branch banking, facilitating the flow of funds from one economic region to another to meet (for example) the demands of seasonal finance. In nineteenth-century England, this type of solution ultimately proved too costly and the path of amalgamation and branch development offered a more appropriate means of integration. Rather slowly, this has tended also to be the path followed in the United States, where branch banking has grown significantly in recent years. None the less, the large number of banks, over half of which are technically still 'unit banks', means that correspondent relationships remain essential. In addition, the federal-funds market has greatly assisted in overcoming the disadvantages of a banking system in which branch development remains somewhat restricted. Its operations help to siphon funds out of sectors of the economy where otherwise they would have remained idle and to put them to work (say) in areas where seasonal demands for finance are at their height. Not only does this market help to correct any maldistribution of funds obtaining as between regions, but its existence also materially assists in diffusing over a wider area than would otherwise have been possible the effects of open-market operations. This is likely to be reflected directly in the federal funds market and, to the extent that they deal in federal funds, banks throughout the country will quickly feel the impact of Federal Reserve operations. In France, there are elements of both systems – some banks have a nationwide network of branches; there is also a grouping of regional and local banks headed by a leading Paris bank; finally, there is the relatively large number of regional and local banks, some of which have developed intimate relationships with Paris banks; alternatively, they may depend for the most part on the services of correspondents. As we have seen, similar 'hybrids' also exist in a number of other countries.

Integration of structure in the senses described above is essential to the development of a money market of whatever kind. Associated with it and partly in consequence of it, there has also tended to emerge a more economical use of available cash resources. In some contexts, this has resulted in the development of a more stable behaviour pattern with regard to the maintenance of cash ratios. In others, it has led to the acceptance of lower cash ratios. Occasionally, there have been elements of both. The more economical use of cash is without doubt an important by-product of a truly integrated banking strucure. Nevertheless, full advantage is unlikely to be taken of opportunities to economise cash, unless there also exists a central bank that is capable and willing to act as a fully-fledged 'lender of last resort'.

Of themselves, the arrangements that lead to integration materially assist in economising cash and other liquid resources. This is true both of the growth of call loan and other related markets (such as the federal funds market in the United States) and of the wider application of branch banking or of correspondent relationships. When there exists some mechanism whereby the full employment of such liquid resources as are available can be assured, there is less necessity to hold reserves at high levels and banks can work to a finer margin. That is by no means the whole story, but it is an important part of it. Another essential element is the knowledge that the banks can depend on the central bank as a true lender of last resort. In the final analysis, it is the existence of borrowing facilities at the central bank that makes it possible for them to accept standards of liquidity much lower than they might otherwise conceive to be adequate.

There are many countries where banking business is subject to quite marked seasonal fluctuations. The banks may accommodate this type of situation in one of three ways: (i) they can hold much higher cash ratios than would otherwise have been necessary and allow them to fluctuate in accordance with the demands of business; (ii) they can hold less cash and place a higher proportion of their assets in securities that are readily marketable, so that they can easily adjust their cash position either by compressing or expanding their holdings of liquid assets (other than cash), though resort to this technique may well oblige them from time to time to accept capital losses as a result of sales on a falling market; or (iii) they can hold lower, and possibly stable, cash ratios and have recourse to the central bank against lodgment of security on those occasions when the pressure of demand for loans and/or cash is heavy. Nevertheless, the commercial banks cannot expect to borrow freely from the central bank at all times, unless they are prepared to accept its authority and such discipline as the central bank may feel constrained to apply, e.g., by determining the price at which it will make accommodation available to borrowing banks, or by stipulating the composition of their assets structure.

In order to enforce its wishes, a central bank operating in a mature money market will usually intervene from time to time both to influence the amount of cash and other liquid assets available and the prices that apply to the securities dealt in. However, even where appropriate market arrangements exist, a central bank will only be able to undertake 'open-market operations' if it is empowered to purchase and to hold the types of assets that are available in the markets, and if it is adequately supplied at all times with assets that it can sell in these markets. Usually, central banks have been inhibited less by limitations on the types of securities that might be purchased – though such restrictions have sometimes existed – than by a shortage of 'ammunition'. Indeed, both in the United Kingdom and in the United States, prior to the development of the Treasury bill as a popular and convenient means of government borrowing, an embarrassing dearth of saleable assets was a not infrequent experience. Historically, governments have usually obliged quite handsomely by providing convenient instruments in adequate – and sometimes more than adequate – amounts. Even in the absence of an accommodating government, central banks have not always been powerless and, on occasion, they have themselves created appropriate instruments. Thus, the Central Bank of Argentina in the 1930s issued a security of its own for sale to commercial banks and, at a later date (in the 1950s), the Central Bank of Ceylon decided to supplement government issues by offering short-term paper specially created by itself, because its 'own portfolio was very limited'. The Bank of Norway has issued its own money market paper since 1978.[9] And there have been other examples. At the same time, let it be understood that a dearth of ammunition appropriate for the carrying out of open-market operations, while it may prove greatly inconvenient to a central bank, by no means precludes disciplinary activity of a more direct kind (e.g., by requiring the maintenance of minimum cash-reserve or liquid-assets reserve ratios, or the holding of special deposits with the central bank).[10] The existence of a strong, active central bank will serve to stimulate integration by fostering the growth of the right sort of environment, but the precise character of the discipline imposed can vary a great deal.

The more economical employment of cash – permitting the maintenance of either relatively stable or lower cash ratios – may be brought about in several ways, but an essential prerequisite is again a strong central bank. In England, for example, it was the growth of the bill market which made possible the achievement of relatively stable cash ratios, since this market provided an outlet for temporarily surplus cash that was invested by the discount houses in a relatively liquid security. It was not, however, until the discount market's own liquidity was in effect underwritten by the Bank of England's complete acceptance of its responsibilities as a lender of last resort that the joint-stock banks could safely hold their cash ratios at what became a conventional minimum of approximately 10 per cent. After the abolition of 'window dressing' in 1946, this was reduced to a more or less constant 8 per cent, which the authorities now expected the banks to observe. This was associated with a minimum liquid-assets ratio of about 30 per cent (latterly 28 per cent). Subsequent developments have already been described (see pp. 265-6); here the important point to emphasise is that it has been possible for the banks to maintain – even to increase – economy in the use of cash.

The policy that obtained in England of maintaining a more or less fixed cash ratio was something of a special case. In the large number of countries where commercial banks are required to maintain minimum cash reserves, these minima can usually be varied within specified limits. It will obviously be less likely under these conditions that fixed cash ratios will obtain, but the technique does tend to impose a more standard type of behaviour than previously existed and to mould the commercial banks to a pattern. Only when excess reserves obstinately remain at high levels is large-scale non-conformity possible. Thus, in the United States, where the existence of excess reserves had on a number of occasions in the past enabled the commercial banks to act somewhat independently of the authorities, more recent experience has demonstrated what can be done when the authorities are prepared to put on the pressure in the open market. Moreover, this pressure has on the whole been exerted successfully, despite the widely divergent practices of commercial banks in the United States with regard to secondary reserves.

In countries which neither apply a fixed cash ratio nor minimum reserve requirements, the general experience has been a tendency for cash ratios to fall. This has certainly been true of a number of European countries, where banks have become accustomed to work to much finer margins of cash than at one time was regarded as appropriate. In terms of the preceding discussion, it is argued that this, too, assists in providing conditions favourable to a greater degree of integration.

Much of our recent argument has been concerned with the behaviour of the banks' cash-reserve ratios, whereas the authors of the Radcliffe

Committee Report in the United Kingdom (published in 1959), felt that emphasis should be placed on the 'wider structure of liquidity in the economy' and many economists agreed with them. One of the chief means of influencing this wider structure of liquidity is by controlling the liquidity of lending institutions which by contributing to the 'ease with which money can be raised' influence the liquidity of the economy as a whole. Among these institutions the banks hold a special position, because for most borrowers they are much the most convenient institutional source of short-term funds that is available (often the only source). Yet other institutions, like hire-purchase finance companies, though they may not 'create credit', also effectively stimulate the flow of monetary resources and their activities have similar effects. If, therefore, there is a case for controlling the liquidity of the banking system, it would seem desirable to control the activities of these other financial institutions as well.

It is the common experience that 'mature' money markets tend to be characterised by a degree of specialisation. There is nothing remarkable in that. It has been a function of growth. Until the volume and continuity of transactions is such as to justify full time concentration on a particular type of activity, there is no purpose in specialisation. But the specialist is bound to emerge as soon as a sufficient demand develops for his services.

Thus, private banking was at first merely a sideline of business in less liquid chattels. The early 'bankers' were merchants, or goldsmiths, or sometimes manufacturers. Only when their banking business grew to such proportions as to make it impossible to combine conveniently these two sets of activities did the choice have to be made and the banker was obliged to become a specialist. Within the banking field, too, there was scope for specialisation as soon as a sufficient demand for specific types of service became evident. For example, the need of the country banker in England for an investment outlet for his surplus funds led to the concentration of certain houses on billbroking. They acted as intermediaries between those who wanted to borrow on bills and those who wished to invest in bills. In due course, these houses were to become dealers in bills and to carry a stock-in-trade as principals, financed to a large extent by funds borrowed from the banks. On this basis, the modern discount houses began to evolve, providing, in addition, a retail market in bills and other instruments, which enabled the banks to obtain the particular maturities they required from time to time for the purpose of maintaining secondary reserves of a currently suitable maturity distribution. Latterly, they had also assisted in 'making' the market for short-dated government securities and, by concentrating maturing stocks and bonds into a few hands, materially facilitated the conversion operations of the authorities. Another example drawn from London relates to the merchant bankers, some of whom for a time and in a limited sense still acted as merchants. One of their functions became financing the movement of goods. This they did by 'accepting' a bill of exchange on behalf of a client known or recommended to them, thereby facilitating its negotiation. In this way, the accepting houses became specialists in marketing reputation and integrity, as well as experts in the relevant financial techniques. Nevertheless, they also acquired a number of other important functions and activities (for example, as issuing houses). In addition, with the development of much wider money markets, the discount houses likewise became less specialised than they were.

New York is the only other money market in the world comparable with London in importance and sophistication, but there the degree of specialisation has always been rather less marked. Money-market institutions, including the banks, generally straddled several fields. With deregulation, straddling has tended to increase. Yet there has been a certain amount of specialisation. Thus, dealings in government securities may not be the exclusive activity of any single firm in the market, but there are nevertheless certain firms which concentrate more particularly on such dealings. Likewise, there are a small number of houses that could claim to be specialists in the placement of commercial paper, though again this is by no means their main business. With the same qualifications, specialist expertise has been built up in handling bankers' acceptances, certificates of deposit, and federal funds.

In Australia, the banking system has been integrated for many years, but the emergence of a money market that made use of specialist institutions came rather slowly. Formerly, the banks themselves tended to provide the entire range of services. The only long-standing specialization was in the field of agricutural credit – even that was incomplete. Latterly, specialists made their appearance in the capital market and a number of companies were also established for the purpose of providing hire-purchase facilities. Ultimately, too, facilities were devised on the basis of repurchase agreements by certain stock-exchange firms in Sydney and Melbourne in order to meet the needs of clients, who wanted the security of government paper, but whose funds were unlikely to be available long enough to justify an outright purchase. Moreover, government securities with only a few months to run to maturity were not normally available in large amounts. Not until February 1959, however, by which time there already existed an 'unofficial' market of appreciable size, did the central bank begin to provide lender-of-last-resort facilities to 'authorised dealers' in the short-term money market.[11]

India repesented an interesting contrast. In Bombay and Calcutta, which are still its two main money-market centres, there had long been a number of specialist brokers active either in placing money for short periods or in arranging the rediscount of hundis (an indigenous credit instrument rather like a bill of exchange). There was also the endorsing shroff. It was he who actually rediscounted hundis with certain of the larger commercial banks and, in this way, provided such links as existed between the central money market and the indigenous sectors, though this is less so now – and less necessary. These were essentially money-market specialisms and their existence demonstrated a degree of maturity and of sophistication that non-Indians found surprising. Yet the Indian authorities did not in fact choose to build on this basis and their bill-market schemes were more specifically concerned with the problem of how best to deal with the acute financial stringency that regularly develops each busy season. Also, over more recent years, the main emphasis on the institutional side has been further to develop the commercial-banking structure on the basis of widespread branches.

The advantages of specialisation need little elaboration. With the accumulation and concentration of experience comes the development of expertise and it is this that provides the ultimate justification of specialisation of function. Nor must specialisation be confused with 'compartmentalisation'. The purpose of developing specialisms is not to build up separate kingdoms, but to construct bridges between the several parts of the money market. Arbitrage operations, for example, are more likely to achieve their effects in promoting consistent price relationships if they are carried out by experienced operators than if left in less expert hands. Specialisms need imply no tendency towards monopoly, nor isolation of parts of the money market. The specialist holds his place in virtue of his acquired skill and experience. He has no other claim to his position and may be forced from time to time to face new competition for his chosen type of business. The growth of specialisms should on the whole favour the development of fuller and more complete integration of the several markets that constitute the money-market complex – by facilitating the flow of funds both between as well as within markets – and, indeed, if the specialist fails to perform this function, he serves little useful purpose.

Finally, what are the implications of maturity in money-market structure (as here defined) from the point of view of central bank control? Firstly, where a money market is compact and integrated (as in the United Kingdom), the effects of any action taken by the authorities at the centre will percolate rapidly through the whole of the central money market and from there will spread to the country at large. For this to be possible, there must be a market mechanism through the agency of which the authorities can operate and the centre must be linked more or less directly with the rest of the national economy either by means of a wide spread of bank branches, or of a developed correspondent system as in the United States (or a combination of both).

Where, as in India, the central money markets have long been well developed, but the links with the indigenous sectors were still somewhat tenuous, the effects of operations in the central markets only filtered through slowly to the farther corners of the system as a whole. Alternatively, as was the case for many years in Australia, the banking system itself was well integrated, yet in the earlier years no central money-market mechanism really existed through which the authorities could operate effectively. In this kind of situation, relations between the central bank and trading banks tended to be direct and, whether by agreement or by compulsion, liquid-assets ratios and interest rates tended to be determined by direct communication between the central bank and the constituent members of the banking system.

This may also happen in a mature money market, either as a supplementary means of control or – where a cheap-money policy has been followed and traditional weapons have been blunted – in substitution for action in the markets. Thus, if an appropriate market mechanism exists, the central bank has a choice of techniques and may intervene indirectly as the 'hidden hand' or, at its discretion, apply the methods of direct action. In the absence of a true central money market – whether the banking system is integrated or not – direct action is the only practicable method and, in recent years, it has been employed increasingly to apply a measure of credit control to institutions which – given their local environments – would otherwise lie beyond the reach of their central banks.

Secondly, there is the question of the extent to which the commercial banks have developed attitudes with respect to holdings of cash and other liquid assets that renders them more amenable to effective central bank control. Where cash and other liquidity ratios are subject to fairly predictable behaviour patterns (whether these have been imposed by the authorities or not), it ensures that the commercial banks will be dependent on the central institution for their marginal requirements of cash (and, it may be, of other liquid assets also). It then becomes possible for authorities to evoke responsive action on the part of the commercial banks by exerting the minimum amount of pressure. At the same time, the central bank's willingness to act as lender of last resort is a prior condition of the commercial banks' readiness to observe such patterns of behaviour. Unless the banks are confident that assistance will be made available as necessary, they will fight hard to retain a degree of independence by keeping substantial reserves in liquid form.

Thirdly, some specialisation of function, if a less essential requirement, also operates to the advantage of the central bank. Under these circumstances, pressure can be brought to bear easily and rapidly at whatever point is considered to be most strategic in terms of current policy and in the knowledge that there will be repercussive effects in related markets. Thus, where a specialised group of markets exists for short-dated paper of various kinds, it is possible for the central bank by purchase or sale to make cash more or less readily available in whatever sector of the money market it currently desires to influence directly, leaving market forces to spread the effects of any such action and to restore consistency in price relationships throughout the system as a whole.

The point of impact may well be as important a policy consideration as the degree of pressure to be applied (or withdrawn), since the consequential effects of such action will take a little time to work themselves out and may not immediately affect other markets to anything like the same extent. There may be occasions when it is desired to apply a differentiated pressure (particularly on rates) and the efficacy of such shock tactics will not be vitiated by subsequent adjustments elsewhere. The primary effect will have been achieved where it was most wanted. Over the course of time, there will undoubtedly be secondary effects, but these will be more diffused and the consequences therefore less direct. In this way, the existence of specialised markets can assist the central bank to take calculated and specific action to achieve objectives that might have been ill served by a general withdrawal from (or addition to) the cash base (e.g., by raising or lowering reserve requirements).

In addition, the central bank may exert its influence by conferring directly with the respective groups of interests. The leading example of this practice occurs in London, where the Governor of the Bank of England can at any time call in for informal discussion the respective chairmen of the Clearing Bankers' Association, the Accepting Houses Committee, the London Discount Market Association, or the Issuing Houses Association. Similar arrangements exist in the United States, where consultations regularly take place between the Federal Reserve System and appropriate specialist organisations. Other countries that have developed this technique include Japan and a number of West European countries, where regular consultations take place between the authorities and associations representing banking and financial interests.

Yet, in this matter, the absence of specialisation may not handicap a central bank too greatly, provided an integrated commercial-banking structure already exists. Thus, in Australia, prior to the emergence of specialised institutions, the banks were accustomed to undertake a wide range of different types of business. At the same time, because of their small number and the fact that their head offices (or in the case of the then Anglo-Australian banks, principal Australian offices) were mostly situated in one or other of the two main centres (Sydney and Melbourne), it was not a matter of great difficulty to establish contact and to provide for close and continuous consultation on a great variety of matters between central bank and trading banks. Furthermore, the Australian emphasis on branch banking facilitated the rapid transmission of the results of these deliberations to all parts of the economy.

Arrangements such as these are usually described as 'moral suasion', or 'central bank leadership' and resort to it is greatly facilitated by the emergence of specialist groups of institutions. Many American and some British economists would argue the disadvantages of direct action (e.g., the difficulty of establishing standards on the basis of which to interfere with individual decisions), though this need not necessarily follow upon consultations with the central bank. Yet those of a more authoritarian turn of mind might argue that a central bank should be free to employ every available means of implementing its declared policy and, in consequence, they might well regard 'moral suasion' as one of the most effective control techniques of all.

Notes

1. J.S.G. Wilson, 'The Money Market in Canada', *Banca Nazionale del Lavoro Quarterly Review* (June 1972).
2. See J.S.G. Wilson, *Monetary Policy and the Development of Money Markets* (London, 1966), pp. 321-3.

3. See ibid., 'The Canadian Money Market Experiment', pp. 270ff. and J.S.G. Wilson, 'The Money Market in Canada'.

4. See J.S.G. Wilson, 'The Australian Money Market', *Banca Nazionale del Lavoro Quarterly Review* (March 1973).

5. Actually, there was no deliberate decision to shift from Treasury bills to bank bills – it was really an accidental by-product of a sharp increase in the size of operations needed to balance the banking system's cash and a decline in the stock of Treasury bills available in the market to meet it.

6. There is no need here to discuss London money-market arrangements in great detail, since it has been adequately discussed elsewhere. (See, for example, J.S.G. Wilson, *The London Money Markets* (SUERF, 1976) and Wilson, 'Recent Changes in London's Money Market Arrangements' in *Banca Nazionale del Lavoro Quarterly Review* (March 1983).

7. For a detailed study, see Marcia Stigum, *The Money Market*, newly revised edition (Homewood, Illinois, 1983). For a shorter survey that might still serve as a useful introduction, see J.S.G. Wilson, 'Money Markets in the United States of America', *Banca Nazionale del Lavoro Quarterly Review* (December 1970).

8. 'This technique may be chosen to enable the market position on future days to be smoothed out – e.g., a day of expected surplus could be offset by choosing it as a repurchase date. They may be used on days of large shortage when houses are unable to sell sufficient 'outrights' to 'take out' the shortage. On some days, the Bank may be prepared to 'repo' bills, which because they are not within 90 days of maturity would be ineligible for outright purchase. Again 'repos' may be used when the market is particularly reluctant to sell bills of certain maturities to the Bank, because of interest rate expectations. Occasionally, there may be a policy purpose – e.g., switching between techniques to prevent a particular rate structure from becoming too firmly entrenched' (J.S.G. Wilson, 'Recent Changes in London's Money Market Arrangements', p. 96).

9. See the *Bank of Norway Economic Bulletin*, 4 (1983), p. 286.

10. Special deposits were extensively resorted to by the Bank of England between 1960 and 1980. They were a means of siphoning off and immobilising additional bank cash. Calls to special deposit might be regarded as a means of varying the cash ratio, but it would probably be more appropriate to regard such calls as a variation of the minimum liquid-assets ratio.

11. For further details, see J.S.G. Wilson, 'The Australian Money Market'.

10 THE PRINCIPLES OF CENTRAL BANKING

The underlying philosophy of central banking gradually emerged in response to the recurrent British financial crises of the nineteenth century and, in the latter part of the century, techniques were developed by the Bank of England in an effort to overcome the worst consequences of these crises. Over the years in Britain as elsewhere, patterns of behaviour came to be established, which enabled the institutions that became central banks to cope fairly successfully with situations and problems that whenever and wherever they occurred seemed to have much in common.

Modern market economies were seen to be subject to a considerable degree of instability. Although the causes of these fluctuations were many and various, there was little doubt that the ability of banks to create new money had frequently had the effect of reinforcing the strength of forces already making for instability. Commercial banks will generally attempt to preserve a nice balance between their pursuit of profit and the necessity to maintain the degree of liquidity sufficient to ensure that they can repay deposits on demand or when required to do so. Nevertheless, there are also wider considerations. Although a bank may be shrewd enough adequately to safeguard its own liquidity position, the expansion or contraction of the money supply to which it contributes may not in fact be in the general interest. Hence the argument that there should exist some disinterested outside authority that can view economic and financial developments objectively and without being motivated by the considerations of profit and loss.

Such an institution should also be capable of acting to offset the effects of forces originating outside the economy as well as within it. External factors making for instability may be essentially similar to those that operate internally, but the attempt to control destabilising influences that originate elsewhere is much more difficult. Instability in a 'closed' economy will generally be occasioned by tardy adjustment to changing market phenomena, complicated by the exaggerative effects of variability in money flows. Substantially, the same is true of the 'open' economy, i.e. one in which trading relationships with the rest of the world contribute significantly to the earning of its national income. Again, there will be the necessity to adjust to changes in market conditions, but on this occasion the relevant markets will be in other countries. So also may be the monetary complications. There will therefore be an effective widening of the area of necessary adjustment. In addition, there will be a significant difference in the character of the adjustments that can be made, since political boundaries normally preclude the infringement of another country's autonomy. By and large, an 'open' economy must accept as largely beyond its own control patterns of market behaviour external to itself. Hence, the primary adjustments must generally be unilateral (the alternative is international cooperation, but that is rarely more than partially successful).

To the extent that market forces produce their own tendency towards 'equilibrium', they will have repercussions over the wider area and despite the existence of national boundaries. Even so, the existence of national boundaries must introduce additional 'frictions' and further barriers to effective adjustment. When account is taken of such arbitrary arrangements as protective tariffs, subsidies, import and export quotas, and the apparatus of exchange control, the degree to which free-market forces can operate over the wider field is likely to be even more severely restricted. Hence, the central bank must not merely concern itself with the problems of economic instability within its own domestic economy. It must also take into account the repercussions of developments elsewhere.

It is useful in discussing the general principles of central banking to consider what have become the accepted responsibilities of such institutions. Most obviously, a central bank must concern itself with the maintenance of a soundly based commercial-banking structure and, indeed, nowadays its interests tend to comprehend the operations of all financial institutions, including the several groups of non-bank financial intermediaries. Nevertheless, the commercial banks remain the most important of the relevant institutions and it is therefore with their operations that central banks are primarily concerned. Action in this field will generally be the means whereby it contributes to the overall stability of the national economy. It is also a recognised convention that the central bank should cooperate closely with the government of the country concerned. Indeed, in the majority of cases, government (through the Treasury or Ministry of Finance) and central bank have become so intimately associated in the formulation of policy that one frequently refers to the 'monetary authorities' rather than to the central bank as such, when indicating the source of regulatory action.

It is appropriate to consider the relationships between the central bank and the commercial banks. Undoubtedly, over the years, one important source of economic instability has been monetary. Even in relatively well-behaved banking systems, the banks have frequently expanded credit to such an extent that real resources have become more than fully employed, with the consequent development of inflationary pressures. Quite apart from the danger of lending excessively in the pursuit of profit, there may have been a lack of judgement in the making of certain loans, which subsequently have either become frozen or resulted in outright loss. Almost as an inevitable reaction, following a period of relative over-expansion in bank lending leading to a liquidity crisis, there has been a phase of undue caution in the making of loans, with deflationary consequences. Frequently, in the past the turning point was associated with a financial crisis and, in former years, bank failures were a not uncommon experience. Even today, failures occur from time to time and reconstructions become necessary. However, such crises did not merely eliminate banks that had been incompetently managed. Because of the general loss of confidence, they often also threatened the continued existence of institutions whose condition was essentially sound. Hence the necessity for some intervention by the authorities to prevent complete collapse.

The willingness of a central bank to offer support to the commercial banks and other financial institutions in time of crisis was greatly encouraged by the gradual disappearance of the weaker institutions and the general improvement in bank management, The dangers of excessive lending were now more fully appreciated and the banks also became more experienced in the evaluation of their risks. In some cases, the central bank itself has gone out of its way to educate the commercial banks in the canons of good behaviour, as in the United States where the Federal Reserve System maintains a regular examination of commercial-bank books and policies as well as a range of frankly educational activities. In developing countries such as India and Pakistan, central banks have also set up departments to maintain a regular scrutiny of commercial-bank operations and, in this way, have prepared the ground for the more active and continuous support of the commercial banks in time of need.

The most obvious danger which might beset the banks was that of a sudden and overwhelming run on their cash resources in consequence of their liability to depositors to pay on demand. In the ordinary course of business, the demand for cash was found to be fairly constant, or subject to seasonal fluctuations which could be foreseen and guarded against. As we have seen, it became a matter of sound banking practice to carry a reserve of cash and of assets readily convertible into cash sufficient to meet all reasonable demands. There neverthless remained in the background the possibility of a general loss of confidence and the danger of a run on their resources, which the commercial banks might be unable to meet. It therefore became the recognised responsibility of the central bank to protect those banks that had been honestly and competently managed from the consequences of a sudden and unexpected demand for cash. If any such bank were so threatened, it was accepted that the central bank should be prepared either to buy certain of its assets, or to lend against the security of such assets, so that all demands for cash could readily be met and the confidence of depositors restored. In other words, the central bank came to act as the lender of last resort.

To do this effectively, it was necessary that the central bank should possess certain powers. It was imperative that it be permitted either to buy assets or to make advances against the security of the type of assets commercial banks would usually have available. Furthermore, it was necessary that the central bank should have the power to issue money which was acceptable to bank depositors. If, however, a central bank was to be expected to assist a commercial bank in an emergency, it was only reasonable that the central bank – or some related authority – should be allowed to exercise a degree of control over the way in which that bank conducted its business and the manner in which the investment of its funds was distributed between the several classes of banking assets. This implied that the central bank should be in a position to impose its wishes either in virtue of its moral leadership or – more formally – by regulation of a statutory character, and that certain classes of bank assets be 'eligible' at the central bank either for purchase or as security for an advance.

Nevertheless, any tendency to discuss the relations between the central bank and the commercial banks merely in terms of the central bank's being a lender of last resort, upon which the commercial banks can depend with confidence in times of acute strain, obscures the continuing nature of central bank activity. Only occasionally are banking systems today subject to sudden shocks to confidence and panic demands for cash by depositors. Nevertheless, discontinuities in the supply of cash can prove markedy inconvenient both to business and to the economy generally (e.g., withdrawals of money due to tax payments). There has been much evidence in recent years to suggest that most (if not all) central banks have now come to accept day-to-day 'smoothing out' operations as a definite responsibility. The Bank of England, for example, has been increasingly in the market for this purpose, even during periods of credit restriction. It also lends regularly to the discount houses, supplementing their resources whenever the commercial banks feel the need to call back moneys they have on loan to them. In the United States, too, the Federal Reserve System has operated in a similar way through the open market (buying and selling securities) and by lending to the non-bank government-securities dealers on the basis of re-purchase agreements; in addition, the System lends to the commercial banks through the 'discount windows' of the various Federal Reserve Banks. Examples could also be drawn from other countries. The techniques employed may have been rather different, but the objective in each case seems to have been essentially similar. At one time, it may have been true that central bank activity was largely confined to crisis and near-crisis. Irregularities in the money supply were on other occasions often left to look after themselves. Nowadays, however, central banks attempt – with varying degrees of success – to regularise the flow of money throughout the economy at all times and they make a considerable effort to avoid foreseeable hold-ups in the monetary circulation.

Acceptance of the view that there are rights and responsibilities and the evolution of working arrangements on that basis implies a community of outlook among both commercial bankers and central bankers, which in many cases is relatively recent of achievement. The whole concept of a central bank responsible for the stability of the banking system pre-supposes mutual confidence and cooperation. Evidence of such a state of affairs must include a willingness on the part of the commercial banks (frequently supported by a statutory requirement) to hold their reserve balances with the central bank; otherwise, it would be possible for the commercial banks to pursue a credit policy independent of that favoured by the authorities and possibly conflicting with it. Not only does such a concentration of reserves enable the central bank to keep a watchful eye on the positions of the commercial banks and to help them in case of need. It also assists the central bank in fulfilling its more general responsibilities for safeguarding overall economic stability.

It is difficult to over-emphasise the importance of mutual trust and cooperation. To this end, it is most desirable that the central bank should cultivate throughout the financial community a sense of participation in the formulation of credit policy. For this reason, contact between the central bank and the commercial banks must at all times be maintained. The commercial banks must be encouraged to feel that the central bank will give careful consideration to their views on matters of common concern. However, once the central bank has formulated its policy after a full consideration both of the facts and of the views expressed, the commercial banks must be prepared to accept its leadership. Otherwise, the whole basis of central banking would be undermined.

A second set of central-bank responsibilities relates to the national economy as a whole. There is first the question of trading and financial relationships with other countries. No modern economy is completely self-contained. If goods are bought from a foreign country, there will be a demand for foreign exchange to pay for them. Alternatively, if goods are sold abroad, foreign exchange will be acquired that ordinarily the seller will wish to convert into his own domestic currency. These two sets of transactions will usually pass through the banking system, but there is no necessary reason why – over the short period – they should balance. Sometimes there will be a surplus of purchases and sometimes a surplus of sales. Short-period disequilibrium is not likely to matter very much, but it is rather important that there should be some tendency to balance over the longer run. On the one hand, it is difficult to continue indefinitely as a permanent borrower; on the other, if a country persistently tends to buy less abroad than it sells, it will build up a command over goods and services in the world's markets which in effect it is refusing to exercise. Short-period disequilibrium can be met very simply by running down or building up balances of foreign exchange. If a country has no balances to run down, it might borrow. But normally it will at least carry working balances. Moreover, if the commercial banks find it unprofitable to hold such balances, the central bank itself is available to carry them. Indeed, it may insist on the bulk of the country's foreign-exchange resources being concentrated in its hands, or in the hands of an associated agency, leaving the commercial banks with no more than the working balances necessary for their everyday business.

However, there is still the problem of achieving equilibrium in the longer term. A solution may be approached in three different ways: by inducing relative price movements; by exchange revaluation (appreciation or depreciation), including the possibility of a 'floating' rate; or by means of exchange control.

When people buy and sell abroad rather than in the domestic market, they do so because it is profitable. Their activities in external markets can therefore be controlled, if it is possible to influence their profits from this source. This can be achieved by inducing relative price movements. For example, if it is desired to stimulate imports, the monetary authorities can induce a relative rise in home prices by encouraging an expansion of bank credit. If additional exports are necessary in order to achieve a more balanced position, the authorities will attempt to force down home costs by operating to restrict credit. In this context, it is relative prices that matter – the home country's prices in relation to prices in other countries. In times of general inflation, therefore, it is a question of whether one country's prices go up more or less rapidly than another's.

Yet the objective may be achieved more directly by revaluing a country's exchange rate. Depending on the circumstances, the rate may be appreciated or depreciated, or it may be allowed to 'float'. In effect, adjustment is sought by varying the price of one's own currency in terms of the currencies of other countries. Appreciation means that the home currency becomes dearer and that its exports become more expensive for foreigners to buy. Exports are thereby discouraged and imports encouraged. Depreciation involves a cheapening of the home currency as a means of lowering prices of export goods in the world's markets. Exports are encouraged and imports discouraged. In both cases, however, only a temporary stimulus will be given. For this reason, the authorities often seek to maintain as far as possible stability in exchange rates even at the cost of some fluctuation in internal prices, though latterly there has been rather more interest in 'floating' rates, where the rate of exchange finds its own level from day to day and there is less of a tendency for internal prices to fluctuate.

In a number of cases and at various times, the disinclination to jeopardise stability has led the authorities to prefer some form of exchange control (sometimes combined with import licensing). This is a means whereby foreign exchange earned by exports is allocated more or less directly in payment for specific imports. At times, a considerable apparatus has been assembled for this purpose and, despite 'leakages' of various kinds, it has proved reasonably efficient in achieving its stated objective of ensuring balance on external-payments account. In addition, it has been possible to vary the intensity of the control to accord with current developments. Its chief disadvantage is the extent to which its general use interferes with normal market processes, thereby encouraging rigidities, reinforcing vested interests, and operating to restrict the growth of world trade. Hence, the tendency now for the authorities to operate in the market (buying and selling the several currencies on the basis of the funds they hold) in order to offset embarrassing movements in exchange rates.

Whatever the method chosen, it is regarded as desirable that the process of adjustment should be supervised by some central authority – usually the central bank, or some institution closely associated with it – which can assemble the information necessary to ensure that responses to changing conditions external to the economy are made with sufficient rapidity and to the required extent.

There is also the problem of the incidence of economic fluctuations. This likewise concerns the community as a whole and it is a matter for which the central bank must accept some responsibility.

It is generally accepted today that monetary influences are at least an important contributory factor in causing economic fluctuations. An expansion in bank credit makes possible – if it does not cause – the relative over-expansion of investment activity, which is characteristic of a boom. Furthermore, many still maintain that control of the boom is a condition of avoiding depression. Insofar as monetary policy can assist in mitigating the worst excesses of the boom, it is the responsibility of the central bank to regulate the amount of bank lending and (sometimes) lending by other financial institutions as well. Also, though there is less general agreement about this, the central bank may feel it necessary to influence in some degree the direction of lending.

It would be wrong, however, merely to emphasise the central bank's responsibility for the regulation of expansionary influences. Indeed, there have been times when a central bank has been thought of primarily as an agency concerned to combat the possibility of a slump. Recessions, when they occur, are often in the nature of an adjustment, an attempt on the part of the body economic to eliminate the waste products of relative over-expansion. Such adjustments are necessary to restore economic health, but at times the process of readjustment has tended to go too far and a 'secondary' depression has supervened. Depressive factors have been reinforced by a general lack of confidence and, once this has happened, it has sometimes proved extremely difficult to stimulate recovery. In these circumstances, prevention is likely to be far easier than cure and it has therefore become a recognised function of the central bank to take such steps as may be necessary to preclude, if possible, any such general deterioration in economic activity.

It used to be the view – whether it was socially desirable or not is another matter – that relatively high unemployment levels in effect operated as a kind of discipline in the economy. Nowadays, however, unemployment – though it remains a major social problem – in a number of countries no longer bites in the way it used to do. Almost certainly this is because of changes that have taken place in the social fabric. Whether inactivity is due to redundancy or strikes, the worker (and his family) is now usually protected in a number of ways – e.g., income-tax rebates and social-security payments of various kinds. In addition, in a situation where prices were rising fairly rapidly and persistently, the effects of expectations had to be taken into account. In particular, the expectation that prices would continue to rise resulted at least for a time in a continuing upward pressure on wages – to offset or more than offset rising prices – and this was likely to happen whatever the unemployment situation might be. Again, there has been the 'revolution of rising expectations', which generated pressure for higher real take-home pay, whatever the levels of unemployment.[1] But rising expectations had a much wider significance. As societies became more affluent during the 1960s, with employment maintained at high levels over much of the decade, domestic consumption was also likely to be at high levels. Rising expectations were also translated into the increasing expenditure of central and local governments on items like social-security services, cultural and leisure amenities, the maintenance of medical and health services, educational reforms, and better communications. The investment level may not have been as high in some countries as compared with others, but it was obviously as necessary because of the technological revolution and the incidence of obsolescence. In general, the pressure on scarce resources that characterised much of the World War II experience is sufficient to explain a good deal of the upward pressure on prices that developed after World War II. The economic system was already vulnerable to exogenous shocks long before the impact of higher oil prices beginning in 1973. It could be argued, too, that greater fiscal and monetary discipline was likely to discourage investment and to induce higher levels of unemployment, though it is somewhat doubtful whether in fact such discipline has always been as wholeheartedly imposed as politicians would have us believe.

More generally, for the central bank effectively to regulate the volume and distribution of credit so that economic fluctuations may be damped, if not eliminated, it must at least be able to regulate commercial-bank liquidity (cash and near-cash), since this is the basis of bank lending, Moreover, over more recent years, the monetary authorities in a number of countries have begun to resort increasingly to monetary aggregates as a basis of policy. This does not mean an uncritical acceptance of monetarist philosophy, rather what P.W. Volcker has called 'practical monetarism'.[2] But, in addition to the Federal Reserve in the

United States, there have been a growing number of West European countries that have adopted the practice of setting growth targets for the money supply and/or other monetary targets (like domestic credit expansion), though usually allowing for some variation between a range of limits. Japan has had reservations and has preferred to indicate monetary projections or forecasts, partly because of the difficulty of changing a set target, should this become necessary. Nor is there any great degree of consensus as to which target or aggregate to employ. In general terms, choice of a particular aggregate as a basis for reference would be linked to the theories – more or less explicit – on which the actions of a particular central bank are based; it will also depend on the state of a country's economy and the financial environment of the country concerned. Where there are publicly declared targets, these can have an important announcement effect.

There is nowadays little dispute about the broad objectives, though the techniques of control will be various and will depend at least to some extent on environmental factors. It is sufficient to emphasise here the nature of the central bank's responsibility for the monetary health of the economy. To this end, it must place itself in a position to recognise the phase of the business cycle (boom or recession) through which the economy is passing. On the basis of this diagnosis, it can then take action to 'cushion' the economy against the effects of fluctuations in the national income, whether the source of the disturbance be at home or overseas. It would be incorrect to suppose, however, that the actions of the central bank can, unaided, achieve a high degree of income stability. It can by wise guidance contribute to that end, but monetary action is in no sense a panacea and, at all times, the degree to which it is likely to be effective depends on the provision of an appropriate fiscal environment.

There is next the question of ensuring that banking services are adequately supplied to all members of the community that have need of them. In certain countries, particular areas may be 'under-banked' (e.g., the rural areas of India, and the northern and more remote parts of Norway) and at various times central banks have attempted – directly or indirectly – to meet such needs. Indeed, it was such an attitude which prompted the early extension to the provinces of branches of the Bank of France. In India, as we have seen, the authorities encouraged both the opening of 'pioneer' branches first by the former Imperial Bank of India and after 1955 by its successor the State Bank of India and, indeed, latterly, the general extension of bank branches to rural and semi-rural areas by all the nationalised banks (under the 'lead bank' scheme). On other occasions, the central bank has assisted in the establishment of a separate institution, which would help fill the gaps in the national coverage of the banking system. The active part played by officials of the State Bank of Pakistan in the foundation of the semi-public National Bank of Pakistan is a case in point.

A somewhat different type of problem arises when the business methods of existing banks do not accord with minimum standards. In such circumstances, a system of bank inspection and audit organised by the central banking authorities (as in India and Pakistan) or of bank 'examinations' (as by the Federal Reserve and other authorities in the United States) may be the appropriate answer. Alternatively, the supervision of bank operations may be handed over to a separate authority, such as a Banking Control Commission (as in France) or a Registrar of Banks (as in South Africa).

In recent years, there has also been some tendency in the developing countries to lay upon central banks a responsibility for financing development. It depends on what one means by 'development'. If it is intended to convert the central bank into an engine for investment, there is a grave danger that its primary functions may be subverted. Responsibility for schemes for development properly belongs to a central planning authority, though without doubt staff from the central bank may well play a useful advisory role, especially on financial matters.

If, however, one means by 'development' the closing of gaps in the financial infrastructure (by setting up new institutions and extending financial services to a wider public), this is certainly a field in which one would expect the central bank to give a lead. In particular, one might expect the central bank to encourage the establishment and growth of specialist institutions (like agricultural credit or industrial finance corporations and savings institutions), in order to improve the mechanism of tapping existing liquid resources and of supplementing the flow of funds for investment in specific fields.[3]

Finally, central banks have over the years acquired a number of well-defined responsibilities as bankers to their respective national governments. As a matter of history, some institutions developed into central banks substantially because they were in origin bankers to the government. In the case of the Bank of England, for example, this would not seem too exaggerated a statement and, in some respects, there are parallels in the evolution of the former Commonwealth Bank of Australia as a central bank (after 1959, these functions passed into the hands of a separate Reserve Bank of Australia). More recently, it has been the rule to require a new central bank as a matter of course to accept responsibility for the financial affairs of its government. The reasons are not far to seek. Government transactions have become of increasing importance in influencing the working of the economy. Government balances may swing within wide limits and the flow of money to and from the government could have most disturbing effects. The institution that holds the government's account is in a strategic position for the purpose of cushioning the commercial banks against the impact of large movements of cash originating in this way. Furthermore, as banker to the government, it is the obvious responsibility of the central bank to provide routine banking services, such as arranging loan floatations and supervising their service, renewal, or redemption. It will also usually provide the note issue. Equally important are the central bank's responsibilities as a specialist adviser. Much government action and related legislation will at times have important monetary consequences. For example, to budget for a deficit during a boom would obviously exaggerate the economic expansion already in progress. It is the function of a central bank to advise the government on the probable consequences of any proposed action and, where necessary, to suggest appropriate alternatives. In this role, it is desirable that the central bank should scrutinise the government's proposed actions with a certain amount of objectivity and, at times, to offer positive criticism. Moreover, if a central bank is to play its full part in the informed discussion of government policy, it must retain its right to state its point of view with vigour. Nevertheless, once a decision has been taken, the central bank will be expected to cooperate with the government in carrying out that policy, for which the government alone is ultimately responsible. In this context, it is appropriate to quote Montagu Norman's famous dictum (when speaking of the role of the Bank of England in 1926):

> I think it is of the utmost importance that the policy of the Bank and the policy of the Government should at all times be in harmony – in as complete harmony as possible. I look upon the Bank as having the unique right to offer advice and to press such advice even to the point of 'nagging'; but always of course subject to the supreme authority of the Government.

Many central banks are now nationalised and this reflects the increasingly general recognition of the central bank as a servant, if not a creature, of the government. It is also in a way a final recognition of the central bank as a responsible public institution, whose function it is to serve the community as a whole, untrammelled in its judgement by the narrow dictates of profit and loss. The irony of the situation is that in fact most central banks make very handsome profits indeed.

Notes

1. By the early 1980s, in certain countries (e.g., the United States and the United Kingdom) because of the recession, wages in some sectors tended to be either relatively stable or to evidence even a downward trend; however, by 1984, there were signs of renewed pressure, which began to edge wages up again.

2. P.W. Volcker, 'A Broader Role for Monetary Targets', *Federal Reserve Bank of New York Quarterly Review*, (vol. 2 Spring 1977), p. 15.

3. In this context, see also J.S.G. Wilson, 'Building the Financial System of a Developing Country', *Lloyds Bank Review* (July 1969).

11 THE TECHNIQUES OF CREDIT CONTROL

The principles of central banking have a general applicability, but when we come to consider the means adopted to influence, regulate or control the activities of commercial banks and other financial institutions, there is in fact a considerable degree of variety. At the same time, one can usefully group into categories the several 'weapons of control' that have been employed from time to time.

The reasons for this variety of technique are not far to seek, since the means of control adopted by the central bank in question must obviously depend primarily on the environment within which the monetary authorities must operate. More specifically, the choice of method will be conditioned very largely by the degree of development of the money market, within the framework of which the central bank has to formulate its techniques. On occasion, the choice of technique will also be influenced by the policy being followed by the government (e.g. if a cheap-money policy is favoured, obviously it will not be possible to employ the weapon of high interest rates to curtail credit).

The types of credit control, which may be employed for the purpose of influencing the quantity of credit made available through the agency of the banking and near-banking systems, may be divided into (i) the so-called 'classical' or indirect techniques and (ii) the various 'direct' controls that may be used.

The 'classical' techniques are based on open-market operations in certain types of assets that are eligible for central bank purchase or sale, or as security for central bank advances. These operations are invariably associated with related changes in one or more 'strategic' rates of interest, the most influential of these rates being the minimum rate at which the central bank will do business (Bank rate, or discount rate), since other rates tend to move in sympathy with it. Indeed, where this 'classical' technique is employed, it is impossible to discuss its quantitative aspects without at the same time invoking price considerations as well. Thus, if the emphasis is quantitative in character, it is important to achieve an appropriate and consistent price (or interest-rate) structure. Alternatively, if a particular price (or rate) structure is desired (e.g., prior to a new government security issue, or to induce a change in the emphasis of institutional investment, say, between long-term and short-term securities), it is frequently necessary to precondition the relevant market(s) by means of open-market operations. For either of these purposes to be achieved, it is essential that the central bank should possess (if it is selling) or be willing to absorb (if it is buying) the appropriate types of securities. It is further implied that the central bank may be obliged to operate in more than one market, though this is not a view that has always been fully accepted.[1]

The purpose of direct quantitative credit controls is generally either to influence the cash and liquidity bases of commercial-bank lending by the freezing or unfreezing of their liquid resources, or to impose general or sectional 'ceilings' on bank loans. The circumstances in which direct quantitative controls will usually be preferred to the 'classical' techniques are of two main kinds: (i) where open-market operations cannot be employed because markets in the relevant securities do not yet exist (alternatively, such markets may exist, but they may not yet have developed sufficient width to take the strain of transactions of the size that may be necessary from time to time to make quantitative action effective); and (ii) where the banks have not yet formed firm habits with regard to the maintenance of cash and liquid-assets ratios, it will be difficult to predict their reactions to any given change in their reserves as a result of open-market operations. Until established patterns of behaviour have emerged with respect to the maintenance of liquid-assets ratios, use of the 'classical' techniques will be subject to obvious limitations and the tendency will be to employ more direct methods.

Nevertheless, there may well be occasions when direct methods of control will be employed even within the framework of a mature and sophisticated money market, and where the 'classical' techniques are already long established as an appropriate means of control. In this event, direct methods will tend to be employed, whenever necessary, as a supplemental measure. For example, this would doubtless now be the purpose of varying the required minimum reserves of the commercial banks in the United States.

Open-Market Operations and Discount Policy

The way in which open-market operations influence first the cash reserves and through them the general liquidity of the commercial banks is essentially very simple. If the central bank buys securities in the 'open market', the cash it offers in exchange adds to the reserves of the banks; if the central bank sells securities in the 'open market', the cash necessaryto pay for them is either withdrawn from the banks' reserves, or obtained by running down holdings of other assets (with the possibility of capital losses in consequence of these sales). It does not matter whether this buying and selling takes place between the central bank and the commercial banks, or between the central bank and other financial sectors, including the public at large, since these are the customers of the commercial banks.

If the process of creating stringent conditions (with higher rates of interest) is pushed far enough and if the banks still fail to come into line, the authorities can virtually force them to conform. The authorities are able to do this by squeezing bank liquidity and obliging the banks to face the possibility of heavy losses in consequence of having to sell securities. In other words, the attack can be made via the banks' profits. The fact that banks may now be faced with the necessity to sell securities at a substantial loss if they go on expanding their loans will make them feel relatively illiquid and cause them to consider carefully the extent to which they can still pursue a policy of credit expansion.

Again, by 'managing' the national debt, it is possible for the monetary authorities to induce movements in interest rates and, by this means, also to bring about changes in liquidity. Provided only that the authorities avoid putting out an over-supply of short-term paper, holders of debt will have to consider from time to time the extent to which some of the longer-term securities remain liquid, in the sense that they can still be sold for cash without substantial loss. On those occasions when financial institutions are obliged to fall back on the 'cushion' of their longer-dated securities by selling for the purpose of obtaining the liquid resources necessary to support their lending programmes, they will become sensitive to any operations that affect the medium- and long-term parts of the rate structure. It is in this way that debt management can be used by the authorities to influence the wider structure of liquidity.

The difficulties about this prescription are the danger that the authorities may be led into 'monetising' too large a part of the national debt, and that, although it may be relatively easy to increase general liquidity by pushing bond yields down, it will be much more difficult to decrease liquidity by forcing them up, since even at attractive prices banks and other financial institutions may not want to buy the securities that are being offered for sale. However, the degree of dependence on the technique of debt management may be reduced by resorting to a variety of supplementary measures.

In London, the discount houses effectively put to work the revolving fund of cash that circulates through the British banking system. If temporarily there is an inadequate supply (due to money leaving the commercial banking system and passing into the hands of the authorities as a result of tax payments, gilt-edged purchases by the public from the Government broker, increases in the note issue, payments of oil royalties, foreign-exchange settements, etc.), the Bank of England will either lend on a short-term basis, or buy some of the assets held by the discount houses, or it may be these are held by the clearing banks, which then make the relevant moneys available to the discount market. Since November 1980, there has been a shift of emphasis from lending to open-market operations by dealing in bankers' acceptances. Alternatively, if there is a surplus of money in the market, the Bank of England will sell Treasury bills to the discount market (or to the banks) in order to 'mop up' the excess. These are in the character of 'smoothing out' operations.

As from August 1981, the system of lending at a Minimum Lending Rate (which had replaced Bank rate in October 1972) was suspended. Linked with this were certain changes that affected discount market arrangements. It seemed that the Bank of England wished to give the money market more say in the determination of interest rates rather than themselves to impose a structure. Under the new system then introduced, short rates (say up to 7-14 days) were to be kept by the authorities within a range – the so-called 'unpublished band'; longer rates were to be allowed to fluctuate more freely. 'Decisions as to the band will be taken in accord with the same range of considerations as would have determined decisions about MLR, so that the new arrangements imply a change in techniques, rather than in the objectives of monetary policy.'[2] This meant scrapping the old structure of Treasury bill-dealing rates whereby the Bank of England were not only ready to lend overnight at Minimum Lending Rate (which had now been suspended), but also to buy Treasury bills of different maturities at predetermined levels. (Incidentally, since the Bank of England had hardly lent to the market since November 1980, MLR, though perhaps retaining a psychological inflence, had virtually ceased to have any operational effect on rates.) The announcement of bill-dealing rates a week ahead was one of the first things to go. The next stage – in terms of day-to-day operations – was the decision in November 1980 to shift the emphasis from lending to open-market operations especially by dealing in bills. In practice, this meant primarily eligible bank bills, i.e. bankers' acceptances issued by accepting houses, the clearing banks, some Commonwealth banks, and (from August 1981) certain foreign banks. Actually, there was no deliberate decision to shift from Treasury bills to bank bills – it was really an accidental by-product of a sharp increase in the size of operations needed to balance the banking system's cash and a decline in the stock of Treasury bills available in the market to meet it.[3] When there was a shortage of credit and discount houses were obliged to sell bills to the Bank of England, they were now required to name a price; if the Bank of England did not like it, it could turn them down. The Bank of England still set the rates, but it was the market that proposed them.

What the Bank of England was now trying to do was to:

> smooth out day-to-day shortages or surpluses of cash by means of open-market operations, rather than by direct lending to the discount market. In dealing with shortages, the Bank has usually either bought bills outright or, if the shortage was to be followed before long by a day of prospective surplus, it has bought bills for resale on that day. When the market has been in surplus, the Bank has sought to sell Treasury bills set to mature on a day of prospective shortage. Where large transactions could be estimated in advance – notably oil tax payments or calls on part-paid gilt-edged stocks already sold – operations have been framed accordingly . . . All these operations were conducted within the context of a general objective for very short-term interest rates. Where the Bank dealt in longer-term bills, it did so to change the market's cash position on the day of the transaction and hence to influence very short-term interest rates. The Bank did not aim to affect rates on longer-term bills themselves but, rather, operated at appropriate market rates to avoid giving a signal which could otherwise have had undue influence on the market.[4]

However, this system will no doubt be subject to modification, when the Bank's new proposals for market arrangements are introduced in 1986.[5]

As we have seen, the Bank is also responsible for managing the national debt (these transactions go through the Government broker, who operates on the London stock exchange) and, whether the object is to influence the flows of money or not, such transactions will in fact have monetary effects. Indeed, the one function, managing the money supply, merges into the other, managing the national debt, though clearly the latter likewise has the effect of influencing both the general liquidity of the economy and the structure of interest rates.

In the USA, the Federal Reserve System is responsible for regulating the money supply, debt management being the responsibility of the Treasury. At several levels, there is effective liaison and regular consultations between the two. Within the Federal Reserve System, it is the Federal Open Market Committee (FOMC) which is the most important single monetary policy-making body. It is presided over by the Chairman of the System's Board of Governors, with the President of the Federal Reserve Bank of New York as its permanent Vice-Chairman; he serves on a continuous basis. Other members include the Governors of the System, and four of the Presidents of the other Federal Reserve Banks serving one year in rotation. Rotation is conducted so that each year one member is elected to the Committee by the Boards of Directors of each of the following groups of Reserve Banks: (i) Boston, Philadelphia, and Richmond; (ii) Cleveland and Chicago; (iii) Atlanta, St Louis, and Dallas; and (iv) Minneapolis, Kansas City, and San Francisco. The other Presidents and a number of staff officers also attend, though without votes. The latter are selected from among the officers and employees of the Board of Governors and the Federal Reserve Banks. Officers include: a Secretary to maintain a record of actions taken by the Committee on all questions of policy; economists to prepare and present to the Committee information regarding business and credit conditions and domestic and international economic and financial developments; General Counsel to furnish such legal advice as the Committee may require; and a Manager and Deputy Managers of the System Open Market Account to execute open-market transactions and to report to the Committee on market conditions.

The law requires that meetings of the FOMC be held at least four times each year in Washington, DC, upon the call of the Chairman of the Board of Governors or at the request of any three members of the Committee. Typically, meetings are held once every four to six weeks in the offices of the Board of Governors in Washington, according to a schedule tentatively agreed upon at the beginning of the year. If circumstances require consultation or consideration of an action between these regular meetings, members may be called on to participate in a special meeting or a telephone conference, or to vote on a recommended action by telegram or telephone. At each regular meeting, the Committee votes on the policy to be carried out during the interval between meetings; at least twice a year the Committee also votes on certain longer-run policy objectives.

Prior to each regular meeting of the Committee, written reports from System staff on past and prospective economic and financial developments are sent to each Committee member and to non-member Reserve Bank Presidents. Reports prepared by the management of the System Open Market Account on operations in the domestic open market and in foreign currencies since the last regular meeting are also distributed. At the meeting itself, oral reports are given by staff officers on the current and prospective business situation, on conditions in financial markets and on international financial developments. Oral reports on transactions in the System Open Market Account since the previous meeting are given by the Manager or Deputy Managers of the account.

Following these reports, the Committee members and other Reserve Bank Presidents discuss policy. Typically, each participant expresses his or her own views on the state of the economy and prospects for the future, and on the appropriate direction for monetary policy. Then each makes a more explicit recommendation for policy for the coming inter-meeting period (and for the longer term, if under consideration). Finally, the Committee develops a consensus regarding the appropriate course for policy which is incorporated in a directive to the Federal Reserve Bank of New York – the Bank selected by the Committee to execute transactions for the System Open Market Account. The directive issued by the FOMC is cast in relatively specific terms so as to provide concrete guidance to the Manager in the conduct of day-to-day open-market operations– e.g., the Committee's objectives for longer-term growth in certain key monetary and credit aggregates, as well as short-term operating guides for rates of growth in the monetary aggregates (as represented by M1 and M2) and associated ranges of tolerable changes in money-market conditions (as represented by the federal-funds rate).

Thus, the main responsibility of the FOMC is to decide upon the timing and amount of open-market purchases or sales of government securities and, since open-market operations must obviously be consistent with other aspects of monetary and credit policy, it is in the Committee that broad agreement is reached on matters such as changes in discount rates or reserve requirements which are strictly outside its sphere of decision. While all that emerges formally from the Committee is a set of written instructions to the Fed in New York for the operations required in the government-securities market, and any related statement of policy or technical arrangements, the New York representatives also take back with them the 'feel' of the meeting.

As indicated above, the Treasury is responsible for debt management in the sense that it will largely itself decide on the types of securities to be issued and the terms on which they will be offered. It will also be responsible for refundings. In other words, it is primarily responsible for changes in the composition of federal debt. The Federal Reserve, which undertakes purchases and sales in the open market, is concerned to determine where that debt shall be held as a result of which it can – and does – influence monetary flows within the terms of what is decided within the FOMC.

Meanwhile, whether from a debt-management point of view it attempts to maintain 'neutrality' or not, the Federal Reserve in its role as a central bank will be operating to influence monetary flows by undertaking transactions in the open market, which have become the main basis of quantitative credit regulation in the United States. For the most part, the Fed will deal in Treasury bills and, indeed, this is also often the common medium elsewhere. But the Fed likewise operates in other securities of longer maturity as and when this proves to be appropriate.

One of the big differences between London and New York is that the central-banking authorities in New York maintain direct relationships more or less continuously both with the non-bank government-securities dealers and with the commercial banks themselves.

So far as the dealers are concerned, the Federal Reserve Bank of New York may make temporary accommodation available to some 35 primary dealers (including certain banks) under a 're-purchase agreement' (where securities are sold to the Fed under an agreement that they be re-purchased after a stipulated time). These agreements are made only at the initiative of the Fed with the dealers for the purpose of supplying reserves to the banking system, but from the dealers' standpoint they are helpful in financing portfolios. The technique has the advantage of placing funds where they are most needed. Since early 1966, the Fed has also been prepared to mop up money by undertaking reverse RPs. The dealers act as intermediaries for commercial banks with temporarily surplus moneys that they are prepared to place against bills, subject to the Fed re-purchasing them a few days later. Meanwhile, the commercial bank concerned lends the dealer the money to finance the holding of the bill. Reverse RPs are also done direct with the bank dealers.

In addition, all member banks of the Federal Reserve System may have direct access to the 'discount window' of their Federal Reserve Bank (one to each of 12 districts). It is always emphasised that this is a privilege and not a right. In the early years of the System (established in 1913), the emphasis was primarily on the actual discount of eligible paper. Nowadays, the banks usually seek an advance at the prevailing discount rate from their Federal Reserve Bank (each bank has the power 'to establish from time to time, subject to review and determination of the Board of Governors' the rates of discount to be charged and the rates of the different banks tend to move together). This advance would be made against a pledge of government securities (or of 'federal agencies') held in safe custody with the Federal Reserve Bank in question. The Fed will lend for a number of purposes, but always at a time of general stress. It is assumed that as the pressure abates, every effort will be made by borrowing banks to repay their indebtedness as quickly as possible. Under ordinary conditions, the continuous use of Federal Reserve credit by a member bank over a considerable period is not regarded as appropriate.

Following the passage of the Monetary Control Act of 1980, the Board of Governors of the Federal Reserve System adopted a major revision of its Regulation A (effective 1 September 1980), whereby discount and borrowing facilities were now extended to all 'depository institutions' (member and non-member commercial banks, US branches and agencies of foreign banks, Edge and Agreement corporations, savings banks, savings and loan associations, and credit unions) provided they offered transactions accounts or non-personal time deposits that were subject to reserve requirements. These facilities were now extended to them on the same basis as to member banks.

Under Regulation A as revised to implement the Act,[6] Federal Reserve credit was now offered under two major programmes – adjustment credit and extended credit.

> Adjustment credit accounts for most Federal Reserve lending. It is made on a very short term basis to help depository institutions adjust to sudden changes in their need for funds. Extended credit is designed to help institutions cope with such needs over somewhat longer periods. It includes seasonal credit to accommodate the needs of smaller institutions, and other extended credit for institutions facing particular problems. Problems of this latter type may arise from the particular circumstances of a given institution, or from general difficulties affecting a broader range of institutions.

With respect to non-member institutions that have access to special industry lenders such as the Federal Home Loan Banks (for savings and loan associations), credit union centrals, and the Central Liquidity Facility of the National Credit Union Administration, the Fed may provide 'for temporary adjustment credit to such institutions where they are unable to gain timely access to their special lender and for consultation and coordination with the special industry lender'. It was expected that usually such funds would be repaid the next business day, when access to the usual source of funds had been secured. At the same time, the Federal Reserve Board made 'the possible use of a discount-rate surcharge a permanent addition to the System's discount lending rules applicable, according to circumstances, to both adjustment and extended credit'. Such surcharges had been used during 1980 and 1981 as part of the credit-restraint programme. Latterly, the penalties were relaxed on extended credit to assist in resolving the Continental Illinois crisis.[7]

In a number of countries, resort to open-market operations has become a much more important means of regulating the supply of money than was formerly the case. Because of space limitations, however, only one or two examples can be given. Thus, in France beginning in the late 1960s, Bank of France operations in the open market largely replaced the earlier system of *plafonds* on central-bank accommodation. Day-to-day liquidity problems are settled in the money market (on an *en pension* basis through the Paris discount houses). In this way, the Bank of France 'injects into the banking system the liquidity that it requires'. If the Bank of France wishes to 'mop up' money (which is exceptional) it may borrow *en pension* on a day-to-day basis from the money market.[8] It is through its open-market operations, too, that the Bank of France is able to adjust money-market interest rates.[9]

In West Germany, the main traditional instruments of liquidity management are variations in minimum reserve ratios and rediscount quotas. However, both of these instruments (especially the former) have been used somewhat less frequently since about the mid-1970s.

> Since banks require time to adjust their position to changes in these instruments, the Bundesbank can hardly use these instruments for influencing banks' liquidity position in the very short run, that is, within a calendar month. Moreover, their use is frequently associated with undesired signaling effects at home and abroad. The Bundesbank has therefore tended to rely more heavily on 'fine-tuning' measures in the open market . . . in recent years to drain reserves from the banking system or accord temporary assistance to the money market. In exceptional circumstances, quantitative ceilings have also been imposed on the use of the Lombard facility. Under

> such conditions, 'fine-tuning' measures assumed additional importance since it was left to the Bundesbank to satisfy banks' residual reserve demands through ad hoc intervention in the interbank market.[10]

'Fine-tuning' operations or 'reversible assistance measures' are employed mainly to cushion short-run fluctuations in bank reserves or to influence in the desired direction (but not too conspicuously) key money-market rates, but always with the possibility of ready reversal. Such measures have been used more actively and systematically since about 1979 and the range of instruments available for short-run intervention has been widened. Thus,

> Reserve-absorbing measures include the sale of bill-type money market paper issued by the Bundesbank, foreign exchange transactions under repurchase agreements, and the sale of Bundesbank discount paper with maturities ranging from 6 to 24 months. Reserve-creating measures comprise the day-to-day lending of Federal government cash funds to the money market, foreign exchange swaps, open market transactions in commercial bills and bonds under repurchase agreements, and redemption prior to maturity of Bundesbank discount paper.[11]

In 1982, to quote an example, operations relating to 'reversible assistance' or 'fine-tuning' covered periods ranging from less than a week to four to six weeks.

Direct Credit Controls

The so-called 'classical' techniques of credit control, namely, open-market operations and discount policy, can only be employed where there exists a sufficiently developed complex of markets in which to buy and sell assets of the type that commercial banks will ordinarily hold. Direct credit controls have a wider range of application. They may be applied to institutions that form part of a developed market either as a substitute for the 'classical' techniques, or as a supplementary measure. But direct controls are more likely to be resorted to under conditions in which a sufficiently developed money-market mechanism is absent. In these circumstances, a central bank can only impose its authority by means of direct action. Frequently, this is the situation that faces a newly established central bank. It may take many years to evolve an appropriate market mechanism and to establish a central-banking tradition. The authorities may therefore feel that they cannot afford to wait. They may adopt the not unreasonable view that a central bank without positive powers is without purpose. They may therefore provide the central bank from the first (as in Pakistan, the Philippines, Sri Lanka and Malaysia) with very full powers to control the banking system.

The purpose of imposing a direct quantitative regulation of credit is to curb the inflationary pressures that may be occasioned by an expansion of commercial-bank lending. This objective can be achieved in five main ways:

(i) the commercial banks may be required (a) to maintain stated minimum reserve ratios of cash to deposits; or (b) they may be required to maintain a stated liquid assets ratio; or (c) a combination of (a) and (b);
(ii) part of the cash resources of the commercial banks may be immobilised at the discretion of the central bank, though sometimes only within a range of stated limits;
(iii) ceilings may be imposed on the amount of accommodation to be made available to the commercial banks at the central bank (these are sometimes also referred to as 'discount quotas');
(iv) an attempt may be made to prescribe a ceiling within which commercial bank lending must itself be held; and
(v) a kind of ceiling may be imposed on the growth in interest-bearing deposits, such that any 'excessive' growth in such deposits may be siphoned off into non-interest-bearing supplementary special deposits.

Minimum Reserve Requirements

Variation of minimum cash-reserve requirements as a direct means of quantitative credit control has become increasingly general in recent years and the inspiration has frequently derived from American experience. It is only fair to point out, however, that in its origins the American insistence on stated minimum cash-reserve requirements for commercial banks was really only a means of prescribing minimum standards of sound behaviour. It was not until rather later that variation of such ratios was seen to be a useful supplementary quantitative credit control. This has also been true elsewhere (as in India and New Zealand).

In fact, the power to vary the cash reserves of the commercial banks in the United States was first accorded, under emergency conditions in May 1933, by the Thomas Amendment to the Federal Reserve Act. However, this was only a temporary provision and was superseded by the powers incorporated in the Banking Act 1935. The new instrument of control was employed for the first time during the boom of 1936-7 and periodic variation of minimum reserve requirements subsequently came to be recognised as an appropriate technique for preventing 'injurious credit expansion or contraction'.

At times, the Federal Reserve Board's decisions were subject to considerable criticism but, as it became more experienced in the use of this technique, variation in reserve requirements, when combined with other measures, came to be regarded as a useful means of cushioning the economy against the repercussions of a fall in activity. On the other hand, there was evidence to suggest that when the reserves of the commercial banks were at higher levels, the upper limit to the increase in reserve requirements proved to be too low, if effective action was to be taken to regulate credit expansion. It is only fair to add, however, that as long as a 'stable bond market' was accepted policy, it was unreasonable to expect that variation of reserve requirements within the prescribed limits could be completely effective. Latterly, following the 'accord' between the Treasury and the Federal Reserve Board in March 1951, much greater emphasis was placed on the use of open-market operations and the variation of minimum reserve requirements as a means of controlling the credit base then tended to be pushed into the background. The technique of requiring the maintenance of minimum reserve ratios has a wide following and is in fact employed nowadays in a large number of countries thoughout the world.

In a number of countries, the authorities require the maintenance of minimum liquid-assets ratios. This is often associated with minimum requirements for cash reserves, though this has not always been the case (as witness France, where until 1966 there were no minimum cash-reserve requirements but a *coéfficient de trésorerie*, dropped in favour of such requirements as from January 1967). Where prescribed minima relate to liquid assets and not to cash as such, reserves will be held in the form of earning assets and, from the point of view of the commercial banks, this is an important distinction.

In the United Kingdom, an important step towards a uniform and explicit minimum liquidity ratio for the London clearing banks was taken in 1951, when the Governor of the Bank of England indicated to the banks that a liquidity ratio of from 32-28 per cent would be regarded as normal but that it would be undesirable for the ratio to be allowed to fall below 25 per cent as an extreme limit. By 1957, a 30 per cent minimum had become more rigid (and was reduced to 28 per cent in 1963). It should be noted, too, that after 1946 and within these ratios, the London clearing banks (but not the Scottish banks) observed a more or less fixed cash ratio of 8 per cent. A new element had been introduced in 1960, when the Bank of England launched its system of 'special deposits' as a means of reinforcing other methods of credit control. Calls were now made from time to time on the London clearing banks to deposit with the Bank of England by a specified date some specified percentage of their gross deposits; similar arrangements applied to the Scottish banks, but the calls were smaller. This lasted until 1971, when – under Competition and Credit Control – a new 12½ per cent minimum reserve ratio (excluding till cash) was introduced. This related to 'eligible liabilities' (primarily sterling deposits of up to two years' maturity, including sterling certificates of deposit). When called upon to do so, the banks could also be required to place special deposits with the Bank of England. These arrangements were replaced in August 1981 by, firstly, a voluntary holding of operational funds with the Bank of England by the London clearing banks ('for clearing purposes') and, secondly, a uniform requirement of ½ per cent of an institution's eligible liabilities that would be applied to all banks and licensed deposit-takers with eligible liabilities averaging more than £10 million; this was the non-operational requirement and was to be set twice a year in relation to average eligible liabilities in the previous six months. In calculating eligible liabilities, inter-bank loans and secured call money placed with discount houses, money brokers, and gilt-edged jobbers in the stock exchange were treated as an offset. Window-dressing was to be avoided, since it would be 'contrary to the objective of these agreed arrangements for any institution to reduce its eligible liabilities deliberately or artificially on reporting dates'. The Bank of England accordingly reserved the right to make spot checks. Also, as from 20 August 1981, the date when the new changes came in, all banks that were eligible acceptors were normally required to hold an average equivalent to 6 per cent of their eligible liabilities either as secured money with discount houses or as secured call money with money brokers and gilt-edged jobbers, but the amount held in the form of secured money with a discount house was not normally to fall below 4 per cent of eligible liabilities. This was to be monitored by the Bank of England, to which banks would make monthly returns of daily figures. This money became known as 'club money'.

The use of minimum reserve requirements as a means of credit control may take many different forms. As a means of achieving restriction, it can, if pushed far enough, undoubtedly produce results, especially when the requirements relate to the holding of cash balances. As a method of countering recession, it suffers from the obvious deficiencies of any quantitative action, i.e. the possible unwillingness of the banks to lend, or of their customers to borrow. Moreover, at all times, it is a somewhat clumsy technique, and it is difficult to allow for the special needs of different institutions. If a wholehearted attempt were made to discriminate between individual banks, either the control would tend to founder in complicated formulae or, if separate ratios were established for each institution at the discretion of the central bank, its actions might be open to misinterpretation.

Immobilisation of Cash Resources

The second group of direct quantitative credit controls relates to those arrangements in which a portion – as distinct from a proportion – of the cash resources of the commercial banks is immobilised at the discretion of the central bank, though possibly subject to some limitation of this discretion. Two leading examples of this technique were the wartime and post-war use of the Treasury Deposit Receipt (TDR) in the United Kingdom and the 'special-account procedure' adopted in Australia in 1941 and not modified substantially until 1953.

Both were means of ensuring that the increased banking liquidity deriving from wartime government expenditure was in fact immobilised as efficiently as possible and on a continuing basis. To this end, the direct issue of TDRs at a nominal rate of interest to banks in the United Kingdom was begun in July 1940. TDRs were issued with a life of six months; later, there were also five- and seven-month maturities. They were not negotiable in the market, nor transferable between banks, but they could be tendered as cash in payment for government bonds (and tax certificates) and hence during the war years (when bills were 'on tap') had a limited degree of liquidity. The Bank of England communicated to the banks collectively the amount of the weekly call, which was divided between them in proportion to their deposits. There was a limited possibility of rediscount with the Bank of England. After the war, TDRs were replaced by Treasury bills and, in order to reduce the consequent high liquidity of the banks, there was a 'forced funding' of £1,000 million of Treasury bills in November 1951, which were now invested in Serial Funding Stocks.

The special-account procedure introduced by regulations in Australia in 1941 had a similar objective. The surplus investible funds of the Australian trading banks, which were defined as the amount by which each bank's total assets in Australia at any time exceeded the average of its total assets in Australia in August 1939, were to be placed in special deposit accounts with the Commonwealth Bank (which at that time was also the central bank) at a nominal rate of interest. A trading bank was not to withdraw any sum from its special account, except with the consent of the Commonwealth Bank and, during the war years, it was generally the practice of the Commonwealth Bank to direct the trading banks to lodge in their special accounts each month an amount equal to the increase in their total assets in Australia during the preceding month. There was provision for withdrawals from these accounts, subject to Commonwealth Bank consent, but as a rule during the war years a lodgement was not requested when it was known that a rise in assets would be followed by an early fall. Legislation replaced the relevant regulations in 1945 and special-account procedures were used as a means of general credit control (e.g., to curb inflation). But there was an upper limit on special deposits – the amounts transferred from wartime special account, plus any increase in the banks' assets following the implementation of the Banking Act 1945. Withdrawals might again be permitted (possibly, subject to conditions) and, at times, substantial withdrawals were permitted in the early post-war years, thereby introducing a degree of flexibility into the control. Alternatively, the banks could be required to sell government securities, or they might at times borrow from the central bank. This was the system which was operated until 1953, when a more complicated formula was introduced, later to be superseded by resort to reserve ratios (in early 1960). In recent years, too, open-market operations have become of increasing importance.

Discount Quotas

A technique that has been employed on several occasions in recent years is the use made of 'ceilings', in the sense of a limit on the amount of accommodation that the central bank is prepared to make available to the commercial banks. The difficulty of operating this type of quantitative credit control is how to discover a method of making it effective, while adapting it to take into account changes in the economy. Its most obvious use is as a means of checking an inflationary process, but if the upward pressures on prices are sufficiently strong, there is always the temptation to increase the ceilings and the restraint often then becomes little more than a temporary check.

The post-war experience of France was a case in point and it was not until borrowings in excess of the primary ceilings were made subject to increasingly heavy penalties that the French authorites were able to make this type of control effective. Usually, it is only when a control begins to hurt and to hit bank profits that the banks become really sensitive to changes in credit policy and the implementation of a control becomes truly effective.

Plafonds, or 'ceilings', were first introduced in France in October 1948. Rediscount ceilings (or discount quotas) were fixed for each bank, though some categories of paper were excluded. Ceilings could be increased or (after 1957) reduced. But discounts that fell outside the ceiling were relatively illiquid, since funds were tied up until the paper matured and, as the banks were at that time obliged to borrow almost continuously from the Bank of France, the dangers of illiquidity were considerable.

From the authorities' point of view, the chief difficulty in operating this control was the persistent building up of pressure against the ceilings. This was met partly by upward revisions in the ceilings themselves and partly by instituting a number of 'safety valves'. The degree of elasticity required, particularly during a period of rapidly rising prices, constituted the chief weakness of the ceiling technique. In all the circumstances, some upward revisions were unavoidable, but which claims were legitimate and which were not? The central bank was constantly under pressure to adjust the ceilings upwards and much bilateral bargaining took place between the Bank of France and individual commercial banks. Yet the commercial banks continued to complain that the strictness of the control was excessive and that the technique lacked flexibility.

The inadequacies of the *plafonds* technique in its original form became very apparent when prices began to rise rapidly during the Korean War boom and even the built-in safety valves failed fully to accommodate the related pressures on bank liquidity. The need for some strengthening of the mechanism was obvious. This was attempted in October 1951. Previously, rediscounts had frequently exceeded the ceilings during the course of the month and were only brought within the *plafonds* by special action (e.g., through the open market). This situation was brought under control by introducing a secondary ceiling to which a penalty rate of interest was applied. This was extended in 1958 to permit rediscounts even beyond this secondary ceiling, provided a further penalty was imposed. But this assistance was not unrestricted, since each application was scrutinised by the Bank of France.

This was the system that existed until about the spring of 1964, though it did not finally disappear until 1968, being largely replaced by Bank of France operations in the open market. From early 1967, the French banks were also subject to minimum reserve requirements.

Plafonds (or 'discount quotas') have likewise been employed in West Germany. They were first introduced in 1952 and were greatly strengthened in 1955. Quotas may be reduced from time to time (after 1964, also to discourage institutions from borrowing abroad). Again, there were safety valves (though less generous than in France) and the possibility of extra accommodation (Lombard credits) at a higher rate. In certain circumstances, supplementary quotas may be approved for periods of up to six months. A bank may also seek to raise funds through the money market, though it may find this source rather more costly. Discount quotas are still an important basis of credit control in West Germany.

Other countries that have employed this technique have included Sweden, where for a time the central bank imposed formal or informal ceilings on banks, sometimes on finance companies. If the banks failed to observe the ceiling, a penalty was applied based on the amount of the excess borrowing and its duration. Also, in Finland, commercial banks have at times been able to borrow limited amounts from the Bank of Finland by way of traditional credit quotas. Beyond these quotas, funds could formerly be obtained as supra-quota credit but at a higher rate. Now if the banks require additional funds, they are forced into the official call money market. Denmark, too, has permitted borrowing from the central bank in tranches, with higher (penalty) rates applying after the first tranche of the loan quota has been resorted to; this can be expensive.

Credit Ceilings

One must consider the attempts that have been made to prescribe a general ceiling within which the quantity of commercial bank lending must itself be held. This is even more difficult to achieve. An early example of an attempt to place a ceiling on bank loans was the adoption of a 'rising ceiling' by Chile in September 1953. All banks were then required not to expand the volume of their loans to businesses and individuals by more than 1½ per cent per month (which was presumably the then current estimate of the rate of increase in prices), using as their basis the average of a bank's advances on selected dates in 1953. At the same time, certain types of loans were forbidden and bank resources were to be directed to 'productive and distributive activities which really contribute to the expansion of the national economy'. The banks were also placed under an obligation to provide information on the destination of their loans, the ceiling control being reinforced by a qualitative control. In succeeding years, adjustments were made on several occasions in the maximum permitted credit increase, which was expressed either as a percentage of advances or sometimes simply as a definite peso figure for the banking system as a whole. On 1 April 1959, all quantitative credit restrictions in force up to that time were removed and banks were permitted to advance funds up to their financial capacity provided they operated within the regulations established under the general banking law. There was no evidence to suggest that these controls were particularly effective, but the major problem in Chile has in any event long been fiscal rather than monetary.

A ceiling on loans may be imposed merely as a temporary measure as by agreement in Canada in 1951-2; also in the Netherlands (1957-8).

A country that has had a great deal of experience of this type of ceiling is the United Kingdom, where it was first introduced as a temporary measure in 1955, when the banks were asked to bring their advances down on average by 10 per cent. At a later stage, the attempt was made to impose a true ceiling, such that bank advances did not exceed the average of the months October 1956 to September 1957. This ceiling was continued until July 1958. Again, in 1961, the authorities indicated that the banks must aim at checking the rate of rise in bank advances and this came to be interpreted as a request that the level of advances at the end of 1961 should be no higher than in the previous June. Also the banks were not to encourage an increase in the volume of commercial bills. This request was modified in May 1962 and largely withdrawn in October, but it was back again in May 1965, when the clearing banks were requested not to increase their advances to the private sector at an annual rate of more than about 5 per cent in the 12 months to mid-March 1966; similarly with commercial bills. Other financial institutions were requested to observe a comparable degree of restraint. For 12 months after March 1966, advances and discounts, allowing for seasonal factors, were not to rise above the levels set for March 1966. In fact, this represented an intensification of the credit squeeze, since advances could not be expanded even though prices were rising. However, because of a falling off in business confidence as a result of credit restriction, towards the end of 1966 bank lending was well below the official ceiling. From April 1967, the authorities announced that there would now be an emphasis on making calls to special deposits. This was welcomed by the banks, which were however to be disappointed. Ceilings were back by November 1967. Apart from finance for exports and shipbuilding, there was to be no increase in bank advances to the private sector except for seasonal reasons. But in May 1968 a new ceiling was instituted that comprehended all such lending, including credit related to exports and for shipbuilding. The clearing banks were now asked to restrict the total of this lending, after seasonal adjustment, to 104 per cent of the November 1967 figure, which was roughly the then existing level, with priority to be given to finance for exports and for activities directly related to improving the balance of payments. The restrictions also extended to other types of credit. Although later fixed-rate lending for exports and shipbuilding was excluded from the ceiling, credit became even tighter, when by March 1969 the ceiling was reduced to 98 per cent of the November 1967 level. Similarly for the Scottish banks. The banks experienced considerable difficulty in meeting this new requirement and agreed merely to 'do their best'. Advances nevertheless increased above the ceiling and, as a fine, interest paid by the Bank of Engand on special deposits was halved. Not until late autumn 1969 did it become clear that the authorities were prepared to abandon their long campaign to get bank loans down to the target figure. Although no formal announcement was made to this effect, it seems that the Bank of England eventually settled for the banks keeping their figures within reasonably close distance of the then existing level. The policy of squeeze moved into a more flexible phase and, by 1971, was replaced by Competition and Credit Control, when the ceiling was dropped altogether.

The advantage of this type of credit control is no doubt its relative informality, but its successful implementation obviously depends on the very full cooperation of the commercial-banking community as a whole and it is no secret that in the United Kingdom use of this technique was without exception heartily disliked by the commercial banks. It is a form of control that also has real weaknesses, especially in a country like the United Kingdom that bases much of its lending on the overdraft technique, where customers have agreed 'limits' up to which they can overdraw.

In France, on the other hand, the *encadrement du crédit* as it was called, first imposed in 1958-9 and thereafter from time to time, became a regular feature of credit control from the first half of 1973 onwards. Subject to certain exclusions, the mechanism chosen was to permit a certain percentage rate of growth in bank credits in relation to a particular month in the previous year, these limits being fixed quarterly and subject to variation from time to time (e.g., by way of gradual reduction; or on other occasions when a degree of economic expansion was desired, to permit of some increase).[12] Subsequently (in early 1975), reference was made to a fixed base equal to an index of 100, in relation to which base the index might be increased (or decreased) and credit expanded (or contracted) accordingly. The system was further refined to vary the rate of change of credits within different types of financial institution and over the years it was subject in the interests of flexibility to many amendments.[13] In effect, there was a combination of quantitative and qualitative credit controls. It should be noted that when the ceilings were exceeded the banks concerned were required by way of penalty to maintain supplementary compulsory reserves with the Bank of France. The *encadrement* system was phased out at the end of 1984. It had become increasingly cumbersome and ineffective. The growth in the money supply was now to be regulated by a mechanism based on depositing bank reserves at the Bank of France calculated on the basis of both deposits and credits. It was anticipated that there might now be greater flexibility in interest rates. Also, bank lending potential would now depend more directly on increases in the banks' capital resources and their issues of bonds.

At times (e.g., in the 1970s) in Belgium, too, the monetary authorities have had recourse to the direct limitation of bank credits and have also imposed an *encadrement du crédit*.

A somewhat similar tool of monetary control, which when suitable is used in Japan, is 'window-guidance', i.e. direct controls on bank lending to the private non-bank sector.

> Window guidance is fast and certain especially when supported by interest rate operations in the inter-bank market. Bank lending to the private nonbank sector in Japan is indeed declining in relative importance, but still far exceeds other sources of money supply increases, such as inflow of funds from abroad or underwriting of government bonds by banks. Hence, window guidance can still be an important method of monetary policy.
>
> But precisely because window guidance is a method of direct control, its harmful effects – such as ossification of market shares of banks and limitations on freedom to compete – are many. Thus, in money supply management, interbank rate operations are the main tool, and window guidance is only a supplementary or stopgap measure. With this attitude, and in response to the growing monetary relaxation since the middle of 1980, the Bank of Japan has per-

mitted city banks, long-term credit banks and all other financial intermediaries to lend as they wish. But this statement carries the implication that window guidance will be reimposed if future movements of the money supply and other variables make this necessary.[14]

Ceilings on Interest-bearing Deposits

Another technique that has been employed in the United Kingdom (and briefly emulated in the United States) was a ceiling on interest-bearing deposits – a 'corset' – with penalties if the ceiling was not observed, any 'excessive' growth in such deposits being siphoned off into non-interest-bearing supplementary special deposits with the Bank of England, with the object of improving the authorities' control over the money supply and bank lending. This Supplementary Deposit Scheme, which was announced in December 1973, was applied both to banks and to deposit-taking finance houses, with the Bank of England specifying a maximum rate of growth for interest-bearing eligible liabilities. Any institution whose interest-bearing eligible liabilities grew faster than the rate specified had to place non-interest-bearing special deposits with the Bank of England to an extent related to their excess interest-bearing eligible liabilities. Moreover, the rate of call for special deposits was progressive, to a point at which it quickly became virtually prohibitive. Latterly, however, if a bank which had incurred a penalty came back within its limits, the non-interest-bearing special deposits were repaid. When it was not required, the scheme was suspended (e.g., in March 1975); it could equally quickly be reinstated (as in November 1976). It was not greatly liked by the banks and was finally phased out in June 1980.

Temporarily, a somewhat similar scheme was introduced in the United States on 25 October 1979, when the Federal Reserve Board announced the establishment of a 'marginal reserve requirement' (initially of 8 per cent) on increases in 'managed liabilities' in excess of a base amount. These were liabilities that had been actively used to finance a rapid expansion in bank credit. This requirement was applied to all increases in managed liabilities of member banks, Edge Act corporations, and US agencies and branches of foreign banks. To the extent that these institutions increased the aggregate level of their managed liabilities above a base amount of either $100 million or the average amount of managed liabilities held by such institutions as of the two statement weeks ending 26 September, 1979 (whichever was the larger), the relevant institutions would be required to put up an additional 8 per cent reserve against their deposits. Subsequently, the base was varied, but much the same principles applied. Managed liabilities included large time deposits ($100,000 and over) with maturities of less than a year, Euro-dollar borrowings, re-purchase agreements against US government and federal agency securities (except those entered into with similar institutions), and federal funds borrowings from a non-member institution. The marginal reserves were to be additional to any other reserve requirements already in place for member banks and Edge Act corporations. (Large time deposits of $100,000 or more (also obligations of affiliates, and ineligible acceptances) were already subject to a supplementary reserve requirement of 2 per cent put in place on 2 November 1978, plus a basic reserve ranging from 1 per cent to 6 per cent depending on maturity. This lasted until 24 July 1980.) It should be mentioned, too, that these marginal reserve reqirements that were introduced in the United States were part of a package, which also included an increase in the Fed's discount rate and a change in the method used to conduct monetary policy placing greater emphasis in day-to-day operations on the supply of bank reserves and less emphasis on confining short-term fluctuations in the federal funds rate. The marginal reserve requirement was increased to 10 per cent from 3 April 1980, was decreased to 5 per cent from 12 June 1980, and was reduced to zero from 24 July 1980.[15]

Qualitative Credit Controls

In addition to regulating the quantity of credit, central banks have sometimes attempted to influence the directions in which the commercial banks lend. And in the field of qualitative control of credit likewise, there has been much emulation of experience elsewhere, though there are important differences of degree. Thus, a loose system of control prevailed in the United Kingdom during World War II and afterwards, based initially on directives from the Capital Issues Committee and later on requests from the Bank of England. Meanwhile, a highly formalized technique was employed in Australia during the war and earlier post-war years; detailed and specific instructions were given to the trading banks, marginal cases being referred to the central bank (as a result of which there developed a kind of 'case law'). The system of Voluntary Credit Restraint in the United States in 1951 was similar. As a matter of interest, the more formal controls seemed to have been no more effective than the looser system employed in the

United Kingdom and, in more recent years, most countries have come to depend much more on qualitative guidance and the more formal type of control has been abandoned. Moreover, at no time can qualitative controls assume the whole burden of suppressing inflation[16] and nowadays qualitative controls are regarded merely as a supplementary measure, which may be included in the 'policy package' as announced from time to time by the authorities. In some instances, too (e.g., housing in Sweden),[17] qualitative agreements may be entered into as an instrument of social policy.

Somewhat similar are the 'selective credit controls' imposed, for example, on hire-purchase finance (instalment credit) as in the United States (up to 1952) and elsewhere (e.g., by stipulating the percentage of deposit required and the length of the term over which repayments may be spread). Even when these are not varied in order to serve as a control over credit, there is a case for insisting on such requirements for prudential reasons. Again, the USA, under the Securities Exchange Act 1934, the Fed can fix 'margins' and vary the percentage of the price of a security that the buyer himself will be called upon to find in ready cash, thereby limiting the extent to which he could borrow for this purpose. Credit extended against real estate was likewise controlled for a period in the early 1950s.

Regulation of Interest Rates

Another form of direct control that has been employed from time to time relates to the regulation of interest rates – ceilings on deposit rates, as under Regulation Q in the United States, or in France.[18] Other countries that have regulated interest rates – either by direct control or by agreement – include Australia (on both deposits and advances),[19] New Zealand,[20] Norway (where over a number of years a low-interest-rate policy was favoured)[21] and Japan (where rates were subject to 'guidance' until the mid-1970s).[22] In other countries (e.g., formerly in the UK), there was a degree of self-regulation by means of 'cartels', though most – if not all – of these have now been abolished. Likewise, in all the countries referred to (with latterly some temporary retreat in New Zealand),[23] interest rates have over recent years been liberalised and this has been consistent with a general reliance very much more on persuasion and less on authority; in short, there has been a much greater emphasis on guidance than on direct controls.[24]

In conclusion, what are likely to be the most effective means of credit control? There is no simple answer, but there is a clear case for selecting whatever combination of measures seems within a particular institutional environment to be most appropriate at the time, to exclude none that even in a small way is likely to help towards the final objective, and to act promptly. This is the technique of the 'package deal' with a variable content. Within this framework, the emphasis might well be on quantitative credit controls (including open-market operations and the application of penalty rates to excessive borrowing from the central bank), which on the basis of experience seemed to be the most effective types of measures that can be adopted. At the same time, it is essential, if monetary policy is to have any chance of success, that an appropriate fiscal environment be provided. Indeed, one might go further. Monetary policy cannot be either formulated or considered in isolation; it is properly to be regarded as merely one aspect of a more general economic policy, operating as part of a coordinated whole.

Notes

1. See, for example, the 'Bills Only' Controversy of the early 1950s in the USA (J.S.G. Wilson, *Monetary Policy and the Development of Money Markets* (London, 1966), pp. 169-71 and 177).

2. See *Bank of England Quarterly Bulletin* (September 1981), p. 312.

3. See *Bank of England Quarterly Bulletin* (June 1982), p. 181.

4. *Bank of England Quarterly Bulletin* (September 1981), p. 333. For the relevant background and additional detail, see J.S.G. Wilson, 'London's Money Market Arrangements'.

5. Bank of England, *The Future Structure of the Gilt-Edged Market*. The Bank of England's dealing and supervisory relationships with certain participants (November 1984).

6. See Federal Reserve Bank of New York Circular No. 8899 (22 August 1980).

7. See *Financial Times*, 21 November 1984.

8. The *pensions* are done in *effets privés*, which have maturities up to 90 days and three signatures. The Bank of France will also offer a rate at which it will buy Treasury bills *(bons du Trésor) en pension* (say for seven days) and banks can sell eligible paper to the Bank of France on a tender basis (*adjudication*).

9. See Robert Raymond, 'The Formulation and Implementation of Monetary Policy in France' in Federal Reserve Bank of New York, *Central Bank Views on Monetary Targeting* (1983), pp. 108-9.

10. See Hermann-Josef Dudler, 'The Implementation of Monetary Objectives in Germany – Open Market Objectives and Credit Facilities' in ibid., p. 19.

11. Ibid., p. 20.

12. Later to accord with the monetary target, which was first adopted in 1977.

13. In recent years, the most important of these was to authorise a distribution of credit outside the ceilings, provided there was a simultaneous growth in

the 'permanent' resources (bonds and capital) of the bank concerned.

14. Reiichi Shimamoto, 'Monetary Control in Japan' in *Monetary Targeting*, p. 83.

15. See Board of Governors of Federal Reserve System, *Annual Statistical Digest 1981*, pp. 218-19.

16. As the French at one time thought; see J.S.G. Wilson, *French Banking Structure*, pp. 378 ff.

17. See *Sveriges Riksbank Quarterly Review* 1 (1984), p. 50. The reverse can also be true, with banks being asked 'to be strict with credit for housing'. See *Bank of Finland Monthly Bulletin* (August 1982), p. 26.

18. See J.S.G. Wilson, *French Banking Structure and Credit Policy* (London 1957), pp. 66-7. There are still some restrictions. Before September 1981, the return on term deposits was free of regulation for amounts in excess of FFr 100,000 fixed for more than one month. The amount was than raised to FFr 500,000, but the moneys had to be fixed for more than six months. Deposits fixed for over 12 months were free of regulation whatever the amount.

19. See R.F. Holder, 'Australia' in W.F. Crick (ed.), *Commonwealth Banking Systems* (1965), pp. 75, and 88-9.

20. R.S. Deane, P.W.E. Nicholl and R.G. Smith (eds.), *Monetary Policy and the New Zealand Financial System*, 2nd edn (1983), *passim*.

21. See R.S. Sayers in *Banking in Western Europe* (Oxford, 1962), pp. 312-13.

22. For a summary of more recent developments, see Shimamoto, 'Monetary Control in Japan', pp. 82-3.

23. The Interest on Deposit Regulations have now been removed. See *Reserve Bank of New Zealand Bulletin*, October 1984, p. 467.

24. See J.S.G. Wilson, 'Fashions in Central Banking', *South African Journal of Economics* (September 1979).

12 CONCLUSION

It is appropriate now to draw our discussion together and to establish what kinds of conclusions emerge. Broadly speaking, one can say that over the years – because of much emulation of practice elsewhere – there are now fewer differences than formerly existed in the operations and techniques both of commercial banks (and similar institutions) and of central-banking (and related) institutions. In addition, if one looks back over a period of (say) fifty years, there have undoubtedly been fashions in central banking, such that the policies followed and the techniques employed have over different periods been rather similar, largely due to the increasingly free interchange of information and ideas between central bankers. In the commercial-banking field, on the other hand, competition has tended to be the driving force, with one bank imitating the packages offered by other banks – even when one bank has a new idea and innovates a new type of service or package, it does not remain a new idea for very long. And yet what one bank offers can frequently still be different from what is offered elsewhere, since not everybody will be as receptive as the others when an innovation is first introduced, often by a new entrant. Even when subject to the drive of competition, many bankers can remain somewhat cautious and conservative.

Together with the emergence of an increasing degree of similarity in commercial-banking operations, there has also been much technical development over the years. We may not yet have attained the cashless society that was first adumbrated quite some time ago, but as a result of the switch to new technologies particularly in the electronics and information fields, many new techniques have been introduced which have provided much more convenient servicing of bank customers, increased speed and efficiency in transmitting monetary items, as well as an increasing range of ancillary packages. The systems do not, however, always work perfectly and computer and electronic breakdowns are not uncommon. One suspects, too, that computer breakdown is not infrequently an excuse for the development of faults elsewhere in the system. Even more worrying is the rapid growth in cheque-card and credit-card fraud, the criminal abuse of computer technology, and the like. The Brave New World has not achieved its successes without a measure of social and financial cost.

In pressing ahead with these new technologies – sometimes before all the bugs had been eliminated from the systems employed – competition was undoubtedly the driving force. Yet not only has there been an increase in the degree of competitiveness between institutions in the same financial sector (e.g., commercial banks), there has also been a considerable extension of competition as between different financial sectors. Thus, commercial banks and savings banks have been invading each other's fields of activity over a period of many years. Increasingly, too, savings and loan associations (in the United States) and building societies (in Britain) have offered an extended number of services in competition with the commercial banks. In the process – and in a number of countries – banks and similar institutions have become 'universal banks' or, alternatively, have formed themselves into financial services groups, often with a large commercial bank as the leader, but comprehending as well merchant banking, leasing, factoring, computer services, even latterly (in the United Kingdom) links with stock exchange firms and discount houses. Indeed, at the time of writing, frontiers between financial sectors are shifting with disconcerting rapidity and there have been some financial experts who fear the process may be in danger of going too far, or certainly of moving too fast.

Moreover, with the internationalisation of banking and of financial services, not only have foreign banks moved into a number of countries (where permitted) in direct competition with domestic banks (though sometimes in a relatively restricted or specialised field), but they have also begun to build up similar groups in competition with domestic groups. Competition is again the driving force, but it would not have been possible without increasingly efficient international communications of all kinds. In a widening range of countries, too, the authorities have been willing to accept these developments – partly in the interest of encouraging greater competition with domestic banks (some of which could only benefit from an invasion of new ideas and a more aggressive approach), but partly also from a need to develop a greater degree of reciprocity as between different countries. And, on balance, the internationalisation of banking and financial services has provided both advantages and often (but not always) greater profits.

In the search for increased profitability, there can be no doubt that the more sophisticated techniques of assets and liabilities management, which are rapidly spreading to an increasing range of countries, have had a major impact. In order that institutions enjoy the full benefits, access to internationally important money and capital markets (including latterly markets in financial futures) is essential, but there is much that can be achieved even within the framework of a less highly developed money-market complex. Indeed, the trend is increasingly towards greater interest in the active management both of liabilities and of assets – sometimes with more emphasis on one side rather than the other (depending on current circumstances), such that greater profits are sought by obtaining access to new and expanding sources of liabilities (at appropriate prices) for advantageous investment, whether in loans and/or securities, including money-market assets; assets (like loans and mortgages) may also be sold to other holders. One can expect these trends to continue, though they have at times given occasion for concern, when banks and other financial institutions have sought too aggressively to push their profits to higher levels.

That is why there is a need for monetary authorities – like the central banks – to promote discipline (and especially self-discipline) in the expansion of business and the pursuit of profit. Moreover, some of the changes outlined above have obvious implications for the role that the authorities must fill. Thus, competition both within and between different financial sectors, including foreign institutions, needs to be monitored continuously. Even so, financial crises have a habit of recurring and there needs to be in addition the support of depositor protection or deposit insurance. Both the increasing degree of competition – favoured by a greater addiction to market-oriented policies – and the shifting frontiers between financial markets have posed some awkward problems for the monetary authorities.

Thus, the rapid growth of new financial sectors – thrift institutions (savings banks, savings and loan associations, and building societies), as well as hire-purchase or instalment-credit companies, unit trusts and mutual funds, and credit unions – has caused concern. What does one do about it? The authorities have not always been very sure. For example, in the United States, statutory power to impose controls over consumer credit were only made available on a temporary basis; after resort to these controls during the inflation arising out of the Korean War, the power to impose them was not renewed and, after a lengthy enquiry into Consumer Instalment Credit, following a direction by President Eisenhower in February 1956, the Federal Reserve Board of Govenors showed no desire to reintroduce it, largely because of the administrative difficulties. This is not what deterred the Radcliffe Commitee in the United Kingdom reporting in 1959. What seems to have inhibited them was the feeling that the further growth of new financial institutions would soon render any register out of date and any attempt at control ineffective. It is true that one control tends to breed more control, but surely it is better to regulate – by prudential means – the growth of new institutions rather than to wait until the situation looks like getting out of hand. This is a problem that has only increased over the years and, in some quarters, it is now being maintained that deregulation, which has had such popularity in the United States (in the interest of encouraging competition and thereby – it is hoped – greater efficiency) has already gone too far. Certainly, there is need of monitoring growth and, ideally, of encouraging self-discipline, fostered – where it will work – by self-regulation. None the less, there is a strong case for also maintaining a framework of statutory powers, even though these may remain only in the background.

One of the problems to which both the growth of new types of institutions and the innovations that they introduced gave rise was their effects on the measurement of the monetary aggregates used as a basis of policy. The several types of new accounts (in the United States, NOW and Super-NOW accounts, money market mutual funds, etc.) in effect produced new kinds of 'money'. In these circumstances, serious concern has been expressed as to the continued reliability of monetary aggregates as economic indicators, and their usefulness for monetary policy. Would some money-supply indicators now become subject to large and unpredictable changes that would largely vitiate their usefulness in attempting to frame policy?

On the basis of long years of study, in matters of credit policy, the author has already come down on the side of quantitative credit controls. In his view – and experience largely confirms it – these are likely to be the most effective of those available in the central-bank armoury in restraining inflationary pressures (if not in stimulating demand when recession supervenes). Within this category, direct credit controls may still need to be employed where markets through which to operate are largely absent; such controls may also be used – as they still often are – in a supplementary fashion. But where developed money and capital markets already exist, there is a strong case for employing open-market operations and a discount (or related) policy in order to influence the level of interest rates. This is consistent with the recent emphasis in a number of countries on market determination of the allocation of resources, both financial and other. Also, in addition to 'freeing' interest rates, there has been a retreat from 'captive markets' (e.g., in government securities, where institutions were required to take up and hold a certain quantum of new issues). But it must always be remembered that – even when they operate through markets – the actions of central banks (e.g., in terms both of the volumes in which they operate and of their pricing) are by their very nature arbitrary. Nevertheless, the responses of the institutions the behaviour of which they seek to regulate or influence will be determined through the agency of a market; they therefore retain freedom of action and of decision. That is the difference.

Finally, there has been an increasing emphasis over the years in central bank policy on 'guidance' and 'leadership' and a greater degree of liberalisation. Both the United States and the United Kingdom had by 1951 broken free from the rigidities of the war years. Deregulation in the United States proceeded apace after the passing of the Depository Institutions Deregulation and Monetary Control Act of 1980, though latterly there have been some signs of re-regulation (e.g., in the matter of banks' building up more adequate capital ratios). In the United Kingdom freedom was short-lived and from about 1955 until 1969 the operations of the banking system were constrained very largely by the imposition of credit ceilings, with more complete freedom (at least until the advent of the 'corset') after the introduction of Competition and Credit Control in September 1971. Although subject to detailed prudential supervision, banking has long been deregulated in West Germany – even a foreign bank or broker can secure ready entry. Indeed, a high degree of competition has been encouraged since the late 1950s. Liberalisation, or the 'freeing' of interest rates, dates from 1967. Evidence of this greater liberalisation also began to appear in France, where during the late 1960s and following a period of considerable *dirigisme*, there was an increasing emphasis on resort to open-market operations and much greater freedom for interest rates. Countries where there was considerable scope for the deregulation of interest rates were Australia and New Zealand. In Australia, the special account procedures were finally abandoned in 1960 and, even in the 1950s, some progress had already been made in securing acceptance for a conventional liquidity-type ratio to deposits (later to become established as the LGS ratio). This is now being replaced by a Prime Assets Ratio. In addition, and despite initially narrow markets, the central bank gradually became more active in terms of open-market operations, with obvious implications for interest rates, which were progressively freed. More generally, the authorities came to rely as much as possible on persuasion and as little as possible on authority, with a much greater emphasis on guidance rather than on direct controls. Again, in New Zealand after March 1976 (though with some subsequent interruption), there was a move away from a system of direct controls over interest rates and towards greater reliance on market forces. In the case of Canada, the few interest-rate controls that had existed had been removed much earlier (in the late 1960s). The main developments in Canada were (i) the introduction and spread of new types of instruments (e.g., following the lead of the near-banks and smaller chartered banks, daily interest savings accounts, which offered the small saver the opportunity to earn near-market rates of interest on liquid assets available for only short periods of time); this was followed by daily interest chequing accounts and the gradual spread of an 'all-in-one' account during 1981-2; on the corporate side, cash-management packages were offered first to very large companies and large governmental organisations and then to intermediate-sized companies; and (ii) as elsewhere, the tendency for the various financial sectors to invade each other's traditional territories. In South Africa, too, the expectation was that the de Kock Commission on the Monetary System and Monetary Policy would likewise report in terms of encouraging the development of more liberal attitudes by the monetary authorities there. In Japan, as well, similar moves were afoot. Certificates of deposit were introduced as a new money-market instrument and interest rates were gradually liberalised. Banks and related financial institutions again began to invade each other's territories and once more frontiers were shifting. Exchange control was removed and there was now much external investment (e.g., in US securities). In short, in these several areas of experience, banking and financial systems seemed to be on the march and were largely keeping in step.

POSTSCRIPT – AUSTRALIA

Since the writing of the main text was completed, the LGS ratio (see p. 268) has been phased out and a new Prime Assets Ratio introduced. As part of the prudential management of trading bank liquidity, all trading banks subject to the Banking Act 1959 have agreed with the Reserve Bank of Australia that they will hold at all times a tranche of high quality 'liquifiable assets'. These assets were described as 'prime assets' and comprise notes and coin, balances with the Reserve Bank, Treasury notes and other Commonwealth Government securities, and loans to authorised money market dealers secured against Commonwealth Government securities. The minimum Prime Assets Ratio (PAR) was set at 12 per cent of each trading bank's total liabilities in Australian currency (other than shareholders' funds) within Australia. Funds held in Statutory Reserve Deposits (SRDs) up to the equivalent of 3 per cent of a trading bank's deposits are counted as prime assets for the purpose of meeting this obligation. The agreement on the Prime Assets Ratio replaced the LGS convention between the Reserve Bank and the major trading banks, which had operated for a number of years. If, under the new arrangements, a bank were in danger of breaching the PAR requirement, it would now be required to correct the situation promptly under the supervision of the Reserve Bank. At the same time, the Reserve Bank aims to ensure that there are sufficient funds available in the market to meet the banking system's need for liquid assets and, given the development of Australian financial markets, individual banks should normally be able to handle their liquidity requirements without recourse to the Reserve Bank. Any assistance that was in fact provided by the Reserve Bank would be at its discretion.

The new 12 per cent minimum PAR requirement meant that, initially at least, most banks would need to hold a slightly smaller amount of liquid assets and government securities than they previously needed to hold under the LGS convention. The new PAR requirement is therefore being phased in gradually, adjustments in banks' assets to conform to the PAR arrangements being made under Reserve Bank direction as conditions permit. As already indicated, part of the funds held in SRDs may be counted towards the Prime Assets Ratio, though they have not been transferred from the SRD account. Apart from that no changes have been made to the Statutory Reserve Deposit arrangements nor to the existing SRD ratios. New banks authorised in terms of the Federal Treasurer's statement of 27 February 1985 are to be subject to the same PAR and SRD requirements as existing trading banks. (See Reserve Bank of Australia Press Note, 8 May 1985.)

July 1985

INDEX

Aarhus 217
Abrams, Richard K. 131n.
'Accelerator Clause' 287
Acceptances 222
Accepting Houses 19, 401
Accepting Houses Committee 383
'Accord' (US Treasury/Federal Reserve 1951) 410
Act on the Supervision of The Credit System 182+n.
Adjudication (Tender) 422n.
Adjustment Credit (USA) 406, 407
Advances 222, 278ff.
African Banking Corporation Ltd 49
'Agencies' (USA) 368, 373
Agreement Corporations 105, 106, 406
Agricultural Credit Corporation (Ireland) 56
Agricultural Mortgage Corporation (UK) 279, 333
Åland, Bank of 215
Åland Islands 215
Alberta 43
Algemene Bank Nederland 180
Allen, A.M. 202n.
Allen, G.C. 205n.
Allgemeine Finanz- und Waren Treuhand AG 168, 203n.
Allied Irish Banks Ltd 54
Allied Irish Investment Bank Ltd 55
'All-in pricing' 287
'All or nothing' Principle 318-19
'All Purpose Banks' (Austria) 161, 163, 165
Alsace-Lorraine 15, 139, 160
Almanij 203n.
Amalgamations (of Banks)
  Australia 24-5
  Austria 167, 170
  Canada 43, 46
  England 16-17, 18, 281, 374
  Germany 154
  Ireland 54
  Japan 196, 343
  Norway 206, 208, 209-10, 211
  Scotland 13, 17-18
  South Africa 49
  Treasury Committee on 16
  USA 66, 374
American Banks
  in Austria 163
  in Belgium 175
  in Ireland 55-6
  in London 20
American Express 122
American General 123
Amsterdam-Rotterdam Bank 180
Amsterdamsche Bank 180
Andelsbanken 217
Anglo-Egyptian Bank Ltd 61n.
ANZ Banking Group (New Zealand) Ltd 38+n.
Arbitrage Operations 178, 180, 380
Argentina 257-8, 321
Arkansas 72
Arndt, Dr E.H.D. 49+n., 50, 62n.
Arndt, H.W. 327n.
Artigiancassa 187
Ashton, T.S. 329n.
Asian Development Bank 35
Asian Dollar Market 250
Assets (of Banks) 260ff.
  Eligibility of 264, 265, 388
  Mobilisation of 264, 272
Assets and Liabilities Management 346ff., 425-6
  Definition 346
  and Funds Management 354, 357
  Marginal Adjustment 354-5, 356, 357-9
Associated Banks (Ireland) 54, 56+n.
Association of Austrian Banks and Bankers 161
Association of Raiffeisen Banks (Austria) 161
Association of Volksbanken 161
Associazione fra le Casse di Risparmio Italiane 186
Atlanta 403
Australia 2-3, 4, 11, 21ff., 65, 126, 223, 224, 225, 227, 229-30, 243-4, 251, 263, 267-8, 304-6, 350, 354, 355, 356, 357, 358, 365, 367, 379-80, 381, 383, 420, 421
  Federation 24, 65

Australia and New Zealand Bank 24, 25+n.
Australia and New Zealand Banking Group (PNG) Ltd 32, 33
Australia and New Zealand Banking Group Ltd 25, 32
Australian Bank of Commerce 24
Australian Bank Ltd 26
Australian Banks' Export Re-Finance Corporation 27
Australian Industry Development Corporation 27
Australian Resources Development Bank 26, 27, 306
Austria 161ff., 224, 243, 250, 313-14, 340, 355, 357, 358
Austrian Savings Bank Association 161
Automatic Transfer Services (ATS) 112, 122, 131n.
Automobile Paper 290, 317
Autres Effets 308
Aval 222, 312
Avances 308
Aziende di credito 185, 204n.

Bache 123
Baer, Julius 189
Bagehot, Walter 3, 95+n.
Bahamas 106
Balance of Payments 322
Ballarat Banking Company 59n.
Balogh, T. 327n.
Banca Commerciale Italiana 185
Banca Nazionale dell'Agricoltura 185
Banca Nazionale del Lavoro 185
Banche di Credito Ordinario 185
Banche d'interesse nazionale 185
Banche popolari cooperative 186
Banco di Napoli 185
Banco di Roma 185
Banco di S. Spirito 185
Bank Balance Sheet 222, 347
Bank Card 305, 306
Banker-Customer Relationship 260, 320
Bankers' Acceptances 234, 245, 287-8, 368, 372, 373, 379, 401-2
Bankers Trust 234
Bank Failures 387
  Australia 29
  Canada 46
  Germany 153, 154, 155
  Japan 196, 343
Bank für Arbeit und Wirtscheft 162
Bank Holding Companies
  USA 73, 74ff., 78-9
Bank Holding Company Act (USA)
  1956 – 67, 68, 75, 78-9, 128n.
  1970 – 75-6, 78-9, 110, 123, 128n., 132n.
Banking (Bank) Acts
  Australia 1945 – 413; 1959 – 26
  Austria 1979 – 161, 162, 165
  Belgium 1935 – 171
  Canada 1871 – 42; 1900 – 46; 1913 – 46; 1980 – 243
  Finland 216-17
  Germany 1976 (1985) – 203n.
  Italy 1936 – 184, 204n.
  Japan 199, 200
  South Africa – Banks Act 1917 – 49
  Switzerland 190
  UK 1979 – 256
  USA 1933 – 78; 1935 – 410
Banking Bureau (Ministry of Finance – Japan) 201-2
Banking by Mail (USA) 72
Banking Commission, Belgium 171, 179, 341, 342
Banking Control Commission (France) 231, 347, 395
Banking – Defined 221
Banking Habit 251
Banking Ordinance
  Switzerland 190
Banking Reforms (Belgium 1934-5) 171, 341
Bank Inspection Board (Sweden) 213+n.
Bank Inspectorate
  Denmark 218
  Finland 217
  Norway 207
Bank Merger Act (USA) 67, 68
  1960 – 67, 68, 84
  1966 – 67, 68, 88ff.
Bank Nationalisation 202n., 224
  Austria 163
  France 135, 138, 140, 141
  India 142, 143, 144, 148, 149, 150
Bank Notes
  Canada 41+n.
  Scotland 13+n., 262

Bank of Adelaide 25
Bank of America 68, 126n., 224
Bank of Australasia 21, 23, 24, 25
Bank of British Columbia 43
Bank of Canada, Montreal 42
Bank of China 59n.
Bank of England 256-7, 279, 298, 300, 301, 318, 372, 373+n., 377, 382, 384n., 385, 388-9, 395, 396, 401, 402, 410-11, 417, 419, 420
Bank of Finland 215, 216, 217, 317, 332n., 415
Bank of Ghana 268
Bank of Ghana Ordinance 1957 328n.
Bank of Helsinki 214
Bank of Italy 225
Bank of Ireland 54
Bank of Japan 194, 197, 202, 418-19
Bank of Korea 205n.
Bank of Lebanon 255
Bank Leu 188
Bank Mees & Hope 181
Bank of Montreal 41-2, 46
Bank Negara Malaysia 268
Bank of New Brunswick 60n.
Bank of New South Wales 21, 23, 24, 25
Bank of New York 60n.
Bank of New Zealand, 25, 38
Bank of North America 126n.
Bank of Norway 207-8, 250, 376
Bank of Nova Scotia 46
Bank of Papua New Guinea 31, 33, 34
Bank of Queensland Ltd 25
Bank of Scotland 12-13, 17
Bank of South Australia 21
Bank of South Pacific Ltd 31, 33
Bank of Stockholm 9
Bank of Sweden (Riksbank) 9, 213
Bank of Taiwan 195
Bank of Tokyo 199, 201
Bank of Upper Canada 41, 42
Bank of Victoria 25
Bank Rate 2, 299, 398, 401
Banks of 'National Interest' (Italy) 185, 187, 188
Bank Stock Corporation (Milwaukee) 86
Bank Trade Unions (India) 151
Bank van Leening (Lombard Bank) 48
Bank voor Nederlandsche Gemeenten (Bank for Netherlands Municipalities) 181
Banque Belge pour l'Étranger 177
Banque Canadienne Nationale 44
Banque(s) d'Affaires (France) 135, 138, 139, 152, 224+n., 245, 334-6, 336
Banque de Bruxelles 176+n., 204n.
Banque de Bruzelles Lambert 177
Banque(s) de Crédit à Long et Moyen Terme (France) 135
Banque de France (Bank of France) 136, 267, 372, 394, 407, 414-15
Banque de l'Indochine 139
Banque de l'Indochine et de Suez (Banque Indosuez) 32, 139
Banque de l'Union Européenne 140
Banque Lambert 204n.
Banque Nationale de Paris 25, 138, 139
Banque de Paris et des Pays-Bas (Paribas) 138, 181
Banque Parisienne de Crédit 140
Banque Provinciale du Canada 44
Banque Vernes 140
Banque Worms 140
Banques Inscrites 230, 231, 309
Banques Populaires 136, 231, 309
Barclays Bank 16, 17, 18-19, 298
Barclays Bank DCO 48+n.
Barclays Bank (Dominion, Colonial & Overseas) 49
Barclays Bank International Ltd 18-19
Barclays (Canada) Ltd 43
Barclays National Bank Ltd 48, 49
Baring Crisis 261
Base Rate(s) 2, 299, 398, 401
Bavaria 160
Bayerische Hypotheken- und Wechsel-Bank 157
Bayerische Landesbank 157
Bayerische Vereinsbank 157
Bearer Discount Notes (Canada) 242, 354
Beckhart, Benjamin Haggott 6n., 205n.
Belgium 170ff., 224, 225, 249, 250, 251, 311-12, 341-2, 355, 357, 358
Beneficial Corporation 123
Bengal 134
Bergen 207, 208
Bergen Bank 206, 208, 210, 211
Berlin 152, 153, 154
Berliner Grossbanken 152

Berliner Handelgesellschaft 160
Berne 188, 190
Bihar 145
BIKUBEN (Denmark) 218
Bill Brokers (England) 374, 378
Billet à ordre 309
Bill Market (England) 14, 15-16
Bill Market Schemes (India) 380
Bill of Exchange (also Bill Finance) 7, 9, 39, 222, 281, 282, 303, 305, 307-8, 309-10, 311, 314, 315, 316, 317, 354, 356, 358, 366, 376-7, 379
  Accommodation (Finance) 38, 307-8, 316
  Trade 38, 307-8
'Bills Only' Controversy (USA) 422n.
Bimetallism (in Japan) 194
Blainey, Geoffrey 58n., 59n., 324n.
Boerenbond (Belgium) 174
Bombay 144, 361, 367, 371, 380
Bonds, Issues of (also of Debentures)
  Austria 164
  Belgium 173
  Finland 215
  Germany 339
  Italy 186, 187
  Japan 199, 200, 344
  of National Government 344
  Sweden 212
  Switzerland 342-3
Bons de Caisse
  Belgium 179, 312
  France 230, 231
Bons et Comptes à Echéance fixe 230
Bons du Trésor 372, 422n.
Boston 61n., 403
'Bought' money 231, 233f., 352, 353
Bowsher, Norman N. 128n.
Branch Banking 3, 12ff.
  Australia 21ff., 383
  Austria 167, 169
  Belgium 170-1+n., 175
  Canada 40ff., 47-8
  Denmark 217-18
  England 281
  Finland 214-15
  France 139
  Germany 153, 155
  India 143-5, 148, 380
  Ireland 54ff.
  Italy 185-6
  Japan 199, 201
  New Zealand 38ff.
  Norway 207-8, 209-11
  Papua New Guinea 32-3
  South Africa 48ff., 50
  Sweden 213
  Switzerland 188, 189
  USA 66, 69ff., 82-3, 127n., 294, 375
Branches (Pioneer) 32
Brazil 321
Brennan, Mr Justice 87
'Bridging' Finance 306
British Columbia 43, 61n.
British Linen Bank 17
British North America Act 1867 42
Brittany 140
Brock, Bronwyn 131n.
Brown, Donald M. 129n.
Building and Loan Associations (Germany) 157+n.
Building Societies 349, 425, 426
  Australia 28
  Austria 161, 166, 167
  Ireland 57
  New Zealand 39
  South Africa 51-3, 62n.
  UK 20, 239+n., 257, 350, 351
Building Societies Protection Fund 257
Bundesbank 310, 407-8
Bürgschaftsfonds 164
Business Development Loans (UK) 298
Business Groups Act 1974
  Papua New Guinea 34
Butlin, S.J. 58n., 59n., 324
'Buy-Backs' 373

Caisse des Dépôts et Consignations (France) 136, 309
Caisse Générale d'Épargne et de Retraite 173-4
Caisse Nationale de Crédit Agricole (France) 135-6, 140, 141
Caisse Nationale de Crédit Professionel 174
Caisses de crédit mutuel
  Switzerland 189
Caisses d'Épargne
  France 231, 309
Caisses Populaires
  Canada 44
Calcutta 144, 149, 361, 367, 371,

380
'Calendar' (France) 335
California 40, 68, 69, 71, 101, 109, 126n., 292
Call Loan Market 371, 375
Call Money 264, 265, 272, 366
Call Money Market(s) *see* Call Loan Market
Campbell Committee Inquiry 59n.
Canada 4, 40ff., 126, 242-3, 271, 296, 354, 364-5, 416, 429
  Confederation 42, 43, 46, 47
Canadian Bank of Commerce 43, 46
Canadian Commercial Bank 43
Canadian Co-operative Credit Society 44
Canadian Imperial Bank of Commerce 43
Cantonal Banks (Switzerland) 188-9, 190, 191, 312-13
Cape Cod Banks 100
Cape of Good Hope Bank 48
Capital
  Gains 271, 369
  Losses 271, 272, 273, 276, 375, 400
Capital Adequacy 347
  Belgium 172
  France 141
  Japan 201
  Switzerland 190
  USA 223, 224, 338-9
Capital (Inc. Bank Capital) 82, 221, 222ff.
Capital Issues Committee (UK) 420
Capital Ratios 222-4, 352
  Belgium 172
  France 141, 337
  Japan 201
  Papua New Guinea 33
  USA 428
Capital, Shortage of Available 336, 343, 344
Captive Market(s) 272, 427
Carlsen, Morten 219n.
Cartells 153, 237, 348-9, 421
Carter, President 115
Cash 222, 260ff.
  Revolving Fund of 264, 362, 364, 371, 400-1
Cash Credit 281, 311n., 314
Cash Credit Bond 281
'Cashline Deposit Accounts' 229
Cash Ratio(s) 260-4, 375
  England 261-2
  Scotland 262
  USA 269-70
Cash Reserve(s) 260ff., 377,
  Economical Use of 367, 375, 377, 381-2
  Fixed (UK) 262, 377
Casse di Risparmio e Monti di Credito su Pegno di 1° Categoria 186
Casse rurali e artigiane e monti di Credito su Pegno di 2° Categoria 186
Caste (India) 146, 147
Ceilings (on Loans) *see* Credit Ceilings
Ceilings on Interest-bearing Deposits
  UK 419
  USA 419-20
Central African Federation 269
Central Bank Act
  Ireland 1942 54
Central Banking 358, 426
  and Banking Services 394-5
  and Commercial Banks 386-90, 393
  and Development 395
  and Exchange Rate 391-2
  and Government 395-6
  and Money Markets 381-3
  Consultation 389-90
  Examinations 387, 395
  External Policy 385-6, 390
  Fashions in 423n., 424
  Leadership 383, 389-90, 428
  Moral Leadership 383
  Nationalisation 397
  Principles of 385ff.
  Responsibilities 386ff.
  as Special Adviser 396
Central Bank of Argentina 376
Central Bank of Ceylon 376
Central Bank of Ireland 54, 55
Central Bank of Malaya 268
Central Bank of Malaya Ordinance 1958 328n.
Central Bank of Nigeria 268
Central Bank of Nigeria Ordinance 1958 328n.
Central Bank(s) 2, 6, 265, 367, 375
Centrale des Caisses Rurales 204n.
Central Reserve City Banks 328n.
Centre de Chèques Postaux 231
CENTRO Internationale

Handelsbank AG 203n.
Ceriani 204n.
Certificates of Deposit 348, 349, 354, 355, 368
Australia 243-4
Austria 248
France 359n.
Germany 248
Italy 326n.
Japan 232, 247, 429
New Zealand 244
Secondary Markets in 233-4, 237-8, 240, 242, 244, 245, 246, 247+n., 248, 355
Spain 245
Sterling 237ff., 349; forward market 349
Sweden 246-7
UK 20, 237-40
USA 113, 114, 233-5, 236, 373, 379
Chain Banking (USA) 127n.
Chandigarh 144
Change in Bank Control Act (USA) 68
Chartered Bank(s) – Canada 40ff. *passim*
Charterhouse Industrial Development Company 333
Charters 41-2, 43
Chase Manhattan Bank 216
Chase Manhattan Overseas Banking Corporation 180, 234
Cheap Money (UK) 277, 381, 398
Chef de file 335
Chemical Bank 224, 234
Cheque(s) 8, 259
Chèques Postaux 260
Chicago 99, 104, 127n., 236, 287, 288, 294, 361, 372, 403
Chile 415-16
Chit Funds (India) 143
Chlepner, B.S. 203n., 345n.
Chosen Bank 195+n.
Christiania Bank og Kreditkasse 206, 208, 211
Chrystal, K.A. 131n.
Citibank (also Citicorp) 68, 216, 224, 232, 303, 419
Citibank of New York 68
Citizen's Federal Savings and Loan Association 110-11
City Banks (Japan) 199, 200, 201
City of Glasgow Bank 14
Clark, Ramsey 93
Clayton Act (USA) 84, 86, 87, 90, 91-2, 93
Clearance of Cheques
USA 97-8
Clearing Bankers' Association 383
Cleveland 288, 403
Cline, W.R. 332n.
Clinton, New Jersey 129n.
'Closed' Economy 385
'Club Money' 266 +n., 411
Clydesdale and North of Scotland (Clydesdale Bank) 17
Clydesdale Bank 17
Coastal Express (Norway) 207
Coéfficient de trésorerie 410
'Collateral Note', 287
Collection of Proceeds
USA 97-8
Cologne 160
Colonial Bank 61n.
Colonial Bank Act 1925 61n.
Colorado 68-70
Co-maker 291
Comecon 321
Comité de la Réglementation Bancaire (France) 136
Comité des Établissements de Crédit (France) 136
Commercial Bank(s) 349, 425
Austria 161-3
Belgium 173, 174-5, 177
Denmark 217-18
Finland 214-15
France 135, 139-40
Germany 152ff.
India 142
Italy 184-6, 187
Japan 193ff., 198-201
Netherlands 180-1
Norway 206-7
Papua New Guinea 31-3
South Africa 48-50, 52
Sweden 211
Switzerland 188-9
USA 68-9, 124, 270, 373
Commercial Banking Company of Sydney 21, 23, 24-5
Commercial Bank of Australia 24, 25
Commercial Bank of Scotland 17

Commercial Bills 222, 272, 368
Australia 305
New Zealand 307
Spain 245-6+n.
UK 281, 401-2+n.
USA 287-8
Commercial Investment Trust Finance Corporation 100
Commercial Paper (USA) 100-1, 234, 366, 368, 373, 379
Canada 296
France 372
Commerzbank 155, 156, 157
Commission de Contrôle des Banques (commission bancaire)
France 136
Commission on Money and Credit Report 1961 115, 127n.
Commitment Fee 287, 295, 300, 305, 307, 312, 313, 314
Committee on Banking (Papua New Guinea) 30-1
Committee on Banking Structure (Norway) 209-11+n.
Committee on Finance and Industry (Macmillan Committee) 324n.
Committee of Inquiry into the Australian Financial System 331n.
Committee to Review the Functioning of Financial Institutions (Wilson Committee) 325n.
Committee on the Working of the Monetary System (Radcliffe Committee) 324n., 326n., 327n., 329n., 330n.
Commonwealth Banking Corporation 25+n., 26
Commonwealth Bank of Australia 2, 395-6, 413
Commonwealth Development Bank 26
Commonwealth Savings Bank 26, 229
Commonwealth Trading Bank 25, 31, 32, 36, 224
Commonwealth Development Finance Company (UK) 279
Communications 12-13, 15, 66, 114, 208, 370, 425
Community Reinvestment Act (USA) 79
Compagnie Financière de Suez 139, 140
Compagnie Générale d'Électricité 141
Compagnies Financières (France) 136
Companies Act 1976 (Papua New Guinea) 34
'Compensating Balances' (also Compensatory Deposits)
Japan 232
USA 287, 325n., 348
Competition 4, 19, 424, 425, 426
Australia 22
Belgium 176
Germany 153, 159
South Africa 49-50
UK 20, 319+n., 349
USA 80, 85, 89, 93-4, 114, 127n., 293-4
Competition and Credit Control (UK) 238, 241, 265-6, 296, 298, 299, 327n., 349, 411, 417, 428
Compte-titres 334
Comptes à Échéance 230
Comptes à Terme 230
Comptes à Vue 230
Comptes Courants 230
Comptes de Chèques 230
Comptes Débiteurs 308
Comptes d'Épargne à Régime Spécial 230
Comptes Spéciaux 230
Comptoir National d'Escompte de Paris 26
Comptres Ordinaires 230
Comptroller of the Currency, Federal (USA) 67, 86, 87, 88, 95, 130n., 224
Computerisation 424, 425
USA 114
Concentration (of Banking Business) 5, 12, 77
Australia 25-6
Austria 167, 168, 170
Belgium 170, 176-7, 179
England 12ff.
France 139
Germany 3, 154, 156-7, 161
Italy 184-5, 187
Japan 196-7, 199, 200; Deconcentration 197-8; Reversed 198
Netherlands 180
Norway 209
Scotland 12

South Africa 49-50
Switzerland 188
USA 93-5, 130n
Conféderation Nationale du Crédit Mutuel 136
Confidence 9, 10, 251, 254, 263, 264, 277, 387, 388
Conflict of Interest 126
Conseil National du Crédit (National Credit Council)
France 136
Consortium Banks 219+n.
Consumer Credit Act 1972 (Netherlands) 183
Consumer Loans
Australia 305
Belgium 177, 178, 179
Finland 215
Italy 186
Netherlands 183
Sweden 212, 315
UK 285
USA 289-91
Continental Illinois 92, 321, 407
Continental Illinois Bank (Conill) 234
'Conventional' Mortgages 289
Coöperatieve Centrale Boerenleenbank 181
Coöperatieve Centrale Raiffeisen Bank 181
Coöperatieve Centrale Raiffeisen Boerenleenbank 181
Cooperative Banks
Austria 161, 165-6
Belgium 174
Denmark 218
Finland 214, 215, 258
Germany 156, 157, 160
India 142-3, 148
Italy 186
Japan 200
Netherlands 180-1+n.
Sweden 211, 212
Switzerland 189, 191
Cooperatives Act 1965
Papua New Guinea 34
Copenhagen 217
Cordell, David M. 128n.
Corporate Cash Management Services (USA) 112
Corporation Tax Act (Ireland) 55
Corporation Treasurers
USA 233
Correspondent Balances 103, 227
Correspondent Banking 3, 15
Fees 103-4
Germany 152-3
Japan 201
Minimum Balance 103, 104
Norway 209
Purchase and Sale of Banks 102+n.
USA 67, 95ff., 130n., 131n., 318, 372, 374, 375, 381
'Corset' (UK) (Supplementary Deposit Scheme) 419, 428
Country Banks (USA) 104, 269
Buying and Selling 102
'Country Risk' 321-2, 323
Coutts 18
Créances Commerciales 308, 309
Credit 9, 10
Creation 9, 10, 349, 385
Distribution 420-1
Regulation of 398ff.
Crédit Agricole (France) 136, 231, 308
Credit Analysis (and Information) 101-2, 283, 292-3, 312, 313, 320
Creditanstalt-Banverein 162, 163, 170, 340
Credit Cards 212, 296n., 305, 306, 424; *see also* Bank Card
Fraud 424
Credit Ceilings 415-19
Canada 416
Chile 415-16
France 417-18
Japan 418-19
Netherlands 416
United Kingdom 416-17, 428
Crédit Commercial de France 139, 140
Crédit Communal de Belgique 174
Credit Control, Techniques of 398ff.
'Classical' 398-408, 427
Direct 376, 381, 399, 408-20, 427
Package Deal 415-16, 420, 421, 422
Crédit Cooperatif 136
Crédit du Nord 139
Credit-Export (Belgium) 174
Crédit Foncier
France 136

crédit fonciers 189
Crédit Général SA de Banque 176
Credit Guarantee Loan Scheme (Papua New Guinea) 37
Credit Industrial and Commercial 137, 139, 140
Credit Information
 Switzerland 332n.
 UK 320
 USA 101-2, 292-3
 see also Service Central des Risques
Credito Italiano 185
Crédit Lyonnais 138, 139, 181
Crédit Mutuel 136, 231, 309
Crédit National (France) 136, 141, 308, 309
Crédit Suisse 188
Credit Union Centrals (USA) 406-7
Credit Unions 349, 426
 Australia 28
 Canada 44
 Ireland 57
 New Zealand 40
 USA 235, 270, 406
Crick, W.F. 58n., 327n., 330n., 423n.
Crore 202n.
Currency Exchanges (Chicago) 72+n.
Currency Reform (Western Germany, 1948) 337
Current Account(s) 7, 349, 352
Current Account Lending
 Belgium 311+n.
 Sweden 315-16
 Switzerland 312
Curtin, Dr P.W.E. 30
'Customer Banks' (Belgium) 178, 180

Dacey, W. Manning 329n.
Dai-Ichii Bank 205n.
Dai-Ichi Kangyo Bank 199
Daimyo 192, 193
Daiwa Bank 199
Daiwa Securities 200
Dallas 99, 256, 403
Dalton, Hugh 329n.
Danmarks National Bank 218
Dark, L.J.H. 202n.
Darmstädter Bank 153
Davies, Glyn 327n.
D – Banks (Germany) 153
Deane, R.S. 326n., 327n., 423n.
Debentures 349
 Japan 199, 344, 345n.
Debt Service Ratio 322
Deeds, Loans Against (Japan) 303-4
De Kock, Dr M.H. 50, 429
De Kock Commission on the Monetary System and Monetary Policy (South Africa) 62n., 429
Delhi 144
Delinquency (and Loss) Ratios (USA) 290
Delors, Jacques (Minister of Finance) 139
Demand Deposits 252-3
Den Danske Bank 217
Den Danske Provinsbank 217
Denmark 217ff., 225, 250, 355, 358, 485
Den Norske Creditbank 206, 208, 210-11, 219+n.
Department of Industry (UK) 300
Department of Justice (USA)
 see Justice, Department of
Deposit Account 228, 229, 253-4
 Deposits at Notice 228, 232, 253, 299, 349
Deposit Banking 334, 336
 Austria 163
 Evolution of 7ff., 221, 222
 Germany 152
Deposit Banks
 France 135, 138, 139, 140
 Germany 152
Deposit Insurance 254ff., 426
 India 254-5
 Lebanon 255
 UK 256-7
 USA 254
Deposit Insurance and Credit Guarantee Corporation, formerly Deposit Insurance Corporation (India) 254
Deposit Insurance Institution (Lebanon) 255
Depositor Protection 254ff., 426
 Belgium 174
 France 267
 UK 256-7
 see also Deposit Insurance
Depository Institutions Deregulation and Monetary Control Act 1980 (also referred to as Monetary

Control Act) 115ff., 270, 326n., 406, 428
Deposits (Inc. Bank Deposits) 226ff.
Foreign 227-8
Inertia of 227ff., 251-4
Deposits, Index-Tied (Finland) 257-9
Deposits, Large *see* Large Deposits
Deposits, Nationalisation of (Argentina) 257
Deposits, Run on 228
Deposits on 'Special Conditions' 246-7+n.
Deposits, Structure of 227ff., 350-1
Deposit-takers, licensed (UK) 256
Deregulation 427, 428-9
Australia 126, 428
Canada 126, 429
France 126, 428
Italy 126
Japan 126, 429
New Zealand 428
South Africa 429
Spain 126
Sweden 126
West Germany 126, 428
UK 126
USA 109ff., 379
Deutsche Bank 153, 155, 156, 157
Deutsche Genossenschaftsbank 157, 159
Development Finance Corporation (New Zealand) 40
Dickie, Paul M. 60n.
Direct Wire Facilities 103
Dirigisme (France) 428
Discontogesellschaft 153
Discount(s) 278-9
Australia 305
of Bills 281
Japan 303, 310
New Zealand 307
Norway 315
Papua New Guinea 33
Portugal 309
South Africa 51
Spain 309
West Germany 309-10
Discount Corporation of New York 234
Discount Houses 15-16, 238, 240, 264, 265, 355, 366, 371, 372, 377, 378-9, 389, 400-1, 425
Discount Market *see* Discount Houses
Discount Policy 354, 399-408 *passim*, 427
Discount Quotas 409, 413-15
France 414-15
West Germany 415
Discount Rate 398, 406
Discount Window (of Federal Reserve Banks – USA) 118, 353, 389, 405-7
'Discriminant Analysis' 322
District Bank 18
District of Columbia 69, 77
Diwok, Fritz 203n.
Documentary Credits 316
Dollar Exchange Bills 288
Donnithorne, Audrey G. 205n.
Dresdner Bank 153, 155, 156, 157
Drummond & Company 17
'Dual' Banking (USA) 67
Dudler, Herman-Josef 422n.
'Dumb-Bell' Maturity Distribution (of securities) 275, 276
Dunham, Constance 131n., 132n.
Dusseldorf 156, 159, 160

Economic Fluctuations 392-4
Edge, Senator Walter 104
Edge Act Corporations 104-5, 108, 270, 406, 419, 420
Effets Privés 422n.
Egypt 11
Ehrlich, E.E. 205n.
Eisenhower, President 426
Eligibility (of Securities at Central Bank) 277, 388
Empain-Schneider Group 140
Encadrement du Crédit
Belgium 418
France 417-18
England 13-14, 16-17, 18-19, 228, 237-41, 265-6
English, Scottish and Australian Bank 24
En pension 249, 326n., 355, 358, 372, 373, 407, 422n.
Environment
Influence of 1-2, 3
Equities 271, 278

Equity Capital for Industry 333
Erste Oesterreichische Spar-Casse
    162
Établissement(s) de Crédit (France)
    135, 140, 336
Euro-Currency Markets 107, 163,
    164, 175, 238, 240, 242, 249,
    250-1, 349, 353, 354, 356, 358,
    368, 373
    Borrowings 113, 251, 420
    Euro-Dollar 107, 234-5, 240,
        243, 249, 350, 353, 368,
        373
    Liabilities 270
European Investment Bank 57, 187
L'Européenne de Banque 140
Excess Reserves 270, 377
Exchange Banks 370
Exchange Control 390, 391, 429
Exchange Houses (Japan) 195+n.
Exchange Rate(s)
    and Central Bank 390-2
    Depreciation 390
    Floating 390
Exchequer Bills (Ireland) 354, 358
Exogenous Shocks 393
Export Credit(s)
    Austria 164
    France 334
    Netherlands 311
    UK 297, 300, 301
    West Germany 302
Export Credit Guarantee Department
    (ECGD) 300
Export-Financiering-Maatschappij
    181
Export-Import Bank of Japan 200

Facility Letter 299+n.
Factoring (Companies) 288, 425
    Austria 166, 203n.
    Finland 215
    Italy 186
    Norway 208
    Sweden 212
    Switzerland 190
    USA 288
Fællesbanken (Denmark) 218
Farm Development Loan Fund
    (Australia) 27, 305
Farm Development Loan Scheme
    (UK) 298
Faust, Jon 132n.
Federal Banking Commission
    (Switzerland) 190+n.
Federal Deposit Insurance
    Corporation and Act (USA) 68,
    84, 86, 88, 95, 108, 130n., 224,
    254
Federal Funds (USA) 98, 101,
    113, 235, 265, 270, 348, 353,
    366, 368, 373, 374, 375, 379,
    420
Federal Home Loan Bank Board
    (USA) 124-5
Federal Home Loan Banks (USA)
    406
Federal Housing Administration
    (USA) 289
Federal Open Market Committee
    403-5
    System Open Market Account
        404
Federal Reserve Act (USA) 104, 410
Federal Reserve System (USA) –
    Including Federal Reserve Board
    and Federal Reserve Banks 67-8,
    78-9, 84, 86, 88, 94, 108, 116ff.,
    124, 126n., 130n., 224, 235,
    269-70, 372-3, 374, 383, 387,
    389, 395, 403-7, 419-20, 421,
    426
*Fédération centrale du crédit mutuel
    agricole et rural* 136
*Fédération des Caisses Populaires
    Desjardins* (Canada) 44
Federation of Rhodesia and
    Nyasaland 269+n.
Fellesbanken (Norway) 206, 209
Feudal System (Japan) 192, 193
Fforde, J.S. 329n.
Finance Acts
    Ireland 1984 62n.
    UK 1983 20
Finance Committee of Storting
    (Norway) 210
Finance Companies 349, 426
    Australia 27
    Canada 45
    Finland 215
    Ireland 56, 57
    Italy 186
    Netherlands 183
    New Zealand 38
    Norway 207
    Papua New Guinea 35

Scotland 240, 279
South Africa 50
Sweden 212, 246
Switzerland 189-90, 191
UK 279
USA 291
Finance Corporation for Industry (UK) 279, 333
Finance Corporation of Australia 25
Finance Paper (USA) 130n., 234
Financial Crises 387, 426
Financial Futures Markets 236-7, 240, 426
Financial Innovation 109-15, 120-5, 424
Financial Services Groups 126, 425
Financieringsmaatschappijen (Finance Companies) 183
Finanzierungsgarantie-Gesellschaft mit beschränkter Haftung 164
'Fine-tuning' (West Germany) 407-8
Finland 214ff., 243, 257-9, 278, 340-1, 357, 358, 415
Finnish Export Credit 215
Finnish Workers' Savings Bank 215
First Bank of the United States 60n.
First City National Bank of Houston 130n.
First National City Bank of New York 43, 233
First Nationwide Financial Corporation 111
First Nationwide Savings 111
Fiscal Environment 394, 416, 422
Fischer, Gerald C. 88+n., 90-1, 128n., 129n.
Fiskernes Bank 206
Fixed Charge 330n.
Fixed Deposits 228, 229
'Flask' Distribution (Maturity of securities) 276
Floating Charge 284+n.
Floating Rate Notes (FRNs) 352
'Floor Planting' 290
Florida 105, 108, 109, 127n., 133n.
Foreign Banks 4, 19-20, 134, 225, 370-1, 372, 425
Australia 59n.
Austria 161, 163-4
Belgium 172, 175-6, 179
Canada – Subsidiaries 44-5
Denmark 218
Finland 214, 215-16
Germany 126, 159, 248, 428
India 144, 151
Ireland – Subsidiaries 56
Italy 185-6
Japan 199
Netherlands 181
Norway 207+n., 210+n., 211, 219n.
Spain 245
Sweden 212+n., 219n., 247
Switzerland 189, 190+n., 191
UK 19-20, 401-2
USA 270, 406, 419
Foreign Currency Deposits
Norway 332n.
Scotland 241
Foreign Currency Loans 315, 316
Foreign Deposits 227-8
Foreign Exchange 390-2
Foreign Exchange Business (Inc. Foreign Exchange Arbitrage)
Austria 163
Belgium 175, 177, 178, 179
Germany 158-9
Italy 187
Japan 199
Norway 315
Sweden 316
Switzerland 188, 313
Föreningsbankernas Bank 211
Företagskapital AB 213
Formosa 195
Forward Cover 250
France 5, 11, 15, 126, 134, 135ff., 175, 223, 224, 226, 230-1, 243, 249, 250, 251, 266-7, 271, 278, 379, 308-9, 334-6, 354, 355, 356, 357-8, 374, 407, 410, 414-15, 417-18, 421, 428
North 139-140, 160
Frank, C.R. 332n.
Frankfurt-am-Main 159, 160
Frankfurter Bank 160
Fraud 424
Frederickson, J. William 327n.
Free Association of Provincial Mortgage Banks (Austria) 161
Freedman, Arthur M. 126n.

Fuji Bank 199
Fully Drawn Advance
  Australia 304-5, 306, 357
  Papua New Guinea 33
Funds Management 357-8

Gagnon, Joseph E. 130n., 132n.
Garn-St Germain Depository Institutions Act 1982, 120, 122
Garvy, George 326n.
'General Banks' (South Africa) 50, 52, 61n.
General Electric 110
General Mortgage Bank (Sweden) 212
General Motors Acceptance Corporation 100
Geneva 188, 189
Genossenschaftliche Zentralbank AG 161, 162, 165
Gensaki Market 232, 247-8, 355, 358
Georgia 133n.
German Credit Banks 227
Germany (West) 3, 5, 15, 126, 151ff., 161, 227, 229, 248, 250, 251, 271, 278, 279, 301-3, 336-41, 355, 357, 358, 407-8, 415, 428
  Deconcentration Programme 3, 155-6
  Empire 152
  Unification 151, 152
Gesetz über das Kreditwesen
  Germany 203n.
Gestion des Fortunes
  Belgium 204n.
Giannini, A.P. 126n.
Gibson, J. Douglas 61n.
Gilbart, J.W. 330n.
Gilt-edged 401, 402+n., 422n.
Gilt-edged Jobbers 411
Girard Trust Corn Exchange Bank 87, 92
Giro (inc. Postal Giro) 10, 259ff. 349
  Belgium 174
  Denmark 218
  Finland 215
  France 260
  Germany 260
  Netherlands 183-4+n.
  Switzerland 190
  UK – National Giro 260+n.
Girozentralen
  Austria 161
  Germany 157, 158, 160, 302
Girozentrale und Bank der Oesterreichischen Sparkassen AG 162, 164-5
Glyn Mills & Company 17
Goldsmiths (London) 8, 9, 378
Gold Standard (in Japan) 194
Goodfriend, Marvin 131n., 132n.
Gordon, Gavin, 204n.
Gordon, J.J. 330n.
Götabanken 211, 213
Gothenburg 211
Government Broker 401, 402
Government Securities Dealers
  New Zealand 39
  USA 373
Grand Cayman Islands 106
Great Depression (1930s) 46, 155, 170, 233, 341
'Green Revolution' 146
Gregory, T.E. 58n.
Gross National Product 322
Group Banking (USA) 73ff., 127n.
Growth, Economic 12
Guarantee Act (Austria) 1977 – 164
Guarantee(s) 312, 317
  Director's 330n.
Guerin-Calvert, Margaret 132n.
Guffey, Roger 133n.
Gulf and Western 110
Gutai, Ivan 59n.

Hambros Bank 216
Hamburg 159, 160
Hamilton, Alexander 60n.
Han 193
Hand, Graham 359n., 360n.
Hanover 160
Hanover Bank 86
Hansatu 193
Hard Core Borrowing (UK) 301
'Hard Core' Lending 285, 301
Harlan, Mr Justice 87
Harris, C.P. 327n.
Helsinki 215, 216
Herfindahl Index 94+n.

Herman, Edward S. 126n.
Herstelbank 181
Hessische Landesbank Girozentrale 157
Hibernian Bank Ltd 54
Japan 201, 224, 226
'Hidden Hand' 381
Hidden Reserves, of Banks 226
Higgins, Bryon 132n.
Hire Purchase 56, 240, 279, 378, 421
Hokkaido Takushoku Bank 199
'Hold-back' 290
Holden, J. Milnes 329n., 330n.
Holder, R.F. 59n., 423n.
Holding Companies
USA 3, 73ff.
Hollandsche Bank-Unie 180
Hong Kong 264, 371
Hong Kong and Shanghai Banking Corporation 36
Hope and Company 181
Horwitz, Paul M. 129n., 129-30n.
Hotel- und Fremdenverkehrs-Treuhandgesellschaft mbH 203n.
'Hot Money' 227
Household International 123
Housing Board (Sweden) 212
Housing Corporation (New Zealand) 40
Housing Loan Guarantee Scheme (Papua New Guinea) 37
Housing Loans, 179, 215, 314, 317
Houston 83
Hundi (India) 147, 150, 380
Hungary 163
Hybrid Banking 3-4, 5, 134ff., 206ff., 217-19, 227, 374
Local Loyalties; Denmark 217, 218; France 137; Norway 207; Sweden 214
Social Attitudes (France) 136-7
Social Factors (India) 145-7
Hyper-Inflation
Germany 154

Illinois 68, 72, 73, 97, 109
Immobilisation of Cash Resources 412-13
Imperial Bank of Canada 43, 46
Imperial Bank of India 143, 148
Import Licensing 391
Incasso-Bank 180
'Independent Bankers' (USA) 67, 69, 71, 128-9n.
Index-Tied Deposits (Finland) *see* Deposits, Index-Tied
India 5, 11, 15, 134, 141ff., 224, 251, 264, 271, 276-7, 281, 363, 380, 381, 387, 394-5, 409
All-India Rural Credit Survey (1954) 148
Language(s) 146-7
South 134, 143
Indigenous Bankers (India) 143, 147, 149-50
'Indirect Route' (London) 372
Indosuez 135, 138, 216
Indosuez Niugini Ltd 32, 33
Industrial Bank of Japan 195, 199, 344, 345n.
Industrial Banking 333ff.
Ireland 56
Italy 186-7
Industrial Banks
France *see Banques d'Affaires*
Germany 154
Spain 245
Industrial Bonds and Stocks (Holdings by Banks) 163, 339-40
Industrial and Commercial Finance Corporation (UK) 279, 333
Industrial Credit Company Limited (Ireland) 56
Industrial Development Act 1981 (Ireland) 62n.
Industrial Equities, Bank Holdings of
Austria 163
Belgium 171
Germany 339-40
Industrial Finance 333ff.
Italy 186-7
Industrialisation Fund of Finland 215
Industrikredit (AB) 213
Industry Act (UK) 333
Industry Bank (Norway) 207
Inertia, of Deposits 228ff., 251-4
Inflation 252, 387, 391, 393, 413
Finland 257-9
Germany (Inc. Hyper-inflation) 154
Inflation, Rates of 322, 347, 351

Japan 198
Switzerland 191
USA 113, 116
Individual Retirement Accounts (IRA) 120
Instalment Credit (*see also* Hire Purchase) 56, 240, 279, 289-91, 378, 421, 426
Instalment Credit Sales Act 1961 183
Institut Belgo-Luxembourgeois du Change 172
Institut de Réescompte et de Garantie 174
Insurance Companies 57, 190, 200, 212, 215, 218, 289, 294-5, 314, 369
Insurance Export Company 334
Inter-American Development Bank 342
Inter-Bank Market(s) 265, 348, 349, 353, 354, 355, 357-8, 359, 366
Austria 165
Belgium 178, 249, 311
Canada 242
France 249
Germany 408
Hong Kong 265
India 265
Ireland 56
Japan 248, 265, 418
London 238, 239, 241-2, 264-5, 300, 353
Singapore 265
Inter-Company Market 350
Interest Adjustment Act 1966 (USA) 131n.
Interest Rate(s) 113-14, 115, 179, 292, 295, 297, 301-2, 303, 317, 323, 401, 402, 407, 427, 428, 429
Arbitrage 357+n,
Ceilings 350
Expectations 271, 351, 353
Fixed 299, 301, 302
Futures 236-7, 353-4, 356
Nominal 347
Real 257-9, 351
Strategic 398
Volatility of 347, 369
Interest Rate Cartel(s) 153, 237, 348-9, 421
Interest Rate Sensitivity 348, 350, 353, 354
Interest Rates, Liberalisation of 428-9
Interest Rates Order
Germany 159+n.
Interest Rates, Regulation of 118, 421-2
Deregulation 348, 421, 423n.
Interim Credit 334
International Banking 104ff., 178, 342
International Banking Act 1978 (USA) 105, 106
International Banking Facilities (IBFs) 107-9
International Debt Crisis 321
International Development Association 35
Internationalisation of Banking 425
International Lending 320ff.
Inter-State Banking (USA) 125+n., 132-3n.
Intra Bank 255
Crisis 227, 255
Investment Advice
Germany 159
USA 98
Investment Bank of Ireland Ltd 55
Investment Banks
Germany 159
Investment Portfolios
USA 98
Investments, of Banks, 222, 271ff., 277
As residual 278, 354
Austria 163
Belgium 171
England and Wales 273-4
Germany 339-40
in Subsidiaries 347
Investment Trusts
Switzerland 190
Investors in Industry (UK) 279, 333
Iowa 68, 69, 70, 72
Ireland, Republic of 54ff., 355, 358
and European Monetary System 54
Labour Disputes (Banking) 63n.
Issuing Houses Association 383
Istituti di categoria 204n.
Istituti di credito di diritto pubblico 185
Istituto Bancario Italiano 185

Istituto Bancario S. Paulo di Torino 185
Istituto di Credito delle Casse di Risparmio Italiane (ICCRI) 186
Istituto di Credito delle Casse Rurali e Artigiane (ICCREA) 186
Istituto Mobiliare Italiano (IMI) 186
Istituto per la Ricostruzione Industriale (IRI) 185
Italy 126, 184ff., 224, 225, 226, 243, 249, 250+n., 355
  Central 184
  North 184
  South 184-5

Jamaica 269+n.
James, Marquis and Bessie Rowland 126n.
Jamieson, A.B. 61n.
Jämtlands Folkbank 211
Japan 6n., 126, 134, 175, 192ff., 224, 225, 232, 243, 247-8, 250, 252, 271, 278, 303-4, 310, 320, 343-5, 354, 355, 356, 357, 358, 383, 418-19, 421
  De-concentration 197, 198
  Restoration (1868) 193
  Restoration of Sovereignty (1952) 198
Japan Development Bank 200
Japanese Banks, in London 20
Johnson, Harry L. 129n.
Joint Account Basis (Norway) 209
Joint Family Ownership (India) 146, 147
Joint Stock Company (England) 14
Joint Stock Ownership
  England 13, 14
Jura 188
Justice, Department of (USA) 86, 87, 88, 92, 93, 94, 129n., 130n.

Kansallis-Osake-Pankki 214
Kansas 68, 70, 71, 97, 128n.
Kansas City 99, 286, 403
Karachi 371
Karnataka 149
Kas-Associatie 181
Kennedy, Robert 86
Kentucky 100
KEOGH Depositors 120
Key, Sydney J. 131n.
Kimball, Richard C. 131n.
Kirkenes 207
Kjøbenhavns Handelsbank 217
Koch, Donald L. 132n., 133n.
Koko (Finance Corporations – Japan) 200
Kommunkredit AB 213
Kommunlåneinstitutet AB 213
Korea 45, 205n.
Korean War 414, 426
Kredietbank 171, 176, 177
Kreditanstalt für Wiederaufbau 331n.
Kreditkasse/Fiskernes Bank 206, 207, 208, 210, 211
Kreditwesengesetz (Austria) 161
Kyowa Bank 199

'Laddering' (of Securities) 272, 273, 275
Land and Agricultural Bank (Land Bank – South Africa) 53-4
Lantbrukskredit AB 212
Large Deposits 350, 354, 355, 358
  Australia 244
  Austria 248
  Belgium 249
  England 239
  Finland 250
  Germany 248
  Italy 249
  Scotland 229
  USA 420
Launceston Bank for Savings 26
'Lead' Bank
  Germany 338
  India 144
  Switzerland 342
Leasing 35, 54, 56, 186, 212, 215, 296, 306, 307, 425
Lebanon 227, 264
Leipzig 154
Lender of First Resort (Finland) 358
Lender of Last Resort 265, 367, 375-6, 382, 388
Lending Limit(s), to Single Customer
  USA 98-9, 347
Lexington, Kentucky 86, 88, 91-2, 129n.
LGS Ratio (Australia) 3+n., 268, 428

Defined 328n.
Liabilities (of Banks) 222ff.
Eligible 266, 411
Liabilities Management 346, 348, 352, 354
see also Assets and Liabilities Management
Liberator Building Society 257
Licensing (of Banks) 347
Life Insurance (Assurance) Offices 29, 39, 45, 57, 124, 200
Limited Liability 14+n.
Liquid Assets 222, 264ff., 367
see also Liquidity
Liquidity 1, 10, 33, 172, 182, 190, 260ff., 271, 347, 385, 393, 402
Papua New Guinea 33
Wider structure of 378, 400
Liquidity Preference 251-2
Liquidity Ratios 410
England 265-6, 410-11
France 266-7, 410
Literacy (India) 146
Lloyds Bank 16, 18, 19, 38, 298
International 19, 32
Loan(s) 222, 278ff., 352
Against Deeds (Japan) 302-3
Agricultural Loans 291-2, 321
Automobile Loans 290, 317
Cattle Loans 286
Construction 289, 314, 315, 317
Cotton Loans 286
to Directors 347
Energy-related 321
Formality (in USA) 285, 287
Grain Loans 286
Home Improvement Loans 290, 314, 316
'Joint Account' Basis (Norway) 209
Oil Loans 286
Pre-payment of 295, 302, 314
Produce Loans 285
Property 321
Real Estate 288-9
Secured 283-4
Self-liquidating 281-2
Shipbuilding Loans 300, 314, 417
to Single Borrower 347
Timber Loans 285, 286-7
Tobacco Loans 286
Unsecured 283
Whiskey Loans 286
Loan Account(s) 8, 281-2, 284-5
Loan Associations (Norway) 207+n.
Loan Fund for Education (Norway) 207
Loan Substitution Securities 330n.
Local Authorities 369
Belgium 174
Netherlands 181-2
Local Banker (Local Banks) 14, 15
Australia 21, 23
Belgium 176, 178, 180, 204n.
Denmark 218
France 134, 139
Germany 154-5
Norway 207, 208, 209
Sweden 211, 213, 214
USA 95-7, 286
'Localisation' – Papua New Guinea 36
Lombard 310+n., 407, 415
Lombard Odier 189
Lombard Rate 415
London 235, 255, 264-5, 357, 361, 366, 368, 371, 379, 400-1, 405
London Clearing Banks 19, 20, 126, 238-9, 255, 273-4, 372, 401, 410-11
London Discount Market Association 383
London Inter-Bank Offered Rate (LIBOR) 107, 299, 349
London and South African Bank 48
Long-term Credit Bank Law 1952 (Japan) 199, 343
Long-term Credit Bank of Japan 199, 344
Long-term Credit Banks 199-200, 232, 419
Long-term Finance 337, 338
see also Term Loans
Los Angeles 83+n.
Louisville 286
Lower Canada 41
'Lumpiness' (of Maturity Distribution) 272, 274
Luytjes, Jan 132n.
Luxembourg 302

McGee, John S. 127n.
Mackay, A.G.L. 58n
Madhya Pradesh 145
Madras 144

Maine 100
Maisons de Réescompte (France) 135, 139, 372, 407
Malaysia 264, 409
'Management Accounts' 320
Management Expertise 347
Manchuria 195
Manufacturers Hanover 86
Manufacturers Hanover Bank 224
Manufacturers' Trust 86
Marginal Reserve Requirement (USA) 419-20
Maritime Provinces (of Canada) 43, 47
Marketability (of Securities) 271, 277
Market Concentration (USA) 93-4, 130n.
 Herfindahl Index 94+n.
Marseilles 160
Martins Bank 18, 19
Marwari(s) 367
Massachusetts 60-1n., 115
 Cape Cod Banks 100
Matsukata (Count) 194, 195
Maturity Distribution(s) – of Securities 273-7, 353
Mediocrediti Regionali 187
Mediocredito Centrale 187
Mees, R. & Zoonen 181
Melbourne 361, 379, 383
Memorandum of Deposit 284
Memphis 99, 286
Mercantile Bank of Canada 43
Merchant Bankers, 7, 15, 331n. 378, 379, 425
 Australia 27
 Ireland 55
 Italy 186
 New Zealand 38
 Papua New Guinea 36
 South Africa 51, 52
Mergers (of Banks)
 Australia 165
 Belgium 170-1, 172, 176
 Canada 46, 47
 Denmark 218
 France 140
 Germany 154, 160
 India 145, 151
 Italy 187
 Netherlands 182
 Norway 206, 208, 209-10, 211
 Sweden 212
 USA 66, 80ff., 293
Merger(s) of Business Firms, Arrangement of 336-7
Merrill Lynch 122, 123
Mexican Dollars 193
Mexico 321
Michigan 71
Middle East 189, 227
Midi 140
Midland Bank Limited 16, 17, 54, 285, 296-7
Milwaukee 101
Minimum Lending Rate 401
Minimum Reserves 409-12, 415
 USA 399
Minneapolis 100, 129n., 286, 403
Minnesota 68, 70, 71, 74, 97
Missouri 68, 69, 70, 71, 72, 73
Mitchell, W.A. 330n.
Mitsubishi Bank 195, 196, 199
Mitsui Bank 195, 196, 199
'Mixed Banking' 184, 341
Monaco 135, 139
Monetarism 393
Monetary Aggregates 116-17, 121-2, 132n., 393, 394, 427
'Monetary Authorities' 386
Monetary Control Act 1980 406
 see also Depository Institutions Deregulation and Monetary Control Act
Monetary Policy 346, 385ff., 394, 398ff., 418, 422, 427
Money Brokers 239, 242, 250, 266, 355, 371
Money-Changing 7
Moneylenders 370
 India 147-8, 150
Money Management 239-40, 242, 270, 328n.
Money Market Assets 277
'Money Market' Banks
 Belgium 178, 180
Money Market Deposit Accounts
 USA 120, 121
Money Market(s) 346, 361ff., 398, 426
 Australia 365, 379-80
 Austria 165
 Bazaar Markets (India) 363, 370
 Berlin 152
 Channels of Communication 369

Characteristics 361
Defined 361, 366
Developed 366
Frictions 369
Impersonal Relationships 361-2
Integrated Structure 367ff., 381-3
London 361, 378-9, 400-2+n.
Mature 367, 376, 378, 381ff.
'Money-Market Corporations' (Australia) 27
Official 358
Organised Sector (India) 363, 367-8, 370
Papua New Guinea 36
Preconditions for 362-6
Revolving Fund (of Cash) 362, 364, 371
Shifting, Costs of 369
Short-term Money Market Dealers (Australia) 27
South Africa 363
Specialisation of Function 367, 378-80, 382-3
Undeveloped 366
Unofficial 358, 368, 380
USA 361, 372-3, 379, 403-5
Money Market Mutual Fund (USA) 110, 116, 350, 351, 427
'Money Trust'
UK 16
USA 66, 67, 69
Monopoly, Distrust of (USA) 67, 69, 80
Local 70
Montreal 361
Montreal City and District Savings Bank 44
'Mopping Up' (of Cash) 372, 401, 407
'Moral Suasion' 383
Morison, Ian 327n.
Mortgage Bank of Japan 195
Mortgage Banks
Austria 165
Germany 302
Netherlands 182
Mortgage Broking 160
Mortgage Credit Associations (Denmark) 218
Mortgage Credit Banks (Finland) 215
Mortgage Lending
Netherlands 183
Switzerland 188, 189
UK 20, 241
Mortgage Societies (Sweden) 212
Moving Average 323
Multani Shroff (India) 149-50 367
Multi-Bank Borrowing 318-20
Munich 154, 159, 160
Municipal Bank (Norway) 207
Municipalities, Financing of
Netherlands 181-2
Norway 314-15
'Municipals' (USA) 274, 275-6, 329n.
Munster and Leinster Bank Ltd 54
Murphy, Antoin E. 63n.
Mutual Funds 426
Mutual Savings Banks (USA) 68, 111, 115, 117, 118, 270

National and Commercial Banking Group Ltd 17+n.
National Bank 17+n.
National Bank for Agriculture and and Rural Development (India) 142
National Bank of Australasia 24, 25
National Bank of Belgium 171, 173
National Bank of Canada 44
National Bank Ltd (Ireland) 54
National Bank of New Zealand 38
National Bank of Pakistan 395
National Bank of Scotland 17, 18
National Bank of South Africa Ltd 49
National Banking Acts (USA) – 1863 and 1864 47+n.
National Banks 67
National Banks (Japan) 193-4
National Banks Ordinance (Japan) 193
National Commercial Banking Corporation of Australia Ltd (National Australia Bank) 25, 31-2
National Commercial Bank of Scotland Ltd 17+n.
National Credit Union Administration (USA)
Central Liquidity Facility 406
National Debt, Management of 400,

402, 403, 404-5
National Enterprise Board (UK) 333
Nationale Investerings Bank 181
National Finance Corporation (South Africa) 365
National Giro (UK) 10, 260+n.
National Investors' Scheme (also National Investment and Development Authority) Papua New Guinea 37
Nationalisation of Banks *see* Bank Nationalisation
National Pension Insurance Fund (Sweden) 212, 326n.
National Provincial Bank 16, 18
National Savings (UK) 351
National Steel Corporation 111
National Westminster Bank, 18, 54, 181, 298
Native Economic Development Act 1951 – Papua New Guinea 34
Nazi Era 155, 337
'Near Cash' 351, 371, 393
Nebraska 69, 70, 100
Nedbank Ltd 48
Nederlandsche Handel-Maatschappij 180
Nederlandsche Middenstandsbank 180, 183
Nederlandse Credietbank 180
Nederlandse Overzee Bank 181
Nederlandse Participatie Maatschappij 181
Negotiability (of Credit Instruments) 9, 10
Negotiated Order of Withdrawal (NOW) – USA 111-12, 117, 119, 121, 122, 427
Netherlands (The), 175, 180ff., 224, 227, 249, 250, 251, 278, 311, 340, 354, 355, 356, 357, 416
Netherlands Bank 311
Netherlands Bank of South Africa 49
Nevin, Edward 329n.
New Brunswick 43
New Coins Ordinance (Japan) 194
New England 111, 112, 130n.
Newfoundland 61n.
New Hampshire 115
New Issues (of Capital) 338, 341, 379
New Jersey 71, 111, 115, 128n., 129n.
Newlyn, W.T. 61n.
New York (State of) 69, 71, 77
New York 99, 105, 109, 111, 115, 233, 234, 236, 287, 288, 294, 361, 366, 368, 371, 372, 373, 379, 403, 405
New Zealand 37ff., 224, 225, 243, 244, 263, 271, 306-8, 354, 355, 356, 357, 358, 364, 409, 421
Nicholl, P.W.E. 326n., 327n., 423n.
Nidhis (India) 143
Nikko Securities 200
Nippon Credit Bank 199, 344
Niugini-Lloyds International Bank Ltd 32, 33
Nomura Securities 200
Non-Associated Banks (Ireland) 55-6, 57
'Non-Bank Bank' (USA) 132n.
Non-Bank Financial Institutions 60n., 349, 378
Non-Member Banks (of US Federal Reserve System) 126n.
Non-Par Banks (USA) 98, 103
Non-Scheduled Banks (India) 142
Non-Utilisation Fee *see* Commitment Fee
Norddeutsche Landesbank Girozentrale 157
Nordic Bank 219
Norinchukin Bank 200
Norman, Montagu 396
North and South Wales Bank 261
North Cape (Norway) 207
North Carolina 71
North Dakota 72
Northern Bank Ltd 54
Northland Bank 43
North Sea Oil 300
Norway 4, 206ff., 225, 243, 249-50, 314-15, 355, 358, 394, 421
Note Issuance/Revolving Underwriting Facility (NIFs) 352+n.
Note Issue 396, 401
Notes (Bank) 8-9
Notes and Coin

USA 101
Nova Scotia 43

Oesterreichische Creditinstitut 163
Oesterreichische Exportfondsgesellschaft mbH 164, 203n.
Oesterreichische Investitionskredit AG 164, 202n.
Oesterreichische Kommunalkredit AG 164, 203n.
Oesterreichische Kontrollbank AG 162, 164, 203n.
Oesterreichische Länderbank 162, 163, 170
Oesterreichische Volksbanken AG (OEVAG) 166
Ohio 71
Oil Prices 393
Oklahoma 69, 70, 71
Okobank 215
Omaha 99
Ontario 47
'Open Credit' System 282
'Open' Economy 385
Open Market Operations 2, 354, 358, 372, 374, 376, 377, 398-408 *passim*, 402, 404, 413, 414, 415, 422, 427-8, 428
  in Bills 401-2
  Smoothing Out 388-9, 401, 402
Ordinary Banks (Japan) 194, 196
Ordinary Banks Ordinance (Japan) 194
Ordinary Credit Banks (Italy), 185, 188
Ordinary Deposits (Japan) 232
Oriental Development Company 195
Orissa 145
Osaka 193, 199
Oslo 206, 207, 208, 211
Oslo & Akershus 206
Oslobanken 219n.
Oulu 214
Overdraft(s) (also Current Account Lending) 8, 9, 253, 278+n., 281-3+n., 310, 311, 357, 417
  Arbitrage 239, 357+n.
  Australia 304-5
  Austria 313
  Belgium 311
  Denmark 317
  Finland 317
  Japan 303
  Netherlands 311
  New Zealand 307
  Norway 314
  Papua New Guinea 33
  Sweden 315-16
  Switzerland 312
  USA 286
'Overlines' 81, 99, 103, 130n., 318

Pakistan 251, 271, 281, 387, 395, 409
Papua New Guinea 29ff.
  Currency 31
  Exchange Rate 31
Papua New Guinea Banking Corporation 31, 32, 33, 36
Papua New Guinea Development Bank 35-6, 37
Paribas 135, 138, 140
Paribas International 181
Paribas-Warburg 181
Paris 372
Parliamentary Banking Committee (Finland) 216
Parliamentary Finance Committee (Finland) 216
Parthemos, James 131n.
Participation(s)
  in Capital 271, 334, 335, 337, 339
  in Loans 99+n.
Pastoral Finance Companies Australia 28-9
Penn Square 101
Pennsylvania 71
Pension Funds 190, 218
People's Banks (Italy) 186, 187, 188
Personal Loans
  Australia 304-5
  Austria 313
  Belgium 312
  Denmark 317
  England 285
  Italy 184
  Japan 304
  New Zealand 307
  Papua New Guinea 33
  Sweden 316-17
  Switzerland 189
  USA 290
Philadelphia 403
Philadelphia National Bank 87, 88, 92, 129n.

Philippines 409
Pictet 189
Pierson, Heldring & Pierson 181
Plafonds (France) 266, 407, 414-15
Plancher (France) 266-7
Plans d'Épargne-Logement 231
Poland 163
Political Risk 321, 322
Pontolillo, Vincenzo 204n.
Portefeuille-Effets 308-9
Portfolio Management
 Germany 338
 Switzerland 189
Portugal 224, 309, 357, 358
Postal Bank, Proposed (Netherlands) 183
Postal Cheque Office (Belgium) 173, 175
Postal Cheque System (Switzerland) 190
Postal Savings Bank
 Austria 161, 162, 166-7, 203n., 340
Postal Savings Bank Act 1969 (Austria) 166
Postipankki 215, 216, 332n.
Post-och Kreditbanken (PK banken) 211, 213
Post Office National Giro 10
Post Office Savings Bank
 Ireland 56
 Netherlands 183
 New Zealand 38
 Norway 207
 Switzerland 190
Postsparkasse (Austria) 166-7
Precautionary Balances 351
Presbisch, Dr 257
President's Commission on Financial Structure and Regulation (Hunt Commission), Report 1971 115
Pressnell, L.S. 329-30n.
Primary Dealers (New York) 405
Primary Industry Bank of Australia 26, 27, 306
Prime Assets Ratio 428, 430
Prime Rate
 USA 292, 295
Prince Edward Island 61n.
'Priority' Loans
 India 149
Privatbanken 217
Private Banks 378
 Austria 163
 Belgium 341
 Germany 154, 157, 159-60, 338-9
 Switzerland 189, 190, 191
Private Placements – Netherlands 249+n., 354
 Switzerland 342
Private Savings Banks Act (New Zealand) 60n
Project Risk 321-2
Promissory Note(s) 287, 296
Protection of Depositors Act 1963 (UK) 256
Provident National Bank 130n.
Provincial Banks (Germany) 152-3, 154
Provincial Bank of Ireland Ltd 54
Proxmire, Senator William A. 131n.
Prudential 122, 123
Prudential Supervision 224, 346, 347n., 421, 427
 Austria 161
 Belgium 172
 Denmark 218
 Finland 217
 Germany 126, 428
 Japan 201-2
 Sweden 213+n., 315, 316
 Switzerland 190, 192
 UK 256
Public Law Banks (Italy) 185, 187, 188
Public Sector Banks
 Australia 25+n.
 India 142
Public Sector Institutions
 Belgium 173-4
Public Service Investment Society (New Zealand) 60n.
Punjab 134, 149
Punjab National Bank 149

Qualitative Credit Control 416, 418, 420-1
Quantitative Credit Controls 398-420 *passim*, 427
Quebec 44, 47
Quebec Bank 42
Quebec Savings Bank Act 44
Queensland National Bank 25

Rabobank Nederland 180, 181

Radcliffe Committee (UK) 296+n., 324n., 377-8, 426
Rae, George 261+n., 327n., 328n.
Raiffeisen Banks
  Austria 161, 165-6, 167
  Belgium 174, 204n.
  Italy 186
  Switzerland 189, 191
Raymond, Robert 422n.
Real Estate Loans 286, 421
Real Rates of Interest 258
Recession 392, 394, 412, 427
Rediscount Quotas 407
Redundancy 393
Regional Bank(s) 134
  Austria 161, 162-3, 165-6
  Belgium 178, 179
  Denmark 218
  Finland 215
  France 137, 139
  Germany 157, 160
  India 141, 149
  Japan 199, 200, 201, 232, 303
  Norway 207, 208, 209, 210
  Sweden 211, 213, 214, 247
  Switzerland 189, 191
Regional Bank Ordinance 1975 (India) 142
Regional Committee of the Association of Norwegian Savings Banks 210+n.
Regional Development Fund (Sweden) 215
Regional Rural Banks
  India 142, 148, 149
Registrar of Banks (South Africa) 395
Regulation A (USA) 406-7
Regulation Q (USA) 118, 231, 233, 234, 350, 421
Reichsbank 152
Reid, Margaret 256, 326n.
REIT (Real Estate Investment Trust) Loans (USA) 101
Renault 141
Representative Office(s)
  Austria 163-4
  Finland 215, 216
  Japan 199
  Netherlands 181
  Norway 207
  Sweden 212
  USA 106
Repurchase Agreement(s) (RPs)
  Australia 379
  Finland 250
  Germany 408
  London 384n.
  Reverse RPs 270, 373, 405
  USA 98, 112-13, 235-6, 270, 353, 373, 389, 405, 420
Reserve Bank of Australia 2, 30, 31, 268, 305, 396
Reserve Bank of India 143, 144, 149-50, 276
Reserve Bank of India Act 142, 255
Reserve City Banks (USA) 269
Reserved Liability 58n.
Reserve Requirements 113, 115, 116-17
Reserves, Bank 222ff.
Resources and Investment Finance Limited – Papua New Guinea 36
Retail Banking
  Austria 163
  Belgium 170, 178, 179
  Canada 242, 296
  Finland 216
  France 138
  Germany 158, 159
  Italy 184
  USA 82
Retail Loans 289
'Retail' Money 349
Reuss, Representative Henry S. 131n.
Reverse Yield Curve 351
'Reversible Assistance Measures' 408
Rhoades, Stephen A. 129n., 130n.
Rhodesia and Nyasaland, Federation of 269+n.
Rhône-Alpes 139
Rhône-Poulenc 141
Richmond 403
Rights Issues 225
Rising Expectations, Revolution of 393
Risk(s) 352, 369
  Distribution of 190, 337
  Spread of 15, 24, 41, 49, 153
Rogaland 206
Rothschild 140

Rotterdam 181
Rotterdamsche Bank 180
Royal Bank of Canada 46
Royal Bank of Ireland Ltd 54
Royal Bank of Scotland 17, 18, 229
Royal Bank of Scotland Group 18
Run on Bank Cash 264, 387-8
Rural and Artisan Banks (Italy) 186, 188
Rural Banking and Finance Corporation (New Zealand) 40
Rural and Industries Bank of Western Australia 26
Rutz, Roger D. 129n.

Safe Custody
  USA 98, 104
Saint Gobain 141
St Louis 99, 403
Saitama Bank 199
Sale and Repurchase Agreement(s) *see* Repurchase Agreements
Sales Finance Companies (USA) 291
Samurai 192, 193, 194
San Francisco 105, 288, 361, 403
Sankin-Kotai 193
Sanwa Bank 196, 199
Saving(s) 20, 302-3, 351
Savings Accounts 231, 232, 303, 338
Savings Bank of South Australia 26
Savings Bank of Tasmania 26
Savings Banks 349, 350, 425, 426
  Australia 26, 229-30
  Austria 161, 164-5
  Belgium 173, 177, 178-9
  Canada 44
  Denmark 218
  Finland 215, 258
  France 136, 309, 324n.
  Germany 154, 155, 156-7, 158, 159, 160
  Italy 186, 188
  Netherlands 182-3
  New Zealand 38+n., 244
  Norway 206, 207, 209, 210, 211
  South Africa 50
  Sweden 211, 212, 213-14, 316
  Switzerland 189, 190, 191
  USA 235, 270, 406
Savings and Loan Association(s)
  USA 112, 119, 125, 235, 270, 349, 350, 406, 425, 426
Savings and Loan Societies
  Papua New Guinea 33-5
Sayers, R.S. 58n., 61n., 219n., 324n., 327n., 329n., 423n.
Scandinavia 224
Scandinavian Bank 219
Scheduled Banks (India) 142
Schull, Joseph 61n.
Schweiger, Irving 127n.
Scotland 9, 12-13, 17-18, 228-9, 230, 262, 274, 281, 300-1
  Agents 13+n.
Scott, Ira O. Jr 131n.
Scottish Agricultural Securities Corporation 333
Scottish Clearing Banks 20, 238, 240-2, 255, 300-1, 372, 401, 411
Scriveners (Money Scriveners) 8
SDS (Denmark) 218
Sears, Roebuck and Company 110, 122
Seasonal Fluctuations 375
Seattle 286-7
Secondary Banking Crisis 1973-75 (UK) 255+n., 256
Secondary depression 392
Secondary Market(s) – in CDs 233-4, 237-8, 240, 242, 244, 245, 246, 354
Securities and Exchange Commission 198
Securities Companies (Japan) 200, 247
Securities Co-ordinating Liquidation Commission (Japan) 198
Secrurities Exchange Act 1934 (USA) 421
Securities Houses (Japan) 200, 247
'Security' Credit Institutions (Netherlands) 183
Security, for loans 283-4
  Accounts Receivable 284, 288
  Assignment of Life Insurance Policy 284
  Chattel Mortgages 284, 291-2
  Floating Charge 284
  Guarantee 284
  Hypothecation 284
  Mortgage(s) 283-4
    of Ships 284
  Mortgage Debenture 284
  Pledge 284
  Stocks and Shares 284

Security Portfolios 271ff.
Select Committee on Banking Legislation (South Africa) 50
Select Committee on Constitutional Development (Papua New Guinea) 30
Selective Credit Control 421
Self-Financing 281, 337, 344
'Semi-Wholesale Money' 355
Serial Funding Stocks (UK) 412
Service Central des Risques 320
Shann, Edward 324
Share Drafts (of Credit Unions in USA) 111
'Shell' Branch
USA 106
Sherman Anti-Trust Act (USA) 84, 86, 87, 90, 91, 92
's-Hertogenbosch 181
Shifting Frontiers (in Financial Markets) 126, 425, 426, 429
Shimamoto, Reiichi 423n.
Shinyo-kinko (Shinkin) – Japan 200
Shinyo-kumiai (Japan) 200
Ship Mortgage Finance Company (UK) 279, 333-4
Shogun 192
Shoko Chukin Bank 200
Shroff 149-50, 380
Silver Standard (Japan) 194
Singapore 371
Skandinaviska Enskilda Banken 211, 213, 216, 219
Skopbank 215
Slavenburg's Bank (NV) 181
Smaistrla, Charles J. 128n.
Smith, R.G. 326n., 327n., 423n.
Smith, William French 94
Smoothing Out Operations 388-9, 401, 402
'Social Control' of Banking (India) 143
Société de développement régional 309
Société Générale de Banque 170, 176, 177
Société Générale pour Favoriser le Développement du Commerce et de l'Industrie en France 138, 139
Société Nationale de Credit à l'Industrie 174
Société Nationale d'Investissement 174
Sogo (Mutual) Banks (Japan) 200
Solicitors' Nominee Companies (New Zealand) 39-40
Solvency (Solvability) 172, 182, 260, 347
South Africa 4, 48ff., 363, 365, 395
Union 49
South Carolina 133n.
'Sovereign Loans' 320, 323
Sovereign Loan Risk 321ff.
Soviet Union 1, 2, 10, 163
Spain 126, 175, 243, 245-6, 250, 354, 355, 356, 358
Sparebanken Vest 206
Sparbankernas Bank 211
Sparkassengesetz (Austria) (Savings Bank Act) 161
Special Account Procedure (Australia) 412-13, 428
Special Deposit Accounts 249-50
Special Deposits (UK) 249-50, 355, 358, 384n., 411
Special Reserve Deposits (Australia) 413
Specie 8
Payments (in Japan) 194
'Spectral Analysis' 323
Sri Lanka 251, 271, 409
Stable Bond Market Policy (USA) 277, 410
Staffing, of Banks (India) 148-9
Standard Bank of South Africa Ltd 48, 49
Standard Life Assurance 17
State Bank of India 142, 143, 148, 149, 150, 202n.
State Bank of New South Wales 26
State Bank of Pakistan 395
State Bank of South Australia 26
State Bank of Victoria 26
State Banks
Australia 26
Norway 206-7
USA 67
State Housing Bank (Norway) 207, 314
State Investment Fund (Sweden) 215
'Statutory Interest Groups' (Austria) 161, 162
Statutory Reserve Deposits (Australia) 267-8

Stavanger 207
Stellenbosch District Bank Ltd 49
Stewart, Mr Justice 87
Stigum, Marcia 325n., 384n.
Stock Exchange(s) – and Firms 126, 425
  Belgium 172
  Denmark 340-1
  Finland 340
  France 335
  London 264
  Netherlands 340
  New York 265
  Spain 245
  Switzerland 342
Stockholm 211
Stock and Station Agents (New Zealand) 39
'Straight Loans' (Belgium) 311, 357
Structure of Banking
  Effects of Climate and Geography 206ff.
Subordinated Debt 225-6
  Belgium 172
  France 141
Sukbat, E.B. 59n.
Sumitomo Bank 195, 196, 199
Summers, Bruce 131n.
Sun Banks of Florida 133n.
Sundvallsbanken 211
Super-NOW Accounts (USA) 120, 121, 427
Supervisory Board (of Company) Bank Members (Germany) 340
Supplementary Deposit Scheme ('Corset' in UK) 419, 428
Supra-quota Credit (Finland) 415
Surplus Investible Funds (Australia) 413
Suviranta, Professor 258
Sveabanken 213
Svenska Handelsbanken 211, 213
Svensk Exportkredit (AB) 213
Swaps 248, 249, 251, 288, 315, 354, 355, 356, 408
  North Bound (Canada) 243
  South Bound (Canada) 243
Sweden 126, 211ff., 225, 243, 246-7, 315-16, 355, 357, 358, 415, 421
Swedish Export Credits Guarantee Board 213
Swedish Investment Bank 213
Swiss Bank Corporation 188
Swiss National Bank 190-1, 342
Swiss Volksbank 188
Switzerland 188ff., 224, 227, 250, 251, 278, 312-13, 342-3, 354, 356, 358
  Federation 188
Sydney 361, 379, 383
Syndicates
  Austria 313
  France 335
  Germany 338
  Sweden 316
  Switzerland 342-3
  UK 299
  USA 294
Syron, Richard F. 132n.

Taiyo Kobe Bank 199
Tamagna, F.M. 205n.
Tamil Nadu 149
Tanker Finance Limited (UK) 279, 334
Tanshi Houses (Japan) 247+n.
Task Group on Regulation of Financial Services (Bush Task Group) 129n.
Tatom, John A. 132n.
Taylor, F.S. 57-8n.
Tax losses (on Securities) 276
T-Distribution (Maturity of Securities) 275
Technologies, New (in Banking) 424, 425
Term Loan Fund (Australia) 27, 305
Term Loans 221, 238, 240, 242, 280, 294ff., 311, 312, 313, 314, 315, 316, 317, 349, 354, 357
  and Equity Interest 331n.
  Balloon 295
  Bullet Loan 295
  Formal Term Loan Agreement 295, 298-9+n., 301, 305, 307, 311, 313, 314, 315, 317
  Mismatch of Maturities 300, 301, 303
  Refinancing Facilities 301
Terms of Trade 362
Texas 68, 70, 71, 97, 128n., 292
Third World 320, 321, 323, 352
Thirty Years War (1618-48) 336
'Thomas Amendment' (USA) 410
Thomson-Brandt 141
Three Banks Group 17

Tillet, Paul 327n.
Time Deposits 350
  France 230, 231
  Germany 338
  Japan 232, 343, 344-5
  Scotland 241
  USA 231-2
Time Series 322, 323
Titres participatifs (France) 141, 226
Tokai Bank 199
Tokugawa, House of 192
Tokyo 199, 371
Toronto 361
Toronto and Dominion Bank 43
Trade Unions, Bank (India) 151
Trading Bank(s)
  Australia 23ff., 357
  New Zealand 37ff.
  Papua New Guinea 30
Trading Portfolio (of Securities) 271, 275, 278, 338, 342
Transactions Demand for Money 251
Transamerica Corporation 128n.
Transferable Certificates of Deposit (New Zealand) 244, 354, 358
Travelers 123
Treasury Bills 272+n., 354, 358, 359, 363, 364, 365, 366, 368, 372, 376, 384n., 401-2, 405, 412
  Canada 242
  France 308
  India 277
  Papua New Guinea 33+n.
  UK 402, 412
  USA 101, 233, 270
Treasury Deposit Receipt (UK) 412
Tripura 145
Tromsø ('Capital of the Arctic') 207
Trondheim 207
Trust and Loan Companies (Canada) 45
Trust Banks (Japan) 200
Trust Company of Georgia 133n.
Trustee Savings Banks
  Australia 26
  Ireland 56
  New Zealand 38
  United Kingdom 350
'Truth in Lending' (USA) 119-20
Twentsche Bank 180

Ulster Bank Limited 54
Uncertainty 251-2, 272,351, 369
Underwriting (of Bond/Share Issues) 334ff.
Unemployment 351, 392-3
Union Bank of Australia 21, 23, 24, 25
Union Bank of Finland 214
Union Bank of Scotland 17
Union Bank of Switzerland 188
Union de Banques à Paris 140
Union des Assurances de Paris 140
Unit Banking 3, 4, 21, 64ff., 95, 97, 170, 208, 227, 374
United Kingdom 4, 12ff., 175, 224, 226, 227, 233, 237ff., 252, 279, 280-1, 296ff., 318-20, 333-4, 335, 381, 410-11, 416-17, 420, 421 428
United States of America 2, 3, 4, 15, 64ff., 189, 223, 224, 227, 231-2, 233, 261, 264, 269-70, 274-6, 279-80, 285ff., 318, 320, 321, 350, 355, 372-3, 381, 387, 389, 403-7, 409-10, 426, 428
  Federation of 64-5, 66
Unit Trust(s) 339, 426
'Universal' Banks 135, 184, 425
  Austria 163, 165
  Belgium 179
  Finland 215
  Germany 156, 158, 338
  Netherlands 182
  Switzerland 189, 190
Unsecured Loans 283, 287
Unused Limit Fee *see* Commitment Fee
Uplandsbanken 211
Usury 7, 118-19
Uttar Pradesh 145

Valais 188
van Lanschot Bankiers 181
Vasena (Senor) 257
Vaud 188, 189
Velocity of Circulation 254+n.
Veterans' Administration (USA) 289
Village Economic Development Fund – Papua New Guinea 37
Volcker, P.W. 393+n.
Volksbanken (Austria) 161, 166, 167
  Association of 161
Volkskas Beperk 48, 49
Voluntary Credit Restraint (USA) 420
Vontobel Holdings 189

Voorschotbanken (Credit Banks) 183
Vrabac, Daniel J. 132n.

Wadsworth, J.E. 58n., 327n., 330n.
Walker, Ernest W. 129n.
Warehouse Receipts 312
'Warehousing', of Mortgages 289
Washington Savings and Loan Association 110
Watkins, Thomas G. 128n.
Wechsel 309-10, 314, 357
Welch, Jane 327n., 359n.
Wermlandsbanken 211
Wertpapier-Emissionsgesetz (Austria) 161
West, Robert Craig 128n.
West Bengal 145
Westdeutsche Landesbank Girozentrale 157
Western Australian Bank 24
Westminster Bank 16, 18, 298
Westpac Bank – PNG– Limited 31, 32, 33
Westpac Banking Corporation (formerly Bank of New South Wales) 25, 31,38+n.
West Side Federal Savings and Loan Association 110
West Virginia 70-1
Whale, P. Barrett 202n.
Whitaker, T.K. 62n.
Whitehead, David D. 132n.
Whittlesey, Charles R. 126n., 327n.
Wholesale Banking
  Belgium 178, 179
  Finland 250
  Germany 158
  USA 82, 289
Wholesale Money 222, 233ff., 250, 299, 348, 349, 355
'Window-Dressing' 262, 266, 377, 411
'Window Guidance' (Japan) 202, 418-19
Williams Deacon's 17
Williams & Glyn's Bank Ltd 17+n., 255
Wilson, J.S.G. 127n., 129n., 202n., 204n., 323n., 325n., 326n., 327n., 329n., 330n., 331n., 332n., 345n., 383n., 384n., 397n., 422n., 423n.
Wisconsin 68, 69, 70, 101
Working Capital, Provision of 282
World Bank 342
'Wrapped Money' 193+n.
Wyoming 70

Yamaichi Securities 200
Yasuda 195, 196
Yedo (Tokyo) 193
Yield 271
Yokas, Steve 132n.
Yokohama Specie Bank 195
Yugoslavia 163

Zaibatsu 196, 197+n., 198
Zentralsparkasse, Vienna 162, 203n.
Zürcher Kantonalbank 188
Zürich 188